the Growth
of the Church
in AFRICA

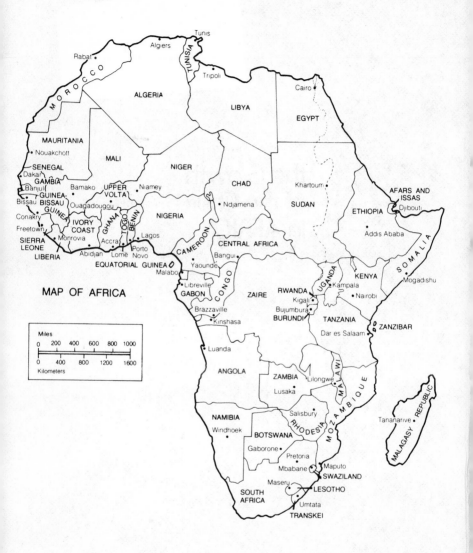

MAP OF AFRICA

Peter
Falk

the Growth
of the Church
in AFRICA

**ZONDERVAN
PUBLISHING HOUSE** OF THE ZONDERVAN CORPORATION
GRAND RAPIDS, MICHIGAN 49506

THE GROWTH OF THE CHURCH IN AFRICA
Copyright © 1979 by The Zondervan Corporation

Library of Congress Cataloging in Publication Data

Falk, Peter, 1921-
    The growth of the church in Africa.

    (Contemporary evangelical perspectives)
    Bibliography: p.
    Includes index.
    1. Missions—Africa. 2. Africa—Church
history. I. Title.
BV3500.F3   276   78-11982
ISBN 0-310-37585-1

Printed in the United States of America.

To my wife, Annie,
and children, Leola and Marvin,
who have shared years
of ministry with me

Contents

10

Foreword

The story of Christianity in Africa is truly remarkable. At the turn of the century the church in Africa (all branches) could claim a mere 3 percent of the population. By now, though, only three-quarters of a century later, membership is over 30 percent and could possibly reach 50 percent by the year 2000. By that time "Africa may well have become in the main a Christian . . . continent, and the home of one of the largest Christian communities in the world."*

Euroamerican Christians have seen "The Dark Continent" as spiritually benighted, largely lacking the light of the gospel of Christ. To be sure, that light had shone for a time to the north of the Sahara. But it had apparently been stamped out by the coming of Islam. Eastern Christianity had gained and maintained a foothold in Ethiopia. But to Euroamerican Christians that light seems dim and flickering at best. And the rest of the continent appears to be spiritually dark.

And African Christians themselves, participants though they have been in this remarkable Christward movement, have often been "in the dark" concerning the dimensions of that movement. It has been easy for them to get so enmeshed in the practical problems of Christian life and witness that they have failed to see the broad picture. Even missionaries, those who have given their lives to bring this story into being, have often remained ignorant of any but their own part of the drama.

It is the broad understanding of this Christward movement in Africa that Dr. Falk seeks to bring to our attention. This is the story of dedicated Euroamerican Christians who could not ignore

---

*See David B. Barrett, "AD 2000: 350 Million Christians in Africa," *International Review of Missions* 59 (1970): 39-54. Quote from page 39.

15

the spiritual needs of African peoples. So when explorers and traders began to find their way to Africa, Euroamerican Christians sent missionaries along. From the beginning the toll was heavy. Many did not survive their first year on African soil. Of those who lived, many could not master the strange languages and cultures. Enormous mistakes were made but, by God's grace, glorious victories were won. And through it all God planted His church, the bearer of gospel light, in thousands of African villages, towns, and cities.

This is also the story of the receiving people—people who, though often exploited, mistreated, and enslaved by Euroamericans, were able to hear and respond to a message that Euroamericans did not always live by. It has seldom been easy for African Christians to stand for Christ. But it is the magnificent dedication and perseverence of Africans, plus the increasing demonstration of the ability of Africans to lead creatively, that is primarily responsible for the success of Christianity in Africa. African efforts, too, have often been marred by mistakes. But, by God's grace, the work of God in Africa today thrives largely in African hands.

It is the story of a long struggle. The harvest being reaped today is not necessarily the result of recent plantings. Dr. Falk takes us back to pre-Islamic North Africa, the introduction of Coptic Christianity into Ethiopia, to find the earliest plantings. But most of the story of Christianity in Africa is less than two centuries old. The major focus is, therefore, on this period.

Dr. Falk is a missionary to Africa. He is a personal bridge between Euroamerica and Africa and has, therefore, a concern that this story be known in both places. For better than two decades he has taught African church history and otherwise ministered to Africans in Zaire. He has found a need for African Christians, at their end of the bridge, to come to better understandings of their roots in the history of the Christian movement in Africa. But appropriate materials are often not available. There are works of great detail that are available only in the more complete of the theological libraries of Africa. There are partial treatments of various kinds, of primary benefit only to those whose special interests they serve. Dr. Falk seeks here to provide a brief and nontechnical treatment of the history of African Christianity continent-wide that will be suitable as a textbook for courses on that subject in English-speaking Africa.

At the Euroamerican end of the bridge, there is a similar need. Those who have sent Dr. Falk and thousands of others to Africa need to know what has become of their investment. And those preparing to go need to know what has framed the context in which they seek to minister. For these and other interested persons—pastors, teachers, and laymen—this volume meets the need for something brief and nontechnical yet comprehensive.

Dr. Falk has undertaken an enormous task, requiring broad reading and an ability to synthesize mountains of data and to identify and communicate the key points in accurate yet simplified fashion. Both the extensive bibliography on and the concise presentation of his topics throughout the volume testify to his ability to carry out his difficult assignment effectively. This book represents a large amount of dedicated work by a devoted and able servant of Africa. It is my prayer that the continuing history of God's working in Africa will be greatly enhanced both by the publication of this record and by the involvement of you, the reader, in that continuing history.

CHARLES H. KRAFT

Acknowledgments

It would be impossible to include all the people who should be recognized in this brief acknowledgment. Many Christians and church agencies throughout Africa, from the Mennonite Central Committee in Morocco, to the Church of Christ in Zambia, to the Mission Romande in South Africa, have shown most gracious hospitality and shared information concerning the history of the church in Africa. Church headquarters and libraries in Africa, America, and Europe most cordially made their records available for the research.

I am indebted to many African Christians who expressed the need of the churches for such a history and to many teachers who encouraged me to make this material available to them. Frederic L. Holland, Arthur F. Glasser, and Charles H. Kraft, professors in the School of World Mission at the Fuller Theological Seminary, provided encouragement in advising that this writing be undertaken. The facilities of the McAlister Library at the Fuller Theological Seminary, with the large selection of theses written recently, the U.C.L.A. Research Library in Los Angeles, and the African Library of the California Institute of Technology in Pasadena provided a unique opportunity for research.

Finally, I must acknowledge two people without whose assistance this study would not have been written. Dr. Charles H. Kraft's appreciative comments provided inspiration to proceed in the writing. My wife, Annie, by typing the original draft, relieved me of much tedious work and released my time and energy to move ahead, making the completion of the work much more feasible. Thank you!

the Growth
of the Church
in AFRICA

Introduction

Two amazing and significant facts of history are the sweep of Christianity over North Africa during the early centuries of the Christian era and, after a millennium of difficulties and setbacks, its flowering throughout Africa south of the Sahara in the nineteenth and twentieth centuries. Christianity was established in North Africa during the times of the apostles; it spread rapidly, won the allegiance of the overwhelming majority of the population, and contributed most significantly to the ministry of the Christian church during the first five centuries. From its ranks came able leaders, teachers, apologists, theologians, and writers, who witnessed to their faith with a dynamism that eventually won the support of the Roman state, causing Christianity to become the predominent religion of the Greco-Roman civilization.

The church experienced one of the most disastrous calamities of its history in the invasion of North Africa during the seventh and eighth centuries. It survived with much difficulty in Egypt and became practically nonexistent in northern West Africa. As a result of the fall of the Roman Empire and the decay of the Greco-Roman civilization, the Roman and Byzantine churches chiefly devoted their efforts to evangelize the peoples of Europe. Their attempts to minister in North Africa were opposed by the Muslims. The church strove to establish itself in Ethiopia and to guard the country against Arab invasion. Consequently the Christian ministry in Africa accomplished little until the nineteenth century.

A resurgence of spiritual life in Western Europe in the sixteenth century inspired interest in missions and brought missionary agencies into existence. In the fifteenth, sixteenth, and seventeenth centuries Christianity was planted on the fringes of Africa south of the Sahara. Protestant contacts with Africa attained a significant dimension during the latter part of the nineteenth century and produced a flowering forth of Christianity in sub-Saharan Africa in the twentieth century. The Roman Catholic Church was somewhat later in its missionary thrust in this part of Africa, but when it renewed its efforts, it sent a large staff into the ministry.

The Africans south of the Sahara readily accepted the Christian faith and spontaneously proclaimed it to their fellow-men. They assumed responsibility for the ministry of the church, integrating the Christian teaching in their life and culture. Indigenous churches grew out of the missionary efforts, and independent churches were established by individuals, attracting many adherents. Christian councils were formed in many countries. Some churches formed the Association of Evangelical Evangelicals of Africa and Madagascar and others formed the All-Africa Council of Churches (AACC) to establish fellowship among the churches and strengthen their common witness. The churches of Africa assumed their places in the world-wide Christian fellowship.

During the past decade Christian educators, pastors, and laymen have expressed the need of a brief record of the coming of Christianity to Africa. This study presents a brief history of the coming of the church and of its ministry in every country of Africa in order to enable the reader to attain some essential information concerning the church. It presents the concerns of the pioneers of the gospel ministry to bring the Christian faith to the people; the acts of God in the midst of the people of Africa, bringing them, by His divine grace, into fellowship with Himself; and the development of indigenous churches, which are assuming their place in the universal Christian brotherhood.

Although the dedication of Christians to proclaim the gospel to the people of Africa should not be underestimated, the cultural and sociological factors of the African people has significantly influenced the growth of the church. The encounter of the African culture with the Christian revelation and the acceptance of this revelation was very important in the development of the church. The emergence of the church in the African setting is a fascinating story. God is working a miracle of grace in the lives of multitudes in Africa. The church is rapidly being established. The coming of Christianity to Africa has meaning and purpose within God's sovereign redemptive revelation.

1

Christianity in North Africa: A Promising Beginning

North Africa played a prominent role in the early civilizations of the world. The records of Narmer-Menes indicate the existence of the Egyptian civilization at the time of the Sumerians in Babylon and their contribution to the civilization of their day. From the second millennium B.C., Egypt had intimate ties with Palestine and Syria. Throughout the centuries Egypt has been in constant contact with the civilizations of the Middle East and Europe.

The Israelites lived in the land of Goshen in Egypt for nearly four centuries. During Alexander the Great's reign the city of Alexandria gained importance, becoming a significant center of commerce. Many Jews made it their home, building synagogues in it and introducing the worship of Jehovah and the instruction of the Torah to the people. The prominence of the Jewish faith and teaching in Alexandria led to the translation of the Septuagint (LXX) in that city. The Septuagint greatly promoted the diffusion of the teachings of the Old Testament among the Greek-speaking peoples, including those of North Africa. The teaching of the Old Testament in the Greek in synagogues of the cities of Egypt, especially Alexandria, prepared the people for the coming of Christianity.

EARLY BEGINNINGS

Egypt

It is certain that the gospel came to Egypt very early, particularly to Alexandria; but it is not known when the earliest church came into existence. The constant contact with Palestine, the flight of Joseph and Mary with the young child (Matt. 2:13-15), and the journey of the Ethiopian to Jerusalem by way of Egypt would tend to indicate that the gospel came to Egypt during the early years of the church.

Eusebius accepted a tradition of his day that John Mark was an active missionary in Egypt and established churches in the city of Alexandria. Historians, however, have not been able to verify this report. Apollos, an Alexandrian Christian, came to Ephesus as a missionary preacher before Paul carried out his ministry in that city (Acts 18:24ff.). Christians were reported in Alexandria during the reign of Hadrian (c. 125). The famous catechetical school of Alexandria was founded by Pantaenus about 180. Clement succeeded him, and Origen succeeded Clement.

Reliable records concerning the existence of Christianity in Egypt date to the episcopate of Demetrius of Alexandria (A.D. 189-232) The church was then established and the bishop of Alexandria seems to have been at its head. Demetrius apparently appointed three other bishops and the number increased to twenty-three under his successor,[1] indicating the expansion of the church during this time.

North Africa

Although the records of the entrance of Christianity in Africa are not complete, it is evident that the gospel came very early to northern West Africa. Simon of Cyrene carried the cross of Jesus Christ; it is thought that he became a believer, for his sons Alexander and Rufus are among the people known to those to whom the Gospel according to Mark was written (Mark 15:21; Rom. 16:13). Cyrenians are listed among the people present at Jerusalem when God's revelation on the Day of Pentecost took place (Acts 2:10). Cyrenians and Cyprians brought the gospel to Antioch; so it appears that the gospel had been planted in Cyrene (Acts 11:20). The records of the development of the church in this area have not been preserved. However, according to Synesius' letters there were half a dozen bishoprics in the area in 410.

The Berber tribes were the earliest inhabitants of the provinces of North Africa. Later, during the height of their trade and expansion, Phoenicians settled at strategic places especially at Carthage. There has been speculation concerning the extent of the contact Carthage maintained with the people of the West African coast. Carthage was a prominent city of the early civilizations. The Punic Wars (264-146 B.C.) reveal the stage of development and the strength of Carthage. During the centuries some Jewish communities also appeared. The Roman element of the population came as a result of the occupations. It consisted mainly of discharged soldiers who remained in Africa when their services were terminated. They became small landowners and the standard-bearers of the Roman civilization.

Agriculture was the main occupation of this region. Africa supplied Italy with much wheat, oil, wine, fruit, and vegetables. The Roman population was interested in expanding the agricultural area to increase the supply of agricultural products. The expansion of the agricultural area was opposed by the nomadic tribes living on the less fertile soils toward the interior, and it became necessary to guard against conflict between the two communities.

Lybian, Punic, and Latin religious elements were present in the population of this region. The Berbers still venerated the spirits of natural objects on which life depended. To these the Phoenicians added their deities. Later the Romans introduced the gods of the Roman pantheon. North Africa witnessed a significant development in material culture during the Roman period and became effectively Romanized.

Little is known of the beginning of Christian church and its early growth until the end of the second century. The earliest reliable records reveal a well-established church, whose leaders called upon the emperors to consider the validity of their faith and provide tolerance for it. Justin Martyr, the philosopher from Asia Minor, spent some time in North Africa. Dressed in his philosopher's cloak, he argued for the reasonableness of the Christian faith according to philosophic thought. From North Africa, he went to Rome where he died a martyr's death in 166. Tertullian (born c. 155), an apologist of the Christian faith, presented his apology to the emperor, hoping to promote a greater understanding of the Christian faith.[2]

As commerce with Rome was quite well established and there was a flow of emigrants between Rome and Carthage, Christianity likely came to North Africa from Rome.[3] The names of early Christians indicate that they probably were servants who had been taught by their masters. The martyrdom of twelve Christians in A.D. 180 reveals that they were of the Romanized population of Numidia. This indicates the spread of the Christian faith among the people of North Africa toward the end of the second century.

Nubia

Early Egyptian voyages were made down the east coast to Somaliland in the neighborhood of Cape Guardafui and beyond. These voyages were made quite regularly during the Greek and Roman periods. Egyptian influence extended to various degrees south during its early history, and Egypt's contacts and trade relations extended beyond its sphere of political influence. Trade along the Nile River was an important factor in Egypt's history.[4]

The dramatic conversion of the Ethiopian, "a minister of Candace, the queen of the Ethiopians" (Acts 8:27 RSV), figures in the planting of Christianity in North Africa. This Ethiopian probably did not come from the Abyssinia of today, but rather from a kingdom that was then located on the Nile River and had Meroe as its capital. Certain monuments discovered at Meroe, Naga, and Musswourat indicate the Roman influence on the architecture of these cities.[5] Candace was a title borne by the queen-mother, who was the effective authority in the country. The story of the Ethiopian leads us to believe that he was a literate proselyte who went to Jerusalem to worship at the temple. His reading in the Septuagint implied that the teaching of the Old Testament had reached the southern kingdom by means of the Jews who had migrated along the Nile. We would like to think of him as a herald of the Good News to his people, but we have no reliable evidence of this. Several centuries later, Jewish communities existed in this region and also farther south, but no records concerning a Christian community have been discovered.

DEVELOPMENTS IN EGYPT (100-640)

Christianity won its first adherents among the God-fearing people of Alexandria. As it spread in Egypt, it came into contact with people of cultural differences. On the one hand the Greek-speaking population of the Delta was acquainted with the Septuagint. They were influenced by Greek philosophy and Platonic ideals. In harmony with the interest for learning, the catechetical school of Alexandria offered theological instruction to Christians and prepared them to confront the population with the Christian message. This missionary endeavor was mostly directed toward them and less to win the population of the interior.

The language and cultural differences between the people of the Delta and those of the interior hindered the natural diffusion of the gospel among the people of Middle and Upper Egypt, where the Coptic language, the dominion of the priests of the popular Egyptian religion, and the Old Egyptian religion stood in the way. However, the persecution of the Christians in Thebias under the Emperor Septimius Severus, following his edict of A.D. 202 forbidding conversions to Christianity and Judaism, indicates that Christianity had advanced into Upper Egypt as early as the latter part of the second century.[6] The persecution was largely confined to Egypt and North Africa. Dispersion through persecution led to further expansion of the church. The Christians fled to the south to the cataract regions and to the west into Libya, proclaiming the gospel to the people. The church soon became rooted in the native populations; the Coptic language was employed and the church took on a national character.

The early Gnostics presented the Christian faith to the intelligentsia of Alexandria as a superior philosophy giving a more coherent explanation to the universe than the Oriental religions. This teaching was widespread in Alexandria during the first part of the second century. Basilide, Valentin, and Carpocrate were prominent leaders of the movement.

Educational Pattern

In order to strengthen the church and to combat the false teaching of the Gnostics, Christian instruction was emphasized. This led to the establishment of the catechetical school of Alexandria, which played a significant role in the life of the church. Pantaenus founded the school about A.D. 180. Clement of Alexandria succeeded him and gave able leadership to the school as well as rendering service in the church. He was also a gifted writer. His "Exortation to the Heathen" is an apologetic treatise; his "Instructor" is the first treatise on Christian conduct and presents valuable information on the customs of the age; and his "Stromata" is a collection of profound thoughts on religion and theology.

Origen continued Clement's work when the latter was driven from the city by the persecution in 203. Even though his father became a martyr for the faith, Origen remained a courageous believer. His scholarly activities, in which he presents a theological system, have been very valuable for the church throughout the

centuries. Origen devoted much attention to biblical textual criticism and exegesis. Among his productions are the *Hexapala*,
giving the Hebrew and four parallel Greek translations of the Old
Testament; a series of valuable commentaries; *De Principiis*, a
systematic presentation of Christianity, which had a large influence on the Greek dogmatic thinking; and *Against Celsus*, which
was the keenest and most convincing defense of the Christian faith
written during the early period of the church.[7] Origen's thoughts
and methods completed the process that had long been interpret-
ing Christian truths in terms of Hellenistic thinking and gave the
Christian system of thought the fullest scientific standing. He
spent the last years of his life in Caesarea, teaching, writing, and
preaching. He died probably in 251 as a result of suffering during
the persecution under Decius.

Persecution and Growth

The church went through a number of persecutions. During the
persecution under Septimius Severus in 202, Clement and many
other Christians were forced into exile, whereas Origen's father
and others became martyrs of the faith. Decius' edicts against
Christianity (250-251) caused many Christians to compromise by
purchasing statements attesting that they had burned incense in
compliance with the Roman religion; thereby they secured safety
from persecutions. When the persecution was over, the more
pious members of the church regarded those who had denied their
faith with disdain. This attitude caused considerable tension in the
church. Dionysius, bishop of Alexandria, and others were exiled to
Libya in 250 and again in 258 under Valerian. Dionysius courageously witnessed to his faith and was instrumental in planting the
church in Libya. The basic cause for the persecution seems to
have been a pestilence that drove the terrified people to the altar of
the gods and led to hysteria against Christians. The latter, because
of their neglect of the gods, were singled out and commanded to do
homage to the old gods of the empire. The persecutions attempted
to deprive the church of its leadership and thereby cause the
termination of the ministry of the church.

The last and most severe persecution of the church came in 303
during Diocletion's reign, having been instigated by his son-in-law
Maximin Daia. The persecution was intensified in 311. After Maximin's death the persecution was stopped, and two years later (313)

Constantine issued the Edict of Milan, granting freedom of worship to Christians.

Monastic Emergence

Although ascetic tendencies have been present in the church from its beginning, monasticism was unknown in the first two centuries of the Christian era. From the first days of the church, intimate fellowship with the Lord was recommended and fasting was an accepted discipline. It became customary for widows who did not remarry to devote themselves to the service of the church. Celibacy was early held in esteem within the church, many basing their thinking on 1 Corinthians 7. Men like Origen who were ascetics had a profound influence on many prominent members of the church in Egypt.

During the third century, asceticism began to influence many church members. Ascetic ideals grew in the church. Men and women, without leaving their homes, were practicing asceticism. The persecutions forced Christians to seek refuge in unfrequented places. There in isolation they were able to worship God in peace and seek intimate fellowship with Him. This furthered the monastic spirit.

As a result of persecution, the gospel was proclaimed in new regions and many people came into the church. As the church grew, the teaching and perfecting of the believers was not fully accomplished. Since the condition in the church did not meet the ideals of the pious, they moved toward a more ascetic life.

Another factor in the development of monasticism was the ascetics' concept of the world. To them, the world was filled with sights that offended Christian morality. From such influences the ascetics desired to flee. Some people wanted to be free from the burden of civic obligations. Political and economic disorders may have bred a sense of insecurity. Thus, as the cities grew larger the tendency to escape the noise, crowds, and moral corruption by seeking the isolation of the countryside also increased.

Toward the close of the third century, as the church was established, its public worship became more formal and rigid. This led to a desire for a freer and a more personal approach to God. The geography and climate of Egypt favored the ascetic life, whether solitary or in community. The fertile valley of the Nile was flanked on either side by a desert void of population, where rain was infrequent; there the ascetic could live alone with little shelter. Thus, motivated by these factors, Christian hermits by the end of the third century were scattered over the isolated areas of Egypt. Monasticism began as a laymen's movement in search of a more pious life.

Although Paul of Thebes was probably the first monk, Anthony is considered the founder of Christian monasticism. He was born in Koma, in central Egypt, about 250. Impressed with Christ's message to the rich young man, he gave up his possessions as a young man and took up the ascetic life outside his native village. He worked with his hands, spending part of the return for food and giving the rest to the needy. He spent much time in prayer and meditation and visited other like-minded persons, learning more about the perfect ascetic life of love, kindness, self-denial, and endurance. Some fifteen years later he withdrew to a ruined fort on a mountain and there lived alone for nearly twenty years. He soon had many imitators who built cells for themselves in the mountains and emulated him in the solitary life.

Other monks preferred a modification of the hermit's way of life. These monks had individual dwellings sufficiently near one another to make fellowship possible. The largest of these groups were in the deserts of Nitria and Scetis. These monks, whether living alone or in groups, were at their own discretion in the degree of self-denial and the form of worship that they practiced.

The modified form of hermit life was not pleasing to the monks who desired a more regulated life and a closer fellowship with other monks. Pachomius (c. 292-346), a younger contemporary of Anthony, came to their assistance. Having observed the kindness of Christians, he became a believer and adopted the hermit life. However, he was dissatisfied with its irregularites; so he established a monastery at Tabennisi in southern Egypt about 315-320.[8] It became so popular that several others were established. Pachomius ruled over them from a central monastery. This gave rise to the third type of monasticism, the cenobitic, in which rules were drawn up by which the life of inmates was regulated. The monks were assigned to work, had regular hours for worship and rest, wore similar dress, and lived in cells close to one another. They lived together in a closely regulated community. Before his death, Pachomius appointed a successor. At his death in 346 there were ten monasteries in Egypt.

In conjunction with his sister Mary, who directed it, Pachomius established a convent for women. This practice spread to other parts of Christendom and played a major role in the spread of Christianity in Europe and Asia Minor.

Monasticism quickly spread to Asia Minor and later to Europe. Rules were gradually developed for the operation of the community. By the end of the fourth century monasticism was stabilized and established as a system of religious life. Each monastery was surrounded by an enclosure. Within this enclosure were the houses in which the monks lived. Every monk had his private room. Every house had a common room for meetings. The monasteries were enlarged during the Middle Ages, especially in Europe, and included a compound with a church, a refectory, a library, a kitchen, a bakery, various workshops, and an infirmary.[9] The monastic system provided for meditations, study, and work. Extreme asceticism was discouraged. Strict obedience to the superiors was required of all. Chastity and poverty were compulsory. Monasticism greatly appealed to the people. By the time of the death of Pachomius, some three thousand monks had joined the system, and this number increased to five thousand by the end of the fourth century. Monasticism contributed to the spread of the gospel and to the ministry of the Christian church in North Africa.

Church Extension via the Patriarchate

The patriarchs of Alexandria played a significant role in the universal church during the period beginning in 313, when Constantine, by the Edict of Milan, declared religious liberty for the entire Roman Empire, until 451, when Dioscurus was deposed for having accepted the Monophysite doctrine. During the fourth century the church in Egypt made considerable progress through the rapid establishment of monasticism and the faithful ministry of the monks. The Scriptures were translated into the Coptic language, services were conducted in the same, and an indigenous Coptic Church, which took its place in the history of the church of the first centuries, was established.

The patriarchate of Alexandria gained importance because of its role in relation to Arius and Nestorious. The unity of the church was threatened by the teaching of Arius of Alexandria. Through the teaching of Tertullian and Novatian, the church in the West had reached practical unanimity regarding the unity of substance between Christ and the Father. However, this was not the case in the East. Origen had given the church the most systematic presentation of theological thought; however, he had not presented the nature of Christ as clearly as Tertullian had done, and this caused some uncertainty in the church on this important matter of faith.

The controversy began when Arius, a presbyter in charge of the church known as Baucalis at Alexandria, began to dispute with his bishop, Alexander, concerning the nature of Christ. Arius maintained that Christ was neither fully God nor fully man. He was like God but not of the same substance as God. Bishop Alexander, however, maintained that the Son was eternal, like in essence to the Father. Arius did not heed the bishop's warning to correct his teaching, but defended his position. Consequently, Alexander called a regional synod at Alexandria in 320 or 321. The synod condemned the teaching of Arius and his sympathizers. Arius appealed to Eusebius of Nicomedia and soon found a refuge with him. Alexander wrote widely to fellow bishops explaining the false teaching of his presbyter. The church in the eastern part of the empire was in turmoil.

Constantine was concerned for the unity of the empire and counted on the church to serve as a unifying factor. The turmoil in the church, which threatened the unity of the church, was also a threat to the unity of the empire. Therefore, Constantine was anxious to have the matter settled. He sent his ecclesiastical advisor, Bishop Hosius of Cordova, to Alexandria with an imperial letter advising that the dispute be settled. The attempt failed. Consequently, Constantine called a general council of the church to be held at Nicaea in 325; to this he summoned all the bishops of the church in the entire empire, there being 318 in number. They traveled and were lodged at the expense of the state. The church was no longer being persecuted, nor was it maintaining its full freedom to serve under the lordship of Christ.

The Emperor himself opened the church council and pleaded for the unity of the church. But the task to establish the unity was larger than he had expected. A vigorous and difficult debate ensued between the Arians, led by Eusebius of Nicomedia, and the supporters of the Nicene faith, led by Athanasius, a deacon of the church of Alexandria and the private secretary of Bishop Alexander. A third party, led by Eusebius of Caesarea, was not well informed about the question at stake.

The church was confronted with the task of carefully and critically defining and presenting its faith. Early in the deliberations of the council, the Arians presented a creed, which was rejected. Eusebius of Caesarea offered the creed of his church, a confession dating from before the controversy. It was amended to clearly state that the Son was "begotten, not made" and "of one essence with the Father." Athanasius was the strong supporter of the Nicene Creed. He illustrated the relationship of the Son to the Father by using the analogy of the rays of the sun. The rays present the light and consequently the sun, but they cannot be distinguished from the sun. Similarly, in his opinion, the Son manifested the Father, but was of the same essence and one with the Father. Athanasius used the Greek term *homoousion*. This term had been used in the West, and the thought was not altogether strange. The debate in the council was intense, but the term *homoousion* was accepted by the majority of the representatives.

Constantine was more concerned about the unity of the church than about theological exactness. Under his influence, all but two bishops and Arius signed the Nicene Creed. The three were banished. The church had now adopted a universally recognized creed. The unity of the church was, however, more apparent than real. The Arian reaction created serious tensions that greatly impaired the effectiveness of the church's ministry and marred its testimony.

Eusebius of Nicomedia and his Arian sympathizers tried to reassert the Arian teaching and to restore Arius to his position. Eusebius won considerable favor with Constantine and used his influence in favor of Arius. Athanasius, the champion of Nicaea, became bishop of Alexandria after the death of Alexander in 328. Eusebius considered Athanasius the real enemy. He tried to secure the discomfiture of Athanasius and the restoration of Arius. Arius, having returned from banishment, presented a carefully written creed to Constantine. Constantine seemed satisfied with Arius's attitude and asked Athanasius to restore him to his position in the church at Alexandria. When Athanasius refused to comply, Constantine was displeased with his action; in 335 Constantine, banished Athanasius from Alexandria.

Arius died in 336, but the struggle continued until the death of Athanasius in 373. Some of the sons of Constantine supported the Nicene Creed, while others supported the Arian doctrine. Consequently, Athanasius was banished five times, but finally died with honor at Alexandria in 373, and the Nicene Creed was maintained by the church. The church continued to reconsider its faith. At the Second General Council at Constantinople in 381, further precisions were added to the Nicene Creed, stating that there was one divine essence, which manifests itself in three persons.

Three strong bishops in turn served Alexandria after Athanasius from 385 to 451. Theophilus, Cyril, and Dioscurus brought the episcopal seat into international recognition and, through Dioscurus's wrong judgment and unethical behavior, it again lost its ecumenical influence.

In 391 Theophilus carried out Emperor Theodosius's (379-395) edict to close all the pagan temples, which were still quite numerous and influential in Old Egypt[10] and were supported by the Neoplatonic philosophy. This school of thought, however, continued until 529 when it was terminated by the order of Justinian. Many statues and temples were torn down throughout the country. This apparent victory of Christianity over paganism enhanced the prestige of the patriarch of Alexandria.

Cyril, Theophilus's nephew, succeeded him in 411. He was anxious to exert his influence in ecumenical relations as well as in the ministry of the church in Egypt. When the weakness of the teaching of Nestorius, bishop of Constantinople, came to light, Cyril vigorously opposed him. He placed the emphasis on the divine nature of Christ. Yet he maintained that in the interchange between the divine and the human natures each is a complete nature, and the two natures form one personality, which is divine. Thus he emphasized the divine over the human nature in Christ.

An ancient designation of Mary, the mother of Jesus, was "Mother of God." This expression had been freely used in the East, except for the representatives of the school of Antioch, who were concerned about the implication and used it very carefully. Nestorius came to Constantinople from Antioch and during his ministry there became disturbed about the implications of the term. He advocated that the Greek term *Christokos*, "Mother of Christ," be used, for that which "is born of the flesh is flesh." In preaching against the expression "Mother of God," he had touched the rising religious reverence for the Virgin Mary. Opposition soon emerged. Cyril saw the opportunity to humiliate his rival. An exchange of critical letters between Cyril and Nestorius followed. Cyril then attacked the patriarch of Constantinople openly.

One of the most repulsive contests in the history of the Christian church ensued. Cyril was motivated by personal ambition and jealousy. He appealed to the emperor and empress and to the bishop of Rome, Celestine I. The empire was soon involved in the dispute. A general council met at Ephesus in 431. The two parties vigorously opposed each other. John of Antioch and the bishops of Asia Minor supported Nestorius. The emperor, Theodosius II, was at a loss as to what to do. Nestorius retired to a monastery. Theodosius imprisoned Cyril and Memnon, bishop of Ephesus, as troublemakers, but they were soon allowed to return to their sees. In 433 Cyril signed the creed drawn up by John, bishop of Antioch. Although Nestorius withdrew from public ministry, his supporters found much support in Syria and Persia.

In Egypt, Cyril was considered the victor of the dispute, and he enhanced his authority through it. The monks supported his cause and continued to struggle against the ancient religions of Egypt. Cyril died in 444 and was succeeded by Dioscurus, a person of less intellectual acumen and religious motive, but very ambitious to advance the authority of the Alexandrian see. Like his predecessor, he tried to increase his prestige through ecumenical relations. The occasion presented itself when the teaching of Eutyches, an abbot near Constantinople, was censored. Eusebius of Dorylaeum exposed his incorrect teaching that Christ had two natures before the Incarnation, but after the Incarnation he had only one nature. Eutyches was summoned before the regional council at Constantinople.

Another ecumenical dispute began. Dioscurus came to Eutyches' defense. But Leo of Rome came to Flavian's support, presenting his famous *Tome* of 449. At the stormy meeting of the general council at Ephesus in 449, Dioscurus refused to permit the reading of Leo's tome and succeeded in condemning Flavian. Flavian died shortly after the meeting. However, Leo denounced the procedures of the meeting. Another meeting was convened at Chalcedon in 451. Dioscurus was deposed and sent into exile; he died in exile three years later. Through this incident the prestige of the see of Alexandria was greatly reduced. The Monophysite doctrine, which emphasized the divine nature of Christ over against His human nature, was condemned, and Leo's tome became the basis for the Chalcedonian creed of 451.

Although the Fourth Ecumenical Council accepted the creed, the opponents to Chalcedon continued to maintain and propagate their concept of the nature of Christ. The churches of Syria and Egypt were greatly influenced by the Monophysite doctrine. A lengthy struggle took place in the Egyptian church, producing two factions in the church. As time passed, partly because the Chalcedonian faith was supported by the West and the Monophysite faith was considered Egyptian, the latter gained the majority of the Egyptian Christians and eventually became the faith of the churches of Egypt and Ethiopia.

Emperor Justinian (527-565) realized that the schism could inspire further division in the church and the empire, so he made a strong attempt to bring about a reconciliation, but he was unable to do so. Other emperors had no more success, and the division remained. The idea of the supremacy of the divine nature of Christ may have been influenced by the mystic tendencies and the concept of judgment that the Egyptians had attained through the worship of Osiris. Yet the reason for the rejection of the Chalcedonian faith by the Egyptian church was probably more cultural than doctrinal. Dioscurus's banishment destroyed the hope for the Egyptian people to regain a significant recognition as a people among the nations.[11]

From the time of the Council of Chalcedon in 451 until the Arab conquest in 639, the religious controversies continued almost constantly. For some time both the orthodox and the Monophysite believers in the church wanted to control the patriarchate of Alexandria. The controversies between the Greek and the Egyptian elements continued and sometimes broke into riots. But the Egyptian element continued to gain influence and support until it became predominant. It was compelled to face the onslaught of Islam when it came.

DEVELOPMENTS IN NORTH AFRICA (100-640)

Its Earlier Strength Through Dynamic Leaders

Tertullian—Apologetic Undergirding. North Africa, as well as Egypt, has given significant leaders to the church. Tertullian, born about 155 to pagan parents in Carthage, became one of the most remarkable personalities of the ancient church. Beginning about 197, he gave leadership to the church in Carthage and North Africa. He studied law and practiced his profession in Rome. He also possessed a wide knowledge of philosophy and history and devoted himself to the study of Christian literature. He was converted in 195 and returned to Carthage, where he devoted himself to the ministry of the church until about 222-225.[12] A talented polemicist, he formulated with precision the theological conceptions that had been vaguely apprehended and presented by the church. He is sometimes considered the father of Latin theology.[13] For him Christianity was primarily knowledge of God and was not to be compared with the existing philosophical systems. His presentation of the Christian faith, with a call to a rigorous moral application, and his defense of the faith greatly contributed to the establishment of Christianity in North Africa despite the persecution by Septimius Severus.[14] He wrote to encourage the Christians and to uphold Christianity in the face of its opponents. Pleading for it against the cruelties of the proconsul, he indicated that the blood of the martyrs is the seed of the church and that the Christians were in every town, and the more the government persecuted them, the more numerous they became. The church, which counted from seventy to ninety bishoprics at the time of the demise of Tertullian at about 220, counted some 150 bishoprics at the beginning of the fourth century.[15]

The church in North Africa passed through a number of persecutions during the time of its establishment from 180 until Constantine proclaimed the Edict of Milan in 313.[16] In 202, during the ministry of Tertullian, Septimius Severus persecuted the church. Among those who suffered martyrdom was a young lady of the aristocracy, Perpetua, and five catechumens from Carthage. Perpetua's father was greatly disturbed to learn that his daughter had accepted the Christian faith and that she would bring disgrace upon him by becoming a martyr. He begged her to renounce her faith. But in spite of his pleading, she remained true to her faith and, together with the others, courageously faced death in the arena. The serenity and peace they manifested was a powerful witness to the reality of the Christian faith and led others to accept it. Under Caracalla (211-217) a persecution again raged in North Africa. Alexander Severus (222-235) was favorable to the church.

Chapels were constructed during his reign and Bibles were placed in some of them. From 235 to 248 the policy for or against the church was largely determined by the sentiments of the local officials. The laws, however, deprived the Christians of legal protection.

The celebration of the thousandth anniversary of the founding of Rome in 248 brought the ancient traditions and splendors to the memory of the people at a time when the empire was threatened by a barbarian attack. The cause of the sad state of affairs was attributed to the Christians' neglect of the Roman gods who had given Rome its splendor. Decius (249-251) issued an edict in 250 that initiated a universal and systematic persecution of Christians.

The Decian persecution was the worst trial that the universal church had experienced. The objectives were (1) to remove the leaders from the congregations by imprisonment, exile, or death, and (2) to compel the Christians by torture, imprisonment, and fear of death to sacrifice to the gods and burn incense before the image of the emperor as a testimony of their fidelity to him. Some Christians thought it a small matter to make obeisance to the gods and to the emperor in order to ward off the persecution. They burned incense or procured certificates indicating that they had worshiped. When the persecution was over, many of these people who had denied their faith requested to be readmitted into the fellowship of the church. Church leaders were divided on the question. Some readily readmitted them, whereas others were more hesitant and wanted to see evidence of sincerity. An influential party, led by Novatian, requested a sincere manifestation of repentance. When the church at Rome did not heed their request, they withdrew, and Novatian became the bishop of the new party. The Novatian party was supported by a large segment of the church in North Africa, and it soon formed a strong organization.[17]

Cyprian—Organic Unification. Cyprian was chosen bishop of the church at Carthage in 259. During the years he gave leadership to the church in North Africa, he was kind and sympathetic with the people in need; at the same time he showed high executive ability. After the Decian persecution, Novatian led a group in the church who placed strict conditions on readmitting the church members who had denied their faith. Cyprian led the party that maintained that these people, the *lapsi* ("lapsed") as they were

called, should be admitted to penance. The agitation of the Nova-
tians caused some tension in the church, but Cyprian's party won
the day.[18] Cyprian contributed greatly to the establishment of the
church—the communion of the saints, as the body of Christ in
which God's grace is offered to people through the proclamation of
the Word. Thus the church becomes the medium for salvation.
Through his presentation of the ministry of the church, Cyprian
strengthened both the role of the church and the role of the
bishops, who gave guidance to the church. It is necessary to
consider Cyprian's ministry in the light of the tension that existed
in the church because of the persecutions. A clear directive by the
church would reduce the danger of divisions.

During the persecution in 250, Cyprian was able to save his life
by withdrawing to a village in the neighborhood of Carthage.
Valerian (253-260) renewed the persecution with much severity in
258. Church services were forbidden and property was confiscated. The Christian leaders were to be executed, and the Christians disgraced and banished, and their property confiscated. The
church in North Africa was dispersed. Cyprian became a martyr of
the faith. The persecution was carried out to please the gods and
bring success in the war against Persia. But in 260 Valerian became the victim of the greatest disgrace to which a Roman emperor could be submitted by becoming a prisoner of the Persians,
having to serve the Persian general, and finally coming to a dis-
graceful death at the hands of the Persians. The defeat was a
tremendous shock to the Romans. They asked themselves whether
it had been caused by the displeasure of the Christians' God.
Valerian's son and successor, Gallienus (260-269), returned the
confiscated property and showed a degree of favor to the church.
The laws against Christianity were not repealed, but the church
ministered in peace until 303.

During the period of peace from 260-303, the church expanded,
reaching the people of the interior of Numibia and the
Mauritanias. The church was the strongest in the cities and in the
Latin-speaking portions of the population. The faith was most
strongly rooted in this element of the population, which was a
minority. The rich Christian literature of North Africa, which
influenced the Occident, came from this group. The Punic stock of
the population became Christian only in part. Only a small minority of the bishops seem to have been of Punic origin.[19] The conver-

sion of the Berber element of the population seems to have been even less profound. The Latin language was the vehicle for preaching, and the Scriptures were not translated into the language of the people. Consequently, the Punic and Berber populations became Christians only to the degree that they became Latinized. The fact that Christianity did not become thoroughly rooted in the indigenous population may in part be the reason why Christianity suffered a greater loss in North Africa than in Egypt when the Muslim invaders came to conquer.

Its Later Weakness Through Doctrinal Controversies

Neoplatonism. Several religious tendencies arose during this period. Neoplatonism was founded in Alexandria by Ammonius Saccas (c. 245) and was developed by Plotinus (205-270). Neoplatonism held that God was a simple, absolute, perfect existence from whom the lower existences come. The Nous, or mind, emanates from God. From the Nous the world-soul derives its being, and from it the individual souls derive their beings. Matter comes from world-soul. Salvation was in the rising of the soul in mystic contemplation to God. Neoplatonism had some influence on Christian theology, but it was not accepted by many people.[20]

Montanism. During the second century many Christians awaited the fulfillment of Christ's promise of the Comforter (John 15:26). Montanism presented the thought of the special dispensation of the Holy Spirit and of an early return of Christ. Although the early church maintained this idea, in about 156 Montanus deviated from the proclamation and indicated that he was the passive instrument through whom the Holy Spirit spoke. Two prophetesses, Prisca and Maximilla, soon joined him. They proclaimed that the heavenly Jerusalem would be established in Phrygia and called the believers to practice strict asceticism. Tertullian was influenced by this teaching in 207. Its influence was felt in Carthage until the time of Augustine. It appealed to a tendency present in the church that later expressed itself in monasticism.[21]

The church was confronted with the necessity to define its doctrine, since many Christians did not have a clear understanding of the doctrine of the person and work of Jesus Christ. The christological discussions seem to have had an indirect result on monasticism and gave rise to the Monarchians, who asserted the unity of God. They constituted two very unlike groups. One group's members maintained that Jesus was the Son of God by adoption and were called Dynamic Monarchians. The other group maintained that Christ was but a temporary form of manifestation of the one God, who revealed Himself as Father, Son, and Holy Spirit at different periods in His divine self-revelation to man. They are known as Modalistic Monarchians. The Modalistic Monarchians were more numerous than the Dynamic Monarchians in North Africa, for the people were concerned to confess the unity of God. Tertullian expounded the christological doctrine. Novation expounded Tertullian's teaching in the third century. The church expressed its faith in the Nicene Creed in 325.[22]

Manichaeism. Manichaeism, founded by Mani of Persia between 242 and 277, was based on the old Persian dualism of light and darkness, which they thought were eternally at war. They viewed the human body as basically a prison house of the realm of evil; in it a portion of the realm of light was confined. Salvation was the ascetic rejection of all that belongs to the realm of darkness. The members were of two classes: the perfect practiced full austerities, while the hearers accepted the teaching but did not rigorously apply it. Manichaeism spread rapidly through the empire, especially during the fourth and fifth centuries and became a strong rival of Christianity. Its influence became apparent time and again in the church during the Middle Ages. It was Donatism, however, that divided the church in North Africa during the fourth century.[23]

Donatism. The Roman Empire experienced a period of internal difficulties. In 284 Diocletian, a strong and able administrator, became emperor. He was determined to reorganize the administration of the empire and arranged for a government of four: two "Augustuses" of higher position, one in the East and one in the West; and two "Caesars," each of whom was to succeed the Augustus in his area upon the latter's death.

Diocletian did not oppose Christianity, but he was anxious for all people to participate in the well-being of the empire. He was not altogether pleased that the Christians, increasing rapidly in number, refrained to a certain degree from participation in politics. His son-in-law, Galerius, the Caesar of the eastern part of the empire, provoked him to persecute the Christians by indicating that they were undermining his empire. Diocletian did not conceive that a force like Christianity would remain neutral in the empire. Consequently he attempted to bring it into subjection to the empire with its religion. The persecution began in 303. In 304 all Christians were required to offer sacrifices. The severity of the persecution varied with the attitude of the magistrates. It was rigorously applied in North Africa, and many Christians sacrificed or purchased certificates attesting that they had sacrificed.

Thus when peace was again restored and the Christian faith was recognized by the Edict of Milan in 313, the church in North Africa more than ever before had to deal with the problem of restoring to fellowship those who had denied the faith during the persecution. Some Christians felt they should be readmitted upon the confession of repentance, whereas others thought they should be rebaptized. The difficulty became especially acute because some church leaders had purchased security from persecution, while many lay Christians had remained faithful and some had suffered martyrdom. The faithful Christians did not want to receive the sacraments at the hands of ministers who had denied their faith during the persecution by purchasing certificates attesting that they had worshiped the Roman gods. The faithful did also not wish to acknowledge the ordination of another person by such a minister.

The schism in North Africa arose out of a complicated affair. The strict religious group maintained that Caecilian, who became bishop of Carthage in 311, had received consecration at the hands of Felix, who was accused of having surrendered copies of the Scriptures to the civil authorities during the persecution. The strict group emphasized that Felix was not qualified to serve as bishop, therefore Caecilian's consecration was not valid.[24] The Donatist group of Carthage was supported by certain bishops. In 312 they consecrated another bishop, Majorinus, who was succeeded by Donatus in the same year, causing a schism in the church in North Africa.

Constantine wanted the church to be a vital unifying factor in the empire. He viewed disharmony and schism in the church with much disfavor and used his influence to bring about unity whenever possible. Under the Edict of Milan certain imperial benefactions were to be distributed to the "catholic," or universal, church of North Africa. When the Donatists received no share, they appealed to Constantine. This gave him an occasion to attempt a reconciliation of the two parties. During the next seven years five investigations of the matter took place. In 314 he summoned a synod of his portion of the empire to meet at Arles, in southern France, at public expense. The large church council declared the consecration at the hands of an unworthy cleric valid and rejected the contentions of the Donatists. It also recognized heretical baptism and approved the Roman date for Easter. The Donatists again appealed to the emperor, who once more decided against them in 316. When they refused to comply with his mediation, he closed their churches and banished their bishops. A period of suppression of the Donatists followed. The church in North Africa was in turmoil and suffered very much through it. Realizing that the suppression, rather than unifying the church, caused the Donatists to spread and become more numerous, Constantine inaugurated in 322 a period of tolerance that lasted until 347.

The civil servants, themselves Christians who were responsible for the region, attempted to bring about a reunion of the two factions of the church but were unsuccessful. They resorted to suppression for some time, but when no success came from it, they desisted.

The Emperor Constantine was disturbed by the rivalry of the two churches and by the activities of the rural population who, having lost their land, had formed themselves into bands called Circumcellions and had became a menace to the peace of the country. He sent troops to bring them to order. However, the troops did not effectively distinguish between the Donatists and Circumcellions and brutally suppressed both.

In 362 Emperor Julian lifted the ban on the exiled Donatists and allowed them to occupy their churches. The rivalry between the Donatists and the Catholics began again. The desire of the Donatists and the Catholics to outdo each other and gain the majority of the population caused them to intensify their activities. The result was that bishops who did not always have the highest qualifications were consecrated. Some priests changed their allegiance if in so doing they could become bishops of the other church.[25] At the time of Augustine, the Donatists outnumbered the Catholic members of the church.

Donatus died in 355 and was succeeded by Parmenianus, who

undertook the struggle against the Catholics with the help of the Circumcellions. In 363, the Kabyles revolted against the Roman government. The Donatists joined them in the struggle, taking on the image of a national church. The insurgents gained some territory, but jealousy and treason in their own ranks brought about their defeat.[26]

The Donatists survived the incident with relative strength and 310 bishops were present at the Council at Bagai in 394. However, Primianus, the successor of Parmenianus, did not possess the gifts to guide such a large movement and maintain its inspiration for sacrificial witness. The Donatists were approaching a period of decline.[27]

Augustine came to the scene at a time when the Donatists had largely spent their original inspiration, dedication, and vigor. They were less able to sustain Augustine's intellectual challenge than they had been able to support the attacks of force by the Roman military. Augustine (353-430), a native of Tagaste near Carthage, became one of the church's most outstanding leaders. He contributed greatly to Western Christianity, and through his efforts it attained its greatest height since apostolic times. His writings have significantly guided the church whenever it has taken note of them. He was basically the spiritual predecessor of much of the Reformation, standing between Paul and Luther in proclaiming salvation by grace through faith in Jesus Christ.

Augustine's father was not wealthy, but he gave his son an opportunity to get a good education. His mother, Monica, was a pious Christian who was much concerned about her son. Augustine pursued his studies in rhetoric in Carthage and became professor of rhetoric in that city. He was influenced by Manichaeism and followed them in his search for spiritual satisfaction for nine years. He finally acknowledged the moral and intellectual inadequacies of Manichaeism; disillusioned with it, he became a skeptic. He fathered a son, Adeodatus, by his faithful concubine. His mother prayed that he might come to true faith in Christ. Much against her will and without her knowledge of his intentions, Augustine went to Rome. However, he did not find contentment. In his search for peace of heart, he went to Milan to attend the services conducted by Ambrose, the bishop of Milan.[28]

While in Milan, Augustine experienced a crisis in his life. Through the preaching of Ambrose he came under an effective presentation of the gospel. At the same time he was exposed to Neoplatonism. The Bible was a new revelation to him. In it he saw the spiritual world as the real world and God as the source of all reality. Man finds fulfillment in knowing God. Evil is alienation from the will of God. In his *Confessions*, Augustine presents the agony of soul that he experienced. He realized that his conduct was short of his ideals. He was unable to improve his conduct. In his need he turned to the Scriptures and received peace of mind through faith in Christ. His life was transformed by a divine power for Christian living and for service. In 387 he was baptized, together with his son, Adeodatus, and his friend Alypius. With his mother, who had followed him to Milan, and his son, he set out to return to Tagaste. But his mother died while they were waiting for passage across the Mediterranean and he was obliged to bury her in Italy.[29]

While in Tagaste, Augustine delved into studies relating to the Christian faith and presented his discoveries in writing. His early writings opposed Manichaeism. After the death of his son, Adeodatus, Augustine went in deep grief to Hippo in early 391 with the intention of founding a monastery. But the church called him to the priesthood, and four years later he was ordained colleague-bishop to Valerius of Hippo. He founded a monastery and developed it into a training center for the clergy.

No sooner had Augustine returned to North Africa than he was deeply involved in the struggle with the Donatists.[30] He perceived an element of "works righteousness" in the Donatists' emphasis on the "pure life," and thus he forcefully presented the grace of God. His treatise on *Grace and Freedom of Choice* presents the greatness of the grace of God. He challenged the Donatists, declaring that they had both missed the love of God and broken the unity of the church by rejecting the Catholics and beginning a separate church. Augustine did not seem to consider that the Donatist branch of the church was an adaptation of Christianity to African thought and that the Donatist Church was in fact the national church of North Africa. Augustine's victory over the Donatist Church came through presenting it as heretical. The Donatists had no theologian capable of defending their cause against so able a person as Augustine. The theological debate was followed by a conference held at Carthage in 411 under the direction of an imperial commissioner. There were 286 Catholic and 279 Donatist bishops present.[31] The Donatists were ordered to return to the Catholic Church and an edict was pronounced to enforce the return. A violent suppression of the Donatists followed. The Catholic Church, together with the state, persecuted fellow Christians. This was one of the sad periods in the history of the church in North Africa. Churches were destroyed and the faithful were put to death or dispersed. By 413 the Donatist Church had virtually disappeared. The Catholics, however, profited little from this victory, for in 429 the Vandals, holding the Arian faith, crossed the Straits of Gibraltar and began the conquest of North Africa. Augustine wrote his *City of God* while the Vandals were marching against Carthage. He died on August 28, 430.

The tragedy of the divided church and of the government's intervention, forcing the Donatists to conform to imperial order, can only be seen in the light of history. The Donatist Church might have played a significant role in the establishment of Christianity in Africa. Christianity was established in Egypt because the Coptic Church became the national church. The Donatists appeared as the African national party and won many people from the rank and file of the Berber society. One of the reasons why they won the Berbers may have been their opposition to the Roman authority and the expression of racial and national independence. This stand may be observed in part, in their close relations with the Circumcellions. One may well ask what the future of the church might have been if the church had remained unified.

Pelagianism. The church was concerned to expound its faith not only regarding the person and work of Jesus Christ, but also regarding the efficacy of the work of Christ on man's relation to God. The Latin church was occupied with the anthropological and soteriological questions of sin and grace. The christological and anthropologico-soterio-logical concepts are vitally related, since Christ became man in order to redeem man. Pelagianism virtually denied man's need of redemption. The church generally agreed on the moral accountability of man, the effects of sin on man and his relation to God, and the necessity of redeeming grace; but it failed to clearly define the state of man because of sin and the relation of human freedom to divine grace in the work of regeneration.[32] On the one hand, the Greek fathers emphasized the indispensable cooperation of human freedom with divine grace in the work of redemption. On the other hand, the Latin fathers stressed the hereditary guilt of man and the sovereignty of God's grace, without denying the freedom and accountability of every person.

Pelagius, a monk from Britain, in 409 was at Rome where he wrote a commentary on the Epistles of Paul. Accompanied by Coelestius, he went to North Africa in 411, at the time Alaric's invasion threatened Rome. From there he proceeded to Palestine. He taught that every man is created with perfect freedom to choose between good and evil; that sin is purely a matter of will; that each soul is created pure and has the freedom to do good or evil;[33] that unbaptized children are saved[34] and therefore the practice of infant baptism is unnecessary; and that, through divine grace, which is with every person, and by choosing the good, there have been sinless people even before Christ.

Augustine, in contrast, taught that God created man faultless and with the free will to choose good or evil. But Adam sinned and, through Adam's original sin, his limitations to choose good have been passed on to his posterity and all need salvation. Through baptism the guilt of this original sin is removed, but not sin itself, and man needs the divine grace to enable him to will the good.

Augustine opposed Pelagianism at the synods and through his writings. He exposed its errors and presented his views on the biblical teachings concerning the effects of Adam's sin on his posterity and the efficacy of the redemptive work of Christ for those who believe. Through the influence of Augustine and his friends, two synods were held in North Africa in 416 in order to expose the errors of Pelagius. They condemned the Pelagian teaching and appealed to Innocent I of Rome (402-417) to confirm their judgment. Another synod was held at Carthage in 418 affirming their earlier judgment. Through Augustine's clear and forceful presentations, Pelagianism was rejected by the Western church.[35]

Although Augustine's teaching was basically maintained by the church, his contemporaries were not ready to accept his strong emphasis on the inner Christian life, with less emphasis on the external ceremonies. This attitude gave rise to Semi-Pelagianism, an attempt to reconcile the systems of Pelagius and Augustine. This remained a mechanical and abitrary combination instead of becoming an inward, organic coalescence. It did not really satisfy either party. It appealed, however, to the legalistic and ascetic piety of the Middle Ages.[36]

Its Encounter With External Peoples

Evidently, Christianity did not penetrate North Africa beyond the Roman frontier. In Romanized Africa, Christianity witnessed the greatest success among the Roman and the Romanized population, which was a small and wealthy segment. It reached many of the Punic inhabitants, but this was also only a small part of the entire population. It won only a few of the Berber people, and this was chiefly accomplished by the Donatists. When they were suppressed, the church virtually lost contact with the indigenous element of the population.

Another factor that hindered Christianity from taking strong roots in Africa was the use of Latin. Instead of the language of the people, Latin was used in the services and in the preparation of literature. The Bible was translated into Latin but was not made available in Punic or in the Berber language. Punic was used in preaching, but few priests were fluent in it.[37] Consequently Christianity basically reached the Roman and Punic elements of the population and did not become the religion of the indigenous people. The Berbers won by the Donatists belonged to areas such as Numidia. Thus, as we shall note later, when the Muslims struck and the Roman and Romanized population fled from North Africa, the church was not ready to meet the long and difficult suppression.

Vandals (430-534). North Africa was divided when the Vandals appeared. The Circumcellions were displeased with the Roman government and opposed it. After more than a century of division, the Catholics, with the help of the state, had just crushed the Donatists, bringing the religious life in North Africa to a low ebb. The Barbarian invasions had destroyed the power of the Roman Empire in Europe. Consequently it was unable to defend its interests in North Africa. The Vandals, under Genseric, crossed the Straits of Gibraltar in 429 and settled in Mauretania. By a treaty in 435 the Roman Empire recognized the settlement of the Vandals. Then, by a move that surprised the empire, the Vandals took Carthage in 439. In 442 the Roman emperor recognized Genseric as an independent ruler. The Vandal kingdom in Africa survived until Emperor Justinian of Byzance tried to reestablish the Roman Empire and sent his able commander Belisarius against North Africa. Belisarius took it for the Byzantine Empire in 533; however, after Justinian, the Byzantine Empire declined and the rule in North Africa came to an end.

The Vandals were Arian Christians, as were most of the barbarians who invaded Europe during the fifth century. Some of the Vandal kings were ardent Arians and imposed their faith on the people. Genseric established an Arian church in Carthage. It was dependent on the king, who appointed the bishops and authorized the synods. Genseric dispossessed the Catholic priests and entrusted the churches and church properties to the Arians.[38] The Vandal language was used for church services, whereas the Latin was retained for commerce and diplomatic transactions.

Genseric had political ambitions. In 455 he took Rome, and this virtually terminated the existence of the Roman Empire in the West. The Vandals took the important cities in North Africa in 475. Genseric basically occupied himself with Tunisia and gave little attention to the interior of the country. His attention was directed toward the Mediterranean, where his fleet exercised much control. The mountain people established several kingdoms and declared their independence. In 476 Emperor Zenon the Isaurien of Constantinople recognized Genseric's authority over Corse, Sardinia, Sicily, and the Beleares. Being master of Carthage and Rome and of the islands of the Mediterranean, he was therefore master of the western part of the Mediterranean. He was at the height of his power when he died in 477.

Huneric (477-484), the successor of Genseric, was an ardent Arian and soon began to persecute the Catholics. Some fled to Sicily, while others fled to the interior of the country and disappeared among the Berbers or in the desert regions. The services were conducted in the Vandal language, basically by Vandal priests. Once again Christianity was not made an integral part of the indigenous culture and there was no significant outreach to the Berber population.

Gunthamund (484-496) relaxed the persecution. Thrasamund (496-523) was a cultivated and liberal king, who offered certain rights to all citizens. The Vandal empire, however, was losing its vigor. In 520 the nomads' force from Tripoli, led by Cabaon and mounted on camels, defeated the Vandal army. Ten years later the Vandals were again defeated. Hilderic was deposed by his army, and Gelimer assumed the authority.[39] Both religiously and politically, North Africa was a divided country.

Byzantines (534-647). Justinian, the emperor of the Byzantine Empire (527-565), wanted to restore the Roman Empire to its greatness of previous centuries. Having signed a peace treaty with the Persians in 532, he moved against the Vandals in North Africa. His general, Belisarius, defeated Gelimer's army at Tricamarum in 533 and then took Carthage. He proceeded to conquer the islands of the Mediterranean, the positions of importance on the coast of Spain, and finally also several positions in Italy.[40]

Justinian decreed the restoration of all church buildings and church property and recognized the bishop of Carthage as metropolitan of the independent diocese. The Arians, Donatists, Jews, and pagans were subjected to a new rule. But Justinian thought of the church as an arm of the state; in propagating the Christian faith, the church was strengthening the imperial power. The emperors of Byzance have always had a large influence on the church, and this was especially the case with Justinian. He put forth considerable effort to bring all people of the empire under the influence of the Christian faith. He requested that the African chiefs and people be encouraged to accept the Christian faith and bestowed honorific titles on the chiefs who became Christian.[41] The church succeeded in bringing a number of Berber peoples under the influence of Christianity. A renaissance of Donatism occurred, especially in the regions occupied by the Byzantine army. This was, in part, a nationalistic reaction against the Byzantine occupation. It was also true that some of the Catholics of the cities became disillusioned with life in the church and the practice of simony and therefore joined the Donatists. These circumstances, however, did not cause the church to become thoroughly rooted in the North African society.

The population did not want to submit to the new foreign rule. No sooner had Belisarius returned to Constantinople, following his victory at Carthage, than the people of the southern part of Tunisia and of Numidia revolted. The revolt was put down by Solomon. The Catholic Church criticized the government officials for their greedy treatment of the people, thereby causing dissatisfaction. In 545 another revolt was led by Antalas of Tunisia and Lowata of Tripolitania. It took the Byzantine general, John Troglita, two years to subdue them. In 653 Constantinople was obliged to send an army to crush a revolt of the people of Numidia. In 587 the Berbers almost succeeded in regaining Carthage. Thus the Byzantine government of North Africa was a precarious one and did not contribute to the stability and progress of the country.[42]

North Africa needed a devoted statesman and Christian to lead it out of its state of decadence, but no such leader arose. New problems were, however, added to the already critical situation. Justinian was an earnest adherent of the symbol of Chalcedon and ardently sought the unity of the church. But he tried to satisfy the monophysite leaders and establish unity by condemning an edict known as the "Three Chapters": Theodore's writings, Theodoret's writings against Cyril, and Ibas's letter to Maris.[43] This, however, antagonized the bishops of North Africa. Some were deposed and others were set up in their places by imperial order. Finally, in 553, Justinian called a council at Constantinople, but this did not end the controversy.

As a result of the activities of its leaders, the Monophysite doctrine, already strongly established in Egypt, was also introduced in North Africa. Although it did not gain many adherents, it added to the disharmony already existing in the church. Catholics, Donatists, Arians, and Monophysites were represented in the church in North Africa. This division weakened the cause of the church, making it less able to resist the Muslim domination.

DEVELOPMENTS IN ETHIOPIA (100-640)

According to the national legend of Ethiopia, the history of the Axum kingdom begins in the tenth century B.C. with King Menelik, who is supposed to be the son of the queen of Sheba and Solomon, the Israelite king of that period. This tradition has been maintained by the Ethiopians and has served as a source of national pride and stability in the political leadership. It has also influenced the close relationship between the church and the state in Ethiopia. With an occasional interruption, the Solomonic dynasty, until recently, has ruled Ethiopia since that time. Emperor Haile Selassie claimed to be a descendant of that dynasty.

The kingdom of Axum is in the northern part of Ethiopia, impinging on the Red Sea. The capital, Axum, is situated in the Tigre province. Until the twentieth century the kings of the country were crowned on an antique throne dating back to pre-Christian times. Axum became an important commercial center in the first century A.D. Egyptian influence in the city was quite prominent. The inhabitants of the Axumite kingdom traded quite widely with the

countries of the Middle East and developed a distinct civilization
of their own.

Lying on the Red Sea, this region had contacts with the countries around this body of water, as it offered a means of communication. The languages spoken in this region indicate that a migration
from southern Arabia may have taken place at about the fifth
century B.C. The languages used in Ethiopia—as Tigre, Tigrinya,
and Amharic—are Semitic languages. The early Sebean influence
in Ethiopia is evidenced by the similarity of the carvings and
inscriptions on their monolithic stelae to those found in the southern region of Arabia. It is also conjectured that these contacts gave
rise to the similarities in religious symbolism.

The Ethiopian tradition also asserts that Jewish migrations,
probably preexilic, have taken place. Thus the Jews propagated
their faith among the people. These influences from the Jewish
peoples were reflected in the Ethiopian patterns of worship and, no
doubt, had an effect on the form Christianity was to take when it
was adopted by Ethiopia. The adherents of Judaism, however,
were not numerous. Some historians think the monotheistic form
of Sabean worship had its origin in the queen of Sheba's visit to
Israel.[44]

During the third century A.D. voyages to India via the Red Sea
became more frequent. Also, contacts with the Hellenistic civilization increased when the seaport, Adoulis, was established. Trade
flowed through it to Egypt, Arabia, India, and as far as Malasia.[45]
The kingdom of Axum, or Abyssinia, became prominent in world
affairs, establishing relations with Persia, Constantinople, and
Rome. In the fourth century, Ezanas enlarged his kingdom by
bringing the Bedja of the north and the Meroe kingdom of the
cataract region in submission to him.

The introduction of Christianity into this region is connected
with the testimony of Frumentius and Aedesius, members of the
crew of Meropius of Tyre who had set out to visit the lands
bordering the Red Sea and probably also India. On the return
journey the ship put into harbor for supplies. The people were
hostile and put all but the two youths to death. These were taken to
the king, who appointed each one to a position of trust. The king
was pleased with their service and granted them their freedom.
Through their testimony, a Christian community came into being.[46]

Aedesius returned to Tyre. Frumentius, however, was burdened for the Christian community; he went to Athanasius, bishop of Alexandria, and requested that a spiritual shepherd be sent to these Christians. Athanasius thought no one was more qualified to serve this Christian community than Frumentius himself, who had presented the faith to them. Frumentius was consecrated bishop and returned to Ethiopia during 341 or shortly after this date. The king accepted the Christian faith and established Christianity in his kingdom. The gradual evolution of his religious policy can be deduced from his coins. The early coins bear the symbol of the crescent and disk, whereas the later coins bear the cross. Although Christianity became the official religion of Ethiopia at an early date, the country was not readily evangelized. A century and a half after the official acceptance of Christianity, the masses were basically unaffected by the new faith.

A large part of the population was evangelized only during the latter part of the fifth and during the sixth century by a party of monks from the Syrian church. They translated the Scriptures from the Antioch version into Ge'ez, the language of the Axumites. This translation is relevant for the history of the church, for it contains several apocryphal books that seem to have been used by the church during the fifth and sixth centuries. As the Syrian church accepted the Monophysite faith after the Council of Chalcedon, these monks likely introduced this faith into Ethiopia. Consequently the Ethiopian church has adhered to it.[47]

During the sixth and seventh centuries, Christianity made considerable progress. Monasticism had a certain influence, and monasteries and convents were established. Through their ministry Christianity became more thoroughly rooted in Ethiopia. The monks took the Christian faith to the non-Semitic peoples of the south. Their ministry also served as the practical source for spiritual vitality within the Ethiopian church. They studied the literature written in Egypt[48] and nurtured the people as a result of their study.

The Coptic Church of Egypt followed the precedent set by Athanasius in appointing Frumentius as bishop of Abyssinia and continued to appoint the abuna (chief bishop of the Ethiopian church) from among the Egyptian clergy. Many of these men did not speak the language of the Ethiopian people nor were they acquainted with their culture. (In 1951 S.M. Haile Salassie abolished this custom, making the Ethiopian church completely independent.)

In 615 a few Muslims, driven from Mecca by the Qoraichites, arrived in Axum and were cordially received by the king. In 655 the Arabs conquered Persia and defeated the Byzantine navy. The Red Sea came under Arab influence and Christian Ethiopia was isolated from the other Christian countries and was obliged to struggle for its existence until the latter part of the sixteenth century.

DEVELOPMENTS IN NUBIA (100-640)

The active commerce between Egypt and the kingdoms to the south provided opportunities of contact and of evangelism. The First Cataract, and including the island of Philae, was the ethnological as well as geographical boundary between Egypt and the kingdoms to the south. To the south lay the region of Nubia, sometimes also spoken of as Ethiopia in ancient times. This region, between the First and Second Cataracts, where much information could be attained through archaeological studies, has been affected by the Aswan Dam. The geographic setting has been greatly altered. The people of the Nubian culture were of mixed Hamitic and Negro descent. Philae was an important center for the worship of Isis in Roman times.

The historical records concerning Nubia for the first centuries are very fragmentary. There is no evidence of the effective establishment of Christianity there before the sixth century when Julian, a presbyter of Alexandria, was sent by the Empress Theodora. He was well received by the Nobadae people and won them to the Christian faith. They were placed under the Monophysite patriarch of Alexandria. Having served for several years, Julian returned to Alexandria. Some twenty years later Longinus came and continued the ministry with much success. After five years of service, he visited Alexandria. Upon his return, he undertook a ministry among the Alodaei to the south of the Makorites. This ministry proved effective in establishing the Christian faith among them.

A mission of the Orthodox Church of Constantinople, sent by Justinian, ministered to the neighboring people, the Makorites, and succeeded in winning some converts to the Christian faith.

The Christian faith continued to win adherents in the region from Aswan to Dongola and became the prevailing faith in the region. Congregations were established and churches were built in the region. Although the missionaries were in close relationship with the patriarch of Alexandria, most of them were of Byzantine origin and used the Greek rather than the Coptic language in the liturgy and for funeral inscriptions.[49] The country experienced economic prosperity during several centuries.

SUMMARY

The God-fearing people of North Africa were the first to receive the Christian faith. Having received the faith, they applied it in their daily life, articulated it in theological terms, and retained it in spite of persecution. The God-fearing people were Old Testament believers. When the message of Christ's coming in fulfillment of prophecy was proclaimed to them, they accepted Christ as the Messiah. Since they were already familiar with the Old Testament message, the revelation of Jesus Christ was not another religion but the completion of the religion to which they adhered.

In order to strengthen the church and combat the false teachings, Christian instruction was emphasized and catechetical schools were opened, of which the Catechetical School of Alexandria was one. The early church was blessed with some faithful leaders who taught the Christian faith and presented their understanding in writing to the churches. These treatises have been invaluable sources for the church throughout the centuries.

Led by faithful pastors, the early Christians testified to the sincerity of their faith and preserved the church through periods of severe persecution. From A.D. 64 until 311 the churches passed through many persecutions. Tertullian expressed a significant truth when he informed the civil authorities that the blood of martyrs is the seed of the church. The more the Christians were persecuted, the more they multiplied.

The persecutions in Egypt caused the Christians to flee to the interior of the country. They spread the gospel message in the Coptic language and planted churches wherever they went. During this time monasticism began as a laymen's movement in search of a more pious life. The monks contributed significantly to the establishment of indigenous Christianity in Egypt.

The theological controversies greatly weakened and retarded the Christian ministry in Egypt. The Arian controversy involved an important doctrinal understanding. But the Egyptian patriarch could have rendered a greater service to the church if there had been a more sincere search for the truth, plus the humility to accept it.

Although North Africa has given significant leaders to the church, the church never became thoroughly rooted among the people. North Africa has witnessed a number of invasions, and as a result of these invasions a heterogeneous society has come into existence. The Berber peoples, indigenous in this area, experienced the invasions of the Phoenicians. Later the Romans conquered the country and a Romanized minority in the society came into existence.

Christianity did not penetrate North Africa beyond the Roman frontier. It witnessed the greatest success among the Roman and Romanized element of the population, which was a small and wealthy segment of the population. Christianity also reached many members of the Punic element of society, but this was only a small part of the entire population. It won only a few members of the Berber people, and this was chiefly accomplished by the Donatists. When they were suppressed, the church virtually lost contact with the indigenous element of the population. A country is not really evangelized unless the church becomes an indigenous church.

Another factor that prevented Christianity from taking strong roots in North Africa was the use of the Latin language, instead of the language of the people, in the services and in the preparation of Christian literature. The Bible was translated into Latin but was not made available either in the Punic or in the Berber language.

North Africa was the scene of theological, cultural, and political divisions. Neoplatonism, Montanism, Manichaeism, Donatism, and Pelagianism, one after another, plagued the church. The long strife between the Catholics and the Donatists, the suppression of the latter group by force, left the church in a weak state. To this was added the Vandal invasion, the persecution of the orthodox Christians, and the imposition of the Arian faith. The tables turned once more when Justinian I, emperor at Constantinople, reconquered North Africa in an effort to reestablish the old Roman Empire and reimposed the orthodox faith. The Greek control was of short duration and the Vandals again assumed power. Thus in the latter part of the sixth century, Christianity in North Africa was divided among Catholics, Donatists, and Arians; it lacked the unity and force to resist the Muslim suppression.

Study Questions

1. Outline briefly the beginning of the Church in Egypt and in Northwest Africa.
2. Indicate the effects of the persecutions of the third century on Christianity in Egypt.
3. What contributions did the Catechetical School of Alexandria make to Christianity in Egypt?
4. What contributions did Origen make to the growth of the church?
5. Indicate the causes for the rise and results of monasticism.
6. How did the patriarchs establish the Church of Alexandria during the fourth century?
7. Explain the error of Arius's teaching and the decision of the Council of Nicaea.
8. Explain the error in Nestorius's teaching.
9. What error did Eutychus teach?
10. What do these ecumenical disputes indicate concerning the Christology of the church?
11. Tertullian is sometimes considered the father of Latin theology. Describe Tertullian's contributions to the establishment of the Christian faith.
12. How did the persecutions affect the church in Northwest Africa?
13. What contributions did Cyprian make to the ministries of the church?
14. (a) Describe briefly the basic teaching of Neoplatonism, Montanism, and Manichaeism.
    (b) How did these teachings affect the church?
15. (a) What factors gave rise to Donatism?
    (b) Evaluate the church's dealing with Donatism.
    (c) Describe the effects of Donatism on the church.
16. Augustine is sometimes thought of as standing between the apostle Paul and Martin Luther. Describe briefly his contributions to the Christian faith.
17. Describe briefly the error in Pelagius's teaching and describe the teaching the church maintained.
18. What were the basic effects of the Vandal rule in Northwest Africa on the church?
19. How did Emporer Justinian's attempt to restore the Roman Empire affect the church and the state in Northwest Africa?

20. Describe the beginning of Christianity in Ethiopia.
21. What contribution did the monks make toward establishing Christianity in Ethiopia?
22. Describe the beginning of Christianity in Nubia.
23. Indicate the strengths and weaknesses of Christianity in Egypt and Northwest Africa.

2

Christianity Encounters Islam: A Millennium of Darkness (640-1652)

THE ARAB CONQUEST (640-1275)

Beginnings in Arabia

At the beginning of the seventh century, the Coptic Church in Egypt was establishing itself as the national church and penetrating every region of the country and every strata of society to a greater degree. Monasticism greatly influenced the church, and the large staff of monks carried the Christian faith to the distant parts of the country. The teaching of the Scriptures in the language of the people in the church helped Christianity take root in Egypt.

Although Christianity had come to North Africa several centuries earlier and should have reached the entire population, it had experienced a number of reversals instead of continuous growth and establishment. It had been subjected to Roman, Vandal, and Byzantine rule, each group imposing its unique ideas on the people. The church was divided among Catholic, Donatist, and Monophysite parties. It did not possess the Scriptures in the language of the people and had not really become the church of the people.

While Christianity was becoming the major faith of the Mediterranean world, Islam began in Arabia through the dreams and visions of Muhammad. He was born in 570 in Mecca, a caravan town located on the main trade route between Egypt and India. Though a member of the ruling Quarish tribe of Mecca, Muhammad was illiterate. He lost his father early in life and grew up in a poor home. He married an economically independent woman, who

61

was somewhat older than he was. She encouraged him to devote himself to the visions he began to have at forty years of age. The visions constituted his call to the service of Allah, the "all-powerful." According to Muhammad, the angel Gabriel appeared to him and summoned him to serve as the messenger of Allah. Consequently, Muhammad preached to the inhabitants of Mecca and to pilgrims who came to the city. He challenged them to accept a new morality and a monotheistic faith.

Muhammad's first disciples were members of his own family. In the early days of the movement, more converts were gained among the poor than among the influential people of the palace. Muhammad apparently regarded temporal power essential to his religious purposes. Persecution broke out, and Muhammad fled from Mecca to Medina in 622. This event, known as the Hijira, marks the beginning of the Muslim calendar. At Medina, Muhammad welded into a religious community the disciples from Mecca and from Medina. He also formed them into a political entity through which he ruled at Medina until his death in 632. During this time Mecca and a number of Arab tribes capitulated to him.

It is difficult to determine the extent to which Muhammad was influenced by Christianity. He referred to the Christians and Jews as people of the Book and he may well have drawn his emphasis on the coming judgment from Syrian Christianity. He was concerned to supply religious texts for his followers to substantiate his message. The fact that some of his followers took refuge in Abyssinia in 615 when they were persecuted in Mecca denotes their trust in the Christian kingdom to offer refuge to them.

The predominant idea of Muhammad's religious conception was the sense of God's exaltation and the sense of utter dependence of all creatures on the Almighty and Incomprehensible. Therefore, devotion to Him without reservation is requested. He further maintained that God had given man many revelations, which he lost except for the law of Moses, the psalms of David, the gospels of Jesus, and the Koran. Muslims believe the succeeding revelation is greater than the preceding one. Therefore, the Koran is the most authoritative revelation. Muhammad considered Christ to be a prophet like Moses and others, but himself to be a greater prophet than Christ. Consequently, the Muslims do not accept the deity of Christ nor His redemptive ministry. Muslims strictly observe the prescriptions for religious activities.

After Muhammad's death, his followers in rapid succession conquered, unified, and converted to Islam the warring and plundering tribes of Arabia. Having become a military force, the followers of Muhammad looked for greater returns for their military ambitions. Their zeal was enhanced through the conquest of Damascus in 635. They rapidly moved on to conquer Antioch in 636, Jerusalem in 638, and Caesarea in 640. By 650 they had destroyed the Persian Empire. The Muslims do not consider these conquests as events of the past, but as a vital part of their religion.[1]

Advance Into Egypt

Egypt was readily accessible to the Muslims. The fertile valley presented a strong temptation to a people who were attempting to find their substance on the desert regions of Arabia. Egypt was to them a granary of wheat to be exploited as much as possible. They crossed the Red Sea and were quite at home with the Egyptian climate, people, and language, as in all these things Egypt had a close affinity with Arabia. The Arabian merchants had traveled across Egypt to other parts of North Africa and were well acquainted with the entire region and the resources available in it. Furthermore, Egypt was unhappy with the Byzantine rule. Since 631, Cyrus had applied a repressive policy toward the Coptic Church. Therefore, they did not resist the Arab invasion, for they hoped the Arabs would drive the Greeks out of the country. Thinking that the Arab occupation would be temporary, as the Persian occupation had been, they supposed they would be independent after the Arabs withdrew again. Consequently, the Arab army under Amr ibn al Ac invaded Egypt in 640 without encountering strong resistance. They took Alexandria and rapidly conquered Egypt to the first cataract. However, the Egyptians were badly deceived, for the Arab occupation became permanent.[2]

The Arabs applied effective conquering policies. The people were obliged to pay tribute to the conquerors, but this was not heavier than the imperial demands had been. At first they granted religious toleration. The Coptic patriarch was restored to office, and the church was permitted to retain its property. They did not exert pressure to produce converts. It was basically a military occupation in which the Arab tribes asserted themselves, breaking through the frontiers that their neighbors were either unable or unwilling to defend.

After the Arabs were in full possession of the country, their attitude changed. The Christians were soon treated as second-class citizens, lacking equal privileges with the Muslims. The second caliph, Omar, stipulated that in addition to paying tribute, the Christians were to show hospitality to the Muslims, which meant contributing to their sustenance. They were not permitted to erect new churches or monasteries, or to exhibit any Christian practice that would present the Christian faith, such as wearing a cross. Omar demanded distinctions between Christians and Muslims in dress, saddles, the use of weapons, and the height of the houses.[3]

By the end of the first century of Muslim occupation, a poll tax, a land tax, and various requisitions for the army and for other purposes were imposed on the Christians, whereas there is no evidence that a tax was imposed on Muslims. The poll tax amounted to three or four dinars per adult male. The difficulty the poll tax imposed on the laborer, whose annual earning was sixteen dinars, is evident. Furthermore, the land tax was even larger than the poll tax. Many peasants with small land holdings were unable to pay the tax and deserted their land holdings. The Arab government introduced a pass system to prevent the peasants from leaving their land. In due course, in order to increase the revenue, the government subjected the Muslims to a land tax. The difficulties were accentuated by officials who regarded their appointment to office as an opportunity for personal benefit and made exactions from the people, increasing their already-heavy burden. Converts to Islam were automatically exempt from poll tax. In order to escape from this financial pressure, so many people claimed to have accepted Islam that a policy making converts pay was introduced to support the revenue. In 744 the governor of Egypt again offered tax exemption to converts. It is estimated that in response twenty-four thousand Christians became Muslims.[4]

Although Omar forbade the building of churches and monasteries, the law was not enforced under the Umayyads (661-750). Churches, convents, and monasteries were built. However, the Abbasids enforced the regulation and ordered new churches to be destroyed, though they permitted a measure of freedom of worship.

Because of the pressures and restrictions placed on them by the Arabs, the Egyptian Christians revolted a number of times, attempting to throw off the Muslim yoke. They failed, however, and became subject to severe persecution by the Muslims. Churches and monasteries were destroyed. The Coptic Christian community existed under very trying circumstances and became sadly reduced.

The pressure and persecution inflicted on the Christians by the Muslims also to a large extent stopped the training of the believers. There were not enough pastors to continue the ministry of the church. Some of the leaders retired to monastic life. Consequently, the Christians did not find the bond of fellowship to sustain them in the persecution and difficult situations. There was a significant reduction in the number of Christians. Only a remnant of genuine Christians remained true to their faith through centuries of pressure.

Occupation of North Africa

The Arabs were attracted to Egypt because the wheat fields of the Nile valley offered the sustenance they badly needed. They were further attracted to North Africa by the grain fields and the wine and olive groves. As early as 647 they made an expedition into North Africa and defeated Gregory of Carthage, but withdrew with their loot.

Whereas the Egyptians offered little resistance to the Arabs, the Berber-Arab kingdoms as semi-independent from the calif. Carthage, the main center of North Africa, was not taken until 697, country helped the Berbers in their struggle. They could retreat into the mountains or the deserts when pressed by the enemy and, at an opportune moment, strike again. It was not until 710 that the Arabs gained a measure of control over the country. Even then the Berbers rejected the Arab administration and established Berber-Arab kingdoms as semi-independent from the calif. Carthage, the main center of North Africa, was not taken until 697, when an army of forty thousand was sent against it, and it was finally secured by power at sea. The Arab success against North Africa came after the Byzantines lost control of the seas and could not intervene.[5] In 708 Musa ibn Musair took control. He succeeded in getting the cooperation of several Berber leaders, notably Tarik, who led him to his victory over the country. The Arab victory brought North Africa into the sphere of economic influence of the Arab-occupied world, which included Persia, Mesopotamia, and Syria—the sources of ancient civilizations. The pilgrims and merchants passed from one country to another.

In the preceding chapter we observed that the Christian faith penetrated mostly the Roman element of society and hardly affected the Berber population. Then the Romans were pushed back by the Vandals, and the Vandals in turn were pushed back by the Greeks. As parts of North Africa fell to Arab conquerors, members of the upper strata of society embarked for Italy and Spain. Their departure weakened the church.

The Arabs applied much pressure on Berber chiefs. Some chiefs embraced Islam under the threat of death. Kusaila is an example. He was taken prisoner and evaded death by adopting Islam. His conversion, however, was probably a matter of convenience, for he died fighting the Arabs. Kahina, another leader, led her people in a heroic fight against the Arabs. After her defeat and death, the people accepted Arab rule and Islam.[6] Further Islamization was promoted by the Arab scheme of assimilation. Practicing polygamy, the Arabs took Berber wives and brought about a rapid racial intermixture. Also, Berber women were sent in large numbers to oriental harems.[7]

As in Egypt, the Christians were subjected to economic pressure, which they could not support. If a Christian, for convenience, stated that he was a Muslim, he was obliged to send his children to Muslim teachers for instruction. An apostate to Islam who became Christian a second time had no choice, for he had to either embrace Islam or die. Thus, through suppression and persecution, the church was greatly reduced.

There was also a gradual permeation of Islam by methods similar to the Christian monastic system. Muslim agents went to remote areas practicing the religious routine of the devout Muslims. Muslim merchants were soon found in many hamlets, carrying their religion with them and planting it in the hamlet through the harems they established. There was one temporal power and it imposed its religion on the people.

When the Arab conquest had been completed, Christianity had been reduced to a small part of its former state. Whereas there had been approximately seven hundred bishoprics at the time of the Vandal conquest, there were not more than thirty or forty at the end of the seventh century, and only a few remained at the end of the eleventh century.

In addition to the suppression of the church by the Arabs and the flight of many Christians to Europe, the rapid disappearance of the church in North Africa was no doubt also due to its not having thoroughly taken root in Berber population. This resulted in part because the Scriptures had not been translated, and the liturgy had not been prepared, in the language of the people. Furthermore, the Donatist Church, which ministered to the Berber population, was suppressed by the imperial edict. The church was divided because of the theological controversies and was not enthusiastically supported by the people. Thus it disappeared, leaving hardly a trace of its existence in the region during five centuries.

Assaults on Ethiopia

After the Arabs had occupied Egypt and controlled the Red Sea, the Ethiopian church was separated from other Christian communities. It was obliged to provide for its inner resources, while on the one hand warding off hostile Arab forces who were constantly striving to penetrate its domain and on the other hand resisting the nomadic Bedjas, who were progressively expanding in the Eritrean plateau.

The records of the Ethiopian history from 700 to 1270 are incomplete and unreliable. During the eighth century the Axum kingdom extended its borders to the south and moved its capital to a more southerly location, probably as a result of the dangers that existed on the northern frontier. In the ninth century its power declined noticeably. During the tenth century the Agaos were in a state of revolt, but they were finally converted through the faithful ministry of the monks.

Little is known concerning the Agao dynasty and of the activities of the famous king Lalibela, who is said to have ruled at the beginning of the thirteenth century and constructed magnificant churches in his capital called "The New Jerusalem." Reliable records of the Ethiopian history date to 1270 when Amlak founded a new dynasty, related to Menelik, the supposed son of Solomon and Sheba.

Southward Into Nubia

In 652 the Arabs invaded Nubia as far as Dongola, the capital, and destroyed the church. A treaty was drawn up whereby the

Nubians would receive corn, oil, and clothing in return for an annual delivery of slaves. This state of affairs continued for some time. Arab traders moved back and forth. During the latter part of the tenth century, Muslim settlers from Egypt secured land in the north of the kingdom.[8]

In the thirteenth century the Muslim rulers intervened in the affairs of the kingdom. In 1275 Dongola, the capital, was taken; the king was carried off to Egypt, and an Egyptian was placed on the throne. The Nubian Christians continued to carry on for several centuries under Muslim rulers. But the immigrant Arab chiefs increased their influence, and by intermarriage the native inhabitants were assimilated by the Arab tribes.[9]

Soba was the capital of the Alwa kingdom to the south of the Makorites. It is described as a beautiful city with monasteries, churches rich with gold, and fine gardens. The people of the country were Christian. The bishops were appointed by the patriarch of Alexandria. In the thirteenth century Abu Salih, an Armenian, spoke of four hundred Monophysite churches in the kingdom.

Even though the Alwa kingdom was farther removed from Egypt, similar influences were at work in this region as in the northern kingdom. Toward the close of the sixth century a significant immigration from Yemen brought people of Arabic and Persian origin into these regions. This migration of the Yemen people to the west probably explains why some peoples of the Sudan attribute their origin to Yemenite migrations. The Christian communities were subjected to Arab political domination and the effects of Arab settlements. However, Christianity continued to prosper until the fall of Dongola. After it was taken, the Muslims intensified their pressure on the Christians in the general area and also in the Alwa kingdom to the south. Separated from contacts with other churches, unable to train or receive leaders from abroad, and restricted in its ministry, Christianity began to decline.

Invasion of the Sudan

The Berber people were reluctant to accept and propagate the Muslim religion. The tribes on the fringes of the desert were no more anxious to receive Islam and Arab rule than the people of the coast had been. But when Berber independence under their own Islamized dynasties was secured, it became a part of the people and was carried by them wherever they went. It was carried across the desert by the trade routes to Western Sudan, gradually converting large Negro kingdoms to Islam. West Africa has had sustained contact with the civilization of North Africa since the time of Christ.[10] In the eleventh century a Sanhadja chief from the Senegal border made a journey to Mecca and invited a Muslim teacher to his region. When the tribesman disregarded the teaching, Abu Bekr, a chief of the Sanhadja, waged war against the old kingdom of Ghana in western Sudan in 1076; victorious, he forced Islam on the people.[11] The city of Ghana lay on the western caravan route that ran from Morocco to Taghaza in the desert, which was famous for its salt mines. Islam moved eastward from Taghaza and Ghana and westward from the Makurra and Alwa kingdoms of the southern Nile region and eventually spread over the Sudan.

The Muslims, Arabs, and Berbers impressed the Negro people with their trade and at the same time transmitted their faith to them. They settled among the people and intermarried with them, and on numerous occasions they became the dominating element in the society. The prospect of booty, which caused the Arabs to cross over to Africa, was also a motivating factor in the spread of Islam and in the destruction of some of the kingdoms of the forest belt. Timbuktu was founded by Muslim Taureg who moved south and north with the seasons and finally settled on the northwestern point of the Niger bend. With navigation on the Niger at their disposal, they were readily able to reach other parts of the vast country through which the river flows.

Baramendana, one of the first rulers of the Mali empire, was converted to Islam. He made a pilgrimage to Mecca. Making pilgrimages to Mecca became a practice followed by his successors, among whom was Mansa Musa. Musa's pilgrimage became famous and promoted the spread of Islam through the empire. By the fourteenth century Islam had reached Kano on the trade route to Tripoli. From there it spread to the other Hausa kingdoms.

Islam spread westward from the Nile region in the thirteenth century when the kingdom of Kanem held the hegemony of central Sudan. There was considerable contact between Kanem and Cairo. As the northern kingdoms of Nubia held to Christianity, Islam did not reach the southern Sudan until the sixteenth century. It became the state religion of Darfur of the southern Sudan only during the reign of Ahmad Bokhor (1682-1722).[12]

Although Islam became the religion of many of the rulers, and Muslim traders and clerics were found in many towns, the masses of people remained animists. The Islamization of the people continued through the nineteenth century and was abetted by the policy of religious neutrality of France and Britain. During the twentieth century Islam has continued to spread more by migration than by conversion. The Muslim traders have moved into the cities of the southern regions. There they have found satisfying opportunities; so relatives and friends have followed.

More recently, Pakistani missionaries of the militant Ahmadiyyah Mission have established themselves in many of the coastal cities in the English-speaking countries. They are now beginning to open schools and clinics and engage in social service. The common people of the Sudan belt are mostly illiterate, and many are open to educational and religious instruction.

STRENGTHENING CHRISTIAN REMNANTS THROUGHOUT NORTH AFRICA (1275-1652)

Egypt

The Coptic Church in Egypt was able to retain its independence and continue a ministry to its members during the centuries of Muslim domination, even though its numbers were greatly reduced and evangelism was forbidden. The church had legal status and continued its ministry under the direction of the patriarch. The national character of the church, the use of the Bible in the Coptic language, and the unity of the church under the leadership of the patriarch helped the Coptic Church to survive twelve centuries of Muslim domination.

In its noble struggle for existence, the Coptic Church failed to train leaders adequately for the church and to instruct the laity in the Christian faith. This situation, in addition to the restrictions on evangelism imposed by the civil authorities, caused the church to lose its vitality. The services became more ritualistic and the vibrant testimony of a relationship with Christ became less evident.

North Africa

During a millennium following the Muslim invasion, the Christian witness was practically nonexistent in North Africa. Small communities, generally in isolated places of the mountains or deserts, survived the Muslim invasion and pressure. Some rulers were more tolerant, permitting the communities a relatively peaceful existence, even though their activities were restricted. The Christian communities of Draa and Bugia of Mauretania had some contacts with the outside world. The king of Bugia permitted the person appointed to be bishop to go to Rome for consecration. But the Christian communities were not permitted to evangelize and could only present a Christian presence in the communities.[13] The sultans of Morocco and Tunisia welcomed the service of Christian soldiers, for they felt more secure with bodyguards who were above local rivalries. Christian merchants were allowed to live in assigned areas of towns, but any attempt to propagate the faith was speedily put down.

Occasional efforts to establish Christian missions were undertaken at a considerable risk of the messengers' lives. The attempts of the Fourth Crusade to regain North African territory caused the Arabs to be even more careful not to permit an European presence there. A Franciscan mission to Tunis in 1219 failed. Realizing the hostility of the Muslims, Christian merchants sent the Franciscans back to Europe. Five friars became martyrs in Morocco in 1220.[14] The Dominicans ministered to the Christian soldiers and Christian slaves with a measure of success. They visited the discouraged Christians and the apostates in order to revive their faith, and they also offered instruction to interested Muslims. Because they were careful to retain the favor of the authorities, they were able to function in a limited capacity. Raymond Lull made several visits to North Africa. He gained several converts at Tunis, but was stoned to death at Bugia.[15] When the coast of Africa and other continents were "discovered," Catholic missionaries went to other places and effective missions to North Africa were resumed only during the time of French influence in the region.

Ethiopia

From 1270 to 1527 the Christian emperors of Ethiopia formed its Christianity and defended it against Muslim attacks. The characteristics of Christianity in Ethiopia were developed during this period of its history.[16] Ethiopia's isolation has played a significant role in its cultural, economic, and spiritual development. Its elevated tableland served as a natural fortress when the country, surrounded by the forces of Islam, was forced into an independency that was later reflected in its religious life and its cultural, economic, and social structures. Muslim traders settled along the northern frontier of Ethiopia. Because of the wealth they acquired, they had a marked influence on the less-fortunate peasants. The Ethiopians, however, were able to defend their country against Muslim invasion. As a result of the attacks on its northern frontier, the center of the empire was transferred to the southern provinces. The church reached new areas of the kingdom during the following centuries.

The emperors of the fourteenth and fifteenth centuries were able to create a national unity, with Christianity as a unifying factor. The Ethiopian church experienced a revival through the ministry of Tekle Haimanot, known as the "Saint of Ethiopia," who died at about 1312. The church and the state stood together for religious and national preservation during the strong Muslim attempt to conquer Ethiopia from the fourteenth to the sixteenth century. Zara Ya'kob (1434-1468) engaged in communications with the pope in an effort to seek help in his struggle with adversaries of the church. Lebna Dengel (1508-1540), with the help of the Portuguese, was able to defend his country from Muslim conquest.[17] Thus Ethiopia was able to remain independent until the resurgence of the Christian faith and European nationalism changed the religious and political scene.

Nubia

Christianity prospered remarkably in Nubia for several centuries even though it was surrounded by Muslims and its contacts with the Christian churches of the Mediterranean world were very limited. The ministry of the monks at Dongola was important for the church. But in 1275 Muslim forces from Egypt took Dongola, and in 1317 the large church was transformed into a mosque. During the fourteenth century Arabic nomads migrated into the country, moving towards Kordofan and Darfur where they played a historic role. Soba survived Muslim pressure until 1504.[18] In the sixteenth century the Portuguese reported that Christians in this region were seeking help from the king of Abyssinia. When missionaries came to this region during the following century, the Christian witness had disappeared.

The survival of Christianity in Nubia for a thousand years even though it was surrounded by Muslims and under Muslim influence during a large part of the time indicates that it had taken strong roots among the people. The use of the Nubian language for the production of Christian literature also testifies to this fact. However, the failure of the Nubian church to evangelize the peoples to the south and west indicates that it did not possess the power of the Spirit that caused the early church to go forward. There are three main reasons why the Nubian church was not able to survive the Muslim influence: (1) it probably lacked inner vitality, (2) it had no stimulating influence from other Christians, and, (3) the monasteries having been closed by the Muslims, it failed to produce Christian leaders who were able to nurture the believers and guide them through the centuries of Muslim influence.

EXPLORING UNEVANGELIZED AREAS ON THE WEST COAST (1275-1652)

Toward the end of the thirteenth century, Europe witnessed an awakening of a search for knowledge in religion, exploration, science, and industry. The invention of the compass, the new knowledge and skills of navigation, and the larger and stronger vessels encouraged the people to venture to unknown regions. The reports of the voyages of Marco Polo (1271-1285) greatly inspired European seamen. The discovery of the Canary Islands by Lanzarote Malocello in 1312 marked the beginning of European contacts with the peoples to the south. From 1364 to 1387 ten expeditions were sent to the coast of Africa. The Little Dieppe was established on the coast of Sierra Leone.

Franciscan missionaries sailed with the Portuguese expeditions to Madeira (1420), the Azores (1431), and the Cape Verde Islands (1450).[19] By the 1450s the Spaniards had established themselves on the Canary Islands and claimed a part of the mainland. Everywhere else along the West African coast the Portuguese ruled. During the fifteenth century Portugal disputed the possession of the islands with Spain, but in 1490 she finally accepted Spanish authority over them. For the most part, the Roman Catholic missions to black Africa during the fifteenth through the seventeenth centuries were under Portuguese auspices.

The discoveries by Vasco da Gama and Christopher Columbus made a profound impression on the European mind and gave the

Christian church a new outlook. New lands, previously unknown, lured Western explorers. A new route to Asia that circumnavigated the trade routes controlled by the Muslims had been found. It is important to note that in addition to trade the explorers and rulers had two great purposes in view: One purpose was to bring the gospel to the people to whom it had not been proclaimed; the other was to communicate with the Christian churches that were thought to be in existence in those lands and thus foster a world alliance of the faithful, through which the Muslim power would be destroyed.[20]

Cape Bojador: Henry the Navigator

If any individual could be credited with instigating a desire to discover the unknown areas of the coast of Africa, he would be Prince Henry of Portugal, known to history as Henry the Navigator. He had a strong desire to find a sea route to India. He also had a concern to thwart the influence of the Muslims, enemies of the Christian faith, and to bring the faith to the people of other countries. He built an observatory on the extreme southwest coast of Portugal, overlooking the Atlantic. For forty years he studied maps, made plans for journeys of exploration, and sent his captains on expedition after expedition down the African coast. Henry had to overcome major conceptions of his day, which maintained that evil awaited any person who passed beyond Cape Bojador.

Through Henry's efforts, his captains soon discovered Madeira and sailed to Cape Bojador. But for twelve years he could get no one to explore the regions beyond it. At last in 1434 Gil Eannes explored the coast beyond Cape Bojador. His move stimulated further discovery. In 1445 the Senegal River and Cape Verde were discovered. In 1451-1452 Cabo Mesurado, where Monrovia now stands, was attained. By 1470 explorers had reached Elmina on the Guinea coast. In 1472 Diogo Cam discovered the mouth of the Zaire River. In 1487 Bartholomew Diaz passed around the Cape of Good Hope, opening the route to Asia and the islands that Vasco da Gama found in 1498 after having proceeded north along the eastern coast of Africa and discovering such notable places as the Quilimane River, Mozambique, Mombasa, and Malinda.

At first the Portuguese only sought food and pilots in the African settlements and made no attempt at conquest. But before long the struggle for influence between the Arabs and the Portuguese began. This was the beginning of the Portuguese influence on the east coast of Africa that continued till the seventeenth century. The Portuguese established themselves at Mombasa, Malinda, Kilwa, and Sofala.

Henry the Navigator was not only interested in exploration, he was also concerned to bring all the people to faith in Jesus Christ. Although Henry died in 1460 before the great discoveries that he inspired were accomplished and before evangelistic missions to the people of Africa had attained his vision, the Catholic Church undertook missions at a number of places along the African coast. By virtue of the patronage system that Pope Nicholas introduced in 1454, dividing the new world between Portugal and Spain, Portugal was responsible to Christianize Africa.

The Roman Catholic Church sent missionaries to the islands off the West Coast of Africa, beginning with the fifteenth century. Then it used these island bases as springboards for missionary efforts on the mainland. The islands had good harbors. Before long, adequate ports with good shipping facilities were established and ships from Europe called regularly with provisions and equipment on their way to and from the East. In contrast to the unhealthy climate on the mainland, nearly all the islands had an ideal climate and the missionaries could return from the mainland to regain their health.

The Canary Islands

The Canary Islands were visited by European expeditions before the Spanish occupation. In 1402 Spain sent John of Bethencourt and Gadifur de la Salle to the Canary Islands to bring the Guanches under Spanish rule. Some agricultural families from Caux, who were to develop the islands, sailed with the expedition. This was the first attempt at colonization.[21] The expedition also included a priest, John Le Verrier, and a monk, Peter Bontier. In 1406 Rome erected the diocese of St. Maritial de Rubincon with headquarters on the Lanzarote Island. The first bishop, Albert de las Casas, was a Franciscan.[22] The earliest missionary activities were directed toward the Guanches of the Canaries. Spanish Franciscans are said to have evangelized four of the larger islands by 1476. Intermarriage between Spaniards and Guanches eventually produced a common stock.[23] In 1459 Rome asked the Franciscans to attempt to work in Guinea on the mainland.

The Azores, the Madeiras, and the Cape Verde Islands

Before the Europeans discovered the Azores, the Madeiras, and the Cape Verde Islands, the first two groups, and probably the third, were without inhabitants. In the fifteenth century a beginning was made to colonize the islands. The first settlers were Portuguese and immigrants from the Guinea coast. The Franciscans were active on all three groups of islands.[24] In 1462 Alphonso of Bolano, a Portuguese Franciscan who had served on the Canaries, was appointed prefect for Guinea. Several contacts were made in Senegambia. A chief and his twenty-five companions received baptism in 1489, but there was little progress to report.[25]

The Sierra Leone Coast

In Sierra Leone, Portuguese Jesuits were active from the beginning of the seventeenth century. They reported to have baptized the king, his sons, and many other people.[26] The Andalusion friars are reported to have worked with some success during the latter part of the seventeenth century. Some work was also carried on in the kingdom of Benin. But no permanent Christian communities seem to have arisen from these early ministries on the African coast.[27]

The Guinea Coast

The Protestant churches made contacts with the peoples on the African coasts at a much later date. Portugal led in the discovery of the coasts and retained the monopoly of the trade along the coasts for some time. Pope Alexander VI had entrusted the evangelization of the African peoples to Portugal. But after the Netherlands gained their independence, they developed important trading companies and challenged the Portuguese authority. As a result of their conflict with Spain and Portugal and the development of their sea power, the Dutch began to make contacts with the coast of Africa and struck at the Portuguese trading posts. In 1637 they seized the famous Portuguese post on the Guinea coast, St. Georges of Elmina, and in 1642 they took St. Anthony of Axim, second in importance. Other European countries also moved into the trade and established trading posts on the African coast and applied their influence wherever possible.

The Dutch West India Company acknowledged its responsibility to evangelize the people it dealt with. Chaplains were sent to minister to the personnel of the company. They naturally came into contact with the native people as they worked at the post or as others came to séll their produce. However, the chaplains did not seem to follow a systematic effort of evangelization and so the results of their contacts with the people were negligible. Several efforts were made to train African individuals in Europe with the hope that they might take the gospel to their people, but these individuals stood alone, and the efforts did not produce important results. A Dutch merchant purchased a Negro boy, who was a native of the Gold Coast (now Ghana). When he returned to Holland, he took the lad, whom he called Jacobus Elisa Johannes Capitein, with him for an education. After five years of study at the University of Leyden, Capitein was ordained to the ministry of the Dutch Reformed Church and returned to the Gold Coast as chaplain at St. George d'Elmina. He translated the twelve articles of the Apostles' Creed into the Fanti language. Even though he married an European lady, he was not well received by either the Europeans or his own people. He died after a short and unhappy career at the age of thirty.

Another young African boy, Anthony William Amo of Axim on the Gold Coast, was taken to Europe and became the protégé of the Princess of Brunswick. He studied at Halle, in Saxony, and also at the University of Wittenberg, where he received a doctor's degree. However, when his benefactress, the princess, died, he was overcome by deep depression. He returned to Axim, but lived a solitary life and accomplished little.

The Protestants did not make concentrated efforts to evangelize the peoples until the eighteenth century, and lasting results were not seen until the nineteenth century.

CHRISTIANIZING THE CONGO KINGDOM (1484-1652)

The story of the Roman Catholic missions in the Congo is very interesting and merits serious study. Through these missions a large part of the country was brought under Christian influence during a period of several centuries. After this, the work virtually disappeared. Except for Ethiopia, the Congo is the only African country south of the Sahara that had intimate and prolonged relations with the Christian faith prior to the missionary activities of the last centuries.

Diogo Cam discovered the mouth of the Zaire River in 1482. At this time the king resided at Mbanza Kongo, the San Salvador of today, and ruled an almost rectangular region extending from the Benga River to the Zaire boundary and from the ocean to the Kwango River. Relations between Portugal and the kingdom of Congo were soon established. In 1484 Diogo Cam took some natives of the country back to Portugal with him, leaving some Portuguese as security for their safe return. In 1485 John II of Portugal sent them back with gifts to the king of the Congo.

Through his tactful dealings, Diogo Cam won the esteem of the people. The king was sensitive to the knowledge of the Portuguese regarding the countries of Africa and Europe and concerning the art of shipbuilding and navigation. He asked for someone who might teach his people. Cam left a priest to teach the people. In 1481 an embassy of the Congo was sent to Portugal and in 1491 the first party of missionaries arrived, including masons, carpenters, and other skilled craftsmen, who were to construct a part of the capital. The king, his wife, and his oldest son, Alphonso, were readily baptized. Alphonso was sincere, but the king was not so stable; his second son reacted against the Christian influence.

Alphonso became governor of the province of Nsudi in 1504 and welcomed a new group of missionaries. Among them were schoolteachers and music directors. In 1506 he sent his son Henry to Portugal for training. Alphonso succeeded to the chieftainship in 1507 as a Christian. He devoted his efforts to the development of his country. He supported the work of the missionaries and fresh parties arrived from time to time.[28]

The relations between Lisbon and the Congo capital were excellent during these years. In 1512 Manuel, king of Portugal, sent five ships with masons, carpenters, and building materials to construct churches in the Congo. A significant development took place in the Congo during Alphonso's reign. There were at least six churches at San Salvador, and churches and schools were found in other provinces of the country. The king became a Christian, and his secretary produced public documents in the European style.

Henry, the son of Alphonso who was sent for training to Lisbon in 1506, was consecrated bishop in 1518 and was appointed vicar apostolic of Congo. He returned to the Congo in 1521, but was handicapped by delicate health and did not exercise a significant influence in evangelizing his people. He died in 1530, nine years after his return. Some other Africans were ordained priests. But the effort to create an indigenous clergy apparently was unsuccessful.[29]

Even though Alphonso energetically supported the Christian mission and many people were baptized, little evidence of radical change among the population could be noted. After the death of Alphonso the kingdom declined rather rapidly. A number of Catholic societies served in the Congo during this period. It is thought that Canons of St. John the Evangelist, and probably also Franciscans, were among the early missionaries. As a result of the tropical diseases, the death rate among the Catholic missionaries was very high, while others returned to Europe because of ill health, causing a very rapid turnover of workers. The Jesuits arrived about 1548 and were in the Congo at intervals during much of the remainder of the sixteenth century. The first party consisted of three priests and a brother. Reports indicate that they baptized five thousand people in three months.[30] As they were unable to follow up, instruct, and nurture these believers, a large number of them abandoned the faith and returned to their previous way of life. The Franciscans reappeared toward the end of the sixteenth century. Several hundred Capuchins came to the Congo and Angola in the seventeenth century.[31] From 1673 to 1701 fifty-five died and only forty-six were able to complete seven years of service.

To the south of the kingdom of Congo was the territory of Angola. Its chief was a vassal of the king of the Congo. The Portuguese devoted progressively more time to Angola and less to the Congo and established their authority at San Paulo de Loanda. The Jesuits began a ministry there in 1574 and within ten years baptized the king and many subjects. A cathedral was constructed in San Paulo de Loanda. Pope Clement VIII made Angola an episcopal see in 1596. From that time on, the bishops resided at Loanda rather than at San Salvador. From 1599 to 1624, four bishops in succession resided at Loanda.

The Portuguese established themselves at Sao Philip of Benguella in 1617. But they did not move into the interior until 1685. By establishing a post at Caconda, they made contact with the Ovimbundu, the largest ethnic group in Angola, which constitutes approximately 1.5 million of the total population of 4 million of Angola. But the missionary activities had little success.

The political situation in the Congo and Angola became strained and a number of disturbances took place. The Portuguese residing in the Mbamba province were massacred. Yet the Jesuits established a college at San Salvador in 1624, and a number of Congolese were ordained following their training. A civil war erupted between King Climpanzu and King Chmulaza, which lasted forty years. In 1678 San Salvador was destroyed, the royal palace was burned to the ground, and the Jesuit college and churches were destroyed.

The Portuguese did not maintain the quality of the effort to evangelize and bring European civilization to the kingdoms of the Congo and Angola. Whereas the early efforts to develop the Congo were made at Portugal's expenses, in the sixteenth century the Portuguese turned to slave trade. At first people were hired to work in the plantations on the island of Sao Tome, but the request for laborers in their plantations in South America tempted them into the slave trade.

The already-problematic political situation was further disturbed through the hostile relations with the Dutch and Spaniards. The Dutch drove the Portuguese from the West African coast and, for a few years, until the Portuguese could reassert themselves, even from the Angolan and Brazilian coasts. The African kings established relations first with one foreign power and then with another. This caused some confusion in the country. Finally the civil wars brought the kingdom to its destruction.

The ministry of the Catholic Church in the Congo and Angola gradually deteriorated and dwindled to an insignificant presence in several coastal cities. From these cities a priest made an occasional visit to one of the towns of the interior in order to baptize those who presented themselves or the children whom parents brought. However, the people became quite ignorant of the Christian teaching, and the rituals that some observed had little meaning for them. Although exterior factors contributed to the disappearance of Christianity, the basic reason for this sad outcome of several centuries of "Christian" presence is probably the life of the Catholic Church itself. Even though a few men were trained for the priesthood in Portugal, priests were not trained in proportion to the large number of people who were baptized. The baptized were not thoroughly taught in the Christian faith and readily deserted it. Christianity did not become a part of the life and culture of the people.

CONTACTING THE EAST COAST (1500-1652)

Portuguese and Arabs

The records of the history of East Africa until the tenth century are incomplete. Although the extent of the contacts between East Africa and Asia have not been determined, there are indications that certain contacts existed. The Arab contacts with the east coast of Africa seem to have come during the period of Arab expansion. According to traditions retained in Arabia and East Africa, the earliest Arab colonists in East Africa were eighth century Shi'ite refugees from Oman. Others followed and established trade along the coast. The period of prosperity on the East African coast was from the middle of the thirteenth century until the coming of the Portuguese.[32]

Vasco da Gama's success in discovering a route to India around the Cape of Good Hope and via the eastern coast of Africa was viewed with disfavor by the Arabs who were in control of the Red Sea and of the eastern coast of Africa as far south as Zanzibar. As a result of the demand for spices, gold, ivory, and slaves, the Arabs had developed a lucrative trade between Africa, Asia, and Europe. They controlled the commerce between Kilwa, near the mouth of the Zambezi River, and Calicut, on the Indian coast. In 1500 the king of Portugal sent Cabral with a fleet to India, with the instructions to establish friendship with those who were willing to engage in commerce and become Christians. The Portuguese soon developed trade along the eastern coast of Africa and clashed with the Arabs in doing so. In 1505 they decided to establish forts along the coast. Kilwa was easily occupied. But Mombasa resisted a Portuguese establishment and was taken with difficulty. At Malinda, Mombasa's rival, they were welcomed. Sofala, to the south, was occupied without opposition.

The struggle for the sovereignty on the eastern coast of Africa had erupted and developed to a crisis at a naval battle in the Indian Ocean in 1509 when the Portuguese engaged an Arab fleet under the flag of the Egyptian sultan. The Portuguese victory led to a century of uncontested control of the eastern seas.[33] In order to have free access to the Red Sea, the Portuguese destroyed Brava, Berbera, and Zeila, cities of Somalia, and established a garrison on the island of Sokotora.[34] The Arab traders who attempted to penetrate the northern territories of Ethiopia were basically looking for slaves whom they sent in large numbers to Arabia and India. They launched an attack from Somalia in order to conquer Ethiopia. Unable to defend the country against Arab intrusion, the Ethiopians appealed to the Portuguese for help in 1541. The Arabs were finally defeated in 1543, but the country had been ruined. A large part of the population had been massacred or carried off as slaves, and the treasuries of the churches and monasteries were carried off to Arabia and India.[35] It was some years before Ethiopia could recover, to a degree, from the war. However, because of the Portuguese assistance, it was able to remain independent.

The Arabs did not accept the Portuguese presence on the eastern coast without challenge. The Arabs of Mombasa and Kilwa strove for liberation from the commercial monopoly of the Portuguese and attempted to regain the prosperity they had during the fifteenth century. They were supported by the sultan of Moscat, who established himself on the Arabic coast of Oman to the south of the Gulf of Persia. By 1631 the Portuguese power was waning in Europe and consequently also in the overseas territories. The people of Mombasa rebelled and reestablished their independence. The Imam of Moscat drove the Portuguese out of Malinda and Kilwa, and this reduced the Portuguese holdings to Mozambique and Sofala. From 1622 to 1650 the Arabs reestablished, to a large degree, the slave trade between the coast and India. In 1698 they virtually controlled the coast north of the Cape of Delgado. Finally in 1752 both the Portuguese and the Arabs recognized two zones of influence: that of the Arabs to the north of the Cape of Delgado and that of the Portuguese to the south.[36] The Arabs carried on an extensive slave trade between the African coast and India until it was restrained through the efforts of J. Kirk, the British consul at Zanzibar.

The Portuguese occupation of the Zanzibar coast of Africa left no significant mark. The Portuguese interests had been essentially commercial and maritime. They supplanted the Arab seaborne trade.[37] Through their presence, however, the Ethiopian kingdom had been preserved and the Arab occupation of East Africa retarded.

When Vasco da Gama accomplished his voyage to India in 1499, the passages via the Near East ceased to be the only possible routes to the East. Before long other European nations sought the

African route to the spices of the East and established trading posts along the coast of Africa. The Dutch became the rivals of the Portuguese on the West African coast. In 1637 they took Elmina from the Portuguese and established their authority on the west coast. Other European countries, notably Britain and Denmark, soon established trading posts on the West African coast. The Dutch pushed their way around the Cape of Good Hope and established trade with the East. They soon realized the importance of the Cape for provisions for the voyages. As a result of a shipwreck off the Cape, they discovered that the climate was suitable for Europeans and that the people were peaceful and could be evangelized. Consequently, they founded Cape Town in 1652.

Roman Catholics

Behind Sofala, on the coast south of the Zambezi, lay the tribe of Makalanga. The Mashona of Rhodesia are descendants of this tribe. The kingdom of the chief, known by the title Monomotapa, was the magnet for the Portuguese, for its trade in gold passed through Sofala.

The pioneer missionary effort in East Africa was made at this point when Father Goncalo da Silveira and two priests of the Society of Jesus began a ministry in 1560. Moving inland from Sofala, they made contacts with a chief in the neighborhood of Inhambane. The chief and about four hundred of his tribe were converted and consented to baptism.

However, Monomotapa was the objective of the Catholic mission, and in September Silveira and his companions moved inland to Sena, a Portuguese post on the Zambezi. Here they found some Portuguese and some Indians who were already Christians. Father Goncalo da Silveira ministered to them, and, while waiting for permission to go to Monomotapa, also baptized about five hundred Bantu. The king sent the permission with gifts on Christmas Day. The king, his mother, and a number of the court accepted the Christian faith and were baptized. But the Muslims, seeing large numbers turning to Christianity, accused Silveira of being a spy of the viceroy of India. Silveira became aware of their plot to kill him and could have left the court, but he chose to stay and was put to death in 1561. His death brought the Jesuit mission of the sixteenth century to an end. Its influence disappeared and was not found by later missions.

In 1577 two Dominicans began work in Mozambique. Before long, their ministry spread to Sofala, Sena, and Tete. They cared for the spiritual welfare of the Portuguese and worked for the conversion of the local people; they soon baptized large numbers of them. Dos Santo baptized seventeen hundred persons at Sofala between 1586 and 1590. In 1612 a "Prelature Nullius" was organized; it extended from Cape Guardafui to the Cape of Good Hope, with the administrator's headquarters at Mozambique.[38]

The Dominicans' success in the kingdom of Monomotapa came after Manuza became king in 1631. Manuza was baptized in 1652 and took the name of Philippe. By 1667 there were sixteen places of worship on the lower Zambezi, of which nine were Dominican, six were Jesuit, and one was under a secular priest. However, as the century closed, both the Dominican work and the revived work of the Jesuits in the Zambezi valley were on the decline and gradually came to an end. The Portuguese also made some attempts to plant Christianity in Madagascar, and the French congregation of the mission made courageous attempts to do so in the seventeenth century. None of these efforts, however, produced permanent Christian communities.[39]

In 1652, the year Manuza was baptized, Jan van Riebeeck with the first Dutch settlers landed at Table Bay and began the settlement that became Cape Town. Thus 1652 marks the division of the Roman Catholic endeavor and the Protestant settlement in southern Africa.[40]

SUMMARY

The gospel was proclaimed to the people of the interior of Egypt, and the church became established throughout the country. The Scriptures were translated into the Coptic (Egyptian) language and services were held in the Coptic language. The church became a national church united under a patriarch. These factors helped the church withstand the Muslim invasion and suppression.

The Muslims did not permit the Coptic Church to offer Christian education to its members, especially to church leaders under pain of persecution. This was one of the main reasons for the decline of the Coptic Church. The Christians did not find the spiritual nurture to sustain them in the difficult situations and encourage them to witness to their faith. Therefore, only a remnant of genuine Christians retained their faith through centuries of pressure.

The North African population contained three distinct cultural elements: the indigenous Berber, the Punic, and the Roman. The Romans had ruled them and imposed their culture on them. When difficulties arose, most of the Romans returned to Europe.

Politically, North Africa was a divided region. The Phoenicians invaded and dominated North Africa for centuries. Then the Romans ruled until Rome fell under the Barbarian invasion. The Vandal rule was challenged by Justinian I of Constantinople. However, the Byzantine rule did not last and North Africa returned to Vandal rule. But by the latter part of the sixth century the Vandal rule began to disintegrate.

The Berber population had only limited strength to resist the Muslim pressure. This was true for the following reasons: (1) Christianity had not thoroughly taken root in the Berber population, (2) it was divided theologically, (3) the Bible had not been translated into the Berber language, and (4) the country was divided politically.

Although the abuna was appointed by the patriarch of Alexandria, the Ethiopian church was indigenous and united. The Scriptures had been translated into Ge'ez. Services were conducted in the languages of the people. The state and church fought against Muslim invasion and together survived.

As the centuries passed, the Egyptian church continued to resist Muslim pressure; but it did not retain its vitality and failed to supply leaders to guide the church. The life of the church became more tradition than a real life-giving force. Under Muslim pressure the Christian witness became almost nonexistent throughout North Africa.

The Christian agencies failed to consider adequately the Arabic culture and adapt their methods to it. They denounced the Muslim religion, and so created opposition instead of providing bridges of communication. Later Cardinal Lavigerie took a new approach by ministering basically to needy children who were ceded to his organization, but Christianity gained few adherents in the Muslim countries.

From the fifteenth to the eighteenth century, Roman Catholic missionaries sailed with many Portuguese vessels to various places along the coast of Africa and began missionary enterprises. However, even though a large population in the Kingdom of Congo (now a part of Angola) was influenced by the gospel, permanent, indigenous, reproducing churches were not established through these efforts. The Catholic missionaries baptized many people, but they prepared few leaders in comparison to the number baptized. The church did not become indigenous in the society and was not thoroughly established. Christianity did not become rooted in the culture and rapidly disintegrated when it was no longer sustained by missionaries.

The ethics of the Europeans frequently did not substantiate the Christian faith, but greatly hindered its progress. Although in the beginning the Portuguese established friendly relations with the people of the Congo and sent carpenters and masons and building supplies to the country, later they ruined their trust by engaging in slave trade. The reader cannot help but compare the striking difference between the results of the Roman Catholic work in the Congo and on the east coast of Africa with those of the London Missionary Society in Madagascar in the seventeenth century. The former work disintegrated without persecution, whereas the latter grew in spite of persecution.

Study Questions

1. Describe the beginning of Islam.
2. What were Muhammad's basic teachings?
3. Why was Egypt an attractive area for exploitation for the Muslims?
4. Describe the Muslim rule of Egypt.
5. Describe the Arab conquest and the conditions of the Christians under Muslim rule in North Africa.
6. What factors helped Ethiopia repulse Arab assaults?
7. Describe the Arab pressure on Nubia from 652 to 1275.
8. To what extent did Islam penetrate the Sudan during this period?
9. What factors helped the Coptic Church survive under Muslim pressure?
10. What assistance were the Western churches able to give the Coptic Church during this period?
11. Describe the Christian witness in Northwest Africa from 1200 to 1652.
12. What were the characteristics of Ethiopian Christianity?

13. Evaluate the strengths and weaknesses of Christianity in Nubia.
14. How did the Portuguese exploration influence missions on the west coast of Africa?
15. Describe the success of the Franciscans' missionary efforts on the Canary Islands.
16. Describe the Roman Catholic missionary policy in West Africa during this period.
17. Describe the strength of Christianity in the Congo Kingdom during King Alphonso's reign.
18. Explain the causes for the rapid decline of Christianity in the Congo Kingdom.
19. Evaluate the effects of Portuguese establishments in East Africa on the expansion of Christianity.

3

Missionary Interest Revived in Western Christianity

The resumption of the proclamation of the gospel to the un-evangelized peoples and the world-wide spread of Christianity in the fifteenth century are significant factors in the history of the Christian church. The church of Europe had been blocked off from contacts with Eastern peoples by the Muslim occupation of the Near East and North Africa, which closed the trade routes to the East. The discovery of unknown lands and new routes to the East opened an entirely new world to the church. The invention of the printing press aided the diffusion of the gospel message. Thus the revival of interest in missions and the resumption of the proclamation of the gospel to the unevangelized peoples was of monumental importance.

ROMAN CATHOLIC MISSIONARY INTEREST (1300-1700)

The development of the Roman Catholic missions coincided with the discoveries of parts of the world previously unknown to Europeans and the expansion of the overseas empires of Portugal and Spain. The governments and the Catholic Church were both concerned about discovery and evangelism. The discoveries had a profound influence on the European mind and on the outlook of the Catholic Church. In addition to trade with the East, two important purposes motivated the explorers and the rulers who made the voyages possible. First, they wanted to bring the gospel to the peoples to whom it had not been proclaimed; second, they wanted to establish contact with the Christian churches they thought existed in those lands. The pope expected Portugal and Spain to evangelize the peoples they had placed under their rule. In 1456

Pope Calixtus III gave to the Great Prior of the Order of Christ of Portugal the spiritual supervision of all existing dominions of the crown of Portugal.[1] Spanish rule in Latin America is an example of this idea put in practice. Catholic priests were generally a part of the exploratory expeditions. Wherever these powers established their rule, the work of the church and the activities of the civil authorities were closely related.

Formation of Missionary Orders

During the later Middle Ages a number of orders of the Catholic Church were founded in order to serve the needs of the church. These orders became the mission agencies in the Catholic Church's missionary endeavors during the modern period. The existing ones were called upon to serve in various countries, and new ones were founded to meet the needs as they developed. The Cistercians began with Robert, a Benedictine monk who attracted a number of hermits and withdrew to Citeaux in France in 1098. The movement came largely out of a need to strengthen the devotional life of the church and received much inspiration through the ministry of Bernard of Clairvaux, who became abbot of the fourth of the Cistercian houses in 1115.[2] The Carthusians were founded by Bruno in 1084. The Cistercians and the Carthusians devoted themselves to work, meditation, study, and the preparation of Christian literature. The Franciscans and the Dominicans, however, were founded for the purpose of instructing the people. Francis of Assisi (1181-1226) began the society in 1209. He was the first founder of a monastic order to make the ideal of missionary service an integral part of the religious life of the order. The Dominicans were founded in Toulouse in 1216 by Dominic of Caloroga in order to combat the ministry of the Cathari and the Waldenses. The Carmelites, the Augustinians, and a number of other orders soon came into being. Later, in the eighteenth and nineteenth centuries, additional missionary orders, such as the Holy Ghost Fathers and the White Fathers, were founded. The Franciscans and the Dominicans shared a large part of the burden of proclaiming the gospel on the coasts of Africa and on the nearby islands during the fifteenth to the eighteenth centuries. The Holy Ghost Fathers, the White Fathers, and other orders have shared this responsibility in the latter part of the nineteenth and twentieth centuries.

Service of Missionary Orders

Missionary activity had remained a principal feature of the Franciscan vocation. In the thirteenth century it penetrated into Asia. John of Monte Corvine (c.1246-1329) was the founder of the Catholic missions in China. In the sixteenth and seventeenth centuries they ministered along the coast of Africa. The Dominicans played a major part in the missionary movement associated with the Portuguese and Spanish expansion of the sixteenth century.

Other orders were founded in later centuries to fulfill certain needs and accomplish certain ministries. The Jesuits, founded in Paris by Ignatius Loyola in 1534, were aggressive in their missionary endeavor and in teaching the people. Among their early missionaries were Matee Ricci, who began a ministry in China, and Francis Xavier, who served in several eastern countries, notably in Japan. The Holy Ghost Fathers were founded in 1703 by Claude Francois Poullart des Places (1679-1709) for the training of students for pastoral work in Paris. They served in North Africa and later in Uganda and in other countries of Africa.

The Roman Catholic Church called on these orders to fulfill the services it considered essential to undertake. The members of the orders had committed themselves to serve the church. Consequently, by papal request the church could deploy these servants to any country and any ministry it deemed essential. Thus, wherever Spain and Portugal established colonial strongholds, the Catholic orders carried the gospel to these countries and claimed large numbers of people for the Catholic Church. The approach of these two powers to the newly discovered countries was that of conquest, settlement, and evangelization. The peoples of these countries were to be brought under the permanent dominion of the Christian kings. This dominion was to be maintained by a considerable number of Europeans as permanent settlers.

The Roman Catholic Church arranged a system of comity to avoid duplication and competition by the orders. Certain orders were assigned to certain countries. In order to unify the missionary activities of the Roman Catholic missionary agencies, Pope Gregory XV in 1622, created the Sacred Congregation for the Propagation of the Faith. This body was constituted of cardinals chosen by the pope. Its purpose was to handle all matters connected with missions, as well as matters of training missionaries and an indigenous clergy.[3]

PROTESTANT MISSIONARY INTEREST (1521-1792)

Their new understanding of God's revelation in Jesus Christ and of the Christian life in fellowship with Him did not prompt the Protestant churches of Europe to proclaim the gospel to the unevangelized peoples. Whereas the Catholic Church engaged in missionary efforts during the period of world exploration, the Protestant churches were occupied in establishing themselves. They had been compelled to fight for their existence until the Treaty of Westphalia was signed in 1684. When they finally received civil status, they were exhausted from the years of war. Their material resources were depleted, and they had lost the spiritual strength of the early years of the Reformation. They made some efforts to evangelize the Muslims who had penetrated Europe along the Danube River. But the strife between the Catholics and the Protestants compelled the Protestants of Hungary and Transylvania to seek the protection of the Muslim forces. Consequently, their evangelistic efforts produced no effective results.

During the early period of world discovery, the Protestants were not in contact with unevangelized people in Africa, Asia, or the Americas. Spain and Portugal, both Roman Catholic countries, were the exploring and colonizing powers of the post-Reformation period. They enjoyed the mastery over the seas and the monopoly of world trade. Wherever their ships went, they carried merchants and missionaries. The kings of these countries were committed to the Christianization of their overseas colonies of which they took possession. When the Dutch and the British undertook their exploratory and commercial ventures, one of the objectives of the Dutch was to plant the Reformed faith in its territories, which they did notably in South Africa, Indonesia, and Brazil. Their work in Brazil took place during their brief occupation of the territory. The British East India Company was opposed to missionary work. The company refused to transport missionaries on its ships and forbade them to reside in its territories. Consequently, the early Protestant missions encountered considerable difficulty in establishing missionary enterprises. As late as 1793 William Carey was refused passage on the ships of the British East India Company.

Individuals Reveal Missionary Interest (1531-1792)

The vision for missions and the concern for the unevangelized peoples of the world was largely lacking in the Protestant churches of the seventeenth and eighteenth centuries. Hadrian Saravia (1531-1613), a Dutch pastor at Antwerp and Brussels, later professor at Lyde, and finally dean of Westminster, maintained that the Great Commission applied to all generations and that without a doubt the church had a missionary responsibility.[4] However, significant segments of the Reformation did not accept this position. The Lutherans generally maintained that the apostles had fulfilled the Great Commission by taking the gospel to the then-known world. If later generations were without the gospel, it was because of their unbelief. Certain predestinarians were preoccupied with the sovereignty of God and expected Him to bring about a miraculous conversion of the people without the effort of the Christians. Thus, to the time of William Carey, they maintained that if God wills the conversion of the heathen, they will be saved without human instrumentality. Extreme predestinarians believed that if God does not desire the salvation of the heathen, it is useless for man to intervene.

Justinian von Weltz (1621-1668) was one of the early advocates of missions. He labored and wrote for an uplifting of the Christian life and for a practical manifestation of the Christian faith by the proclamation of the gospel to unevangelized peoples. He saw the Christian life and missions as interrelated. Beginning in 1663, he wrote a number of treatises in which he challenged the German churches and especially the Christian students to missionary work.[5] He called for the organization of a missionary society that would be responsible for this ministry and advocated the opening of a school to train missionary candidates. However, the churches lacked missionary vision, and his appeal seemed unfruitful. Nevertheless, he had brought three very important factors to the attention of the churches, and the German Pietists soon gave expression to these ideas.

Among the early European Christians to become interested in the evangelization of the nations were the Pietists of Germany. They were concerned to share their religious life with others. They were never numerous and never carried out vast missionary enterprises, for their missionaries went in small groups to various countries. Yet they inspired other churches of their time with an interest in missions. Through their inspiration no fewer than six important missionary societies were formed in Germany.

Pietist Movement's Missionary Interest (1694-1792)

The Pietists opened a school at Halle in 1694 to train Christian workers. Philip Spener (1635-1705) gave direction to the school for ten years. After Spener's death in 1705, August Francke (1663-1727) guided this important ministry. Halle became the educational center of Pietism and the fountainhead of the missionary enterprise of the eighteenth century. Many students of the university of Halle dedicated themselves to proclaim the gospel to unevangelized people and went to various parts of the world. Bartholemew Ziegenbalg and Christian Schwartz gave valuable service in Tranquebar during the first part of the eighteenth century. Hans Egede went to Greenland in 1721.

Of special significance in creating a missionary spirit in the Protestant churches was Halle's relationship with the administration of the Danish East India Company. King Frederick IV was concerned to provide religious services for the colonists and also to evangelize the indigenous population. In 1705 he assigned Dr. Franz Lutkens, court chaplain at Copenhagen, to provide for this ministry. Finding no volunteers in Denmark, Lutkens appealed to Halle for recruits. Bartholomew Ziegenbalg and Heinrich Plutschau were the first volunteers. Francke gave the venture his devoted support. This led to the formation of the Danish-Halle Mission, a forerunner of Protestant missionary societies.

Ziegenbalg gave fifteen years of devoted service to the mission. After the departure of Ziegenbalg, Christian Schwartz, one of his younger colleagues, continued to give guidance to the ministry. During his furlough in 1715, Ziegenbalg traveled widely in Europe and created much interest in missions, especially in Denmark, Germany, and England. He met and greatly influenced Zinzendorf, who was instrumental in organizing the Moravian missions.

Moravian Church's Missionary Interest (1732-1792)

The Moravian Christians were inspired by Zinzendorf, who during his travels met several converts from the unevangelized peoples of Greenland and the Antilles. Zinzendorf was greatly influenced by these meetings. He became bishop of the Moravian Church in 1739 and for thirty years devoted himself to promote missions and to support those who went to a foreign country. The Moravians may be considered the first Protestant missionary church. During the period from 1732 to 1862 this church sent out more than two thousand missionaries; by 1887 it counted about eighty-three thousand converts.[6] The Moravians' first efforts in Africa south of the Sahara were in West Africa and at the Cape, beginning in 1737. Both the Danish-Halle and the Moravian missions led the Protestant churches in the missionary enterprise throughout the eighteenth century and caused other churches to reflect on the missionary mandate of the church.

Formation of Missionary Societies (1649-1792)

Some early Protestant missionary efforts were undertaken largely by individuals rather than by church organizations. The Protestant churches had no missionary societies or orders to promote the missionary endeavor, support missionaries, and provide continuity in the ministry. Men like John Eliot sensed a responsibility to proclaim the gospel to those who were not acquainted with its message. These men did much to foster an understanding of the missionary mandate—an understanding that eventually resulted in the founding of missionary societies. A significant breakthrough in the Protestant missionary effort came only when a number of missionary societies were formed at the close of the eighteenth century.

During the eighteenth century the European knowledge of medical science and of tropical diseases did not qualify them to undertake missionary enterprises in tropical regions. The Moravian attempt in Ghana came to an end with the deaths of all the members of two parties, as will be indicated later. Nevertheless, the Moravians served in many countries and before long the Moravian Church had three members abroad for every one at home. Their contribution to the life and ministry of the churches in Europe and America should be recognized. They were radiant, witnessing Christians wherever they went, and they inspired others to a greater devotion. Peter Boller ministered to John Wesley in one of the latter's moments of discouragement. Wesley found the joy of the relationship with Christ that guided him to a very fruitful ministry. Through his visit with Zinzendorf at Herrnhut, Wesley attained a greater understanding of the missionary task of the church. He transmitted this new understanding to others through his ministry and in this way he inspired missions.

The Protestant missionary awakening came as a result of the Pietist movement in Europe and the evangelical awakening in Britain. Although some missionary efforts had been made earlier, the beginning of the modern missionary movement is often attached to William Carey's ministry and the founding of many missionary societies.

The Society for the Propagation of the Gospel in New England, a branch of the Church of England, was founded in 1649 for the purpose of propagating the gospel among the Indians of North America. Its first missionary was John Eliot. Born in England, Eliot came to the New World in 1631 and began his work among the Indians the following year. Eliot was effective in the evangelization of the Indians and organized schools for their education.

The Society for Promoting Christian Knowledge was organized in 1698 as an independent mission within the Anglican Church. Its original purpose was to strengthen the religious life of the colonists of the New World. However, it has branched into different parts of the world and become a missionary agency.[7]

The Society for the Propagation of the Gospel in Foreign Parts, commonly known as SPG, was founded by royal charter in 1701 as a specific missionary agency of the Anglican Church. The SPG had the twofold purpose of ministering to the spiritual needs of the English settlers and of evangelizing the indigenous population. However, during the eighteenth century its ministry was mostly confined to the American colonies and the West Indies.[8]

Following these forerunners of the seventeenth and eighteenth centuries, a multitude of missionary societies undertook ministries of evangelization towards the close of the eighteenth century and in the nineteenth century. As a result of William Carey's plea, the Baptist Missionary Society (BMS) was organized in 1792, and Carey himself became the first missionary, going to India in 1793. William Carey's momentous plea for missions is generally regarded as the stimulus for modern missions. Denominational and interdenominational missionary societies were formed in rapid succession, and missionary enterprises were launched in many countries.

MISSIONARY CONCERN OPPOSES SLAVE TRADE

History of Slave Trade

Slavery was practiced during the time of the early church. People became slaves through economic default as well as by seizure as captives in war. Slave trade was carried on in the northern countries of East Africa from the early centuries of the Christian era and it gradually moved further south. The Arab traders requested slaves more than anything else from Ethiopia. When the Portuguese established posts along the coast of East Africa, they found a regular traffic carried on by Arab traders. When the Arabs conquered Egypt and moved south to Nubia, they requested trade in slaves for wheat and oil from Egypt. Slaves were a significant factor in the commerce that passed across the trade routes of the Sahara in West Africa. The captives of tribal wars were held as slaves. Many became the servants of the captor tribe. Some succumbed as victims of human sacrifices. The fate of those who were sold to slave traders from the north was also dreadful. Caravans moved through Timbuktu and Gao on the long trek to the northern cities. During the late fifteenth and early sixteenth centuries, slavery was an institution in parts of the Mediterranean world. The Turks and the Moors held Europeans, Arabs, and Africans in bondage.[9]

Slavery was a constituent part of the social system in West Africa. Whether in the Niger Delta, in Ibo country, or in Yorubaland, slaves were the principal source of investment to indicate wealth. The possession of slaves was regarded as adding dignity to a man and enhancing his social status, much as did the custom of having several wives. In Yoruba country the work on the farms and in the households was basically done by slaves. Slaves dominated Yorubaland and outnumbered the Ijaw and Efik people.[10]

The period of slave trade was characterized by an acceleration of the pace of change, especially on the coast of West Africa from Senegal to Cameroon, in the Angola region, and on the coast of East Africa from Mozambique to Kenya. The slave trade took different forms and had different effects in various parts of the continent. It was most complex in West Africa, and its effects were most profoundly felt in Nigeria, the Ivory Coast, Dahomey, and Ghana. Whereas in the past the slave trade had been carried on almost exclusively in the north, it now shifted from the trans-

Saharan routes to the sea routes of the south, causing the Sudanic cities like Timbuktu and Gao to decline, while the coastal cities like Accra and Lagos boomed. Through the acquisition of firearms, some of the coastal people acquired a new power. There was persistent warfare among West African peoples. Traditional political systems with complex checks and balances in the use of power became transformed into slave-raiding war machines, such as those of the Dahomean kings of the eighteenth century.[11]

Portugal inaugurated the slave trade between western Africa and Europe. Probably the first slaves taken from West Africa by Europeans were brought to Portugal by Antonio Gonsalvo in 1443. Portugal had the first of many chartered companies to trade in African gold and slaves. The slave trade grew rapidly. A few Negro slaves admitted to the West Indies proved such a success that the traffic grew enormously. In 1516 Charles V granted a Flemish trader permission to import four thousand slaves annually to the West Indies. From 1550 to the close of the seventeenth century, one by one, the leading nations of Europe began to get footholds on the African coasts, especially on the west coast. Portugal was gradually pushed out.

Extent of Slave Trade

The Portuguese and Spanish explorers had originally set up provisioning stations for ships sailing south around the African continent en route to the East Indies and mainland Asia. With the discovery of the New World and the development of its vast resources, there was a demand for laborers for the mines and the plantations. African slaves, who could be readily obtained, were carried overseas to the New World. The provisioning stations of West Africa became slave-trading forts. The new market greatly encouraged slave-raiding. The chiefs of the Benin Coast took the opportunity to enrich themselves by the slave trade and by bargaining with the competing European powers. There were for a time no exterritorial European forts.[12] The tribes that had long-standing hostilities toward one another took the opportunity to sell members of the neighboring tribe as slaves. Wars of aggression specifically to secure slaves were promoted. There arose a class of African middlemen who secured slaves in the interior and brought them by land or water to the trading posts.

The trade routes between Europe, West Africa, and the New

World soon formed a triangle. From the European posts manufactured goods were shipped to West Africa and traded for slaves. The slaves were carried to the countries of the New World and traded for such produce as sugar, coffee, tobacco, cotton, silver, and gold. This cargo was then sold in the European markets.[13]

The slave trade developed into an enormous blemish on modern history. Greed dominated the scene and power ruled; there was no consideration for the next person. African chiefs and European and Arab traders used their power for material gain without compunction for the lives lost, the families disrupted, and the agony of parents who lost their children. The world was seemingly struck with blindness and failed to perceive the inhumanity of the slave trade.

Elimination of Slave Trade

The revival of Christianity in Europe and America during the eighteenth century brought about an effective renewal of Christian enterprise in Africa. It was the motivating power behind far-reaching social reforms at home and produced an amazing record of self-denying service overseas. As a result of the new conception of social justice, some Christians were appalled at the evils of the slave trade and exposed them to the public. The Society of Friends were pioneers for the abolition of the slave trade and of slavery as an institution of society. The first recorded protest was made by Friends, probably from Holland, issued in 1688 at Germantown, Pennsylvania. However, no action took place. In 1758, at the Friends' Yearly Meeting, John Woolman voiced his protest against shelving the issue. The assembly was moved by a sense of their neglected duty. A committee was appointed and began aggressive work.

In Britain the Friends also organized support for abolition and made plans to educate the public on the subject. In 1773 they appointed a committee for this purpose. As a result of this effort, the Society for the Abolition of Slave Trade was formed; Thomas Clarkson and Granville Sharp were members of the standing committee. Granville Sharp (1735-1813) became intensely interested in the suffering Negro slaves who were brought to England by visiting West Indian planters. He studied the law on the subject and eventually succeeded in securing from the chief justice the famous judgment of 1772 regarding the forcible detention of a slave. According to this judgment, as soon as any slave set foot on English soil, he became a free man.[14] From that time on all slaves in England were recognized as free men. Thus slavery was deleted from the British Isles.

Granville Sharp was joined in his struggle against slavery by William Wilberforce, John Venn, Zachary Macaulay, James Stephen, Charles Grant, and others. They are often known as the Clapham Sect because they met in the house of Henry Thornton at Clapham Common. They worked zealously for the abolition of slavery. It was no small matter. In 1787 William Wilberforce took up the parliamentary leadership of the campaign for abolition. Before the supporters of abolition were able to succeed in having the bill passed in the House, the French Revolution broke out and delayed further action. The abolition bill was passed by the British Parliament in 1807 and came into effect on January 2, 1808. The enforcement of the law became the task of the British navy. As a result of its patrol of the West African coast, captured African slaves were restored to the African coast.

Later, England persuaded other powers in Europe to follow her example. The fight to abolish slavery was officially considered accomplished in 1833, but traffic persisted. It should be noted that the success of the antislavery movement was not only an achievement of Christian men, but also an indispensable prerequisite for the planting of the Christianity in Africa.[15]

In 1827 the British obtained permission from the Spanish to occupy the island of Fernando Po, twenty-five miles off the Cameroon mainland, for the purpose of controlling the shipment of slaves from this area. The Man-o'-War Bay, which lies between Victoria and Bimbia, is a reminder of the efforts made by the British to suppress the nefarious slave trade. This suitably situated bay sheltered anchorage for the men-of-war of the British navy as they lay in wait for slavers plying the coast of West Africa. Because of the length of the coast, the task was no small one. For fifty years the antislavery campaign was carried on. Whenever slaves were found on a ship, they were liberated and taken to a colony established for liberated slaves. They were confronted with the Christian faith and given an opportunity to receive an education.

The slave trade along the east coast of Africa had been carried on by Arab traders for centuries. They not only purchased slaves at the coastal ports but also penetrated the continent with their forces. They followed three main trade routes from the coast to the lake region; from there they penetrated as far as Kisangani in Zaire, raiding villages and marching the captives to the coast. David Livingstone came upon them at Kasongo on the Lualaba River. George Grenfell encountered their devastating activities on the Zaire River below Kisangani. During the greater part of the nineteenth century, the sultan at Zanzibar used many slaves for the clove plantations on the island and approved the slave trade in general.[16] The Arab traders attacked mission stations when they offered refuge to runaway slaves. John Kirk became the British vice consul at Zanzibar in 1868. He applied every effort to improve the conditions for the people at Zanzibar and on the coast. The sultan, fearing foreign intervention in Zanzibar, issued a law forbidding slavery in his domains in 1873. Even though the slave market was closed on the island, the slave traders tried to sneak slaves away along the coast. The British navy patrolled the coast and succeeded in reducing the traffic, but it continued until the Arabs were defeated on the mainland in 1888-1891. The peoples' conscience had been awakened to the inhumane practice and, as one nation after another turned against it, the evil trade finally disappeared.

SUMMARY

The renewal of Roman Catholic missions coincided with the European discovery of previously unknown parts of the world. The orders that were created became the missionary agencies of the Catholic Church. The ideal of missionary service was an integral part of the Franciscan Order. The Roman Catholic Church was able to call on the members of the religious orders for service and entrust regions of service to them.

The missionary vision became general in the Protestant churches only in the latter part of the eighteenth century. During the seventeenth century certain individuals advocated missions, and others undertook missionary efforts. The Moravians were among the forerunners in Protestant missions. However, when the Protestant churches acknowledged their responsibility to proclaim the gospel to all men, many missionary societies were organized and many missionaries undertook service in Africa.

Having acknowledged their responsibility to proclaim the gospel to all men and also the equality of all men before God, some

Protestants became concerned about the evils of slave trade. They labored untiringly for many years, presenting their convictions to peoples and governments, until the evil practice was abolished.

Study Questions

1. Explain the significance of the Roman Catholic orders for the missionary endeavor.
2. Describe briefly the beginning of Protestant missions in West Africa.
3. What contributions did the Moravian Church make to world missions?
4. Distinguish between the Protestant missionary societies that were agencies of churches and the independent agencies.
5. To what extent was slavery a constituent part of the social system of West Africa?
6. Describe the effects of slave trade on the African peoples.
7. Describe briefly the struggle to terminate slave trade.

4

Missionary Efforts
on the West Coast (1652-1884)

The Roman Catholic missionary agencies established themselves on the islands, which had a healthy climate, off the coast of
Africa. They then approached the mainland from these bases.
Therefore, contacts with the people on the coast were generally at
the regions of the trading posts in the proximity of their base. They
were, however, obliged to live in the unhealthy climate of the coast
in order to attain lasting results. Similarly, the Protestant missionary agencies began their ministries at strategic centers on the
coast, generally at seaports. After having proclaimed the gospel in
those regions, they moved to close the gap between the points of
contact in order to reach all the people.

The Roman Catholic agencies were most active from 1402 until
1772; then a change took place toward the latter part of the
eighteenth century. The Portuguese influence on the coast dwindled rapidly, and this affected the Roman Catholic efforts. The
Dutch, British, and Danes augmented their trade, increasing the
Protestant presence along the coast. But of greater significance
was the renewal of missionary interest in the Protestant churches
and their concern to stop the slave trade. The concentrated missionary activities by the Protestant churches began with the settlement of freed slaves on the West African coast. Because of its
geographic proximity, West Africa was the scene of most of the
early missionary efforts in black Africa. The early contacts were
made when scientific knowledge of tropical diseases was almost
nonexistent. Therefore, West Africa became the "white man's
grave," and relatively few results came from the early work of the
missionaries. Most missionaries, as will be seen below, were able

to devote only a brief time of ministry before they were incapacitated by a tropical disease.

MIGRATION AND EVANGELIZATION

Settlements in Sierra Leone

The judgment of the British Chief Justice Lord Mansfield in 1772, liberating the slaves in the British Isles, created a social problem. The liberated slaves were homeless and needed to be incorporated into the society. Many of them were unable to find employment. A similar problem arose in America after the end of the War of Independence in 1783. Many American Negroes had fought on the side of the British in the war and could not return to the United States. Some were settled in Nova Scotia, but they found the Canadian climate too severe. Others were settled in the Bahamas. Some came to England, increasing the already-existing number of homeless and unemployed there.

A settlement in West Africa seemed a reasonable solution for the problem the freed slaves were confronting. A return to the African continent seemed natural. However, the effort soon encountered many problems the philanthropists had not envisioned. The African chiefs had sold the slaves and were not willing to accept freed slaves of other tribes in their territories. A neutral territory had to be found or purchased for the settlement of freed slaves.

To the advocates of the settlement, Sierra Leone seemed an appropriate place. The first attempt was made in 1787. A party of 411 persons sailed for the West African coast. The party arrived in the area of Freetown. Captain Thompson arranged for twenty square miles of land by treaty with a local chief. But the party arrived during the rainy season and found it difficult to construct shelters and to find food. Disease took its toll of the settlers. After already suffering much hardship and loss of life, in 1789 the little settlement was attacked and burned by a neighboring chief. About sixty settlers were found and resettled at Granville Town by the Sierra Leone Company, newly formed for the purpose of resettling freed slaves. Granville Sharp was very disappointed that some of the settlers had deserted the colony and joined the slave traders.[1]

In 1792 the settlers were joined by 1,196 "Nova Scotians" who had been resettled there after their liberation, but had found the Canadian winter unfavorable and wanted to migrate to a warmer

climate.[2] Through a new arrangement with the chief Temne, these
settlers were colonized at Freetown. Zachary Macaulay governed
the colony from 1794 to 1799. In 1800 a party of 550 Maroons,
former slaves from the West Indies, arrived.[3] To these three
groups were added, after 1808, increasing numbers of liberated
Africans from along the African coast. It is estimated that approximately 114,000 liberated people were settled in the villages
around Freetown from 1808 to 1877.

A number of factors affected the establishment of the Sierra
Leone Colony. Granville Sharp, who was the motivating force
behind the settlement of the liberated slaves in Sierra Leone,
instigated a legitimate commerce of products of the land to provide
a livelihood for the people. The English government desired to
establish a naval base at Sierra Leone from which to patrol the
West African coast for slave traders. After the French raid of the
settlement in 1794, the directors of the Sierra Leone Company
realized that protection of the settlement was a necessity. In 1804
they proposed that the settlement be transferred to the British
crown. Consequently, Sierra Leone became a crown colony and a
naval base in order that the Royal Navy could enforce the new law.
The slaves it captured were brought to Freetown, and the slaves,
now called liberated Africans, were set free. They came from as
far north as Senegal and as far south as Angola, but the majority
were from the Yoruba and Ibo tribes in Nigeria. Very touching
scenes were witnessed at Regent's Town when the resident people
found members of their families among newly liberated slaves who
arrived from time to time.

The Christian agents and the government were concerned to
bring the benefits of Western civilization to the socially uprooted
people. At first the settlers, who had received some education and
were mostly Christianized, remained aloof from the liberated Africans. But gradually, as the latter acquired some education and
accepted the Christian faith, the differences between the two
groups diminished; they developed into a more homogeneous unit
and were called Creoles.

Most of the settlers who arrived from Nova Scotia in 1792
professed to be Christians. They had come under the proclamation
of the gospel in the American colonies and in Nova Scotia. Some of
them were Baptists, some were Methodists, and some adhered to
the Countess of Huntingdon's Connexion. There were preachers

among the settlers, and on arrival at the settlement, they organized their religious life. David George, a Baptist preacher, was quite influential among the settlers. Moses Wilkenson guided the Methodists. They were emotional in their services. Visions and dreams played an important role. The members of the Countess of Huntington's Connexion had a profound religious sentiment. Upon their arrival, they returned thanks to God for His guidance. The first building they constructed was a house of worship.

The liberated Africans, uprooted from their culture, constituted a responsive group for missionary activities. They were more open to listen to the gospel than the people of the tribes who were more secure in their tribal setting and lacked the freedom to act independently. Bichersteth, a representative of the Church Missionary Society (CMS), came to evaluate the possibilities for missionary work in Sierra Leone. He realized that these representatives of many tribes of West Africa could be evangelized and serve as a tremendous force to bring the gospel to their people throughout West Africa.[4] Nine villages were established around Freetown by liberated Africans from 1816-1819. William Johnson from Hanover had an effective ministry of evangelism and instruction among them. The church witnessed significant growth.

In addition to their ministry to the colony, the missionary societies were constrained to bring the gospel to the people of the interior and the coastal regions. Various societies made four unsuccessful attempts to establish a ministry to the people of Rio Pongas, the Banana Islands, and the Bullom shore. Then the Church Missionary Society turned its attention to these people. Using Freetown as a base to launch such an endeavor, Melchior Renner and Peter Hartwig, both of the John Jaenicke's Missionary Seminary in Berlin, were sent to Sierra Leone in 1804. From 1808 until 1814 their work was basically limited to schools for children. Because of the hostility of the local chiefs who wanted to continue the slave trade, the work was abandoned in 1916. Nylander started a work on the Bullom shore across the estuary north of Freetown. He produced a grammar and vocabulary of Bullom and translated some chapters of the Gospel according to Matthew into the language. But the slave trade disrupted the Christian ministry to the extent that the society withdrew from the same and devoted its efforts to the Sierra Leone Colony.

In the colony, the society made a special effort to teach the people. In 1827 the "Christian Institute" became the Fourah Bay College, where hundreds of catechists and teachers who served in Sierra Leone and in other countries of West Africa were prepared. The first African priest of the Anglican Church was ordained at Freetown in 1852. During the next decade some twenty men were ordained to the Christian ministry.[5] In 1864 one of the Fourah Bay students, Samuel Adjai Crowther, was consecrated bishop at London. He and many others dedicated themselves to take the gospel to the people of Africa. While at college they studied the vernacular languages with a view to translating the Bible and Christian literature.[6]

Missionary J. F. Schoen studied the Ibo and Hausa languages and prepared a grammar for the Hausa language. Samuel Crowther did the same for the Yoruba language. The Gospels according to Matthew and Luke and the Acts of the Apostles were translated into Yoruba.

Among the important literary contributions was Dr. S. W. Koelle's famous *Polyglotta Africana*. Koelle, a Semitic scholar, pursued investigations into the African languages with the object of preparing the way for missions to the interior of the continent. He produced the *Polyglotta Africana*, a comparative vocabulary of the hundred words and phrases in 150 languages and dialects. His work received recognition by the secretary of the Royal Asiatic Society and received the Volney prize from the French Institute in 1853. The latter honor was gained in 1877 by the Hausa studies and translations of J. F. Schoen.[7] These efforts to reduce the languages to writing and to translate portions of the Scriptures were a great asset in launching the Niger River and Yoruba missions.

In 1851 Henry Venn recommended principles whereby an indigenous church would be established. The significant factor was to train African church leaders and to entrust the churches and the evangelization of the people to them. The society would then move to new regions as soon as the ministry could be entrusted to the African leaders. In 1854 the society began to apply these principles. A council of pastors under the guidance of the bishop and the church councils became responsible for the church's ministry. In 1860 the constitution that Henry Venn had drawn up for the church in Sierra Leone was approved by the archbishop of Canterbury.[8] The Anglican Church of Sierra Leone was organized in 1861 with a membership of approximately twelve thousand.[9]

The Fourah Bay College; the Annie Walsh School for girls, which was established in 1845; and the missionary posts remained the responsibility of the society. The national church assumed the responsibility for the village schools in 1854, including the payment of the teachers.

In its effort to train indigenous leaders, the society affiliated the Fourah Bay College with the University of Durham in 1876; this arrangement permitted the African students to study for a degree in their own land. In 1880 three students received the Bachelor of Arts and five the Bachelor of Theology degree. Students from other parts of the west coast entered the college. In 1886 two students from Lagos were admitted. Many of the Fourah Bay students entered the Christian ministry and had a far-reaching influence in the English-speaking part of West Africa.[10]

In 1896 the British government declared the hinterland a protectorate under its rule, without consulting the chiefs. The boundaries were drawn according to the line of latitude and river watersheds, not according to the tribal boundaries. The government decided against annexing the country to the colony and forcing English law on people who knew nothing about it. In the protectorate, which was separated from the colony, the chiefs still ruled but were guided by European district commissioners.

The Church Missionary Society had some difficulty in establishing a Christian ministry among the tribes of the interior. A work among the Temne at Port Loko was begun in 1840. But the Muslim influence was strong, and the response did not come until 1895. Within a year, European and Creole missionaries opened more than a dozen stations in the main towns of the western part of Temneland. However, the Hut War Tax in 1898 closed the work, and only Port Loko was reopened after the war. Several other efforts were made to evangelize the people of the tribes; but the response was minimal, and in 1912 the Sierra Leone Church relinquished the efforts to evangelize the tribes. The churches that remained had become Creole, and the society's further ministry was among these people.

It is noteworthy that graduates of the Fourah Bay College went to minister in other parts of West Africa such as the Niger River region, Dahomey, and Nigeria, and were successful in establishing indigenous churches. But they failed to gain credibility for the communication of the gospel to their neighbors in Sierra Leone since they went as messengers of the gospel to their own people and they were unable to bridge tribal barriers in this neighboring clan. Consequently the Church Missionary Society felt compelled to reopen its missionary enterprise with other personnel in Sierra Leone.

The English Methodists entered Sierra Leone in 1811. After several failures, they succeeded in establishing a continuing work. They developed a significant educational ministry, having eleven hundred pupils enrolled by 1837. In 1840 two men were ordained to the ministry. One of them, Charles Night, continued an effective ministry for thirty-seven years. In 1843 they established the Wesleyan Educational and Theological Institution to train their members for the ministry and for general service in the church. They hoped that the institution would be instrumental in spreading the evangelical truth throughout the colony and the regions beyond the colony. They experienced a unique response among the liberated Africans similar to that experienced by the Anglicans. There was a large Creole ingathering until 1857. The people voluntarily turned from their worship of idols and sought instruction in the Christian faith, It has been suggested that the decline of church growth after 1857 was due to the implementation of the catechumenal system, the reduction of funds from England, and the fact that in 1857 the colony was well churched.[11] The church witnessed gradual growth from 1857 to 1920.[12]

The Methodists divided their congregations into small classes, which were conducted by laymen. Effective instruction and pastoral care could be given to small groups. The church planned to evangelize the colony by having each pastor visit all the towns and villages around his post until churches were planted in them. The pastor, responsible for a circuit, made quarterly visits to each class or group to give suitable advice to them.[13] In 1854 the 6,828 Methodist members were divided among thirty-four chapels and four circuits. In 1867 the Sierra Leone district was placed under native administration. But the office of chairman and general superintendent was filled by a missionary, who was appointed by the conference in England.

The results of the Methodist ministry among the Creoles of the colony were similar to those of the Church Missionary Society. In 1877 efforts were made to establish a ministry among the tribes. Within four years missions were begun in three different language areas. However, the relations between the Creoles and the indigenous populaton did not promote evangelization. The population did not trust the Creoles, and the society eventually realized that in order to succeed in winning the people it would have to send missionaries to develop a new work.

The members of the Countess of Huntingdon's Connexion, who came with the settlers from Nova Scotia, were led by three Negro preachers. In the beginning they continued their ministry independently and did not establish relations with the society in London until 1839. They began a ministry on the Sherbro Island and along the Scaries River in 1852. The church community was counting 1,044 members and was organized into districts in 1856. During the same year two pastors, Anthony Elliot and S. R. Wright, died. John Trotter guided the church and opened a school for the training of church leaders. The church began some congregations in the interior, but because of comity agreement, they have been turned over to other churches in recent years.

The Baptists who came with the Nova Scotia settlers confined their fellowship to their group. Consequently they did not win others and remained a small, ingrown community.

The West African Methodist Church is a small church of liberated Africans who separated from the Methodist Church.

The Evangelical United Brethren Church initiated work in Freetown in 1855. The first mission was established at Shenge. In 1875 the ministry began to make progress. The church was organized in 1880. In 1883 Thomas Tucker, the first convert of the mission, became a preacher of the gospel. The society used the school approach in its ministry. Although this approach was instrumental in drawing pupils to the schools, in time the society realized that the schools did not bring about significant church growth. The English language was used in the colony. Later it was also used in the provinces, but communication in English with the indigenous population was not effective.

The Roman Catholic ministry in Sierra Leone was quite minimal during this period. Joseph Koeberle of the Holy Ghost Fathers arrived in 1864, and Father Blanchet followed in 1865. Several Sisters of the St. Joseph of Cluny came in 1866.[14] Freetown was the only center of activity until the 1890s and little progress was registered.

Efforts in Guinea

The missionary societies were constrained to evangelize the people of the interior from the colony of liberated settlers in Sierra Leone. The first attempts made by the Baptist Missionary Society (BMS) in 1795 and next by the Glasgow Missionary Society in 1796, failed. In 1797 the Glasgow and Edinburgh societies, in cooperation with the London Missionary Society (LMS), made another attempt at establishing a mission among the native people, using Sierra Leone as the base. Each society sent two missionaries. Greig and Brunton of the Edinburgh Society went to work among the Susu tribe on the Rio Pongas about sixty miles north of Freetown, where they began a school. Greig was able to establish a good relationship with the people and attain a working knowledge of the language. Unfortunately, he was murdered by Fula traders, who seem to have coveted his belongings.[15] Brunton became a colonial chaplain, but soon left because of sickness. Ferguson and Graham of the Glasgow Society went to work in the Banana Islands, where they died after seven months. Russel and Cappe went to the Bullom shore, across the estuary from Freetown. Russel died after six months and Cappe returned to Britain.[16]

The first continuing work in this region was initiated by the Church Missionary Society. The society appealed to the Missionary Seminary in Berlin, directed by John Jaenicke, for missionaries. Mechior Renner and Peter Hartwig volunteered and were sent to Sierra Leone in 1804. It was the first mission the Church Missionary Society had begun. In 1808 the society established work among the Susu of the Rio Pongas. Their efforts mainly concerned children, and they were unsuccessful in reaching the people.[17] In 1816 this undertaking was abandoned, and the mission moved to Sierra Leone to work among the liberated Africans. A significant reason for the withdrawal of the mission was the Susu chief's desire to continue with the appalling slave trade, which the missionaries' presence discouraged. A second reason was the high mortality of missionaries: between 1804 and 1816, sixteen out of twenty-six died.[18] Nylander commenced work on the Bullom shore across the estuary to the north of Freetown. He produced a grammar and a vocabulary of Bullom and translated some chapters of the Gospel according to Matthew.

The Anglicans from the West Indies took up the ministry in the

1850s. H. J. Leacock from Barvados and a colleague arrived in 1855. They selected a field on the Rio Pongas. Unfortunately, Leacock died within a year. Reinforcements arrived, some of whom were trained in Codrington College under Rawle. In 1874 the Church of the West Indies made this field their special responsibility. However, as a result of the French occupation, they transferred their major effort to the British territory in Sierre Leone.[19]

In the eighteenth century the Roman Catholic Church gave spiritual care to the personnel of the French trading post and erected a prefecture for St. Louis and Gorée in 1765, but no systematic attempt was made to reach the native people.[20] The Sisters of St. Joseph came to St. Louis in 1819 and to Gorée in 1823.[21] They established a hospital and conducted a girls' school. In 1842 three American Jesuit priests arrived at Cape Palmas in Liberia. Dr. Barron was asked to take charge of Upper Guinea. However, in 1845 Barron was in Rome to submit his resignation. The Holy Ghost Fathers entered the work in this part of the continent in 1833. In 1863 the Vicariate Apostolic of Senegambia became their responsibility. They commenced a ministry on the Rio Pongas among the Susu in 1878 through an opening resulting from educational opportunities given to sons of chiefs. A ministry was begun at new centers, and a small work gradually developed.

Contacts in Senegambia

In 1843 Gambia became a British colony and a British protectorate in the valley of the Gambia River, flanked on both sides by Senegal. Bathurst is the only city of importance. The Wesleyan Methodists pioneered in this country in 1821. William Fox joined the mission in 1833 and for nine years pleaded that the mission had possibilities and should not be overlooked. As in other countries of this region, the climate is unhealthy, and death and disease continually depleted the European staff. In 1870 the ministry was carried on at St. Mary's and at McCarthy's Island, with a church membership of 715.[22] A training institution was established in 1875 and it contributed to the preparation of church workers.

The Catholic Church assigned this territory to the Holy Ghost Fathers, but their ministry made little progress.[23] Their schools received government grants. In 1872 three priests and two brothers were instructing at the boys' schools and several sisters were teaching the girls at the St. Mary's girls' school.[24]

The movement of the peoples and religions of North Africa also affected the peoples of Senegal and the neighboring countries on the west coast. Although the Negroes constitute the majority of the population, Moors and Berbers are included in it.[25] Having occupied Mauretania on the northern border of Senegal, the Muslims soon crossed the border into Senegal and influenced its people. The Portuguese discovered the Senegal River in 1455, but they made little contact with the people.

Although the Portuguese and Spanish regimes along the upper west coast of Africa ceased during the eighteenth century, the Roman Catholic bishops, from their island sees in the Atlantic, continued to send priests to visit the Christians on the mainland. But the old missions gradually disintegrated.[26]

A new era in the history of Roman Catholic missions began when societies from the northern countries of Europe assumed the missionary challenge. In the beginning of the nineteenth century, the Holy Ghost Fathers and the Cluny Sisters were active in the Senegambia region. However, due to the limited number of workers, intensive efforts were not made until the latter half of the century.[27]

In 1846 Pope Pius IX added Senegambia to the territory of the Two Guineas. The vicariate of the Two Guineas now included all the territory between the prefecture of Senegal and the diocese of Loanda. In 1849 the pope named Father Bissieux as vicar apostolic of the Two Guineas. Bissieux made his headquarters at Libreville in Gabon, where he had labored for several years, and left his coadjutor, Bishop Aloysuis Kobès, at Dakar to guide the propagation of the faith in that region.

The Holy Ghost Fathers and the Sisters of the Immaculate Conception entered the field. The main activities were centered at St. Joseph de N'gazobil. But Kobès also directed the opening of new stations. He encouraged the founding of an institute for nuns. This institute became known as the Daughters of the Holy Heart of Mary. It was the first institute for Negro nuns to be established in Africa.[28] Kobès was concerned to develop an agricultural settlement with which industrial training was to be associated. When France annexed Senegal in 1847, Kobès applied for and was granted a concession of one thousand hectares from the French government for a cotton plantation. The initial project was a success but it was abandoned after locusts devastated the land for nine years. Schools, however, were maintained, and Kobès directed his attention to the training of an African ministry.[29]

The Société des Missions Evangéliques de Paris, a united endeavor of a number of Protestant churches, entered Senegal in 1862. Its staff was never large. For the first sixty years, the majority of the men sent out either died or were compelled to leave after a few months of service because of ill health. The work was difficult and converts were few. The multiple demands of the various areas of service were staggering. The society was unable to minister to all the needs; so it limited its work in Senegal to a church, a dispensary, and a bookstore in Dakar. Other societies did not enter the field until after World War I.

Ventures in Liberia

The Republic of Liberia is unique among the countries of Africa in that it has not been colonized. It had its origin in 1816 when the American Colonization Society was given a charter by the United States Congress to send freed slaves back to Africa. The philanthropic scheme was mainly instigated by J. S. Mills. In order to understand the Liberia of today, it is necessary to consider its origin and to distinguish between the minority, Americo-Liberians, and the indigenous population, the Africano-Liberians, who constitute the large majority. The Americo-Liberians live mostly in or near Monrovia.

As in the case of many other African countries, the geographic and climatic conditions have had a marked influence on the development of the country and on its population. It was the only country entirely covered with virgin forest. The Liberian coastal climate was very unhealthy. The Portuguese called it the "Pepper Coast" and hardly came near it. The Galhinas River and Cape Mount near the Sierra Leone border and the Gastos River in the Bassa country about 120 miles south of Monrovia were points of slave trade. But slave trade was not as extensive there as on the coast of Ghana. There were very few Liberians among the liberated Africans who returned to Sierra Leone and Liberia from 1822 to 1867. Although a small country with a population of approximately 1.5 million, it wields an influence on African and world affairs. Its internal problems, however, still include a high illiteracy rate, a high infant mortality rate, a low per capita income, and low production. In the coastal areas the people have had more educational opportunities, whereas the people of the interior are mostly illiterate. The tribes of the interior largely retain their traditional way of life. English is the official language, and the country's educational program has been conducted in English even though few people understand that language.

The British effort to settle freed slaves in Sierra Leone influenced the Americans to make a similar effort at another locality. Many people in America voiced strong opposition to slavery from its beginning. Even many slaveholders had guilty consciences and left wills freeing their slaves. The idea of a colony in Africa where freed slaves could settle was advocated by some people before the Revolutionary War. Thomas Jefferson was among those who urged that freed slaves be assisted to return to Africa.

The first contingent arrived in 1820. Under the guidance of Christian Wiltberger and with the counsel of W. A. B. Johnson of Sierra Leone, a territory 140 miles long and 40 miles wide was purchased at Cape Mesurado. The climate at the coast was unfavorable. Consequently they moved partly inland to a higher elevation where Monrovia is now located. In response to a suggestion from General Harper in 1824, the country was called Liberia, indicating liberty, and the capital city was called Monrovia.

In 1822 another party of fifty-three people arrived, under the leadership of Jehudi Ashmun. Ashmun may be considered the real founder of Liberia. He directed the colony for six years until it was well established. More settlers arrived during the following years. Leaving a colony of twelve hundred people, Ashmun returned in 1828 to the United States of America because of ill health. He died during the course of the year.

Between 1820 and 1840, 4,456 people returned to Liberia. Scientific knowledge concerning tropical diseases was limited, and medical services in the colony were almost nonexistent. Consequently malaria, dysentery, and yellow fever took the lives of many of the newcomers.[30] By 1847, 6,100 persons were settled between Cape Mount and the Large Cess, of which 1,300 were at Monrovia.

In 1847 the independent Republic of Liberia, with a constitution like that of the United States, was proclaimed. Britain and France were among the first countries to recognize the new nation, but they did not take its independence seriously. Because of its declaration of independence and the distance that separated it from America, some American statesmen felt little moral obligation to

Liberia. When European powers encroached on the Liberian territory, America only voiced diplomatic objections.

From the very beginning, the indigenous tribes were hostile to
the newcomers and made frequent raids on the settlement. On a
number of occasions the very existence of the colony came into
question. The hostilities were the roots of fear and suspicion,
vestiges of which remain and constitute a disruptive influence in
the society. The settlers separated themselves from the indigenous
population, and this caused political and social difficulties and
retarded or even obstructed the evangelization of the indigenous
population. Therefore, as in Sierra Leone, it became necessary to
carry on two distinct ministries.

Most of the Negro colonists who came from the United States
already adhered to one of the Protestant denominations. Therefore, it was not necessary to evangelize them, but rather to establish self-sufficient, reproducing churches. A number of churches
devoted themselves to this ministry. Among the immigrants were
members of the Baptist denomination. The African Missionary
Convention (AMC) was an auxiliary of the General Baptist Convention of America, which was founded in 1814. This society sent two
Negro ministers, Lott Carey and Colin Teague, to Liberia in 1821.
Lott Carey was a gifted leader. He ably assisted Ashmun in establishing the colony and directed it after Ashmun's departure. He
guided the ministry of the church, the program of education, and
also the care of the sick. The society sent eighteen missionaries to
Liberia between 1833 and 1840, of which fourteen died. After 1856
they sent only black missionaries, hoping that they might adapt
more satisfactorily to the climate. However, this was not the case.
In 1846 the foreign mission board of the Southern Baptist Convention appointed missionaries to Liberia, but transferred them to
Nigeria in the 1870s in order to concentrate on the Yoruba country.[31] The two black missions, the Lott Carey Baptist Foreign
Mission and the National Baptist Convention, continued their
ministry in Liberia. The Baptists outnumbered the other
denominations.

In response to an appeal Ashmun made for missionaries, the
Basel Evangelical Missionary Society sent five missionaries to Liberia
in 1828. G. A. Kissling began a ministry to the Bassa tribe. H. H.
Wulff died and the other three returned to Europe. In 1830, J. F.
Sessing returned to Liberia with three new recruits. But all three

died within four months. Sessing went to Sierra Leone. Four months later Kissling, having baptized the first Bassa convert, also left Liberia. Thus ended a noble effort in the unfavorable climate that brought many other projects to a quick and fruitless end.

The year 1833 witnessed the beginning of the Methodist, Presbyterian, and Congregational ministries in Liberia. Melville B. Cox, the first American Methodist missionary, died within four months of his arrival. Miss Sophronia Farrington, a member of a party of five who arrived on New Year's Day, 1834, encouraged the society to continue the ministry in spite of the heavy loss of missionary lives. John Seys and Mrs. Ann Wilkins were among the reinforcements who helped to establish the ministry.[32] Concerned to train local leadership, they founded the College of West Africa at Monrovia in 1839. This college is the oldest institution in Liberia. For a period in the second half of the century the mission was at a decline, but Bishop William Taylor arrived at an appropriate time, in 1884, and kindled new courage and devotion at many stations in various districts. Bishop Joseph Hartzell succeeded Taylor in 1896 and was instrumental in strengthening and establishing the ministry. The mission was concerned to evangelize the indigenous population as well as the liberated Africans.[33] A ministry was begun at several centers and in 1898 the church counted 2,667 members.[34]

John B. Pinney, the representative of the Presbyterian Church, attempted to give agriculture its proper position in the establishment of a colony. He returned to the United States for recruits in 1834, and, within four months of their return to Liberia, three of the four were dead. He returned to America with Finley. In 1839 he was back with three new helpers. They were soon victims of the climate, and Pinney retired from Liberia.[35]

John Leighton Wilson of the American Board (Congregational) began a ministry at Cape Palmas in 1834 and gave seven years of dedicated service. He reduced the Grebo language to writing and started translating the Bible, even while his colleagues died of tropical diseases. Added to the problems of climate for the missionaries, there was continual tension between the settlers and the tribes. In 1841 the board transferred the mission to Gabon.[36]

John Payne, the first missionary of the American Episcopal Church, arrived in 1835. He was consecrated bishop in 1851 and served until 1871. The mission prospered under his long and able leadership. Bishop Samuel Ferguson (1884-1916), a capable leader, developed an outstanding educational system. Cuttington College and Divinity School trained personnel for the scores of village and church schools.[37]

The United Lutheran Church began its ministry in 1860. Morris Officer established the station at Muhlenberg, twenty-five miles up the St. Paul River, and began the central boarding school there. David and Emily Day made a significant contribution. The mission, however, seemed unsuccessful in reaching the indigenous people. The children that were taught in the central boarding school tended to gravitate toward the Americo-Liberian society instead of taking the initiative and assuming the responsibility to reach the indigenous population. The leadership of the church largely fell to foreign missionaries. The work did not begin to show signs of expansion until toward the end of the century, and even then its growth was relatively small. The further development of the ministry in Liberia will be observed later.

NATIVE RULE AND EVANGELIZATION
Endeavors in Ghana

Missionary societies made their early contacts at strategic points on the long coast of West Africa. Then later, as they undertook to bring the gospel to all the people, they went to the regions that had been neglected. The early missionary effort in Ghana came as a result of commercial contacts of the seventeenth century. The Portuguese began to trade with the coast in the fifteenth century. Later the Dutch, English, Danes, French, Swedes, and Brandenburgers followed. The Moravians, under Zinzendorf's leadership, were indefatigable in bringing the gospel to all unevangelized people. An opportunity to bring the gospel to Ghana presented itself after Christian Protten, whose father was a Danish soldier at Christiansborg and whose mother was a member of the royal family of Anecho, had been sent to Copenhagen to receive an education.

In 1735 Zinzendorf met Protten at Copenhagen and invited him to Herrnhut. Protten volunteered for work at Elmina, Ghana, where Zinzendorf wanted to establish a Christian ministry. Henry Huckuff of the Moravian Church volunteered to accompany him. They arrived in 1737, but Huckuff died within two months of his arrival. Protten turned his attention to teaching in a school for

mulatto children and presented his plans to Governor General
Martog of the Dutch post for approval. However, because tensions
existed between the Dutch and the Danes, Protten was suspected
of being a Danish spy and was kept under disguised arrest until
April 1739.[38] He returned to Europe and, after a lengthy stay at
Herrnhut, went back to Christiansborg, the Danish post. He married Rebecca, the widow of a Moravian from the Antilles, and
served as a teacher. In 1764 he prepared a grammar in Fanti, in
which he included selections from the Bible. He died in 1769.[39]

The Moravian Brethren attempted to continue his endeavor. A
party of five led by Meder arrived at Christiansborg in 1768. But
three members of the party died within two months. In 1770 four
more recruits came. They selected a site at Christiansborg, but
every member of the staff died within two years and the endeavor
was terminated. No further missionary effort on this part of the
coast was made until the nineteenth century.

The Basel Evangelical Missionary Society, in association with
the Danish trading interests on the coast, began their noteworthy
ministry with the coming of four pioneer missionaries in 1828 in a
region controlled by the Danes. The workers were from Switzerland and Germany. The last member of the party died in October
1831. Three other missionaries arrived in 1832, but by the end of
the year Andreas Riis was the only survivor to continue the ministry. After three years he received permission to move to a better
climate in the Akwapim Mountains. A station was established at
Akropong, which became the administrative center of the mission. Two missionaries and Riis's bride-to-be joined Riis in 1837.
Death again disrupted the ministry, taking the two missionaries
from the field in 1838 and leaving Riis and his wife to carry on
alone.[40] They went on furlough in 1840 and returned in 1843 with a
group of Moravian Christians from Jamaica. They survived and
formed the nucleus of the first Protestant church in Ghana. The
first converts were baptized at Akropong in 1847 and at Aburi in
1856. Reinforcements came from Europe. Johann Zimmerman
came in 1850. That same year the Gold Coast government was
given a separate status, independent from Sierra Leone. The
Danes transferred their posts to the British in return for ten
thousand British pounds. In 1852 the legislative assembly suggested a poll tax. In 1854 resistance to the payment of the poll tax
came to a head in Accra. The British bombarded the city. As a

result of these unfavorable circumstances, Zimmerman and August Steinhauser moved from Accra to Abokabi. In 1857, Mohenu, a leading pagan priest became a Christian. He and his family were baptized. For thirty years Mohenu carried on an effective preaching ministry, supported by a worthy Christian life.[41]

A ministry was begun at Odumase among the Krobo people west of the Volta in 1857. Under Zimmerman's leadership it became a head station for a successful ministry of evangelization of the Krobo people. After a Christian community had been established, the ministry soon spread to include eight districts with twenty-four congregations and 1,851 members by 1869 and 4,000 members by 1878. The society made a vital contribution in the training of indigenous leaders for the church. Schools for boys and girls and for the training of catechists were opened.

Several members of the Basel Evangelical Missionary Society made distinguished literary contributions. Johann Zimmerman devoted himself to study the Ga language, and J. G. Christaller became a prominent authority on the Twi and Ashanti languages.[42] He completed the translation of the New Testament in 1864 and of the entire Bible in 1871. He also produced a dictionary and published 3,600 Twi proverbs.[43]

Zimmerman had ideas of agricultural development in the suitable climate of the Akwapim Mountains. But circumstances prevented him from carrying out his plans. Through the efforts of families from the Antilles, however, coffee and cocoa plantations were introduced. The climate of Ghana was conducive to the growing of cocoa. Cocoa plantations thrived instantly, and by the end of the century Ghana was the largest cocoa producer in the world.[44] This produce has become an important export and a large source of income for the people and the country.

The ministry of the Methodist Missionary Society began in 1834 as an outgrowth of grants of Bibles to schoolboys in the British Cape Coast Castle by the British and Foreign Bible Society, and this created a remarkable interest in learning more about the Christian faith.[45] Two couples, the H. O. Wrigleys and the P. Harrops, went to serve in this capacity but soon became victims of the West African diseases. Thomas Birch Freeman was the son of a Negro father from the East Indies and of an English mother (Anny Birch). Hearing of the challenge, Freeman, who had received an education in England, volunteered for service.[46] His wife died after six weeks in Africa.[47] Freeman was bereaved but, confident of God's will for his life, he continued without hesitation. His extraordinary services of long duration laid the foundation for a continuing Methodist ministry.

Through Freeman's contacts, the Methodist Church was able to begin a ministry among the Ashanti tribe in 1838. War between the Fanti of the coast and the Ashanti had been common until 1826. Freeman ventured to visit Kumasi (1839), Abomey, and Abeokuta. It was the first visit by a Christian missionary.[48] His courtesy, friendliness, and respect for the chiefs won the confidence of the people and he received a cordial reception by the king of the Ashanti.

Freeman had exceptional missionary plans and proceeded to begin work even though the conditions were not altogether appropriate and the necessary preparations had not been made. He visited much of West Africa, founding schools and congregations wherever people were interested in English schools and the English faith.[49] He visited Abeokuta and planned a missionary station there. Later he contacted the king of Dahomey and called at Anecho and Whydah. He also traveled to other parts of the coast of West Africa carrying on an effective ministry wherever he went.

Freeman realized the necessity for indigenous leadership to establish the church. He arranged for schools and the training of a native pastorate. On his second visit to the Ashanti king, he raised the question of a school. This policy has been continued by the Methodist Church, and its educational ministry has become quite important. Freeman also acknowledged the prominent part Christians could play in spreading the faith through their testimony and their participation in the services.[50] Between 1834 and 1844 there was steady growth in church membership. The Methodist Church had its largest growth in the central and western sections of the country.

Beginnings in Togo

The North German Missionary Society, also known as Bremen Mission from the city in which its headquarters were located, began its activities at Peki to the east of the Volta, in the southwestern part of the Ewe country in 1847. It chose an area for service to the east of the Basel Mission and later took charge of the latter's ministry to the east of the Volta. As in many other endeavors in West Africa, malaria took a heavy toll. By November, Lorenz Wolf was the only survivor of the party of four.[51] He continued courageously, but was forced to return to Germany in 1851. The society's attempt in 1853 to launch a ministry with Keta on the coast as a base was successful. It undertook to explore the country in order to bring Christianity to the people and assist them to develop the country. Christian Hornberger made several exploratory voyages from Keta to the interior, until then unknown to the missionaries. On one of these voyages he visited Atakpame and Wegbe Ho.[52] He carefully noted the geography of the country and the life of the people and in this way made an important contribution to the knowledge of the geography and ethnography of the Ewe country. The ministry was extended to Waya in 1855, to Anyoko in 1857, and to Wegbe Ho in 1859.[53]

In 1861 Steinemann and Haupt made an exploratory voyage from Wegbe Ho to Anfoin and called at Avatimé on their way and again on the return voyage. The society encouraged the commercial agents F. M. Victor and Sons to provide legal commerce for the country so that the people would have a regular and fair market for their products.[54]

The ministry was interrupted at Wegbe Ho and Waya by the Ashanti aggression of 1869-1874.[55] After peace had been restored in 1874, the society reconstructed and enlarged Wegbe Ho and established ministries at Peki and Amadzofé on the Avatime. The ministry entered a period of progress in which it grew and was established. As slave trade was finally brought to an end and the British prohibited the institution of slavery after the Ashanti war (1874), the missions faced a new situation. They ministered to a society in which every person was free to choose his or her destiny. This freedom had a positive effect on the ministry of the church. Those who chose to serve the church did so because of spiritual conviction.

Zahn, the Bremen Mission inspector, was influenced by Henry Venn of the Church Missionary Society to strongly advocate independent churches as the goal of evangelical missionary work and to train an indigenous leadership to guide the churches in their ministry. Schools for children and for catechists were founded. Although their motives were not always strictly evangelical, the youth pressed into the schools and came under evangelical influence with gratifying results. The contribution of catechists and pastors in planting Christianity in Africa cannot be over-emphasized. Joseph Tawia from Gbadzeme in Avatime was baptized at Maiera, an outstation of the Basel Mission and a purely African congregation. He returned to his region and began to preach. In 1876 he came to Ho with five persons who wanted to become Christians. Joseph Tawia was encouraged to continue the ministry, and a Christian village was formed.[56] Many similar contributions have been made which served as a dynamic factor in planting Christianity in towns, villages, and hamlets throughout Africa south of the Sahara.

The Bremen Mission sent more than one hundred missionaries to this region during the forty years of its ministry before the German colonization of the country. More than one half of them died while in service. Their contribution to the geography and ethnography of the country and the quality of their faith demand respect.[57]

Thomas Birch Freeman, the Methodist missionary strategist, visited the coast of Togo in 1843, preaching and making contacts wherever he went. But a continuing enterprise was not established until the 1870s, and, after a decade of preparatory work, the ministry began to witness growth, beginning in the latter 1880s.

As a result of earlier contacts Catholics made with the people of the coast, some Roman Catholics with Portuguese names could be found at the beginning of the nineteenth century. Portuguese priests visited them occasionally, but no continuing ministry was established. In the 1880s the Society of African Missions maintained a station in the region and cared for the few Roman Catholics in the country, but, finding an unfavorable attitude, they withdrew again. The Society of the Divine Word began an uninterrupted work in 1892, which made noteworthy progress from its commencement to 1914.[58]

Difficulties in Dahomey

The Spanish Capuchins made the first effort to plant Christianity in Dahomey in the seventeenth century, but it had no lasting results. Although the Catholic and Protestant churches expected the European trading forts to Christianize the people with whom they had contact, little evangelization took place. A few individuals took one of the natives into their homes and provided the individual with an European education.

Thomas Birch Freeman's visit to Dahomey in 1843 paved the way for continuous missionary endeavors in that country. King Dahomey was not willing to discontinue his warfare and slave raiding, but he agreed to discontinue human sacrifices. Freeman established relations that provided further opportunities to communicate with him. Freeman visited him again in 1854, but Dahomey was not favorably inclined to have missions in his territory. However, an African agent was stationed at Whydah on the coast. From 1857 to 1866 P. W. Bernasko served there. In 1862 the Dahomeans attacked and destroyed Ishagga and took the Christians as prisoners. Dahorty, the catechist of the Church Missionary Society, was among the prisoners. They crucified one of the Christians in Abomey, thinking he was the catechist. Dahorty was released in 1866. Bernasko was virtually a prisoner until 1866, when he was able to withdraw from the region. Whydah remained without a Methodist representative for some years.

The Catholics began a ministry in the region between the Volta and the Niger rivers. Borghero visited King Gréré in 1861 and received permission to remain in Dahomey, but not to baptize. He appropriated the old Portuguese fort and gathered the Christians from Portuguese days, mostly mulattoes and some liberated slaves, into a community. The Roman Catholic Church established the vicariate of the Coast of Benin in 1870.[59] From 1871 to 1884 the center was abandoned because of the opposition of the witch doctors, and the ministry did not achieve substantial gains until the 1890s.[60]

Advances in Nigeria

In the campaign against slave trade, Thomas Fowell Buxton and his associates envisioned the possibilities of legal commerce that would provide the African peasant with a respectable livelihood and restore his dignity. The 1840s were times of high expectations and great disappointments in Africa. Buxton and his associates attempted to bring to realization their plans to open Africa to the plow and the Bible. From 1854 to 1873 David Livingstone continued to emphasize this need. The largest effort put forth in the 1840s was the Niger expedition promoted by Buxton. Although the first voyage was not successful, subsequent voyages opened the Niger area to philanthropic efforts and inspired subsequent endeavors in other parts of the continent in later years, such as the

African Lakes Company in the Lake Nyasa region and the East Africa Scottish Industrial Mission in Kenya.

The course of the Niger River had been discovered by Mungo Park (1771-1806) and other explorers, and it was known that this river held the key to vast and populous areas. An enterprise combining commercial and philanthropic objectives for the introduction of European civilization on the Niger was undertaken in 1841. In the joint endeavor of church and state, the party included the missionary J. F. Schoen from Sierra Leone, Samuel Adjai Crowther,[61] and several Christians like Thomas King and Simon Jonas who originally were from this region and were to serve as interpreters. They were well received by the Ibo people. The reception from the Engara, even though less enthusiastic, permitted them to install elements of a model farm among them. The voyage had been undertaken during the dry season and the low river did not permit the expedition to attain the Nupe. On the return voyage, Schoen assigned Thomas King as catechist to the Engara. Although the expedition brought new knowledge about the possibilities for a philanthropic enterprise, it proved too costly. When the expedition finally returned to Fernando Po, forty-one members of the party had died. Therefore no further attempts to develop the Niger region were made until 1854.

The expedition up the Niger coincided with the return of slaves from Sierra Leone to western Nigeria, notably to the Yorubaland.[62] Between 1839 and 1842 several hundred former slaves returned to their own people whom they found some distance inland from Lagos and Badagry, especially at or near Abeokuta.[63] The return of liberated slaves was soon in full process. However, extensive slave trading continued at Lagos and those who passed through that port encountered much difficulty. Consequently the people soon went via Badagry. They wrote to the emissaries of the Church Missionary Society to inform them of their happy discoveries and to request spiritual nurture.

The Methodist Church responded to the appeal from their believers by sending T. B. Freeman to visit the people at Badagry and Abeokuta. Freeman arrived at Badagry in September 1842[64] and sent a message to Shodeke, the chief of Abeokuta, informing him of his intended visit. The chief not only responded cordially, but sent an escort with a mount for Freeman.[65] Shodeke was a noble spirit; he received refugees from many tribes in his town.

William de Graft, a Methodist missionary, was made responsible for the ministry at Badagry and Abeokuta. As these towns feared an attack from Dahomey, Freeman decided to visit the king in order to secure their safety and that of the mission in that area. Apparently the king was favorably impressed by the visit. He agreed to stop making human sacrifices; however, he gave no assurance concerning the safety of the Yoruba, and he refused to allow missionary activities in his country.[66]

Henry Townsend of the Church Missionary Society visited Abeokuta in 1842 and 1843. Shodeke was pleased at the return of his people from slavery and requested that Townsend write to the governor of Sierra Leone to express his thankfulness to the British government for their assistance. He expressed his desire to suppress the slave trade and to have missionaries and legal merchants in his country. He strove for peaceful relations with Dahomey and objected to the slave raiding at Lagos. After some consideration, he stated that the Christian faith was the true religion and offered the missionaries full liberty for their ministry.

In 1844 Townsend returned to Abeokuta with C. A. Gollmer and his wife and Samuel Crowther to commence a ministry in Abeokuta. Crowther met his mother and sisters after having been separated from them for more than twenty years.[67] Crowther's mother, Afala, wanted to make a special sacrifice to her gods in gratitude for the reunion with her son, but Crowther instructed her that she owed this mercy to the Christian God.[68] His mother and sister were among the first converts, and Crowther translated the baptism service into Yoruba for his mother.[69] Crowther also served in other capacities, but the Yoruba mission occupied most of his time.

Shodeke, chief of Abeokuta, died in 1844. Several days after his death Dahomey took the Egba post on the route to Badagry, closing transportation between Abeokuta and the port. This situation retarded the progress of the two societies. The Church Missionary Society concentrated its efforts at Abeokuta, while the Methodist Mission worked at Badagry.

Shodeke's favorable attitude opened Yoruba country to missionary work at a time when Dahomey rejected missions. At the same time Kosoko usurped the power from his uncle, Chief Akitoye of Lagos. Kosoko was concerned to benefit from slave trade. The testimony of the liberated slaves, the kindness of the missionaries, and the assistance of the British government opened the country for the Christian ministry. Many liberated slaves found members of their families, whom they had not seen for some years. Sierra Leone merchants purchased the produce of the country at Badagry. A British trading firm, Thomas Hutton and Co., soon opened factories and stores in Abeokuta and Badagry.[70] Some chiefs recognized the advantages of civil order, lawful commerce, and the Christian ministry but opposed the traffic of slaves; other chiefs wanted to benefit from slave traffic. When Townsend left for England in 1848, the chiefs sent a letter with him to the queen, expressing their gratitude for the measure of peace in their country and indicating their concern about the situation at Lagos. The queen cordially responded to the letter.[71] However, the slave trade at Lagos continued until it brought about a tribal war in 1851 and was only eliminated in 1861.

Samuel Crowther's contribution to the planting of Christianity in Nigeria deserves special mention. He participated in three journeys up the Niger River and his reports and his efforts played an important role in the establishment of a ministry on the Niger. In 1851 he went to England in connection with his Yoruba translations. While he was there, he was received by Prince Albert and the queen. On another occasion he was received by Lord Palmerton, who was amazed that the well-dressed clergyman was a former slave. While Crowther was at the Church Missionary House, he met Sir Henry Leeke, the captain who had rescued him from slavery. Sir Henry invited him to his country house in Kent and arranged for him to bring a message in the parish church. When he was asked to address a gathering of men at Cambridge, he pleaded with them to help Africa. Wherever Crowther went, he promoted the missionary cause and inspired others to do likewise.

Crowther had made an unusual literary contribution in the preparation of a Yoruba grammar, a Yoruba-and-English dictionary, and Yoruba versions of many books of the Bible. Therefore Henry Venn suggested to the vice-chancellor of Oxford that the D.D. degree be conferred on him; this took place in 1864 shortly before he was consecrated as bishop. On June 19, 1864, in a ceremony conducted in Canterbury Cathedral, Crowther was consecrated as bishop of the Niger territories. He served the church in this region until his death in 1891.

In 1854 the English government undertook another voyage up

the Niger River. The *S.S. Pleiad,* under the direction of Dr. Baikie, ascended the river to the junction of the Benue River and then followed the Benue for 250 miles without losing a voyager. As a result of the success of this voyage, Macgregor Laird proposed that annual voyages be made. Samuel Crowther, who had accompanied the *Pleiad,* published his voyage journal and encouraged the churches to undertake missionary endeavors along the river.

In 1857 the government sponsored another voyage and invited the Church Missionary Society to participate in it. The purpose of the voyage was to acquire a more complete knowledge of the river, conclude commercial treaties with the chiefs, and open the region to missionary service. Samuel Crowther and J. C. Taylor, consecrated Ibo pastor at Sierra Leone, were sent by the Church Missionary Society. The voyage was made in the *S.S. Dayspring.*[72]

J. C. Taylor stayed at Onitsha for twenty months to commence a ministry. Crowther made arrangements for ministries at Abo, to the north of the Delta; at Idda, north of Onitsha; and at Gbebe, at the confluence of the rivers. The voyage was continued to Rabba in the Nupe country, where a Muslim Fulani governed. They were cordially received and decided to continue. However, the current was too strong for the motors of the vessel. Pushed back against a rock, the vessel sank. Happily all the passengers were saved. They erected a camp on the shore and waited for assistance. After some time another vessel, the *Sunbeam,* arrived and the party embarked. Crowther stayed at Onitsha and returned later by canoe as far as Rabba, where he visited the chief of Ilorin and presented the gospel to him.[73]

Thus the Niger Mission was started. The ministry had commenced at Onitsha and other churches had been inspired to undertake missionary efforts. The society sent five men for this mission in 1859, but three were engaged at Sierra Leone and at Abeokuta and the other two became ill. Consequently the early opportunity on the Niger River was not redeemed.

After Kosoko usurped the power at Lagos, Akitoye, the lawful ruler, went to reside at Badagry and was recognized as the legitimate ruler by the Abeokuta chiefs.[74] Kosoko raided Badagry and burned a large part of the town. Akitoye requested the British naval commander to support him. A force landed at Lagos. Akitoye regained power and agreed to terminate the slave traffic through Lagos and make the port accessible for legitimate trade with the Yoruba country. At the request of the commodore and the consul, a mission was immediately established and a catechist, James White, was placed there.[75] Slave trade, however, was not totally eliminated until 1861.

The missionaries presented the vastness of the country to their society, indicating that a dozen large villages could be reached. When Townsend visited Ijaye, a Yoruba town of some forty thousand people, the chief invited a missionary to his town but was unwilling to assure his protection. The chief of Ketu opposed slavery and asked Crowther to send missionaries, assuring their protection. Thus some chiefs extended a sincere invitation to missionaries.

The Church Missionary Society took immediate steps to provide indigenous leadership for the congregations in Nigeria. In 1854 it consecrated two deacons, and two years later ordained three ministers. It gave priority to evangelism and church planting but was also conscious of the people's poverty and encouraged agriculture and commerce, especially of cotton and palm oil. Commerce increased rapidly and became profitable after Lagos was taken and the River Ogun was accessible for lawful commerce. Later the Ijebu declared that their country had benefited from economic advantages. Henry Venn presented samples of produce to brokers in England and stimulated trade, especially in cotton. By the end of the century, an important cotton industry was developing.[76]

The measure of security and prosperity greatly influenced the chiefs. The traffic of slaves was greatly reduced. A number of chiefs made mutual agreements not to capture members of the other tribe. The prisoners at Ibadan were returned to Abeokuta. The Yoruba mission witnessed much success. David and Anna Hinderer made an initial visit to Ibadan in 1851 and returned in 1853 to commence a work there. They devoted seventeen years to this ministry. Hinderer also received an invitation from the Oni of Ife to teach him "the new way of happiness."[77] In 1853 A.C. Mann began a work at Ijaye. In 1856 a teacher was placed at Oyo, the political headquarters of the Yoruba people. In 1855 Mann made a journey to the northeast. He visited Ogbomosho and secured a site for a mission center. He proceeded to Ilorin on the Hausa frontier, which was under Muslim rule. He interviewed the Emir several times but failed to receive permission to work there.

The Southern Baptist Convention was the third society to undertake a mission to the Yoruba. The first representatives of the society—Thomas Bowen, Hervey Goodale, and Robert F. Hill—arrived at Monrovia, Liberia, in 1849 while en route to Nigeria. Hill discontinued the endeavor, and Goodale died in December. Bowen was left alone to begin the ministry. He proceeded to Badagry from where he planned to continue to Igboko, about two hundred miles north of Lagos. However, because of Yoruba wars, the road was closed, and he could only proceed to Abeokuta.

The effects of the wars on the church may be illustrated by the following incident. During the Dahomey attack on Abeokuta, John Baptist Dasalu, a servant of the Lord, disappeared and was reported dead. Some time later a ransomed Egba prisoner reported that Dasalu was in captivity at Dahomey. But all efforts to find him or to obtain his release failed. In 1855, a party of emancipated slaves arrived in England from Cuba. They reported that Dasalu had arrived in Cuba and informed them about the Dahomey war with Abeokuta and of the conditions in Nigeria. The Church Missionary Society asked the British government to secure his release. After arriving in England in August, 1856, he was warmly welcomed by the society and sent back to his native land.[78] Dasalu was found because he was a known church worker, but many people remained slaves because no one interceded for them.

Bowen studied the Yoruba language at the Church Missionary Society's station at Abeokuta while waiting to proceed to Igboko. Because the road to Igboko was still closed in 1852, he arranged for a ministry in Ijaye, a city with a population of approximately forty thousand. Then he returned to the United States to marry his fiancée, to report on his work, and to secure recruits for the ministry.[79]

In 1853, Bowen returned with his bride and two other couples. However, upon arriving at Abeokuta, they contracted malaria. The J. L. Lacys were incapacitated and sent home, and the J. S. Dennards both died within a year. Bowen and his wife were the only survivors to establish the Baptist Yoruba Mission.[80] When they arrived at Ijaye, they learned that A.C. Mann of the Church Missionary Society had returned to Ijaye and commenced a ministry there. Since the city was large and was bordered by a vast unreached region, they decided to remain and work there also. In 1854, W. H. Clarke joined the Baptist work, and the Bowens proceeded to begin a ministry at Ogbomosho. From Ogbomosho,

Bowen made several visits to Ilorin, the Muslim center, but was unable to receive permission to establish a mission there.[81] His health obliged him to retire in 1856. In the meantime J. M. Harden, a Negro from Liberia, had begun a work in Lagos. Recruits came and the society undertook ministries at Abeokuta in 1857 and at Oyo in 1858.[82] Mission comity apparently was not observed in Nigeria as strictly as it was in many other countries of Africa. As in Abeokuta, several churches ministered in the same cities almost from the commencement of the missionary endeavor.

In 1860 a difficult period for the missionary enterprise in Nigeria began when one of the numerous wars broke out in Yoruba country. The war basically involved the Egbas of Abeokuta and the people of Ibadan. The Egbas wanted control of the trade to the coast, whereas the Ibadan wanted a through route to the coast. The Dahomeans took advantage of the situation and destroyed Ishagga, allied with Abeokuta. Ibadan destroyed Ijaye, which was also allied to Abeokuta. A British officer rescued A.C. Mann and his wife, but Mrs. Mann died as a result of the difficulties. Edwin Roper insisted on staying with his congregation at Ijaye, but was carried away as prisoner to Ibadan.

Because the slave trade, which still flowed through Lagos, was partly responsible for the war, the British annexed Lagos in 1861 to completely terminate the evil trade and also eliminate its secondary effects. In 1865 the Abeokuta people attacked Ikorodu, near Lagos, which had associations with Ibadan. But the British forces demanded their retreat. Irritated by this rebuff and further restraints by the British, they expelled the missionaries from Abeokuta in 1867. This was an unexpected turn in a town considered the focal point for spreading the gospel in central Nigeria.[83] But the church survived and witnessed to the transforming grace of God under the guidance of three native pastors—Moore, Allen, and Williams. In 1870 the situation stabilized and further missionary endeavors were undertaken, although Abeokuta was not definitely reoccupied until 1880.

As the ministry developed in Nigeria, the importance of the location of Lagos became evident and so the Church Missionary Society made the old headquarters of slave trade the headquarters of its missionary enterprise in Nigeria.[84] The ministry of the church expanded significantly. Early in 1869, the Lagos Christians began to relieve the society of the support of the schools, and in

1870 efforts were made to form a native pastorate. Bishop Cheetham vigorously promoted these plans. Four Yoruba Christians were ordained to the ministry in 1871 and three more in 1876. The church did not attain the measure of independence that the Sierra Leone church achieved, but native pastors were in charge of many congregations and other functions of the church.

Crowther took up residence at Lagos and guided the large ministry entrusted to him from this central location. His work in the southern part of Nigeria was more successful than in the northern part, but he did not neglect the work in the north. He traveled from the Delta to Nupeland, and the evangelists who served under his direction made contacts at various towns.[85] Crowther worked in close cooperation with the merchant companies, for he thought the success of the Niger Mission depended on the success of legitimate trade.[86] The Niger Mission was sustained in its early days by the vision of men like Crowther and Baikie. Soon signs of progress convinced others of the validity of the project.

While the Church Missionary Society and the Methodist Mission began ministries on the Niger River and inland from Lagos, the United Presbyterian Church of Scotland began a mission in Calabar, to the east of Lagos, in 1846. This ministry was instigated by a presbytery in Jamaica. Hope Waddell, the pioneer of the group, had been a missionary to Jamaica. The initial party included Jamaicans and Scottish missionaries who had served in Jamaica.[87] The local chief welcomed the party and supported the missionaries in many of their endeavors, even though another section of the population feared they would disrupt the slave trade. The Jamaican representatives were well received by the people, though the people had not always welcomed Jamaicans before.[88]

The ministry was begun in a busy center of trade, where slave trade played a major role, liquor was in demand, and life was cheap. The belief regarding the future life required attendants to be put to death and buried with their deceased chief to serve him in his future life. Witchcraft was prominent and caused a heavy death toll among the people.[89] The destruction of newborn twins and the killing of the aged were customs routinely practiced. The mission had a significant influence in instilling a respect for life, which eventually brought an end to the ritual extermination of human life.[90]

The society made an important literary contribution. Hugh Goldie, who arrived in 1847, compiled a dictionary of the Efik language. William Anderson translated portions of the New Testament, and Goldie completed the New Testament in Efik in 1862. Alexander Robb completed the translation of the Old Testament in 1868. Robb's translation of *Pilgrim's Progress* was greatly appreciated by the people.[91]

A church was established among the Efik people, and in 1872 Esien Ukpabio, the first convert and catechist, was ordained to the Christian ministry. For some years the mission was confined to the Efik people. The people who held a monopoly on trade with the interior disapproved of missionaries contacting other tribes for fear that their lucrative trade would be spoiled. In 1874 a Christian succeeded the deceased chief. Then in the 1880s the territory was made a British protectorate, and contacts with the interior were soon possible.[92]

The Presbyterian Mission's intention had been to proceed up the Cross River to the interior. These hopes began to materialize. A ministry was begun at Ikotama in 1887 and at Unwana, just over one hundred miles from Calabar, in 1888, James Luke investigated possibilities to expand their work up the river.[93] However, war, disease, and death of the workers kept the society from expanding further at that time. Nevertheless, the influence of the mission in the region was considerable. Mary Slessor, frequently called "The White Queen of Calabar," had a very fruitful ministry and was instrumental in bringing the gospel to the people of the interior. In 1888, after twelve years of service at Calabar, she was assigned to the Okoyong, a tribe that disrespected the laws and the rights of its neighbors. Her influence on the people was unusual and her decisions were recognized by the chiefs and the people.[94] After five years of service among the Okoyong, she moved on to the west of Cross River to the Aro. Fearless and undaunted, she visited people who had kept away from contact with outsiders, both whites and blacks, and established her base at Itu. The society was not ready to expand its ministry; nevertheless, due to Mary Slessor's influence, in 1907 the chief of all the Aros announced that he would rule in God's ways. Near the end of her ministry Mary accepted an invitation from Ikpe and planted a church in the old slave center on the Enyong Creek.[95] Having carried the gospel, by which slave-raiding tribes changed their life patterns, deep into the inte-

rior of the Cross River regions, she died on January 13, 1915, and
was buried in Calabar.

Antonio, who had come from Sao Tomé and had been brought up
in a seminary in Bahia, was sold into slavery in Brazil. After his
emancipation, he began the Catholic ministry at Lagos. When the
first missionaries of the French Catholic missionary body, the
Society of African Missions, arrived in Dahomey in 1861 and also
visited Lagos, they found a Catholic community there. Father
Broghero directed the Catholic ministry on the coast. Some Brazilian and Cuban emigrants came to Nigeria. When Bouche was
sent to take charge of the church in 1867, he reported about five
hundred Catholics.[96] The emigrants influenced the missions to
undertake a ministry in Nigeria and became an integral part of
the missionary movement, serving in various capacities. In turn,
their contacts with the churches kept them from disappearing
among the people and helped them retain their faith.

POLITICAL AMBITIONS AND EVANGELIZATION

Changes in Cameroon

The Christian ministry in Cameroon originated in the desire by
British Christians to stop the slave trade on this part of the coast.
In 1827 the British obtained permission from the Spanish to install
themselves on the island of Fernando Po, twenty-five miles off the
Cameroon mainland, for the purpose of controlling the traffic of
slaves. Soon, liberated Africans were settled on the Fernando Po
island. A sense of obligation toward these people and the opportunity to minister to them prompted the beginning of the mission to
Fernando Po and to Cameroon.

As early as 1814 the Baptist Christians of Jamaica expressed
their interest in bringing the gospel to Africa. The first party of
missionaries of the Baptist Missionary Society arrived at Fernando
Po in 1843. Members of the group were Dr. G.K. Prince, a medical
doctor, and two Jamaicans of West African ancestry, Joseph Merrick and Alexander Fuller. Arriving five months later were John
Clarke, a missionary to Jamaica since 1836; thirty-nine Jamaicans;
and Alfred Saker, a missionary recruit.[97] The ministry among the
liberated Africans was promising. Services were held and classes
of instruction conducted. But before long the Spanish began to
harass them and finally requested their departure. Many of the
Jamaicans returned to the West Indies. Joseph Merrick, however,

visited the people on the mainland, and in 1845 he and his wife settled among the Isubu at Bimbia. He not only learned the language and reduced it to writing, but also translated the Gospel of Matthew, the Book of Genesis, and selections from the Gospel of John. He began regular church services and opened a school. In 1849, because of poor health, he set sail for Europe; but he died during the voyage.[98]

In 1845, Alfred Saker established residence at Duala with the purpose of evangelizing the Duala tribe. Even though the results were not immediately apparent, through his faithful ministry of more than thirty-five years the church was firmly planted in Cameroon. He had a unique influence on the people. He strove to improve their conditions by opposing slave trade and providing for a more satisfactory economic situation. After several years of devoted ministry in the Duala language, the first convert was baptized in 1849. Soon others were added and a church was organized. Saker ordained the first two pastors of the Cameroon church. Thomas Johnson was consecrated in 1855, and George Nkwe was consecrated in 1866.[99] Saker translated the Bible into Duala and through his ministry more than eighty thousand coastal people heard the gospel in their language. As a result of Saker's presence, Victoria became an important center where Protestants from Fernando Po settled. Saker was concerned about thoroughly instructing the new believers and establishing a sound, even if small, church. Some of his colleagues preferred to move to more receptive people of the interior of the country.[100] After thirty-one years of fruitful service, he left Cameroon in 1876 and died in 1880.

George Grenfell succeeded Alfred Saker in the ministry in Cameroon. Grenfell was troubled by the slow progress the church manifested and directed his efforts toward exploring the interior of the country and proclaiming the gospel to the other tribes.[101] His thinking had been influenced by the Basel Mission's experience in Accra, where the people of the interior were more receptive, while the people of Accra were looking for material gain. Grenfell made a number of exploratory voyages up the branches of the Cameroon River as far as it was navigable. His service in Cameroon was terminated rather early and unexpectedly through the opening of a new mission by the Baptist Missionary Society in Zaire. George Grenfell and Thomas Comber were among the pioneers to launch the new endeavor in 1878.

In 1884 the German government sent representatives to Cameroon. They secured the signatures of several chiefs along the
Cameroon River and annexed Cameroon on July 14, 1884, hoisting
German flags over the Bell, Akwa, and Dido towns along the
river.[102] The British missionaries suddenly found themselves
under a German administration that did not favor a strong British
influence in the country. This placed the Baptist missionaries in an
unfortunate situation. The Baptist Missionary Society therefore
transferred the Cameroon enterprise to the Basel Evangelical Missionary Society and concentrated its efforts on the work in Zaire.
The Basel missionaries arrived at Duala in 1886. At the time of the
transfer there were 203 church members in the Baptist congregations and 368 children were enrolled in the schools.[103] In reflecting
on their ministry, Thomas Lewis observed that they had not prepared the church leaders to assume the responsibilities to guide
the young church to become a self-sufficient, reproducing church.

Whereas the Baptist Missionary Society observed the congregational polity, granting considerable autonomy to the congregations,
the Basel Mission was guided by a more centralized authority. The
pastors were somewhat uncomfortable with the new emphasis,
feeling that their authority was being restricted. The Basel Mission
did not oppose the practices, but the Christians were reluctant to
accept the mission's authority in matters of discipline, of the
parish life, and of liturgy. A schism occurred, involving the Duala
and Victoria churches, and through the division an independent
Baptist church was formed. The German administration was inclined to view the native Baptist movement as a political, independent movement.

After a short time of independence, the Baptist churches of
Cameroon desired the assistance of an European Baptists organization. Arrangements were made with the Baptists in Berlin for a
cooperative ministry. In 1891 the German Baptists appointed the
first missionary, August Steffens, an American Baptist. With this
appointment, the cooperation of the American Baptist General
Missionary Society with the mission in Cameroon began. As a
result of the new arrangement, the ministry of the Baptist
churches was strengthened. The new missionary activity of the
1890s produced encouraging growth.[104] The Baptists of Victoria,
however, split in 1894. Pastor Wilson established a separate work.
Finally in 1898 the missionaries separated from the Victoria

church and concentrated their efforts in East Cameroon, where the greatest growth was taking place.

The ministry of the Basel Mission progressed rapidly. The society opened nine new stations between 1887 and 1897, among them Bonaberi, Mangamba, Lobethal, and Edea. Twenty-two missionaries were engaged in the ministry of the society. The Christian community grew from 172 in 1888 to 1,473 in 1897, and the Christian day schools instructed many children in the Christian faith. The people soon realized that the missionaries were their friends and were serving in their interests, even though they imposed a rigorous discipline. However, due to the rapidity of church growth, many new members were not thoroughly instructed in the Christian faith and continued some of their former practices of which the church disapproved. The mission, therefore, decided to desist from expanding for a time and concentrate its efforts on instructing members. The society opened a Bible school at Beréa, as well as several teacher training schools, to strengthen the teaching ministry of the church. Some of the students returned to their villages as Christian teachers. Many young people received a Christian education in a mission school and witnessed to the people of their villages. This testimony opened new opportunities for the proclamation of the gospel. In 1903, after the Christian community had been more thoroughly established, the society was able to respond to requests to open new centers to the north. This phase of its expansion will be observed later.

Uncertainties in Gabon

The American Board of Commissioners made the initial attempts to evangelize Gabon and the surrounding territories of French-speaking Africa. Using Cape Palmas, Liberia, as their base, they launched the first Protestant missionary effort in the lower areas of the Gabon River in 1842. J. L. Wilson and Benjamin Griswold established the first center of activity at Baraka near the present city of Libreville. At Baraka trade was active and some vessels from England and America called. The river was navigable for thirty miles; so it was an excellent means to contact the people living along its banks. A successful ministry at the location was anticipated.

In 1843, however, the French tried to secure possession of this territory and in July, 1845, destroyed much property in the town and on the mission. This made the future of a Protestant mission in Gabon uncertain. The mission served under hardships and doubt as to its future. In addition to the work among the Mpongwe people, the workers began a second station some thirty miles inland among the Bakele. In 1854 they opened a third station some ninety miles to the interior among the Bakele, Shekani, and Pangwe.[105]

The Presbyterian Church of the United States undertook a ministry on the island of Corisco, north of Gabon, in 1849. J. L. Mackey and G. W. Simpson and their wives came to begin the ministry. Before long Mackey was the only survivor, but new recruits were sent, and in 1855 nine workers were serving on the field. Attempts to begin a work on the mainland, via the Rio Muni and the Benito, were unsuccessful. The American Board ceded their stations to the Presbyterian Church in 1870. In 1874 hopes for more success appeared when Robert Nassau traveled up the Ogowe River and established a station at Belambila, twenty miles beyond Lambaréné. In 1877 he left Belambila and settled at Kangwe-Lambaréné. This work became the most fruitful, and soon provided evangelists for the Pakuins.[106]

The Presbyterian Church encountered considerable difficulty with the French administration, which was anxious to establish its influence over the country. The Presbyterians were compelled to close the schools because they could not meet the French requirements for teachers competent in the French language. Consequently the society approached the Paris Evangelical Missionary Society to share in the ministry by sending teachers or by assuming full responsibility for the schools. Two French officials, Dr. Ballay and M. de Brazza, who were concerned that French influence be established in Gabon, encouraged the Paris society to assume the responsibility. In 1888, three French missionaries came to participate in the mission's teaching program. However, the Presbyterian Church found the political climate too unfavorable and transferred the work in Gabon to the Paris society. They then concentrated their efforts on the section of their work in Cameroon.[107]

Gabon was one of the main centers of work of the Roman Catholic Church. Jean Remi Bessieux arrived in Gabon in 1844. Three additional recruits came in 1846. In 1848 Bessieux was named vicar apostolic of the two Guineas. In 1849 Sisters of the

Immaculate Conception came to Gabon.[108] In 1852 they were
established at Sainte-Pierre, where the French government hospital is located. In addition to their medical services, they instructed
girls. By the time of his death in 1876, Bessieux had established
the Roman Catholic work in Gabon with a Christian community of
some two thousand members. Bessieux had gained credibility with
the chief and influenced him. Just before the chief died ten years
later, he instructed the people not to attribute his death to an
evildoer or to put any slaves to death on his account. His son who
succeeded him accepted the Christian faith.

SUMMARY

The Roman Catholic missionary agencies established on the
islands off the coast of Africa made occasional contacts with the
people at the European trading posts in the proximity of their
bases. These contacts, however, were too sporadic to be effective.
Work was also established at several bases on the coast, but the
Roman Catholic missionary effort was weak during this period.

Concentrated Protestant missionary efforts began with the return of freed slaves from Britain and America to Sierra Leone and
by the missionary efforts among the slaves freed along the coast of
Africa. Missionary efforts were also soon established at strategic
places along the coast. The liberated Africans constituted a responsive group for missionary activities. They were separated
from their tribal ties and taboos and were obliged to make decisions for the future. Some of those who accepted the Christian
faith received training in mission schools and became effective
missionary agents to their own people. The ministry of Samuel
Adjai Crowther and Thomas Birch Freeman contributed greatly to
establishing the Christian faith in West Africa. The return of
Yoruba Christians to Nigeria played a significant role in the development of the missionary endeavor in that country. Through the
inspiration of Henry Venn, the Church Missionary Society adopted
an enlightened policy of establishing indigenous churches.

Little was known of tropical diseases, and the missionaries
experienced many hazards in the seventeenth and eighteenth centuries; an early death ended the service of many missionaries.
Thus the establishment of the Christian faith was greatly retarded
in many regions. However, additional recruits volunteered for

service, and eventually preventive medicines were discovered; thus the Christian faith took root among the peoples.

The Basel and Bremen Missionary Societies made a remarkable contribution, establishing a rapport with the people, reducing several languages to writing, revealing the ethnography, and establishing Christianity in Ghana and Togo. The Baptist Missionary Society began a ministry on the island of Fernando Po and then in Cameroon. Christians from Jamaica served in launching this venture.

In addition to the missionary interest, a concern for the well-being of the people of Africa was prevalent in Europe. The Niger expeditions were promoted by the British government in order to establish contacts with the peoples of the Niger River territory. Some of the early trading companies came because of a concern to improve the conditions of the people. Henry Venn encouraged trade with the people of West Africa. The Basel Missionary Society introduced cocoa and coffee planting into Ghana.

Protestant missionary work was extended as far as Gabon along the Guinea coast. After France established its influence over the territory, the American missionaries were not welcome. Consequently they entrusted the ministry to the Paris Evangelical Missionary Society.

By 1884 churches had been established at strategic locations along the coast from Guinea to Gabon. In a few cases, the Christian ministry had also advanced into the interior of the countries, but the movement into the interior and the ministry to the unreached areas belongs to the next period. Christian leaders were receiving training, and the evangelization of Africa in the next period largely belongs to them.

Study Questions

1. Evaluate the effort to settle freed slaves in Sierra Leone.
2. Evaluate the contribution the settlement in Sierra Leone made to the expansion of Christianity.
3. People separated from tribal restrictions may constitute a fertile field for evangelism and church growth. Apply this statement to the liberated West Africans.

4. Evaluate the contribution of leadership training to church planting.

5. Henry Venn advocated principles by which indigenous churches would be established. Compare Venn's principles with church-growth principles.

6. How did the cultural barriers between the Creoles and the indigenous population hinder church planting among the indigenous people?

7. Evaluate the adaptability of the Methodist "small classes" for church planting.

8. Evaluate the Evangelical United Brethren's school approach for church growth.

9. Describe the relations between the settlers and the indigenous population in Liberia and their effects on church planting.

10. "Men like to become Christians without crossing racial, linguistic, or class barriers" (McGavran, 1970:198). How does this statement apply to the Christian ministry in Liberia?

11. How can missions avoid the halting of growth essentially due to the effect of "redemption plus lift" of a program of education and aid? (McGavran, 1970:260). How did this concern apply to the ministry of the United Lutheran Church in Liberia?

12. Evaluate the missionary strategy of the Basel Evangelical Missionary Society in Ghana.

13. Evaluate the indigenous principles Freeman employed in the Christian ministry in Ghana.

14. Compare the missionary principles advocated by the Bremen Missionary Society in Togo with those advocated by Henry Venn.

15. Describe briefly the contributions the missionary societies made to Ghana and Togo before Germany took control.

16. What contribution did the Niger expeditions make to the missionary enterprise?

17. Explain the contribution the freed slaves who returned to Nigeria made to the planting of the church in that country.

18. Briefly describe Samuel Crowther's ministry.

19. What steps did the Church Missionary Society take to provide indigenous leadership for the congregations in Nigeria?

20. What factors contributed to the expansion of the ministry of the Presbyterian Church in Calabar, Nigeria?

21. Describe the contribution of the Jamaican Christians in bringing the Christian faith to Cameroon.
22. Evaluate the missionary principles of Alfred Salker and George Grenfell in Cameroon.
23. Distinguish between the church policy of the Baptist Missionary Society and of the Basel Evangelical Missionary Society and indicate how this affected the ministry of the latter society.
24. Describe briefly how the French colonial ambitions interfered in the missionary activities in Gabon.

5

Missionary Efforts in South Africa

During the seventeenth and eighteenth centuries two protagonists, the Negroes and the Dutch, appeared on the scene at the Cape, which until then had been the home of the nomadic Hottentots. The Cape is the only region of Africa where European families settled during the seventeenth century to establish a new society and where the Negro people arrived at such a late date.[1]

The historical records concerning the arrival of the Hottentots and Bushmen in the southern part of Africa are obscure. Historians are not agreed on the date of their arrival nor on the density of the population. From the fourteenth to the seventeenth century, two Negro peoples were moving toward the southern tip of Africa. The Sotho-Ichuana dispersed and settled in the present Transvaal and Orange states. By 1550 the Xhosas, the southernmost tribe, was settled in the Transkei. They arrived at the Fish River, south of East London, around 1650. They met the Dutch in this region in 1775.[2]

The climate and the productive soil, especially east of the Cape, attracted Europeans to this region and contributed to the rapid development of the country and to the establishment of the church. Whereas the death toll of missionaries was extremely high in the tropical regions, in South Africa the favorable climatic conditions enabled them to serve for many years. The disintegration of the tribal life, a result of devastating tribal wars, may have caused the people to be receptive to another religion. The Christianity propagated in South Africa was mostly Protestant. In 1914 the Christians in South Africa constituted more than half the total number of Christians in Africa south of the Sahara.[3]

EARLY BEGINNINGS

Witness of the Settlers at the Cape

Since Vasco da Gama discovered a route to Asia by circumnavigating the Cape of Good Hope, European traders called at the Cape for refreshments. The Dutch were the first to settle at the Cape. This enterprise owed its inception to a shipwreck of a vessel belonging to the Dutch East India Company in 1648. The crew reached the shore, built a few huts, and waited for passage to Europe. The local people soon came with cattle and sheep to barter for goods rescued from the ship. The crew was favorably impressed with their friendliness and, upon arrival in Holland, recommended building a supply station at the Cape for vessels of the company.

In 1652 the company sent Jan van Riebeeck with a number of other people to establish a supply post at the Cape. This community took their faith with them and introduced it to the people of the Cape. Van Riebeeck gave strict orders to his party to treat the native people fairly and establish good relations with them.[4] The population of the Cape was sparse and unable to furnish sufficient supplies for passing vessels. Consequently, the European colonists began to cultivate the soil to raise the needed produce; as they did so they became attached to the land. This was the beginning of colonization. This small party also was unable to produce sufficient supplies, and so additional immigrants were invited to the Cape colony.

The colony purchased the livestock and the produce the Hottentots could provide. Although the market encouraged production, the demand exceeded the supply. As a result, the colony looked for labor to increase production. This created an employer-employee relationship in which the newcomer to the country became the employer and the producer. The colony soon requested slaves. The first party came in 1658 when a vessel from Amsterdam intercepted a Portuguese slave ship and brought 170 persons to the Cape. Since they were mostly girls and small boys, they failed to provide immediate help. A school was arranged and they were instructed. Some of the children accepted the Christian faith, and some girls became the wives of Dutch colonists. During the seventeenth century, many children born to slave mothers had white fathers. The company required that they be baptized and manumitted at a certain age.[5] This was, however, the beginning of the use of slaves in the colony and another source of grievance in later years.

Until 1657 all residents had worked for the company, but in that year they received plots of land and their produce was purchased by the company for a fixed price. Van Riebeeck advocated a farming community of small peasant proprietors cultivating their own land. This plan was not put into effect.[6] As the colony expanded, tensions concerning the occupation of land began and became a major problem between the two peoples in later years. The Hottentots resorted to cattle stealing, justifying their action on the basis that the cattle were raised on their land. The colony tried to maintain good relations and supported provocations for seven years before resorting to repressive measures. In later years these tensions occasionally broke out and became a serious menace to the peace of the country.

As time went by, more Dutch immigrants arrived, and a civil government was provided for the Cape. In 1679 Simon van der Stel was appointed the first governor. The Cape colony became a small settlement, with Hottentots and settlers cultivating the land and herding their cattle and sheep. More settlers arrived in the latter part of the seventeenth century. Among them were two hundred French Huguenot refugees. The company sponsored these people to help the community become agriculturally and militarily self-sufficient. The Huguenot settlers had a French pastor, but their children were obliged to learn the Dutch language in the schools. By 1750, after some years of tension, the French and the Dutch communities amalgamated.[7]

Stellenbosch was the first "inland" community where the concerns of the settlers prevailed over those of the company. A church organization with a church council and a minister was formed in 1685. The population increase fostered the establishment of other communities and towns farther inland. Since much land north and east of Cape Town was available, sons of farmers settled there. Thus in about a century, the settlement expanded from a radius of fifty miles from Cape Town to two hundred miles north and four hundred miles east by 1795, reaching as far as Morsels Bay.[8]

From 1652 to 1665 there was no resident minister at the Cape, and a so-called "sick comforter" was responsible for spiritual services. But according to the regulations of the home church in Holland, he was not permitted to administer the sacraments nor perform certain other functions. Sometimes a clergyman from a ship was available for services while the ship was in the harbor. The church in Holland exercised discretion in its position toward the baptism of native converts. It considered the baptism of children of Christian parents proper because they are already in the covenant. But the baptism of the children of unbelievers was considered unlawful. Therefore, as long as there was no ordained minister at the Cape, evangelization of the native people was not emphasized.[9] Some families instructed their servants or the children they took into their homes. In 1662 the first Hottentot convert to be baptized was Eva, who acquired a good knowledge of Dutch and served as interpreter in dealings with the tribes.[10] She later married the assistant surgeon of the settlement. Some native children were accepted in the predominantly white school of the settlement, but no concentrated effort to encourage them to attend school was made until some years later. Religion was the chief barrier between the Dutch and the native people. Converted slaves who were baptized were manumitted and enjoyed privileges similar to those of the settlers. These circumstances probably created an ulterior motive to the slave to become a believer.

In 1674 a church council for the settlement was organized. The structural form of Dutch Reformed Church administration was followed at Cape Town, but the company was represented by a political commissioner at all meetings and the company engaged and assigned the ministers.[11] The council of policy also approved the election of members of the church council. When the French Huguenots arrived, the close relationship between the church and state was again apparent, for the administration considered the Dutch Reformed Church the only church of the colony. The company permitted a separate consistory for the Huguenots, but important matters were to be referred to the authorities of Cape Town.[12] The population of the colony increased to five thousand persons. The ministers of the Dutch Reformed Church served the congregations at Cape Town, Stellenbosch, and Drakenstein. Since the settlers were spread over a vast region, some of them lived up to three days journey from a church.

Witness of the Moravians

Through the Pietist movement in the eighteenth century, some people in Europe became conscious of their responsibility to proclaim the gospel to unevangelized peoples. Ziegenbalg and

Plutschau stopped at the Cape during their voyage to India in 1706. They wrote to Christians in Holland concerning the necessity of evangelizing the Hottentots of South Africa.[13] When no one in Holland volunteered, a request was made to the Moravian Brethren. George Schmidt had spent six years in an Austrian jail for having visited Protestants. He volunteered for the service. After conferring with authorities of the Dutch Reformed Church in Amsterdam, he was sent to the Cape in 1737 with a letter of recommendation to the governor.[14] Schmidt received a mixed reception at Cape Town. Especially pertinent was a pastor's attitude against baptizing Hottentots. The Dutch Reformed Church was hesitant to baptize the people and was unwilling to grant Schmidt the authority to baptize his converts. Schmidt moved to his proposed center of activity, which later became the famous Moravian mission station of Genadendal.

Schmidt settled among the Hottentots and taught them the rudiments of the Christian faith. He held Sunday services, conducted classes for children and adults, and taught some basic agriculture. The response to the gospel was not enthusiastic, but there were some converts. Schmidt was willing to present his teaching and his baptismal candidates to the church council for approval, but his offer was not accepted. Schmidt presented his situation to his church in Germany. Zinzendorf authorized him to baptize. Schmidt proceeded with his mission and in the following days baptized six persons in nearby streams. He was called before the governor, the council of policy, and the clergy. He was forbidden to administer the sacraments until the Classis of Amsterdam would clarify the matter.[15] Schmidt waited, but no answer came. He was unable to cope with the situation. Upon his request, Herrnhut granted him permission to leave. He went to Europe, hoping to obtain the approval he desired, but was unsuccessful. The Dutch Reformed Church requested that Schmidt serve under its auspices. He therefore stayed in Europe and served as a pastor in a Moravian settlement.[16] The Hottentots waited for his return until they received the sad news of his death in 1785.

The mission in the Cape ceased for nearly fifty years before the Moravian Church reopened Genadendal. Several pastors of the Dutch Reformed Church did much to arouse the conscience of their white congregations. The first one, Van Lier, while a minister at Cape Town from 1786 to 1793, repeatedly presented the neces-

sity of missionary work among the Hottentots and encouraged the
church in Holland to organize a missionary society. In 1794
Michiel Vos, a member of the Cape church, completed his studies
in Holland. He returned to the Cape and was assigned to
Roodezans.

In 1787 Bishop J. F. Reichel of the Unitas Fratrum visited the
Cape. After discussing the situation with Van Lier and others, he
was convinced that the mission among the Hottentots should be
reopened. They were granted permission to reopen the mission
and to administer the sacraments but were requested to refrain
from missionary activities in areas where the official church
existed. In 1792 Marfeld, Schwinn, and Kihnel (a Hollander and
two Germans) arrived and reopened Genadendal.[17] Some of the
people remembered Schmidt and retained notions of the Christian
faith. The Christian fellowship was readily reestablished. The
mission expanded rapidly. The first person was baptized in 1793,
and from that time more were added to the church. By 1798 about
eight hundred Hottentots were living on the station and one-
quarter of them were church members. A church building to seat
one thousand people was erected. The mission received mixed
responses from the European population. But when the governor
visited it in 1803, he was pleased with the good results, and it was
he who suggested that the station be called Genadendal (a valley of
grace). This name has been in use since 1806.[18] The missionaries
taught such trades as smithery, cultery making, and crafts. Cordial
relations developed with European farmers, and a number of them
occasionally shared in the worship service.

As the population at Genadendal grew, it became expedient to
begin another center of activity, and Mamre was started in 1808.[19]
The people settled about the station. By 1818 the Moravians established a third station, Enon, on the White River, a tributary to the
Sunday River. It was close to the frontier of the colony, and since
this displeased the Xhosa, they destroyed it in 1819, but it was
rebuilt later. The Moravians founded Elim in 1824 and took over
the government leper settlement, called Hemel-en-Aerde, in the
Caledon district.[20]

Bishop Hans Peter Hallbeck gave direction to the Moravian
Mission for twenty-three years. In 1828 Shiloh station was estab-
lished to the east of the Cape and served both Hottentots and
Bantu. It was destroyed during the war in 1847 but was rebuilt at

government expense in 1850. By 1842 a total of 3,908 adults and children had been baptized at Genadendal.[21] By 1850 seven stations were established, at which 7,100 members resided and thirteen national workers were active. The ministry expanded and had a profound influence on the people, teaching them both the gospel and the rudiments of agriculture and industry to improve their living conditions. The work of the Moravians was appreciated by natives and the government. Bishop Gray considered their work as one of the best in South Africa. The stations became Christian communities where the principles of Christian living were applied. This missionary strategy seemed effective and was adopted by other missionary societies.

Witness of the Dutch Reformed Church

In 1793, France declared war on a coalition of European states and marched against Holland. In 1795 the Prince of Orange fled to England. He requested the British to protect the Dutch colonies and ordered the authorities at Cape Town to submit to the British. However, the colony at the Cape was unwilling to submit to British rule and resisted the British expedition when it arrived in 1795. It was, however, defeated by the British forces and compelled to surrender to them.[22]

The first British occupation of the Cape lasted from 1795 to 1803. It presented a complicated situation for the established church, which had been supported by the state. The company assigned and remunerated the ministers. Now the church was suddenly under a foreign power and was no longer the recognized, established church. Even though the government was discreet in its encroachment in church affairs and did not give legal status to British missions, it faced a delicate situation when a congregation at Graaf Reinet opposed accepting its minister, because he had taken the oath of allegiance to the British king. The Anglican Church had not taken root in the country during this period. When the Anglican pastors, who had come as chaplains with the army, baptized either Hottentots or slaves, the authorities of the Dutch Reformed Church protested.[23]

In 1802 the war with France came to a temporary halt, and in 1803 the Cape again passed into Dutch hands. The government of the Cape became the responsibility of the governors and the commissioner-general. DeMist, a person of keen perception, was called to the latter office. He recognized the necessity for a community to provide for the maintenance of religion, but this did not mean a monopoly of the state church. Rather, it also included protection of the law for Reformed, Lutherans, Anglicans, Moravians, and others. Since the old relationship between the church and state had been dissolved in Holland in 1795, the church at the Cape was in a unique situation. In 1804 deMist declared that the Cape church was no longer a state church. However, because its membership greatly exceeded that of other churches, it was granted special privileges.

Hostilities were renewed in Europe, Britain again landed forces at the Cape in 1806. The governor, Janssens, resisted the landing of forces but was defeated and compelled to surrender. In 1814, when Napoleon was defeated and the war ended, the British retained the occupation of the Cape. The Anglican clergy were given more liberty. The British increased the English population of the Cape by bringing settlers to the eastern Cape. By 1820 Britain had brought some five thousand settlers, ex-soldiers and their families, into the country and settled them close behind the frontier, hoping to make it more secure by providing British presence among the Boer population.[24] By 1860 the Cape had acquired a British population who regarded the Cape as a permanent home. The authorities tried to find suitable ministers in Scotland when Holland failed to supply candidates for vacant posts in the church. The Presbyterian Church in Scotland was viewed as a suitable source of ministers because it held the Calvinist faith, as did the Dutch Reformed Church.[25]

The coming of the Anglican Church, coupled with the British rule, caused further complications. The Anglican congregations were regarded as pertaining to the Church of England, but a single Anglican Church for the Cape was not established. Consequently, two semiestablished churches, the Dutch Reformed and the Anglican, functioned under special privileges for some time at the Cape.

Witness of the London Missionary Society

At the beginning of the nineteenth century, the London Missionary Society responded to the challenge to evangelize the people of South Africa. It encouraged other societies to join in the worthy but immense task, which instigated a significant expansion of the

Christian faith in the Cape province and later throughout South Africa. It was to be nondenominational and its agents were to preach the gospel without propagating any particular form of church order or government. In 1799 they sent a party of four missionaries to the Cape. Of these, John Edmonds and William Edwards were English, and Johannes Theodorus Vanderkemp (also written Van der Kemp) and Johannes Kicherer were Dutch.[26]

Vanderkemp became the first director of the London Missionary Society's ministry in South Africa. He was born at Rotterdam in 1747, the son of a Lutheran minister. He was a person of varied experiences. After having begun medical studies at the University of Leyden, he joined the army for sixteen years. Then he resigned, married, and terminated his medical studies at the University of Edinburgh. He spoke a number of modern European languages. In 1791, while he and his family were sailing on the Rotterdam River, a sudden summer storm came up, and his wife and daughter drowned.[27] He offered himself to the London Missionary Society for service, was ordained a minister by the Presbyterian Church of Scotland, and served in South Africa. When he returned to Holland, Vanderkemp implemented the founding of the Netherlands Missionary Society.[28]

When the party of London Missionary Society workers arrived at the Cape, two of the members went to work on the northern frontier of the colony. Vanderkemp attempted to work among the people of Gaika on the eastern frontier. However, the tensions between the Xhosa and the Boers created a disturbing situation and hindered effective missionary work. Vanderkemp moved back to Graaf Reinet and in 1801 began a ministry among the Hottentots at Bethelsdorp. By 1808 about a thousand Hottentots, of whom two hundred were Christians, had settled at Bethelsdorp. Vanderkemp wanted to serve all the people's needs. Stone houses, schools, and churches were constructed. Agriculture, animal husbandry, industry, and carpentry were pursued. He required every person at Bethelsdorp to provide for his daily needs. These activities testified to the constructive approach in teaching the people. The colonists, however, wanted the Hottentots as farm laborers and denounced Bethelsdorp as a place of idleness.[29]

Vanderkemp was a person with strong convictions and he did not hesitate to advocate them. He maintained that owning slaves was a sin against God and man. He also said that it was the duty of every Christian to preach to the unevangelized, in their case especially the Hottentots, and bring them into the Christian fellowship. He expected the Boers to remain on their farms and to support missions. He was among those who insisted that there should be equality among Christians. He tried to identify with the people and married a member of his congregation of Malagasy origin. Some of the colonists criticized him, but many of them and some of Vanderkemp's colleagues took Christian girls as wives. Vanderkemp's marriage, no doubt, led to his desire to take the gospel to Madagascar, but he was unable to accomplish this.

Under Vanderkemp's direction, the missionaries of the London Missionary Society became the protectors of the Hottentots. At one time, one-third of the Hottentot population was living at one of the mission stations. The missionaries helped the Hottentots arrange fair working conditions with farmers. This situation became more acute as the colony developed. Vanderkemp died in 1811. After his death, the London Missionary Society appointed John Campbell, a clergyman, to make an inspection tour of all its stations in South Africa.[30]

The London Missionary Society expanded its ministry among the Hottentots by beginning the Caledon Institution at Zuurbrak in 1811. Pacaltsdorp, just west of George, evolved from Read's contacts with a small group of Hottentots. Theopolis grew out of the overflow from Bethelsdorp; it was in the region of the present Port Alfred. These institutions were mainly for the Hottentots, or colored people. A few Xhosas, Damaras, and later also Fingoes and Batswana, came in contact with the missionary endeavor.

The London Missionary Society established several important training institutions at Hankey on the Gomtoos River. W. Philip, son of Dr. John Philip, engineered a 250-yard tunnel to conduct water from the river to irrigate the fields.

The government permitted Hottentots and coloreds to live in the Kat River district, which had formerly been occupied by the Xhosas. Many people moving to this area came from Bethelsdorp or Theopolis. James Read, Jr., the minister from Bethelsdorp, was called to be teacher and copastor with his father. His brother Joseph also became a teacher. Teachers for surrounding villages were instructed at an institution. The work in the area was successful for a few years, but further progress was impaired by the Xhosa attacks in 1835 and 1847. By the time the third attack came in 1851, the morale of the settlement had deteriorated, the zeal for improvement had abated, and the settlement had begun to disintegrate. At Theopolis, the Hottentots got into a skirmish with the Fingoes and also attacked the British. These incidents brought the work to an end.[31] The frequent political disturbances did not permit the church to become thoroughly rooted among the people. Very few colored ministers had been trained. Though a school functioned at Hankey for a few years, its duration was too brief to accomplish significant results.

The London Missionary Society undertook to evangelize the Xhosas on the eastern frontier of the colony. In 1816 Joseph Williams arrived, accompanied by Jack Read and Jan Tzatzoe (also written Tshatshu) of Bethelsdorp, the son of a Xhosa chief. They crossed the Great Fish River and, after conferring with Gaika, chose a site on the Kat River. The people were pleased to have a missionary among them. In a year's time 138 people had settled at the post and attendance at worship services was about 100. Tzatzoe went to Theopolis, where he assisted Barker. Williams devoted himself to his task, but his labors were terminated by his premature death in 1818. After his death, one of the believers, Ntsikana, continued to gather people for worship. The Cape government did not permit the London Missionary Society to send a successor to Williams, but it sent John Brownlee in 1820. The ministry was delayed by the "Fifth Kaffir War," which was between Gaika and his uncle Ndambe. William R. Thompson of the Glasgow Society joined Brownlee in 1821. Ntsikana continued to proclaim the gospel until his death. Realizing that his end was approaching, he encouraged his followers to join the Brownlee mission. Tiyo Soga, the first Xhosa pastor, was one of Ntsikana's disciples. He was ordained to the ministry in 1856 and served his people competently until his death in 1871.[32]

The Glasgow Missionary Society came to serve jointly with the London Missionary Society. William R. Thompson joined John Brownlee at Chumie in the Kat River district, while John Bennie and John Ross began the Lovedale station, eight miles from Chumie. Lovedale became an important training center, offering instruction from the elementary to the university level. Instruction in theology, agriculture, and crafts was offered. William Govan was director of the school from 1840 to 1870; after that Jack Stewart guided it until 1905. It became one of the most significant institutions of learning.

Kicherer and Edwards, accompanied by Cornelius Kramer, a young Dutchman from the Cape, undertook a ministry in the Zak River district in the northern part of the Cape province. This venture came as a result of an appeal by Florus Fisher, a farmer of the district, to whom the Bushmen had appealed for a Christian teacher. Fisher took the Bushmen deputies to Cape Town and appealed to the missionaries to undertake a ministry among them. They accepted the invitation and journeyed to Fisher's farm. They then traveled a week in desert country without meeting anyone.[33] Finally they found some scattered Bushmen settlements along the Zak River; they settled among them and began to establish relations with the people. A Hottentot and his wife, who both spoke Dutch, interpreted for them. They conducted services, taught the children, and instructed some concerning agriculture. The mission was closer to a number of farmers than the nearest Dutch Reformed Church, and occasionally some farmers participated in the worship, especially to celebrate the Lord's Supper.[34] Edwards departed but Kicherer and Kramer were joined by Anderson in 1800. In 1801 Anderson crossed the Orange River and began a station to the north of the river. The ministry was more successful among the Hottentots and the Griqua than among the Bushmen. The Bushmen continued to threaten those who listened to the missionaries. Kicherer made a trip to Europe and took three Hottentot converts with him to Holland and England. They encouraged the people to continue the ministry. Upon his return to the Cape, Kicherer married a Dutch woman at Cape Town and accepted a pastorate at Graaf Reinet. Michiel Vos and his wife and Botma, a farmer, continued the work at Zak River for a time, but in 1806 the project was abandoned. The first attempt to win the Bushmen failed. However, through it the missionaries had been introduced to the Namaqua, Coranna, Griqua, and Bechuana people, and the Hottentot and mulatto converts later became the pillars for the Griqua mission. The Griqua were mostly the descendants of Hottentot and European stock, while the Coranna were Hottentots who had moved to the Orange River area.[35]

Anderson continued his ministry among the Griqua on the Orange River. In 1806 he reported that he and his associates were ministering to about 750 people and attendance at services reached 250. Kramer and Scholtz followed the people to Griqua Town, where water was available, and worked there.

Griqua Town was the western center of activity among the Griqua, while Philippolis was the eastern center. A strife concerning leadership disturbed the peace among the Griqua during the 1820s, and during the 1830s the farmers were constantly bidding for the land. Finally the Philippolis community sold out to the farmers and, during the 1860s, trekked east to Griqualand near the Drakensberg Mountains. Later they also lost most of that land to settlers. Whereas in 1811 there were about 800 inhabitants at Griqua Town, by 1842 there were about 4,800. Many of the Griqua had become literate. But by 1840 the spring, their source of water, was beginning to dry up; and the important mission center and stop en route to the interior eventually disappeared.[36]

In 1806 Christian and Abraham Albrecht and J. Sydenfaden arrived from Holland, crossed the Orange River, and began a ministry to the Namaqua. But they were close to the region of Jonker Africaner, who attacked the Namaqua at Warm Bath. Consequently about five hundred people crossed the Orange River and settled at Pella to the south of the river. The people responded to the gospel message. By 1815 church membership totaled fifty, and six Griqua and Hottentot preachers were serving.[37]

In 1819 Dr. John Philip agreed to accompany John Campbell on a tour of inspection of the work in South Africa and stay for five years to implement reforms in the London Mission. He stayed until his death in 1851 and made a very valuable contribution to the planting of Christianity in South Africa. In his ministry he was chiefly concerned about two matters: first, the continual tension on the frontier between the tribes and the farmers, who were constantly occupying more land; and, second, the conditions of the Hottentots within the colony. Because he addressed himself to these issues, he was accused of interfering in politics. Philip also maintained that in order to work and become responsible citizens of the colony, the Hottentots should receive good instruction. The Hottentots, who had lived off the land, found their way of life disappearing and were confronted with the choice of being farm laborers or vagrants. Neither situation was satisfying to them.

As superintendent of the London Missionary Society, Philip traveled widely in the colony. He received reports and was well informed. He felt compelled to improve the Hottentots' condition. Because the situation was exposed, the government appointed a commission of inquiry. The result of the investigation was "Ordinance 50," issued in 1828, which stated that all people had the same legal rights; the Hottentots were free to work or not to work; vagrancy was not punishable; and the ordinance could be changed only with the consent of the imperial government.[38] The ordinance improved the situation of the native people. However, Philip said that in order for their livelihood to be adequately provided for, they would have to be taught and be provided with land where they could live and practice agriculture. The solutions he advocated greatly improved the situation. Further solutions and adjustments were necessary as the country entered new phases in its development.

Witness of the Wesleyan Methodists

The Methodist Church sent its first missionary, Barnabas Shaw, to South Africa in 1816. Methodist meetings had been held by soldiers at Cape Town since 1806. They encouraged the church to develop a mission in the country. J.H. Schmelen of the London Missionary Society advised Shaw to undertake a ministry to the Namaqua in the northwestern part of Cape Province. On their way to the Namaqua region, Schmelen and Shaw met a Nama chief who was en route to Cape Town to find a teacher for his people. Shaw accepted the invitation as an indication of divine guidance and established himself at Leliefontein on the Kamiesberg. The Namaqua received him with much enthusiasm.[39]

Shaw adopted the principle of giving instruction in the Bible and in agriculture. Because of its elevation, Leliefontein had sufficient rainfall to grow crops. The people were eager to learn, and so Shaw's ministry was successful. By 1817 seventeen adults and eleven children had been baptized. By 1826 a prosperous station was established, with ninety-seven church members. Among the members were Peter and Jack Links, who later became missionaries. Peter served among the Bechuana. Jack Links and John Jager went to evangelize to the north of the Orange River, where they were murdered in a Bushman village.[40] In the outreach from Leliefontein, other centers for evangelism developed. In the latter part of the nineteenth century, the copper mines of Namaqualand and the Kimberley and Johannesburg mines attracted strong men of the community, retarding its economic and social development.

In 1823 Stephen Broadbent established a station among the Barolongs to the east of the London Missionary Society. Because of difficulties with the Bataungs, the ministry was transferred to Ploatberg near the Modder River, where some eight thousand Barolongs settled. Broadbent showed the people how to dig wells to get water. The Barolongs did not have sufficient land at this location and in 1833 some settled at Thaba Nchu on Basuto land. Later some returned and settled at Mafeking. The Methodist Church became the church to the Barolongs.

The Methodist mission in South Africa was confronted with a new challenge as a result of the migration of British settlers to the Port Elizabeth region after 1814. The British government assisted them in migrating.[41] Having landed at Port Elizabeth, they moved into the interior, where the soil was fertile. In 1820 the Methodist Church sent William Shaw to minister to the settlers. Upon landing at Algoa Bay with a party of settlers, Shaw went to the frontier with them and immediately arranged for services. He served all the denominations and all races in the area. There were Hottentots and Methodist soldiers at the British garrison at Grahamstown, and Shaw made this the base for his activities. A church was constructed at Grahamstown. When it was completed, Shaw permitted other denominations to use it as well.

The scattered settlements required more places of worship. The Methodist system of classes and local preachers was suited to the circumstances. Shaw envisioned a chain of stations toward the northeast. With the cooperation of local preachers, congregations were gathered among various groups of natives and white settlers.[42] Members of the Methodist Church were also concerned about evangelizing the people and asked the church in Britain to send missionaries to South Africa. The ministry was rapidly promoted. Wesleyville was established in 1823, Mount Coke in 1825, Butterworth in 1827, Morley in 1829, Clarkebury and Buntingville in 1830, and Shawbury and Palmerton somewhat later. The ministry expanded systematically across the Kei River into Kaffir territory. Shaw hoped the chain of stations would include Natal and Delagoa Bay.[43] Although Shaw's vision was not realized during his lifetime, it was surpassed, for the Methodist work extended beyond Delagoa Bay into Rhodesia. By 1860 there were 132 missionaries serving in this significant enterprise.

Shaw wanted to send a missionary to every chief and establish a school at every station. He energetically promoted the work during the 1820s, when the settlers were concerned about evangelizing

the native people. The church, however, lacked sufficient personnel and funds for such an ambitious program. Nevertheless, Shaw
promoted the ministry at a time when the people were receptive.
Although some work was disturbed by wars in later years, the
church was planted among the people. One of the missionaries,
John W. Appleyard, wrote a Kaffir grammar. Through Appleyard's
initiative, the Bible was translated into the Kaffir language.[44]

The Methodists established their first mission to the Xhosa tribe
at Wesleyville in 1820. They ministered to a number of tribes as
they expanded their work from Port Elizabeth to Delagoa Bay.
Shaw's vision that the Methodist congregations should provide the
personnel and money for missionary enterprises was largely accomplished, and settlers, or children of settlers, comprised most
of the missionaries who served the Methodist circuits. These volunteers were well acquainted with the situation and began their
services while still in training for the ministry.

Witness in Botswana

The population to the northeast of Cape Town was very sparse.
The London Missionary Society formed plans to develop the ministries at Theopolis and at Hooge Kraal, when it realized that the
Namaqua and the Griqua opened the route to the Bechuana. In
1816 Jack Read settled at Lattakoos among the Bechuana.

In 1817 two of the well-known missionaries of the London Missionary Society's work in South Africa, Robert Moffat and John
Philip, arrived on the field of service. After spending several
weeks at Cape Town, Robert Moffat proceeded to the Orange
River in the vicinity of Africaner, whom the farmers feared. The
London Missionary Society had already tried to establish relations
with him. Campbell, the field director, had sent a letter accompanied with a gift to him, and Christian Albrecht, who served on
the Orange River, had contacted him.[45] When Moffat visited him,
he agreed to have a missionary come to his village. Ebner, who was
serving at Pella, was sent to Africaner. As a result of his ministry,
two sons of Africaner were baptized and later Africaner himself.
Moffat gained his confidence and in 1819 took the chief with him to
Cape Town. Africaner's presence created an immense impression
at Cape Town. The government was thankful for the missionaries'
ministry, which had resulted in a remarkable change in Africaner's life.[46]

While at the Cape, Moffat married Mary Smith. The couple, accompanied by John Campbell, proceeded to Kuruman among the Bechuana, where they worked faithfully for fifty years. The first church among the Bechuana was established at Kuruman in 1829. Moffat's aim was to bring the Bible and the plow to the African people.

In 1829 Mzilikazi, the Matabele chief, sent two messengers to Moffat to inquire concerning the truth. Moffat conferred with them and then accompanied them to their village to assure their safe arrival. This generosity convinced Mzilikazi of Moffat's sincere love for the people. When Moffat visited him the second time, the chief agreed to have a missionary come to instruct his people.[47] Moffat's friendship with Mzilikazi opened the Matabele tribe to missionary activities. Moffat later made a reconnaissance tour through the Matabele country as far as the Zambezi River. He translated the Bible into Bechuana. It was printed in 1857. In 1870 the Moffats returned to England for retirement. Mrs. Moffat died the following year and Mr. Moffat died in 1883. After the Moffats returned to England, his son continued the work at Kuruman, which included the Moffat institute for the training of evangelists.

The ministry at Lekatlong, where Helmore served, was relatively successful. Out of a population of twelve hundred residing in the locality, there were six hundred members in 1850. Most of the children, however, left the settlement to work at the cattle posts.

David Livingstone contributed significantly to the promotion of the missionary cause in Botswana and in sub-Sahara Africa. Born in Blantyre, Scotland, he was influenced by Gutzlaff, missionary to China, and by Robert Moffat, whom he joined in Botswana and whose son-in-law he later became. In preparation for missionary service, Livingstone pursued medical and theological studies. He presented his application to the London Missionary Society and arrived at Cape Town on March 15, 1841. He was assigned to serve at Kuruman, together with Hamilton, Ross, and Edwards. The Moffat family was on furlough at the time.[48]

The population at Kuruman was sparse. After several months of service, Livingstone and Edwards traveled approximately 250 miles to the north in search of another field of ministry. The Kwena people were interested in having missionaries in their midst. Livingstone's relationship with their chief, Sechele, began at this time. In order to prepare for a ministry among them, Livingstone stayed with them for six months, learning their language and customs. Before returning to Kuruman, he also visited the Ngwato. However, he was unable to begin a ministry among the Kwenas because of a tribal war. In 1843 he started Mabotsa station among the Khatla to the southeast of the Kwena and approximately 250 miles from Kuruman. In 1845 Livingstone married Mary, the oldest daughter of Robert Moffat. They served at Mabotsa. He later attempted work among the Kwena at Choruane, but lack of water compelled him to move to Kolobeng on the Kolobeng stream. Livingstone had the joy of baptizing Sechele and of establishing a small Christian community at this place.[49]

Livingstone stressed the importance of introducing indigenous workers in the missionary effort and tried to place a catechist east of Kolobeng. The Boers objected to this action; they accused Livingstone of selling ammunition to the native people and requested his expulsion from the territory. Livingstone had a craving to explore unknown regions. In 1849 Livingstone, Oswell, and Murray were the first Europeans to reach Lake Ngami. In 1850 Livingstone attempted to cross the Kalahari Desert with his family and Sechele, but had to return because of malaria and the tsetse fly, which was a source of sleeping sickness. In 1851 Livingstone and Oswell arrived at Lake Ngami and were cordially received by Sebitwane, the Makololo chief. When they reached the Zambezi River, Livingstone had his first direct experience with the evils of slave trade.

Livingstone asked permission of the society to send his family to Europe while he continued to explore the central part of the continent, for he believed it was necessary to explore the continent and open it to Christianity and commerce in order to stop the slave trade. He thought Christianity would teach people the dignity of human beings, while commerce would provide a substitute for the inhumane trade. Therefore he believed his task was to explore the country so that missionaries could follow and plant Christianity among the peoples. After his family sailed for England, Livingstone returned to the Makololos on the Zambezi River and began the Linyanti station. From there, accompanied by twenty-seven Makololos, he marched to the northwest and reached Loanda in May 1854. Edmund Gabriel, the British commissioner at Loanda, received him and offered him passage back to England. But Livingstone refused the offer, for he felt obliged to accompany the Zambezians to their homes. He returned to Linyanti on September 11, 1855.[50]

On November 3, 1855, Livingstone left Linyanti for Quilimane on the Indian Ocean. Sekeletu, Sebitwane's son, now the Makololo chief, supplied him with men and the provisions for the journey. The chief and two hundred members of his people accompanied Livingstone and his men. On November 15 they arrived at the falls on the Zambezi, which Livingstone named Victoria Falls in honor of the queen of England. On November 20, Sekeletu and his people bade Livingstone farewell and returned to their homes. Livingstone followed the Zambezi River because he wanted to ascertain the importance of the river for commerce. Upon his arrival at Tete, the interior post of the Portuguese, he was cordially received by the commander in charge. He left the 120 Makololo men, who had accompanied him, at Tete and proceeded to Quilimane. Livingstone explored Africa from west to east and made his discoveries known to the outside world. It was an historic and decisive event for missions in Africa. The information that Livingstone presented to the world inspired the churches to occupy the previously unknown regions.

Livingstone's concerns were not shared by everyone. Some felt he was more interested in exploration than in evangelization. However, when Livingstone returned to England, he was received with much acclamation. He was asked to report at conferences and to various societies and to write his first book, which he entitled *Missionary Travels and Researches in South Africa.*[51] His presentations in Britain inspired the formation of several missionary societies with the purpose of evangelizing the interior regions off the Zambezi River. Livingstone devoted the rest of his life to this region, moving from Lake Nyasa to Lake Tanganyika and on to the Lualaba River.

Witness in Jeopardy: The Trek

The small provisioning establishment at Cape Town had gradually expanded to become a colony of considerable magnitude. It claimed an area of land that promised significant opportunities to the settlers. In 1679 Simon van der Stel founded Stellenbosch and in 1687, Drakenstein. In seventy years the settlers had moved as far as the Fish River, five hundred miles east of Cape Town.[52] In

1785 they established Graaf Reinet as the administrative center for the immense oriental district between the Gomtoos and Great Fish rivers, which in 1795 they proclaimed the independent Republic of Graaf Reinet.[53]

While the Boers were expanding their land holdings and establishing a colony, the Napoleonic War broke out in Europe and the British army occupied the Cape in order to prevent a French occupation. The British did not approve of an independent Republic of Graaf Reinet; they landed troops at Algoa Bay and by 1799 had taken the republic and imprisoned its leaders. This action was the beginning of the endless hatred between Dutch and British in South Africa. Even when the British withdrew in 1803, the tension between the two groups remained. In 1806 the British reoccupied the Cape, and this occupation lasted for almost a hundred years. The Boers were greatly displeased.

The land problem became a serious threat to peace in South Africa. Whereas the Boers were constantly expanding their land holdings, the government realized the necessity of controlling such expansion and of providing protection for all people. Therefore the government proclaimed the Grand Charter of the Hottentots in 1809. This charter guaranteed certain liberties of work. An ordonnance of 1812 limited the number of acres any one person could possess.

The Dutch were further displeased when the Prince of Orange ceded the Cape to the British in 1814. They resented being British subjects. The British colonization brought many British into the Graaf Reinet district, which the Boers wanted to occupy. Ordonnance 50, promulgated in 1828, permitted the indigenous peoples to possess land, offered equal rights to mulattoes and Europeans, and rejected the use of the Dutch language in the schools and in administration. These actions by the government greatly annoyed the Boers. Furthermore, the government was strong enough to control the activities of the colonists on the frontier, but not to control the activities of the tribes. Consequently, grievances continued and wars erupted. Many Boers decided to leave the colony. With their essentials loaded on canvas-topped ox-drawn wagons, they moved north across the Orange River and beyond the Griqua settlement at Philippolis.

The migrations of the Boers were facilitated by the disturbance and the consequent reduction of the population in the area to which the Boers were going. The disturbance had been caused by Chaka and his followers. Chaka, the real founder of the Zulu, succeeded Dinguiswayo in 1818. In ten years his army devastated the Natal, where the Nguni, Tembu, Ponda, and Xhosa had lived since the fifteenth century. It is estimated that more than a million lives were lost through these wars. In 1828 Chaka was assassinated by his half brother, Dingaan. Three generals then set out to conquer tribes distantly removed from Zululand. Manukosi conquered the country north of the lower Limpopo; Mzilikazi moved west and scattered the Soto and the Tshuana and established himself in the present Orange Free State; Sebitwane directed the Kololo (or Makololo) to the Upper Zambezi, where they settled.[54]

The Boers met Mzilikazi and the Matabele in the Orange Free State. The Matabele withdrew from the region and settled near Bulawayo in Rhodesia. In 1837 and 1838 the Boers gathered at Thaba Nchu. They elected officials and drafted a constitution for a republic.[55] Some of the Boers under Potgieter moved even farther north across the Vaal River and established the Republic of Potchefstroom in the present Transvaal in 1838. Another group under Piet Retief's leadership followed the Drakensberg Mountain passes and went to the Tugela valley. Having arranged to purchase land from Dingaan, the Boers, not suspecting any evil, came unarmed to a meal and all sixty-five were massacred by the Zulus. The other Boers, with Andrew Pretorius as commander, defeated the Zulus in the battle of Blood River and proclaimed the Republic of Natal in 1840,[56] with Pietermaritzburg as its capital. The British, however, did not recognize the independent Boer republics. This fact provoked much bloodshed and disrupted the work of the churches during half a century.

The Dutch Reformed Church advised the Boers not to leave the colony and sent no minister with them. At this time no distinction was made by the Cape church between nonwhite and white members. All had communion together. Erasmus Smit, the brother-in-law to Maritz, went with one of the parties. At Thaba Nchu, James Archbell, a Methodist missionary to the Barolongs, ministered to the Boers; Daniel Lindley, a Presbyterian missionary, ministered to the Matabele and served the Boers wherever he could.

As a result of the conflict between the Boers and the Matabele, the latter moved to Bulawayo in Rhodesia. Hence the ministry in which Daniel Lindley and his colleagues of the American Board of Commissioners had been engaged in since 1835 came to an end. The American Board had also begun a ministry among the Zulu in 1835 in the Natal. This was disrupted by the war.

EXPANSION OF CHRISTIANITY IN SOUTH AFRICA

The map and the history of South Africa changed immensely with the Zulu wars and the Boer trek between 1818 and 1856. The Cape colony had covered a relatively small area. When the Boers moved into the Orange Free State and Natal, the British government suddenly extended the frontiers of the Cape colony and proclaimed the Orange Free State and Natal British colonies. Missionary endeavors were disrupted in frontier situations in the Orange River area and along the Indian Ocean. Some tribes, like the Matabele, moved to an entirely new location, leaving the mission either without a population or in contact with a new people. Consequently, much of the frontier ministry had come to an end and it was necessary to begin again. Although Britain had proclaimed the new Boer settlements British colonies, the political situation was very unsettled.

The Church in the Cape Province

The Methodists had expanded rapidly into the interior of the country in order to serve the settlers and to proclaim the gospel to the unevangelized people. Many Methodist settlers had shared the church's concern for the indigenous population and assisted in the ministry. Through the frontier wars some mission stations had been destroyed, while others were abandoned because there were no funds and no men to continue the ministry; in addition, the settler's sympathies had been alienated. A special appeal for financial help was made in England and the ministry was reviving. Then in 1857 the "cattle-killing" of the Xhosa took place because prophets proclaimed that if the people killed their cattle and destroyed their crops, the spirits of the ancestors would return and drive the white people into the ocean.[57] Although the government and the missionaries tried to help the starving people, their resources were insufficient and many people perished. This was a sad event in the history of the Xhosa and the establishment of the church among them. Colonists settled in the depopulated areas. By 1866 the frontier of the Cape colony had expanded to the Kei

River and eventually the territory between the Kei and Natal was also annexed.

In 1859 the London Missionary Society formed the congregations that had come into being through its ministry in the Cape colony into a Congregational Union, which became a part of the Congregational Union of South Africa in 1883.

The ministry of the Methodist Church was greatly strengthened through the work of William Taylor. Before coming to South Africa, he had conducted evangelistic meetings in the United States, Canada, and Australia. He arrived in 1862 and conducted meetings at Cape Town, Port Elizabeth, and Uitenhagen. At Grahamstown, Charles Pamla interpreted for him and a true revival took place. The two continued their ministry in the major cities of the southeastern coast and into Natal. A new spirit animated the churches and a new period in the history of the Methodist Church in South Africa began. The ministry of Taylor and Pamla was seconded by the Christians who devoted themselves to evangelize their fellowmen. The revival was especially noticeable among the Zulu. Ralph Scott began a ministry among the Asians in 1862. He had served in Asia for eighteen years and spoke Tamil and Hindustani. He served until 1880 without realizing significant results.

The Lovedale Institute, opened in 1841, trained church ministers according to European academic requirements. In 1869 the administration decided to adapt the instruction to prepare indigenous students for the ministry. As a result of the change, the enrollment increased considerably and the institution's contribution to the work of the church was enhanced. In 1877 a school for pedagogical training was begun at Blythswood in the Transkei.

At this time a significant development occurred in the Dutch Reformed Church of South Africa, which was constrained to begin mission work at Smithfield, Winburg, and Bloemfontein during 1849-1850. Andrew Murray was sent to Bloemfontein. Feeling strongly the need to bring the gospel to the people and realizing the need for workers, he encouraged the church to open a training school for missionaries. Such a school was opened at Wellington in 1877. Murray exercised an important influence in the life of the school. He inspired many people and greatly promoted the missionary endeavor of the church. By 1878 the church had begun eighteen congregations in the Orange Free State. These congregations served the people in the communities where they were located.

In response to John Philip's appeal in 1829 to other churches to help in the evangelization of South Africa, the Rhenish Missionary Society launched a missionary endeavor to the Hottentot people in the northern part of the Cape colony at Wupperthal near Clanwilliam and Ebenezer at the mouth of the Olifants River. In addition to the Christian ministry, the mission also taught crafts and farming methods.

From its ministry among the Hottentots, the Rhenish Mission moved on to the Namaqua, occupying the northwestern part of the Cape Province. During the 1840s it assumed the responsibility for the London Missionary Society's stations in this region. As farmers occupied more land, the Namaqua moved farther to the north and the mission with them. Eventually the Rhenish Mission began a ministry in South West Africa and developed a large work there.

The London Missionary Society, feeling the congregations should continue to minister to their people, began to withdraw from the endeavor during the 1850s and discontinued its financial support to the churches in the 1880s.[58] In 1877 the Congregational Union, Church Aid and Missionary Society of South Africa was constituted in order to establish and support the churches and missions of the Congregational Church. It federated the churches of the London Missionary Society and of the American Board of Commissioners.[59]

Bishop Robert Gray directed the ministry of the Anglican Church with devotion and insight. When he arrived in South Africa, the Anglican Church had one diocese; at the time of his death at Cape Town in 1872 there were six dioceses, served by 127 pastors. William Jones succeeded him in 1874 and gave thirty-four years of faithful service to the church during the important period of its development. He became archbishop in 1897.

The Anglican Church's first mission to the Africans was undertaken in 1854 among the Xhosa tribe. Bishop Gray was impressed with the results of the Moravian mission and adopted their mission as his model. He induced the British government to vote forty thousand British pounds per annum during 1855-57 to subsidize educational and industrial work among the native peoples. In 1854 Armstrong arrived to direct the new diocese of Grahamstown. By means of the subsidy three more stations were opened.[60]

By the support of the Episcopal Church of Scotland, the diocese of St. John's, Kafraria, was created in 1873, and Henry Callaway became its first bishop in 1880.

The Catholic Church created a central prefecture for the Cape of Good Hope. The prefecture was under the care of the Missionary Fathers of Lyons from 1873 to 1882. In 1874 Gaudeul and Pasquereau of Our Lady of the Sacred Heart began a work at Pella. In 1882 the Missionary Fathers of Lyons withdrew from this area; the Orange River prefecture was placed under the care of the Oblates of St. Francis of Sales.[61] Moran, the vicar apostolic of the eastern vicariate (1856-70), placed the emphasis on schools. He was succeeded by Ricards, who invited the Trappists to establish a monastery in the Cape colony.[62] They landed near Port Elizabeth in 1880, but the chosen site was not favorable, and they moved to Mariannhill near Durban in Natal.[63]

The Church in Botswana

The Botswana came in contact with the gospel early in the nineteenth century, and a number of stations were established in their area. Robert Moffat translated the Scriptures into Setswana and strove to establish a community of committed Christians at Kuruman. David Livingstone visited the Kwena and Ngwato and organized a small Christian community at Kolobeng, which he left so that he could explore Botswana and find strategic places for missionary work. Helmore had a successful ministry at Lekatlong. But much of the sparsely populated country was not occupied until the latter part of the nineteenth century.

In 1862 the London Missionary Society asked John Mackenzie to minister to the Ngwato at Shushong, a town of thirty thousand, in the eastern part of Botswana. Roger Price served with him until he was sent to the Kwena in 1866. The ministry was successful, and members of the chief's family were among the converts. In 1865 a crisis occurred in the chief's family. The chief, Sekhone, who had been favorably disposed toward the mission, became irritated when his sons refused to accompany him to the circumcision camp. He pronounced himself against the Christian religion because it caused the sons to disobey their parents. His action provoked a division in the tribe. Sekhone lost the respect of his people, left the tribe, and stayed with another chief. His son, Khama, became chief. He lived to a ripe age and permitted Christianity to gain considerable influence in the Ngwato tribe. Khama did what he could to prohibit drinking in his territory. Christian ethics were gradually observed to a greater degree.[64]

Robert Price ministered among the Kwena, where Sechele was chief. Sechele had guided affairs since Livingstone's departure and felt he should have supervision of the church as well as other institutions of the tribe. The mission, however, thought Sechele had syncretistic tendencies and tried to guard the church against them.

In response to a request from Moremi, the chief of the Lake Ngami area, the London Missionary Society began a ministry at Lake Ngami in 1875. J. D. Hepburn, serving at Shoshong, responded to the request. Accompanied by his wife, three children, and two evangelists, he traveled to Lake Ngami and began the ministry. In 1880 he reported that the people were responsive.

After his trip to Angola and back along the Zambezi to the east coast, Livingstone encouraged the London Missionary Society to give attention to the larger populations of the Makololo on the Zambezi and the Matabele in the Bulawayo region. Because of his friendship with Mzilikazi, the Matabele chief, the society asked Robert Moffat to accompany his son, John Moffat, William Sykes, and J. M. Thomas to the Matabele in order to establish a ministry there. Mzilikazi was hesitant to accept strangers in his territory, but Moffat gained his confidence and work was begun in Inyanti. However, the tribe remained closed to the gospel,[65] and a permanent work in the tribe was established later.

The ministry of the Dutch Reformed Mission at Mochudi has met with good response by the Bakgatala people. The chief, Lentswe, became a church member in 1892 and promoted the Christian ministry. By 1908 a school system had been organized that offered elementary education in the villages and middle school education at Mochudi.[66]

The Roman Catholic Church has only recently begun a ministry in Botswana. Several priests are offering high-school training at a boarding school near Gaberones.

The Church in the Orange Free State

The ministry of the Wesleyan Methodist missionaries Samuel Broadbents and Thomas Hodgsons among the Barolong at Ploatberg, plus the migration of the people to Thaba Nchu, then back to the Vaal River, and finally their settlement near Mafeking, has been mentioned earlier. Thaba Nchu became the center of the Methodist ministry along the Caledon River, where the society established a number of stations among the Barolong, the Koranna, and the Griqua. To the northeast, the society began a ministry among the Batlokwa, who had not migrated from this region.

Tribal wars between the Barolong and the Basuto, and between the Batlokwa and Basuto, brought about a disturbed condition during the 1840s and destroyed the Christian ministry in the region. The Barolong attacked Umpukani, a station among the Koronna that was started by Edwards in 1836. They killed the Fingo, Koranna, Griqua, and Botswana Christians, except those who hid in Schreiner's house. After the attack, the Schreiner family and the remaining Christians left the station, which was destroyed in their absence. The Methodist Mission closed the other stations in the region, except at Thaba Nchu. This was the only station operating after twenty-five years of effort.

Jack Allison began the station at Imparani among the Batlokwa, who were paying tribute to Dingaan. Allison was able to establish peace between Sikonyela, the Batlokwa chief, and Dingaan and the Boers when Dingaan claimed someone had stolen cattle from him. When the Swazi chief heard of Allison's good work, he sent a delegation to Allison to invite him to begin a ministry among his tribe. In 1839, when a Christian community was being established, a Christian was accused of causing the measles epidemic and was put to death. The Christians were obliged to leave Imparani. After a brief stay at Thaba Nchu, Allison and some of the converts began a mission in Swaziland.

The political situation normalized to a degree, and the churches undertook to minister to the people in the region. In 1851 the Methodist Church began to establish a ministry by locating in the cities that were coming into existence: Bloemfontein, Smithfield, Fauersmith, and Kimberley. The ministers in the cities served both the settlers and the indigenous population. In some cases several catechists served in surrounding villages.

In 1847 the Reformed Church of the Cape appointed a commission to investigate the conditions of the ministry to their members who had moved to the north of the Orange River. The commission found that the communities there were spiritually neglected. As a result, consistories were established at Smithfield, Harrismith, and Bloemfontein, in addition to the one at Winburg; and pastors were sent to Bloemfontein and Winburg in 1849 and 1850 respectively. By 1878 eighteen congregations had been started in the Orange Free State. These congregations established sister congregations. In response to a request from a local chief, a mission was begun at Witzie's Hoek, where eventually a school for the training of African church leaders was founded.

A deacon of the Anglican Church served in Bloemfontein from 1850 to 1860. The archdeacon Merriman from Grahamstown visited the work at Bloemfontein. In 1863 the church created the diocese of Bloemfontein and consecrated John Mackenzie as bishop of the Orange Free State. However, Mackenzie died during a visit to Malawi, and Edward Twells served as bishop from 1865 to 1869. Twells aimed to establish congregations among the European and the indigenous population. He also tried to establish the Anglican Church among the Basuto and the Barolong. His actions were not appreciated by the Paris Mission and the Methodists who were serving these tribes. The Anglican Church was not able to develop the ministry among these peoples. A small work was eventually established among the Basuto.

In 1851 the Catholic Church sent Hoenderwangers to work among the English soldiers and the Dutch Catholics in the Orange Free State. He established residence at Bloemfontein and visited Catholics in the state and in Lesotho until 1869, when an accident necessitated his return to Belgium. As a result of the discovery of diamonds, by 1870 most of the Catholics of the Orange Free State had moved to Kimberley. The two priests who had been assigned to the state moved there also. Schools were opened at Bloemfontein and Kimberley, and in 1886 the vicariate of the Orange Free State was created.

The Church in Lesotho

In response to an invitation from John Philip, the Paris Evangelical Missionary Society sent its first missionaries to South Africa in 1829.[67] Isaac Bisseau accepted an invitation by the Huguenots to serve in their area, while Samuel Roland and Prosper Lamus, after visiting Robert Moffat, went to serve the Bahurutsi at Mosega. But the Bahurutsi were attacked by Mzilikazi, and the missionaries were compelled to withdraw.

When Casalis, Arbousset, and Gosselin came in 1833, they went to the Basuto at Thaba Bosiu, where Moshesh was chief. When the Basuto had been threatened by Chaka's armies during the Zulu wars of expansion, they took refuge in the Drakensberg Mountains where they were able to defend themselves. Moshesh had sent a message to Philip requesting missionaries, and he received them cordially. They established a station at Morija, which became the central station for the work of the society, with schools and a print shop located there. The London Missionary Society ceded their work at the confluence of the Caledon and Orange Rivers to them. In 1837 Casalis began a ministry at Thaba Bosiu, the capital of the tribe. A mission was also begun at Mekuatling.[68]

The Boer farmers who settled in the Caledon River valley came in conflict with the Basuto because of the land. Tensions erupted in 1858, 1864, and 1867. From 1865 to 1868 it became a question whether the Basuto, the Boers, or the British would rule the region. In response to the counsel of the missionaries, Moshesh asked that Lesotho become a British protectorate, and it was able to maintain its independence.

The Basuto were receptive to the gospel and the believers assumed responsibilities. In 1863 the ministry of the stations was entrusted to them, and they became responsible for the evangelization of their fellow-men. From nine stations in 1870, the work developed to sixteen in 1889. An indigenous church was formed; it had 5,984 members in 1880. Considerable progress was made and the ministry was enlarged at various outstations, especially among the Basuto living in the eastern part of Griqualand.[69] The people frequently settled near the church school.

The society established a printing press at Morija in 1841, and it became an important center for the diffusion of Christian literature. In 1864 Mabille began to edit the paper *Leselinyana* (The Small Light) in the Sesothe language. In 1881 the Bible was revised and printed. The printery has continued to function throughout the years and has made a significant contribution to the ministry.

In order to train workers for school and church activities, a high school to train teachers and evangelists was established in 1868. A girls' school was begun in 1871, and later an industrial school with a smithery, a carpenter shop, and a shoe factory. In 1880 a Bible school began to train the future pastors for the church. From 1883 to 1914 the school work developed and contributed to the establishment of the church, furnishing it with a number of worthy leaders.[70]

During this time the Lesotho Church was interested in undertaking its own missionary effort. It considered a ministry to the north of the Transvaal, but there were disturbances in the region. Finally, under the direction of Frances Coillard, a ministry was begun among the Barotse along the Zambezi River near Victoria Falls. However, it soon became apparent that the distance between the two regions made it difficult for the Lesotho Church to be responsible for this ministry; so it became a separate mission project of the Paris Evangelical Society.[71]

From 1914 to 1939 the society had financial difficulties and was unable to send as many missionaries to Africa as it desired. Nevertheless, the interest in learning, which became very prominent, gave rise to a large educational enterprise. The girls benefited more from formal education than the boys, who were required to herd cattle at the early age of eight years and spend much time from the fourteenth to the eighteenth year of their life in circumcision camps. Because of the poverty of the mountainous country, many young men went to work in the mines at Johannesburg, especially to acquire money for the bride price. The church conducted several youth centers where the gospel was presented to them and where they could find Christian fellowship. The church became autonomous in 1964.

Bishop Gray of the Anglican Church visited Moshesh in 1850 and from 1865 to 1869 Twells tried to establish congregations among the Lesotho to the west. But effective work was not undertaken until the 1870s at Modderpoort in the Orange Free State. In 1875 work was begun at Mohale's Hoek in the south and at Leribe in the north. Later another station was begun at Butha Buthe. Twells and Webb caused some hard feelings by their attitude toward other missions, but John Widdicombe respected the work of other societies and cooperated with them. The Anglican Church in Lesotho is not large.

In 1862 Bishop Allard and Father Gerard of the Roman Catholic Church promised Moshesh that they would teach reading, writing, sewing, and weaving if they were permitted to open a work. Moshesh permitted them to establish themselves at Roma, twenty miles from Thaba Bosiu.[72] In 1865 the Sisters of the Holy Family arrived to teach the girls how to sew and weave. The work has progressed since that day but it is not large.

The Church in Natal

In 1824 a group of traders from Grahamstown came to Durban (then Port Natal), looking for ivory. In addition to the trade in blankets, pots, beads, etc., they traded guns and ammunition to acquire the ivory they desired. Chaka granted the traders land rights at Durban. Later Dingaan extended rights to the north and south along the coast. As many men had been killed by the Zulu wars, some of the traders took many wives and became the chiefs of new tribes. They began to fill the vacuum and established an exceptional authority in the region.

Allen Gardiner of the Anglican Church came to Natal in 1835. He readily realized that no permanent church work could be accomplished while such conditions existed and returned to England to persuade the British government to establish order in the region.[73] He returned to Natal in 1837, accompanied by Francis Owen. But their efforts were unsuccessful. In 1838 the Boers, under Pieter Retief, arrived in Natal. A party of Boers was massacred and several years of war followed, destroying any impression Gardiner and Owen may have made.

Upon his arrival in Natal, Henry Callaway found the missionaries discouraged. He felt that the work would be more successful if the Zulu language was used and started to translate portions of the Scriptures into Zulu. The missionaries of the American Board had begun the translation of the New Testament. As a result of the collaboration of the two societies, the New Testament was published in 1872 and the Bible in 1883. Callaway also emphasized the training of native pastors. The St. Alban College was opened for this purpose. The first two students were ordained in 1871.

Venable, Lindley, and Wilson, missionaries of the American Board, began a ministry at Umlozi near Durban in 1837. However, because of the wars, no successful work could be done, and they were obliged to withdraw from the region for several years. Adams and Lindley began ministries at Adams and Inanda. The British government annexed Natal in 1843, but actually ruled only after the Boers moved into the Transvaal in 1845. The first convert in this region was Mbulasi at Amamzimtoti. She sought refuge at the

Adams home when Chaka killed her husband. Her testimony greatly influenced the Makhanya people to accept the Christian faith. By 1850 a group of thirty-two believers had been gathered at Amamzimtoti.[74] This was the beginning of a lasting ministry. Adams and Lindley also stressed the importance of the people's settling on the land. They were appointed to the land commission which reserved land for the indigenous population.

The society sent fifteen couples to the Zulu work between 1846 and 1860 and established twelve stations. A revival took place in the church, and the Zulu Christians became missionaries to their own people. In response to this interest an interior mission was organized, a school to offer pedagogical training was begun at Amamzimtoti in 1864, and a girls' school was started at Inanda in 1869. In its effort to establish autonomous churches, the society ordained two men and placed them in charge of these congregations. Jack Dube rendered an effective ministry as pastor of the Inanda congregation.

The Methodist Church sent Jack Archbell to Pietermaritzburg in 1846. In 1847 Allison, having been obliged to leave Imparani, came with some Batlokwa and Swazi people and began a ministry at Indaleni and another at Edendale. He instructed his followers to be evangelists and teachers. They established the Methodist ministry in Natal.[75] The Methodist and American Board Missions wanted to divide the area between them, but the Methodist workers were enthusiastic and did not want to limit their field of activity. The American Board, to a large degree, adopted the Methodists' principles.

Hans P. Schreuder began the work of the Norwegian Lutheran Church in the independent Zululand at Umpumulo in 1848. He hoped that the chief, Mpande, would permit the proclamation of the gospel in his region. But Mpande persecuted the Christians and they were obliged to seek refuge in Natal. Cetshwaya succeeded Mpande and continued his policy. The Christians passed through a difficult period. In 1879 Cetshwayo attacked the British. As a result of this disturbance, Zululand was incorporated into the British Empire. By 1881 the Norwegian Society had established ten stations between the Tugela and Umfalozi rivers.

The Berlin Mission sent W. Posselt to work among the Zulu and the Germans in the Durban area. Ministries were begun at New Germany several miles from Durban, at Emmaus at the foot of the

Drakensberg Mountains, and near Bergville which was established by Guldenpfennig in 1846.

The Hermannsburg Mission began a self-supporting mission in which they cultivated the soil to support themselves. Eventually some devoted their full time to the work of the mission, whereas others became farmers. The society gave useful industrial training to the people among whom they worked. The American Lutherans of Buffalo Synod came and assumed the responsibilities for several small projects.

Beginning in 1889, the various branches of the Lutheran Church held meetings that finally led to the union of the Lutheran groups in this part of South Africa into the Evangelical Lutheran Church.

J. W. Colenso, the first Anglican bishop of Natal, arrived in 1854. He advocated the baptism of polygamists, and this caused some reaction. Being influenced by German scholars, he caused more dissension through his textual criticism. He was dismissed from office, but refused to accept the action and remained in his position until his death in 1883. The division was not reconciled until 1901. Nevertheless, the work grew steadily and the diocese of Zululand was created in the 1860s. The St. Alban's training college at Estcourt has supplied many pastors, catechists, and teachers. Successful mission work was also carried on among the immigrants from India in the Durban area. The important centers of the diocese of Zululand are Kwa Magwaza, where a hospital and a training college for teachers and catechists were opened, and St. Augustine, whence the ministry has extended to many annexes.

Missionaries of the Society for the Propagation of the Gospel of the Anglican Church came to Zululand in 1860. By 1874 they had established five stations. The Zulu chiefs regarded their work with suspicion, for they questioned the possibility of simultaneous allegiance to two entities—the church and the tribe. They considered the missionaries rivals to whom the believers gave their loyalty. The believers were persecuted. The ministry suffered and a number of stations were destroyed during the Zulu War (1878-1879). After the war the work was reestablished and began a normal growth.

The Roman Catholic Church erected the vicariate apostolic of Natal in 1850 and appointed M. F. J. Allard of the Oblates of Mary Immaculate as the first bishop. He arrived in 1852 and gave priority to the establishment of the work among the Roman

Catholics in Durban and Pietermaritzburg, where he found about two hundred Catholics. The French-speaking priests had to learn the English and the Zulu languages. The early work among the Zulu was unsuccessful and Allard turned his attention to the Basuto.

Work among the Zulu began when the Trappists from Bosnia established a monastery at Mariannhill near Durban.[76] In four years Pfanner, the abbot, collected 130 priests and brothers and raised money to build monasteries, farms, schools, and industrial projects. Pfanner's idea was to build a Christian community first, hoping that the people would become Christians by participating in the Christian community. He began a number of monasteries. His projects were expensive and failed to produce the results that were expected. Finally a new order of Religious Missionaries of Mariannhill was created as a separate order in 1909.[77] The order emphasized religious, agricultural, and industrial training, organizing cooperatives among the people. The Mariannhill Fathers extended their ministry to the southern part of Natal and to the Transkei.[78] The Oblates serve in the other parts of Natal. In the 1880s they established work among the Indians who came as sugar-cane workers.[79] Beginning in the 1920s, the mission work produced good results.

The Church in Transvaal

The region between the Vaal and Limpopo Rivers was disturbed by political rivalries during most of the nineteenth century. As a result of the raids by Chaka and his successors, many people lost their lives and many others fled from the region. From 1818 to 1828 life was very insecure and most normal activities were neglected. Then, beginning with 1836, the Boers clashed with the tribes, and later the British fought the Boers and the tribes.

Due to the friendship Robert Moffat had established with Mzilikazi, a ministry was begun among his people, the Matabele. The Paris Evangelical Mission began a work at Mosega among the Bahurutsi in 1831. But in 1832 Mzilikazi attacked the Bahurutsi, and Mosega was destroyed. The Bahurutsi fled southwest and the work was continued at Motito near Kuruman.

In 1836 Venable, Lindley, and Wilson of the American Board began a work among the Matabele at Mosega. But in 1837 the tensions between the Matabele and the Boers erupted. Mosega was again destroyed, the Matabele moved to the Bulawayo region in Rhodesia, and the missionaries went to work in Natal. The political situation was less complicated north of the Limpopo River. The Batswana were in the western part and the Mashona and Matabele were in the northern part of this region.

Four congregations, scattered from Potchefstroom to Soutpansberg, were founded by the Boers. The Cape church engaged in considerable dialogue with these congregations, hoping that they would become a part of the Dutch Reformed Church. But in 1856 these congregations formed the Hervormde Kerk, which claimed its independency from the Cape church. In 1860 it was declared the official state church of the Republic of Transvaal.[80]

The Reformed Church of South Africa in 1853 appointed a Committee on Interior Missions, which was to further the evangelization of native people. Henry Gonin and Alexander McKidd arrived in the Transvaal in 1861. McKidd began a work among the Si-Pedi at Zoutpansberg and Gonin went to the Khatla near the Botswana border. He had a very effective ministry for forty-five years, and the tribe accepted the Christian faith.[81]

The Berlin Mission began a ministry in the eastern part of Transvaal in 1860, but effective work was not possible because of tribal disturbances. In 1864 the Swazi attacked the Kopa and the latter moved south. The Botschabelo station among them became a prosperous work where teachers were trained and industrial instruction was offered. By 1876 it reported a Christian community of 1,057 members. The endeavor witnessed significant expansion in which twenty-three stations were established between Pretoria and Zoutpansberg from 1865 to 1880. The Hermannsburg Mission established a ministry among the Kwena between Pretoria and the western frontier. Eventually the Hermannsburg and the Berlin Societies united to form the Evangelical Lutheran Church.

Sekukuni, the Bapedi chief, attacked the Transvaal republic. Shepitone responded to the incident by annexing the Transvaal in 1877. The settlers were displeased at this action and organized the Insurrection Committee, which was under Kruger, Jubert, and Pretorius. The Boers defeated the British at three occasions, especially at Mojuba Hill in 1881. The Pretoria Convention was signed, and for all practical purposes, this gave the Boers autonomy.

Gold was discovered on the Witwatersrand in 1886; the discovery caused a most rapid economic and demographic revolution. Johannesburg, which was only a village in 1886, had over 102,000 inhabitants by 1896.[82] The British took measures to incorporate the Transvaal. War broke out in 1899. Britain sent reinforcements to the extent that in 1901 a total of only 22,000 Boers fought against 275,000 British. The Boers fought to the last. But their families were starving while the men were fighting and they finally had to submit. The Orange Free State and the Transvaal were proclaimed British colonies. The Boer War of 1899 to 1902 caused a heavy loss of life and created an enmity between Boers and British that still exists and is a part of South Africa's intricate problems.

The Boer War caused much damage to the churches. Many congregations were disrupted, some members were killed, and some fled to other regions. The people had also been disturbed psychologically; mistrust and hatred had been sown. The British government was suspicious of the Dutch and German missionary societies. Five of the stations of the Berlin and Hermannsburg Societies, serving to the east and west of Pretoria, were destroyed.[83] The work was not resumed at several stations because the people had left the districts.

Swiss Reformed churches supported the ministry of the Paris Evangelical Mission, but in 1885 they undertook their own missionary endeavor in the northern Transvaal among the Magwamba people. Ernest Creux and Paul Berthoud, who served with the Paris Society in Lesotho, and three Basuto evangelists began the ministry at Valdezia. The Basuto evangelists made a unique contribution to the work. In 1879 the first four Magwamba were sent to the catechist school at Morija. The second station, Elim, was begun in 1882. Valdezia was in the tropical climate and malaria soon became an obstacle to the workers. There were six deaths during the first five years of activity.

The Boer War did not affect the northern Transvaal where the Swiss Mission labored, but the mission was unable to receive the supplies, especially medicines, during the war. The mission rendered an important ministry in Transvaal. It established the church, prepared Christian literature, and made ethnographic studies. The missionaries realized that the Magwamba were of the same ethnic origin as the Tsonga people, of which the majority are in Portuguese East Africa. They extended their work across the border and established an important work in southern Mozambique.[84] The mission also extended its work southward as far as Pretoria and Johannesburg.

The Anglican Church sent J. B. Wills to Pretoria in 1870 to gather the members of the Anglican faith, some of whom were farmers; some, miners; and others, businessmen. The first congregations were gathered near Barberton. Bishop Wilkinson consecrated some deacons to serve these congregations. In 1878 the Transvaal diocese was created and placed under Bishop Bousfield's charge. The work began to prosper, but was stopped during the Boer War. The Community of the Resurrection came to serve in the spiritual ministry, social welfare work, educational work, and theological training.[85] They befriended those in need and in the school, and the boys felt loved and accepted.

The Methodist Church employed the principles introduced by William Shaw and witnessed significant growth. It established its ministries in cities, such as Potchefstroom, Pretoria, and Lydenburg. African Christians contributed to the advancement of the gospel. David Magatha began the church at Potchefstroom and Samuel Mathabathe, having studied under Allison at Pietermaritzburg, returned to work in the Transvaal. But he was not permitted to do so during Sekukuni's chieftainship. The Methodists had much success among the miners, even though many of the miners stayed a short period. The miners returned to their homes in Zambia and Malawi, taking the gospel message with them. The church served those who settled in the towns and became a new African proletariat. The women's groups, called Manyanos, met for prayer and visited the sick. They greatly contributed to the ministry of the church among the women.[86]

As a result of the heavy concentration of the population in the mining districts, almost all of the churches established ministries in them as they sought to follow up their church members and reach others. The American Methodist Mission, serving the Batswa in Mozambique, considered it expedient to arrange a ministry to its members at the mines in the Transvaal.

The attitude of the people of Swaziland to the Europeans changed at different periods. It remained static during the colonial period. The king granted land concessions to those who brought gifts to him, especially guns and ammunition, until two-thirds of the land had been ceded. Then he began to realize that they would not have sufficient land for the Swazi. Pressed for more land by the settlers, the king and his counselors asked the British administration for help. The Concession Partition Act was passed in 1907, reserving the rest of the land for the Swazi. The Swazi ruler, the sister of the former king, was disappointed. Realizing that the land would not be returned free of charge, she began in 1913 to encourage the young men to acquire funds by working in South Africa and then to buy land. By means of this policy several million acres of land were bought by the Swazi.[87]

The missionary work in Swaziland was affected by the attitude of the rulers. In 1860 the Berlin Mission sent two men to Swaziland. Umswazi, the chief, told them he was not interested in anything but guns and ammunition.[88] Consequently, they went to work at Lydenburg in eastern Transvaal. The Anglicans won the approval of Umbandzeni through their work at two farms, one in Transvaal near the border and the other in Swaziland. Umbandzeni often sought the advice of Jackson. The Anglicans hoped that the royal family might accept Christianity, but this did not happen. Many of the women became Christians, but the men remained indifferent.[89]

THE INDEPENDENT CHURCHES IN SOUTH AFRICA

Christianity has made a profound impact on sub-Saharan Africa during the last century. The effect may be compared to the impact of Christianity on the Roman Empire in the first centuries.[90] The indigenous leadership and separate churches testify that Christianity is taking root in the African culture. Independent churches exist throughout sub-Saharan Africa but are especially numerous in South Africa. They have experienced a phenomenal numerical growth and reveal an unprecedented proliferation of ecclesiastical divisions.

The separatist churches in South Africa began in the latter part of the nineteenth century. One of the first secessions took place in Lesotho where in 1892 about 150 members separated from the Mount Hermon congregation of the Paris Evangelical Missionary Society. The schism, however, was not permanent. Then in 1884 Nehemiah Tile, a Methodist minister, founded the Tembu National Church. In 1892 the Methodist minister, Mangena Mokoni founded his Ethiopian Church in the Transvaal. He gained adherents rapidly. Mokoni aimed to make the Ethiopian Church a church for all Africans in the subcontinent.[91] Before long, divisions occurred in this church, and this marked the beginning of a proliferation of separations and divisions. By 1967 some 3,200 secessionist groups existed.[92] By 1966 one-quarter of the Bantu Christians of South Africa adhered to separatist groups.

The independent churches of South Africa are classified as Ethiopian, Zionist, and Messianic. These are general groupings that indicate certain characteristics of each group. The latter two groups reveal strong syncretistic tendencies.

The term *Ethiopian* implies African, according to the New Testament (cf. Acts 8:27). The basic motive of these churches is to establish independent African churches.

The Zionist churches are led by a prophet who has received his call from God and is head of the church. But the authority is transmitted from father to son. Most of these churches have separated from the former group through the instigation of a prophet. They are also called Churches of the Holy Spirit because the Holy Spirit is said to direct the prophet. In West Africa they are known as praying churches. They emphasize faith healing, the baptism of adults by immersion, and the eminence of the second coming of Christ. They maintain that revelations and healings are manifestations of the Holy Spirit.[93]

The Bantu Messianic Movement has many affinities with the Zionist churches, but the prophet assumes a greater importance. Special powers are attributed to him in order to indicate his identification with Christ. He guards the keys to heaven and becomes the savior and mediator to the degree of replacing Christ.[94]

As a result of a number of rebellions by separatist groups, the government has regarded the separatist churches as politically dangerous. Police dispersed the group called the Israelites near Queenstown in 1920, and a large number were killed in the ensuing fight. The government has been reluctant to grant recognition to new groups. However, since the existence of such groups is not considered illegal, the restrictions are not preventing the formation of new groups.

Little Christian fellowship has existed between the separatist churches and the older denominations. The separatist churches coveted independence and separateness, while the older churches basically considered them a menace to church work. However, as these churches are becoming more established and known by the older churches, they are more readily accepted. As the leaders of many separatist churches are receiving more education and church members are being instructed in the Christian faith, many separatist churches are presenting a dynamic Christian witness that is acceptable to the older churches.

The separatist churches have the potential for phenomenal church growth. They draw the ordinary people to their meetings and fellowship. They communicate with the people according to their understanding. A vital spirit of renewal is manifest in some independent churches and they are carrying out the Lord's commission.

THE CHURCH IN THE UNION OF SOUTH AFRICA

The Union of South Africa, effectuated in 1910, inaugurated a new period in the history of the country which offered new possibilities to the people. The Boer War of 1899-1902 caused much destruction and loss of life. The new political arrangement challenged the people to coexist peacefully and develop the country.

The churches suffered extremely during the war. Mission stations and church property were destroyed. People fled from their homes and the lives of many church members, especially those of the Dutch Reformed Church, were lost. The Afrikaner nationalism was most prominently expressed in the churches of the Afrikaner republics. Since 1948 the Dutch Reformed Churches have had close ties with the Nationalistic Party.

Although the Dutch Reformed Church of South Africa suffered immensely in the republic during the Boer War, it witnessed a remarkable recovery. It devoted itself to evangelization in South Africa and in other countries of Africa. Through its missionary efforts, it established churches in Rhodesia, Malawi, and Nigeria. In 1950 it began to cede its ministry in Nigeria to the Christian Reformed Church of the United States—a process that was completed in 1961.

South Africa has witnessed large church growth in the twentieth century. Through the earlier efforts to proclaim the gospel, many people had become familiar with the Christian faith. The normalized political conditions of the twentieth century provided an opportunity to bring the people into the congregations and plant new churches throughout the country. The trained clergy greatly contributed to the expansion of the Christian faith. Under their leadership new churches were planted and assumed the responsibility for the Christian ministry. This relieved the missionary personnel for ministry in other parts of Africa. The London Missionary Society reduced its foreign staff as early as 1850.[95]

After the congregations had been founded and leaders trained to guide them in worship and mission, the missionary societies introduced measures to establish autonomous churches. In 1865 the Paris Evangelical Missionary Society entrusted the pastors with the responsibility for the local congregations, and in 1894 the first synod of the Lesotho church was held. In 1869 the American Board of Commissioners presented its program to transfer the responsibilities to the local church. The Zulu pastors were responsible for the churches. The Bantu Presbyterian Church of South Africa, the fruit of the missionary services of the Glasgow Missionary Society, inaugurated its first general assembly at Lovedale in 1923. The Baptist Union of South Africa was formed in 1881. It created the South African Baptist Missionary Society in 1892, and the congregations that were established formed the Bantu Baptist Church in 1927.[96] The growth and development in some churches was more rapid than in others; nevertheless, there was a general movement toward independent churches. It should be noted, however, that the tendency was to form semiautonomous congregations where each group had freedom of self-expression.

The concern to fellowship with other churches and to unitedly present the church of Christ led to the formation of the South African General Missionary Conference in 1904. This was a significant event at the time when missionaries everywhere were realizing the necessity for a closer relationship in the mission of the church. It led also to the Missionary Conference at Edinburgh in 1910. Except for the Roman Catholic and the separatist churches, all the churches of South Africa participated in the conference. Eight sessions of the conference were held between 1904 and 1932. The conference established cordial relations among the denominations and gave consideration to the evangelization of the unreached peoples.[97] In 1936 the Christian Council of South Africa replaced the Missionary Conference. Its functions, however, were to promote fellowship in thinking and planning, and the work was to be consultative and advisory. Unfortunately, the Dutch Reformed Church and the Church of the Province of South Africa withdrew from the council in 1941.[98] The effort for fellowship on the national level has not been implemented on the regional level, and regional councils have not met regularly.[99]

The consolidation of the International Missionary Council with the World Council of Churches inspired further considerations during the 1960s. Efforts were made to establish closer relations and cooperation with the Afrikaans churches, the Roman Catholics, and with some separatist churches, which have formed the African Independent Churches Association. The more intimate relationship between the Roman Catholic and the Protestant churches during the 1960s has had a positive influence.

In South Africa, as in many other countries of Africa, the program of education grew out of the missions' efforts to evangelize through Christian education in order to develop a literate laity and prepare church members for service. Eventually the churches left Christian education basically to elementary schoolteachers. When the government assumed the supervision of the schools, the churches were obliged to prepare materials and restructure their Christian education program.

The churches had established training institutions to prepare workers for every phase of its ministry. The theological faculties frequently were a part of a college. When these institutions were placed under government control, the churches' program of leadership training was greatly affected. The Anglicans, Methodists, Presbyterians, and Congregationalists founded the Federal Theological Seminary at Alice, to train their clergy. The government revoked this privilege and assumed control of the seminary in 1974. The Anglicans also train workers at St. Bede's College in Umtata. The Lutherans train their personnel at the school at Umpumulo in Natal and at Marang in the Transvaal. The Moravians provide theological training at Port Elizabeth. Theological faculties provide education for the Afrikaans-speaking churches at Stellenbosch, Pretoria, and Potchefstroom. The Roman Catholics receive theological education at Hamanskraal in the Transvaal, at Pietermaritzburg, and at Pretoria. The Rhodes University and the University at Roma in Lesotho also have theological faculties.[100]

Some independent churches do not provide theological training and hesitate to send their candidates to other schools. Consequently they lack trained personnel. Some churches are sending professors to assist them in training leaders for these churches.

The coexistence of blacks and whites in South Africa has posed serious problems. The churches face insurmountable problems in the race relations and the apartheid policy. They desire fraternal relations among the people and protest the policy, but they have had little success. The gospel has been proclaimed and most of the people adhere to a church. Yet a greater manifestation of Christ's kingdom among men is to be desired.

THE CHURCH IN NAMIBIA

Namibia (South West Africa) was formerly a German protectorate but in 1919 the League of Nations assigned it as a mandate of the Union of South Africa. In 1968 the United Nations General Assembly changed the country's name to Namibia and appointed an eleven-nation council to be responsible for the administration of the country and to guide it toward independence. However, South Africa has continued to interfere with this development. The population is about 690,000 and includes Nama (Hottentots), Ovambo (Bantu), Bushmen, whites, and others.[101]

The London Missionary Society and the Wesleyan Methodist Mission ministered to the Namaqua in the northern Cape Province. However, they ceded their work to the Rhenish Missionary Society. From its ministry in the Cape Province, the Rhenish Missionary Society followed the Namaqua to the north of the Orange River and extended its ministry into the southern part of Namibia.

The society encountered considerable political difficulty in its early ministry in Namibia. Jonker Africaner acted friendly to the missionaries, but he stole cattle. The presence of the missionaries was not convenient for Africaner's activities. In 1851 he asked missionary Knudsen to leave his territory. Knudsen had made contacts with Paul Goliath's clan and devoted himself to this clan. Kroenlein and Hohn did likewise. In 1860 they reported having established a faithful Christian community at Beersheba.[102] Kleinschmidt's ministry at Rehoboth was successful, and a church of some two hundred members came into being. The chief was one of the members.

In 1844 the society began a ministry among the Herero people north of the Namaqua. Hugo Hahn, the pioneer of this endeavor, appealed to tradesmen to come and instruct the people. He opened a training school for catechists and evangelists.[103] The work, which was progressing satisfactorily, was greatly hindered from 1863 to 1870 by war between the Namaqua and the Herero. Jonker

Africaner had died in 1861 and had been succeeded by his son
Christian, who started the seven-years' war. After the war, the
Namaqua feared and mistrusted the Herero. This situation affected the church's ministry. But the work was reestablished and
expanded, and by 1875 the society reported good progress.

At the close of the war in 1870, the Finnish Missionary Society
responded to Hahn's suggestion to undertake a ministry among the
Ovambo, a large tribe in northern Namibia and in Angola.[104] A
party of ten people, among them tradesmen, were sent. Although
the Ovambo had invited Hahn to settle among them, they probably
did so because of the security he would bring; they were not
necessarily ready to receive the missionaries' message. The missionaries taught and witnessed for twenty years before significant
progress was observed.[105]

The Germans took over Namibia in 1884. Efforts were soon
made to develop the country. Geological, botanic, and ethnographic researches were launched. A railway was laid to the copper
mines at Octavi (1900-1901), and the mines were developed.[106]

The stability and the progress in the development of the country
influenced the work of the missionary societies. In 1903 the
Rhenish Society reported 5,000 members among the Namaqua and
5,100 among the Herero. By 1914 the work of the Rhenish Society
was progressing well. Its ministry was carried on at twenty-two
stations, and it reported a church membership of 25,000.

The Jesuits wanted to begin a work in 1878. However, they had
not asked the chief's permission, and Maharero expelled them
from his territory.[107] For some time the Holy Ghost Fathers attempted a mission to South West Africa. But they were also
unsuccessful and gave up the endeavor.[108] In 1892 the Catholic
Church entrusted the territory to the Oblates of Mary Immaculate
who at first ministered to the scattered Roman Catholic settlers
and the Batswanas who had come from the British territories.
Their work among the Herero was interrupted during the war
(1903-1907) and only became successful after 1907.[109] The trade
school at Windhoek won some favor for the Catholics. German
Franciscan nuns, who had trained as nurses, opened a hospital at
Windhoek. By 1914 the church reported about two thousand
members among the local people.[110] The Roman Catholic missionaries were not interned during the war, but the work was disrupted
somewhat by the war and by the recruiting of soldiers.

By 1945 the Roman Catholics were active at three stations in Ovamboland and a sisterhood for native girls was established. The first national, Gerald Molekekwa, was ordained a priest in 1942.[111] The ministry has grown significantly during the last decades.

The ministry of the Rhenish Mission experienced new problems during World War I. The Allied forces occupied Namibia. The mission was unable to receive funds from Germany. The Rhenish Mission at the Cape came to its assistance by surrendering the mission farms at five centers in the Cape Province for funds. Some of the German missionaries were permitted to continue their services until 1918. Then the Treaty of Versailles required the repatriation of German nationals. The congregations carried on for several years with little support in personnel and funds.

After the war the territory was mandated to the Union of South Africa, and a number of Herero reserves were created. During the 1920s the German missionaries were permitted to return and contribute to the work directed by the Christians during their absence. The church grew to a membership exceeding one hundred thousand, and a literate laity took its place in the church and in society. In 1957 it became the Evangelical Lutheran Church of South West Africa.

The Finnish Mission, however, had been able to continue its ministry among the Ovambo. By 1918 a staff of thirty-six was actively engaged and the church membership was approximately three thousand. Two Bible schools and a seminary prepare workers for the Ovambokavanga Church, which became independent in 1954 with some two hundred thousand members.

The Finnish Mission brought a large missionary and native staff into its service. By 1950 the society offered services at ten high schools, ninety elementary schools, nine hospitals, and eleven dispensaries. Some other churches entered the field later, but more than 90 percent of the Protestant Christians adhere to the two Lutheran Churches.[112]

The Anglican Church administers its work in Namibia from the Damaraland diocese in the Province of South Africa. The larger part of its ministry is among the Ovambo in the northern part of the country. Its membership is about fifty thousand. The Dutch Reformed Church has extended its ministry to Namibia and has established a church of some forty-five thousand members.

A number of separatist movements have come into existence in Namibia. Some four thousand members of the Evangelical Lutheran Church joined the African Methodist Episcopal Church. In 1955 the Herero of the Evangelical Lutheran Church founded the Oruuano Church. This group has split several times.[113]

SUMMARY

Missionary interest was aroused by the Moravian Church. The London Missionary Society followed. John Philip encouraged other societies to join in the missionary effort. The Methodists, under the inspiration of William Shaw, opened a chain of preaching places from Grahamstown to the northeast. The Paris Evangelical Missionary Society devoted its ministry to the Basuto, while the Congregational, Lutheran, and Anglican Churches established ministries along the east coast.

The British occupation of the Cape Province caused the Boers to move towards the northeast in order to establish independent colonies. The British moved armed forces into these territories and occupied them. This caused much bloodshed and disrupted the work of the churches during half a century. In the eastern part of South Africa, permanent missionary work was actually established only after the Boer War (1899-1902).

Independent churches became numerous throughout South Africa and witnessed a phenomenal numerical growth. By 1967 there were some 3,200 religious groups that may be classified as Ethiopian, Zionist, and Messianic. Generally, they have emphasized spontaneous inspiration, but have failed to train church leaders. Recently some groups have sent future leaders elsewhere for training.

South Africa has witnessed large church growth in the twentieth century. The trained clergy greatly contributed to the expansion of the Christian faith. Under their leadership new congregations were planted. The Lutherans from Germany and Finland made significant contributions to the Christian ministry in Namibia. The churches in Namibia are a vital influence in the life of the country.

Study Questions

1. State the factors that brought about the European settlement at the Cape.

2. Compare the attitudes of the Dutch Reformed Church and the Moravian Mission toward the people in Cape Province.
3. Describe the results of the British colonial ambition in South Africa.
4. Describe the results of the missionaries' efforts to protect the rights of the people in South Africa.
5. Evaluate the results of William Shaw's principle of using volunteers in extending the Christian ministry.
6. The Bible and the plow were emphasized in the ministry of the churches in South Africa. Evaluate the churches' efforts to minister to the total man.
7. Describe the contribution of the leadership training at the Lovedale Institute and other schools of training for the establishment of the church.
8. Evaluate the missionary spirit among the Basuto, the Zulu, and other Christians in South Africa.
9. Church growth is along tribal lines. Indicate how the ministry of the Swiss Reformed Churches substantiated this statement.
10. Evaluate the contributions, strengths, and weaknesses of the Independent Churches.
11. Indicate to what extent the fellowship between the churches in South Africa advanced the Christian cause.
12. Describe the churches' struggle with the government's apartheid policy.
13. "No practical priority on earth is higher than that of discipling out to its fringes a people which under the leading of the Holy Spirit turns responsive" (McGavran 1970:213). How does this principle apply to the ministry among the Ovimbundu tribe?

6

Missionary Efforts in Southeast Africa (1652-1975)

EXPANSION OF CHRISTIANITY FROM THE SOUTH

Rhodesia and Zambia came under British rule chiefly through Cecil Rhodes's ambitious plans to link South Africa, Egypt, and Sudan by a block of territory. He extended the influence of the British South Africa Company into the Zambezi basin through a number of treaties with the chiefs of the region. The company administered the region from 1895 to 1923; it was governed by a responsible government from 1923 to 1953; and it was a part of the Federation of Rhodesia and Nyasaland from 1953 to 1963.[1] In 1964 the three territories of the Federation—Rhodesia, Zambia, and Malawi—became self-governing, and in 1965 Ian Smith unilaterally declared Rhodesia an independent state in which he rules with a minority government.

The missionaries' influence, in which Moffat and Livingstone were pioneers, came to south-central Africa by land from the south. It also came from the east by way of the Zambezi, where Livingstone was again the initiator. At the same time the London Missionary Society began a mission at Madagascar (1820) and the Church Missionary Society undertook a ministry at Mombasa on the east coast (1844). Therefore, in the expansion of the Christian faith in East Africa, approaches were made from several directions, and these efforts brought their influences to bear on relationships between people, on slave trade, and on other aspects of society.

Missionary work in Southeast Africa has been obliged to contend with the effects of colonial ambitions. Missionary penetration, the discovery of minerals, and the extension of colonial rule occurred almost simultaneously. Although Livingstone visited the Makololo tribe in 1851 and Moffat contacted the Matabele in 1854, permanent missionary work was not begun at Inyanti among the Matabele until 1859. The prospectors soon followed the missionaries. In 1866 Europeans became aware of gold deposits in Rhodesia. Mzilikazi died in 1869 and 1871 his son, Lobengula, granted permission to dig for gold, with the notation, however, that no land would be alienated. Cecil Rhodes was anxious to secure this region for Britain before any other power could annex it. In 1887 the British asked the assistance of J. S. Moffat to conclude a treaty with Lobengula, which virtually placed the Matabele under British protection. In 1888 the chief gave a further concession, which was taken over by the British South Africa Company.

Rhodes also wanted to extend the company's sphere of action to the lands north of the Zambezi. He sent a party to hoist the Union Jack at Salisbury in 1890. He allotted farms to the pioneer settlers and established administrative services. In 1891 a police force of 650 men came to the region.[2]

The Matabele were both a pastoral and a warlike people. The cultivating in the tribe was done by slaves.[3] Every spring for over seventy years the Matabele had made raids on Mashonaland, killing men and women and carrying off the girls as slaves and the boys to be soldiers. In 1893 the British South Africa Company intervened. A fierce battle ensued. Lobengula refused to arrange terms with the company and fled. When he saw the situation was hopeless, he thanked his chiefs and warriors for their bravery and said he would disappear like a needle in the grass. He rode off alone on his horse and disappeared.[4] Under the royal charter granted to the company, Matabeleland and Mashonaland became two provinces of Southern Rhodesia.

The Barotse under Lewanika wanted to remain independent, but the Portuguese were a threat; the British were wooing Lewanika to accept British protection. Coillard was requested to serve as interpreter in the land negotiations with the representatives of the British South Africa Company. An agreement was reached, and in 1887 a representative of the company took up residence at Mongu.[5] British rule was thereby extended north of the Zambezi River. In 1897 R. T. Corydon became the first resident.

In 1878 the supporters of the missions in Malawi formed the African Lakes Company to combat slave trade by introducing legitimate commerce. The company soon came into collision with the Arabs, especially around the northern shore of Lake Nyasa and around the southern end of Lake Tanganyika.

H. H. Johnston and Alfred Sharpe made treaties with the chiefs between the Zambezi River and Lake Tanganyika. The treaties provided that in return for full mineral and commercial rights, the company would promote Christian missions and education. Sharpe failed to acquire a treaty with Msiri. The Belgians occupied Msiri's domain in connection with the war against slave raids in Katanga, especially on the Lualaba River. Consequently, this region was annexed to Zaire. The African Lakes Company extended its influence in the northeastern part of Zambia through treaties with other chiefs. In 1889 Rhodes acquired the rights of the African Lakes Company, thus extending the influence of the British South Africa Company over Malawi and the northeastern part of Zambia.

Malawi became a protectorate under the colonial office in 1891. Rhodesia was granted responsible government as a British colony. The administration was taken over intact from the British South Africa Company,[6] which administered Zambia until it passed under the administration of the British government in 1924. From 1953 to 1963 the three territories functioned under the federation of the Rhodesias and Nyasaland. The people, however, were not satisfied with this federation. It was dissolved and the countries became separate entities.

The large territory through which the Zambezi flows fell naturally into two distinct territories which were governed as Southern Rhodesia and Northern Rhodesia, now Zambia. The more temperate climate and the discovery of gold in Rhodesia attracted farmers and miners to the southern territory.

Rhodesia

The Matabele were a powerful people who occupied a large part of Rhodesia during the latter part of the nineteenth century. They resided in the southwest area of Transvaal during the early part of the nineteenth century. Robert Moffat visited Mzilikazi in 1829 and again in 1835 and established friendly relations with the Matabele chief while the tribe was in the Transvaal.[7] In 1835 the missionaries of the American Board came to work among the Matabele. However, as a result of the clash with the Boers in 1836, the tribe moved north of the Limpopo River to the Bulawayo region.[8]

Moffat visited Mzilikazi again in 1854 and 1857. In 1859 he accompanied a missionary delegation, of which his son John Smith Moffat was a member, to establish a ministry to the Matabele. Mzilikazi was happy to meet his friend again. Though somewhat hesitantly, he granted the favorable site at Inyanti for the mission. However, the tribe as a unit did not accept the Christian faith, and no individual felt free to act unilaterally. Thus the mission carried on a ministry for some thirty years before any significant results were observed. Finally a change took place and the people requested catechists. From 1900 to 1910 there was a significant increase in the enrollment of pupils in the schools and of church membership. The London Missionary Society was the only society in Rhodesia for thirty years. In spite of the many difficulties it faced, the society carried on and eventually established a church that is now a part of the United Congregational Church of Southern Africa.

The society contributed to the general development of the country through its training efforts. The crafts taught at the Hope Fountain school helped many lads earn a livelihood. G. J. Wilkerson's plan was not to train experts but to give a short course in a variety of trades. A girls' school and a department for teacher training were added to the school, and additional efforts were made at other centers.

In 1851 Livingstone visited Sebitwane, the Makololo chief, at Lake Ngami. He then continued his journey and saw the Zambezi River. Later the Makololo settled in the Zambezi region. Here Livingstone visited them, and they accompanied him on his journey across Africa to Loanda and from Loanda to Quilimane. Upon Livingstone's recommendation, the London Missionary Society designated the Holloway Helmore and the Roger Price families for such a ministry. They arrived in 1860, but the endeavor resulted in the deaths of the members of the two families, except for Roger Price and two of the Helmore children, who returned to Kuruman. Five years later the Barotse of Victoria Falls region massacred the Makololo and virtually exterminated the tribe.

From 1870 to 1890 the Paris Mission, the American Board, and the Jesuits attempted ministries in Rhodesia, but they were unsuccessful.[9] Chief Lobengula rejected the Catholics because he disapproved of having his people taught by anyone who did not believe in wives and mothers.[10]

During the 1890s Britain extended its rule over the region and granted large tracts of land to missionary agencies for their work. In some instances the farms were expected to support the missionary endeavor. In 1890 the Anglican Church created the Mashonaland diocese and appointed Knight-Bruce as its bishop.[11] Bishop Knight-Bruce devoted himself to the service of the people. During the war between Lobengula and the British, Knight-Bruce helped the sick, giving his ox wagon as a place to treat the sick, while he slept on the ground beside it.[12] He traveled widely during his ministry and obtained large tracts of land, which he reserved as settlements for the indigenous population. At first the society devoted its ministry mostly to the Mashona, while the London Missionary Society served the Matabele. But the influx of white settlers prompted it to serve those of its communion, and it created a diocese for the Matabele region. The ministry of the society was successful and the Anglican communion became the largest in the country.[13] The society also had an important ministry among the white population. The efforts of A. S. Cripps are to be noted. As a missionary and poet he defended the right of the indigenous population before the magistrates and endeavored to promote good relations between the races.[14]

In response to the appeal of Cecil Rhodes, the Wesleyan Methodist Missionary Society undertook a mission to Rhodesia in 1891. They received extensive grants of land at Salisbury and Umtali. An appeal for teachers and evangelists was made to the Methodist congregations in Transvaal, and soon strong centers with numerous outstations were in operation. The society served both the indigenous and the white population; both groups were represented in the clergy and in the congregations. The ministry was retarded by the Matabele revolt in 1894 and 1896. One of the missionaries made a valuable contribution as peacemaker; and after order had been reestablished, the ministry made significant progress and became the second largest in Rhodesia. In 1897 they received a large tract of land at Tegwami, and the society began an industrial mission. After 1900 the society established many more stations with outstations and expanded its ministry.[15] At Salisbury it began the Epworth Theological College, which has become a cooperative school of five denominations.[16]

The Dutch Reformed Church, serving in the Transvaal, undertook a ministry near the Zimbabwe ruins in 1891. For twenty years

Stephanus Hofmeyer wanted to proclaim the gospel to the Mashona; he sent evangelists to establish good relations with them. Lobengula, the Matabele chief, refused to permit him to serve there. The society began its ministry at Morgenstern (Morningstar) and soon established six stations between the Limpopo River and Zimbabwe in the region where the visiting evangelists gained credibility with the people. The ministry was an extension of the Transvaal work, and a catechist was responsible for every station.

In 1893 the American Board of Commissioners established a ministry among the Ndau at Mount Salinda on the Plateau River near the Mozambique frontier. Cecil Rhodes welcomed educators and granted a large tract of land for this purpose. The society established elementary, secondary, industrial, and normal schools at Mount Salinda. A nursing school was opened in connection with the Pierce Memorial Hospital. In 1897 a congregation was organized. In 1896 a second station was begun at Chicore and other centers were developed later.[17]

The Seventh-Day Adventists began a ministry at Solusi, about thirty miles southwest of Bulawayo in 1894. They offered medical care at a hospital and a leprosarium and provided training at three colleges. The church membership grew to twenty-eight thousand in 1971.[18]

The Methodist Episcopal Church, under the direction of Joseph Crane Hartzell, began a ministry in 1897. The British South Africa Company was transferring its administrative center from Umtali to Beira on the railroad to Salisbury. It gave its former center, including the buildings, and a large tract of land to the Methodist Church. The church ministered to all the people in the Umtali valley and provided schools for the children. Other stations with outstations were soon established. In addition to two hospitals and several village clinics, a large evangelistic and educational work developed. The general assembly of Rhodesia was founded in 1931. It has created six districts in the Umtali and Salisbury regions and in eastern Rhodesia. The church has witnessed continuous growth. In order to promote the agricultural development of the country, the society operates four large farms.[19]

The Brethren in Christ sent a delegation to Africa in 1897. The conditions for a ministry in Rhodesia seemed favorable, and they began at Motopa Hills in the Matabele region.[20] From there they extended their ministry to Bulawayo and they also undertook a ministry in Zambia. The society's educational work has not contributed to church growth as the society had expected.[21] In recent years Fred Holland has given leadership in theological education by extension in Rhodesia, Zambia, and Malawi.

In 1942 the Evangelical Alliance Mission began work in an area on the Zambezi River, an area almost untouched by the gospel. This mission has been successful and developed ten centers. In addition to ministries of evangelism and elementary education, the society operated a high school, a teacher training center, and a Bible school at Kapfundi, and hospital services at Chirange.[22]

By the end of the nineteenth century, Protestant missions were serving throughout the country, proclaiming the gospel, offering education, healing the sick, and exercising a significant influence in the social and political structures. At first missions encountered some resistance in certain tribal areas, but eventually the people realized that Christianity had something to offer. Furthermore, the value of a formal education and of industrial instruction was realized and the desire for schools soon became prominent. Having accepted the Christian faith, many Christians witnessed to their fellow-men and contributed to spreading the gospel. Some became evangelists, pastors, and teachers and assumed the responsibilities of the church. By 1950 many churches had been established and had become autonomous.

The period of missions from 1890 into the twentieth century was unique in that progress in medical knowledge, the development of better modes of transportation and communication, and the dedication of many Christians for the service of the Lord contributed to the expansion of Christianity. The missions already serving increased their staffs, and other missions came to the country. Advanced training centers aided the native people in preparing for, and taking responsibilities in, the educational and evangelistic program of the church.

The English language has been used quite extensively in church work in Rhodesia. This is one reason why the translation of the Scriptures was not given more emphasis. The Bible appeared in the Shona language in 1950.[23] The New Testament is available in four languages. Because of the existing political tension, literature distribution has been discouraged. The political tension is affecting the church's ministry negatively.

As the church developed, certain differences of opinion and practice and of cultural values became evident. Polygamy was one of the problems about which the churches disagreed. Some Christians abhorred it, while others considered it a social institution. Some church leaders administered the sacraments to polygamists, whereas others refused to do so.

The oneness of the church came into question in Rhodesia. One reason was that the white population with its own cultural characteristics was large enough to constitute separate congregations. Another factor was that in some instances the settlers formed congregations before the gospel was proclaimed, and separate indigenous congregations were established later on. Often the Christians were not comfortable in the existing congregations; so they formed separate congregations even though they adhered to the same denomination. Cultural differences have been a cause of a proliferation of separatist and independent churches and sects. Some of these faithfully proclaim salvation through faith in Christ. Others are syncretistic, and in some sects the prophets basically exalt themselves. The unity of all groups through faith in Christ needs to be sought.

In more recent years the Rhodesian churches were caught up in the political conflict caused by the unilateral declaration of independence by Ian Smith and his party; Smith ruled the country with a minority government. Some churches vigorously opposed this action, but the party in power disregarded their concerns and closely controlled all activities. Church leaders were harassed, beaten, fined, and jailed.

The Southern Rhodesia Missionary Conference, now called the Christian Council of Rhodesia, was organized in 1903. It had seventeen member bodies and six affiliate bodies in 1967.[24] The Christian council has expressed the concerns of the churches on a number of issues involving the country. The government, however, has rejected the churches' suggestions. The churches of Rhodesia are confronted with a very critical situation. Time alone will tell if they will overcome human frailties and live as one brotherhood under the lordship of Christ.

In recent years the Anglican diocese of Mashonaland and Matabeleland, the Presbyterian Church, the Methodist Church, the Congregational Union, and the United Church of Christ have engaged in church union negotiations.

Zambia

The monument to David Livingstone on the banks of the Zambezi River at Victoria Falls is a reminder of his unique contribution in making this region known to the world and bringing the gospel and legal commerce to it. The modern history of Zambia until 1963 was closely related to Rhodesia. It came under British rule and was a member of the federation of Rhodesia and Nyasaland until it was dissolved in 1963. Although Zambia is about twice the size of Rhodesia, the population of the two countries varies only slightly. President Kaunda guided the republic of Zambia according to Christian principles, and the country had a decade of peace and prosperity.

Livingstone and his colleague Oswell, accompanied by Sechele, the Makololo chief, arrived at the Zambezi in 1851. Livingstone was determined to explore the country and find strategic sites for the Christian ministry. He made his historic journey across the continent from 1852 to 1856. Then he presented his findings to the world in his book *Missionary Travels and Researches in South Africa*. As a result of his presentations the Universities Mission, the Livingstonia Mission, and the Blantyre Mission undertook the challenge to bring the gospel to the people of the Zambezi River regions. However, these societies followed the Shiré River to Lake Nyasa and established ministries in Malawi. Having returned to the Lower Zambezi in 1858, Livingstone accompanied the Makololo, who chose to return to their homes on the Upper Zambezi. His further efforts were directed to discover the region of the lakes and the source of the Zaire River.

Fred S. Arnot of the Plymouth Brethren came by way of South Africa and spent about two years with Lewanika, chief of the Barotse, in the Livingstone region. Arnot had a profound influence on the chief, and the latter welcomed a mission among his people but did not become a Christian. Arnot took the position of a guest of the king and assisted at many meetings, announced the gospel, and helped the sick.[25] His relations with the people were effective and he won their respect; but they adhered to their practices and no Christian community came into being during his stay. Nevertheless, his relationship with the people prepared a good reception for the Swiss missionaries. When they were about to undertake the ministry, Arnot went to Bihe in Angola, where he helped the missionaries of the American Board against the intrigues of Braga, a Portuguese merchant, who counseled the chief to expel the missionaries from his territory. Then he went to Benguella to get the merchandise he needed for his work in the interior.[26]

While F. S. Arnot was returning to the interior of the continent, Msiri, the chief of Garanganze (or Shaba of today) in the southeast of Zaire, sent a message requesting that Europeans come to Bunkeya, his town. Arnot met the messenger and accepted the invitation.[27] The chief was well impressed with Arnot's attitude, and a favorable relationship was established between them. Other missionaries came to serve and won the confidence of the people. But Msiri had brought some clans under his rule by force. After his death in 1891, his people dispersed. Later Garanganze was annexed to Zaire, and the people were given orders to return to Bunkeya. The Garanganze Mission, as it was called, extended its ministry from Kalene Hill and Johnston Falls in Zambia and from Kalunda to Benguella in Angola[28] and has organized some two hundred assemblies.

The first continuing mission in Zambia was inspired by the Christians of Lesotho who were concerned to witness to people who had not received the Christian message. They looked for a field of service. Lewanika, the Barotse chief, seemed pleased to have the mission in this area. However, several years passed before missionaries and support were found and the project was started. The distance between Lesotho and Victoria Falls was large; so it was hardly possible for the Lesotho church to maintain the endeavor. Therefore, the Paris Evangelical Missionary Society made the mission to the Barotse a separate endeavor, and it was supported by the society.

In 1885 Coillard began the station at Secheke. Then he went to Lealui, the capital of the Barotse kingdom, and began another station at Sefula.[29] Another station was built at Nalolo, where Mokwai Mosanka, the king's sister, lived. In addition to the elementary schools at every center, the society built a school to train evangelists at Lealui.[30] However, the missionary personnel was hardly sufficient to staff the projects.

The ministry was being established, when some chiefs became concerned to revive their religion. Then the political rule of the region was in question. Lewanika wanted to remain independent, but the Portuguese were a threat and the British were trying to influence him to accept British protection. Coillard was requested to serve as interpreter in the long negotiations with the British South Africa Company. An agreement was reached, and in 1887 a representative of the company took up residence at Mongo.[31] British rule was thereby extended to the north of the Zambezi River.

The construction of the railway to Salisbury at the close of the century greatly facilitated travel for the missionaries in the northern region. The fourteen new missionaries who arrived in 1899 were able to travel to Bulawayo by train. Although the unhealthy living conditions compelled many missionaries to withdraw from the work, the society continued a ministry from eight centers surrounded by many outstations.[32]

The evangelists of the Livingstonia Mission who served in Malawi ministered in villages removed from the centers of missionary activities, initiated bases of extension and established groups of believers. Consequently, the society followed up this ministry and founded four stations in Zambia. In 1895 it established the station Mwenze. In 1905 David Kaunda, the father of President Kaunda, began the Lubwa station.[33] In honor of the missionary-explorer, David Livingstone, in 1906, his nephew and his grandson, Malcom Moffat and R. Hubert Wilson, founded a station at Chitambo, the place where Livingstone died.[34]

People in Europe were moved by the death and the funeral service of David Livingstone. Robert Arthington of Leed, England, presented five thousand British pounds to the London Missionary Society for work in the Tanganyika area, which Livingstone had explored. The London Missionary Society's expedition left Zanzibar in 1877; after a difficult voyage, it arrived at Ujiji on Lake Tanganyika.[35] The society built several stations in Tanzania; and in 1887, beginning with Fwambo and Niakolo, it extended its ministry in Zambia among the Mawbwe, Lungu, Bemba, and Lunda tribes.[36]

In order to further its ministry around Lake Tanganyika, the society undertook the formidable task of transporting a steamer, in sections, overland to Lake Tanganyika, then assembling it and launching it on the lake. Because the climate around the lake was unhealthy, the society ministered to the people on the highlands south of Lake Tanganyika. It opened elementary, secondary, industrial, and medical schools. It contributed substantially to the training of personnel through these efforts in education. The church that was founded through the ministry of the society became one of the largest in the country. It participated in the work of the United Mission of the Copper Belt, serving the miners who came from the various parts of Zambia and from the neighboring countries.

Toward the close of the nineteenth century, a number of Protestant missionary societies were serving at strategic centers in the country, proclaiming the gospel, instructing the people, healing the sick, and helping people with their economic problems. As the missionaries brought the gospel and new knowledge to the people of Central Africa, they encountered opposition from the slave traders, especially in the Lake Tanganyika area. (The subject of slavery will be treated in relation to the ministry in Tanzania.)

The African Lakes Company, which operated in Malawi, extended its trade into Zambia and around the southern end of Lake Tanganyika and made trade agreements with many chiefs. In 1889 Cecil Rhodes acquired the rights and property of the African Lakes Company for the British South Africa Company, thereby extending the influence, if not rule, of his company to Lake Nyasa and Lake Tanganyika. Rhodes wanted to occupy the territory and welcomed the contribution missions made in serving the medical needs of the people and in offering schooling. In South Africa the people, especially the Hottentots, settled on or around the mission stations, and the missionaries intervened for the indigenous people to reserve land for them. In Rhodesia, Zambia, and Malawi, Cecil Rhodes granted tracts of land to mission stations. These tracts were large enough to provide locations for a number of villages. The Catholic Missions adopted the policy of the mission farms to a greater degree than the Protestant Missions.

The White Fathers of the Roman Catholic Church commenced work near Lake Tanganyika in 1879. They extended their ministry southward and in 1891 made contacts with the people in northern Zambia. However, they secured permission only from Mwamba, the Bemba chief, to establish work among his people in 1898. After 1902 they extended their ministry into the Alunda tribe, founded a number of stations in the Lake Bangweulu region, and created the Bangweulu Vicariate Apostolic.[37]

The Jesuits began work at Chickuni near the railway line on the plateau between the Kafue and the Zambezi in 1905. At a later date the Polish Jesuits planted stations between the Kafue and the Luangwas. The girls' school at Chikuni, conducted by the Sisters of Notre Dame, taught weaving, spinning, basketry, beadwork, and stitchwork. The agricultural work included a model farm. J. Torrend did valuable linguistic studies.[38] In 1910 the Jesuits transferred their work from Miruru in Mozambique to Zambia. They enlarged their work in Zambia, establishing a station in Lusaka in 1922 and at Broken Hill in 1923. The prefecture apostolic of Broken Hill was instituted in 1927, and the Zambia work was separated from that of Rhodesia. The name was changed to Lusaka in 1946, and the prefecture was raised to vicariate; in 1959 an archdiocese was established. The prefecture of Fort Jameson was established in 1937 and was raised to a vicariate in 1953.[39]

A number of missionary societies came at the beginning of the twentieth century and participated in the ministry in Zambia. The Baptists of South Africa chose the Luangwas district in the northern part of Zambia for ministry in 1905. They reduced the language to writing, gave medical care, and opened schools, which also offered training in manual labor.[40] The Kafulafuta station was founded in 1910. The society made Ndola the center of its activities in 1924. It also established a ministry at Kitwe, Lusaka, Chingola, and Luanshya.[41] The development of the mines in the district confronted the society with the unique challenge to proclaim the gospel to all the mine workers.[42]

The Universities Mission to Central Africa was created in response to David Livingstone's appeal for missionary work in Central Africa. In 1858 the mission made an attempt to establish a ministry at Magomero, below Lake Nyasa. But after the deaths of a number of the party, the rest withdrew to Zanzibar. From the Zanzibar base the mission launched a ministry on the Rovuma River in 1875. In 1909 the mission also established a diocese in Zambia. It formed five dioceses in East Africa. It established eight stations, beginning with Livingstone in 1910 and founding Fiwila in 1924.[43] In 1935 the society participated in founding the United Mission of the Copper Belt and in the ministry to the mine workers. The work has seen a significant expansion, but the society lacked workers to minister to the people at a time when they were desirous of spiritual assistance. Its appeal for priests improved the situation considerably, but a certain need remained.[44] In the 1960s it built a cathedral in Lusaka and ministered in the nine urban parishes.

The Seventh-Day Adventists founded the station at Rusanga in 1905, at Musofu to the east of Ndola in 1917, and at Chimpempe near Lake Mweru in 1921. They established a ministry at Muchenje in the Lusaka district. They located their headquarters for Zambia in Lusaka.[45]

In 1899 the Primitive Methodists came to work among the Mashukulumbwe, a tribe ruled by the Barotse. They waited at Kasungulu for three years for permission from Lewanika to begin this work. Failing to receive the permission, they finally went to work among the Ba-Ila people. A second party began a ministry at Nanzela in 1895. In 1905 the work was extended east of the Kafue to Nambala, and a number of stations were founded among the Batonga during the following years. J. R. Fell began a training institution at Kafue. The students in the teachers' course also received training in carpentry, animal husbandry, and agriculture. The society has ministered to the Ba-Ila and the Batonga.[46] The work was difficult and the results were not encouraging.[47]

The Wesleyan Methodists extended their activities northward from Rhodesia in response to an invitation from a chief who had become a Christian while working in the mines in Rhodesia.[48] They have extended their ministry to Broken Hill and in the Luano valley and to the Zambezi River to the south.

In 1932 a synod was created to combine the ministries of the Primitive and the Wesleyan Methodists in Zambia. The church is engaged to work in the southern and central provinces and has joined other churches to form the United Church of Zambia.[49]

The Brethren in Christ, with work in the Bulawayo region in Rhodesia, also established a work in the Choma district in Zambia. They began a ministry at Macha on the Batoka plateau in 1906. In 1923 their work was extended to Sikalongo and another ministry commenced at Nahumba. The society emphasized the educational ministry. More recently, realizing that it has not produced the church growth they had expected, they have accentuated the strengthening of congregations through theological education by extension.

The South Africa General Mission began its ministry at Chisalala in 1910 and later extended the same to Lulafuta, Mukinge Hill, Kaba Hill, and Luampa. The society reached an agreement with the Paris Evangelical Mission in 1923 whereby the former would serve the people between the Kabombo and Zambezi Rivers. In 1964 the society changed its name to Africa Evangelical Fellowship[50] and has extended its ministry to the Copper Belt and to towns along the railroad. The church is making good progress and is serving the people from widely scattered centers.[51]

Recently a number of other societies began to serve in Zambia. The Southern Baptist Convention began its work in Zambia in 1959. It concentrated its efforts in Lusaka and in the towns along the railway leading to the Copper Belt. Its seminary for training church workers is located in Lusaka, as is also the recording studio for the preparation of braodcasting tapes. They have maintained an active staff and the ministry is showing good progress. The work of the Church of Christ (Disciples) in Zambia was begun in 1923 by an evangelist who came from Rhodesia to work at Sinde, north of Livingstone. Several other stations were begun in the region. Then in 1962 the Zambia Christian Mission also began a ministry. The two agencies have established a ministry in the Livingstone, Lusaka, and Copper Belt regions.

The African Methodist Episcopal Church commenced work in the Copper Belt in 1930. The Scandinavian Independent Baptist Union began a ministry around Ndola in the Copper Belt in 1931. In 1955 the Pentecostal Assemblies of Canada came to the Fort Jameson area and extended their outreach to the Copper Belt.

A survey of Rhodesia, Zambia, and Malawi readily indicates the rapidity with which Christian agencies penetrated these countries and validated Livingstone's vision to open the continent to Christianity and commerce. Christian missions had done little in East Africa before the death of Livingstone in 1874. But as has been indicated, from this date on, large sections of the countries were reached with the gospel.

The societies serving in Zambia generally adopted the traditional methods of establishing schools and helping the sick, in addition to proclaiming the gospel. The people were illiterate, and the societies thought it was essential to establish a literate Christian community and prepare leaders for service. The people were benefitted through the educational and medical services. Bible lessons were taught, and many of the students became members of churches. But the educational ministry did not produce substantial church growth or strong reproducing churches.

The Christians of various churches were serving in intimate fellowship and close cooperation with one another. They were motivated with the same concern and confronted with the same obstacles. These factors brought them closer together. Thus the United Church of Zambia is the product of missionary action. All the mission societies serving in Zambia participated in a missionary conference. In 1914 the conference considered the partition of the spheres of activities between the various societies.

In 1925 the rich deposits of sulfide ores were discovered in the Copper Belt in the northeastern part of Zambia. Mining plants and compounds for mine workers sprang up almost overnight. Thousands of men from all parts of the country went to work in the mines. The copper mines soon became the basis of the Zambian economy.

The societies serving in Zambia encountered a difficulty caused by the movement of men from the villages to the mining areas. These men were absent from their families for lengthy periods of time—from six months to several years, and sometimes even longer. They lived under poor housing conditions. Under these circumstances it was difficult to maintain a dynamic church program, a high moral standard, and a strong spirit of evangelism. It was also rather difficult to secure and train leaders for the congregations.

The Baptists, serving at Ndolo, Kitwe, and the Copper Belt in general, were confronted with the extremely large and intricate task of serving all the mine workers who came from many denominations.[52] The other denominations, however, felt responsible to serve their members. Closer cooperation in the ministry in the Copper Belt was necessary. After long negotiations, the Baptists, Presbyterians, Methodists, Anglicans, and Congregationalists formed the United Mission of the Copper Belt in 1934.

The missionary activity, however, chiefly concerned the education of the children, social ministries among the women, and counsel for the men in their work in the mines. It was practically impossible to arrange for a cooperative program in evangelism. The negotiations that began in 1930 finally terminated in the formation of the United Church of the Copper Belt in 1936. However, the Southern Baptist Convention and the Anglicans refrained from becoming members of the United Church.[53]

Ecumenical relations were forming in other parts of the country. In 1945 the Presbyterians and Congregationalists serving in the Northern Province met at Chitambo in order to create the United Church of Central Africa. This action vitally influenced the other churches serving in Zambia. The United Mission of the Copper Belt inspired the ecumenical establishment at Mindolo, a center for conferences and various short training institutes. It also offers regular courses in writing, journalism, agriculture, homemaking, and art. A school of theology has been instituted. The Africa Literature Center is located at Mindolo. It plays a vital part in aiding the churches in Zambia, and its widespread influence reaches other countries.

Collin Morris has worked persistently for a further union of churches in Zambia. In 1958 a church union committee was constituted of which E.G. Nightingale was the secretary. It presented a constitution for a school of theology in which the churches were encouraged to participate. The proposal was accepted in August 1960. Thereupon a pastoral session was organized that brought the pastors of the Methodist, Presbyterian, Moravian, and Congregational churches together for study and fellowship. Some Baptist pastors from Igreja and central Angola associated with the endeavor.

Negotiations to create a United Church of Zambia were carried on. The Anglican and Methodist churches were somewhat undecided about the union. In time, however, the Methodists of Zambia became convinced that union was essential. Their position influenced the Anglicans and gave new impetus to the union movement. Then the Methodist committee in England hesitated. At their 1964 conference, the Methodists gave permission for union. In 1964 the Baptist Church and the Evangelical Reformed Church of Barotseland also joined the communities already united.

On January 16, 1965, delegates, visitors, and honored guests from all parts of the country and the world gathered in the Mindolo church to officially celebrate the union of the Church of Zambia. It was an impressive service and an occasion of extraordinary significance for the church in Zambia. His excellency, the president of Zambia, Dr. Kenneth Kaunda, read the Old Testament lesson. Rev. C. M. Morris, who had tirelessly worked for union, delivered the sermon. After the service, President Kaunda, Rev. A. F.

Griffiths of the London Missionary Society, and the archbishop of Central Africa extended greetings to the United Church of Zambia.

EXPANSION OF CHRISTIANITY FROM THE EAST
Malawi

David Livingstone, above all others, may be credited with opening central Africa to missionary work and legitimate trade and bringing to the people a new way of livelihood. Through his continuous travels in the lake regions, his important geographical discoveries, his careful observations, accurate recordings, and his dynamic presentations on Africa, the Christians of Great Britain and other countries attained a new understanding of, and a vital concern for, the people of Africa. Many people were unable to ignore the challenge. Having crossed the continent from west to east, Livingstone thought the Shiré Highlands and the lake area were suitable to apply his vision to restructure the life of the people by replacing the slave trade with Christianity and commerce.

David Livingstone stirred a missionary interest on behalf of the people of Malawi during his furlough in 1856, after having crossed Africa from Loanda in Angola to Quilimane on the Indian Ocean. As a result of his appeal, the Universities Mission of Central Africa undertook a ministry in the Lake Nyasa area. The African Lakes Company followed them to Lake Nyasa, introducing legitimate trade and offering the people an opportunity to provide for their livelihood.

Livingstone received a royal welcome in England in 1856. The Royal Geographical Society received his report with great interest, awarded him the gold medal, and made him a Fellow. The universities of Oxford and Glasgow conferred degrees on him. He gave many lectures and created much interest in Africa. The prince consort honored him with a personal interview. He was received in personal audience by the queen. Livingstone was appointed British consul of Quilimane and returned to Africa at the head of an expedition for which the British government had voted five thousand British pounds. The party included John Kirk, Thomas Baines, Mrs. Livingstone, their son Oswell, and Livingstone's brother Charles. The group arrived at the mouth of the Zambezi River in 1858. After some difficult experiences with navigation, climate, and disease, Livingstone discovered Lake Nyasa on Sep-

tember 17, 1859.[54] In May 1860 he left for Linyanti to accompany
the Makololos, who came with him in 1856, back to their homes.
After his return to the coast, he had the joy of welcoming the first
representatives of the Universities Mission to Central Africa. They
came under the leadership of Bishop Charles Mackenzie early in
1861.[55] The missionaries founded the station Magomero on the
Upper Shiré. Before long the early death of Mackenzie and Barrup
interrupted the effort.[56]

The other members of the party decided to locate at Shupanga,
nearer to the coast. The climate was unhealthy. Mrs. Livingstone
died in 1862. This was a difficult blow for Livingstone. Scudamore
and Dickenson died in 1863. William Tozer, who had been appointed to succeed Mackenzie, considered the climate unsuitable
for Europeans and withdrew the missionary party to Zanzibar.
Livingstone was most disappointed at this action. He felt the
Christian cause had been abandoned.

In 1864 the British government recalled the expedition. This was
a. shock for Livingstone. But he was obliged to submit to the
circumstances and return to England. During his stay in England
he wrote the book *The Zambezi and Its Tributaries* in which he
forcefully presented the needs of the peoples of East Africa. The
Royal Geographic Society asked Livingstone to head a small expedition to discover if the sources of which he had spoken were the
source of the Nile River.

He arrived at Zanzibar in 1866; departing from there, he proceeded up the Rovuma River to Lake Nyasa. From there he
continued the route to Lake Tanganyika. It was a country ravished
by famine and occupied by unfriendly tribes. In addition to the
numerous difficulties, Livingstone's medicine box was stolen.
Without it his life was in danger. But Livingstone continued his
expedition. He discovered Lake Tanganyika on April 1, 1867; Lake
Mweru on November 8, 1867; and Lake Bengweulu on July 18,
1870. Because he had no medicine with him and the food he
received was meager, his health began to fail. He went to Ujiji and
rested for four months.

During the next two years, from 1869 to 1871, Livingstone
traversed the Maniema. He arrived at Bombare on September 21,
1869, and at Nyangwe on the bank of the Lualaba River on March
31, 1871. He constructed a hut for himself. However, the slave
raids were of the worst nature in this region. On July 15 he saw the
slave raiders massacre women who came to market. Throughout

this area, from Ujiji to Bambarre and to Nyangwe, the slave traffic was of the vilest form. Livingstone returned to Ujiji on October 23, 1871, and found that the supplies he expected had been stolen. He was discouraged. But at this time Henry Morton Stanley, who had been sent to look for him, found him. Livingstone was greatly encouraged by Stanley's visit and the supplies he brought with him.[57]

For four months Livingstone and Stanley lived and traveled together. Stanley wanted Livingstone to return to Europe with him, but Livingstone wanted to complete his task. He accompanied Stanley to Unyenyembe on the route to Zanzibar. Livingstone stayed there and waited for the men and the supplies Stanley would send to him from the coast. They arrived on August 14, 1872. Jack Wainwright was among the men.

Livingstone undertook to complete a circuit around Lake Bangweulu in order to determine whether a river flowed into it from the south. Due to the marshes in this region and the torrential rains, the undertaking became a difficult one and Livingstone was exhausted. They arrived at Chitambo's village on April 29, 1873. The next day he rested and asked Susu about the region. Early in the morning on May 1, 1873, his faithful servants found him kneeling in prayer, but there was no movement. They gently entered the tent and learned that he had completed his life's journey.

Livingstone had not been able to complete the exploration of the source of the Nile River nor to ascertain that the Lualaba was the stream that flowed through the heart of the continent to become the Zaire River with its tremendous waterways and finally empty into the Atlantic Ocean. But his discoveries were the key by which Central Africa could be discovered, by which the country torn by the slave traffic could be opened to the world, and by which Africa's wound could be healed. Livingstone's ministry stirred several mission societies to continue the ministry in Central Africa to which he had devoted himself.

Livingstone's faithful men carried his body to the coast, from where it was sent to England. David Livingstone was buried in Westminster Abbey on April 18, 1874. His funeral stirred the Christians of Britain, as his lectures had done. James Stewart of the Lovedale Institute of South Africa, who had accompanied one of the groups to the Zambezi during Livingstone's third voyage,[58] took the initiative to begin a ministry in the Lake Nyasa region. He was on furlough in 1875 and, having attended the funeral service for Livingstone, he raised the question about continuing Livingstone's work. The Free Church of Scotland founded the Livingstonia Mission.

Lieutenant E. D. Young, who had spent two years with Livingstone in this region, was to guide the first group to its ministry.[59] Young successfully directed the party to Lake Nyasa. He supervised the transport of the steamer to the lake and chose a site for the mission. During their voyage up the Shiré River, they passed the graves of Mrs. Livingstone at Shapungu, of Bishop Mackenzie at Ruo, of Scudamore and Dickenson at Chibisa, and of Thornton at the Falls. At the Murchison cataracts the *Ilala*, as the steamer was called, was dismantled and its parts carried some fifty miles up the river to be reassembled. The work was done by the Makololos who had accompanied Livingstone and settled at Chibisa. On October 12, 1876, the missionary party entered Lake Nyasa on the steamer *Ilala*. They chose a site on the western side of Cape Maclear to establish themselves. Before long they began a school. The majority of the pupils were Makololo boys.[60]

One month after their arrival, Young, Laws, Macfayden, and Baker made a voyage around the lake. They cruised northward along the eastern shore and observed evidences of slave trade. They saw villages in ruins on the shore. The Arabs whom they met seemed disturbed by the presence of a British steamer on the lake. As they approached the northern part of the lake, they saw the gigantic mountain range that is over one hundred miles long and averages ten thousand feet in height.[61] Young called this range the "Livingstone Mountains." These men were the first Europeans to tour the lake, which is approximately four hundred miles long. They were also the first to see the northern part of the lake.

The society had arranged for Young, a marine officer, to direct the travel and transport to Lake Nyasa and to choose a site for a mission. Then James Stewart would come to direct the work. Young had successfully accomplished his charge. Therefore he returned to Europe upon the arrival of Stewart.

The second stage of the establishment of the mission began with the coming of Stewart and four men; a doctor, an agriculturist, an engineer, and a weaver. A party representing the Church of Scotland came with them. Stewart also brought with him four students of the Lovedale Institute—William Koyi, Isaac Wuchope, Shadrach Ungunana, and Mapassa Ntintili. Shadrach Ungunana was the first teacher at Lake Nyasa. Unfortunately, he died a year after his arrival. Isaac Wuchope suffered from malaria and had to return to South Africa. William Koyi was instrumental in reaching the Ngoni and normalizing relations between them and the neighboring tribes. Having accomplished his assignment of giving guidance to the establishment of a mission, Stewart returned to his responsibilities at the Lovedale Institute. Robert Laws became the chairman of the Livingstonia Mission and gave leadership to it for fifty-two years. In 1881 the station was moved to Bandawe, a site near the middle of the western shore of the lake where more people could be readily reached and a strong work developed.[62]

The mission made contacts with the Tonga and the Ngoni. Robert Laws established friendly relations with Mombera, the Ngoni chief, and was able to avert a war between the Ngoni and the Tonga.[63] After the mission was moved to Banawe, William Koyi was sent to work among the Ngoni. As he was a Xhosa and had a common ethnic origin with the Ngoni, he was already acquainted with their language and customs and was eventually able to begin a ministry among them.[64] His ministry also contributed to establishing a peaceful relationship between the Ngoni and the Tonga. The mission devoted itself to evangelize and teach the people. The Nyanja language was reduced to writing, a grammar was produced, and books that were essential for the ministry were translated.[65] Laws was instrumental in establishing the Livingstonia Institute near Florence Bay in 1895. The program of this institute resembles the one of the Lovedale Institute; training was offered in many branches, including industries and handicrafts.[66] During the first decades of its ministry, the society had to contend with the slave trade and tribal wars. Consequently progress at the beginning was slow. However, the mission strove to establish an indigenous church and ordained six elders and deacons at Bandawe in 1895. In 1899 the first congregation among the Ngoni was constituted. After the people realized the value of a formal education, a remarkable change took place and the report for 1974 indicated 9,517 church members and 57,000 pupils in the schools.[67]

The Church of Scotland was also stirred to action by

Livingstone's death. It formed the Blantyre Missionary Society to serve the people for whose cause Livingstone had spent many years of sacrificial effort. The society sent Henry Henderson with the Livingstonia party in 1875 to select a suitable location for a ministry. He spent several months with the Livingstonia Mission during which he surveyed the surrounding country and chose a site on the Shiré Highlands as a place for a ministry and called it Blantyre after the birthplace of Livingstone.

The first group of six missionaries of the Blantyre Missionary Society arrived on October 23, 1876. Among them were Macklin, a medical doctor, and John Buchanan, an agronomist who introduced the coffee plantation into East Africa.[68] In 1877 James Stewart, a cousin to the one who served with the Livingstonia Mission, came to Blantyre. He was an engineer and gave leadership in the building of the station and the digging of a canal that brought water to the station. He also directed the construction of a sixty-mile road, which connected the Lower Shiré with the Upper Shiré and passed by Blantyre.[69]

In 1878 Duff Macdonald, an ordained missionary, became the director of the new undertaking. His wife was the first European woman to reside in this part of the country. Macdonald studied the Yao language and translated the Gospels according to Matthew and Mark and the historic sections of the Old Testament into Yao. He also studied the African culture and wrote the two volumes of his *Africana*.

Being located in the area of slave traffic, Blantyre soon became involved in the slave problem, which affected many missions in East Africa. Refugee slaves sought and received asylum at the station. The slave traders were displeased and on several occasions attacked the station and seized whomever they could. The mission also was confronted with the problem of governing the refugee community, which consumed the missionaries' time. The society became concerned about the consequences of this policy. Macdonald resigned and was succeeded by David Clement Scott, whom the society instructed to refrain from offering asylum to refugee slaves.[70] However, in order to assist the refugee slaves, the society adopted a policy of redeeming the slave, who in turn paid the ransom through services at the station.[71]

Scott applied the new policy regarding refugee slaves and developed a strong program of industrial education and religious work at Blantyre.[72] Even though he became an invalid, he continued to direct the ministry until 1898. His Nyanja dictionary made an outstanding contribution to the ministry.

Alexander Hetherwick succeeded Scott in 1898. For thirty years he guided the ministry according to the principles adopted by Scott. The ministry witnessed a remarkable growth. Other stations were opened and the ministry was extended into Mozambique. At the training institution, named Henry Henderson at Blantyre, teachers, artisans, clerks, and overseers of plantations were trained. The overall effort contributed significantly to the development of leadership in all phases of the society's ministry.

In response to the missionary vision of Andrew Murray, the Dutch Reformed Church of South Africa began a ministry in Malawi in 1888 in collaboration with the Livingstonia Mission.[73] It established itself south of Blandawe in the district of the Ngoni chief, Chiwere. Eventually it had more missionaries than the Livingstonia Mission and assumed the responsibility for its southern stations. It emphasized the ministry of national workers in the church. In addition to the evangelistic ministry, the society also conducted schools and offered medical services and instruction in agriculture and village industries.[74] As with the ministries of other societies, through these services a limited number of people advanced economically. But the time that missionaries were able to devote to village evangelism and church planting was limited by the station ministries.

The Livingstonia Mission and the Blantyre Mission were both formed by Scottish Presbyterian churches and worked in close cooperation in Malawi. In 1924 the Church of Central Africa, Presbyterian, was constituted by the Christians of these two bodies. In 1926 the Christian community of the Reformed Church also joined the Church of Central Africa, Presbyterian.

David Livingstone advocated legitimate commerce to combat slave trade and provide opportunities for the development of the regions. The supporters of the missions in Malawi soon recognized the validity of this idea. They formed the Livingstonia Central African Trading Company in 1878 in order to relieve the missions of the burden of transportation into the interior and to develop the commerce and resources of the region.[75] The company's agents were chosen for their Christian character and became willing helpers of the missions. They worked side by side with the missionaries for the people's welfare. The company used one steamer, the *S.S. Lady Nyasa*, for transport on the Zambezi and the Lower Shiré. They used the *S.S. Ilala* to transport the merchandise on the Upper Shiré. The administrative headquarters of the company were at Blantyre, one mile from the Blantyre station.[76] The company's contribution in establishing legitimate trade and thereby influencing the development of the country was noteworthy. Through missionary effort and through legitimate trade, the Scottish churches took up the challenge Livingstone had placed before them. The missions ministered to the physical and spiritual needs of the people. Consequently, the services of the commercial company served the overall effort of the missions. It checked, to some extent, the traffic in slaves.[77] It offered cloth, pots, and many other items for daily use to the people in exchange for ivory and the produce of their gardens and fields. Whereas in the past the chiefs had purchased these items with slaves, the missions and the company refused to accept slaves, obliging the people to cultivate the soil instead of capturing slaves. Consequently, the legitimate trade had a restraining effect on the slave traffic in the area from the Lake Nyasa region to Lake Tanganyika. The company signed trade agreements with many chiefs. When the African Lakes Company was taken over by the British East Africa Company, the latter used these agreements to further its influence in Malawi, Zambia, and the Lake Tanganyika region.

The missionary efforts improved the economic and social life of the people. The slave trade, tribal wars, and famine were greatly reduced. The emphasis on planting crops for sale increased the supply of food. Sufficient food and medical services improved the people's health. Some of the people took on village industry and became carpenters, masons, blacksmiths, tailors, or even printers. They acquired tools with which they could work more efficiently. They cultivated larger gardens, made furniture, and constructed larger houses. They began to make soap. Because of improved roads and a measure of order in the country, the people were able to travel about and engage in industry and trade.[78]

Harry Johnston, the British consul at Quilimane, visited Blantyre in 1890 and was surprised at the progress he observed in the area where the mission served. The people possessed chickens, cattle, and horses, and the children were well nourished and healthy. In 1891 Merensky, the director of the Berlin Mission, gave a similar report. During his visit he had seen good houses, schools, and a chapel. There was a good road between the Katanga station on the Lower Shiré and Matope on the Upper Shiré and the secondary posts at Domasi and Magomero. Bridges of stone and wood had been constructed, and carts were drawn by oxen. On the large plantations people were growing coffee, tea, sugar, vegetables, pineapples, and oranges. Native masons and carpenters were constructing a girls' school with bricks they had prepared themselves. A paper was printed in English and in Yao at the mission press. Johnston had observed the press at Livingstonia printing portions of the Scriptures. Also printed were reading books, lessons in history and geography, and other materials for the schools conducted in the Nyanja, Tonga, Ngoni, Nyankusu, and Konde languages. The growth of the Christian community from 1890 on was encouraging.

When David Livingstone crossed Africa from the west to the east, he came upon the Portuguese trading post at Tete. In 1856 Livingstone returned to East Africa as British consul of Quilimane. The spheres of British and Portuguese influence were not defined. The British missions and the trading company were striving to develop the more solubrious Shiré and Lake Nyasa region, but the Portuguese exerted their influence at the mouth of the Zambezi. In 1883 the British began to establish their authority by sending Captain Foot to act as British consul of the region and to stop the slave trade at its source. He made his headquarters at the Blantyre Mission. His successor, A. G. S. Hawes, moved the headquarters to Mount Zomba.

The Arab slave traders, especially Mlozi, an Arab half-caste, were plundering the villages. Under his direction the men and boys of a Konde village were massacred and the women and girls were marched off as slaves. The British presence was a threat to his nefarious livelihood and in 1887 he attacked the African Lakes Company trading center at Karonga. He was repelled by the employees of the company. His stronghold was besieged and burned to the ground, and Mlozi was executed. The armed confrontation of the slave traders called for a stronger government to establish order in the region. Harry Johnston was sent to Malawi as British consul with the mission to arrange a treaty with the slave traders by which the plundering of local peoples would cease.

The African Lakes Company extended its activities into Zambia and around the southern end of Lake Tanganyika, signing trade agreements with many chiefs through which a certain relationship was established and the company acquired trading privileges. In 1889 Cecil Rhodes acquired the property and rights of the African Lakes Company, thereby extending the influence of the British East Africa Company to Lake Nyasa and Lake Tanganyika.

The Nyasa Industrial Mission extended its ministry from Zambia into Malawi, introducing its services at Likubula on the Shiré Highlands in the early 1890s.[79] The leaders of this mission desired to teach the people how to raise better crops and engage in simple village industries. The mission hoped to create an interest in the Christian faith through its services to the people. The Australian Baptists who began the Mission ceded it to the British Baptists in 1896. In 1898 the latter established a second station at Cholo. In 1905 a significant peoples' movement to Christianity began.

As a result of the initial difficulties to establish a ministry on the Shiré Highlands, the Universities Mission withdrew to Zanzibar, hoping to evangelize the people of the mainland by training evangelists at Zanzibar and sending them to the mainland. In 1875 the mission, under the direction of Bishop Steers, undertook to establish a ministry to the northeast of Lake Nyasa, approaching the country by the Rovuma River. Chuma, Livingstone's faithful servant, directed the transport.[80] In 1876 it commenced a ministry among the Yaos at Masasi to the north of Rovuma. The mission extended its ministry southward to Newala in 1878 and to Nataka in the lake region in 1880. Through W. P. Johnson's instigation, a steamer was placed on Lake Nyasa in 1885 to serve in contacting several tribes. The mission established its headquarters on Likoma Island.[81] With the island as its focal point, the mission established a ministry at many posts on the lakeshore and eventually extended its witness into Mozambique. In accordance with its policy of missions, it engaged in an educational ministry in which the teachers' college gave leadership. St. Andrews Theological College at Nkwazi on Likoma Island trained candidates for the ministry of the diocese of Malawi. The local Christians were ordained as priests and deacons and were encouraged to participate in the ministry. Nationals were placed in charge of three posts founded in 1890.[82]

The White Fathers of the Roman Catholic Church established themselves near one of the stations of the Reformed Church in

1901. In 1907 they baptized the first believers. By 1911 they were laboring at five centers. In 1913 the Catholic Church created a separate vicariate apostolic for the Nyasa region.

The De Montfort Fathers, another French order, came to the south of Lake Nyasa in 1910. They expanded their ministry and it was made a separate vicariate apostolic in 1914. The Roman Catholic missions came at a time when the people were responsive and an interest in education had developed. However, their ministry did not witness significant growth until after 1914.[83]

As a result of several decades of ministry of missions, a marked interest in education was expressed throughout the southeastern part of Africa. The enrollment in the schools increased sharply and the missions undertook to instruct the gospel message in the schools. Many pupils became church members, but they did not all become witnessing Christians.

Joseph Booth came to Malawi from Australia in 1891 to establish an interdenominational and self-propagating industrial mission. He acquired a large tract of land near Blantyre and later opened additional centers. The enterprise endeavored to combine agricultural development and Christian witness. It sought to support itself by means of large coffee and cotton plantations and was able to establish several Christian communities.[84]

The Seventh-Day Adventists founded a mission in Malawi in 1902. It has had a successful ministry and established a church of over twenty thousand members.[85]

A number of other societies have entered Malawi in recent years. Missionaries of the Assemblies of God came to assist several existing groups. They opened six centers of activity in various parts of the country and soon developed a flourishing work through the emphasis on the ministry of evangelists trained in the Bible school. The national workers soon outnumbered the missionaries and assumed the responsibility for the church.

In 1942 the Malawi Christian Council was formed.[86] It is a member of the All-Africa Conference of Churches, but has no other outside connections. The Evangelical Association of Malawi is affiliated with the Association of Evangelicals of Africa and Madagascar. In recent years talks concerning church union have been taking place between the Church of Central Africa, Presbyterian, the Anglicans, and the Churches of Christ (Disciples).

Mozambique

Mozambique is a large country on the east coast of Africa through which the great Zambezi River and its tributaries flow. It has two good harbors—Lourenco Marques, to the south, and Beira, farther north, through which many products from and to the Transvaal and Rhodesia are shipped. The land is fertile, and the rainfall is abundant.

The territory was under Arab domination for several centuries before it was reached by Vasco da Gama in 1498. When da Gama came to this area, the Arab slave trade was exercised freely and dominated the northern part of the country. The Portuguese established their authority in 1505. However, instead of suppressing the notorious trade, they also traded with slaves, transporting some of them to plantations in Brazil. Consequently, they have not developed the country as some other European powers have done. Indian and Arab traders carried on some small business enterprises along the coast, but Portugal has not developed the economy through large industries nor provided large labor opportunities. Portugal has now granted independence to Mozambique.

Medical services and educational opportunities were limited. Consequently, malaria, tuberculosis, sleeping sickness, and leprosy claimed many lives every year. Venereal diseases also caused much illness and unhappiness.[87] Only a small percent of students have attained a high school education. Many young men annually work in the mines of South Africa to secure revenue for the heavy taxes. The movements of the laboring men have not been conducive to Christian work. Families are broken up for unreasonable periods of time.

The efforts of the Catholic orders in East Africa during the sixteenth and seventeenth centuries and their subsequent decline have been observed. The expulsion of the Jesuits in 1759 and the suppression of the religious orders in the second quarter of the nineteenth century caused a severe setback to the Catholic work in Mozambique. Because it was without qualified leadership, it virtually disintegrated. The Catholic missions were in a state of decline during the earlier part of the nineteenth century. The Jesuits returned in 1881 and revived the weakened Roman Catholic witness, which had been maintained by a few seculars from Goa. The Jesuits opened a number of posts. However, climate and disease took a heavy toll of their personnel and they were obliged to close several centers. They devoted their ministry chiefly to the small white minority. The Seminary of Sernache provided Portuguese seculars for its ministry. When Portugal became a republic in 1910 and adopted an anticlerical attitude, the Jesuits were again expelled from the country. The Society of the Divine Word replaced them, but their relatively small staff did not develop a large work.

The Portuguese Franciscans opened a mission in 1898 and the Fathers of Mary of Montfort joined them. They located in the Inhambane area.[88] They prepared Christian literature in the vernacular, including a translation of the Bible and a catechism.[89] Because of the vicissitudes in the country and in the ministry of the Catholic orders, the Catholic membership in Mozambique did not exceed five thousand by 1914.

The secular Fathers of the Portuguese Institute of National Missions had developed the largest ministry by 1936, serving at twenty-seven of the forty Catholic stations.[90] The country has experienced considerable economic progress since then, which is also reflected in the growth of the educational program and of the church in the country.

The Protestant churches were restrained in their activities in the Portuguese territories. After the declaration of the republic and the separation of church and state in Portugal in 1910, the Protestants had the possibility of working in Portuguese territories, but their activities in Mozambique were restricted and could not be administered freely.[91]

The early Protestant attempts to reach the non-Christians of Mozambique were unsuccessful. The British Methodists placed a missionary at Delagoa Bay in 1820. But because of the unhealthy climate, the enterprise was again abandoned. For half a century no further effort was made to evangelize Mozambique.

The Swiss missionaries, Paul Berthoud and Creux, of the Mission Romande, serving in the Transvaal to the west of Lourenco Marques and Inhambane, had frequent contacts with the people of southern Mozambique. They realized that the main body of the Magawamba tribe, whom they were serving in the Transvaal, was resident in Mozambique. The Christians from the Transvaal visited friends and relatives in Mozambique and vice versa, whereby the gospel was diffused in the tribe and people became Christians.

One of the Christians from Transvaal went to serve as evangelist in Mozambique in 1881.[92] When Berthoud went to Lourenco Marques in Mozambique in 1887, he found a community of a hundred believers in one locality. This is another example of the diffusion of the Christian faith through the testimony of believers. The spontaneous expansion of the faith has moved across boundaries and political barriers. This community had grown to 725 members by 1889.[93] The mission intensified its ministry in Mozambique, adding to the work in Lourenco Marques, a center at Rikatla in 1889 and another at Antioka in 1890. Thus the mission entered a period of effective ministry.[94]

In the 1880s a native of Lourenco Marques, who had joined the Wesleyan Methodist Church while in South Africa, proclaimed the gospel to his people. He was deported in 1896 and went to South Africa. British missionaries were placed in charge of the ministry he had begun. By 1893 a community of 230 believers had been gathered. The mission, however, did not maintain a strong staff, and this deterred the progress of the ministry.

The American Board of Commissioners undertook a mission to Mozambique in 1879, but they suffered several failures before they were able to establish a work at Inhambane in 1883.[95] However, the port was insalubrious; so in 1888 the mission moved over the border into Rhodesia to a higher altitude and a more favorable climate. The missionaries ministered to the people of Mozambique from their centers in Rhodesia. E.H. Richards remained with the people whom he had served until the Methodist Episcopal Church came and he joined that mission.

As a result of their contacts with the American Board and their desire to plant stations across Central Africa, from Loanda to the east coast, the American Methodists settled across the bay from Inhambane. Under the direction of Bishop William Taylor, they continued the witness abandoned by the American Board. A number of native people had been converted while they were working at Johannesburg. When they returned to Mozambique, they participated in the ministry. The American Methodists have served faithfully in Mozambique and in Angola and have developed recommendable work, even though the government placed many restrictions on their ministry. The church is not large but it is well established and is autonomous. The ministry of the church is divided into six districts. Services are held at over nine hundred places. The first African bishop was elected in 1964.

The government restricted the educational ministry of the society. It was not permitted to open many high schools.[96] The Central Training School, the Hartzell School, Keys Memorial School, and a nursing school have made a significant contribution in preparing evangelists, teachers, nurses, and technicians. The two hospitals and the leprosarium have given valuable services.[97]

In 1893 the Anglican Church consecrated W. E. Smyth as the first bishop for the diocese of southern Mozambique. He established residence at Inhambane. He was joined by several clergy and they began a ministry at several centers. At first their ministry was chiefly to the Europeans residing in the area.[98] But in 1895 they began a ministry to the Lenges at Mtsova. It was conducted by a faithful African Christian. This has become a significant work, reaching also the Chopi, a people related to the Lenges.[99]

The Africa Evangelical Fellowship has a small work in Mozambique. Although it has had workers in the country at certain periods, none have resided there since 1960, and the work is basically guided from Malawi. The church is growing and has trebled its membership within the last decade.

The Church of the Nazarene began a successful ministry in Mozambique in 1954. They proclaim the gospel at more than three hundred places and about one-third of these places are already self-supporting. They prepare evangelists for their places of worship at three Bible institutes.

The Pentecostal Assemblies of Canada came to Mozambique early in the 1950s. Their work expanded rapidly and by 1965 about three hundred assemblies, served by national workers, were functioning. The membership has grown to approximately ten thousand, and the work is indigenous and self-supporting. Their ministry has also been effective among the Portuguese population. Two multiracial churches, one at Lourenco Marques and one at Beira, are led by Portuguese pastors.

Many catechists, evangelists, and pastors in Mozambique have received some training in a Bible institute. The Swiss Mission ceded its station at Rikatla to the Christian Council for a Union Theological Seminary and Ecumenical Center. Although the seminary is basically supported by the Swiss Presbyterians and the Methodists, students from the other churches are invited to attend.

The Congregational Church, the Presbyterian Church of Mozambique, the Scandinavian Baptist Mission, the Church of God, World-wide Evangelization Crusade, and the Seventh-Day Adventists are also serving in Mozambique.

The Christian Council of Mozambique was organized in 1944.[100] It aims to coordinate the ministry of the churches and missions and is publishing a paper that serves as a unifying factor. Nearly all the Protestant churches and missions are members of the Christian Council.

EXPANSION OF CHRISTIANITY ON ISLANDS OFF THE EAST AFRICAN COAST

Madagascar

Madagascar, the third largest island of the world, lies 250 miles off the coast of Africa and has basically a Malaysian population. The language is Malay-Polynesian. Although ethnic and cultural elements have been introduced by immigrants from Africa and Arabia, the homogeneity of the Malagasy language and culture is remarkable. It therefore seems evident that the first inhabitants came from the Malayo-Indonesian archipelago. It has been suggested that the inhabitants arrived between 300 B.C. and A.D. 200.[101] It has been further stated that Indonesians had relations with Madagascar until the thirteenth century, when they were replaced by the Arabs.[102] Finally, Madagascar was made known to Europeans by Diego Diaz in 1500.

The Roman Catholic Church made an abortive attempt to plant a church on the island in 1613. The Portuguese landed near Fort Dauphin, but the king would not assure the safety of the Jesuits. Consequently, they chose to leave. From 1642 to 1674 the French maintained a trading post at Fort Dauphin and French priests came to the post. But as the people were hostile to the colony, the priests left in 1672 and the enterprise was abandoned in 1674.[103]

The history of Christianity in Madagascar began in 1820. It may be divided into two periods: (1) the period of English influence from 1820 to 1896, during which time English-speaking missionaries were vitally engaged in the ministry; and (2) the period of French influence from 1896,[104] when Catholics and French-speaking missions were given preference.

In 1820 missionaries of the London Missionary Society landed at the seaport Tamatave on the eastern coast. The party consisted of

David Jones and Thomas Bevan and their wives and two children. It was the hot, rainy season, and malaria soon took a heavy toll. A few weeks after landing, David Jones was the only survivor.[105] Encouraged by a cordial reception from King Radama I at Tananarive, Jones asked the mission to send more missionaries and artisans. The mission responded to the request by sending six ordained and eight artisan missionaries from 1820 to 1828.

The first recruit to join Jones was David Griffith.[106] The mission instructed its workers to give priority to the translation of the Scriptures and present them to the people in their language as soon as possible. Several books of the Old Testament were translated, and in 1830 the New Testament translation was completed.[107] The missionaries proclaimed the gospel and opened several schools to train catechists for the Christian ministry. Members of the royal family were among the first pupils. The king erected a school building.

Radama I was interested in advancing his country and sent ten Malagasy boys to England. He set out to bring about a social and intellectual reformation. In 1827 more than four thousand people were able to read and write and workmen were being trained in European craftsmanship.[108]

In 1928 Radama I died, and one of his twelve wives, Ramano, became queen under the name Ranavalona I. She ordered the massacre of the royal family. With some conservatives in the government, she rejected the reforms introduced by her husband. She ardently adhered to ancestral reverence and was influenced by sorcerers and the conservatives. She undertook to return the country to former traditions and rejected European civilization. During the first years of her rule, she permitted the missionaries to continue their ministry. The first baptisms took place in 1831 with her permission. However, before long she prohibited baptisms and the celebration of the holy communion and requested the missionaries to teach something useful like making soap or gunpowder rather than teaching reading and writing.[109]

In 1831 Queen Ranavalona became hostile toward the Christians. She prohibited soldiers or scholars from becoming Christians and began a persecution that continued until her death in 1861. The aggravations increased. Christianity was outlawed, and the missionaries, one after another, were expelled from the country.[110] The Bible was printed in 1835 before the last missionaries departed. They left on the island a young church with the Bible in its language. But no pastor had been consecrated and no church organization had been adopted. Nevertheless, the Christians met in their homes and encouraged each other in the Christian faith.

The persecution was intensified. The imprisonments, executions, and burnings of Bibles and other Christian literature became more numerous.[111] During this long period the young church persevered faithfully. Families continued to meet to read the Bible and, through the inspiration of the Scriptures, the life of these Christians resembled that of the Christians of the early church.

Rekoto succeeded his mother, taking the name Radama II. He was not a Christian but was favorably inclined to Christianity and granted full religious freedom.[112] The missionaries returned and were overwhelmed to find a vital church that was much larger than when the mission was suspended, even though approximately two hundred Christians had become martyrs.[113] The people desired to hear the gospel, and the church grew very rapidly.

When the news of the interest in the gospel at Madagascar reached England, both the Society for the Propagation of the Gospel and the Church Missionary Society undertook to send missionaries to Madagascar. The Society for the Propagation of the Gospel extended its ministry from Mauritius to Tamatave, the chief port on the east coast of Madagascar,[114] to serve other tribes than the Hòva. The Society for the Propagation of the Gospel sent a bishop to Madagascar in 1874, but the Church Missionary Society withdrew at this time. The bishop settled at Antanànarivò, and a cathedral was constructed.[115]

French Roman Catholic missionaries came to Madagascar during this time and were supported by the representatives of the French government. The Jesuits tried to win the king to their faith.[116] But the Protestants were known and respected on the island, having brought the gospel to it. The French government wanted to increase its influence on the island and consequently supported the Jesuits.[117]

Radama II frequently made hasty decisions. He was influenced by unscrupulous men and became unpopular. A rebellion broke out in the palace on May 12, 1863, and Radama was murdered. His widow succeeded him under the name Rasoherina. She remained faithful to the ancestral customs, but did not oppose the Christian faith. During her reign the development of the country progressed remarkably.

The church grew rapidly during this period. It adopted a church organization known as Six-Monthly Meeting, and became more fully established. Under the supervision of J. M. Sibree, five chapels were constructed at Tananarive in memory of the martyrs of the persecution. The Christian communities also erected many houses of worship. Church attendance was about 40,000.[118] In 1873 the church took on missionary activities and attempted to proclaim the gospel in parts of the island where it was not known. By 1880 the Christian community reported 248,108 adherents.[119] Considerable effort was made to provide Christian literature. Beginning in 1866 a Christian paper appeared regularly.[120]

In 1867 the Friends Foreign Missionary Association agreed to assist the London Missionary Society. The Association devoted itself to an educational ministry. But it also constructed a hospital and opened a medical school where doctors for the island were trained.[121]

In response to an invitation by the London Missionary Society, the Norwegian Missionary Society sent two missionaries to Madagascar in 1866. They began a ministry at Antanànarìvo and established a work among the Bètsilèo tribe to the south of Imerina. Later the society extended its ministry to the Bara tribe, south of the Bètsilèo.[122] The United Norwegian Lutheran Church, an American communion, assisted the Norwegian Missionary Society in its ministry and in 1892 assumed the responsibility for the southern part of its field. In 1894 the Lutheran Free Church assumed the western part of this field.

In 1868 Rasoherina died and was succeeded by her sister Ranavalona II, who married the prime minister. Both Ranavalona and her husband were baptized on February 21, 1869, by a Malagasy minister. The queen was sincere in becoming a church member. A chapel was constructed in the palace and the royal idols were removed.[123]

Christianity spread rapidly among the Hova people. The church was unable to supply the towns and villages with evangelists and catechists. Volunteer teachers were enrolled by the hundreds. The Hova sang Christian hymns by the hour, thus propagating the faith. This method has been very effective in proclaiming the gospel in other parts of Africa also.

In 1883 Ranavalona III became the queen of Madagascar at the age of twenty-two. She was the first sovereign to have received her education in a mission school. Unfortunately, her reign was troubled by French colonial ambitions. France looked for an excuse to interfere in Madagascar's activities, especially to wrest the commerce with the island from the British. The Malagasy monarchy tried to conserve its independence. But in 1883 the French, through a military maneuver, received commercial privileges. They readily increased their activities on the island. In 1895 another French military expedition appeared, and Ranavalona III was compelled to accept French protection. Thus Madagascar virtually became a French protectorate.[124]

The Protestant churches encountered many hardships under French rule. The Jesuits did their utmost to destroy the Protestant ministry. They provoked the French officers to scandalous actions. They told the French officials and the Malagasy people that the Protestants were English and consequently were not loyal to French and Catholic authorities. More than five hundred Protestant chapels were seized and ceded to the Catholics. The people revolted and tried to regain their independence.[125]

The London Missionary Society appealed to the French Protestants for assistance. The Paris Evangelical Missionary Society sent H. Lauga and F. H. Kruger. They were cordially received by the Malagasy church and readily dampened the Jesuit propaganda. The French administrator M. H. Larache also received them cordially. But he was not able to restore order in the country and was replaced by General Gallieni, who became governor general and governed until 1905. Gallieni was favorably inclined to the Protestant churches. The French administrators, however, had communication difficulties, as the educated Malagasy spoke English.

In 1897 the Paris Mission sent twenty-seven missionaries to Madagascar. They assumed responsibilities in education. They requested the return of the Protestant chapels.[126] General Gallieni was impressed with the ministry of the Protestant churches and wished to restore order. The Jesuits returned the chapels and classrooms to the Protestants. The Protestant work was reestablished. It offered elementary-to-university education.

The Protestant work was being reestablished when anticlericalism became influential in France. School subsidies were suppressed in 1903. Then, in 1906, the new governor general of Madagascar, Augagneur, in the name of free thinking, closed all the catechist schools and even some church schools in which the local language was used. He insisted that education not be offered in buildings used for religious services. He allowed only teachers with a French certificate, who knew the French language, to give instruction.[127] By these regulations he closed about 75 percent of the Protestant schools. He applied every possible measure to obstruct the Protestant ministry, even to the point of prohibiting church services, Christian Endeavor Societies, and Young Men's Christian Associations. But in spite of all the obstructions, the ministry of the Protestant churches continued, and the Christian faith gained many adherents through the testimony of dedicated Christians. The Six-Monthly Meetings drew multitudes, who returned after the meetings to their ministry with fresh inspiration.[128]

Rainisoalambo, a layman from the Bètsilèo people, founded the Disciples of Christ, a laymen's organization. It sent its members, two by two, to proclaim the gospel in the rural areas. During five years they followed the trails of the island. The movement spread to other churches in other parts of the island. Through this ministry prayer cells were constituted throughout the island.

The ministry of the churches was arranged in districts, which functioned in relation to the autonomous churches. Pastors became responsible for the larger congregations, whereas the smaller ones were served by catechists.

The missionary conference that met at Tananarive in 1913 emphasized closer cooperation among the communions. A permanent committee was elected and charged with the responsibility to guide the common ministries. This working together was profitable for all the agencies concerned and furthered the growth toward oneness in Christ.[129] In 1934 the majority of the societies accepted a common name, the United Protestant Church of Madagascar, preserving, however, their identity and form of ecclesiastical government.

World War I (1914–1918) had negative effects on the Christian ministry in Madagascar. Several missionaries were mobilized. French and Norwegian missionary societies could not support their work. However, the churches rallied to the task and considerable progress toward self-sufficiency was made. The Hova Christians, especially, dedicated themselves to proclaim the gospel. Hundreds of clergy and lay preachers were active. In the 1920s religious awakenings swept through the country. Malagasy women served as deacons and lay preachers.[130] The depression, beginning in 1929, affected the ministry in Madagascar noticeably.

As in other parts of the world, missionary activities were limited during that time. But the Malagasy Christians assumed additional responsibilities and called more men to the ministry. The churches were recovering from these difficulties when they were repeated from 1939 to 1945 during World War II. Then, in 1947, a rebellion took place that delayed progress in the Christian ministry for some time.[131]

The Soatanana revivalist movement, founded in the 1890s, worked closely with the churches. But recently one section has formed an independent church. Several other independent groups also have been formed. In addition, a number of Pentecostal churches, the Conservative Baptists, and the Jehovah's Witnesses are represented in Madagascar.

The Roman Catholics greatly increased their personnel on the island at the turn of the century. Additional orders and societies came to Madagascar. In 1896 the Lazarists assumed the responsibility for the southern part of the island, while in 1898 the Holy Ghost Fathers began to serve in the northern part. As has generally been the case, there was no consideration of comity between the Roman Catholics and the Protestants. The Roman Catholics began work beside the Protestant endeavors. Favored by the French government, the Roman Catholics made considerable progress. But during the 1920s few Malagasy Christians entered the priesthood. The European personnel have always been numerous. But they have not trained a large Malagasy staff for church work. In 1971 about one thousand workers from overseas were serving in Madagascar, whereas about two hundred Malagasy priests were in the Catholic service.[132]

In 1939 the Roman Catholic Church entrusted the newly created vicariate apostolic to the Malagasy clergy and consecrated one of them as bishop.[133] Today the Roman Catholic organization is directed by Malagasy archbishops and some bishops are Malagasy.

The Church of Christ of Madagascar is the fruit of the ministry of the London Missionary Society. The Episcopal Church of Madagascar has been independent for some time. Its ministry constitutes three dioceses, which are served by its own bishops and clergy. The Norwegian Missionary Society and the two American Lutheran Missions united to form the Malagasy Lutheran Church in 1950. In 1968 in the northern part of the country the churches that have been established as a result of the ministries of the London Missionary Society, the Paris Evangelical Missionary Society, and the Friends Mission formed the Church of Jesus Christ in Madagascar. Their educational ministry has already been placed under one direction. The pastors receive training in one school of theology, and the paper *Fanasima* is serving all three communities.[134] Most of the churches on the island belong to the Christian Council of Madagascar.

The Malagasy Republic was created in 1958 and independence was declared in 1960. The autonomous churches are serving in relation with the government. They play a large role in education, but also manifest a continuing concern for evangelism. The Protestant community is estimated at 1.5 million and the Roman Catholic at 1.2 million. Together they represent 40 percent of the population. The churches have a vital influence on the moral and social life of the society.

Mauritius

Mauritius, a small island off the east coast of Africa and not far from Madagascar, was uninhabited when it was discovered by the Portuguese in 1505. The Portuguese, Dutch, French, and British have in turn governed the island. The Dutch christened it Mauritius in honor of Prince Maurice; but during the French occupation (1715-1810), it was called Isle de France. When the French discovered that the climate of Mauritius was suitable for sugar production, they began large sugar plantations and imported African slaves for labor. Mauritius was further populated by Creoles from the island of Bourbon or Reunion, which France governed. After the emancipation of the slaves in 1834, the plantation owners hired Indian laborers in large numbers. Many Indians returned to their homes after working on the island; however, the descendants of these laborers now constitute about two-thirds of the total population. The small island is now one of the most densely populated areas of the world.[135]

The Europeans who came to the island were mostly Roman Catholics; they propagated their faith among the people, especially among the Negro population. Jacques Desire Laval (d. 1864) of the Holy Ghost Fathers, a missionary to the island, is said to have baptized many people. The Jesuits came later. The Roman Catholic diocese of Port Louis was created in 1847.[136]

Mauritius came under British rule in 1810 during the Napoleonic

Wars. After the emancipation in 1834, the Society for the Propagation of the Gospel of the Anglican Church and the London Missionary Society opened schools for the Negroes and the Creoles. Because of Roman Catholic opposition, however, little was accomplished until the Anglican bishopric of Mauritius was established in 1854 and Vincent W. Ryan was placed in charge.[137] Under his auspices the Society for the Propagation of the Gospel and the Church Missionary Society united their ministries under the guidance of one bishop. The spiritual interests of several thousand members of the Church of England were cared for, and the Society for the Propagation of the Gospel found Christians of their fellowship from South India among the Indian colonies. These Christian groups formed the nuclei for congregations on the island. The Indians were open to the gospel, and soon many of them were baptized. By 1873 nearly two thousand had been baptized. The majority of the Indian converts returned to their native land.[138]

In 1860 the government established an orphan asylum and an industrial school at Powder Mills. Indian orphans and Negro slave children liberated by the British naval patrol were taught with good results. In 1862 sixty of them received baptism upon their confession of faith.

The work of the Anglican Church developed at Mauritius and became a base for the mission to Madagascar and East Africa. Liberated slaves were received and instructed. In 1864 Bishop Ryan ordained five missionaries for services to Madagascar and to the East African coast and consecrated St. Paul's Church, Port Louis. There were people of English, French, Creole, Eurasian, African, Bengali, Madrassi, Malagasy, and Chinese extraction represented in the assembly. In 1867 the society founded St. Paul's Theological College to train men for the priesthood.

That same year a fever epidemic swept away 10 percent of the population of the island. Five missionaries of the Society for the Propagation of the Gospel were among them. The next year, 1868, a hurricane devastated the island. It took years for the island to recover from the disaster. Then another hurricane struck the island in 1891. Many lives were lost and one-third of the capital city was destroyed. The cathedral at St. Louis served as a hospital for three weeks until the emergency was over.[139]

By the beginning of the twentieth century a native clergy was

largely responsible for the pastoral work, which had been arranged
in six districts. Church growth, however, has not been large. In
1907 the Church Missionary Society began a gradual withdrawal
from the ministry, while the church assumed the responsibilities.[140] The ministry of the Society for the Propagation of the
Gospel, which served together with the Church Missionary Society, is of similar significance to that of the latter.[141]

The island was little affected by World War I. But from 1919 to
1939 the church lacked ministerial candidates and funds to expand
its ministry. The society sent support for local mission priests.[142]
The church tried to reach the children by conducting services in
the schools. The Protestant ministry has not maintained its vitality, and the church community has remained a minority on the
island.

SUMMARY

Revival of missionary concern for the salvation of the people
prompted the churches to push forward to new areas and unknown
peoples, even at the risk of their lives. Livingstone's urge to
penetrate Africa with the gospel and open it to legal commerce
also motivated those who came after him. Undoubtedly mistakes
were made, but there have been some important contributions to
the evangelization of the continent. The present generation will do
well to grasp the spirit of the Christian pioneers.

The missionary endeavor was obliged to contend with European
colonial ambitions. Robert Moffat and David Livingstone established relations with the Matabele and the Makololo tribes, and
Coillard with the Barotse. These contacts could have resulted in
the evangelization of these tribes in their cultural setting, with the
tribal culture being preserved. However, because of colonial ambitions, European rule was forced upon these tribes. The significance of their cultures disappeared, and to a certain degree they
were culturally uprooted. Colonial agencies have offered services
to missionary societies and in turn have taken advantage of them
to advance their colonial aspirations. The British South Africa
Company followed the missionaries into Rhodesia, Zambia, and
Malawi, using the friendly relationships missionaries had established with the people as stepping stones to establish their
authority.

The allocation of land has been a serious problem for Southeast

Africa. When land was not reserved for the Hottentots in South Africa, they were soon without land and John Philip interceded for them. As settlers moved into Rhodesia, the land question again became an issue. The more productive land of Rhodesia was soon occupied by the settlers, and the native peoples' agricultural opportunities were limited.

Missions have ministered to the needs of the total man. Through the advancement of medical knowledge and the medical ministry of missionary societies, the life expectancy of the people has increased and much suffering has been prevented or relieved. The education offered by the societies has brought new opportunities to the people; yet at the same time it has caused the disintegration of the African culture. The agricultural and industrial knowledge and assistance have provided new means of livelihood and contributed to terminate the slave trade.

God is the Creator. The soul of man is not fully satisfied until it rests in God. Christian missions have brought the divine revelation to the people, and through this revelation God comes to them and they may encounter God in their culture. The history of the church reveals that the gospel is adequately proclaimed only when it is incarnated in the human agency.

The importance of proclaiming the gospel to the ruling class and of presenting the Scriptures to the people is especially observed during the early years of the establishment of the Christian faith in Madagascar. Members of the ruling class accepted the Christian faith, dedicated themselves to proclaim it to their fellow-men, retained it under persecution, and readily established many congregations after the persecution ceased. Christianity assumed an indigenous character and this contributed to a people movement and rapidly advanced the Christian faith.

The divisions among Christian communities and the political ambitions of European countries and rivalries among them conflicted with the gospel message and greatly hindered the establishment of the Christian faith. Nevertheless, the liberating power of the gospel brought Christians from various tribes and ethnic backgrounds into Christian communion.

Study Questions

1. Describe the effects colonial ambitions have had on the Christian ministry in Southeastern Africa.
2. Indicate the importance of establishing credibility with the people for an effective Christian ministry.
3. What effects did Cecil Rhodes' policy of giving large tracts of land to missions have on the Christian missions?
4. What effects did the desire for education have on the Christian ministry?
5. Describe the effects the cultural differences in Rhodesia have had on the churches.
6. Evaluate F. S. Arnot's missionary policies.
7. Evaluate the unification of the United Church in Zambia and its ministry.
8. Describe the results of David Livingstone's efforts to open Africa to the proclamation of the gospel and to legal trade. To what extent did the Livingstonia Mission and the African Lakes Company apply these principles?
9. Missiologists emphasize the importance of the key personality in a movement of a people to Christ. Substantiate this statement by the ministry of the Swiss Mission in Mozambique.
10. Indicate the importance of presenting the Scriptures to the Christians in their language and of working towards indigeneity during the early stages of a church's existence.
11. Describe how colonial ambitions greatly interfered with the Christian missions in Madagascar.
12. In what way do the people movements in Madagascar verify church-growth principles?

7

Christianity in East Africa
(1652-1975)

The east coast of Africa from the Somali Republic to Cape Delgado constituted a cultural block. It is the cradle of the Swahili language and civilization.[1] From the thirteenth to the eighteenth century, Arab and Islamic influences on the coast were quite significant. The use of one language was actually the only common factor among a population anthropologically quite diversified, being the result of a racial mixture of Negro, Arab, Persian, and Indian stock that has continued for over a thousand years. The people eventually acquired a sentiment of adhering to a distinct cultural unit. However, no trace of a national consciousness was present. The Kiswahili was chiefly the language of a small coastal area. The population of the east coast was not as large as in some other parts of Africa, like Nigeria. The population between the Tona and the Zambezi River was estimated at sixteen million.[2]

INTRODUCTION OF CHRISTIANITY TO EAST AFRICA

The Protestant ministry on the coast of East Africa was begun in 1844 by Johann Krapf, a native of Basel, Switzerland, who served with the Church Missionary Society. Krapf came to East Africa after serving in Ethiopia for three years, where he acquired a knowledge of the Amharic language. During his service in Ethiopia, he was concerned to proclaim the gospel to the Gallas people of southeast Ethiopia and hoped a mission to the Gallas would be instrumental in diffusing the gospel in East Africa. He thought the Gallas could readily be reached from the east coast. In 1842 he went to Egypt to meet the woman who had come to be his bride.[3] After the wedding, Krapf and his wife sailed for Zanzibar with the intention of beginning a mission to the Gallas.

233

Krapf was well received by the British consul at Zanzibar, who introduced him to the sultan, the political authority on the east coast. Krapf presented his plans to begin a mission to the Gallas to the sultan and received permission to undertake the enterprise. The sultan wrote a letter to the authorities on the coast informing them of his approval of Krapf's proposal. Krapf embarked on an exploratory voyage. He visited Pemba, Tanga, and Mombasa and chose the latter town as a base for a mission on the coast. He returned to Zanzibar and a few weeks later, in May 1844, he and his wife reached Mombasa to begin the missionary endeavor.[4]

In July both Krapf and his wife became seriously ill with malaria. Mrs. Krapf died, and he was temporarily incapacitated. After he regained his health, he studied the Swahili language and began to translate the New Testament. He arranged some four thousand words of a Swahili-English dictionary.[5]

During 1844 and 1845 Krapf made several excursions to the interior to find a suitable location for a mission station among the Nyika. He learned that the climate on the higher altitudes in the interior was more favorable than on the coast. But he also became aware of the difficulties of travel in the area.

In 1847 Johann Rebmann came to join Krapf. They chose Rabai Mpia as a center for work among the Nyika and from there they made several attempts to reach the Gallas. During these journeys they discovered Mount Kadiaro and to the east of Mount Kadiaro they met the Taiti people. In 1848 Rebmann traveled west of the Taiti for five days and came to the Chagga tribe. During this journey he saw Mount Kilimanjaro.[6]

In 1849 Krapf visited the Kamba tribe to the northwest of Mombasa. The Kamba chief, Kivoi, invited him to settle in his region. During his travels in Kamba country, Krapf met several Kikuyu people and saw Mount Kenya. Because of Kivoi's invitation, the favorable climate in the region, and the possibility of contacting the tribes in the interior, Krapf recommended that several stations be founded in the region.

In 1849 J. J. Erhardt and Johannes Wagner came to join Krapf and Rebmann in the ministry. But Wagner died on August 1. Krapf and Erhardt undertook to explore the East African coast to the south of Mombasa and to become acquainted with the routes that missionaries could take to bring the gospel to the interior. During this voyage they became aware of the extent of the notorious slave trade of which the city of Kilwa Kivinje was the coast terminus. It has been estimated that some twelve thousand slaves passed through this town every year. Krapf and Erhardt sailed to the mouth of the Rovuma River and returned to Rabai Mpia in March 1850.[7]

Krapf had not been in Europe since he left for service in Ethiopia. In 1850 he returned to reestablish his health and to find recruits. Krapf was honored for his services. He was received by the prince consort in England, and in Berlin the king of Prussia granted him an audience.[8] In his report to the committee of the Church Missionary Society, Krapf suggested that a chain of mission stations be planted across the continent from east to west. The committee authorized the establishment of two stations, one in Usambara and one in Ukambani, and commissioned five men for this service.[9]

During his furlough Krapf presented some translations to the press. He had translated the Gospels, the Acts, and Genesis into the Galla language during his service in Ethiopia. While he was in East Africa, he had prepared a Swahili grammar and a comparative vocabulary in six African languages. He had also translated several portions of Scriptures in Swahili. These were printed with his counsel.

Krapf returned to Rabai Mpia in 1851 with new recruits. But one of them, a man by the name of Pfefferle, died within a month after landing in Africa, and three others returned to Europe. Shortly after his return to East Africa, Krapf went to Ukamba, where a station was to be founded among the Kamba tribe. Chief Kivoi received him cordially. Krapf and Kivoi undertook to explore the Tana River. With several Kamba attendants, they had journeyed four days when they were attacked by robbers, and Kivoi was killed. Kivoi's people fled and Krapf had to return alone. This was a great shock for Krapf and for the Kamba people. The Kamba blamed Krapf for not protecting his friend and host. The unhappy incident terminated the cordial relations between the two parties, and Krapf abandoned his project to plant a mission among the Kamba.[10]

In 1852 Krapf visited the Tanga people, whom he had visited in 1848 to the southwest of Zanzibar. The Tanga chief, Kimweri, received him hospitably, as he had on Krapf's previous visit, and gave permission to establish a ministry among his people. The town of Usambara presented possibilities for a fruitful ministry. The people were well disciplined, and the children observed the tribes' teaching. Krapf was confident they would give serious thought to the Christian message. Krapf returned to Rabai Mpia in September 1852. Because of ill health, he was unable to pursue this opportunity, but was obliged to return to Europe.[11] Krapf spent most of his time in linguistic efforts. He did not return to the ministry of the Church Missionary Society. Erhardt went to Usambara in 1853 and labored there until his health compelled him to return to Europe in 1855. The ministry at a second station had to be interrupted.[12] There was no one to respond to Kimweri's invitation, and so a significant opportunity to plant Christianity among the Tanga people was lost.

As a result of the discoveries Krapf and Rebmann made and the reports they sent to Europe, the British government sent Burton and Speke to East Africa to discover the large lake Krapf had written about. On February 13, 1858, they arrived at Ujiji on Lake Tanganyika. Speke continued the exploration and came to Lake Victoria Nyanza on August 3.

In 1860 Speke, accompanied by Grant, undertook another expedition. They arrived at Lake Victoria Nyanza, discovered the Kagera River, and visited Mutesa, the king of Buganda. From there Speke went east and discovered Ripon Falls, by which Lake Victoria Nyanza empties into the Nile River. Speke and Grant decided to return to Europe. As they were leaving the region, they met Samuel Baker and his wife, who had come from Cairo. Baker discovered Lake Albert in 1863, and then proceeded to the Murchison Falls. They returned to Khartoum in May 1865.

Johann Rebmann faithfully continued his ministry at Rabai Mpia for twenty more years. He put three languages into writing and arranged a dictionary for each language. The Paris Geographical Society conferred silver medals on him and Krapf for their literary contributions.[13] Finally, broken in health and practically blind, Rebmann returned to Europe in 1875, leaving Rabai Mpia in charge of the national Christians. During the thirty-one years since Krapf first came to East Africa, the Church Missionary Society had not sent recruits to establish a strong ministry.

Zanzibar

The island of Zanzibar was the home of Sultan Seyyid Said, who controlled the coast of East Africa during a large part of the nineteenth century when Christianity was planted in East Africa. Consequently the island played a large role in the political and religious affairs of that period, and the Christian missions had to reckon with the Islamic attitude of the governing authority. Zanzibar was the center of authority of navigation and of commerce.

After the discovery of the route to the East around the Cape of Good Hope, the Portuguese influence on the coast was prominent as far north as Mombasa from 1498 to 1698. But during the latter part of the seventeenth century, the Turks moved southward along the east African coast, replacing the Portuguese as far south as Mozambique. In 1805, Seyyid Said ibn Sultan acceded to the throne of Oman and ruled for half a century. In 1840 he established himself on Zanzibar and became powerful.

The Americans, British, and French traded with him and appointed consuls to the island in 1837, 1840, and 1844 respectively. The geographic position of the Oman's territory brought him into contacts with the British government in India. Seyyid Said encouraged the immigration of Indian bankers to influence the development of his territory. They came as British subjects and increased the British influence in East Africa. The American commerce with East Africa amounted to approximately 250,000 pounds sterling in 1856.[14]

The political situation on the island was uncertain for some time. The British had established a significant rapport with the government. Then the French came to the island and before long began the construction of what the British suspected might be a garrison. The French government, however, maintained the establishment was for missionary purposes and, in 1862, entrusted it to the Holy Ghost Fathers. It included a hospital, a pharmacy, and workshops. A school chiefly attended by freed slave children was begun.[15] From Zanzibar they began a ministry at Bagamoyo on the coast in 1863. Bagamoyo served as a base for the mainland ministry, which eventually extended to Mount Kilimanjaro.[16]

The Protestant missions were in contact with the island from the beginning of their work in East Africa; but they did not develop permanent ministries on the island until the latter half of the nineteenth century, Krapf came to Zanzibar in 1844, but his destination was the Galla tribe and he left the island without attempting a ministry on it. In 1863 the Universities Mission, under the direction of George Tozer, withdrew from the Shiré Highlands in Malawi and established itself on Zanzibar.

Tozer proposed the policy of training African men and women on the island and sending them to evangelize the mainland, hoping that they would be more resistant to the tropical diseases.[17] For this purpose, the society opened a boys' and a girls' school and also St. Andrews College. Later Miss Allen had a remarkable ministry among the women and girls at Zanzibar.[18]

Zanzibar was under Muslim government and influence, and only limited mission work was accomplished before 1873. The mission was concerned both to check the slave trade and to provide a place of refuge for freed slaves. It followed up Krapf's contacts with Kimweri, the Tanga chief, on the mainland, with the intention of establishing a ministry there. However, Kimweri was cognizant of the political implications and advised the missionaries to open their station near the coast. In 1867 they began their activities at Magila, located inland from Tanga. The mission also opened a village for freed slaves at Mbeni, a few miles south of the Zanzibar capital. The missionaries were drawing continual attention to the evils of the slave trade; consequently the government was under increasing pressure to check the evil practice.

Seyyid Said developed large cacao, palm, and clove plantations.[19] The clove plantations produced approximately three-quarters of the world's supply of cloves in 1850.[20] The plantations required a large amount of manual labor, for which Said employed slaves from the east African coast. Zanzibar was a large slave trading center. In 1872 a hurricane struck the island, destroying two-thirds of the island's plantations. All the vessels in the port, except one, were either destroyed or sunk. The hurricane destroyed practically the entire Catholic mission. Only four buildings, of about fifty, remained to provide some shelter. The hurricane also struck the coast and destroyed the town of Bagamoyo, which was a slave trading center. The destruction of the plantations, which required much slave labor, helped the British consul, John Kirk, to achieve the closure of the slave market at Zanzibar in 1873. The sultan signed the decree one month after Livingstone's death. The Universities Mission constructed a cathedral on the location where the slave market had been. The cornerstone was laid on Christmas Day, 1873, and the Christ Church Cathedral was consecrated on Christmas Day, 1879.[21]

In 1873 George Tozer resigned from his services and was replaced by Edward Steere, who had served with the mission since 1863. In 1875, under Steere's leadership, the Church Missionary Society undertook to establish a ministry in the northeastern part of the Lake Nyasa region, approaching it via the Rovuma River. A work was begun in 1876 at Masasi, north of the Rovuma River, and in 1878 another center was begun farther south at Newala. The society served both in Malawi and Tanzania. The ministry is further presented in relation to these countries.

THE PLANTING OF CHRISTIANITY IN TANZANIA, KENYA, AND UGANDA

Tanzania

Kimweri was the strong chief of the Tanga people when Krapf visited him in 1848 and 1852. He became chief in 1840 and ruled from the coast to the western side of the Usambara and Pare Mountains. The Pagani River was the southern border of his domain. He was chief of approximately half a million people, whom he ruled with complete authority. Kimweri offered Krapf a site for a mission in Vuga, the capital. However, the society did not respond to the opportunity.

The Universities Mission to Central Africa returned to the Lake Nyasa area from Zanzibar by way of the Rovuma River. In 1876 it began a ministry among the Yao tribe at Masasi, north of the Rovuma and behind Cape Delgado. The society's work among the Yao and Nyanja tribes to the east of Lake Nyasa, with its headquarters on Likoma Island, was observed in its Malawi ministry. The society extended its activities into Tanzania on the northeastern side of Lake Nyasa. In the early period of missionary work in Tanzania, it had the largest Protestant staff and the largest number of believers in Tanzania.[22]

The Church Missionary Society penetrated the country and founded the Mpwapwa station on the south shore of Lake Victoria in 1876. Two years later, in 1878, it opened a center at Mamboia. It continued its ministry at these two places during the disturbed period until 1900. The society entered upon a period of expansion in 1900. It added a station during each of the first three decades of the twentieth century.

Robert Arthington, the rich philanthropist of Leeds, England, was greatly interested in furthering missions. In 1875 he wrote to the London Missionary Society that the Churches of Scotland had undertaken the evangelization of the Lake Nyasa region and the Church Missionary Society, the Lake Victoria region. He suggested that the London Missionary Society undertake the evangelization of the Lake Tanganyika region. He offered to contribute five thousand pounds sterling for such an endeavor. In response to this appeal, the society sent Roger Price, the survivor of the tragic mission to the Makololo tribe on the Zambezi River, to explore the possibilities. The society undertook the mission, and the first five representatives arrived at Ujiji in August 1878. But two members of the party died soon after arriving at Ujiji. Price returned to consult with the directors in England. A second party was accompanied by Joseph Mullens, the foreign secretary of the society; the group arrived in 1879. Mullens died at Mpwapwa, the Church Missionary Society's station, on the way to Ujiji. E.J. Southon, a medical doctor, accepted an invitation from Chief Mirambo to begin a ministry at Urambo, east of Lake Tanganyika. W. Griffith went to Uhuga, west of the lake, while E. C. Hore made a survey of the lake and appraised the opportunities for evangelization around it. The region southwest of the lake, where Livingstone spent his last days, became the society's Central African field of ministry.[23] The society's decision to undertake work on Lake Tanganyika changed the mission's practice of working on the coast to moving to the interior and establishing a connection in the missionary endeavor at Lake Nyasa in Malawi with Lake Tanganyika.

The society realized that a steamer on Lake Tanganyika would be very valuable in reaching a large population on the shores of the lake. But the access to Lake Tanganyika was much more difficult than to Lake Nyasa. In 1882 the African Lakes Company, by way of Lake Nyasa, transported a steamer to Lake Tanganyika for the use of the London Missionary Society. This was an outstanding accomplishment in the evangelization of East Africa and testifies to the sacrifices societies made to bring the gospel to the people. Hore continued to visit the towns and villages around the lake.

Kenya

Mombasa played a significant role in the political scene of East Africa when the Portuguese came in contact with it in 1505, and it continued to do so. The ministry of Krapf, Rebmann, and Erhardt at Rabia Mpia, inland from Mombasa, has been observed. By reducing several languages into writing, preparing dictionaries and translating portions of the Scriptures, and establishing friendly relations with several tribes, they opened the country for mission work. During the last years of Rebmann's solitary work at Rabai Mpia, the British exerted their influence to suppress the slave trade in East Africa. The year Rebmann returned to Europe, the Church Missionary Society founded Frere Town.

In 1873, Sir Bartle Frere suggested to the Church Missionary Society that they start a settlement for freed slaves at Mombasa. Thus the society would resettle slaves as the Universities Mission in Zanzibar and the Roman Catholics at Bagamoyo were also doing. The Church Missionary Society accepted the challenge. It purchased a site near Mombasa in 1875 and received 302 liberated slaves in September of that year. With the opening of this settlement, called Frere Town, a new epoch began for East Africa.[24] Efforts to suppress slave trade and to seize slave vessels were intensified. Slaves fled to the havens of refuge, and the missions came in confrontation with the slave traders.

While Krapf was in Europe, he was instrumental in guiding the United Methodist Free Churches to a ministry in East Africa. He accompanied the first Methodist party to Mombasa in 1862.[25] Ribe, about fifteen miles north of Mombasa, was chosen as a base station for their ministry. By the end of the year, Thomas Wakefield was the only survivor. Charles New joined him the following April.

In 1866 Wakefield and New undertook a journey to the Galla people. However, there was hostility between the Masai and the Galla. They also learned that the Galla tribe was smaller than they had expected. Consequently they returned to Ribe. Charles New visited the Chagga tribe in 1871 and again in 1874. He died in 1875 without having established a work among them. Wakefield served alone until 1877. Then he returned to Europe and the ministry discontinued temporarily.

Uganda

The church in Uganda has a unique history. It has reached a large part of the population and has gained converts in every age and social group: men, women, children, chiefs, and slaves. The Christian message has had a profound influence on the country in the past. The church in Uganda is largely the fruit of the ministry of the Church Missionary Society.

The missions in Uganda owe much to the friendly relations Henry Morton Stanley established with Mutesa, the king of Buganda, which was one of the states of Uganda. Stanley was inspired by Livingstone's dedication and his vision to Christianize Africa. After Livingstone's death, Stanley undertook to complete Livingstone's unfinished task: to discover the source of the Zaire River. He arrived in East Africa in November, 1874. On his way to Ujiji, where he had found Livingstone the previous year, Stanley explored the Lake Victoria area and visited Mutesa, the king of Buganda. Stanley spent several months at the court of Mutesa. During this time he gained some information concerning Africa and won the respect and friendship of the king.

In 1857 at the age of eighteen years, Mutesa had succeeded his father, Suna, to the throne. Suna left sixty-one sons as candidates to the throne. Mutesa was chosen king by the palace officers and his sixty brothers were liquidated.[26] Mutesa soon took power into his hands and ruled the country.

Stanley had a number of interviews with Mutesa in which they discussed various issues. Mutesa was interested to learn the secret of the white man's civilization. The Arabs tried to convert Mutesa to Islam. Stanley indicated that the Christian religion was superior and taught him some of the principles of the Christian faith. He also translated some portions of Scripture for the king. Mutesa thought the white people were better than the Arabs because of their inventions and because they did not enslave people; so he chose the Christian religion. Stanley wrote to the *Daily Telegraph* and the *New York Herald* respectively, challenging the churches to bring the gospel to Buganda.[27] Thus, Mutesa's decision to accept the Christian way opened his country to the Christian witness.

The Church Missionary Society responded to Stanley's appeal and in 1876 sent eight men under the direction of George Shergold Smith, R.M., to Buganda. On their way to Buganda, they founded a halfway station at Mpwapwa, some 250 miles from the coast, which became the society's first station in this part of Tanzania. Four members of the party proceeded to Lake Victoria, and from there to Buganda. The first representatives arrived at Rubaga, Mutesa's capital, on June 30, 1877,[28] and were cordially received by Mutesa. However, sickness and tragic events rapidly removed members of the party from the scene of action. At the end of 1878, only Alexander Mackay and Charles Wilson were in Buganda. Four additional recruits arrived in 1879.

Alexander Mackay rendered a worthwhile service. He faithfully proclaimed the gospel during twelve years. Mutesa searched for the truth and regularly attended the worship services, which encouraged his people to do likewise. The people readily received and believed the gospel message, and a Christian community came into being.

Unfortunately, the wonderful opportunity to lead the people to faith in Jesus Christ was greatly hindered by the dissension and rivalry between the Catholics and Protestants. When the report of the Protestant missionaries' reception by Mutesa was received in Europe, Cardinal Charles Lavigerie, then archbishop of Algeria, hastened to send a mission to Mutesa's court. When Dr. Cust heard of Lavigerie's intentions, he went to Algeria and begged Lavigerie to choose an area of service where the gospel was not being proclaimed. But Lavigerie would not be dissuaded. Representatives of the White Fathers went to East Africa in 1878. They proceeded from Bagamoyo on the coast to Tabora, where they founded their first station. Then five of them went to Bukumbi, on the shore of Lake Victoria, where they began a second station. From there two representatives continued to Mutesa's court. From Tabora another group went to Lake Tanganyika and established themselves at Kibanga on the peninsula over against Ujiji.

The White Fathers at Rubaga, Mutesa's capital, came to the Protestant service, but refuted the message.[29] Mutesa was disturbed. The conflict that swept through Central Africa had been launched; it lasted until Vatican II (1962-1965). Furthermore, Mutesa was soon confronted with English, French, and Arab political ambitions. Each group sought political concessions. Mutesa realized the dangers with which he was confronted. He carefully evaluated the situation and endeavored to retain his independence.[30] Unfortunately, while Livingstone and others like him strove to bring Christianity and legal commerce to the peoples of Africa, others yielded to greed and political ambitions.

Protestant missionaries believed that the Bible in the language of the people served to establish the church. In 1879 Mackay began to translate the Scriptures in Luganda. Before long the people read the portions that were available, and many who could not read had others read the Scriptures to them. Although some people had confessed their faith in Christ before the Catholic priests came, the Protestants instructed the believers and the first ones were baptized in March 1882. By then the Catholics had already baptized some people. Recruits joined the Protestant missionaries and the work progressed.

CONFLICTS IN EAST AFRICA

The political scene in East Africa during the 1870s and 1880s was quite unsettled. The sultan from Zanzibar was the authority on the coast, and his agents did as they pleased wherever they went, collecting ivory and enslaving people. Otherwise, the chiefs were virtually independent, especially farther inland. The slave traders operated under the sultan's auspices, but became despots; they exercised power according to their ambitions, without consideration for human life. European colonial ambitions were added to this disturbing situation. The British South Africa Company advanced from South Africa; it incorporated Rhodesia, Zambia, and a large part of Malawi and proceeded to the border of Zaire and Tanzania. The Portuguese and the British were vying for a monopoly of the Zambezi River area. The spheres of influence in this region had not been clearly defined. The French and the British suspiciously watched each other on the Zanzibar, Madagascar, and Mauritius islands. The Germans, the French, King Leopold of Belgium, and the British carefully observed the political situation at Zanzibar and on the coast opposite Zanzibar.

Under the impression of sincere philanthropic intentions, King Leopold II of Belgium advocated a united effort to abolish slave trade and to bring Central Africa into contact with the outside world. He called an international meeting of all who were interested in this cause in 1876. The Africa International Association was formed. It was to serve as an intelligence agency, establishing posts at strategic intervals across Central Africa to promote exploration and civilization on the continent. Leopold was the president of the association.

The first expedition of the association arrived in East Africa in 1877 on its way to Lake Tanganyika and Zaire. Three of the four leaders were Belgians. Cambier alone reached the interior and established posts at Tabora and Karema on Lake Tanganyika in 1879.[31] In 1880 Leopold requested a foothold on the coast for these activities, but the sultan refused to grant it. Four more expeditions were sent between 1879 and 1884. In 1877, Stanley completed his journey across the continent from the east coast, following the Zaire to its mouth. This was a momentous discovery. Leopold turned his attentions to the west coast and sent further expeditions by way of the Zaire River.

The French interest in East Africa was revealed through an expedition sent into the mainland in 1878 under Debaize. But the expedition came to an end with the death of Debaize at Ujiji in 1879. The next year a French trading company asked Sultan Barghash for a concession to build a railway to Ujiji. However, influenced by John Kirk, the sultan rejected the proposal.

The British consul at Zanzibar was quite influential with the sultan, and the Imperial British East Africa Company was engaged in developments in Kenya. The British government was exerting its influence through the sultan but made no official claim to Tanzania.

In 1884 a German expedition led by Carl Peters arrived at Zanzibar and then crossed over to the mainland, where it concluded treaties with twelve chiefs. In 1885 Germany announced its claim to Tanzania and sent Rohlfs as German consul to Zanzibar. The sultan, however, was not willing to cede any territory and was indignant, claiming the chiefs had no authority to cede the territory. Nevertheless, Germany further made a treaty with Witu, who controlled a region north of the area in which the Imperial British East Africa Company was exerting its influence. Thus the area of British monopoly was between two regions of German influence. The British were displeased with this situation. An agreement was reached in 1886 in which both countries recognized the sultan's authority over Zanzibar and a coastal strip; Britain recognized the German claim to Tanzania; and Germany recognized the British claim to Kenya.

By the 1870s the missionary influence in East Africa was beginning to make an impact and the Arab slave traders were greatly disturbed. They were annoyed at the missionary presence around Lake Nyasa and as far as Lake Tanganyika. They were even more agitated at the freed slaves resettlement centers that were opened during the 1860s and 1870s. The Church Missionary Society received some slaves at Rabai Mpia, which was opened in 1844, but its effect was minimal. During the 1860s pressure was exerted to check the slave trade. The Methodists opened Ribe near Mombasa in 1862. The slave traders of Mombasa vowed they would make soup of the missionaries' livers. The Holy Ghost Fathers opened Bagamoyo on the coast opposite Zanzibar in 1863. They redeemed slaves, who in turn paid their ransom in labor. The Universities Mission opened Magila on the coast in 1867 and Bweni on Zanzibar. Later, in 1876, it also settled freed slaves at Masasi on the Rovuma River. The Church Missionary Society opened Frere Town in 1875. The slave traders were perturbed by these settlements near the coast and by the British patrol vessels in the Indian Ocean. But when the missionaries began to penetrate their raiding domains and establish stations at strategic localities, they were infuriated and prepared for a showdown.

By its very nature and its message, Christianity exerted a spiritual, moral, and legal influence. The humanitarian aspect of the mission stations was their presentation of communities in which all peoples' rights were respected. The freed slaves and the refugees worked, planted fields, and legally obtained their livelihood. They studied trades and learned how to use tools they had not known previously. New crops were introduced. Medical care was generally offered, even though in some cases it was rudimentary and limited. The settlements provided a sense of security, whereas the villages were frequently attacked and pillaged by the slave traders. Consequently the stations were respected by the people. But these freed slave stations were despised by the Arab slave traders and the chiefs who wanted to profit from the ignoble trade. The traders threatened to annihilate a number of these places. Governments and trading companies were obliged to interfere and protect them.

The Catholic Missions adopted the missionary-farms or missionary-colonies principle. At these places they accepted the freed slaves, the refugees, and the children whom the tribes brought to them. The life at the missionary farms was disciplined. Evangelization and education were given priority. Manual labor to provide for the livelihood was assigned. A communal life was organized. When the children who had come to the colony became of marriageable age, a house and a plot of ground to cultivate their fields was assigned.

The Catholics thought the missionary farms offered greater opportunities for evangelism than the villages. These people had been separated from their tribe and were obliged to decide their future for themselves. The restrictions and guidelines of the tribe were remote. Consequently, they accepted the Christian faith more readily than the villagers did. Because they participated in the life of a community in which Christian principles were the guidelines, they were influenced by Christian ethics.

Soon however, both Protestant and Catholic Missions realized that they could not change the structure of the society. The church's responsibility was to minister to the world. They began to direct their ministry more directly to the village people.[32] At the beginning there was little response to the evangelistic ministry in the villages. Furthermore, the missionaries were at a loss as to where to build permanent stations. The problem was that when a famine struck a region, or one tribe threatened another, or a succession of quarrels erupted, the village moved to another locality, leaving the mission station in a locality without villages.

The Protestant societies also recognized that the tribes considered the missionary colonies only another civil order in competition with the tribe. Therefore it was difficult to establish good relations with them. Furthermore, it was necessary to govern the colonies, and this required much time for civil administration and reduced the time available for evangelization. The greatest difficulty, however, was encountered by offering refuge to slaves who fled from the Arab traders. The traders considered them their property and reclaimed them. In some instances they attacked the station that gave refuge to slaves and, if they were not defeated, they seized whomever and whatever they could.

Although the missionary staff in East Africa was quite small, they had penetrated the most important domain of the Arab slave traders. The wealth of the Arabs in East Africa was based on slaves and ivory. The sultan needed slaves for his plantations at Zanzibar. Thus caravans traversed the country in search of elephant tusks and for slaves to carry them to the coast. They followed basically three main routes. The central route led from Bagamoyo to Tabora, an Arab post founded about 1830. At Tabora there was a fork in the route, one branch leading northward through Karagwe to Lake Victoria and the other leading westward to Ujiji on Lake Tanganyika. Here Livingstone became depressed by the Arabs' inhumane treatment of the village people. Beginning in 1856, the Arabs crossed the lake, went to the Lualaba River, and established large slave trading centers at Niangwe and Kasongo, from where they raided a large part of eastern Zaire.

The southern slave route led from Kilwa toward Lake Nyasa. From there it led westward to the Lunda kingdom and to Kasembe on the shore of Lake Mweru. The Ngoni tribe west of Lake Nyasa cooperated with the Arabs, raiding neighboring tribes and selling the people they enslaved to the Arabs. The southern route was used considerably around 1865, when Msiri established his Garanganze kingdom in Shaba, located in southeastern Zaire. At that time commerce moved from the east coast to the west coast, and vice versa, via Msiri's kingdom, until his death resulting from a skirmish with the Belgians in 1891.

The third slave route led from Mombasa past Mount Kilimanjaro to Lake Victoria. This route was not employed as frequently because the warlike Masai tribe, whom the traders feared, lived to the north of this route. This tribe kept much of Kenya free from the Arab slave raiders.

The slave-raiding caravans were sometimes as large as one thousand men. Slaves were purchased from chiefs or Arab traders in the interior, or villages were raided. The raids were most inhumane. The raiders surrounded the villages at night, fired a shot to warn the people to leave their huts, and then set the grass roofs afire. As the people fled their homes, they were taken captive or shot down as they attempted to flee. The loss of life was immense. Once captured, the slaves were treated brutally. As a result, only about one-fifth of them reached the destination to which they were sent.[33] Eventually the population was depleted and the entire prosperous region of the lakes had a population of only seventeen million.

Sir John Kirk, a medical doctor who accompanied Livingstone on his second voyage to Africa, became the British vice-consul at Zanzibar in 1868 and consul in 1873. He negotiated with the sultan for the suppression of slave trade on Zanzibar and the coast. The sultan, who cultivated the relationship with the British to provide security from rival Arab factions, was afraid of an European intervention in East Africa. He signed a treaty prohibiting the exportation of slaves from East Africa and closing all the slave markets in his domains. But the Arabs secretly marched the slaves northward along the coast. In 1876 he issued a further law prohibiting the exportation of slaves from his domains. But some traders refused to submit to the law. At Kilwa, they gathered an army of three thousand men to resist the enforcement of this law. John Kirk arrived in a British cruiser in time to prevent an uprising.[34] After the Suez Canal was opened in 1869, British naval vessels patrolled the coast; but the struggle against the slave trade was difficult.

The Arabs made an all-out effort to take over East Africa. Because Zanzibar was vulnerable to European intervention, the sultan gave the impression of cooperating with the Europeans to suppress the slave trade; but, together with his agents, he made every effort to take over East Africa.[35] The Arab agents controlled the country from the coast to Ujiji. There Tippu-Tib and Rumaliza had established their headquarters from which they controlled the country around the lakes and westward into the Manyema district and eastern Zaire. The Arab activities and their threats, which disturbed the area, made mission work almost impossible. The London Missionary Society abandoned its station at Ujiji in 1884. Tippu-Tib indicated to Hore of the London Society that he had a plan to put things right in the area around the lake.[36] Some missionaries of the London Society were convinced that the Arabs had received orders from the sultan to bring East Africa under their domination. John Kirk, the British consul, wanted the London Society to continue its ministry at Ujiji in order to serve as a buffer for Arab influence and to observe Arab activities.[37]

Tippu-Tib was a double-dealer. He offered his services to the British to find Emin Pasha, an Austrian agent of the Africa International Association in northeastern Zaire, who had signaled for help. At the same time he threatened a religious war, stating that the Arabs had fifty thousand guns in their possession and would drive the Europeans out of Zaire. Henry M. Stanley fully realized the threat Tippu-Tib posed and, to appease him, Stanley employed him as the agent of the Africa International Association at Kisangani on the Zaire River in 1887.

The political situation in East Africa was aggravated by the Egyptians who threatened Uganda and the lake region. The king of Buganda and the sultan of Zanzibar both looked for British aid to maintain their independence. Furthermore, Sultan Barghash knew he did not possess the resources to develop East Africa and invited Sir William Mackinnon, the founder of the Imperial British East Africa Company, to develop the coast. However, the two could not agree on the terms. While Sultan Barghash was negotiating with the British, Rumaliza, Tippu-Tib, and other Arab agents began tactics to bring the region under their jurisdiction and attacked several European posts.

There were several Germans among the first European explorers and missionaries in East Africa. The German government was interested in East Africa. As a result of the Arab activities, the Germans established several posts with the intention of maintaining law and order and protecting their citizens and their interests in the region. The increase of foreign power in the region was a menace to Arab jurisdiction, and they revolted under Bushiri Un Salim in 1888. Several German officials were killed. The revolt spread throughout the lake region and to the eastern part of Zaire. The Arabs now made an all-out effort to bring East Africa and Zaire under their control. Their movement as far as Kisangani in Zaire is noted in our discussion of that country.

The London Missionary Society maintained its ministry at Urambo east of Ujiji, at Niamkolo, and at Twambo at the southern extremity of Lake Tanganyika. The rebellion did not affect this area. But Arthur Brooks, one of the missionaries who had served since 1882, was journeying to the coast when the rebellion erupted and he was killed by the Arabs.

The White Fathers lived on their terrains, separated from the affairs of the surrounding territory. They did not realize the gravity of the political situation. Fearing the activities of the Arab agent, Rumaliza, many people fled to their missionary colonies for refuge, which increased the mission's responsibilities. In 1886, Father Charbonnier indicated that the movements of the Arabs were threatening. Rumaliza conquered all the tribes north of Lake Tanganyika. He then attacked Rwanda. The White Fathers abandoned the Masansa station. In 1887 they were compelled to leave Ufige and Uvira and go to Kibanga. In December Kibanga was attacked and the White Fathers were arrested. Rumaliza spared their lives, but requested an enormous sum for their release. The Kipalapala station on the route to Tanganyika and Uganda was evacuated. Kalunda, one of Tippu-Tib's subordinates, established himself at the Ulungu station.

The rebellion continued until Germany sent Hermann Wissmann with a military force in 1891. Having established order, the German government declared East Africa (now Tanzania) a German protectorate and sent von Soden to be its governor.

During the Arab rebellion, the Church Missionary Society withdrew the missionary families from the region, but the men stayed to continue the ministry. All communications were interrupted. The reinforcements were retained at Frere Town by order of the British Consul at Zanzibar. When order was reestablished, the Church Missionary Society continued its ministry under German jurisdiction.

THE ESTABLISHMENT OF CHRISTIANITY

Tanzania

The German East Africa Company took responsibility for the development and administration of the country. They approached the matter aggressively without due consideration for the local people's interests and culture. The native people did not appreciate the efforts to develop and westernize their country. They resented the hut tax and the forced labor that was imposed. The coming of settlers caused the greatest aggravation, since settlers took possession of land that belonged to the tribes. For the local people, alienation of land passed on from the ancestors for centuries was unknown. They wanted to be independent and continue their way of life. Consequently several rebellions broke out. The most widespread and devastating one was the Maji-Maji rebellion of 1905-1907, which began on the southern highlands north of Lake Nyasa. The people were misled by the scorcerers, who claimed their fetishes would protect them against the enemy's bullets. This proved to be a fatal error. During the rebellion, the people harvested little. Finally, because of starvation and exhaustion, they were compelled to submit.

As a result of the rebellion, the German government took charge of Tanganyika. The colonial office adopted the policy of developing African agriculture, and land was not readily granted to Europeans. The German population in 1914 was approximately five thousand and was chiefly located on the northeastern highlands. The government distributed cotton seed and promised the people a standard price for their crops. It introduced sisal plants from South America. Through its assistance, 19 million rubber trees were planted.[38] By 1913 cotton, coffee, cacoa, sisal, and rubber production was strengthening the economy. The sisal export in 1912 amounted to 375,000 pounds sterling. A research station at Amani in the Usambara mountains assisted in the agricultural development.[39] The government also built railroads to connect the interior with the coastal cities. The Usambara railway, which was begun in 1896 and led to Karogwe, was completed in 1902; the line to Moshi was completed by 1911. The railway running through the central part of Tanganyika led from Dar es Salaam to Kigoma on Lake Tanganyika.[40]

The Berlin Conference (1884-1885) gave an immense impetus to colonialism and to European nationalism. This also influenced the ministry of the missionary societies. In the past the societies had established ministries wherever they felt called. Missionaries of one nationality served with a society of another nationality. Many Swiss and German missionaries had served with English missionary societies. This freedom, cooperation, and Christian fellowship was affected by the spirit of nationalism that prevailed in the countries. The Church Missionary Society ceded its Moshi station, which was south of the Kenya border, to the Leipzig Mission and concentrated its efforts in Kenya, while the London Missionary Society entrusted its Urambo station in Tanzania to the Moravian Mission and concentrated its efforts in Zambia. France exerted considerable pressure on the missionary societies in the countries it colonized. The London Missionary Society was compelled to appeal to the Paris Evangelical Missionary Society for help against French pressure in Madagascar, and the Presbyterians were obliged to do the same in Gabon. Although the Baptist Missionary Society had begun investigating the possibilities of a ministry along the Zaire River in 1877, the German occupation of Cameroon in 1884 influenced the society to cede its mission to the Basel Society. The Baptist Society intensified its work in Angola and Zaire, which was to be an international zone under the guidance of the Africa International Society, according to the 1876 Brussels meeting where the society was formed. From 1885 to 1914 the governments favored missionary societies of their own nation in the territories they governed.

Several German Lutheran societies established ministries in Tanzania. The death of J. L. Krapf in 1881 inspired the formation of the Society for an Evangelical Lutheran Mission in East Africa, which endeavored to bring the gospel to the Kamba people. The society opened stations at Jimba and Munga. This society later amalgamated with the Leipzig Society. The Berlin Evangelical Missionary Society, known as Berlin III, came to Dar es Salaam in

1887, where it ministered to Germans and native people.[41] From Dar es Salaam it extended its work northward into the Tanga region and then to the uplands of Usambara. In 1903 it ceded its mission in Dar es Salaam to the older Berlin Society and extended its ministry westward. In 1907 it entered Rwanda, west of Lake Victoria.

The Berlin Missionary Society (referred to as Berlin I) and the Moravian Mission entered Tanzania via the Lake Nyasa route and established ministries in the southern part of the country in 1891. They took the River Maka as their common border. The Berlin Society served east and northeast of the river, while the Moravians extended their work northwest of the river toward Lake Tanganyika. They began their activities among the Konde tribe and extended it eastward to the Kinge tribe.[42] The work developed rapidly under the direction of A. Merensky, a veteran missionary from South Africa, and by 1914 the mission was ministering at twenty-two stations, giving medical care, translating the Scriptures, and teaching the people.[43]

The Moravians followed the Rungwe River north to the Rungwe hills and, having received a welcome from chief Makapalile, they began their work near the chief's village. From there they extended their ministry to Utengula in chief Merere's region. They opened five stations in that area during the 1890s.[44] In 1898 the London Missionary Society ceded its station Urambo, which was south of Lake Victoria Nyanza and separated from its field, to the Moravians. The society concentrated its efforts on its work across the border in Zambia.[45] The Moravian work increased satisfactorily and by 1914 they were serving at fifteen stations. The Moravians served north of the Livingstonia Mission in Malawi and east of the London Missionary Society in Zambia, and the Berlin I mission served east of the Moravians. There was good cooperation and intimate relations among the societies. Unitedly they witnessed to the grace of God in an area that had been ravaged by slave trade a few years earlier.

During World War I the Free Church of Scotland came to assist the Moravians. This assistance continued till 1926. During World War II, the British Moravians assumed the responsibility for this field.

In 1885 the Church Missionary Society began a station at Moshi, the Chagga chief's village. When Britain and Germany drew up the boundary beteen Tanzania and Kenya, the Chagga tribe and the Moshi station were in the territory controlled by Germany. The Church Missionary Society ceded the Moshi station, located in the region of Mount Kilimanjaro, to the Leipzig society. The latter was the German society that was serving among the Kamba tribe. The Leipzig society rapidly developed an extensive ministry in the northern part of Tanzania among the Kamba, Chagga, and Masai tribes.[46] By 1911 the ministry was conducted at eleven stations at which medical care, education, and teacher training were offered. The Christian community grew rapidly. The society adopted the principles elaborated by Bruno Gutman in which the church organization was based on the Bantu social structure. The church was established and held its first synod in 1930.

The Benedictines were responsible for the vicariate of Dar es Salaam—a vicariate that comprised the southern part of Tanzania. The ministry was begun in 1888, but Arab and Islamic influences were quite prominent. During a rebellion in 1905 the vicar apostolic was killed and several stations were destroyed. The Benedictines, however, continued their ministry faithfully and rebuilt the work. They emphasized agriculture: planting rice, coffee, cacoa, bananas, and cotton, and raising cattle.

The Holy Ghost Fathers extended their field of service from Bagamoyo north to the Kenya border. Cardinal Lavigerie's presentation of the urgency to send missionaries to East Africa inspired the founding of several German Catholic organizations.[47] Two vicariates apostolic were created, and together they directed twenty-five centers in Tanzania by 1914.

After the Arabs had been subdued and order was restored in the Lake Tanganyika region, the Catholic missionaries resumed their activities. The White Fathers had begun mission work at Tabora and in Buganda in 1878. They assumed the responsibility for the evangelization of a large territory in Central Africa, which included the eastern part of Tanzania, Uganda, Rwanda, Burundi, eastern Zaire, and south into Zambia. Cardinal Lavigerie was the strategist behind the undertaking. Monsignor Livinhac was in charge of the ministry in eastern Tanzania and Uganda during the early years of their ministry.

After the founding of the Congo Free State in 1886, the Roman Catholic Church created the vicariate of the Upper Congo.[48] The missionaries moved south along Lake Tanganyika and also northeast of Lake Tanganyika into Rwanda and Burundi, opening many stations and establishing large educational enterprises. By 1913 four vicariates apostolic had been created in Tanzania.

The Africa Inland Mission came to Tanzania from its work in Kenya. The work was begun among the Kamba people, who were unresponsive. In 1901 C.E. Hurlburt began the ministry at Kijabe south of the Kikuyu station. The work in this area was more successful. The Tanzania work became the third largest of the Africa Inland Mission, being next to their efforts in Kenya and Zaire. In 1968 the society reported a church membership of 110,000 persons.

Christianity was spreading in Tanzania. By 1914 stations had been established at the more strategic places, the gospel was being proclaimed, and large numbers of children were attending the schools. The German government, together with the missions, set an example in providing education for well over one hundred thousand children in 1914.[49] World War I interrupted the work of missions before the churches in Tanzania had been prepared to care for their ministries. Most of the mission work had been eatablished after the Arab rebellion. The Allied occupation of Tanzania began in 1916. The removal of the German missionaries began in June 1916. It was a most trying experience for them. Women and children were sent to South Africa and were repatriated in 1919. The men were sent to camps in Mombasa, Tanga, and Egypt. The southwest region, in which the German Moravians were serving, was occupied by Belgian forces. The missionaries were transferred via Zaire to the south of France. From there they returned to Germany. The African Christians were shocked to observe that the white people, who had brought much scientific knowledge and the gospel to them, were at war with each other. The people in general realized the failure of the so-called Christian countries to live by Christian teachings and principles. The war was a set-back for Christianity. The Christians had to overcome the shock, rethink the Christian faith they had accepted, and then assume the responsibility to nurture the believers and proclaim the divine revelation that supersedes the failures of nations and churches.

Before their departure from Tanzania, the representatives of the Berlin I and the Moravian Missions wrote to Robert Laws of the Livingstonia Mission in Malawi asking the Livingstonia Mission to give some oversight to the Christian communities. However, eventually the Livingstonia Mission assumed oversight of the western region; the Blantyre Mission, of the central region; and the Universities Mission, of the coastal region. This partition of their church was regretted by the Berlin I Mission, especially because the confessional and ecclesiastical position of the Universities Mission, being that of the Anglican High Church, was quite different from theirs.

The American Lutherans of the Augustana Synod accepted responsibility for the stations of the Leipzig Mission in 1922. The work of the Bethel Mission in the southeast of Tanzania was taken over by the Church Missionary Society, while the Belgian Protestants gave oversight to the work in Rwanda.

The German Catholic missionaries and the Catholic communities suffered less because of the war than the Protestants did. However, all communities suffered in the general destruction and the economic depression caused by the war.

The Treaty of Versailles was a dictated, not a negotiated, settlement. Britain maintained control over Tanzania, while Belgium retained Rwanda and Burundi. To the missionaries' disappointment, they were not permitted to return to their churches. Consideration for their return was, however, given in 1924, and the return began with a few representatives in 1925. The financial crisis in Germany was a further cause that delayed the missionaries' return. In this time of need, other churches revealed their Christian concern and gave financial assistance to the German missionaries. For three years a Scottish friend defrayed the cost of Oskar Gemuseus's return.[50] The Bethel Mission supported itself in part through its printing works and carpentry shops.[51] By 1930 German missionaries were again serving in most of their former fields, although some fields were shared with the society that had given oversight to the churches in their absence.

A number of other societies established ministries in Tanzania after 1918. Eventually the Protestants and also the Catholics had representatives in all parts of the country. Seven Lutheran churches of Tanzania came into being in 1937, and all seven societies working in Tanzania have united in forming the Evangelical Lutheran Church in Tanzania with a membership of approximately five hundred thousand.

At the beginning of World War II, some of the German missionaries were permitted to continue their work under certain conditions. However, in October 1940 they were interned. Their responsibilities were shared by church leaders. The Tanzanian ministers were well able to give pastoral care to the congregations. They were less prepared to assume the teaching responsibilities in the colleges and some activities of the hospitals. It was difficult to continue the educational and medical ministries without outside financial assistance and additional qualified personnel. World Action sent relief, through the Augustana Society, to the churches that were no longer receiving outside financial assistance. The government tried to assure the continuation of educational and medical work. It assumed control of the largest hospitals and sent Indian doctors to several hospitals.[52] The Augustana Lutheran Society again came to the assistance of the work begun by the German societies. The Swedish Evangelical Mission shared in the ministry of the Berlin Mission's inland field, while the Augustana Mission continued to represent the field to the government.[53]

A number of societies have begun work in Tanzania recently. The Pentecostal Assemblies of Canada extended their ministry from Kenya to Tanzania when members of the Kenya Church migrated there and requested pastors and Christian leadership. Spiritual nurture was given from Kenya for some years until in 1955 a permanent ministry was established. A church of some five thousand members is served by sixty-seven pastors and twelve evangelists.

The Eastern Mennonite Board of Missions and Charities began its ministry in Tanzania in 1934. It emphasized evangelism, education, and medical work. The Tanzania Mennonite Church was greatly edified by the revival movement and its ministry has been encouraging. It has been independent since the 1950s. During the last decade it has rebuilt the Shirati Hospital and offers advanced medical services. The Leprosy Control Center has been moved to the hospital.

The Assemblies of God extended their ministry from Malawi to Tanzania in 1953 to nurture some of their members who migrated to Tanzania. The work was established on an indigenous basis. Workers are trained at two Bible schools. The church, however, has only approximately one thousand members.

The Southern Baptists began work in Tanzania in 1956. They have committed to this work a staff of fifty missionaries who are serving at seven centers. They are training personnel for the ministry at a Bible school and a seminary.

The numerical growth of the Christian communities in East Africa from 1914 to 1950 was phenomenal. The Lutheran churches of the German societies increased from 20,000 in 1914 to 150,000 in 1949. In the Anglican dioceses the African clergy outnumbered the European by four to one; in the Lutheran societies the proportion was three to one. In contrast the African priests in the Catholic orders who were obliged to take the vows of celibacy were one to five to the ordained European missionaries.[54]

The village evangelists or catechists were the base of the ecclesiastical organization of the Protestant churches. An evangelist or a pastor had the oversight of the ministry of a number of catechists. The members of this fellowship or unit comprised a congregation. The expansion of the Christian faith exceeded the training of pastors. Consequently, sometimes one pastor served several congregations and the believers did not receive the close pastoral shepherding they needed. Nevertheless, the credit for evangelizing multitudes in Africa south of the Sahara goes mostly to the dedicated African catechists, evangelists, and pastors.

Many people accepted the Christian faith with the expectation of finding satisfaction and fulfillment in it. The interpretation of the message was influenced by the people's cultural orientation and understanding, in which God met them. The Holy Spirit revealed the divine revelation to them and inspired them to share the message with relatives and friends. The Africans trusted the messengers of the gospel and gave them a hearing as they presented it.

God has used the testimony of Christians to reveal Himself. These testimonies cannot be replaced by organizations. A feature of the revival movement was the sincere love people had for their fellow-men. Often they were unknown to each other, but Christ's love motivated the Christians to be concerned for other people's needs, and this concern was a real witness to them. Tribal barriers simply disappeared, the Christians became members of one church, and they regarded other people in light of the value of human life. Sincere evangelistic efforts were put forth in addition to the spontaneous witness.

The revival inspired many activities in the Christian communities. Of special importance were the Bible study and prayer meet-

ings. The small group prayer meetings were especially meaningful
to the people. Through the Scripture Union meetings, many young
people were edified and received a deeper understanding of the
Scriptures and the Christian faith. Women's organizations reached
other women in the cities and villages and helped them in their
needs. The concern about the poverty of the neighbors inspired
Christian social action.

The Watch Tower movement of the Jehovah's Witnesses was the
earliest, independent, religious movement, separated from Protestant Christianity, to enter Tanzania. The movement was established in Malawi and Zambia and brought into the southwest of
Tanzania by Hanoc Sindano of the Mambwe tribe in 1919. Sindano
was influenced by the movement while he was working in
Rhodesia. The Watch Tower's proclamation against the powers
that be and against the established churches and its emphasis on
the individual's right to possess and spread the truth, appealed to
him and his friends. The British officials tried to suppress the
movement, but it continued to spread.

The African National Church had a more constructive answer to
the political and social problems of colonialism. It was founded by
Simon Kamkhati Mkandawire, a member of the Livingstonia
Church in Malawi, who had been suspended from fellowship because he took a second wife. He thought that polygamy must be
permitted in the church. Together with some friends who were in a
similar relationship with the church, he formed the Africa National
Church in 1928. They carefully prepared for the movement a
constitution and principles, which have guided it. The movement
proposes to uplift society as a whole and to attack the disunity in
society by Christianizing the total community.

In 1925 the Last Church of God and His Christ was founded by
Jordan Msumbwa and a group of men after they had been suspended from church membership for polygamy. This community
resembles the African National Church. Its stronghold is in southern Tanzania, in the Rungwe area.

The movement toward independence in northern Tanzania dif-
fers from that of southern Tanzania. This movement was connected with the movements in Uganda and Kenya. The leaders
were of the elite and in good standing in the churches. Tensions
arose when several church centers were transferred to another
society. As a result of this tension, the Dini ya Bapali group was

formed, and it separated from the church. Other African leaders felt they should continue to serve in the responsibilities they had assumed and resented the return or the coming of a missionary to assume a responsible function in the church. All too often, tensions have been caused because a person's qualifications were based on the amount of formal schooling he had received, without consideration being given for his practical education through experience or the spiritual gifts by which he was carrying out his ministry.

As years went by, missionaries in Tanzania and Kenya faced a new problem that placed them in an odd situation. Missionaries, trading companies, and government agents had fought for the abolition of the slave trade and for the Africans' welfare in general. But the European countries did not stop by liberating Eastern and Central Africa from the evils of the slave trade. They moved in as rulers of these territories. In doing so, they strove to develop and, to an extent, exploit these countries. Many government agents were not familiar with the African culture and frequently showed little respect for cultural patterns and forms of politeness. The Africans resented the way they were treated. Furthermore, the European settlers, who were increasing in number, were occupying more land. Thus the missionaries, who had been assisted by European agencies to fight for the Africans' welfare, found themselves in a position of defending the Africans' cause against these agencies. Missionaries were obliged to check overly ambitious government and trading-company agents and to defend the African cause regarding the occupation of land. In the position of pastors, they had to win the believers' confidence that they were brothers in Christ.

After a period of German, and later British, rule, Tanzania became an independent country in 1961 (Tanganyika, having been independent since 1961, joined with Zanzibar in 1964 to form the nation of Tanzania). At this time the elite of the country consisted mostly of people who had their training in church schools. They were pastors, teachers, civil servants of middle rank, and technicians in various fields. There were only a few lawyers, doctors, engineers, or economists.[55]

The political difficulties in Mozambique, Rwanda, Zaire, and Sudan during the last decade have brought many refugees to Tanzania. The number has been estimated at thirty-six thousand.

They were faced with starvation. The local churches, through the Christian Council of Tanzania, provided some sustenance for them, but the task exceeded their means to help. Overseas agencies such as Church World Service and the Lutheran World Federation came to the churches' assistance during the war and have assisted in the relief efforts after the war. The Christian Council of Tanzania has also provided a spiritual ministry among them, and a good number of them have accepted the Christian faith.

In 1936 the major Protestant churches formed the Tanganyika Christian Council, which later became the Christian Council of Tanzania. Through this council the churches coordinate the various ministries of the church, and the council gives direction to the work in the local churches. Ministries such as radio broadcasting and giving spiritual nurture to university students are directed by the council.

Since Vatican II, cordial relations have been established between the Roman Catholic and Protestant churches in East Africa. In Tanzania occasional prayer services and evangelistic meetings are conducted jointly.

Kenya

Through the cordial relations between the British consul at Zanzibar and the sultan, the former frequently functioned as adviser to the sultan. The British requested the sultan to suppress the slave trade but did not infringe on the sultan's government. The sultan realized the necessity to develop the domains he controlled and in 1876 requested the help of British capitalists to develop his country and open the interior to trade. The request was accepted by Sir William Mackinnon. But the negotiations between Mackinnon's agents and Sultan Braghash broke down in 1877.

After the British and German spheres of interest in East Africa had been arranged, with German dominance over the former Tanganyika and British influence over Kenya, the British East Africa Company Association was formed for the purpose of developing Kenya. William Mackinnon was chairman of the association, which received a royal charter in 1888 and became the Imperial British East Africa Company. Sultan Khalifa, an ineffective administrator, succeeded Braghash in 1888 and ruled until 1890. He was not respected by either his subjects or the consuls at Zanzibar.

Ali, Hamed, and Hamoud followed in rapid succession, and this frequent change caused some instability at Zanzibar.

When the Imperial British East Africa Company transferred its activities and authority in Kenya to the British government, the Arabs realized that both their political and religious influences were threatened. Consequently, they rebelled and made a last effort to control Kenya. The British suppressed the rebellion and began the establishment of Kenya.

Having assumed the responsibility for Kenya, the British began the economic development of the country. Cotton, sugar, rice, coffee, tea, sisal, maize, fruit, and wheat were soon grown. In order to terminate slave trade and slave labor, railways were considered essential to eliminate the caravans that employed many slaves. Railways would also reduce the cost of transporting products and make agriculture in the interior more profitable. However, the construction of railroads was quite difficult, especially through the Rift Valley. The British government undertook the construction of the railway largely because it wanted improved communications with Uganda.[56] The British imported Indian laborers for the project. Those who wanted to return home after completing their contract were given free passage back to India. Those who preferred to stay were permitted to do so. By 1898 thirteen thousand Indians were in Kenya. The railroad from Mombasa to Nairobi was completed in 1899. The British government placed steamers on Lake Victoria Nyanza before the railroad was completed. They provided transportation to the areas around the lake, especially to Uganda.

The railway to Uganda was an immense expense, paid by British taxpayers. After the railway was completed, it operated at a loss because of Kenya's sparse population, totaling only three million in 1936. Some British advocated settling white farmers. Agreements were made with the Masai and other tribes whereby some land was set aside for white settlers, who came from Europe and South Africa. The economy of the country was improved through these efforts, but in later years the native peoples resented the settlers. The white population had risen to about nine thousand by 1919 and the settlers occupied too much land. It became a serious problem, which the government was obliged to regulate.

In 1888 the Arabs threatened to attack the Church Missionary Society's work at Rabai Mpia and Kisuluntini because they had given refuge to slaves who had run away from the Arab plantations on the coast. G.A. Mackenzie of the Imperial British East Africa Company intervened and persuaded the Arabs to accept a ransom of 25 dollars for every slave who had escaped from their possession. Through this arrangement, 1,422 slaves were liberated and peace was maintained.

The installation of freed slaves in Frere Town was the beginning of a new period in East Africa. The slaves sought refuge on the mission stations, and this annoyed the Arabs. The stations were constantly in danger of being raided and burned to the ground by the Arabs, and station personnel were obliged to be on guard. Thus accepting slaves at a mission station caused certain problems and risks. However, it also offered opportunities and brought some satisfying results. In 1910 Archdeacon Binns was favorably impressed with the homes the people had built at Frere Town, the fact that the Christians brought their children to the services, and the depth of the prayers that were expressed by the Christians.[57]

As in West Africa, some of the freed slaves were among the first leaders in the church. One of these, W.F. Jones, was rescued from a slave vessel and taken to Bombay. He was baptized and received an education at the Church Missionary station at Nasik. In 1864 he and another ex-slave, Ishmael Semler, were sent to Mombasa to work with Rebmann. Both were ordained by Bishop Hannington in 1885. Jones accompanied Hannington on a journey to Uganda, during which Hannington was murdered just inside Uganda. Jones died in 1904. Semler devoted about fifty years to the Lord's work.[58]

The Imperial British East Africa Company was building a road to the interior. The road eventually led to Uganda. In 1888 the company invited the Church Missionary Society to establish mission posts along the route. In 1898 the company invited James Stewart of the Lovedale Institute of South Africa to open a station at Kikuyu, modeled after the Lovedale station, where training was offered for the various ministries in which the mission was serving. However, Stewart chose a site some two hundred miles inland and arranged for the station to be built there. He then returned to South Africa, and David Charters directed the work. The people, however, were unresponsive and the station was moved among the Kikuyu. The Blantyre Mission in Malawi sent personnel to develop the ministry. Consequently a model of the Lovedale and Blantyre missions was reproduced. The Church of Scotland assumed the responsibility for this work in 1900 and enlarged its ministry. An interracial church with Africans, Asians, and Europeans, called the Presbyterian Church of East Africa, has been established and has some twenty-eight thousand communicant members. The church trains personnel at two teacher-training colleges and the St. Paul's United Theological College at Limuru and offers services at three hospitals.

In 1899 the Church Missionary Society created the Mombasa diocese. Uganda became a diocese by itself. In the Mombasa diocese, the society's work among the Kikuyu tribe was opened at Kabete in 1900 and at Nairobi in 1906. In 1906 Kenya was made a province, and administrative centers were established at Fort Halls, Nyeri, and in Embu country. By opening this ministry, the Society could reach some five hundred thousand people. The work in the area between the railway and Mount Kenya was successful, and the society planted five stations between Fort Halls and Fort Embu.[59] The medical services of Dr. T. W. W. Crawford were appreciated by the people and they admitted him to their council of elders. By 1913 a Christian community had been gathered and a Kikuyu Conference was held.

The Holy Ghost Fathers, who were serving at Zanzibar and Bagamoyo, extended their ministry to Mombasa in 1891 and to Nairobi, the capital of the protectorate, towards the close of the century. In 1902 they began work on the plateau. In 1906 the Catholic Church created a prefecture for this area and a few years later a vicariate.

A delegation of the English organization, the St. Joseph's Society of Mill Hill, began a ministry in the western part of the country in 1895, and the church created the vicariate apostolic of the Upper Nile. In the region they found some Christians who had been converted through the ministry of the White Fathers in Uganda. A peoples' movement to Christianity soon began and large numbers came into the Catholic Church.[60]

In 1896 the Society of Friends from England began an industrial mission on the island of Pemba, north of Zanzibar. In 1901 the American Friends organized the Friends' Africa Industrial Mission and began a ministry at Kivirondo on the mainland. The work was mostly among the Lumbwa people[61] and had an industrial emphasis, which was quite successful. The work at the Kaimosi station developed rapidly. Before long, some forty thousand pupils were receiving instruction. They opened a teacher-training school, a Bible institute, a print shop, and a hospital. In 1957 they began the Kamusinga station where the efforts were basically devoted to the high school. The Kenya field became the Friends' largest mission endeavor. The Christian community, known as the East Africa Yearly Meeting, became an independent body in 1964. The membership of the community exceeds thirty thousand, and seventeen monthly and three quarterly meetings have been opened. The yearly meeting offers medical services, and its training program includes theological and agricultural training.

The Africa Inland Mission began its ministry in Kenya in 1875 under the direction of Peter Cameron Scott. Unfortunately, all but one of the party died shortly after arriving in Africa. Consequently the ministry did not progress during the first years. In 1904 a party of twenty-three persons arrived, and the society advanced to the interior. Stations were established among the Kamba and the Kikuyu. The society aimed to reach the Masai and open a chain of stations to Lake Chad. In realization of its goal, in 1907 the Society opened the Kilome station among the Masai people and the Kapropita station among the Tugen people. The Africa Inland Church became independent in 1943. It continued to expand its ministry, and by 1960 it was serving twenty-five stations. It developed large medical and educational programs in which people were trained for various professions and services. The large autonomous church supports its ministry. It trains its personnel at six Bible schools and the Scott Theological College. The church has a large radio ministry that transmits more than one hundred programs a month over the government radio station, the Voice of Kenya. Timothy Kimau has served as radio pastor.

The Church of God commenced work in Kenya in 1919 in a region where the sorcerers were keeping the people under their control. The proclamation of the gospel, the religious instruction, and the medical services the society offered have greatly changed the life of the people. The sorcerers' power has been broken. Among the services the society offered were the high school for girls, the Bible school, the hospital, the print shop, and the library at Kima, and the teacher-training school and the Nora Hunter Memorial Hospital at Mwikila. The society has engaged in education. One of its missionaries, Calvin Brallier, was appointed educational supervisor by the government. As a result of the ministry of the Church of God, a church has been established in which national workers conduct services at several hundred places.

The Pentecostal Assemblies of Canada began their ministry in Kenya in 1921. In the late 1940s work was begun at Nairobi. Work in Kenya has become their largest mission endeavor. Andrea Waudi, the first Kenyan pastor of the church, has served faithfully for many years. The church membership is over one hundred thousand and is growing rapidly. Many new places of worship are opened annually. The leaders of these places receive training through Theological Education by Extension. The church offers pastoral training at the Pentecostal Bible College at the Nyang'ori station. The Evangel Press and the Evangel Publishing House supply much Christian literature for Kenya, Tanzania, Uganda, and Zambia.

In 1909 the Methodist Church was prospecting for a field of service. They were advised to establish a ministry in the Meru district, northeast of Mount Kenya. The district was north of the Embu people.

A number of other Protestant societies have begun work in Kenya in recent years. The Southern Baptists commenced their work in 1956. They have a large staff in the area and the church is developing. The Eastern Mennonite Board of Missions and Charities came to Kenya from Tanzania in 1964. The response to its work in Nairobi has been favorable. The revival, which has greatly edified the churches, has also been a great blessing to their church.

The Protestant societies met in conferences in 1908, 1909, and 1913 to make comity arrangements so that their work would be done most efficiently and harmoniously. The representatives of the societies who met in 1909 recommended the formation of a united church for Kenya, but their constituencies did not accept the proposal. However, in 1918 the Church Missionary Society, the Church of Scotland Mission, the Methodist Missionary Society, and the Africa Inland Mission constituted the Kenya Missionary Alliance.[62] Six years later, in 1924, they formed the Kenya Missionary Council. As more and more churches became autonomous, the Kenya Christian Council was formed in which churches and missions are represented.

The Anglican Church of the Province of East Africa, the Evangelical Lutheran Church of Tanzania, the Methodist Church of Kenya, the Moravian Province of Tanzania, and the Presbyterian Church of East Africa have held some meetings concerning church union.

The East Africa Revival, which began in 1927 and spread to other parts of Africa, has greatly affected and edified the churches. It came to the Nairobi area in the latter 1940s and is still inspiring the churches. In 1937 the first envoys of the revival movement of Ruanda visited Kenya. The team ministered to the Christians around Kabete for several days. A small group of Christians, including an Anglican clergyman, experienced a deep sense of salvation. In 1938 a second revival team from Rwanda held services at Pumwani, a Church Missionary Society station in Nairobi. A number of Christians, including several Anglican clergymen and prominent laymen, were converted. Through the brief preaching tour the revival was begun in Kenya.

From 1937 to 1945, the Revival Fellowship was opposed by the established churches. Its members were not permitted to participate in church services. But after World War II the Revival Fellowship developed rapidly in Kenya and won many members in the Anglican, Presbyterian, and Methodist churches. As a result of its positive, evangelistic influence, it won the confidence of the churches. A division arose in the fellowship when some members said they had received the gift of speaking in tongues but the Revival Fellowship rejected the doctrine of speaking in tongues.

Vast revival conventions of several days' duration were organized in and outside of Kenya. They have been a source of spiritual inspiration for thousands of Christians. Revived churches reinterpreted their faith and gave authentic expression in theological understanding and in living relationships. Salvation was interpreted as the continual transforming work of Jesus Christ. Repentance involved public confession and restoration of strained relationships. The revival expressed itself in a sincere concern for the salvation of fellow-men. The believers witnessed in their daily life and went to contact those who were not in fellowship with Christ and His church. The Christians also became concerned about the social and economic problems of the people.

The members of the Revival Fellowship have remained within the churches. They have no officials and no salaried workers, and no headquarters and no budgets. Their large ministry is carried on by dedicated servants. They finance the conventions, travel inside and outside of Kenya, and help the needy with freewill gifts from the members. These gifts flow through the "Lord's Bag." They and the churches would like for them to remain a fellowship rather than become an organization within the churches.

In 1908 Pope Pius X instituted a significant reform for the Roman Catholic missionary endeavor by removing the older mission fields from the jurisdiction of the Propaganda, the Roman Catholic agency for the propagation of the gospel. Consequently, the staff was able to devote more time to develop missionary activities.[63] The missionary staff in Africa was greatly enlarged. Many orders joined those already in the countries, and new vicariates were created until East Africa was divided into relatively small areas of service.

The Holy Ghost Fathers opened the Bura station in 1891 and expanded westward to Limure by 1899. In 1913 they began the Kabaa station. By 1914 a number of stations had been opened among the Kikuyu tribe. The Consolata Fathers, from Turin in Italy, began a ministry in the Meru district in 1911 and in the Embu district in 1922. The Mill Hill Fathers have extended their ministry in eastern Uganda to include western Kenya.

A seminary was opened at Tuso in 1914. The training of an African clergy was emphasized during this time. In 1927 the first Africans, James Camisassa and Thomas Kemango, were ordained to the Catholic priesthood in Kenya. In 1939 St. Paul's Minor Seminary was opened in Nyeri.[64]

The ministry of the missions and churches in Kenya was not disturbed by the war, as was the ministry in Tanzania, but was able to pass through continuous progress and growth. The growth from 1914 to 1950 was phenomenal. After the initial period of preparation, large crowds came for Christian instruction and asked for baptism. A special desire for education was expressed. Thousands of children came to the Christian schools, received religious instruction, and became church members. The village catechists played a very significant role in offering elementary instruction and in proclaiming the gospel throughout the country.

Christian missions have contributed immensely to the development of education in many countries in Africa. Informal education in traditional African society existed before the coming of Christian missions, but formal education in a modern sense owes its existence in Kenya to these missions. Although the Kenya government has assumed the responsibility for the schools, it has invited the participation of the churches in Christian education. The reference to this matter in the Education Act of 1968 indicates that the Kenya government considers it an important factor. The act and regulations assure the place of religion in the schools. The development of curriculum and the cooperation among churches in religious education has been stressed.

In recent years the separatist movement has been very strong in Kenya. The causes for the formation of these groups have been basically the desire for leadership, racial and tribal tensions, and the revival movements. The African lay movement began in Rwanda in 1927 and spread to central Kenya by 1937. Some groups were no longer comfortable in their churches, and the churches were not comfortable with their presence. Consequently separations occurred. Again, some movements were basically political and nationalistic. Since independence in 1963, these groups have been quite vocal. Before independence they felt there could be no compromise on human rights and justice. Having attained independence, they continue to press these issues. In some cases it would be more beneficial to be less vocal and more helpful to remedy suffering.

The nationalistic churches began in the 1920s and 1930s because some people resented the government's type of education and the proscription of female circumcision and polygamy, and were anxious about the Europeans' appropriation of large tracts of land. The first and largest of these churches, the African Independent Pentecostal Church, was founded in 1929. Out of the same general movement emerged the African Greek Orthodox Church, or the Orthodox Church of Kenya, which is a part of the Greek Patriarchate of Alexandria. A number of smaller churches have separated from these churches; two of them are the National Independent Church of Africa and the Independent African Orthodox Church.[65]

The Africa Christian Church and Schools is one of the secessionist churches. It seceded from the Africa Inland Mission in 1947 over educational policies. It is a member of the Kenya Christian Council and has sponsored students at the St. Paul's Theological College.

Revival-Pentecostal Churches arose out of the revival movement. The Friends of the Holy Spirit, or Roho Churches, were formed chiefly by the Anglican Christians at Fort Hall in the 1940s. A member of the Presbyterian Church formed the Apostolic Faith of Africa in the early 1960s. The Holy Church of the Evangelistic Apostles Faith is the result of the work of a missionary of the Apostolic Faith Mission of South Africa. The ministry of the Pentecostal Assemblies of God and the Finnish and Norwegian Pentecostal Missions has given the Pentecostal movement an inspiration, especially among Christian students. A recently formed church, which has links with the Apostolic Faith of Africa, is the Disciples of Christ in Africa.

The Spirit churches of Kenya trace their origin to the Kikuyu colonial experience. The largest of these is the Holy Ghost Church of Kenya; others are the Christian Holy Ghost Church of East Africa, the Kenya Foundation of the Prophets Church, and the African Mission of the Holy Ghost Church.

The separatist churches could be a vital force for renewal, bringing all peoples of Africa into the fellowship of the church, if they could only overcome the desire for prestige and would work together. The desire for leadership causes them to divide into many small groups whereby their witness is marred. Generally, it is not theological or liturgical differences that are the cause of the division, but rather personal relationships. However, Bible reading and Bible study are emphasized by these churches; and the worship services, relevant to the culture, are well attended.

Uganda

King Mutesa died in 1884 and his son Mwanga was elected by the members of the court to succeed him to the throne. Mwanga had received instruction from Mackay. He was the first Buganda king who did not make vast human sacrifices to Lubare, the ancestor spirit, upon accession to power. The Protestant missionaries hoped his rule would provide favorable conditions for the proclamation of the gospel. But Mwanga was in a difficult political situation and suspiciously watched the moves made by foreign countries. The Arabs had a negative influence on Mwanga. They wanted to control East Africa and opposed the missionaries in their activities. Mwanga was confused as to what to believe and became disturbed by the circumstances.

Mwanga suspected his people, especially those who were in

contact with foreigners. Therefore, when the Christians disapproved of the immorality of his court, he began to persecute them. He seized three Christian lads, mutilated them, and burned them to death. They were the first Baganda martyrs; they died on January 30, 1885, because of their loyalty to the Christian faith. In 1882, the Catholic White Fathers had withdrawn to the southern side of Lake Victoria. But Mackay, who had gained the respect of the people, continued his ministry. Together with Ashe, he prepared Christian literature, which included the translation of the Gospel according to Matthew.

The situation in Buganda became more confused and led to sad events in 1885 and 1886. The Baganda tradition maintained that it would be conquered by people approaching from the east, to the north of Lake Victoria. The newly appointed bishop of Eastern Equatorial Africa, James Hannington, took this road on his way to Uganda. He and his men were seized by the Usoga chief and all but four, who escaped, were put to death.[66]

In May 1866, Mwanga began to persecute the Christians because they refused to participate in some of the activities of his court. He considered this a breach of loyalty. Thus, like the early Christians who were martyred because they refused to worship the Roman gods, the Christians of Buganda were persecuted and some two hundred became martyrs. They gave heroic testimony to the grace of God. When Kidza, a member of the church council, was threatened with death, he firmly confessed his faith. He was clubbed and thrown into the flames. "Wakulaga Nua was burned alive, and died exhorting his executioners to believe in Jesus Christ."[67] The blood of the martyrs was the seed of the church in Buganda, and many people asked for baptism. As a result of the persecution, some of the Christians dispersed in the country, and people in the surrounding areas accepted the Christian faith.

Mackay realized that his presence at the capital increased Mwanga's suspicion against the Christians and brought persecution to them. He arranged with Mwanga that Cyril Gordon would take his place.[68] He left the capital in 1887 and went to the southern shore of Lake Victoria where he continued his ministry for three more years. He died at Usambiro in 1890.

Mwanga tried to free himself of Muslims and Christians and return to Lubareism. His plan failed. The opposition united to depose Mwanga and place his brother Kiwewa in authority.

Mwanga fled to the south of Lake Victoria. The Arabs readily gained control over Kiwewa and the Christians were forced to leave the capital. When Kiwewa refused to submit to the Arab wishes, they deposed him and placed his brother Kalema in charge. The Christian chiefs united, joined with Mwanga's party, drove the Arabs from the capital, and restored Mwanga to power. The Christian chief, Apolo Kagwa, who defeated the Arabs, became prime minister, Thus after years of suffering the Christians regained freedom of worship in 1889.[69] However, Kalema and the Arabs regrouped their forces and drove Mwanga and the Christians from the capital. But assisted by the Catholics and members of the British East Africa Company, Mwanga soon regained the capital. The Arab party withdrew to Bunyoro and attacked again. But they were defeated. The Imperial British East Africa Company helped to restore order to the country.

At the Heligoland Treaty of 1890, Germany recognized British influence in Uganda. Britain maintained its presence in Uganda through the Imperial British East Africa Company. In 1894 the company withdrew from Uganda and the British government declared Uganda a British protectorate. The Imperial British East Africa Company maintained order until the British Foreign Office took charge in 1895.

The Christians brought the gospel to many parts of Uganda and the missionaries came to help establish the work that had been begun. In the 1880s the Christian faith was disseminated by the Christians who fled from Mwanga's persecutions. After the Arabs seized power under Kalema in 1888, the Christians fled to the border regions of the country and organized the opposition in which the Christians gave leadership. The success of the Christians against the Muslims in 1889 brought the Christian leaders into political power and gave the church an important recognition in the country. This political situation spread the knowledge of the Christian faith and brought freedom of religion. Christianity spread and congregations were formed through the zeal and devotion of the Christians.

Alfred R. Tucker was appointed bishop to Uganda in 1890 and served until 1911. He came to Uganda after the period of persecution and civil war when the people greatly desired peace in the country. During his service a spiritual revival began and spread to many parts of the country, bringing new congregations into being.

Tucker wrote of the wonderful work of grace through which self-administering, reproducing churches were coming into existence.[70] In 1897 Tucker set forth a plan for the Native Anglican Church in which national and foreigner would serve according to the gifts he or she had received. He succeeded in implementing only a part of his plan, but he made a positive beginning. After the persecution the church could account for only about two hundred members. When Tucker died, its membership had risen to sixty-five thousand.

George Lawrence Pilkington was one of the missionaries who served from 1890 to 1897, while the church was being established and contributed significantly to the revival and the expansion of the church. An ardent evangelist, he mastered the language and devoted himself to translate the Bible into Luganda, the language of the Baganda people. The New Testament was completed in 1892. Portions of the Old Testament, hymns, and Bible stories were also printed. The Scriptures were widely read by the people, bringing the Christian faith into villages and hamlets. A.B. Fisher observed the people's interest in the Scriptures and arranged for Bible-reading sessions in which the catechists instructed the people in the Scriptures. He was serving the Singo tribe. Pilkington adopted this method and called the church to the missionary task. Eighty-five evangelists answered his call and entered this service. Others followed later.[71] By 1894 Bible-reading sessions and services were held at two hundred places. The proclamation of the gospel spread rapidly. Many people accepted the Christian faith and asked for instruction and baptism. After having been instructed by the catechists, some came to present themselves as baptismal candidates.

The evangelistic zeal with which the early Christians in Buganda were inspired is remarkable. Space does not permit the mention of the ministry of the many faithful servants who have carried the gospel to the people under many hardships. Henry Wright Duta, one of the first clergymen in Uganda, was baptized in 1882 and suffered under Mwanga's persecution. He was one of the first deacons and assisted Pilkington in Scripture translation and in Bible reading. He was ordained in 1893 and served until 1913.[72]

In 1893 the Protestant evangelists went to Busoga on the eastern border of Uganda, and in 1894 the Church Missionary Society opened two stations. The expansion of Christianity was very rapid.

In 1898 the Baganda evangelists went to the Bunyoro and Ankole kingdoms or chieftainships, which were a part of Uganda.[73] The movement spread to the Toro kingdom in the extreme west of Uganda. Kasagama, the chief of Toro, requested teachers for his people. Fifteen teachers were sent in 1896. They established the Christian ministry as far as Mboga, near the Zaire border.[74]

Apolo Kivebulaya was one of the evangelists who went to serve in Mboga. The Batalele mutineers crossed the border from Zaire and destroyed Fort Katwe, burned the Mboga chapel, and devastated the countryside. Apolo Kivebulaya served faithfully and rebuilt the work. His concern for the people motivated him to visit the Batwa tribe, or pygmies, in the equatorial forest of eastern Zaire. Finally he went to minister to them and became the apostle of these shy but dangerous, little people and came to be known as "Apolo of the Pygmy Forest."[75]

When the Sudan Mission was going to commence its work, it appealed to the Buganda church for help. Four of the Baganda clergy offered to go. The man chosen was Yosuwa Kiwavu, a senior pastor ordained in 1899, who had served with exemplary devotion for fifteen years in Busoga. In all, a party of twelve was formed, including five teachers and two wives.[76]

The growth of the churches in Uganda was extraordinary. The government census for Buganda in 1911 indicated a total population of 660,000, of whom 127,000 had registered as Protestants.[77] The ministry in the other kingdoms of Uganda also made rapid progress. The work that was begun in Toro in 1896 counted 9,000 Christians by 1914.[78] The ministry made similar progress in the Ankole kingdom to the south and the Ungoro to the north. The church workers were encouraged by the growth of the church and the possibility for outreach which the witnessing church promised.

The Catholics went through experiences similar to those of the Protestants during the Arabs' bid for power. Father Lourdel advised and assisted Mwanga in regaining power. Therefore, after Mwanga's success, Lourdel became Mwanga's European advisor. Thus the Catholics became the favored party under Mwanga's regime. The chiefs who had no religious preference chose the religion of the king. The Catholic community grew rapidly.

The ministry of the Catholic White Fathers in Uganda was influenced by the peoples' movement and the Bible reading sessions in the Protestant church. When Pilkington began the Bible-reading sessions, the Catholic priests were displeased and described him as a "visionary reverend." But before long they realized that the people were instructing themselves and were zealous for the gospel.[79] The number of the catechumens surpassed their ability to instruct them.

Until 1891 the Catholics had only opened the mission station at Rubaga, the capital of Buganda. From 1891 to 1894 they opened four more stations in Buganda, but none in the other kingdoms. In 1894 the part of former Nyanza vicariate in the British zone was divided. The White Fathers retained the area west of Kampala as the vicariate of North Nyanza, and the Society of St. Joseph from Mill Hill in England (also called the Mill Hill Fathers) took the eastern part as the vicariate of the Upper Nile. In 1902 Franciscan nuns from Mill Hill came to aid them. The Catholics began work in the Toro kingdom in 1894, in the Bunyoro kingdom in 1900, and in the Ankole kingdom in 1902.

After the war with the Arabs, the Catholics sent many priests and nuns to Uganda; the staff numbered 159 priests and lay brothers and 41 nuns before 1914. In the early years the Catholic missions relied less on native workers than the Protestants did. Their first men were ordained after several decades of ministry. In 1914 the Roman Catholic schools had enrolled less than one-third as many pupils as the Protestants. Later they changed their policy, however, and trained many catechists, recruited black sisters, and began training men for the priesthood. Children reared as Christians were considered members of the Christian community. The Christian family was emphasized. In 1914 the Uganda mission of the White Fathers was the strongest of the Catholic missions in sub-Saharan Africa.[80]

The Africa Inland Mission expanded its ministry from Kenya to Uganda. The Church Missionary Society turned its Nasa station in the Usukuna province over to them in 1909. It further opened the Nera and Busia stations in the Usukuma province in 1910 and 1913 respectively. With these stations as bases, it established a ministry in the surrounding area. The Africa Inland Mission proposed to occupy the territory toward Lake Chad. It proceeded northwest and opened the Mahagi station in Zaire in 1912, and the Dunge station on the Upper Uele River in 1913. From there it continued to expand to the northwest, occupying large areas unreached by Christian missions.

The Buganda church did not maintain its vitality and evangelistic zeal. The desire for the Scriptures and the zeal to proclaim the gospel, which animated the Christians from 1890 to 1900, gradually became less evident. The Christians became more interested in remaining at the posts and assuming administrative and office duties than evangelizing unreached areas. The Church Missionary Society was obliged to assign missionaries of evangelism to strengthen this ministry.

Bible reading sessions diffused the gospel message throughout Uganda and brought thousands of people into the churches. These Bible study sessions became village schools headed by catechists. However, as the standard of education improved and schools were perfected through the expenditure of funds from the government, the village schools were neglected and discredited. The parents lost confidence in the village schools. This situation affected the Christian life in the villages, where the catechist was the leader.[81] Furthermore, the government-subsidized schools had a special relationship to the Ministry of Education to which the teachers felt more responsible than they did to the church that had given them their education and had accepted them in its services. They no longer wanted to submit to the supervision of the pastors of the parish but wanted to form an administration for the educational work. They showed little interest in assuming responsibilities in the ministries of the church. The schools that were subsidized by the government became separate entities and were not integrated in the life of the church. As early as 1905, the leaders of the church decided to conduct special meetings to edify the church.

The Buganda church was blessed with a revival at the time the second-generation Christians were losing their first love. About 1935 a revival spread through the churches in Uganda. A teacher of the church, Blasio Kigozi, was sent to Rwanda and became burdened because of the lack of spiritual power in the church. He withdrew from his activities for a spiritual retreat and during one week devoted himself to prayer and meditation. The Lord gave him a special blessing. He returned to his work in the power of the Spirit.[82] His testimony led other people to find the same joy, and a revival began in Rwanda. It spread to the Ankole region and eventually throughout Uganda. From Uganda the revival also spread to several regions in Kenya and Tanzania.

The revival brought new interest into the church. The church rediscovered the inspiration of the Christian life with an African expression. Many Christians continued to meet in small groups for fellowship. The lay people—farmers, civil agents, teachers—invited people to their homes to worship God. The lay people assumed the responsibilities for the work of the church. A real sense of social concern was expressed by the church.[83]

The revival movement has greatly edified the churches and inspired significant church growth. Through the revival there was a remarkable recovery of the indigenous structures of the church, in which Christian groups formed around a leader and these groups served as the foundation of the church. The sense of unity and of sharing each others' needs was strong, and this provided a sense of belonging, of being accepted, and of security. This relationship has drawn people to the fellowships and inspired them to witness to others. An unusual feature of this movement is that it has continued as a movement within the churches in several countries without becoming a separate organization.

An outstanding characteristic of the movement is the members' sense of responsibility to proclaim the gospel. Both the clergy and the laity make special efforts, often at their own expense, to proclaim the message. Evangelistic rallies are organized, financed, and conducted by the revival fellowships. These fellowships minister to university students and the youth in the churches. They have arranged for boys' brigades in order to guide them to faith in Christ and a positive relationship with their fellow-men at an early age. The boys' brigade is supplementing the teaching ministry of the churches. This ministry is further reinforced by the Scripture Union.

Members of the Mothers' Union and the Christian Rural Service express a Christian concern for the everyday needs of the neighbors. Christian Rural Service knows no religious or tribal barriers. Thus the movement expresses itself in concerns for the spiritual, social, and physical welfare of other people.

Uganda became an independent nation in 1962. In recent years the Muslim political leader with a military dictatorship, has not been sympathetic to the churches. The churches have been obliged to give expression of their activities and opinions cautiously. But even when they have done so, they have been persecuted. The bishop of the Anglican Church and other church leaders have been executed. Others have fled the country. Nevertheless, the churches are faithfully continuing their ministry. The Christian community is a majority in the country and is exerting a positive influence in the affairs of the country.

THE EXPANSION OF CHRISTIANITY

Rwanda

Rwanda, a small country between Uganda and Zaire, was formerly a part of German East Africa. In 1919 it became a Belgian trusteeship, together with Burundi, until it became independent in 1962. This small territory is one of the most densely populated areas in Africa south of the Sahara. In 1967 its population was placed at 3,306,000. The population is largely Hutu, but the Tutsi have been in power for several centuries. Since 1959 there have been several wars between the two tribes, with a heavy loss of life to both. Many people have fled to neighboring countries. The history of Rwanda has been very closely related politically to that of Burundi. Some churches administer their work in both countries as one unit.

The White Fathers of the Roman Catholic Church began their work around Lake Victoria Nyanza in Uganda and Tanzania in 1878. From this base they extended their ministry to other countries in Central Africa. They made several abortive attempts to establish a ministry in Rwanda and Burundi in 1879-1881, 1884, and 1891. The people were unfriendly and two Fathers were killed in Rumonge during their first attempt to establish work. However, in 1896 they succeeded in beginning their work at Muyaga. When they were accepted in the country, they proceeded to establish their ministry and began six stations from 1896 to 1912. Rwanda and Burundi became one of the most responsive fields of the White Fathers' work.

The Belgian government and the Catholic Missions cooperated closely in the educational and medical services. The missions assumed the responsibility of offering the services, and the government fully financed the programs. This arrangement brought many children to the Catholic schools and into the Roman Catholic Church, which reported a Christian community of 909,351 in 1966.[84]

The Protestant missions were rather late in undertaking intensive missionary activities in this region. Some Bible readers of the Church Missionary Society found their way to the Toto kingdom in the western part of Uganda in 1896 and to the Ankole kingdom in 1898. Apolo Kivebulaya became the apostle to the Batwe people in Zaire.[85] But the Anglican Mission in Rwanda was not begun until 1926. The blessing that came to the church through the experience Blasio Kogozi had in 1935 has been noted in relation to the church in Uganda. This same blessing came to others and brought about a large-scale response in Rwanda. From Rwanda the revival spread into the Ankole area and in time it came to Kampala. A strong, indigenous church was established on this response in Rwanda. The church has continued to grow and now has some ninety thousand members. The ministry has been extended to Burundi.

The Seventh-Day Adventists have a large and growing work in Rwanda. Teachers are being trained at their Gitwe station. A hospital at Ngoma ministers to the medical needs of the people. Their church membership stands at approximately sixty thousand.[86]

The Protestant Mission of Belgium opened three stations in the early 1920s. The missionaries worked in cooperation with the Evangelical Presbyterian Church of Rwanda, which became autonomous in 1959.

The Pentecostal Churches came to Rwanda in the 1930s and have established a small church. A Plymouth Brethren couple began work in Rwanda in 1961.

The Rwanda and Burundi Churches have experienced periods of revival and war and persecution. The revival began in the early period of the church's history and contributed to the establishment of a vital church that was concerned about the evangelization of the country. The witness of the Christians was very spontaneous. They openly confessed their failures in the church services, found forgiveness and, with renewed joy, went to tell others of the grace they had found. As they told their relatives and friends about the Christian faith, the Holy Spirit used their testimonies to reveal salvation through faith in Christ to them. Throughout the history of the Christian church, God has used the testimony of believers to reveal Himself to unbelievers.

The Christians made sincere efforts to proclaim the gospel and also to help people in physical need. Women's meetings, boys' leagues, Scripture Union, and other activities expressed Christian fellowship and ministered to the people.

After a period of most significant edification and growth, the revival spirit abated. Secularism had a certain influence on the Christians. Then came the concern for independence and the anxiety in each tribe to attain power. Political ambitions led to rivalry and finally to tribal wars and bloodshed. In recent years the spirit of revival has returned to Rwanda, and there is renewed church growth. The political situation in Burundi has been unstable, and many Burundi refugees have fled to neighboring countries, including Rwanda.

Burundi

Burundi is a small, mountainous, East African country, situated between Uganda and Zaire. It is populated mainly by the Tutsi and Hutu tribes. Its relatively dense population was estimated at 3,340,000 in 1967 compared to approximately 4,000,000 for Malawi or Zambia. It was a part of German East Africa until World War I. In 1919 it was mandated to Belgium, and in 1962 it became an independent country.

The first Protestant missionaries to undertake missionary activities in Burundi were from the Neukirchner Missionsgesellschaft in Germany. They came in 1911 and were forced to leave in 1916 when the Allied forces took German East Africa. Unfortunately, no missionary agency came to replace the German mission. When finally the Danish Baptist Church came to this field in 1928, they found only the ruins of some buildings and the favorable attitude of some people whom the German missionaries had contacted.

The early period of missionary activities until 1916 was a preparatory period in which the gospel was made known and the missions worked for credibility with the people. The tension between the Hutu and Tutsi tribes complicated this matter. The White Fathers extended their work from Rwanda to Burundi. They were French and served chiefly the Hutu tribe, whereas the Germans governed by indirect rule the area where the Tutsi were the prominent tribe. The White Fathers emphasized evangelism through the schools. Since they were working among the Hutu tribe, they had mostly Hutu pupils in their schools. The Protestant missionaries, working primarily among the Tutsi tribe, emphasized the proclamation of the gospel.

Under the Belgian trusteeship, the White Fathers of the

Catholic Church had the same privileges in Burundi as in Rwanda. The mission readily established a large educational work and baptized many children after they had received religious instruction in the school. The Catholic Church grew from 5,769 members in 1915 to 1,602,950 in 1965.[87]

The Seventh-Day Adventists entered the northwest of Burundi in 1925. Their work has been mostly confined to the Bubanza province, though some work has also been done to the east in the Ngozi province.

As previously mentioned, the Danish Baptists undertook to establish a ministry in the area where the German Protestants had worked before. They applied for permission through the intermediary of the Belgian Protestants and were granted permission for the mission. They arrived in 1928 and settled at Musema, one of the former German Protestant stations. Later they opened other stations.[88] The Baptists lacked personnel and funds to develop and expand the work readily. An awakening began in 1934 and continued for some years. The laymen engaged in house-to-house visitation. This movement contributed greatly to the establishment of the church.

The Free Methodists came to Burundi in 1935 and were received by the Danish Baptists. The Baptists were unable to staff their stations and ceded Muyembe to the Methodists. The Burundi Free Methodist Church has been established. Many church leaders lost their lives during the tribal war of 1972–1973, which had greatly disrupted the work of the church.

The World Gospel Mission came to Burundi in 1938. The Bible school at Mweya has made a significant contribution to the expansion of its ministry. Students from several other denominations also attend the school. The society offers medical services at the Murore Hospital and at two dispensaries but lacks the personnel to continue in full operation.

The Kansas Yearly Meeting of Friends undertook a mission to Burundi in 1935. The Baptists ceded the old German site of Kibimba to them. They work in close cooperation with the Free Methodists and the World Gospel Union Mission.[89]

The Church Missionary Society wanted to expand its ministry in Uganda and Rwanda to Burundi, but for some time permission to enter the country was refused. Finally in 1935 it began the stations of Buhiga and Matana. The ministry has been successful and an active church has been established. The Anglican Church has a teacher-training college at Buhiga and cooperates with other denominations in the teacher-training college at Kibimba. The church trains its personnel at Warner Theological College at Buye.

The revival affected Rwanda and Burundi. The openness to the gospel was nationwide from 1934 to 1948. With the coming of the government subsidies for school, the teachers became less interested in the evangelistic ministry of the church in the mid-1950s. At the same time a spirit of materialism replaced the revival spirit of many church members in many places. A New-Life-for-All campaign was begun in 1970. A revival began among the young people of the Anglican Church in the early 1970s.

An independent organization formed the Corporation Radio Diffusion "Afrique Centrale," which is located in Bujumbura and broadcasts programs in a number of languages. It began broadcasting in 1964 and gives most of the time to gospel programs. Churches in the surrounding countries tape programs and music, which is aired by the station. The corporation's institute of radio arts and sciences is training personnel in radio programing and technique.

The revival movements have brought the Christians to a fuller understanding of the Christian faith and of their relationship to God and to their neighbors. However, the tribal wars of the last decade indicate that the fullness of the Christian life has not been acknowledged by all people. Christianity counts many adherents. The churches are confronted with the task of leading them to full obedience to Christ and His Church.

SUMMARY

The vision of planting at intervals a row of mission stations in order to proclaim the gospel to all people as soon as possible was a worthy desire. However, more could likely have been accomplished to evangelize East Africa if the principle of using local witnesses had received more emphasis. Fourah Bay College in West Africa became a center for the diffusion of the gospel by training men and sending them out to witness in other areas. Wherever similar efforts have been made, the results have been rewarding.

Krapf was concerned to reach the Galla tribe with the gospel. He also established cordial relations with neighboring tribes and thereby opened their territories for possible mission work, but these contacts were not utilized by the Church Missionary Society. Consequently, they basically served only as exploratory trips. Krapf's missionary strategy was to plant a number of stations in the interior of the country as soon as possible rather than to begin a Christian community with a responsive people who then become the evangelizing agency in the territory.

Krapf and Rebmann made significant literary contributions that have been very helpful to later missionary efforts. However, they did not begin a peoples' movement to the Christian faith. Unless other missionaries had come and used their literary work in planting Christianity in East Africa, the work of Krapf and Rebmann would have had little value.

The Church Missionary Society failed to employ the principle of ministering to responsive people in establishing the gospel in East Africa. If the early, cordial contacts with the Kamba and Tanga tribes had been utilized to plant Christianity among them at that time, many people might have been brought to the faith at an earlier date.

Zanzibar reveals the negative influence that colonial ambitions have had on other peoples. The tension and strife among the European powers certainly has not diffused a spirit of peace and good will among the nations. The friendly overtures of nations could not be trusted, for generally they were inspired by ulterior motives.

The widespread concern to eliminate slave trade and the efforts some people put forth to accomplish this goal during the nineteenth century are remarkable. The termination of the nefarious activity brought a more normal life back to Central Africa.

Christian compassion prompted the missionaries to respond to Livingstone's appeal to bring the gospel to Central Africa, open Africa to legitimate trade, and suppress the slave trade. European countries were drawn into the battle against the slave trade and were instrumental in abolishing it. But instead of continuing to guide the people to an indigenous government, the European countries did not help to reestablish orderly, indigenous rule, but used their superior power to colonize these countries. In many instances the colonizing country was the country from which the missionaries had come. The behavior of the European nations, contrary to Christian principles, was detrimental to the Christian cause. The Christian message of love and peace was com-promised.

The coming of the colonial powers placed the missions in an unfavorable position. Missionaries had been the advocates of lib-erty and social justice for the Africans. Now they were citizens of the colonizing countries, but were obliged to serve as servants of justice over against their countrymen. Because of their experience with the colonial powers, the Africans did not always trust the motives of the missionaries. This situation retarded the work of the Christian missions.

The German colonial office made efforts to develop Tanzania according to European ideology and methods without considera-tion of the African cultural patterns and the desires of the Afri-cans. The Germans took for granted that the people would prefer the changes that were introduced. However, the native people had their own value system and did not necessarily prefer the economic advantages the new government was introducing. Con-sequently, discontent was generated. This is one example of many similar situations where the native peoples' culture was ignored and incoming powers felt their ideas were unquestionably superior to those of the local people.

The 1914-1918 and the 1939-1945 world wars caused much dis-ruption of the missionary activities in Tanzania. Unfortunately, the nations that should have been an example of peace and good will caused much hardship and basically denied the Christian princi-ples that supposedly guide their governments. This unfaithfulness to Christian principles was, no doubt, confusing to the African people.

The confusion caused by the governments was in part rectified by the testimony of the mission societies. By assisting the German missions, even though their countries were at war, the societies witnessed to the truth that the unity of the Christian faith tran-scends national boundaries.

It was especially the national catechists and evangelists who have evangelized Africa south of the Sahara. Missionaries and pastors have often established work that some local Christians or a catechist had begun. The witness of the believers has been very important in spreading the Christian faith.

The missions and churches failed to place sufficient emphasis on the preparation of leadership. Progress in the growth of the

Christian community has been retarded because one pastor or leader was responsible for many congregations. Christian groups were not nurtured and people who were responsive were not evangelized. The Church Missionary Society involved several ex-slaves in the Christian ministry in Kenya after they had received Christian training in India. This policy could have been used to a greater advantage. The training of national workers in East Africa could have received more emphasis.

The East-African Revival has contributed greatly to the diffusion of the gospel and the establishment of the church in East Africa. This is basically a lay movement and as such indicates the importance of the ministry of the Christians. This movement has grown spontaneously. It has continued as a movement within the churches but is not controlled by the churches. It has not separated to form another church, but has continued to edify all the churches and guide them to a greater ministry.

The Christian faith was received in Uganda because Henry M. Stanley established good relations with Mutesa. Also, the Church Missionary Society responded immediately to Stanley's appeal for missionaries and entered the field in an opportune period. On the other hand, the coming of French Roman Catholic missionaries and their effort to win Uganda for a French sphere of political influence caused disunity in the Christian faith and much confusion in the land. Had the foreign agents not pressed their views upon Mwanga, the civil disturbance and the persecution of the Christians might have been avoided.

The growth of the church in Uganda presents several important principles. The Holy Spirit used the Word of God to lead people to a saving knowledge of Christ. The Bible-reading sessions were promoted by lay Christians. The lay believers became the evangelists throughout the country. The gospel spread spontaneously and began a peoples' movement in which many people accepted the Christian faith at the same time. The large movements to the Christian faith have been through multi-individual conversions in people movements.

When a people movement takes place, group Bible-study sessions, short Bible courses, workers' retreats, and Theological Education by Extension will contribute to establishing the believers and uniting them into reproducing congregations. New believers need to be instructed in the Christian faith, and Bible study sessions may be most helpful. Churches have, however, halted people movements by waiting for trained pastors to guide these movements, whereas many of the pastors, after having received advanced training, were unwilling to serve in rural, undeveloped regions.

Study Questions

1. "The receptivity or responsiveness of individuals waxes and wanes."[90] If the church redeems the occasions of responsiveness, significant church growth may take place. Apply this principle to the early ministry of the Church Missionary Society in East Africa.
2. Evaluate George Tozer's policy of training Christians to evangelize East Africa.
3. Describe how the social relationships and structures affected the growth of the church in Uganda.
4. How did Christianity affect the Arab slave trade and contribute to bringing about the conflict that ended the slave trade in East Africa?
5. What contributions did Christian missions make to the social conditions of the people?
6. Describe how World War I interfered with the progress of church work in East Africa.
7. Describe the contribution of the catechist-evangelists in extending Christian witness in East Africa.
8. Describe the East African Revival and its contribution to the churches.
9. Evaluate the contribution of Christian missions to the development of education in Kenya.
10. Evaluate the strengths and weaknesses of the Independent churches in Kenya.
11. How did the Bible-reading classes, arranged by George Lawrence Pilkington, substantiate the principle of discipling out to the fringes a people who under the leading of the Holy Spirit have become responsive?[91]
12. How do the ministries of Apolo Kivebulaya and Basio Kogozi in Uganda and Rwanda illustrate the importance of a key personality in a people movement?[92]

13. Describe the outstanding characteristics of the revival movement in Uganda and in East Africa generally.
14. Indicate the contributions of the revival movement in Rwanda and Burundi.

8

The Church in North Africa
(1792-1975)

The church was established in North Africa during the first centuries and became quite prominent, exercising a significant influence throughout North Africa until the Muslim invasion restricted its ministry. Yet today the percentage of Christians on the continent is the lowest in North Africa. The church almost disappeared in North Africa and its influence is slight. The Coptic Church could have become the evangelizing agent for Africa. Unfortunately, however, instead of engaging in evangelism to its neighbors, the Egyptian church became occupied with internal problems. Lacking the inspiration for evangelism and the unity to resist the enemy, it became incapacitated under the Muslim pressure. The Ethiopian Orthodox Church resisted the Muslim attacks. Various agencies contributed to revive the spiritual life of the church. It continued its ministry in Ethiopia during the centuries of isolation. But it failed to evangelize the tribes of Ethiopia and its neighbors. Thus the African Christians did not evangelize North Africa. Renewed efforts in evangelism were undertaken with the coming of European and American Mission Societies in the nineteenth century.

DIFFICULTIES, BUT SOME CHURCH GROWTH
Ethiopia

The emperor Menelik referred to Ethiopia as a Christian island in a Muslim sea.[1] The coming of Christianity to Ethiopia in the fourth century, its expansion, and finally its establishment as the religion of the country have been observed earlier. The church joined the state in courageously resisting the Muslim attacks. But it lacked the inner power to evangelize the peoples at its borders.

288

Because its contacts with other Christian communities were severed, it was obliged to rely on its own resources.

Ethiopian monasticism made a significant contribution in sustaining the Christian faith during centuries of difficulties and also in preserving most of the cultural treasures of art and literature through the period of the Muslim invasion, even though many monasteries were destroyed. As a result of the withdrawal during the time of persecution, the monastic movement in Ethiopia engaged less in an active ministry to the society.

Old Testament traditions are quite prominent in the Ethiopian Orthodox Church. They have entered Ethiopian history through several incidents, which are considered very significant by the people. The Ethiopian tradition, recorded in the *Nebra Negast* (The Glory of the Kings), states that the royal dynasty descended from King Solomon and the queen of Sheba. Budge states that the queen of Sheba commanded the people to embrace Judaism.[2] This tradition has greatly influenced the history of Ethiopia and has provided the rationale for the close relationship between the state and the church.[3] Ethiopians have considered themselves successors of the Jewish people. Furthermore, the Ethiopian tradition maintains that Menelik, the son born to the queen of Sheba and King Solomon, brought the ark of the covenant from Jerusalem to Aksum. A replica of the ark is placed in every Ethiopian Orthodox Church because God's presence dwells in the ark.[4]

Aspects of Old Testament ritual are obvious in the Ethiopian church. The church teaches that the dietary rules of Leviticus are to be observed. Although its members do not fully adhere to the teaching, pork is considered a taboo. The members of the church circumcise the male children on the eighth day after birth. Circumcision is generally practiced in Africa, but it is an initiation rite during which time the child is taught the traditions of the tribe. No doubt the Jews who migrated to Ethiopia introduced further elements of their religion.

As a result of the Muslim pressure, the emperor of Ethiopia assumed the responsibility of defending the faith. The relationship of church and state was closely interwoven. Ethiopian Christianity was occupied with defending and preserving the faith rather than proclaiming the same. The state assumed a very prominent role in the religious activities of the country, relegating to the monasteries the task of preserving the faith. Some of the Ethiopian emperors thought of Christianity as being the religion of Ethiopia and declared that all subjects were to accept this faith. Theodore (1855-1868) used force to bring some tribes in subjection to the government and to accept the Christian faith. In his opinion state and church were synonymous. However, the monastic movement has not Christianized the tribes that were brought in subjection to Ethiopia during the last century. Whereas the emperors considered Christianity the religion of Ethiopia, the tribes they attempted to subject to it regarded it as the religion of their enemies. This attitude did not promote the expansion of Christianity. Furthermore, the Ethiopian church became formal and failed to witness effectively to the non-Christian tribes.

The Ethiopian church felt its subjection to the Egyptian Coptic Church as long as their abuna, or patriarch, was appointed by the patriarch of Alexandria. There was much rejoicing when in 1948 the Egyptian Coptic patriarch and an Ethiopian delegation signed an agreement giving the Ethiopian church the right to appoint its own abuna.

John II of Portugal, who heard about the existence of an African Christian church, dispatched a small delegation to Ethiopia about 1490. The results of their visit have not been recorded. Some thirty years later, John III sent another delegation, which obtained trading privileges with Ethiopia. In view of commercial arrangements between the two countries, the Jesuits undertook a mission. They began a ministry that promised success, but the Jesuits tried to bring the Ethiopian church into submission to Rome. In 1604 the monarch was induced to make his submission to Rome. This action caused a strong reaction in the country. The king was slain and his son reaffirmed his allegiance to the Coptic Church. The favorable relations had been disrupted; the Jesuits were suspected, and in 1633 they were expelled. As a result of this sectarian action, the former interest that the Ethiopian church had in fellowship with the churches of Europe diminished and it became suspicious of them. For some time all overtures to restore rapport were rejected.[5]

Several Roman Catholic attempts to establish a ministry in Ethiopia resulted in disaster. Three Capuchins were beheaded in Massawa in 1648. Almost two centuries later, in 1839, Italian Lazarists landed in Tigre. In 1846 they were followed by Italian Capuchins, who attempted a ministry to the Galla tribe. However, the political situation was unsettled. When Theodore II gained power in 1855, he expelled the Catholics because they favored his rival, Ubie.[6]

In 1825 the Church Missionary Society sent five missionaries to Egypt. Three of them were sent to strengthen its ministry to the Oriental churches, whereas two were sent to Ethiopia to promote a revival. Samuel Gobat and Christian Krugler arrived at Tigre in 1830, and they were kindly received by the local ruler. They brought with them thousands of copies of the Scriptures. These had been prepared from a manuscript in Amharic that William Jowett had found in Egypt. The people eagerly purchased them.[7] Although the life of the Ethiopian church was not radiant, a godly remnant was there and the missionaries had a rewarding ministry. But Krugler died and Gobat's health compelled him to retire in 1836. Johann Krapf, also a representative of the Church Missionary Society, served among the Shoan Christians from 1839 to 1842. Krapf's desire, however, was to proclaim the gospel to the Galla tribe; so he went to East Africa.

In 1855 Theodore II gave permission to J. M. Flad to establish schools, to preach, and to teach the gospel. He distributed many Amharic and Ethiopic Bibles, New Testaments, and Psalms; established schools; and proclaimed the gospel to Ethiopians and Falasha Jews. The latter were receptive and in 1862 thirty-one Falashas were baptized.[8]

The political situation in Ethiopia was very unsettled from 1860 to 1880. During the last years of his reign, Theodore II became a tyrant. Two English adventurers, Bell and Plowden, became his counselors. The people opposed their influence over Theodore II and killed them in 1860. Because of this incident, Theodore II was even less considerate with his citizens and with foreigners. He rejected the counsel of his ministers and the pastors, and even mistreated the abuna (or patriarch) Salama. He wanted to send a delegation to England, but the reply from England failed to come. Irritated by the situation, he imprisoned Cameron, the British consul. Britain sent an expedition to liberate Cameron. The people took this incident as an opportunity to revolt. Theodore II committed suicide, and four years of anarchy followed.[9] Finally John IV, the ruler of the Tigre area, reestablished order and saved Ethiopia from an Egyptian takeover.[10]

The political situation did not permit intensive church work.

The Catholics had maintained a small work in the northern part of the country, mostly in Tigre. In 1867 Athanasios became the forty-second abuna. He helped John IV gain power and then requested the expulsion of the missionaries for his services. The foreign personnel were expelled. Four Catholic stations were destroyed and the Catholic Christians were compelled to return to the Ethiopian Orthodox Church. The Europeans withdrew to Massawa and tried to maintain contact with some people at the border.[11]

Menelik was a powerful ruler of the Shoa province, of the Galla territory, and of the Kaffa kingdom, during the reign of John IV and had founded a new capital at Addis Ababa in 1883. After the death of John IV, Menelik came to power and ruled from 1889 to 1914. He established order in the country and improved relations with foreign countries. From 1897 to 1900 he enlarged his empire to the west toward Sudan, to the south toward Lake Rudolf, and to the southeast. He took measures to develop the country and arranged with France to construct a railroad from Djiboti to Addis Ababa.[12] European cultural influence became apparent during his reign.

The first permanent Protestant missionary endeavor was undertaken by the Evangelical National Missionary Society of Sweden at Massawa in 1866. From there the work was extended to Galeb among the Mensa. The Swedish Mission was the only mission in Eritrea until 1914. Later it extended its ministry to Ethiopia proper and into the southern part of Somaliland. Carl Cederquist, one of the Swedish missionaries, received permission to begin a work in Addia Ababa in 1904. Through Krapf's suggestion, they succeeded in establishing a fruitful work among the western Galla people.

In 1920 the United Presbyterian Church began its ministry among the Wallaga Galla in western Ethiopia. In 1923 Dr. Thomas A. Lambie opened the George Memorial Hospital at Addis Ababa. The hospital served the people in a most significant manner, and its services were much appreciated by the government. The Italians expropriated the hospital during their occupation from 1936 to 1941. After their departure, the Ethiopian government took charge of it. The Presbyterian church offers services at the hospital at Sayo. It offered education and operated a girls' school in addition to the spiritual ministry.

The Bethel Evangelical Church grew out of the Presbyterian

ministry during the Italian occupation (1935-1942). The Christians were persecuted by the Italians, but they continued their ministry faithfully. Although a large missionary staff returned to continue the work, the membership of the church is relatively small.

The largest Protestant ministry in Ethiopia is the outgrowth of the work of the Sudan Interior Mission. The significance of serving responsive people is revealed by this ministry. The first party was retained at Addis Ababa. When they finally received permission to proceed to the interior, the Omo River was swollen from the heavy rains and they were obliged to stay on the east side. There, however, the governors of Kambatta, Wallamo, and Sidamo, who were acquainted with Dr. Lambie, invited the missionaries to their territories. The missionaries agreed to do so and, once in these various places, they readily studied the languages and translated portions of the Scriptures. By 1937 the society had opened fourteen stations.

In 1937 the missionaries were expelled from the country by the Italians. The Christians went through trying experiences during the Italian occupation, but the church grew to ten thousand members in the Wallamo tribe and five thousand in Kambatta. These churches have continued to grow and have over two hundred thousand members. Both churches had charismatic leaders: Ato Biru was at Wallamo and Ato Abba Gole was at Kambatta. The Sidamo church, however, has disappeared.

Several reasons for the rapid and immense growth of these churches may be observed. The credibility that Dr. Lambie established with the governors provided an open door for the ministry. The people were interested in the gospel message. The churches were planted in distinct ethnic units and the people became Christians within their tribe without being compelled to cross cultural barriers. Through the spontaneous, indigenous peoples' movement, evangelization continued in an effort to reach all the members of the tribe. The church members were nurtured and had opportunities to share in the proclamation of the gospel and develop their gifts through practical ministry. The movement was not stalled by the training of a few elite, but sixty-four Bible schools prepared workers for the many church centers. By 1971 eighteen hundred workers were active in the church. This Christian community is known as the Word of Life Evangelical Church.

A number of Lutheran missions established work in Ethiopia

after 1945. In the beginning they met occasionally for fellowship and to divide the ministry among them, but there was no real unity. Sensing the need for unity, they formed the Ethiopian Evangelical Church—Mekane Jesus (the dwelling place of Jesus). This church grew from 20,000 members in 1959 to 155,192 in 1972. The ministry of mission and church is fully integrated and the missionaries serve according to the needs in the ministry.

A very significant ministry related to the Lutheran work is the Radio Voice of the Gospel (RVOG). This work is sponsored by the Lutheran World Federation and is affiliated with the Coordinating Committee of Christian Broadcasting, which represents the All-African Conference of Churches, the Near East Council of Churches, and the East Asia Christian Conference. The station is located in Addis Ababa and beams programs in sixteen languages to Africa, Madagascar, and Asia. Programs are prepared in various countries and sent to the studio. Efforts are being made to follow up the radio ministry with personal contacts.

The Bible Missionary Society of the Anglican Church has devoted itself to work within the Ethiopian Orthodox Church, teaching Bible and other subjects in the seminaries and convents and preaching the gospel whenever the opportunity presents itself. It began the bimonthly magazine, *Witness to the Light*, which has become the organ of five missions.

Ethiopia is one of the largest fields of the Eastern Mennonite Board of Missions and Charities. The ministry is carried on in cooperation with the Meserete Kristos Church. The church is not large but is establishing a vital ministry. It seeks to diffuse Christian literature through its bookstore. Supported by the American Leprosy Mission and the Leprosy Mission from London, England, the Mennonite Mission gives guidance to the All-Africa Leprosy and Rehabilitation Training Center.

A number of missionary societies began work in Ethiopia after 1945. The Seventh-Day Adventists, with eighty-five hundred members, is probably the largest of these communities.

Several tendencies may be observed in the churches in Ethiopia. The Ethiopian Orthodox Church, although a large community, shows little growth through evangelism. Several religious bodies are growing rapidly and winning many people to the Christian faith. Other communities again report nominal growth.

The churches in Ethiopia are facing a new situation. The

present government has separated the church and state. Thus the Ethiopian Orthodox Church is no longer in a favored position, and all the churches are confronted by the secular society.

Sudan

Sudan, a country in northeast Africa and located south of Egypt, was formerly ruled jointly by Egypt and Britain. It became an independent nation in 1956. In northern Sudan the population is mainly Arabic and adheres to the Muslim religion, while the southern part of the country is inhabited by Negroid Africans who are either Christians or animists.

Christianity was introduced in Sudan in the sixth century. It became well rooted and resisted Islamic pressures for several centuries till it was finally suppressed. However, small groups of believers remained scattered till the nineteenth century.

In 1846 the Roman Catholic Church established the Central Africa Vicariate, which served Sudan, Chad, and Uganda. Its responsibility was to minister to the commercial people who were Christians and to evangelize the unbelievers. When the first group of missionaries came and conducted mass, the native people told them that their ancestors had been Christians; they were a happy people who lived in stone houses.[13]

Toward the end of 1847, some Catholic missionaries arrived at Dongola near the third cataract on the Nile and in February 1948 they reached Khartoum. They established a center at Khartoum, and from there they went to the interior of the country. They began a ministry in a region that had been devastated by the slave trade and where people's normal routine of life had been disturbed. Knoblecher, an Austrian member of the delegation, returned to Europe to look for assistance. The mission appealed to Emperor Francois-Joseph II, who aided them and also sent a consul to Khartoum to be of assistance. A mission station was founded at Lado, near the Ugandan border. After 1873 the Catholics started a number of stations south of Khartoum. Since the climate and living conditions were unfavorable, many of the European recruits died. From 1851 to 1858 there were twenty-two deaths.[14]

From 1881 to 1885, mission work in Sudan suffered because of the activities of the Mahdis, followers of Muhammad Ahmed who claimed to be Mahdi, the expected Muslim Messiah. They proclaimed a holy war in August 1881. The Catholic missionaries tried to flee but they were arrested and imprisoned. Feeble and fatigued, many of them died. Some managed to escape but suffered many hardships.[15] On January 6, 1885, Khartoum was attacked; and Gordon, the British representative, and about four thousand English and Egyptian men were killed.[16] Wolseley, the British field marshal, arrived with reinforcements a few days too late to save Khartoum. The struggle continued. In 1899 the British finally defeated the Mahdists.[17] After the British had restored order in Sudan in 1900, mission work continued. Missionaries went to southern Sudan and in 1911 the first ten converts were baptized.[18]

Toward the end of 1860, several Protestant societies started work in Sudan. The British and Foreign Bible Society worked in Khartoum. The Church Missionary Society attempted to work in eastern Sudan, but because of the political situation, no permanent mission could be established till 1899.

In 1899 the United Presbyterians, who already worked in Egypt, sent two representatives to explore possibilities for missions in Sudan. They recommended establishing a mission for which Egyptian Christians would be responsible. The recommendation was accepted, and in 1900 Pastor Jabra Hanna went to Omdurman.[19] Since evangelization was forbidden in northern Sudan, missionaries directed their evangelistic efforts to the people of southern Sudan. However, educational work was permitted in both north and south, and missions took up the challenge. By 1914 considerable progress was made in the two regions.

In 1899 two missionaries of the Church Missionary Society, J. F. Harper and L. H. Gwynne, were granted permission to go to Omdurman, and a Bible colporteur of the Bible society commenced work there also. In the new section of Khartoum, places were reserved for a Gordon Memorial College, a chapel, and a mosque. However, Christians did not have complete liberty for their work.

The Church Missionary Society established a ministry south of the Presbyterians and in the eastern part of the country; the site was near the Ugandan border, between Khartoum and Mengo. The first representatives of the society arrived at Mongalla on January 8, 1906, and opened three stations. At the same time the society expanded its work in Uganda to Gondokora on the Nile, south of the Sudanese border. After the death of Leopold II, king of Belgium, Lau was annexed to Sudan and the Church Missionary Society extended work to this region. The mission stations of Lau, 47 miles west of the Nile, and Yambo, 250 miles west of Gondokoro, among the Azande, were started in 1912. The same year the cathedral in Khartoum was dedicated. In 1914 the first conversions to Christianity among the Dinka took place.[20] That same year the society started a hospital and several schools in northern Sudan, and there were six converts in the north and 106 in the south.[21]

Though the work in Sudan was difficult, the Church Missionary Society expanded and commenced a ministry at Atbara in 1908. The society began a work at Wad Medana among the Muslims in the north in 1919. Work among the native people in the Nuba mountains was begun at Salara in 1935 and at Katcha in 1939.[22] The mission work in the south was friutful and church membership grew rapidly. The Church Missionary Society was unable to supply enough missionary personnel to meet the demands; so they accepted missionaries from other societies. From 1930 to 1960 much emphasis was placed on evangelism through education. By 1960 there were active churches in six tribes; the churches were served by national pastors who had been trained in the Bishop Gwynne Divinity College. In 1968 the society had 600 places of worship, 110,000 church members, and a Christian community of 150,000.[23]

The work of the United Presbyterian Church in northern Sudan expanded only after 1940, when four new stations were opened.[24] In the southern area the church grew rapidly. The Church of Christ of the Upper Nile was established in 1956 and was served by native pastors. The society operated a printery, the Spearhead Press, which was a valuable aid for the ministry of the church.

Other mission societies have work in Sudan. The Sudan Interior Mission entered Sudan when the Italians prohibited them from continuing their work in Ethiopia. By 1960 they had work at eleven centers in the Blue Nile region and the Upper Nile. The Africa Inland Mission started work in Sudan in 1949 and established four mission stations. By 1968 they had eight places of worship and a Christian community of three thousand people.[25]

In 1946 the Church Missionary Society, the United Presbyterians, and the Mission of Sudan formed a missionary council. The Sudan Council of Churches, composed of Catholic, Protestant, and Orthodox churches, was formed in 1965. It is affiliated both

with the All-Africa Council of Churches and with the North East
Council of Churches.[26]

While the churches of Sudan were witnessing outstanding
growth, the Muslim opposition increased. Children were discouraged from attending church services, and efforts were made to
arrest the spread of Christianity. In 1962 the government started to
expel missionaries, and in 1964 all missionaries were expelled
from southern Sudan. The church in southern Sudan underwent a
severe persecution that was instigated by the predominent northern Muslim government from 1963 to 1971. Thousands of Christians were massacred, and churches were totally disrupted. Many
people fled to neighboring countries as refugees, including some
church leaders, who continued to minister to the refugees. Other
church leaders went in hiding with their people. In 1965 all
theological training centers and many churches were destroyed.
By 1971 a measure of order was restored and, according to the law,
the Christians were to have religious freedom. Practically, however, they have not had complete freedom. The churches encounter many difficulties in their effort to get reestablished. Yet
reports from southern Sudan indicate that there is a vital interest
in Christianity and many new converts are coming into the
church.[27]

Somalia

Somalia is a small country of northeast Africa. It is bordered by
the Gulf of Aden and the Indian Ocean, and to the west it borders
on Ethiopia and Kenya. Formerly it was British Somaliland and
Italian Somaliland, but in 1960 it became an independent nation.
Somalia has a population of 2,666,000 (1967),[28] and many of its
inhabitants have cattle in the areas not suitable for raising crops.
There is some agriculture in southern Somalia. Arab traders established contacts with the region and brought Muslim faith to it at an
early date. Consequently, the people basically adhere to the Muslim religion.

Since Somalia was an Italian protectorate from 1889 to World
War II, Protestant missionaries were not welcome. In 1875 before
Somalia became an Italian protectorate, the Evangelical National
Missionary Society of Sweden started a mission there. For sixty
years, the society worked among the Muslims in an educational
program, in providing medical aid, and in proclaiming the gospel.

The society realized that missionaries from Sweden might not be permitted to return and engaged the assistance of the Waldensian Church of Italy. They organized the church to function independently, should the society be expelled from the country, but the church did not have the opportunity to function independently. In 1935 the Italians expelled the society, and the Catholics took over responsibility for their work.[29]

After World War II, two Protestant societies came to work in Somalia. The Mennonites, who were already working in East Africa, came to Somalia in 1952.[30] By 1971 the society had established several centers where a Christian witness was given. They work in education and have a bookstore. They also have some medical work. One of their missionaries, Merlin Grove, was stabbed to death by a Muslim zealot in 1962. Aggressive evangelism is not permitted, but by person-to-person witness the Christian group had grown to about one hundred by 1975. National workers are permitted to baptize converts.

In 1954 the Sudan Interior Mission commenced a ministry in the capital city, Mogadishu, and at Bulo Burti. In 1958 another center was started. At first the mission had several schools but when problems arose concerning compulsory teaching of the Koran, they moved their emphasis to home Bible study groups and to night schools. Good contacts have been made through these efforts and small fellowship groups of believers are forming. The society has also translated the New Testament into the Somali language and is working on the translation of the Old Testament.[31]

The Catholic Church worked among the Europeans in the section of Somalia that was the Italian protectorate.[32] However, they had little success in contacting the native people of Somalia. The Roman Catholics created a prefecture apostolic in 1904. In 1927 the Capuchins were working at fifty-eight places. They had established a number of schools, eleven dispensaries, and one printing press, and teachers were being trained.[33] In 1965 there were thirty-five hundred Roman Catholics in the country, but they were mostly foreigners.[34]

The British were more reluctant to allow Christian workers in British Somaliland because they feared Muslim opposition. The Catholic Capuchins came to Somalia from Aden in 1892 and concentrated their efforts among the children, whom they gathered during a famine. By 1914 they had won several hundred converts.[35] But there was no Protestant ministry in the territory.

Egypt

Egypt, also called the United Arab Republic, is in northeast Africa, with the Mediterranean Sea as its northern border. Christianity came to Egypt in the first century. Because of the national character of Christianity as it was presented and because of the translation of the Bible in the Coptic language, the Christian faith survived twelve centuries of strong Muslim domination. The patriarch of Alexandria has continued in his position and helped preserve the existence and the unity of the Coptic Church.

The Coptic Church of Egypt has a membership of between two and three million.[36] The Coptics have gained a good reputation in the country and are represented in the parliament. They do not accept polygamy or divorce. Because they put more emphasis on education than the Muslims do, they form a large percentage of the better educated class of society. Though they comprise only 6 percent of the population, they have supplied more than half of the country's teachers till recently and in 1960 they still formed 30 percent of the teaching corps. They also perform an important function in government positions.[37] Protestant missionaries observed, however, that the Coptic priests had a limited knowledge of the Bible. They had been influenced by Islam and consequently there was a weakness in their testimony.[38]

The first Protestant mission work in Egypt during the modern period was undertaken by the Moravians in the eighteenth century, but later they withdrew from the country. In 1815 the Church Missionary Society sent William Jowett to Egypt to explore possibilities of working there. He was cordially received by the patriarch of Alexandria. The society wished to cooperate with the Coptic Church instead of starting a separate evangelistic work. In 1818 they started a printery on the island of Malta and produced literature for Egypt and the Near East.[39] The Church Missionary Society continued their cooperative work with the Coptic Church till 1862, when it withdrew because the work was not producing satisfactory results.

In 1882 the society returned to Egypt and started an independent ministry.[40] They opened several stations and did medical work in Cairo.[41] At the end of the century the work was still in the beginning stages. Women missionaries were teaching, visiting

Muslim homes, and nursing patients in the hospitals. The people seemed to believe, but there were few baptisms. In 1920 the society established the diocese for Egypt and Sudan, but in 1945 a separate diocese for Sudan was started. In 1908, Temple Gairdner commenced the movement called Friends of the Bible. Bible study groups were formed at fifty places. This movement inspired the Sunday school movement of the Coptic Church, which fulfilled an important function. The Church Missionary Society established four parishes in Cairo and one in Menuf. It operated two hospitals and had two schools for girls. In 1960 it had about one thousand members.[42]

The United Presbyterian Church of America commenced work in Egypt in 1854. It established centers from Alexandria to Assiut and by 1875 had about six hundred members.[43] Most of the members came from the Coptic Church, but before 1896 they had baptized seventy-five converts from the Muslim faith. There was some persecution of Christians in Egypt as elsewhere in North Africa; some Christians were in danger, and some were killed by poisoning.[44] However, in 1878 a legal representative for Protestants was appointed, and they were recognized as another legal religious group of the country.

There was remarkable growth in Protestantism between 1880 and 1897; the number of missionaries increased from 22 to 47, that of the Egyptian pastors from 6 to 21, and other church workers from 25 to 42. The number of churches grew from 11 to 39, and the church membership from 985 to 5,355.[45] The most successful work was around Assiut. The United Presbyterian Church had a strong educational work. It established several colleges and a seminary. Then in 1921 Charles R. Watson commenced the American University of Cairo. In 1926 the church had a membership of 25,000 and became autonomous; it was named the Coptic Evangelical Church.[46] The society also had a medical ministry that included hospitals at Assiut and Tanta, a clinic in Cairo, and some dispensaries.

Several other societies have served in Egypt. In 1855 Spittler proposed the idea of establishing a chain of stations along the Nile, reaching into Abyssinia. Three stations were started in Egypt, but conditions in Abyssinia caused Spittler to abandon the project.

In 1856 and 1857, Fliedner, the founder of the Kaiserwerth Institution, established a hospital in Alexandria. In 1870 another hospital was built in Cairo. In 1892 the Mission to North Africa sent representatives to Egypt. Except for a few interruptions, the British and Foreign Bible Society has worked in Egypt since 1818.[47]

The General Mission to Egypt, an independent British mission, started its work in 1898. The first group of seven missionaries devoted their time to evangelistic efforts to reach the Muslims living along the Nile River. They engaged in house-to-house visitation, distributing literature and giving medication to those who were sick. Their medical work was appreciated and they established a hospital and a dispensary. One of the missionary women founded a school for girls. In 1920 a home was founded for housing girls who did not wish to submit to Muslim marriages.[48]

The work of the General Mission to Egypt progressed. After fifty-five years, they had forty-five missionaries and ten stations. All their work was in the Delta area. Three medical doctors and five nurses treated about fifty-thousand patients annually. Because of a law passed in 1948, the society was obliged to close two schools. They made a strong effort in literature distribution. But the Muslims were slow to accept the Christian faith, and in 1957 the churches started by the society had a total membership of only one hundred and fifty.[49]

The Assemblies of God began work in Assiut in 1908 and in Alexandria in 1911. They established a center for evangelism in Cairo, where three thousand copies of the paper *Morning Star* were published annually. By 1929 the society had twelve stations and forty-one national church workers. Most of the members of their church came from the Coptic Church. In 1931 a district council of the Assemblies of God was formed, having national and missionary representatives. An outstanding ministry of the society was the American orphanage at Assiut, directed by Lilian Trasher, who was known as the "Mother of the Nile." The orphanage has grown and is supported by donations from Egyptians and foreigners. Since it was started, more than seven thousand orphans and widows have found refuge in the orphanage. In 1960 it had twelve hundred residents.[50]

The Christian Mission to Many Lands, an organ of the Plymouth Brethren, emphasized educational and medical ministry. At the same time this mission was instrumental in organizing two hundred congregations.[51]

Christian missions in Egypt encountered difficulties in 1956 because of the Suez Canal crisis, a conflict of the Egyptians with Britain and France. British missionaries were expelled and their schools and hospitals were confiscated by the government. Other missions were permitted to continue their work. The crisis caused mission societies to work more diligently toward autonomy, and, to date, national Christians have taken responsibility for the work formerly carried on by missions.

The Coptic Orthodox Church, the Greek Orthodox Church, and the Coptic Evangelical Church are members of the World Council of Churches. Some other churches belong to the Evangelical Fellowship of Egypt, formed in 1966.[52] The Coptic Evangelical Organization for Social Services, with the cooperation of other Christian groups, works in Bible teaching, literary programs, agriculture, and other areas of assistance.[53]

Though the Coptic Church and other Protestant churches have been active in Egypt for a long time, the largest percentage of the population is Muslim. In 1965 statistics showed that the population included 91 percent Muslims, 7.89 percent Christians, and .34 percent Jews.[54]

OPPOSITION AND SLIGHT CHURCH GROWTH

Libya

Libya, also known as the Libyan Arab Republic, is situated in North Africa west of Egypt and is bordered by the Mediterranean Sea to the north. Until 1911 the country was dominated by the Turks. It was an Italian colony from 1912 to 1943, and an independent kingdom from 1951 to 1969, when it became a republic. The country is mostly desert but has made much economic progress in the last two decades due to the discovery of oil. This has enabled it to make improvements in education and medical care and to develop the country in general. The population of Libya is basically Muslim, except for the Europeans living there.

Reportedly, a Franciscan monk won many Muslims to Christianity during the thirteenth century, but no indications of lasting results were found in later centuries. The Catholic ministry has been chiefly to Europeans; it has not been successful in reaching the Muslims.[55]

The North Africa Mission came to Libya in 1888 and has persevered in spite of many difficulties. Its main witness has been through medical service. This mission has also made efforts to have some classes for children. A small Libyan church was finally founded in 1957—the first Libyan church in a thousand years.[56]

The Seventh-Day Adventists established a hospital at Benghazi in 1958. Many other churches working in Libya are working with the European population but are not reaching the Muslims.[57] According to the *World Christian Handbook* report for 1968, there were 40,000 Roman Catholics and 2,651 Protestants in Libya, but these were virtually all expatriates.[58]

Tunisia

Tunisia, a small country in North Africa, borders on the Mediterranean Sea. Tunisia fell into the hands of the Turks in 1574 and was governed in the name of the sultan by a *bey* (provincial governor). Till the nineteenth century, Tunisia was a haven for pirates. To remedy the situation, France took control of Tunisia as a protectorate in 1881. From that time till 1956 it remained a French protectorate. In 1956 it became a monarchy, but the following year it was declared a republic. The city of Tunis is built on the former site of Carthage, which was an important center of the Christian church in the first centuries. But Christianity was extinguished by the Arab invasion in the seventh century. Islam is now the recognized state religion.

The Catholic Church made several early attempts to establish work in Tunisia but was unsuccessful. The French Lazarists and the Italian Capuchins came in the seventeenth century, but the work became well established only in the nineteenth century. In 1843 the Roman Catholic Church established the vicariate of Tunisia. Lavigerie had been active in North Africa, especially in Algeria, since 1867; he was named archbishop of Carthage in 1884.[59] After Tunisia became a French protectorate in 1881, many Europeans came there. Most of these immigrants were Catholics, and the Catholic Church was active in ministering to them. Before Lavigerie came to Tunisia, he had already been instrumental in establishing a French college in Tunis. Since Lavigerie was strongly nationalistic, problems arose with the Italian Capuchins, and they withdrew from Tunisia in 1891.[60] Lavigerie was not only concerned to minister to the Europeans but also had a mission strategy to reach Muslims. He wanted missionaries to learn the language and customs of the people, to win credibility in various ways, and then to witness to them about religion.[61] Another strategy was that of gathering orphans, teaching them, and making converts. These converts would then be agents to reach the Muslims with Christianity.[62]

The London Society for Promoting Christianity among the Jews came to North Africa in 1829. At the time there were about thirty thousand Jews in Tunisia, and the society established a work there in 1834. Though their work had some interruptions, it has continued to witness to the Jews. Much of their work consists of distributing Bibles, New Testaments, and other literature both in the Hebrew and the Arabic languages.[63] The society ministers through the St. George's Church, a bookstore, and several schools that have both Jewish and Muslim students.[64]

The North African Mission began its work in Tunisia in 1882. It established seven centers, ministering to Tunisians and to Europeans. It closed several centers later because of a shortage of personnel. An important part of its ministry is the sale of Bibles, and this often opened opportunities for personal evangelism. However, a report of the society in 1962 showed only twenty-five Christians.[65] The mission has had good response to a Bible correspondence course started in 1962 and headquartered in a bookstore. Due to the ministry's success, the bookstore was closed by the government. The center was moved to Marseilles, France, and from there sends out an average of three thousand lessons a month. The mission has combined the correspondence course with the Radio School of the Bible broadcast.[66]

Among the Europeans in Tunisia, there were some members of the Reformed Church and the Lutheran Church. The state of Alsace supported Lutheran pastors to serve these people. A French Protestant church was organized in 1889 as a result of the ministry of a French army chaplain.[67]

The American Methodists commenced work in Tunis in 1908 and have continued serving at this place. They reported forty church members and a Christian community of one hundred. The Reformed Church serves French Protestants and the Anglican Church serves the English, but they did not attempt to evangelize the Tunisians.[68]

Josephine Planter of the Pentecostal Church came to Tunisia from Bohemia in 1912. She was engaged in personal evangelism and Bible distribution for forty years and won some converts to

Christianity. Another female missionary joined her and then went to work in another city. As a result of this beginning, a Pentecostal church was formed in 1957 with twenty members and other people participating.[69]

The government of Tunisia is not favorable to missions, and direct evangelism is forbidden. The work is difficult and there is little response. In 1964 most churches that continued to work in Tunisia formed the Inter-Church Council, a member of the World Council of Churches.[70]

Algeria

Algeria is a country in North Africa that borders the Mediterranean Sea. After a long struggle of guerrilla warfare, it gained its independence from France in 1962. The native people of Algeria are basically Arab and Berber Muslims. There is a small group of Europeans, mostly French.

The French Lazarist Catholic missionaries ministered to the Christian captives before Algeria was occupied by the French. In 1645 they installed themselves at Tunis and in 1646 they entered Algeria. The king of France had a consul in every city. When relations between France and Algeria were broken in 1827, the Lazarists withdrew from the country.[71]

The Roman Catholic Church recommenced its ministry in Algeria in 1838. Antoine Adolph Dupuch was named bishop of Algeria. At the time there were four priests and several nuns in Algeria. Dupuch ran into difficulties with French authorities because he wanted to evangelize the Muslims. He was released from his position in 1845 but the work continued. In 1856 Bishop Pavy died. In 1866 there were 273 priests in Algeria.[72] Pavy was succeeded by Archbishop Lavigerie, whose interest caused the Catholic Church to undertake missions in East Africa, especially in Uganda. In 1868 he formed the society of missionaries known as the "White Fathers," who contributed much to the missionary efforts of the Roman Catholic Church in Africa.[73]

Early Protestants' mission efforts, begun in 1830 by the McCall Mission and the Basel Mission, to minister to the European population in Algeria, were discontinued. In 1881 Edward H. Glenny, the founder of the North Africa Mission Society, and two of his colleagues, arrived in Algeria. The mission divided their ministry between two districts, with one among the Arabs near the Mediterranean and the other among the Berbers in the Kabylia area.[74] The society was more successful among the Berbers, who had some centuries ago been forced to accept the Muslim religion, than among the Arabs, who were staunch Muslims. The Bible was translated into the language of the people. The Algiers Mission Band, a British mission, merged with the North Africa Mission in 1965.

The Episcopal Methodist Church commenced work in Algeria in 1909 under the direction of Joseph C. Hartzell. The society established medical work, an educational program, and three centers for evangelism.[75] In 1962 the society reported eight places of worship and 400 members. But the work was difficult. In a 1968 report, there were still eight places of worship but only 234 members.[76]

The Christian Mission to Many Lands began its ministry in Algeria in 1910. It established seven stations and eleven assemblies.[77] Several other societies have been working in Algeria, including the British and Foreign Bible Society, which sells Bibles wherever it has the opportunity; the Salvation Army; the Church Mission to the Jews; and the Evangelical Baptists. The Mennonite Church has had industrial training centers and agricultural projects in Algeria, through which they have attempted to witness to their faith.

In 1940 the Evangelical Mission Council in Algeria was formed. This body was reorganized to form the Association of Protestant Churches and Institutions in Algeria, but not all churches belong to it.[78] Though extensive efforts in Christian witnessing have been made, as in other Muslim countries, church growth has been very limited.

RESISTANCE AND LITTLE CHURCH GROWTH
Morocco

Morocco is a country in northwest Africa. It borders on the Atlantic Ocean and the Mediterranean Sea. It was a French protectorate since 1912 but became an independent monarchy in 1956. The original inhabitants of the country are Berbers, but there are also a large number of Jews who came to Morocco centuries ago. Some have emigrated to Israel in recent years. A superficial Christianity had reached Morocco in earlier centuries, largely through Spanish Catholic contacts, but it was virtually wiped out during the eighth and ninth centuries when the country was invaded by Muslim Arabs. Now the native population is strongly Muslim.

The Roman Catholic Church ministered to the European population in Morocco. In 1631 a prefecture was established and it continued to function till 1859 when it was turned over to Franciscan missionaries. The prefecture became a vicariate in 1908. By 1955 there were one hundred thousand Catholics in Morocco.[79]

Several Protestant mission societies have work in Morocco. The London Jews Society commenced its ministry in 1875. The North Africa Mission sent its first workers in 1882. It has work in four North African countries, but most of its missionaries came to Morocco.[80] In 1968 the society had 46 missionaries in that country. They operate the Tolloch Memorial Hospital, where thousands of Muslims receive medical care every year and also hear the gospel in the hospital. There is a nurses' training school connected with the hospital. The society, the largest mission in North Africa, has its headquarters in Tangier. It reported services at ten places, a total membership of 170, and a Christian community of 350.[8]

The Southern Morocco Mission is a Scottish mission that came to southern Morocco in 1888. Though the society had some promising work for a while, by 1958 their personnel had dwindled to fifteen. The ministry among the Muslims is difficult and few results are seen. Dr. Cuthbert Nairn, who had served faithfully in the country for fifty-six years, was murdered near his home by a Muslim.[82] In recent years the Southern Morocco Mission became affiliated with the North Africa Mission. It is of importance to note that in a report of their work no national workers are mentioned.[83]

The Gospel Missionary Union commenced its work in 1894. Some missionaries of the society ministered to Jews and to Europeans. The society translated the Bible into the Arabic language as spoken by the native people. In 1950 a Bible school for men was established and later a Bible school for women also was established. By 1958 the society had formed six congregations with a total membership of one hundred.[84] A 1962 report indicates a membership of two hundred.[85] In 1961, the society initiated a Bible correspondence course and in seven years forty thousand Muslims had asked for courses. This interest may have been the reason why the government expelled the missionaries of this society from the country in 1969.[86]

The Bible Churchmen's Missionary Society started work in central Morocco. Missionaries from this society established two stations, where they were involved in medical work and also held meetings for women.[87] Several converts were baptized in 1940. In 1962 the society had four worship centers and one hundred members, who were served by national lay workers and by two missionaries.[88] The mission experienced problems with the government and some of their stations were closed in 1968; four missionaries were expelled.[89]

Other Protestant societies are working in Morocco. The Mildmay Mission to the Jews sent missionaries in 1889, and they have witnessed faithfully to the Jews. The Evangelical Church of Morocco has four places of worship and a Christian community of twenty-five hundred.[90] The Plymouth Brethren, the Seventh-Day Adventists, the Berean Mission, the Christian Mission to Many Lands, the Southern Baptists, the Worldwide Evangelization Crusade, and the Light of Africa have been or still are attempting to reach the people of Morocco with the gospel. The Mennonite Central Committee has been engaged in social and relief work. In 1972 they had an elementary school and an industrial training center in Casablanca and also an agricultural center at another location.

The Voice of Tangier started broadcasting gospel messages in 1953. After six years of transmitting the programs, the radio ministry was forbidden. However, the society is continuing the radio ministry via Trans-World Radio in Monaco.

In 1963 the Moroccan government adopted a constitution by which most mission work is considered illegal. Efforts to evangelize the Muslims have not brought encouraging results. Statistics of 1968 show a Roman Catholic community of 400,000 and indicate that Protestants have 1,458 communicant members, twenty-seven places of worship and a Christian community of 6,056.[91] Missions have, however, ministered to all groups of people in Morocco through their schools, medical work, and translation and literature work, and by distributing Bibles and personal witnessing.

Spanish Sahara and the Canary Islands

The Spanish Sahara is a region of northwest Africa that borders the Atlantic coast. It lies southwest of Morocco. Except for a small group of Spaniards, who are Roman Catholics, the population of the Spanish Sahara is 100 percent Muslim. There is no Protestant church or any organized mission work in Spanish Sahara.[92]

The Canary Islands are off the coast of northwest Africa near the Spanish Sahara. They form two provinces of Spain and have been under Spanish rule since the fifteenth century. The Roman Catholic religion is dominant on the Canary Islands.

The Worldwide Evangelization Crusade is the only Protestant society that has work on the islands. After a small group of Protestant believers was formed, missionaries were expelled from the islands. They withdrew to Lanzarote Island. From this location they visit believers on the Canary Islands. They engaged in house-to-house visitation; however, they were not permitted to have church services.[93]

Mauritania

Mauritania is an Islamic Republic. It was part of French West Africa before it became an independent nation in 1960. The country is mostly desert but it has rich mineral deposits. The population of 1,100,000 (1967) consists primarily of Arabs and of Berber nomads.[94] There are some expatriates, who are mostly French.

The Portuguese had contacts with Mauritania since 1534 and thus Catholic missionaries have been there at intervals. The Catholic Church is ministering mostly to the expatriates.

Protestants have made some attempts to establish mission work in the country but have been unsuccessful in breaking the strong Muslim barrier. Thus they have withdrawn. The Scriptures are available in the Arabic language used in Mauritania. The Christian world needs to make more concentrated efforts to bring the gospel to the people of Mauritania.

SUMMARY

The Ethiopian Orthodox Church went through several periods of testing during which its vitality was seriously strained. After several of these periods, it was revived through the ministry of the monks, but this was not the case after the Muslim invasion during the sixteenth century. The monks withdrew into the monasteries. Their ministry was mainly to preserve the faith, and so the church neglected its missionary responsibility. Their failure clearly indicates that churches need to beware of becoming solely involved in internal affairs with the result that they neglect to see their missionary responsibility as given so clearly by Christ.

The denominational ambitions of the Jesuits in Ethiopia disrupted a fellowship that could have been salutary and could have greatly furthered the church in Ethiopia. However, as a result of ecclesiastical rivalry, missionary activities received a serious setback. This is one example of the many damaging activities of the Jesuits. Disunity among the Christian communities has greatly retarded the progress of Christianity.

The people movement at Wallamo and Kambatta indicates that if the gospel is brought to a people when they are responsive, and if leadership is given by charismatic, indigenous leaders, large church growth may take place. The ministry in Ethiopia further indicates that unless there is indigenous, spontaneous response, little church growth will occur. Dedicated church leaders who are trained in a culturally relevant situation may contribute to church growth, whereas workers who have been culturally disoriented may stall church growth.

The cooperative effort of the Lutheran Church in the local ministry in Ethiopia and in the radio ministry has brought important results. Cooperation among Christian organizations may increase the effectiveness of their ministries.

The error of the British rule in placing Muslim Arabs and Christian Negroes under one government is seen in the tragic persecu- of Christians in the Sudan during the 1960s. It is difficult to understand why neither Britain nor the United Nations protested the unreasonable blood bath. The question may be whether the church fulfilled its obligation to draw attention to this. Sudan is an incident warning the church serving south of the Sahara of the Muslim attitude toward Christians whenever they control the power of a country.

The contribution of the Egyptian Christians to the education and development of Egypt needs to be underscored. The Christians have been in a minority and because of Muslim pressure, its evangelistic efforts have been limited, but the Christians have made a vital contribution to the country. It is important for churches in other parts of the world to recognize the presence and ministry of the Egyptian church and establish Christian fellowship with it.

Although conversions to the Christian faith in North Africa have been relatively few, some Christians are witnessing faithfully. The lack of coordination of the Protestant efforts is one reason for the ineffectiveness of their efforts.[95] People hesitate to become members of small, weak organizations that are considered peculiar by the community. A federation of the Protestant ministry in North Africa could contribute to the progress of the work.

The Christian ministry among the Islamized peoples has not been successful. The church is, however, established in many parts of North Africa, especially in Egypt. The church will want to rethink its understanding of Islam, its attitude toward it, and its methods of presenting the Christian message to the Muslims. The churches of North Africa will want to pray and work for the manifestation of the Holy Spirit, through whose power Jesus Christ is exalted, and they should seek to present the message of Christ in culturally relevant forms.

Study Questions

1. Indicate the contributions of monasticism in sustaining the Christian faith in Ethiopia during centuries of difficulties.
2. Ethiopian Christianity was occupied with defending and preserving the faith, rather than proclaiming it. How did this situation influence Ethiopian Christianity?
3. Describe indigenous church growth during and after World War II.
4. Describe church growth in the southern part of Sudan and the difficulties the churches experienced during the past two decades.
5. What were the contributions of the Coptic Church in Egypt?
6. Evaluate the missionary policy adopted by the Church Missionary Society in 1882.
7. Evaluate the Presbyterian Church's policy of establishing strong educational work.
8. Which missionary policies have been most effective in North Africa?

9

Christianity in West Africa
(1884-1975)

Very significant changes took place in Africa during the last quarter of the nineteenth century, influencing the development of the missionary enterprise. H. M. Stanley's voyage to the mouth of the Zaire River by way of East Africa in 1877 brought the important phase of the exploration of Central Africa by Europeans to completion and greatly stimulated European and American interest in Africa. Beginnings had been made in the missionary enterprise at various areas in West Africa. In many instances an established work developed and Christianity spread through the participation of African leaders and through the testimony of Christians in their own areas and sometimes in districts where no Christian witness had been proclaimed.

Protestant churches increased their efforts to bring the Christian faith to all parts of West Africa. Many missionary societies participated in the work. An important aspect in the promotion of the Protestant faith was the contribution of the African church leaders. The growth of the missionary concern was manifested in the missionary conference at Edinburgh in 1910, and this further inspired the missionary cause. The renewal of the Roman Catholic thrust through the guidance of the Sacred Congregation of Propaganda Fide was very meaningful, bringing many Roman Catholic efforts that also influenced the everyday life of the people. The overwhelming majority of the schools were begun and maintained by missionaries.

Although the occupation of West Africa by Western powers opened some areas that had been closed to Christian missions, it placed Christian missions in a problematic situation that in the end was not beneficial to the Christian cause. The earlier positive endeavor to establish an indigenous church, especially in the ministry of the Church Missionary Society, was discontinued. Instead, the work was conducted through general evangelistic and educational efforts during which the effective establishment of the church did not receive sufficient emphasis.

Christian missions have generally not been productive among the Islamized peoples of West Africa. The penetration of the interior of West Africa was somewhat slow. Little work was done in some of the northern parts of the coastal countries until the second quarter of the twentieth century and many areas have not been fully occupied. The church is only being established in them at this time.

MINORITY CHURCHES BUT A CHRISTIAN PRESENCE

Senegal

Senegal was a part of the former federation of French West Africa but gained its independence from France in 1960. A large part of the republic's population is of Negro blood. The French influence in the country began before 1800 and became strong during the nineteenth century; however, Islam has remained the prevailing religion. The Roman Catholics have maintained a ministry to Senegal since 1849 and the Protestants since 1862, but their efforts have not been productive.

Senegal has been the most discouraging field of the Paris Evangelical Missionary Society in terms of the number of conversions. The Eglise de Dakar has in recent years assumed greater financial support for the Open Door Center, which was started by two African missionaries and which offers medical care, literacy classes, and youth work. The activities of the Freedom Center were strengthened when a team member from the Netherlands and a couple from Cameroon joined the staff in 1968. Through the financial assistance of the German Protestant churches and la Cooperation Francaise, a dispensary, which ministers to the needs of the people and presents its Christian witness through its service, was constructed by the Centre de Bopp.[1]

The Assemblies of God Mission came to Senegal in 1956. Though it began mission work later than some other societies, it had been more successful, and the church that grew from its efforts is the largest Protestant church in the country, reporting a Christian community of 1,698 in 1968.[2] It has established three stations and opened the Temple Evangelique in Dakar in 1963. A Bible institute was begun in 1964.

The Worldwide Evangelization Crusade began a ministry in Senegal in 1936. In 1970 the society had twenty-nine workers in Dakar and eight in other towns of the eastern part of the country. But after many years of labor the society counted only twenty-five Christians.[3]

The Conservative Baptists undertook work in Thies on the east coast in 1961. They began with enthusiasm, holding street meetings and presenting gospel films outdoors. There was good attendance at these meetings, but there were few conversions to the Christian faith. The society has been plagued with illness, and in 1970 only two missionaries remained at Thies. The bookstore was closed, and publication was temporarily discontinued.

The New Tribes Mission sent missionaries to Senegal in 1955. They established a ministry at Casamance, their only station in the country, where six couples were serving in 1970. The response to the ministry, however, has been minimal. Consequently, there are only several thousand adherents to the Protestant community in Senegal.

The Roman Catholic Church created the vicariate apostolic of Senegambia in 1963. The Holy Ghost Fathers opened a seminary that by 1902 graduated ten native priests.[4] In 1939 the first African-born priest was appointed to be head of a new prefecture apostolic in Senegal.[5] The Catholics developed a congregation for native sisters. They opened additional centers and maintained schools. Although their success has been limited, they had 106,857 adherents in 1965.[6]

The entire Christian community of Senegal is only about 3 percent of the population. The Christian community has not been an influential element in the Senegalese society. A similar situation exists in the western countries of the former French West Africa federation.

Gambia

Gambia is a small West African country surrounded on three sides by Senegal and bordering on the Atlantic. It was a British colony that gained its independence in 1965 and became a constitutional monarchy within the British Commonwealth. It has a population of about 316,000 of which about 79 percent are Muslims and about 16 percent are animists. The Christian population is small.[7]

Though the Wesleyan Methodist Church began work in Gambia in 1821, it was hindered because of the unhealthful climate. While Protestant missions were discouraged and failed to move ahead, Islam made strong inroads and thus hindered effective Protestant work later. Through the Methodist Church has had work in Gambia for more than 150 years, latest statistics show seven places of worship with a total membership of about thirteen thousand. They operate several primary schools and a few clinics.[8]

The United Society for the Proclamation of the Gospel (Anglican) was partly successful in its secondary education program in Bathurst, but most of the students are Muslims. Statistics indicate that they have fourteen places of worship with a total membership of six hundred and a Christian population of about nineteen thousand.[9] The consecration of its first African bishop took place in 1960.

The Worldwide Evangelization Crusade undertook work in 1957. The mission has engaged in medical work, trying in this way to make contacts for evangelization. In 1971-72 only one missionary was reported working in that mission in Gambia.[10]

The Roman Catholic Church assigned Gambia to the Holy Ghost Fathers. Work was begun at Bathurst in 1849. Because of illness and constantly changing personnel, no other post to the interior was opened until recently. The results of the effort have been minimal.

Guinea

Guinea is located north of Sierra Leone, west of Mali, and fronting on the Atlantic Ocean. It was formerly a French colony but it became an independent nation in 1958. The majority of the population adheres to the Muslim faith, but there are some animists in the forest regions. The Fullah, the Malinke, and the Susu are the three large tribes, though there are about thirteen smaller tribes.[11]

The Anglican Church undertook a missionary enterprise in the 1850s but it withdrew as a result of the French occupation.[12]

The Christian and Missionary Alliance came to Guinea in 1918 and started work at Baro in the Niger valley. It developed centers in other parts of the country and established a printing press at

Kankan, where the mission had its headquarters. The mission opened a Bible school at Telkora. In the 1960s the headquarters were moved to Conakry, where an International Protestant Church was started to minister to the English-speaking foreigners. The mission made efforts to translate parts of the Scriptures into five languages; however, because of resistance, it had problems with the distribution of the Scriptures.[13]

Other missions working in Guinea include the Paris Evangelical Missionary Society and the Anglican Church with its work at Conakry as a part of the diocese of Gambia and the Rio Pongas. The Open Bible Standard Mission since 1952 has worked among both Muslims and the animists in rural and urban areas.[14]

The Guinea government ordered American and European missionaries to leave the country before June 1967, so that the missions could be Africanized. Though this was a difficult situation, it was instrumental in bringing various groups of Christians together.[15] Missionaries from the Open Bible Standard Mission, the Anglican Church and the Paris Mission left. After much negotiation, the Christian and Missionary Alliance received permission for twenty-six missionaries to remain to work in the Bible school, in the school for missionaries' children, and at the mission headquarters in Conakry. Missionaries were permitted to work and travel with relative freedom, provided they adhered to the government policy. The church continues to minister in the preaching of the gospel, Bible translation, theological training, and in the preparation of radio programs to be broadcast from ELWA, Liberia.[16] The total Protestant community in Guinea is under three thousand.[17]

The Catholic mission commenced work in Guinea in the eighteenth century. The Holy Ghost Fathers opened a school in Dakar, Senegal, and thus, by providing education for the sons of the chiefs, were able to establish credibility to open a mission station. Later their work was extended and they also provided for industrial and plantation schools.[18]

Portuguese Guinea

Portuguese Guinea is a small country adjoining the northwestern boundary of Guinea, with the Atlantic Ocean to the west. It is a Portuguese colony considered an Overseas Province of Portugal. The Roman Catholic Church has largely a membership of foreigners. Most of the native population is Muslim. The Worldwide Evangelization Crusade started work there in 1939, and in 1973 they had five workers. The Protestant community numbers about 1,320.[19]

OLDER CHURCHES BUT MANY UNDISCIPLED

The political situations have affected the ministry of the churches in West Africa. During the seventeenth century and the early part of the eighteenth, slave trade was rampant. Missions and philanthropists were horrified and labored unceasingly to eliminate the inhumane activity. After the slave trade was brought under control, churches were planted at strategic places in West Africa.

Under the guidance of Henry Venn, the secretary of the Church Missionary Society, indigenous church principles were introduced from the beginning of the ministry. The society offered Christian education at the Fourah Bay College in Sierra Leone and encouraged African Christians to dedicate themselves to the evangelization of Africa. Samuel Crowther, James Johnson, and others served as bishops with the church, extending its ministry in West Africa, notably along the Niger and into the interior of Nigeria. During this period missions served in countries governed by African governments. Positive beginnings were made in Ghana, Nigeria, and Cameroon, and churches were planted before European colonial powers intervened in these countries.

The political pattern of the continent was entirely transformed by the coming of colonial powers. The colonial period was marked by rapid changes in the economic and social structures of the countries and a remarkable expansion of the Christian faith. Unfortunately, however, the emphasis on the immediate establishment of indigenous churches, introduced by Henry Venn, was generally not maintained. Some churches gave consideration to the establishment of indigenous churches; however, basically, indigenization received renewed consideration only toward the end of the colonial period. The movement toward the indigenization of churches also influenced the political scene.

A marked movement toward political independence of the countries and toward the independence of the churches began after World War II and was rapidly accomplished in all but a few countries. It has been a period in which many new churches have been established and the union of some churches has taken place. The All-Africa Conference of Churches and the Association of Evangelicals of Africa and Madagascar have been formed and the independent churches have witnessed tremendous growth. The voice of the African churches has been recognized in the universal Christian fellowship.

Sierra Leone

Many of the freed slaves who came to Sierra Leone were Christians and established churches for the settlement. Near the end of the nineteenth century, there were third- and fourth-generation Christians. Much progress had been made in education. Men trained at the Fourah Bay College became leaders in various countries in West Africa. As early as 1886, two students of the church in Lagos were admitted to the college. The church employed the men trained at the Fourah Bay College and also evangelists with a limited education.[20]

The Anglican Church in Sierra Leone undertook a mission on the Bullum shore in 1897 and in 1898 assumed the responsibility for one in Sherbro among the Mende people. There was considerable progress in the Mende work after 1907. By 1912 fourteen outstations had been started.[21] The Anglican Church of Sierra Leone, however, was not prepared to fill the opportunities and fully minister to the response in the Mende tribe.

The American Missionary Society commenced work among the Mendes in 1840. They began several stations but in 1882 they turned their work over to the United Brethren in Christ. Progress was made in the educational and medical ministries. The society operates the Rotifunk Hospital. Recent reports show that the United Brethren in Christ Church in Sierra Leone has 112 places of worship and 1,726 communicant members.[22]

The churches in Sierra Leone experienced serious problems in 1898. The state put pressure on the tribes in the interior, forbidding slave trade and demanding that taxes be paid. A revolt broke out. Many Christians were killed, including seven missionaries, two of whom were doctors from Rotifunk. Leaders of the Methodist Church at Tikonko were killed and the center was destroyed. At Sherbro the church leaders and more than two hundred Christians were massacred.[23] After the revolt, the work was reestablished.

Various Methodist churches are active in Sierra Leone. They include the United Methodists, the African Methodist Episcopal, the West African Methodist Church, and the Methodist Church. Together they have a membership of about 17,592.[24]

The Christian and Missionary Alliance started work in Sierra Leone in 1890 and continued till 1918, when they left to go to another country. The Missionary Church in 1945 went to work in the area abandoned by the Christian and Missionary Alliance. The Missionary Church did translation work, started a Bible school, and later cooperated in the ministry of the Sierra Leone Bible College. They have 29 places of worship, 240 communicant members, and a Christian community of 1,200.[25]

Seventh-Day Adventists, who came to Sierra Leone in 1907, had slow church growth till 1959. In the following four years, however, their membership increased from 1,017 to 2,054. Olson implies that this growth took place because they made plans for church growth and carried them out. They have a thorough stewardship program. All levels of church workers receive the same salary.[26]

The Assemblies of God have worked in the country since 1907. They opened a Bible school in 1963. The students work part time as farmers to support themselves, and class schedules are adjusted accordingly. The Assemblies of God have enthusiastic church services with much participation. However, church growth has been slow.[27]

There are some independent churches active in Sierra Leone. The God is Our Light Church has no sacraments. Emphasis is placed on regular attendance and obedience to laws. This church prohibits any type of medical aid and teaches faith healing through prayer. The Church of the Lord (Aladura) was active in Nigeria and began a ministry in Sierra Leone in 1947. It is a Pentecostal-type church. Its influence spread rapidly, and "praying groups" were begun in various places. Adejobi began the church; it is called by his name in Sierra Leone. The other churches are not favorably inclined toward this church, but its members desire to be accepted.[28]

The Roman Catholic Church in Sierra Leone puts its major emphasis on schools. Church growth results from conversions in the student body, as the church does not win many tribes people. The membership of the Catholic Church is relatively small.

Many of the freed slaves who settled in Sierra Leone were

Baptists and established Baptist churches near the coast. Efforts to reach the tribespeople were made by the Nigerian Baptist Convention, but not until 1960.

Sierra Leone was the first area in Africa where Protestants had mission work. However, results have been disappointing. Though 70 percent of the Creoles along the coast are Christians, only 2 percent of the tribal people are Christians. Many of these people are Muslims because the Muslims contacted them before Christian missions came into the interior.[29] Language may have been a large part of the problem. Instead of the vernacular, the English language is used. The problem is that many people in the interior do not understand English well. According to reports, the problem of the social classes is also disrupting effective communication between the Creoles and the tribes.

Two ecumenical organizations in Sierra Leone are the United Christian Council, belonging to the World Council of Churches, and the Sierra Leone Evangelical Fellowship. There is also a women's organization first known as the Women's Christian Federation but renamed the Sierra Leone United Church of Women because it stresses church union. A part-time organizing secretary was employed by this organization in 1968.

Through the efforts of the United Christian Council, a new interest in Sunday school work was aroused. The council also considered employing an industrial chaplain to work in a new industrial area. It supports the development of a literacy program and also publishes some magazines.

In 1966 an Inter-Church Conference was held with the theme "God renews His Church through lay participation." That year the New-Life-for-All Campaign was organized with specific goals for evangelization. The aim was for total mobilization of the church.[30]

The Sierra Leone Branch of the Bible Societies of West Africa has established a center at Freetown. The New Testament in the Limba language was completed and made available in 1968. Other literature is made available in the vernacular.[31]

Liberia

Liberia is the oldest independent state in West Africa. It was formed in the 1820s when freed American slaves settled there. The majority of the population, however, consists of the tribes who live in the interior.

Missions continue to work among the Americo-Liberians and among the indigenous population of Liberia. Bishop William Taylor was the director of the Methodist Episcopal Church from 1884 to 1896. He introduced the principle of financially self-sufficient churches. Under his direction, work was established in many centers among the tribes of the interior. But his projects were unsuccessful. From 1896 to 1900, twenty-three American black missionaries came to Liberia. In 1904 an associate bishop was appointed. By 1908 the society had ninety-eight staff members, including local and foreign personnel.[32] An outstanding contribution of the society has been the College of West Africa, founded in Monrovia in 1839. This college has provided personnel for the ministry of the church and for government positions. The society serves the medical needs of the people at its hospitals and leprosarium.

An American Episcopal Church made several early but unsuccessful attempts to start work in Liberia. A continuing mission was started in 1834 by John Payne, who in 1851 became bishop of Liberia. He spoke the Grebo language, translated portions of Scripture into Grebo, and studied the customs of the local people. The church among the tribe grew. By 1916 the educational program was well established. The next bishop was Samuel Ferguson, who immigrated to Liberia as a child. He was the first Negro bishop of Liberia. Under his direction the church grew in numbers. He was also concerned to have trained leadership. This led to the establishment of Cuttington College and Divinity School. However, after Bishop Ferguson's death, the leadership training weakened and in 1944 the church had fewer trained leaders than 1916.[33] Recent figures show the church membership at 7,414 with 145 places of worship and 32 ordained men.[34]

The United Lutheran Church established its first mission station in Liberia at Muhlenberg in 1860. Progress was slow because of the high death rate of missionaries, the short terms of others, and the shortage of national leaders. However, by the end of the century there was sufficient personnel to expand and to establish new stations. The Evangelical Lutheran Church was organized in 1948. The church and the mission merged in 1865 and formed the Lutheran Church of Liberia. The church has had problems in becoming fully autonomous because it has been stunted by too much foreign aid and thus has not developed its own resources, neither in spontaneous lay leadership nor in financial responsibility.[35] The church has a membership of 8,334.[36] In 1967 the Lutheran Church instigated the development of a social center in cooperation with other churches, including the Catholics, at Bomi Hill, a mining center. In recent years the church has experienced growth through group conversions in some villages. They opened a Lay Training Center at Kpolopele.[37]

At the beginning of the twentieth century other societies came to Liberia and contributed to the establishment of the church in the country. Among them were the Assemblies of God (1908), who work at fifteen stations in the southeastern part of Liberia. The society emphasizes the training of men for the ministry. It opened three Bible schools for this purpose. The society does not provide scholarships for the Bible school students. Medical work at Hope Town and a leper colony are avenues of ministering to physical needs. The society also does evangelistic work at two large Firestone Rubber Company plantations. The government required that they open some schools, but their major emphasis is evangelism. Revivals took place in some areas between 1928 and 1936. There were large people's movements where whole villages of tribal people burned their fetishes and became Christians. The church operated on an indigenous basis from the start.[38]

Since 1931 the Baptist Mid-Missions has worked in Central province. The work of this group includes a medical ministry, a Bible institute, and a printing press.[39] Church growth has been slow, figures showing 85 places of worship but only 419 communicant members in 1967.[40] The Worldwide Evangelism Crusade opened the first Christian bookstore in Monrovia in 1947. The church that was begun by this society is called the Liberia Inland Mission.

The Sudan Interior Mission is responsible for Radio Station ELWA, which has the tremendous ministry of broadcasting gospel programs in forty languages to all parts of Africa and the Middle East. It also offers Bible correspondence courses, in which some ten thousand students are enrolled.

Many Baptist churches in Liberia had their beginning with the settlers who came to Liberia from America. In recent years the Southern Baptist mission also has been engaged in a ministry in Liberia. The Baptist churches are generally autonomous and operate on a local congregational polity structure. Most of their work is near the coast with people who have had more educational opportunities than those living in the interior.[41]

In 1973 there were forty-one mission societies or church-related organizations working in Liberia. Of these, at least four have worked for a hundred years or more, and thirteen came in 1960 and later. Theological training has been neglected in Liberia and so the church lacks leaders. Some societies have established Bible schools to cope with this problem.

Catholic missions have concentrated on educational work and gained members through schools. They are working in most parts of the country but do not have a large church membership. In 1967 they made special efforts to reach out in Monrovia and in mining settlements elsewhere in the country.[42]

Ecumenical organizations in Liberia are the Liberia Evangelical Fundamental Fellowship and the Christian Rural Fellowship.

GROWING CHURCHES WITH NEW CHALLENGES

Churches were established in numerous coastal cities and towns during the earlier period of the missionary endeavor. These ministries became more established and contributed to the needs of the people. African Christians received training in the ministries of the church and assumed significant responsibilities in all these endeavors. During this period the missionary societies already established in the coastal regions extended their ministry to the people of the interior, and new societies came to serve the unevangelized peoples. This period witnessed massive historic transitions. Christianity and Western education brought about a new outlook on life and also a new desire to attain new goals, leading to the indigenous ministry in the churches and to political independence for the countries. The new churches assumed their responsibilities in ecumenical relationships and formed national and international councils.

Ivory Coast

Ivory Coast, situated east of Liberia, is largely covered with tropical forests and cut up by rivers and streams bordered by palm trees. It was formerly a part of French West Africa. It became an independent nation in 1960. The traditional religion of the country is animism. Muslims have a following of about 709,000.[43] Ivory Coast was neglected by the first mission societies.

One of the most interesting stories of Christian missions occurred in the Ivory Coast. The "prophet" William Wade Harris, a Liberian of the Berbos tribe, grew up under the influence of Christianity. His uncle was a Methodist preacher in Liberia. At the age of twenty, Harris had a deep religious experience. However, his Christian ministry did not begin until 1910, when he was sixty years old. While on an evangelistic tour in the Ivory Coast and Gold Coast, he dressed in a white robe, wore a white turban on his head, and carried a Bible, a bamboo cross, and a gourd of water. He went from place to place proclaiming the message of salvation in Christ. An estimated one hundred thousand people abandoned their fetishes and turned to Christianity. Harris accepted the hospitality of the converts but refused any donations or gifts. He organized groups of believers and advised them to construct chapels. He placed a pastor in charge and had the group name twelve apostles to direct the church. Some converts were sent to the interior tribes to bring them the message of salvation. Harris told the newly formed congregations that missionaries would come to explain the Bible to them.

After two years of ministry in Ivory Coast, Harris was arrested by French authorities and sent back to Liberia, chiefly because he was an alien. The French feared the new religious movement and attempted to stop it. A movement of its size could easily became a strong political movement. The French were very suspicious and did not permit the Protestant missionaries to move into the interior until after the war.[44] They ordered that the chapels be burned. But this did not suppress the movement. The Christians built better and more permanent chapels. Christians endured persecutions but continued to worship in spite of the danger involved. Fetishism almost disappeared. The movement was a remarkable victory for Christianity.

The Wesleyan Methodists began work in the Ivory Coast in 1924. When the government suppressed the Harris movement, many of the churches organized by Harris joined the Methodists, while some churches preferred to remain independent. The churches that remained independent have formed the Harrist Church, which by 1960 had an estimated seventy thousand adherents.[45]

The Wesleyan Methodists established schools, including the secondary school and a women's training center. The original enthusiasm of the Harris influence has waned. Many people are nominal Christians and some members have returned to animistic practices. Had missions been able to come in to teach the people the Bible during the Harrist revival, the church might have been strong; but in a period of almost ten years, the newly converted, illiterate people were left without anyone to give them deeper, spiritual nurture.

In 1964 the Methodist Church had jubilee celebrations, and the Rev. Samson Nandjui was installed as first chairman of the district. The spiritual life of the church was deepened by a return to serious Bible studies.[46] The church has also expanded its work in Abidjan in order to reach the Protestant university students and to increase its witness to port workers.

The Harrist movement witnessed significant expansion after 1945 through the efforts of Jonas Ahui and Ledjou N'Drin Gaston. The revival of the movement gave rise to many independent churches, including the syncretistic Eglise Deimatiste, which claimed ninety thousand adherents in 1958. The total of independent adherents is about two million.[47]

In 1930 the Christian and Missionary Alliance moved into the interior of the country, where there was no Christian witness. By 1959 they had established forty worship centers around Bouake. They started a Bible school at Bouake. A major contribution of the mission has been the translation of the New Testament into the Manika and the Sonhrai languages, and certain books of the Bible have been translated into other dialects.[48] There was marked church growth. The church became fully independent in 1957 and is called the Evangelical Protestant Church of Ivory Coast. The church has about seventy-five thousand members. It is involved in the union school, the Yamoussourko Bible Institute. The society publishes much literature and is involved in a radio ministry.[49]

The Worldwide Evangelization Crusade commenced its work in Ivory Coast in 1934. It is reaching three tribal areas. The church is known as the Evangelical Mission of West Africa and has a membership of about three hundred, worshiping at twenty-five centers.[50]

Since 1947 the Conservative Baptists have worked among the Senufo tribe in the northwestern part of the country. They have a medical work with a hospital and a dispensary. However, much of their effort focuses on village evangelism, adult literacy, and translation.[51] Church growth has been slow and has resulted in a membership of about 813.[52]

Some other missions have started work in Ivory Coast in recent years. They are the Free Will Baptist Mission (1957), the Unevangelized Fields Mission (1963), and the Southern Baptist Convention (1966). Since 1968 the Sudan Interior Mission has been working with the Intermission Evangelical Publishing Center, taking responsibility for the French magazine *Champion*, which is widely read in French-speaking Africa.

Although Roman Catholic missionary contacts with the Ivory Coast began in 1687, the active propagation of Christianity was not begun on an extensive scale until the 1890s. In 1895 Rome entrusted the region to the Society of African Missions of Lyons. By 1901 the society had established six stations and, as the French extended their authority inland, the society moved into the interior. Even though the French government emphasized the lay state and maintained an anticlerical policy during this period, the Catholics developed schools, as they did in the other territories controlled by France. The society established a printing press in which literature for its use was prepared. By 1913 the ministry was beginning to take root among the people and the society reported a membership of twenty-four hundred.[53] Because of the pressure that was exerted on Harris's followers, about twenty thousand of them were induced to join the Roman Catholic Church. Even though Harris's converts added significantly to the growth of the church, Christianity made much less progress in Ivory Coast than in other parts of West Africa. In 1936 the Christians counted for 4 to 5 percent of the population. Roman Catholics were slightly more numerous than Protestants. In 1934 the Roman Catholics ordained their first native priest of Ivory Coast.[54]

The Roman Catholic community witnessed significant growth after 1936. By 1965 the Catholics had established six dioceses and reported 402,655 adherents.[55] In recent years there has been considerable cooperation between Roman Catholics and Protestants. They work together in an effort to serve the thousands of seamen who pass through the city of Abidjan. In 1967 eight Catholic priests and eight Methodist pastors had a meeting to discuss the role of laymen in evangelism.[56]

Recently an Evangelical Publishing Center was established in Abidjan. It serves as a center for promoting and coordinating the publication of literature related to church work for the French-speaking African countries.[57]

Though there is no national church council in Ivory Coast, there is an Evangelical Federation of Ivory Coast. All evangelical missions cooperate in the Bible institute at Yomoussoukro.[58] Recently a national Baptist association was formed.

Ghana

Ghana, a country in West Africa, was formerly known as Gold Coast and was a British colony. It became an independent nation in 1957. It has a population of 9,600,000.[59] Accra is the capital city.

The Wesleyan Methodist Church reestablished its work in Ghana after the Ashanti War in 1896. They started some new centers at which the work was productive. By 1913 the Ashanti mission had baptized 26,000 members. In 1911 William Griffin made an extensive tour of the interior region, going beyond Tomale, the government center. The chiefs gave him a friendly reception and asked him to send teachers to villages and gave him permission to establish mission stations. As a result of Griffin's report, the synod encouraged the church on the coast to work in the interior of the country.

William Wade Harris, an African prophet-evangelist from Liberia, came to Gold Coast and had an effective ministry in 1914, winning many of thousands converts.[60] The people listened to his instructions relating to their Christian life and modes of worship. They obeyed the twelve apostles who were the church leaders. The Methodist Church invited Harris's followers to join the church. Some groups accepted this fraternal fellowship, whereas other groups chose to remain independent.

The Methodist mission emphasized the importance of training national workers. Thus a strong church, served by national pastors, was formed. In 1955 the church started mission work in the northern territories of Ghana. In a year they established ten church centers. They engaged in evangelism and in education. The church started by the Methodist mission became autonomous in 1961 and is known as the Ghana Methodist Church.[61] As a result of the educational efforts of mission and church, centers for training were established, such as the Freeman College, Trinity College, and Kwadasa Women's Training Center.[62] In 1967 the Ghana

Methodist Church had 69,260 communicant members, 116 ordained pastors, and 272 lay church workers.[63]

The goal of the early missionaries of the Basel Mission, who came to Ghana in 1828, was to reach Kumasi, the capital of the Ashanti tribe; however, it took many years to achieve that goal. The death toll among early missionaries was high. After the war of 1896 and the defeat of King Prempeh, the British took over the Ashanti area and missionaries were able to go to Kumasi. The first missionaries arrived there in February 1896. They started working at Kumasi and also opened stations in the vicinity. By 1914 there were 20 mission centers, 17 schools, and 805 church members.[64] In 1905 the Basel Mission decided to proceed to the interior. The governor of the area requested that they wait till a railway was completed so the state would be able to provide protection in the area. In 1912 a pioneer group, under the direction of Otto Schlimming, arrived at Yendi, the capital of the Dagomba area.

One of the methods of the Basel Mission was to establish separate villages for Christians. These villages were directed by Christian principles and developed a strong church. By 1879 they had four thousand believers with six African pastors, ninety lay workers, nine main stations, thirty-one outstations,[65] and many village schools.

During World War I the German missionaries of the Basel Mission had to leave and the mission was turned over to the United Free Church of Scotland. By that time the membership had grown to 12,000 and African church workers outnumbered missionaries 6 to 1.[66] The church became autonomous in 1960. Today the church is known as the Presbyterian Church of Ghana and has 686 worship centers and 52,547 communicant members.[67] The church belongs to the World Council of Churches.

The Bremen Mission saw significant progress from 1884 to 1914. Franz Michael Zahn, a missiologist and director of the Bremen Mission from 1862 to 1900, furthered the progress of its ministry toward independence. From the beginning, agricultural, educational, medical, and technical work was considered a part of the task of evangelization, ministering to the total person. Much effort was made to establish Christian homes and to relate them to the Christian community. Polygamists were accepted into the fellowship of the church and instructed in biblical teachings. The aim to establish an indigenous church was expressed in the establishment of a seminary in 1864 to train pastors for the work of the church.[68] In addition to the training offered in Ghana, twenty men were sent to Germany for training before 1914. They contributed greatly to the ministry of the church and guided it during World War I when the missionaries were interned.

The work of the Bremen Mission suffered from the two world wars. The Scottish church responded to an appeal for help after World War I and was instrumental in organizing the Ewe Presbyterian Church, largely self-governing and self-supporting. In 1922 the church held its first synod. In 1954 its name was changed to Evangelical Presbyterian Church. Under British jurisdiction in Ghana, the church was obliged to use the English language. The Scottish missionaries helped the German-speaking teachers learn English. The German missionaries returned in 1930, but were recalled during World War II. At this time the Evangelical and Reformed Church of America came to its assistance.

The Evangelical Presbyterian Church made considerable effort to train leadership, offering high school, seminary, teacher training, and nurses' training. It joined with the Presbyterian Church of Ghana and the Methodist Church to establish Trinity College to train pastors in 1943. In 1950 the church began its ministry in northern Ghana in the Yendi area. It established an agricultural school in 1962.

The ministry of the Society for the Propagation of the Gospel was begun in 1751 by Thomas Thompson at Cape Coast Castle. It was continued from 1766 to 1816 by Philip Quaque, one of the three boys Thompson sent to England for training. This ministry gained little support from Britain and only a few converts in Africa until the end of the nineteenth century.[69] The activities were confined to the forts. In 1904 N. J. Hamlyn arrived from Lagos and brought new inspiration to the work. In 1909 the diocese of Accra was created, and Hamlyn became the first bishop. The first deacons were ordained in 1915 and two priests in 1917. The Anglicans established nine centers in various parts of the country. The work was more productive and the church became more fully established among the people, gathering a Christian community of sixty thousand members.

The Christian influence in Ghana by 1936 was quite significant. Although only about 10 percent of the population were Christians, non-Christians participated in Christian festivals, joined in Christian prayers, read the Bible, and considered themselves as belonging to the Christian community.[70] The progress of the Christian cause has often been the result of individual witness by church members as they moved about in the country. The provision of formal education by the missions had exerted a substantial impact on the people.

Until 1940 missionary work was carried on mostly in southern Ghana. That year the Worldwide Evangelization Crusade started mission work, establishing four stations and engaging in evangelism and medical work.[71] They also treated leprosy patients. Eventually they became involved in other areas of ministry, including Bible correspondence courses, literature, and radio programs.

Baptist Mid-Missions came to Ghana in 1946 as a result of an invitation by members of the Baptist Church from Yorubaland who came to Ghana for business reasons. This mission started three stations in southern Ghana and in 1949 also commenced work in northern Ghana.[72] According to 1967 figures, they had 15 worship centers and 188 communicant members.[73]

Various other mission societies are working in Ghana. The Assemblies of God have two Bible institutes for training church workers. They have 180 worship centers and 6,069 church members.[74] The African Methodist Episcopal Zion Church commenced work in 1900 and has grown to 84 worship centers and 6,560 members, 47 ordained persons, and many active laymen.[75] Other missions include the Salvation Army, the Seventh-Day Adventists, the Wycliffe Bible Translators, the Society of Friends, and the Sudan Interior Mission. The Mennonite Church has not founded a mission but assists independent churches in various ways. The British and Foreign Bible Society has done extensive work and in 1967 founded the Bible Society of Ghana.[76] Some of the established congregations in Ghana engage in mission work in various parts of the country, and some have also reached out to neighboring countries.[77]

The Christian Council of Ghana, founded in 1929, served as an advisory council for Protestant churches. It has enabled churches to share in various ministries. In 1956 the council asked its members to form a church-union committee. In 1957 negotiations toward church union began, with participation by the Anglican Church, the Methodist Church, the Evangelical Presbyterian

Church of Ghana, the African Methodist Episcopal Church, and the Ghana Mennonite Church. The Ghana Church Union Committee was formed to guide the matter. Drafts of the text of the basis for union were presented to the churches in 1960, 1961, and 1962. In 1963 a doctrinal commission composed of diocesan bishops and theologically qualified persons was formed to guard the faith. Regular meetings were held in 1964. In 1965 the revised basis for union was presented to the negotiating churches. Much deliberation has gone on in committee meetings and much explanation has been given to the churches. The Declaration of Intention on Church Union has been presented with the hope that the churches will eventually accept it.[78] In 1967 the Christian Council of Ghana appointed an evangelist to minister to eighty thousand people in the Volta Resettlement Area. They also promote Christian witness and service in government hospitals and are concerned with religious education in the schools. The council encourages the Ghana Broadcasting Corporation in its presentation of religious programs and religious television.[79]

Catholic missionaries had contacts with Ghana in the early centuries when Portuguese ships stopped there, but very little mission work was done. When missionaries came to Ghana in the nineteenth century, they found elements of Catholic rituals in a syncretic animism. Like the Protestants, many Catholic missionaries died shortly after they reached Ghana. For those who survived, the work was difficult. Catholic societies working in Ghana are the Society of African Missions, the White Fathers, the Divine Word missionaries, and various orders of sisters. The Catholic Church has done much in education and in medical work. A Catholic school of nursing was started in 1953. The Catholic Church established teacher-training colleges and several seminaries. By 1950 Ghana formed an Ecclesiastical Province. There were thirty Ghanian priests and a Ghanian bishop in Accra. According to recent reports, 13.4 percent of the population of Ghana adheres to the Catholic Church and 29.6 percent are Protestants.[80]

Togo

Togo, a small country in West Africa, was a German colony from the 1880s till World War I. It was then divided, part under British administration with Gold Coast and part under the French in the colony of Dahomey. It became an independent nation in 1960. The population of Togo was two million in 1973.[81]

In 1900 the Bremen Mission advanced to Togo and started a station at Agou and in 1905 another one at the commercial center of Akpafu. It was a strategic move. The German government, then in power in Togo, invited American blacks from the Tuskegee Institute of Alabama to come to Togo to teach the native people how to improve the method of cultivating cotton.[82] The mission was purposely established in an area where the soil was rich. Their aim was to found churches in areas where the local people could produce good crops and have the financial resources to support the church and extend its ministry to poorer areas. The church was founded on a solid basis from the beginning and was progressive, showing marked church growth.

In 1902 the Bremen Mission and the Basel Mission established zones of responsibility, the Basel Mission working in the Tua area and the Bremen Mission among the Ewe. The Basel Mission limited its work to the Anoun area in the English triangle east of the Volta River.[83]

The Bremen Mission started work at Akpafu and Atakpame and ministered to the mountain tribes. These tribes spoke diverse languages, but religious instruction was given in the Ewe language. The deaconesses from Hambourg, Germany, came to start a boarding school for girls.[84] The society made strong efforts to train church workers. The effect of this was obvious when native workers performed an outstanding ministry in areas where Europeans were unable to support the climate. During the Ashanti War (1869) a missionary had liberated a young slave who later became a pastor and was sent to Peki.[85]

In 1890 the Bremen Mission founded a school in western Germany with the purpose of training Ewe men to take leadership in the church. These students had the opportunity for advanced study in Europe and also benefited from contacts with European professors and with the churches in Germany. Between 1890 and 1914, twenty African students attended the school.[86] They became pastors who guided the church through the difficult period of World War I (1914-1918) and later. During World War I the ministry of the Bremen Society was restricted. Some German missionaries were able to continue their work in one area, but other work was turned over to the United Free Church of Scotland.

In 1925 the Bremen Mission was officially permitted to work in British Togo. The church in that area formed the Ewe Presbyterian Church in 1927. In 1954 the church changed its name to the Evangelical Presbyterian Church but since 1957 it is the Evangelical Church of Togo.

In the section of Togo that was a French mandate after World War I, the church was independent because the missionaries had to leave. A good foundation had been laid and the church was self-governing and self-supporting.[87] Nevertheless, in 1923 the pastors Akou and Baeta wrote to the Paris Missionary Society, requesting assistance. The society sent a missionary, who did some exploratory traveling in 1927. In 1929 they sent a missionary technician. Later two women were sent and started a center for women's education at Agou (1931). Though the church had some strong pastors who were dedicated to the task, the responsibility was overwhelming, and the church was unable to redeem its opportunities for growth.[88] In 1931 a Paris missionary opened a boarding school for Kabre youth at Atakpame. Some of the pupils went on to the training college, and in 1937 three Protestant schools were opened in the Kabre country. Faure, a teacher at the Bible institute at Atakpame, visited the schools. He stimulated the translation of hymns and Bible passages in the language of the people and encouraged the Paris mission to send a missionary to Kabre. This was not accomplished till 1945 and was done in the name and on behalf of the Evangelical Church of Togo.[89]

Since 1949, Togolese students have been sent to the theological school at Yaounde in Cameroon. Some have also gone to theological faculties in Europe.

Following the contacts made by Thomas Birch Freeman, who made trips to Togo in 1843 and 1854, the Methodist mission started a ministry in Togo. At first some catechists were sent to the Anecho area, but the work was directed from Lagos, Nigeria. Pastor Byran Roe was installed at Anecho in 1888. After Germany had established its authority in Togo, the relations between the society and the state were not harmonious. Pastor J. H. Willington replaced Byran Roe, but he ceded his place to a German pastor named Muellider. The missionaries of this society left in 1907, and the Christian community preserved only a limited contact with Lagos.

The Wesleyan Methodist Mission was based mainly in Dahomey

and Nigeria. Its work was not greatly affected by World War I. In 1921 a French Methodist pastor, Paul Wood, assumed responsibilities at Anecho. The Anecho church, with surrounding churches, formed a circuit of the Popo district of the Wesleyan Methodist Missionary Society, with headquarters in Lagos. The area was frequently visited by French pastors who served with the society in Dahomey.

In 1924, due to the ministry of the "prophet" Harris, the Methodist mission extended its work to Ivory Coast, thus having circuits in Dahomey, in the Anecho area, and in Ivory Coast. A school to train catechists was established in Porto-Novo, but in 1965 it had only 13 students. In 1957 the Anecho-Lome sector was annexed to form the Anecho-Cotonou, counting 3,447 members and 83 catechumens served by 5 pastors and 4 catechists.

After World War II (1939-1945), the church suffered from the effects of the world economic crisis. The farmers received little for their cocoa, coffee, and palm oil. Consequently the church had to seek financial assistance for its ministry, especially to support the catechists. The missionaries assisted in the spiritual activities of the church and in establishing relationships with churches of other countries, notably with French, Swiss, German, and British Protestants.

The Assemblies of God started work in Togo in 1940, working mainly in northwestern Togo. They have built a Bible school to train church workers.

The Southern Baptists commenced work in Togo in 1964 and by 1972 had eleven missionaries working there. They have a seminary for training church workers.[90]

The Evangelical Church of Togo, formed as a result of the work of several mission societies, launched an evangelistic program in the mid 1960s. Teams were assigned to study various aspects of the church's responsibility. Laymen were involved in the movement. By 1965 more than 250 lay people had volunteered to participate in the vernacular literacy campaign and others served on evangelistic teams to reach new areas. The studies and outreach programs involve many people in the ministry of the church. The church attempts to make the gospel relevant to all of a person's life. It has had the greatest expansion in the East Mono region among the Ewe-speaking peoples. Through the ministry of evangelistic teams, medical teams, agricultural extension, and adult education, over 6,000 persons were added to the church between 1962 and 1969.[91]

The Ewe have considered the Evangelical Church of Togo the national church of the Ewe. The use of the Ewe language in the church makes the church popular and national. The Evangelical Church has become indigenous among the Ewe people and is reaching out into villages and outlying districts. Christianity is gaining numerous adherents. There is a strong feeling of solidarity in the Togo church. In some villages the church occupies a central position. Although the ministry among the Kabre is the work of the Togo church, a greater sense of missionary responsibility and unity on the part of all Christians would strengthen the church of Togo.

The Evangelical Church at Lome established a child evangelism department in 1967. Seminars to study youth movements, courses for religious-education teachers, and studies on conjugal life were also undertaken.[92] The "Union de Femmes Togolaises" (Union of Togolese Women) was inaugurated in the Protestant church of Lome.[93]

The churches are trying to reach the unevangelized by imaginative use of the national radio, by sponsoring discussion groups, and by expressing the truth in culturally relevant forms. Efforts were made to create a Christian Council of Togo to coordinate Protestant work in the country.[94]

In 1965 the total Protestant community in Togo numbered 96,944; the Independent Churches, about 1,000; and Catholics, 303,864.[95]

Although the Catholic Church had made some contacts with the people of Togo during the nineteenth century, it only established a Christian community in the beginning of the twentieth century. After 1860 the Society of African Missions cared for the few Catholics in the country. In 1892 the Roman Catholic Church entrusted the work in Togo to the Society of the Divine Word. The personnel serving with the society were predominantly German. They opened a number of stations and established the work before World War I restricted their activities. In 1914 they reported 19,740 church members.[96] When the German missionaries were repatriated, the work was entrusted to the Society of the African Missions of Lyons.[97] The French jurisdiction had a marked influence on the school system. The secular state school system was introduced. Its leaders had no interest in religion. The Roman

Catholics received more aid than did the Protestants, but they too were outstripped by government schools by 1927.[98]

In 1926 the Roman Catholics began work in the northern part of Togo, among the Kabre people, who were untouched by Islam and Protestantism. They established a network of stations across the north.[99]

The Roman Catholics established four dioceses, and in 1965 they reported 303,864 members.[100] The presence of many European priests, however, caused some people to view the Roman Catholic Church as a foreign element in Togo during the years following independence. This impression is gradually disappearing, and the church is becoming more indigenous.

Dahomey

Dahomey, ruled by a powerful king, was frequently at war with the Yoruba people of Nigeria. It became a French protectorate toward the end of the nineteenth century and remained such until it gained full independence in 1960. It is a poor country, having few resources to develop. Oil palm products account for 75 percent of all exports. The economy did not progress after independence, and Dahomey was compelled to seek foreign aid. It is a small country with a population of about 2,505,000 (1967) and is one of the most densely populated countries in West Africa. Dahomey has many tribes; the four largest—the Fon, the Adja, the Bariba, and the Yoruba—form more than half of the population.[101] Dahomey has no lack of ambitious leaders, a fact that caused considerable political instability during the decade following independence.

The English Methodists started work in Dahomey in 1854 as a result of contacts made by Thomas Birch Freeman. However, because of the war between Dahomey and Abeokuta, there were no Methodist church representatives (or missionaries) in the area for some years. After 1870 the English Methodist Society made an effort to establish work at Porto-Novo. Joseph Rhodes spent some time there at various intervals. He learned the Goun language and translated some songs and Scripture passages into this language. An African pastor, T. E. Williams, came to Porto-Novo in 1873. After Thomas Marshal returned to Porto-Novo in 1876, Williams was installed at Agou.[102]

The Methodists established a region for evangelism between

Anecho and Lagos. Then the Popo area was added, which included Badagry, Quidah, Porto-Novo, and ten other locations. In 1880 the president of the district, John Milum, obtained permission from the king to reestablish work in Quidah. An African teacher and a missionary pastor came there in 1881.[103] Starting in 1888, the Methodists' work in southern Dahomey grew considerably as a result of the Christians' personal witness and the organization of prayer meetings.[104]

Dahomey became a French territory, and in 1892 the Methodists were obliged to use the French language in their schools. By March 22, 1922, the schools were placed under the government educational program.[105] The Methodist society founded a seminary in Porto-Novo in 1926, and pastors and catechists have been trained there for many years. Methodists from Togo and Ivory Coast as well as the Evangelical Church of Togo cooperate in this seminary and send students.

The Methodist Church works in five districts. The latest available statistics indicate 251 places of worship, 7,353 members, and a church community of 313,631. These persons are served by 14 pastors and 49 full-time laymen.[106]

The Assemblies of God, presently working in northwestern Dahomey, emphasizes evangelism by preaching the gospel. Their Christian communities form local assemblies that have no synodical affiliations. In 1962 the Assemblies had 1,708 church members. In 1973 they had 14 foreign workers in Dahomey.[107]

The Sudan Interior Mission started stations at Nikki and at Kandi in 1947, and two years later at Parakou and then Djougou. Later four other centers were established. Emphasis is placed on evangelism and education. Church workers are trained in three Bible schools. The mission operates one hospital and several dispensaries.[108] The Sudan Interior Mission had made contributions in linguistics and has translated the Scriptures into the Pilapila, Dompago Bariba, and Boussa languages. Printing of these materials is done in Jos, Nigeria. In 1962, there were 22 churches with 719 members as a result of the mission's work. In 1968 there were 49 worship centers and a Christian community of 1,850 people.[109]

Early Roman Catholic Missions in Dahomey were not productive. After many setbacks the fathers of the Lyons mission in 1883 started work among the coastal people who had been influenced by Christianity while in slavery in Brazil. During the early years the mission had much opposition from native leaders, but after 1890 it was more successful and eventually became the mission's strongest and most prosperous field in West Africa. The Sisters of Our Lady of the Apostles for African Missions joined in the work.[110] The French authorities encouraged the growth of the Catholic mission, and by 1965 there were 5 dioceses with 322,705 members.[111]

Churches of Africa, Madagascar, and the South Pacific had grown out of the missionary endeavors of the Paris Evangelical Missionary Society. These churches in 1967 launched a joint action for mission, called the Action Apostolique Commune, among the Fon people. Churches in Togo, Cameroon, Dahomey, Tahiti, Madagascar, and Switzerland helped provide staff for this enterprise. Through their witness and that of students of the theological college in Porto-Novo, a varied ministry among the Fon people was begun. The work is supported by the churches involved in it. The congregations being established will adhere to the Protestant church of Dahomey.[112] The growth of this ministry has been restricted by an insufficient number of local leaders and a lack of teaching materials for their work. Nevertheless, the gospel has been proclaimed in thirty-six villages, and thirty-four people were baptized in 1971. The church of Dahomey responded to this ministry and by 1972 supplied three quarters of the members of the team.[113]

Nigeria

Nigeria is one of the largest and most populous countries of Africa. Having gained independence from British jurisdiction in 1960, the country is still searching for a viable political structure with which to maintain the economic advantages of its size and to guide its diverse ethnic groups. In the 356,000 square miles of this country there are grove swamps, tropical forests, savannahs, and desert scrub. Temperature, rainfall, and soil vary greatly, and the people are unevenly distributed, according to the nature of the area.

The overwhelming majority of Nigerians are of Negro blood. There are many tribes and languages, with a Negro-Mediterranean mixture in the north. Despite the ethnic similarities of the tribes, the structure of the Nigerian society, in which many tribes mingle, is quite complex. In the south the Negroes were predominent, while the Hausa and Fulani were widespread in the north. Several strong native states and a score of cities with populations from 20,000 to 65,000 had arisen before the British proclaimed Nigeria a protectorate in 1885. The people of the southern part were mostly animists. Islam had penetrated the northern regions of Nigeria via the trade routes from the southern shores of the Mediterranean and the Nile valley. The Muslims won the allegiance of a portion of the population, especially the ruling classes.

Christianity was introduced into Nigeria following the return of Christian slaves, beginning in 1838. The spread of Christianity was largely determined by the physical geography and the receptivity of the people. The peoples south of the Niger and Benue rivers came into contact with Christianity, Western education, and commercial developments along the Guinea coast. This influenced the formation of a professional elite middle class, who demanded and enjoyed the comforts of urban living. In the north, however, autocratic Emirs preferred contacts with the Mediterranean and with Islam and resisted the penetration of Christianity and Western civilization. Consequently, modern education with its influences penetrated the northern areas only a little.

Preparation for the introduction of Christianity into Nigeria took place from 1841, with the first Niger expedition, to 1885, when Britain proclaimed the protectorate. This period opened the way for the larger expansion that came with the establishment of the churches in the southern regions, the extension of Christianity to regions in which the gospel was not proclaimed, and the expansion of the Christian ministry to the northern regions. Christianity witnessed significant expansion after 1885.

Thomas J. Bowen of the Southern Baptist Convention arrived in Abeokuta in 1850. Since the political situation prohibited him from proceeding to the interior, he began a ministry in Abeokuta. Reinforcements came and several centers were opened, but the work was not productive during the first decades. In 1875 W. J. David and a colleague came to revive the ministry.[114] At the close of the century the mission reported six churches and six outstations. However, the work became gradually more productive. One of the stronger congregations was at Lagos. The churches were encouraged to assume the responsibility to evangelize their people. In the 1880s several congregations withdrew from the association to form an independent Baptist association. The mission proclaimed the Yoruba Baptist Association in 1914. Later the name was changed to Nigerian Baptist Convention. By 1914, there were 31 Baptist churches, of which 14 were independent; a membership of 2,880 had grown out of the ministry.[115] In 1919 they formed the Women's Missionary Union of Nigeria.

The society made significant efforts to train church workers. The theological college at Ogbomosho gave leadership in training personnel.[116] Three Bible schools and a teacher training college also prepare church workers. The churches are self-supporting. The field is divided into three districts: the Eastern, Northern, and Midwestern. In 1960 the convention sent two couples to Sierra Leone as its first missionaries.[117] In 1968 the church reported 65,000 members served by 125 pastors and 223 missionaries.[118]

The Qua Iboe Mission is an interdenominational mission founded by Samuel A. Bill through the inspiration of H. Grattan Guinness. This mission began a ministry in the Qua Iboe River valley in eastern Nigeria in 1887. In 1888 A. Bailie joined Bill and by 1890 a small church had been gathered. In 1891 an interdenominational council of friends from North Ireland decided to support the endeavor. In 1898 the Ibuno church had three hundred communicant members. Additional centers were opened, and national workers were trained.[119] The mission steadily advanced up the river. By 1912 half a dozen stations had been established, of which Abak and Uyo were the farthest north. The most significant development was on the eastern side of the river. At Uyo the mission converged with the Scottish Presbyterians, enclosing the Primitive Methodists in a triangle. However, the Methodists moved some twenty miles northward to Ikotekpene.

In the 1930s the Qua Iboe Mission extended its ministry to the Igala district of northern Nigeria. Later it also undertook a work among the Bassa people, but few of these people have accepted the Christian faith. There was, however, rewarding growth in the Qua Iboe Church, which in 1968 reported 40,945 members worshiping at 853 places.[120]

The Primitive Methodists, serving on the island of Fernando Po, were restricted in their ministry by the Spanish authorities. Consequently, in 1893 they established a work at Archibong, between the Presbyterian field and that of the Basel Mission in Cameroon. Four Christians of the Presbyterian Church assisted J. M. Brown in this endeavor. The Methodists used the Scriptures and literature prepared by the Presbyterians.

In 1896 Brown's successor, Thomas Stones, received an invitation from James Egbo Bassey to serve his people at Jamestown on the west bank of the Cross River. This invitation guided the Methodists to the populous region between the Presbyterians and the Qua Iboe Mission.[121]

The Primitive Methodists moved north to Ikotekpene in the Ibo region. They made Ikotekpene their base for advancing into Ibo country. By 1914 they had come to the railway projected to Port Harcourt and by 1916 had established themselves at Nara. While the Methodists moved northward into Ibo country, the Qua Iboe Mission arrived there in an advance eastward from the Niger.

With the Southern Baptists as coadjutors, Wesleyan and Anglican missions developed the work in Abeokuta in Western Nigeria and extended it to neighboring towns. The Yoruba war disrupted the progress. After the war much rebuilding was necessary. However, while the missions were reestablishing themselves, Methodist Christians, in their travels for trade or business, witnessed to their faith and won fellow believers. This brought about a significant expansion of the Methodist work.

The Lower Niger Mission, based at Onitsha, had a remarkable opportunity among the dense Ibo population of the hinterland. In 1903 T. J. Dennis was well received at Owerri and in 1906 he settled at Ebu. Other extensions were made. The towns and villages requested teachers and evangelists and many outstations sprang up. A training institution for evangelists was begun at Awka in 1904. The population east of the Niger was the densest on the West Coast. The British occupied the hinterland, terminated the Aros' slave-trading practice, and opened the country to foreign contacts.

By 1914 there was a steady advance into Ibo country extending from the Niger to the Cross River. In the beginning of the extended ministry, the Onitsha Ibo version of the Scriptures was used to serve all the Ibo groups. But the Ibo Language Conference at Asaba in 1905 decided to produce a version of the Scriptures that would serve the entire Ibo people more adequately, and the task was given to T. J. Dennis. He concluded the Union Ibo version in 1913.[122]

During this period Roman Catholic missions were moving into new centers. The Upper Niger prefecture comprised the region west of the Niger from Forcados to Lokoja and from there eastward to Yola, with headquarters at Lokoja. This center was erected in 1884 and entrusted to the Society of African Missions of Lyons. The Lower Niger prefecture comprised the region bounded by the Niger and Benue up to the Cameroons. The center was erected in 1889 and entrusted to the Fathers of the Holy Ghost. They strengthened their efforts in Nigeria from their field of activity in Gabon. They emphasized schoolwork to match the Protestant efforts. In the Ibo region converts were made in large numbers. In 1932 the St. Patrick's Society for Foreign Mission came to strengthen the Catholic work in the region.

The Niger Mission realized that its work was not progressing satisfactorily. The catechists who were sent to the frontier towns and cities to proclaim the gospel in unevangelized regions were not strong enough to overcome the influences of the people and present an unquestionable testimony, thereby winning the people to the Christian faith. Consequently, they decided to send national Christians and missionaries together to establish the Christian ministry in unevangelized regions.

In order to advance its ministry into the north, the Niger Mission in 1890 divided the area of work into the Sudan and Upper Niger Mission, and the Delta and Lower Niger Mission. Lokoja became the headquarters for the northern work. This ministry was among the Hausa people who had been influenced by Islam and was not as successful as the society hoped it would be.[123] Some of the first missionaries died while attempting to establish the work, while others were turned back by the Muslim emirs. The Church Missionary Society made three attempts to enter the Sudan and suffered a similar loss of life. Finally, in 1905 Dr. W. R. S. Miller received permission to reside in Zaria, where he opened a small dispensary.[124] Other recruits followed, and the translation of the Bible in Hausa was undertaken. An earlier version of the New Testament was presented to the people, and in 1932 the entire Bible was published.

The coincidental occupation of the central and northern parts of Nigeria by the British and by missionary societies caused the Muslim emirs to consider the two movements as two related aspects of Western influence and control. Whereas the missionaries had established ministries in southern Nigeria before the traders and government agencies arrived, in northern Nigeria it was not so, and the missionaries were viewed as closely allied to the political and financial interests of their country.[125]

In 1897 the Royal Niger Company took action against the Fulani slaving activities in Nupe territory. In 1900 the British flag was raised at Lokoja and the protectorates of Southern Nigeria and Northern Nigeria were established. In 1903, because of the murder of an English officer, Lord Lugard occupied Kano and, a few weeks later, Sokoto. This was the beginning of a new period in Hausaland. However, the British followed a policy of excluding Christian missions from Muslim areas. Discouraged from moving more directly to the Hausa people of the northern territories, societies ministered to the animist tribes between Zaria and the Niger and Benue rivers. These peoples responded more readily to the Christian message than did the Islamized peoples of the northern regions. Britain ruled Northern Nigeria through the local chiefs and their councils, under the guidance of British administrators. The local chiefs were friendly to the missionaries and interested in the ideas they brought. They soon became eager to have their children receive the schooling largely offered by missions and assisted by government grants.

Roland V. Bingham, founder of the Sudan Interior Mission, made two unsuccessful attempts to establish a ministry in Kano. His colleagues, Gowan and Kent, died in the effort. In 1901 the Sudan Interior Mission made a third attempt to establish a work in this region and was successful in entering the Nupe tribe and opening a station at Patigi on the Niger.[126] A. W. Banfield was exceptionally adept in the Nupe language. He translated the Bible, compiled a dictionary in the language, and established the Niger Press, which has prepared much Christian literature in many languages. From Patigi the mission extended its ministry into the surrounding territories. The mission established 57 stations within the Central Belt, and 37 to the north, and 7 to the south of it. Thus the mission served many tribes in these regions. It established a very large ministry in Nigeria where in 1960 it had 650 of the some 1,200 missionaries serving actively with the society.

In 1917 the ministry among the Tangale was begun. In 1923 the SIM opened a station at Jos, and soon a cluster of stations were opened in the region around Jos, which became the headquarters for the society. In 1925 it began work in Kano in the Hausa country. The Kano hospital is famous for its eye surgery through which it meets a significant need in the country. Thus the Sudan

Interior Mission extended its ministry to six provinces of the Central Belt and into at least twenty-seven tribes. The large indigenous church was recognized as the Evangelical Churches of West Africa in 1956.[127]

The Sudan Interior Mission was the first to establish a radio station, ELWA, at Monrovia, Liberia. They also initiated the publication of a Christian magazine *African Challenge*, which was planned to appeal to readers in English-speaking Africa. It appears in Yoruba and English, is appreciated by the people, and has a circulation of 160,000 copies.

The Sudan United Mission was formed in Britain in order to bring the gospel to tribes in northern Nigeria. It commenced its ministry at Wase in 1904. From Wase the mission advanced north into Birom land. A second station, started in 1906, was located at Wukari, south of the river. In 1909 the Wase work was transferred to Langtang and from there it was extended to the highland plateau among the Birom tribe. The ministry of the British Branch of the Sudan United Mission is found in three areas: the Langtang lowlands, the central plateau, and in Bornu and Sardauna provinces, reaching to the tribes around Lake Chad.

Starting as an interdenominational mission, the Sudan United Mission became an international federation of missions with a representative board of directors. Each agency is responsible for its own staff and supplies the necessary finances, but works in cooperation with other missions of the federation.

The South African Interdenominational branch looked for a field of service north of the Benue River. Mr. Judd made exploratory trips in this region, advancing to Bornu and Adamawa provinces where the Sudan United Mission later ministered to many tribes. The South African (Methodist) branch of the Sudan United Mission chiefly served the Mada tribe, working in the southwestern part of the plateau provinces and in the north-central part of Benue Province.

In 1913 the Danish Lutheran Church, as a branch of the Sudan United Mission, began a ministry at Numan in Adamawa Province. The Evangelical Brethren branch of the Sudan United Mission undertook to serve an area of its own north of the Benue River and to the east among the Wurkum and Jukun and later extended its work to the Mumuye. The Church of the Brethren Mission opened a ministry to the Bura tribe in southern Bornu province to the north of the area where the Danish Lutherans work.[128]

Some years passed before the Christian ministry in the Central Belt of Nigeria showed significant growth. In 1930 attendance at Christian worship increased remarkably in the areas of the Sudan United Mission. Between 1935 and 1940 the Nigerian evangelists assumed increasing responsibilities and the outstation ministry more than doubled. This movement continued after 1945.

Representatives of the Dutch Reformed Church Mission of South Africa began a ministry at Saai among the Tiv tribe in 1911. The mission extended its outreach west of the Katsina Ala River establishing schools, a hospital, and a leprosy settlement. The headquarters were established at Mkar. In 1940 the Christian Reformed Church of North America began to work among the Jukun and Kuteb tribes. Pioneers in this work were E. H. Smith and his wife. In time it extended its ministry to other tribes and in 1961 assumed full responsibility of the work of the Dutch Reformed Church of South Africa.[129]

In 1955 the churches established by the missions serving under the Sudan United Mission and the Church of the Brethren and the United Church of Christ in Kaduna formed the Fellowship of the Churches of Christ in the Sudan (TEKAS), which was registered with the government in 1956. This name was changed in 1975 to read "Nigeria" instead of "Sudan" (TEKAN). Pastors for these churches are trained in the Theological College of Northern Nigeria, established in 1957 at Bukuru.

The close cooperation between the Sudan Interior Mission and the Sudan United Mission provided a favorable setting for the emergence of an indigenous church. The first Inter-Mission Conference was held in 1910. At the conference at Miango in 1926 the Sudan United Mission presented a draft of a church constitution hoping for a United Church of Africa. However, at the 1929 conference it was decided that this would not be possible and that a Federation of Missions of the Northern Provinces should be sought. The Northern Missions Council grew out of these consultations, which eventually became the Council of Evangelical Churches of Northern Nigeria (CECNN). The council meets annually to discuss common problems and to express valuable suggestions relating to matters concerning the churches and to maintain a bond of fellowship, but its decisions are not binding on the member bodies.

The establishment of British rule over northern Nigeria gradually reduced the fear of Fulani raids, and the people of the mountains began to spread into the surrounding territories. Many went to Bambur. Missions followed their Christians to other towns and regions, provided services for them, and with them proclaimed the gospel to the populace. The Church Missionary Society turned its energies to the large cities of the north. The Methodists, the Assemblies of God, the Qua Iboe Church, and the Southern Baptists followed their members to the north and established many strong city churches.

The Assemblies of God entered Nigeria in 1930 in response to an invitation by Ibo Christians. The latter had read a copy of the Assemblies of God paper *Pentecostal Evangel* and invited the assemblies to come and help them. They found thirty-two indigenous congregations and established a ministry among them and in the southern Nigerian delta in general. By 1934 railway employees who were members of the Assemblies of God lived in northern cities and held prayer services in their homes. This testimony was followed up by Assemblies of God missionaries who settled in Port Harcourt in 1939. By the early 1950s they had extended their ministry to Kaduna and in 1954 a ministry was opened at Rahama.[130] That same year the Northern Church of the Assemblies of God was formed. In 1961 a Nigerian was made responsible for the leadership of the Assemblies of God in Nigeria. The ministry continued to grow until seventeen centers were opened in Nigeria. The Assemblies of God emphasize the training of church leaders. Their five Bible schools have provided over 500 national workers, who are serving 609 congregations with a total membership of 25,000.[131]

The Lutheran Synodical Conference of the United States began a ministry in Calabar in 1936 in response to an invitation from Christians of the Ibesikpo tribe who seceded from the Qua Iboe Mission.[132] The Lutherans soon opened a teacher-training school, a Bible school, and a seminary to train personnel for the ministries in which the church was engaged. Later a hospital and a clinic were also opened. In 1963 the Evangelical Lutheran Church of Nigeria, with a membership of 12,132, was recognized.[133]

The Salvation Army and the Seventh-Day Adventists have served in Nigeria for many years. They report 9,347 and 18,774 members respectively.[134] The Christian Missions to Many Lands,

United Missionary Society, and Church of God (Cleveland) have small ministries with several thousand members in each fellowship.

The Christian Council of Nigeria was founded in 1930 and has given valuable help to the churches. It has done much to make Christian ideals known and respected in the Nigerian society. It is not affiliated with a world body. The churches of Nigeria were host to the All-Africa Conference of Churches in 1958. The Nigerian Evangelical Fellowship is a member of the Association of Evangelicals of Africa and Madagascar.[135]

The New-Life-for-All campaign was widely supported by all evangelical groups. It has significantly edified the churches and brought about important church growth. The expansion of the Protestant work during the last decades has been quite outstanding. Many new places of worship have been established. Yet in spite of all the efforts that have been made, in 1966 twenty-nine tribes were still unreached by the Protestant churches.[136]

The first proposal for a united church in Nigeria was made by Dr. J. T. Dean of the Presbyterian Church of Calabar in 1919. In 1923 an evangelical union was formed; it was to meet annually and discuss union. In 1932 it became the Eastern Regional Committee of the Christian Council. In 1933 a church union committee was formed in the eastern region and the "South India Scheme" was studied. The Lagos ministers were more hesitant to consider union, but in 1947 the Nigerian Union Committee was formed. At a meeting held in Onitsha, the Anglican, Methodist, Presbyterian churches of Nigeria and southern Cameroon, the Qua Iboe Mission, and the Sudan United Mission considered proposals for union. The Qua Iboe Mission and the Sudan United Mission withdrew when they discovered that the aim was organic union.[137]

In 1950 the Joint Union Committee was formed. Its representatives who have met annually, are from Anglican, Presbyterian, and Methodist churches. In 1957 they published the "Proposed Scheme of Church Union in Nigeria," which was largely based on the South India Scheme. December 1965 was set as the provisional date for union. Because of its problems of presenting the gospel to an Islam-oriented community, the Anglican diocese of northern Nigeria did not continue to participate in union discussions. On November 24 the Methodist churches of Lagos asked for a postponement. The union was thus postponed.[138] In January

1966 the massacre of Ibos in the north began and the flight of over five hundred thousand people from the north followed the secession of the Eastern Region in June 1967. During the civil war the union discussions were discontinued, and the possibility of union became less promising.

The ministry of the Society of African Missions of the Roman Catholic Church at Lagos and the surrounding territory and the efforts of the Holy Ghost Fathers in the eastern region have been observed. The ministry in the Ibo region made notable progress during the episcopate of Bishop Shanahan and school work was emphasized to bring the children under the Roman Catholic teachings. Through this effort the Eastern Region became a stronghold of the Roman Catholic Church. However, after the civil war the people were open to the proclamation of the gospel, and evangelical churches multiplied rapidly in the region.[139]

Although the Roman Catholic work was slow in its development in Nigeria, it witnessed gradual progress after the initial difficulties. The Society of African Missions was responsible for the greater part of Nigeria. This society extended its ministry in the Lagos and Niger regions and by 1913 reported a Roman Catholic community of ten thousand members who were served by one vicariate and two prefectures apostolic.[140]

As it advanced into the interior of the country, the Roman Catholic Church encountered good response in some areas. It had considerable success among the Kwalla tribe and became quite strong in the Madha tribe. In 1950 it established a full hierarchy for Nigeria. By 1964 three archbishoprics—Lagos, Onitsha, and Kaduna—and fourteen other dioceses had been established. In 1967 the Roman Catholic Church reported a Christian community of approximately two million in Nigeria.

Independent churches were formed early in the history of Christianity in Nigeria. This reveals a certain restlessness and dissatisfaction and an attitude of independence in the churches. The reasons for separation into several bodies have been for convenience of function, incompatability of understandings, and personal ambitions. After the death of Bishop Crowther in 1891, the Anglican churches of the Lower Niger recognized the new bishop; however, they formed the Niger Delta Pastorate, which was self-governing and financially independent. In 1891 an independent Native African Church was formed in Lagos by deserters from several Protestant churches. Its membership in 1962 was estimated at twenty thousand.[141] In 1901 members of the Anglican Church in Lagos formed the church commonly known as "Bethelites." In 1917 members of the Wesleyan Methodist Erako Church in Lagos formed the United African Methodist Church. The Assemblies of God and the Lutheran Synodical Conference came to assist separatist groups, and this resulted in the formation of another denomination.

More recently a proliferation of independent churches has taken place. This reveals the restlessness and discontent of some people but also a significant dynamism for the expansion of Christianity. There are some five hundred such bodies, with a membership of approximately five hundred thousand.[142] They have become a vital force within the Christian movement. A closer fellowship between these bodies and the churches established by the missionary enterprise is most desirable. In this survey it will suffice to mention several of the more significant bodies.

In 1915 Garrick Sokari Braide, a catechist of the Niger Delta Pastorate (Anglican), which was under the direction of Archdeacon Crowther, led a revival movement that spread through most of southern Owerri province in less than a year. The revival spread in part because of Braide's healing the sick by prayer. He called his followers to a faithful Christian life, indicating that the native church would move on to rule the country.[143] In 1916 Braide was imprisoned on charges of sedition and extortion. His followers divided to form the Garrick Braide Church and the Christ Army Church, and by 1921 they had 7,280 and 21,155 adherents respectively.

The Christ Army Church has continued to grow, but since 1921 it has divided into many small groups with no central organization. Some of them are syncretistic, adopting non-Christian ideas and practices. This movement gained many of its adherents from the existing churches and also from the non-Christian society. The extent of the movement is revealed in that it had gathered 29,435 adherents by 1921, whereas the membership of the Niger Delta Pastorate in 1912 was 7,374.[144]

The Christ Apostolic Church began through the experiences of Daddy Ali, an elder of St. Saviour's Church, who called fellow believers to prayer meetings. Among other things, they rejected infant baptism and the use of medicine. Bishops Jones and

Oluwole tried to keep them in the church but failed. In 1930 Babalola began a healing revival that transformed the prayer movement into a significant religious movement. In 1958 it reported having 86,313 adherents.

The Church of the Lord was begun in Ijebu in 1925 by Josaiah Olulowo Oshitelu, an Anglican schoolteacher who had a series of visions. The movement spread to Ghana, Liberia, and Sierra Leone. There is considerable uncertainity concerning the strength of this movement. The members are classified according to their devotion to the church. Although syncretism is a danger, the movement basically presents the Christian message for faith and life.

Most of these movements began within a church, have a biblically based origin, and proclaim a literal interpretation of the Bible. Unfortunately, however, some prophets seek their own glorification and fail to guide their adherents to Jesus Christ. It is important for the churches to recognize the religious interests in these movements and to minister to them.

The British government system significantly influenced the political development of Nigeria. Although a democratic system had been introduced by the British, Nigeria followed its own course after independence. Political rivalry shattered respect for the electoral process. The unity of Nigeria was eventually threatened by the disastrous civil war between the Eastern Region (Biafra) and the federal government. Nigerian leaders are still faced with the problems of maintaining law and order, creating a national spirit, and providing adequate communication. The period of reconstruction and recovery from the Biafra war will be long.

The churches of the Ibo people suffered greatly during the civil war. Church activities were disrupted. Church leaders and missionaries were separated from their congregations. There was much loss of life and property. The World Council of Churches, Church World Service, Lutheran World Federation, Mennonite Central Committee, and other agencies assisted the churches during this tragic period. One cause for praise to the Lord was that many people turned to the Lord in the hour of need. Some churches reported a marked increase in membership during the war and in the years following the war.

Nigeria has historically been a country with many cities. During the past fifty years the growth of the cities has been significantly accentuated, and the churches are confronted with a unique phenomenon. Although the city dwellers generally maintain the religion they had practiced in the rural areas, they do not retain the same devotion. Secularism has a strong influence on people in urban centers. In the past the churches have not taken the ministry in the cities seriously and have failed to train men to serve city churches effectively. This will need to take priority in the churches' program. The churches need a clear and confident policy in planning for the future and need to respond to that plan with determined action.

Cameroon

The introduction of Christianity to Cameroon through the efforts of the Baptist and Basel missionary societies has been presented in Chapter 4. Having established the Christian community more thoroughly toward the end of the century, the Basel Evangelical Missionary Society began to extend its endeavors northward in 1903. In 1909 it began the first ministry at Bagam among the Bamileke tribe, constructing a chapel and opening schools and a dispensary. Bagam served as the head station for the ministry to the Bamileke. In 1911 the society extended its work to the Nono tribe, entrusting the station at Bangwa to Striebel together with the following Christians: Ngankou Abraham, Ndeyo Isaac, Pueni Paul, and Ndifo Elia. Due to Striebel's good relations with the chief, Bandjoun Zotso, the latter asked the society to begin a ministry in his town.[145] Because of a continuous effort in evangelization and the systematic efforts in education, the ministry of the society made significant progress. Four men were ordained to the ministry and by 1914 services were conducted at 404 places; the membership of the church had risen to 15,112; and 22,818 pupils were enrolled in their schools.[146]

The German Baptist missionaries devoted themselves to their ministry in East Cameroon. Twenty-three missionaries and Christian leaders served at 6 stations and 49 outposts. The church grew steadily between 1890 and 1914, gathering 3,124 members into the church and 3,623 pupils into the schools, where they received Christian instruction.[147]

The American Presbyterians, coming from Liberia, settled on the island of Corisco in 1849, opposite the mouth of the Gabon

River.[148] Later they also established themselves on the coast of the mainland. In 1871 these two areas of ministry were placed under one organization. This was the beginning of a significant ministry in Gabon, Spanish Guinea, and Cameroon. From their center in Rio Muni, they advanced into French Equatorial Africa and into Cameroon in 1879. During the 1880s they expanded in the southern coast region of what became Cameroon, and during the 1890s they extended their ministry eastward and inland.[149]

Because of the attitude of the French government, the American Presbyterians transferred their ministry in Gabon to the Paris Mission and devoted themselves to their ministry in Cameroon. They centered their efforts around a few well-staffed stations from which extensive preaching was carried on in the surrounding country. In 1889 a station was established at Batanga; in 1892 another was begun at Efulen; and in 1894 still another was opened at Ebolovoe southeast of Efulen. Adolphus Good was the pioneer of the thrust into the interior. He was an able language student and translated the Bible and some songs into the Bulu language. Good chose Elat as the base station for the missionary endeavor and died at his post in 1894. The church was further established at Lolodorf in 1897, at Melet in 1909, at Zulassi in 1916, at Yaounde in 1922, at Bafia in 1924, at Abong Mbang in 1926, at Momjepom in 1935, and at Batouri in 1940.[150]

The Pallotti Fathers of the German Roman Catholics were permitted to begin a work in Cameroon in 1889 on certain conditions. These were that they would not trespass on Protestant territory, that only Germans would serve in the Cameroon and that the executive power would reside in the colony. Henry Vieter, the first prefect apostolic of the prefecture, began a ministry on the Sanaga River. However, the Catholics did not abide by the stipulation not to trespass on Protestant territory. In 1898 they entered Duala where the Baptist and Basel Missions had been working since the mid 1840s.[151] The Roman Catholics followed the practice they were employing in other parts of Africa: collecting and educating rescued slave children in Christian villages. Their work made little progress in the early years. Later they established schools in many native villages in order to instruct and win the children. But still, because of limited funds and personnel, the work made little progress. But by 1912 the society had built up a foreign staff of 94 workers serving at 14 stations and had gathered a Christian community of 202,777 members. The Pallotti Fathers studied the customs of the tribes to which they went and adapted their ministry to them.[152]

The war suspended the activities of the German Baptist Society. All their missionaries but two were interned and returned to Europe. Mr. and Mrs. Carl Bender were also made prisoners of war, marched to, and imprisoned at Duala. But Mr. Bender, an American citizen, fought for his rights. After two weeks of harsh treatment, he and his wife were permitted to return to their work at Sappo. Even though all communications and financial assistance were cut off, they had a very successful work. Many new converts were won and additional preaching centers were opened. The need for leadership caused men like the late Rev. Joseph Ebakise Burnley and Pastor Laban Moky to assume responsibility, and this contributed to the expansion of the work.

The Baptist church at Sappo grew from thirty-eight to fourteen hundred members during the Benders' ministry. The Benders left Cameroon in 1919, and the Christians served alone until 1927. The Lord blessed their ministry, and a significant expansion was made northward into the grasslands. After the war the French government refused to allow the German missionaries to return to the territory under French administration. The British, however, permitted them to return in 1927. Consequently they expanded their ministry to the north from Sappo in the territory occupied by the British in order to evangelize the people of the grasslands and move into the highlands.

The German Baptists of North America shared in the ministry of the German Baptists from the beginning in Cameroon. In 1935 the North American Baptist General Missionary Society for the administration of part of the Cameroon field was organized and was incorporated as Cameroon Baptist Mission (U.S.A.). From 1935 to 1941 each society was responsible for a part of the field. When the German missionaries were interned during the war in 1941 and the German mission was discontinued, the Cameroon Baptist Mission (U.S.A.) assumed the responsibility for the entire field. However, the German missionaries were exiled to Jamaica and American missionaries were unable to leave until after the war. With the increase of personnel came a marked growth of the church. The work was expanded and the number of baptized believers more than doubled between 1945 and 1954.[153]

The Baptist Church of Cameroon became independent in 1954. The Baptist congregations formed themselves into a fellowship called the Cameroon Baptist Convention, which is a voluntary fellowship of Baptist churches. The ministry of the Baptist churches has seen considerable progress, extending to twelve mission areas and growing to nearly five hundred churches by 1971.[154]

The Paris Evangelical Missionary Society stepped in to assist the young churches and continue the ministry of the Basel and Baptist missions in the territory that came under French jurisdiction. Being an interdenominational mission, it was able to supply missionaries of the same denomination for each particular field. The churches to which the Paris mission related, and which came into being through this ministry, formed the Evangelical Church of the Cameroon. It became autonomous in 1957. It grew favorably and by 1967 became a Christian community of a quarter million people worshiping in 1,035 churches.[155]

The war affected the ministry to the Basel missionary society. Its missionaries of German nationality were interned, while those of Swiss nationality were expelled from the country. The Christians were disturbed by these events, but assumed responsibilities for the church and continued the ministry. They opened new places of worship and assigned catechists to them. The morality of the Christians was greatly affected by this time of disturbance. The situation was examined at a general assembly of the church. It decided to exert itself to improve the discipline in the church. The pastors, Joseph Ekolo, Modi Din, and Kuo Isedu devoted themselves to the well-being of the church.[156]

The partition of the country into French and English sectors brought considerable hardship to the Basel Mission. It entrusted its stations of the Upper Sanaga to the Presbyterian Church, while the Paris Evangelical Missionary Society assumed the responsibility for its work and that of the German Baptist Mission in the French sector. But the Paris Evangelical Missionary Society was not able to replace the missionaries of the two societies or to occupy all the stations that were entrusted to its care. In 1925 the Basel Mission resumed the ministry in West Cameroon, but it did not receive permission to return to East Cameroon.[157]

The Presbyterian Church of West Cameroon grew out of the ministry of the Basel and Presbyterian mission. These societies emphasized leadership training as well as the proclamation of the gospel, opening schools to develop leaders. A well-established church of over fifty thousand members grew out of their work.[158]

The ministry of the Presbyterian Church of the U.S.A. was successful and witnessed continuous growth as the number of church workers and members increased after 1940. In 1941 there were forty-one ordained ministers serving the Presbyterian Church. In 1957 the number had increased to seventy-nine serving a church of sixty-nine thousand members organized in three synods and ten presbyteries. The Cameroon Presbyterian Church obtained its autonomy in 1957.[159] The membership increased to sixty-three thousand in the next decade, and the number of pastors and Christian teachers increased considerably.[160]

The Presbyterian Church offered medical services at six hospitals, twenty-five dispensaries, two leprosariums, and six dental centers. Its educational ministry was not less important, as evidenced by the training pastors received at the Dager Theological School and at the United School of Theology at Yaounde, a cooperative venture begun in 1962. The farm school at Kibamba inspired the Evangelical Church and the Lutheran Church to make similar efforts, and the school has drawn the attention of other churches serving in Central Africa. The rural efforts were coordinated by the Committee of the Department of the Evangelical Federation.[161]

A division occurred in the Presbyterian Church during its general assembly in 1967 as a result of a long standing difference of opinion over the church's participation in the ecumenical movement. Seven pastors and fourteen elders withdrew from the church to form the Reformed Presbyterian Church. However, the government refused to grant recognition to the newly formed church, and it suffered many hardships. Some of the dissidents were imprisoned for five months, and after their release they were prohibited from gathering for worship.

The American Lutheran Church began to evangelize the northern part of Cameroon in 1923. Mr. and Mrs. Revne established a ministry at Yagua, and from here the society concentrated its efforts toward the Benu, Kebi, and Logon regions. The first converts were baptized at Bosgoi in 1930. Later twenty-five families were baptized at Dachega. From Yagua, the center of the Masana tribe, the work developed among the Masana of Bongor in Chad.

The mission opened a theological college and a leprosarium at Kaile and started Bible schools at Garua and Yagua. The society translated the Bible into Masana, Musgum, Mundang, and Zupuri. It participated in the radio ministry of "The Voice of the Gospel."[162]

The mission emphasized the Christian life in which believers were called upon to abandon the tribal customs and the young people were to look for Christians as their marriage partners. Through this emphasis and the education offered, the society formed a Christian elite among the people. Revne, the founder of the mission, called the Christian workers together for a period of three months every year for classes of helpful instructions for the ministry.[163]

The American Lutheran Sudan Mission began a ministry at Mbula in 1924 and at Meiganga in 1928. In 1932 the Baya tribe became responsive to the gospel, and the ministry spread into the Central African Republic, reaching the Bulu population of Betare-Oya. A number of the young people of the Baya tribe were converted and received a Christian education. An effort to evangelize the Doaya and the Ichamba in the northern part of Cameroon was made by opening a ministry at Poli in 1938. In 1945 the society received permission to begin work at Tchollire among the Laka and Duru. It was here that Walter Trobisch served. The society opened a Bible school at Baboua in 1950 and, in cooperation with the Norwegian Missionary Society, opened a theological school at Meiganga in 1954.[164]

The Bible school at Baboua significantly contributed to church growth. Having received three years of training, its students served in various capacities and took the gospel to new villages and new areas and guided the believers. The Bible school at Poli attempted to train evangelists for that area of the church's ministry, offering instruction in the Fulani language.[165]

The American Lutheran Sudan Mission established ten stations. However, after the death of its founder, A. E. Gunderson, in 1951, the ministry was incorporated into the American Lutheran Mission.

The Norwegian Lutheran Mission began a ministry at Tibati in 1926, serving especially the Mboum people. In 1931 they extended their ministry toward the Baboute and Bafouk at Yoko, a region where the American Presbyterians had served, and toward the Tibar and Mambila, where the Basel Mission had established the

Ngambe station in 1914. These two regions were entrusted to the Norwegian mission. Due in part to the preparatory work already accomplished and the leaders who had been trained by the Presbyterians, the work had quick results and was extended toward West-Galim and northward to Mbe in the Dourou country. The ministry at Dourou, where the animists are governed by chiefs influenced by Islam, soon encountered opposition. The mission was ordered to close its schools, but evangelization continued, and the number of converts has continued to grow to the present day. In the other regions, however, the educational ministry has had good results. The society has gained the favor of the Muslims by its medical work. Medical services have been offered at Tibati, Ngaoundere, and Yoko. Muslim women who required medical care have been cared for in homes, according to Muslim customs.

The American Lutheran Mission and the Norwegian Missionary Society formed the Evangelical Lutheran Church of Cameroon and Central African Republic in 1960. The two missions continue to assist the African church in its ministry. In 1968 the church membership was 23,135 and the people met at 207 places of worship.

When the German Roman Catholic missionaries were interned during World War I, the Holy Ghost Society assumed responsibility for the Catholic work in the French-mandated territory, while the Mill Hill Fathers from Britain assumed responsibility in the territory mandated to the British. During the time of the French and British occupation, the Roman Catholic work experienced marked growth in church membership. Much of this growth may be attributed to that mission's emphasis on education.

The Roman Catholic hierarchy of Cameroon was formed in 1955, and Yaounde became the center of the archdiocese and metropolitan see for the whole country. By 1961 seven suffragan dioceses had been established. The first African priests were ordained in 1935; by 1963 the number of African priests had risen to 166, and there were 175 African sisters. In 1955 the first African bishops were consecrated, and the first African archbishop of Yaounde, Jean-Baptist Zoa, was installed in 1961.[166] The Roman Catholic Church in Cameroon has continued to grow.

An interest in cooperation has been manifested in the establishment of certain ministries. The American Presbyterian Mission and the Paris Evangelical Missionary Society have cooperated in training teachers at the Normal School of Zulassi and in opening the high school at Libamba. The Lutheran churches have cooperated in the Christian broadcast in the Zulfede language prepared at the Ngaoundere studio. Through the cooperative effort of several churches, the Theological Faculty was founded at Yaounde. It admits students with a baccalaureate degree. The theological education fund gave very significant assistance to the establishment of the Theological Faculty, whose ministry, however, has not been as extensive as was anticipated. Many students received scholarships from European faculties and therefore went to Europe to study.

Some interest in ecumenical relations has been expressed. The Federation of Evangelical Missions of Cameroon and Equatorial Africa was formed in 1941. More recently efforts have been made to replace it by the Evangelical Council of Cameroon, which is to be the official voice of the member churches and will maintain relations with the churches in Rio Muni, Gabon, and Congo Brazzaville. Four of the Cameroon churches are affiliated with the All-Africa Conference of Churches.[167] The American and Norwegian Lutheran missions united to form the Evangelical Lutheran Church of the Cameroon and Central African Republic. In 1964 the Presbyterian Church of West Cameroon, the Evangelical Church of Cameroon, and the Presbyterian Church of Cameroon opened discussion for union. In 1967 the Eglise Protestante Africaine, which separated from the Presbyterian Church in East Cameroon in the 1930s joined the union talks.

The independence of Cameroon was proclaimed in 1960. Because the southern parties did not unite behind one leader, the first president was a Muslim, even though Muslims are in the minority in the country. The churches in the southern part of Cameroon have been little affected by independence. But in the northern part Islam is strong and some officials have acted as though Islam is the state religion. They have opposed the church work in every possible way, closing many Christian schools and prohibiting worship in some areas. In the northern part of the country, life has been uncomfortable, if not difficult, for everyone who is not a Muslim.

While the churches were becoming autonomous, they were preoccupied with internal structures, and evangelistic outreach received little attention. However, after reorganization had taken place, the "Christ for All" movement inspired new concern all through the central part of Africa, and the Cameroon churches engaged in active evangelistic work.

There have been large increases in church membership during the last decade. A significant factor in the development of the churches is the growth of an indigenous Christian ministry that is devoting itself to church building.

The Bible societies have contributed greatly to the Christian ministry in Cameroon by supplying the Bible in three languages, the New Testament in seven other languages, and portions in several more languages. The ministry of the Bible societies in the area began in 1870. Until 1958 it was under the direction of the West African Agency. Then a joint agency was established by the British and Foreign Bible Society and the Netherlands Bible Society. The Bible Society of Cameroon was organized in 1964. Distribution of the Scriptures had increased significantly during the last decade for three reasons. The Protestant churches have sought to bring the gospel to the unreached, distribution has been undertaken by the Roman Catholic Church, and there is increased literacy in the country.

Gabon

Gabon, situated between Cameroon and the Republic of Congo, was formerly a part of French Equatorial Africa, but became an independent republic in 1960. The population is composed of many tribes and peoples, including Negroes, Arabs, Hausa, Fula, and Europeans.[168]

The Paris Evangelical Missionary Society was the only Protestant mission in the country from the time it assumed the responsibilities for the ministry begun by the American Presbyterians until the Christian and Missionary Alliance came to Gabon in 1934. Elie Allegret and Urbain Teisseres served at Talagouga and Lambarene respectively. Felix Faure joined them in 1896. The ministry made gradual progress. Other recruits arrived and they established ministries at Ngomo and Samkita. The Presbyterian missionaries continued the work at Baraka until 1913. They then also ceded it to the Paris mission and withdrew from Gabon. The Gabon enterprise became one of the important ministries of the Paris mission.

At the turn of the century the prosperity of Gabon increased considerably through the lumber industry. Many Christians found employment through this industry. In order to help the people, the Paris society formed an industrial and agricultural agency in 1908. It gave some attention to establishing a plantation of somikita—an African cash crop. The factory at Nomo exploited the natural resources of the forest area. But this prosperity almost came to a standstill during World War I. On the other hand, influenced by the Belgian concession system in Zaire, the French also granted concessions in 1899. The commerical agencies mainly sought rubber and ivory and exerted pressure on the native population to gather these products. The people of France protested this system. Consequently, it was modified but not ended. This exploitation of the people retarded the development of the country.[169]

The Paris society enlarged its ministry in Gabon after World War I. Teachers were trained at the normal school and the educational ministry was enlarged, both at the centers and the outstations. Albert Schweitzer, former dean of the theological faculty of the University of Strasbourg, joined this work in Lambarene. Schweitzer was known for his book *The Quest for the Historical Jesus*. His going to Gabon brought this field to the attention of the public. Being a German citizen, he was interned during World War I and sent back to Europe. He returned to Gabon in 1924 and continued his service to relieve suffering and maintain life until his death in 1965. Many volunteer helpers joined him at Lambarene. Some became disillusioned and disturbed by his out-of-date practice. After his death the hospital was modernized.

The ministry of the Paris society was to the north of the Ogowe River, where it established seven stations. As a result of the ministry of the Paris society, the Evangelical Church of Gabon with a community of approximately seventy-five thousand has been organized.[170] Gabon, with a small population of five hundred thousand, maintained close ties with France after it became an independent republic. Consequently, the Christian ministry has not been disrupted by political tensions. Gabon is among the highest countries in Central Africa in literacy. The government has assumed more responsibility for educational and medical services.

The southern part of Gabon was not evangelized by the Paris society. Consequently, in 1934 the Christian and Missionary Alliance moved into this area from its ministry in Zaire. Bongolo was the first station established and became the central station of this area. The society opened the Central Bible School at this place and emphasized the ministry through native leaders trained there. A regional Bible school was opened at Koula Moutou. A revival began at Bongolo in 1968 and spread to the other stations, bringing many people from all walks of life into the church and greatly edifying and strengthening the church. The indigenous church is known as the Evangelical Church of South Gabon.

The Pentecostals entered Gabon more recently and have established a church community of several thousand adherents.

The Roman Catholic Church created the vicariate apostolic of Loango in 1886 on the coast south of Gabon, which included this territory. The Holy Ghost Fathers were responsible for the entire region. In 1890 the vicariate apostolic of Ubangi was created, embracing a large area to the north of the Zaire River. The Holy Ghost Fathers made considerable efforts to teach the people crafts and agriculture on extensive plantations. They introduced and tested tropical plants at a number of agricultural stations.

Prosper Philippe Augouard was the first bishop of the vicariate of Ubangi. He was an able administrator and the ministry developed under his leadership. The prefecture apostolic of Ubangi-Shari was created in the northern part of Congo-Brazzaville in 1909 and also entrusted to the Holy Ghost Fathers. In 1914 there were nearly 30,000 Roman Catholics in the French-speaking part of Equatorial Africa and the majority were in the vicariate apostolic of Gabon.[171] In 1908 the Holy Ghost Fathers served at some twelve stations in Gabon.[172] They trained native leadership to serve in the ministries of the society. A seminary had been founded in Libreville in 1856. The first ordination to the priesthood, however, was not until 1899. In 1911 a community of native sisters was inaugurated. By 1971 the Roman Catholics had become the largest religious group of the country, counting 232,765 members out of a population of approximately 473,000.[173]

SUMMARY

The progress made by the churches in the last century is quite remarkable. It has taken place despite the superficial understanding of the Christian teaching by some church members, the proliferation of independent Christian groups, racial and political tensions, and the growing influence of secular materialism and Islam. The twentieth century, having witnessed a Christian advance through the storm, may be considered the Christian century. Christianity made rapid advances after the original difficulties of ignorance concerning disease, climatic, geographic, and ethnographic conditions had been bridged and rapport had been established with the people. Then the gospel was experienced by individuals and they in turn witnessed to the faith to their fellow-men. In addition, the African churches began to produce their own leaders for every service in the church and the society.

The Christian community multiplied more than fivefold during the first half of the twentieth century. It has continued to grow since 1950 and has greatly influenced many people who are not baptized Christians. A study of southern Nigeria indicates that even though the number of baptized Christians is limited, from seven to ten million people are unwilling to be called anything but Christian.[174] This presents a great potential for church growth and a most sobering responsibility to the churches. The able body of Christian leaders of indigenous churches promises further expansion and indigenization of the Christian faith.

Christian missions and churches reduced many languages to writing and gave the Scriptures to the people. Although to an insufficient degree, they also provided Christian literature. The Sudan Interior Mission pioneered in Christian radio and popular magazines, inspiring similar attempts by other agencies.

The two world wars brought much hardship to the churches of the German-speaking missions. The Christians were shocked to see their missionaries arrested and interned as evildoers. The churches were compelled to continue the ministry without the personnel and financial resources that had supported them before the wars. German-speaking worship services and educational programs had to be changed to French or English. Finally, the churches were obliged to arrange their own course through the political maze of independence and new national struggles.

During the last decades Christianity in West Africa has witnessed a stirring among the people that has brought many independent churches into existence. Again church leaders have interpreted the faith in their own terms and formed an authentic theology. The adoption of new ideas and principles motivated some people to abandon the ethical principles of the tribe, causing a degree of moral and social disintegration. Morals in the cities became questionable. Christian missions and the emerging churches, in dependence on the Holy Spirit, sought to bring into such a situation a spiritual dynamic through the message of salvation in Jesus Christ.

Study Questions

1. Describe the missionary policy that has been most effective in Senegal, in Gambia, and in Guinea.
2. Evaluate the change of policy in the ministry of the Church Missionary Society toward the close of the nineteenth century.
3. Describe the results of cultural barriers on the Christian ministry in Sierra Leone.
4. Explain how church growth in Liberia has been stunted by too much foreign aid.[175]
5. Evaluate the ministry of radio station ELWA in Monrovia, Liberia, and the more recent effort to evangelize the people of the interior of Liberia.
6. Explain why the ministry of William Wade Harris had such a large influence.
7. Describe the results of the policies pursued by the Methodist and Basel missions in Ghana.
8. Describe the Christian influence in Ghana in 1936.
9. What efforts are being made to evangelize the people of the northern part of Ghana?
10. What results did the Bremen Mission have in training leaders for the Togo church in Germany?
11. Describe the evangelistic efforts of the Evangelical Church of Togo during the past decades.
12. Describe the "Joint Action for Mission" and its ministry.
13. Describe the missionary efforts of the Nigerian Baptist Convention.
14. Describe the extention of the ministry of the Qua Iboe church.

10

Christianity in West-Central Africa

The efforts of the Catholic missions in the Congo kingdom from 1491 to the end of the eighteenth century have been observed in chapter 2. This missionary endeavor appeared to be quite successful for some time, and a Christianized kingdom came into being on the western coast of Central Africa. Unfortunately, however, the ministry of the Roman Catholic Church deteriorated and the Christian community dwindled with surprising rapidity and practically disappeared. A limited ministry was continued at several coastal cities, notably Loanda, Benguella, and Bihe during the nineteenth century. Priests made occasional visits to San Salvador, but no effective ministry was maintained. The administration of the Roman Catholic missions became discouraged with the instability of the work.[1]

Portugal maintained its contacts with Angola. The first relations were of a diplomatic and technical nature. Building supplies and artisans were sent to Dom Pedro V. However, before long, the Portuguese exercised a measure of authority along the coast. They grew significant plantations on the islands of Sao Tome and Principe and began to recruit labor in Angola, which became virtually forced labor. Furthermore, slave trade soon developed and exerted its devastating effects and influence.

Even though the Portuguese contacts with the coastal population of Angola continued for more than three centuries, the interior of the country and of the Zaire basin were not penetrated. The Zaire River basin remained isolated from the outside world. Belgian sources report the efforts by some Belgian Protestants to establish contacts with the people on the southern banks of the Zaire River early in the seventeenth century. However, little is known about the expedition. In 1619 Catholic bishop Manuel Baptiste Soares complained to the pope concerning the efforts of these people.[2] Captain J. K. Tuckey, on behalf of the British Admiralty, led a scientific expedition to the Zaire River area in 1816.[3] Tuckey's expedition gathered valuable information concerning the geography and people of the coastal regions, but fever and exhaustion caused the deaths of fifty-four Europeans. The expedition penetrated only as far as the first cataract of the Zaire River. In 1848 Ladislau Magyar, a Hungarian explorer, made another attempt to learn more about the Zaire River but did not attain the point reached by Tuckey's expedition. Adolph Bastian, a German geographer, visited the region in 1857 and again in 1873. Richard Burton, a British geographer, traversed the region in 1863.

The Christian ministry in Central Africa owes much to David Livingstone, who presented the conditions of the people of Africa and appealed to the conscience of Europeans and Americans. He attempted to explore Central Africa in order to open it to trade and civilization. Livingstone explored the Zambezi and Shire River areas and attracted missionary societies to these regions. Then he devoted the last years of his life to exploring the source and course of the Zaire River. From July 12, 1869 to October 23, 1871, Livingstone was in the eastern part of Zaire. Although he was unable to follow the Lualaba River to its mouth and establish it as the source of the Zaire, his discoveries inspired Henry Morton Stanley to continue the effort. Stanley reached the mouth of the Zaire on August 8, 1877. While Livingstone and Stanley were exploring the Zaire River basin, Protestant Christians and missionary societies became concerned about the people of this region and made preparations to proclaim the gospel to them.

CHRISTIAN MINISTRY RENEWED IN ANGOLA

Robert Arthington, a British philanthropist, had a concern for the evangelization of the people of Central Africa and carefully studied the reports of Livingstone and Stanley and other explorers. Even before Stanley made his historic voyage down the Zaire River, Arthington offered 1000 pounds sterling to the Baptist Missionary Society to undertake a missionary endeavor to the people of the Zaire River basin. The society asked George Grenfell and Thomas Comber, who were serving in Cameroon, to embark upon an exploratory journey to this region. They made a brief visit in

January 1878 and returned in July. At this occasion they visited King Pedro V of San Salvador and decided to make San Salvador their base for a ministry in the Zaire basin.[4] The following year Comber returned with the first missionary party, which consisted of Comber's bride, W. H. Bently, H. E. Crudgington, and J. S. Hartland. They began their ministry at San Salvador.[5]

The Baptist missionaries proclaimed the gospel and established credibility with the people, especially with the boys who lived with them. These young men were greatly influenced by the Christian faith and, even though they had not been baptized, assisted the missionaries in establishing cordial relations with other villages. One of the young men, Matoko, served as interpreter and contact man for Comber and Crudgington when they began the secondary post of Muala.[6] A significant turning to the Christian faith took place during a week of evangelistic meetings in December 1886, and a church came into being.[7]

The Christians from San Salvador soon witnessed to their faith in the surrounding villages. Regular preaching places were established, and people came to the Christian faith through the testimony of the Christians at these places. In 1892 Thomas Lewis reported that five people of Mbanza-Mputu had been converted.[8]

In 1898 the society began a second station at Kibokolo. But the people were attached to their fetishes, and the first recorded conversion did not occur until 1907. A church was organized in 1911. A ministry was begun at Mabaya in 1906, but after several years of service, it was discontinued.[9]

In the course of time the ministries of the church and the school at San Salvador became more fully established. In 1912 a hospital was built. Additional places of worship were opened in the district, extending the outreach to the Zaire border. The ministry and the church membership witnessed continuous growth until 1962, In 1925 the society reported a church membership of 11,728, while in 1962 it reported 39,862 members.[10]

The work of the society was disrupted through the political disturbances in 1962. The Portuguese authorities crushed the independence movement. The Protestant missionaries were in favor of self-determination for the people of Angola. The government, which had always been suspicious of Protestants and now aware of the missionaries' sympathies, refused visas to returning or new missionaries. Those who remained in Angola found their ministry very restricted and virtually impossible. Many members of the Baptist Church fled to Zaire and settled in the Nlemvo, Kimpese, and Mbanza-Ngungu regions. A large number also went to Kinshasa. The ministry of the Baptist Church in Angola practically ceased. Relief agencies came to the assistance of the refugees, helping them during the time of need. Having reestablished themselves, they formed an ecclesiastical unit as a part of the Baptist Church of Zaire.

Two factors prompted the American Board of Commissioners to undertake a ministry in the southern part of Angola. There was an appeal by Major Malan, who had served with the British army in South Africa and observed the work of the society in Natal, and Robert Arthington had made a donation of 1,000 pounds sterling for such a ministry. The society decided to open a center at Bihe, some 250 miles from Benguella. William W. Bagaster, William H. Sanders, and Samuel J. Miller arrived at Benguella in November 1880. In March 1881 they proceeded to Bailundu where Ekuikui II, the Ovimbundu chief, received them. However, he was somewhat perplexed about the purpose of their coming if they were not interested in purchasing rubber, ivory, or slaves. He permitted them to begin a station at Bailundu. Miller began a school. Additional recruits arrived, and the ministry was being established when, in February 1882, Bagaster died.[11]

In April 1882 Sanders proceeded to Bihe and received permission to begin a station. The Ovimbundu tribe is large, and the Umbundu language is used throughout a large region. This fact facilitated the distribution of Christian literature and the ministry of the mission.

In 1884, Sanders and Fay were opening a ministry at Kamundongo near Bihe when Ekuikui suddenly ordered the missionaries to leave Bailundu within eight days. Sanders returned to Bailundu to discuss the matter with Ekuikui, but Ekuikui was adamant. Consequently, the missionaries retreated to the coast. Three days after their departure, Frederick Stanley Arnot arrived at Bihe from the Zambezi. He readily realized that Braga, a Portuguese trader, had made Ekuikui believe that his kingdom would be in danger if the missionaries were permitted to remain. Arnot exposed the duplicity of Braga. When Ekuikui realized that he had been misinformed, he sent an earnest request for the missionaries to return to minister to his people.[12]

The ministry of the society was established, and fourteen people were baptized in 1887. The work expanded through the missionaries' itinerant ministry. The society was confronted with a liquor problem when the Portuguese established themselves at Bihe and traded liquor for rubber. The sale of liquor in large quantities greatly affected the morale of the church, and it was obliged to combat this negative influence. Nevertheless, the church continued to grow. The Congregational Church of Canada joined the ministry in 1886. The mission undertook the translation of the Scriptures. The Gospel of Mark was printed in 1889, and the entire New Testament was presented to the Ovimbundu in 1897.[13]

The period from 1889 to 1914 was a time in which the ministry of the Congregational Church was established. The believers devoted themselves to evangelize their fellow-men and opened many places of worship and village schools.

Protestant missionaries served under the cautious observation of the government authorities. The missionaries were careful to report their movements, the coming of visitors, and the meeting of assemblies. Their services won the favor of the people, and this increased the suspicion of the government. They were accused of creating a foreign and denationalizing influence and of giving too much authority to national leaders. As early as the Bailundu revolt in 1902, the people clearly distinguished the Protestant ministry from that of the state, respecting the missionaries and the mission stations. The methods employed by the Portuguese to recruit workers for the cocoa plantations on the islands of Sao Tome and Principe were hardly distinguishable from slave trade. British agents, with the help of Protestant missionaries, exposed the unjustifiable practice. This effort helped to correct the practice, but it also increased Portuguese suspicion and disfavor toward the missionaries.

After 1914 the growth of the ministry of the two churches increased. New centers were established. The Emmanuel Seminary was opened at Dondi for the purpose of preparing church leaders. The 1938 report indicates a combined staff of 1,568 workers and church membership of about 100,000. The society adopted the village government as the model for church government, with such modifications as it considered essential for the different functions. The local church assumed the financial responsibility for the paid workers. Unpaid workers, two in each village, were responsible for the outstation ministry. The two societies supported education, medical work, industrial training, and the promotion of scientific agriculture.[14] The government, however, did not give favorable consideration to the Protestant educational endeavors. It was very hesitant to grant permission to open high schools or leadership-training schools and revoked the privileges if it found a reason to do so. Consequently the Protestants were compelled to do a fault-less job. A press and publication center were established at Dondi. The medical services were expanded and included five hospitals. The Church Council of Central Angola coordinates the ministry, which has developed around eight centers largely as a result of the efforts of the Canadian churches.[15]

The Congregational churches were not as critically affected by the independence movement and the government crackdown as the Baptist churches. Nevertheless, the government suspected the pastors and missionaries and restricted their activities to the extent that work became virtually impossible. In November 1967 the United Churches (Canada and the U.S.A.) decided to withdraw the remaining missionaries as a protest to the reactionary colonial government in Loanda. The churches continued the ministry under the restrictions placed on them.

The Congregational missionaries established themselves among the Ovimbundu, with Bailundu and Bihe as their main centers. Meanwhile, the American Methodists, under the leadership of William Taylor, began a ministry in the Loanda and Malanje regions, opening five centers of activity in 1885.[16] Taylor wanted to make the endeavor self-supporting. He expected the missionaries to find their subsistence wherever they served. However, because the economic resources in Africa were quite limited and the climate was very taxing on their health, this became a serious handicap, and they found little time for evangelism. The magnitude of the task was increased in that the missionaries brought their families with them. Before long, many of them became discouraged and returned to America.

Taylor had the vision of establishing a chain of mission stations at intervals of one hundred to two hundred miles from the Atlantic coast to the Indian Ocean. Two missionaries were to serve at each station. Taylor was not able to realize his plan, but he launched a significant effort. Although his plans exceeded the possibilities of the early years of the church's ministry, eventually the Methodists established large ministries in Angola, Zambia, Zaire, Rhodesia, and Mozambique.

William R. Summers was among the missionaries who arrived in 1885. After he had opened the station at Malanje, he pushed into the interior of the continent to open another station. His journey brought him into Zaire. He passed Luebo and arrived at Kananga on December 23, 1886. He began a ministry near the former government center. Soon, however, his medical supplies were exhausted and his health began to fail. He therefore decided to return to the coast. But he died not far from Kananga on May 23, 1888.[17] Summers was the first Protestant missionary to serve in the Kasai district of Zaire. Several decades passed before the Methodists undertook to bring Summers' vision to realization.

Joseph Hartzell succeeded William Taylor in 1896. He encouraged the society to concentrate its efforts in the Loanda and Malanje regions. The ministry was established under his leadership. Churches were organized and in 1920 the Conference of the Methodist Church was called into being with its ministry divided into two districts, those of Loanda and Malanje.

The Protestant ministry in Angola has been restricted by the Portuguese educational policies. These policies have complicated the establishment of high schools, teacher-training schools, and the licensing of teachers. Nevertheless, the Methodists' educational efforts made a significant contribution to the work of the church and in the general development of the country. In 1928 the society opened the theological college at Keswa, near Malanje. This college has offered important training to many leaders of the churches. After 1961 the government issued few visas to missionaries. The national pastors assumed the responsibility of guiding the churches in their ministry. In 1968 the Methodist Church of Angola reported a Christian community of 57,137 adherents, who were guided by 110 church workers.[18]

The Plymouth Brethren undertook a ministry in Angola in 1889 as a result of Frederick Arnot's appeal. After his visit to the Congregational missionaries at Bailundu in 1884, Arnot returned to the interior of the country and opened a ministry for the society near Lubumbashi in Zaire. In 1889 he guided the group of Plymouth Brethren missionaries to Angola. They established a ministry from Bihe to the Zambian border and across the border into Zambia. At one time the society constituted the largest foreign staff in Angola.[19] The society made a strong effort to proclaim the gospel, to translate the Scriptures, and to train leaders to guide the congregations. They established many assemblies and preaching places. By 1969 the number of missionaries had been reduced to four. Since 1961 the pastors have worked under much stress because of the close observation by government agents. Many have been imprisoned. The churches have proceeded cautiously in their ministry and have continued serving to the extent possible under the circumstances.

The Presbyterian Church of Canada began a ministry in the central part of Angola. When the United Church of Canada was formed in 1925, it assumed the responsibilities for this work. Toward the close of 1967, the society proceeded to withdraw its remaining missionaries from Angola.

A. W. Bailey of the South Africa General Mission (now known as the Africa Evangelical Fellowship), through the help of Fred Arnot began a ministry at Muie on the Kutsi River in 1918. A second station was begun in 1920 at Catota, where the society opened a hospital, a leprosarium, and a Bible institute, as well as schools on the premises and in the outposts. The ministry of the society made continuous progress until 1964. The Bible institute prepared workers for evangelistic expansion. But the missionaries were compelled to leave Luonze in 1963 and Muie in 1967. By 1969 missionaries resided only at two of the main stations in the south-western region, and the Bible institute was closed because of the departure of the teaching staff.

The Canadian Baptists began a ministry in the northwestern part of Angola in 1957. By 1960 twenty-four missionaries were compelled to leave. Many of them came to Zaire and continued their ministry and relief work among the Angolese who fled across the border.

The Portuguese have been critical of Protestant efforts and motives. The Portuguese also have charged that Protestants disrupted the unity of the Christian faith in Angola by teaching in the vernacular and thus neglecting to promote the Portuguese language and the assimilation of Portuguese culture. The Protestants have sensed an increasing measure of discrimination, particularly in the restriction of their educational work. A peoples' movement to Christianity was especially pronounced in the areas of service of the United Church of Canada and the Congregational Church during the 1920s and the 1930s. African Christians spontaneou propagated the Christian faith, and the Ovimbundu tribe v largely Christianized. The census of 1940 reported 286,000 Protestants in Angola.[20] In spite of the restrictions placed on them by the government, the Protestant churches had a successful ministry until 1961. The Protestant teachings regarding human dignity were considered a cause of the rebellion, and the Protestant churches suffered severely because of the rebellion.

A new period in Roman Catholic missions in Angola began in 1865 when the Capuchins relinquished the area and it was assigned to the Holy Ghost Fathers. Since they were French, the Portuguese authorities distrusted them. They encountered some difficulties in establishing their ministry, but eventually were successful in doing so. In 1873 they began a station at Landana to the north of the Zaire River. They opened schools and a theological seminary and developed some significant plantations. In Angola proper they ministered to the nominal Christians and opened centers of ministry among the non-Christians. In 1879 the southern part of Angola was also entrusted to them.

The first decades were spent in establishing the ministry. After this was accomplished, the mission made considerable progress. After 1914 many missionaries came to Angola and state subventions helped them open additional stations and multiply the schools. They opened a seminary for priests and a novitiate for lay brothers at Huilla. They prepared much literature to promote the ministry. The Roman Catholics in Angola multiplied nearly fourfold during the 1930s. A decree of 1926 and a concordat of 1940 between the Vatican and Portugal provided further privileges for the Roman Catholic missions and assured them of state subsidies. According to the census of 1940, there were 714,000 Roman Catholics in Angola.[21] The significant growth of the Roman Catholic Church continued until the independence movement in 1961. Its close association with the government has, however, placed it in an unfavorable relation with the people.

CHRISTIAN MINISTRY ESTABLISHED IN ZAIRE

Zaire, the former Belgian Congo, became an independent nation in 1960 and was known as the Republic of Congo until it was renamed in 1971. Located in a central position in Africa, it is the second largest country on the continent, with a population of

18,300,000.[22] Christianity has made strong inroads, but Islam has not gained a foothold in the country.

The Zaire River basin remained unknown to the outside world while other parts of Africa were being explored. The efforts to explore this region had little success, since these efforts terminated in the region of the first cataracts. The establishment of the Christian ministry in Zaire owes much to David Livingstone, who drew the world's attention to Central Africa. Livingstone died before he was able to accomplish his goal. Henry Morton Stanley continued the efforts of Livingstone and followed the Zaire River from its source to its mouth in 1877.

Commercial companies of different nationalities established themselves at Banana and Boma on the banks of the Zaire River and on the coast to the north and the south of the Zaire River. A Dutch commercial agency had established a thriving commerce with approximately two hundred trading agents in its service carrying on an important trade in ivory, rubber, and palm oil some one thousand miles along the Atlantic coast.[23]

Christians in Europe and America were deeply concerned for the people of this region and considered bringing the gospel to the people even before the success of Stanley's trip was known. As a result of the missionary interest of the Baptist pastor of Cardiff, Alfred Tilly, and Grattan Guinness and his wife, the Livingstone Inland Mission was formed in order to launch a missionary endeavor in Zaire.[24] Robert Arthington, the philanthropist from Leeds, England, was concerned about the people of Africa and offered five thousand pounds sterling to the London Missionary Society to establish a ministry on the shores of Lake Tanganyika and offered one thousand pounds to the Baptist Missionary Society to begin work in the Zaire River region even before Stanley completed his voyage down the Zaire River. In response to this encouragement, the society asked their missionaries in Cameroon, George Grenfell and Thomas Comber, to explore the possibilities of such a mission. They made brief exploratory trips to Zaire in January and in June 1878 visited King Dom Pedro V of San Salvador in Angola and recommended a mission to Zaire with San Salvador as the base for the operation. At the same time, the Baptist Missionary Society and the Livingstone Inland Mission recruited personnel for mission efforts in the Zaire River region.

In February 1878 the representatives of the Livingstone Inland

Mission, Henry Craven, and the Danish mariner Stroem arrived at Matadi and began a missionary endeavor at Palabala.[25] James Telford and Johnson joined Craven in the ministry of the Livingstone Inland Mission at Palabala. Later in the year they began a second center of activity at Mbanza-Manteke.

In 1879 the representatives of the Baptist Missionary Society, Mr. and Mrs. Comber, W. H. Bentley, J. S. Hartland, and H. E. Crudgington, established themselves at San Salvador, which was to serve as the base for their ministry to Zaire. This was the beginning of their Christian ministry in Zaire and of the effort to penetrate the country with the gospel and establish a chain of mission stations along the Zaire River—an effort that was eventually to connect with the ministry in East Africa.

Under the direction of King Leopold II of Belgium, the International Association of Congo was formed. His agents soon arrived in Zaire and attempted to explore the country and to obtain commercial and land concessions from the chiefs along the Zaire River and its tributaries. Stanley returned to Zaire in the service of King Leopold II and undertook to construct a road from Matadi to Kinshasa. In order to do so he established camps at Isangila and Manyanga.

The British Baptist missionaries made repeated efforts to reach Stanley Pool on the Zaire River where Kinshasa is now located. They were turned back each time by the Makuta people, who wanted to maintain full control over their country and the trade between the interior and the coast.[26] Finally, on January 29, 1881, W. Holman Bentley and H. E. Crudgington made the journey to Stanley Pool by way of the north bank of the Zaire. Having found a route to Stanley Pool, they established posts at Matadi, Isangila, and Manyanga in 1881, and in 1882, at Kintambo just below Stanley Pool.[27] This was a significant move toward penetrating the country with the gospel. The Baptist Missionary Society and the Livingstone Inland Mission engaged in a ministry between Matadi and Kinshasa. River transportation provided many opportunities to make contacts with the villages. In 1884 the Baptist Missionary Society sent the steamer *Peace* and the Livingstone Inland Mission sent the *Henry Reed* to promote the ministry around Stanley Pool and on the Zaire River above "the Pool."[28]

The Berlin Conference of 1884-1885 established the boundaries of the Independent State of Congo and later permitted the Belgian

king to assume the title of "sovereign" of the vast territory. Consequently, the Protestant missionary societies were suddenly under
the jurisdiction of a Roman Catholic state. However, as the Berlin
Conference had requested religious tolerance, they were able to
continue their ministry.

The Livingstone Inland Mission and the Baptist Missionary Society undertook to establish work on the Zaire River above Stanley
Pool. The Livingstone Inland Mission opened a station at Bolenge,
on the Ikelemba River, among the N'kundu people in 1883,[29] while
the Baptist Missionary Society opened one at Lukolela in 1884.
This was the beginning of George Grenfell's significant ministry of
exploring the territories and making contacts with the people of
the Zaire River and its tributaries. Grenfell made very accurate
observations. His maps are still in use. Through his observations
of the people, he was able to give valuable advice to other missionary societies that wanted to undertake ministries in Zaire.

The Svenska-Missions-Foerbundet seconded personnel to the
Livingstone Inland Mission. In 1884 the Livingstone Inland Mission found its resources insufficient both to push farther inland and
to maintain the established stations. This mission decided to hand
the entire work over to the American Baptists. At this time the
Svenska-Missions-Foerbundet assumed the responsibility for the
Mukimbungu station.[30] In 1886 it established a separate ministry.
Nils Westlind, a capable linguist, translated the New Testament
into Kikongo in 1891. The society soon began a ministry at Matadi
on the northern bank of the Zaire River. A mission press was
established at Matadi in 1892 and began publishing *Minsamu
Miayenge*, the first periodical of Zaire. The society extended its
ministry to the north of Matadi, occupying the Zaire territory north
of the Zaire River. It pushed on into Congo-Brazzaville, occupying
the southern part of that country. Large churches were established
in both regions.

Kinshasa on the shore of Stanley Pool became the headquarters
for navigation on the Zaire River and its tributaries and rapidly
became an important center to furnish supplies for the missionaries in the interior. Consequently, both the British and the
American Baptists located their headquarters in Kinshasa.

The British Baptists, inspired by Robert Arthington and encouraged by his financial support, made efforts to establish a chain of
stations along the Zaire River.[31] They adopted this policy to dif-

fuse the gospel rapidly into the interior of the continent and to as many tribes as possible. They also wished to open the interior to contacts with the outside world and counteract the devastating activities of the slave traders. Grenfell devoted himself untiringly to this task. As a result of his explorations and encouragements, a ministry was begun at Bolobo in 1888, at Mpoto and Monsembe in 1890, and at Yakusu, near Kisangani, in 1895, forming a chain of stations along the Zaire River to Boyoma Falls. Grenfell continued his efforts to explore and evangelize the entire country. In 1905 he followed the Uruwimi to its headwaters and then continued his voyage to Nyangwe and Kasongo in the region where Livingstone exerted his last efforts to open the continent to the gospel. Largely because of Grenfell's influence, the Baptist Missionary Society established some thirteen stations in the interior above Stanley Pool. The society has continued a ministry in the regions of the lower, middle, and upper Zaire and has established three distinct parts of its church. It has opened schools and hospitals to serve each of the areas and participated in the training offered at Kimpese and at the School of Theology in Kinshasa.

The American Baptists concentrated their efforts in the lower Zaire region, moving eastward into the interior. One of its early missionaries, Dr. Aaron Sims, gave valuable services to nationals and foreigners who sought his help. The Baptist ministry was greatly furthered through a significant turning to the Christian faith at Mbanza-Manteke in 1886. The policy of the society was to concentrate its efforts in one locality and expand as the ministry developed. In 1910 it began its ministry in the Kwango, and this became a large work. The movement to the Christian faith in the Vanga region brought about 25,000 members into the church between 1938 and 1957. The church reported 113,116 members in 1968.[32] It has trained its church workers at the Bible institute at Kikongo, at Kimpese, and at the School of Theology at Kinshasa, and its medical personnel at the Vanga and Kimpese hospitals.

In 1884 the Christian and Missionary Alliance sent four young men to Banana, at the mouth of the Zaire River, to begin a ministry there. The climate retarded the early development of the enterprise, but in 1888 signs of progress became evident. The society established its headquarters at Boma and by 1896 it opened six stations in a radius of sixty-five miles from Boma in the coastal plains of the Mayumbe territory.[33] The mission emphasized and developed a strong Christian fellowship. In 1928 it granted a large degree of autonomy to the church. During the period from 1940 to 1960 it made considerable progress in Christian education and in its medical services. During the 1960s the work was hampered by internal dissensions. But the ministry of the Bible school and the Theological Education by Extension program have edified the church and strengthened its ministry.

The founders of the Livingstone Inland Mission had ceded their ministry in Zaire to the American Baptists in 1884. They were soon disappointed that the Baptists were occupied with the region south and west of Stanley Pool and did not penetrate the country with the gospel. Consequently, in 1889 they organized the Congo Balolo Mission and sent John McKittrick, who had served one term at Bolenge, and seven others to begin a ministry in the Equator Province of Zaire. The climate was unhealthful and the people were somewhat unresponsive. But the society established four stations on the Lulonga, Maringa, and Lopori rivers before the end of the century and eventually had a chain of stations from which they ministered to the region.

The Disciples of Christ came to begin a ministry in Zaire in 1897. But the Belgian administration was unwilling to grant new areas of service to Protestant missions. Consequently, the American Baptists ceded to the Disciples of Christ the Bolenge station, which was located on the upper Zaire River and isolated from their field of ministry. The Disciples of Christ extended their ministry from Bolenge to the east along the Ruki River and its tributaries, occupying the region south of the Congo Balolo Mission. The two missions cooperated in preparing Christian literature. A small printing press was brought to Bolenge in 1907 and in 1929 a larger one was put into use. The Bible was printed in Mongo-Nkundu in 1930.[34] The Disciples established a large ministry and were serving seven stations in 1950. River transporation has been used quite extensively by the society. A school for the training of pastors and teachers called the Congo Christian Institute was opened at Bolenge in 1929. It has also served the Congo Balolo, the British Baptists, and the Evangelical Mission of the Ubangi, as well as the Disciples of Christ. After fifty years of ministry the church reported 77,275 members.[35] In addition to the medical ministry, the society offered treatment to lepers at three colonies. The ministry of the Church of Christ in Congo, as it was called in 1963, has been divided into twelve regions. The church reported some 230,000 members in 1969.[36]

Most of the missions entered Zaire by way of the Zaire River. However, Frederick Stanley Arnot, a member of the Plymouth Brethren, had spent some time near Victoria Falls and crossed Angola to Bihe. He returned to the interior of the continent and began a ministry at Bunkeya, the capital of the chief, Msiri. This was in 1886 at a time when the chief ruled the territory independently. Arnot and his colleagues extended their field of ministry to the south and southeast from Dilolo in the west. They penetrated to Chibambo in the east and then north to Kalamie. Known as the Garanganze Evangelical Mission, according to the former name of the territory, the society established its ministry at some eighteen centers. It has become one of the society's largest fields. Dan Crawford was instrumental in extending the ministry into the Luapula valley. Crawford and others translated the Bible into Luba-Sanga, and Alexander Clarke completed the Luba-Katanga Bible.[37] In 1962 the church had 13,625 members.[38]

The American Presbyterians established their first mission at Luebo in Kasai district in the south-central part of Zaire. Samuel N. Lapsley and H. W. Sheppard, having consulted with the British missionaries at Kinshasa, chose to establish their ministry in this immense unoccupied territory. This was the beginning of the penetration of the interior of Zaire with the gospel.[39] Luebo was on a slave-trade route. It soon developed into a large community as thousands of Baluba settled around the mission. The people were responsive to the Christian message, and many became faithful Christians. A constituency was rapidly built up and a large ministry developed with Luebo and Bulape to the west and north and Kapanga and Kakinda to the south and southeast. Approximately two million people live in this area and most of them speak the Tshiluba language. The educational and medical ministries of the mission were successful. A press was established at Luebo and a large supply of Christian literature and many schoolbooks were printed. The Bible was translated by William M. Morrison and others and was widely circulated and read.

The Presbyterian mission provided steamboat transporation until commercial shipping services were developed. The society strongly protected the rights of the people and trained men for various religious and civil responsibilities. The pastoral school at

Luebo and the Institute Morrison at Kakinda have trained church workers. The normal school at Bibanga and the medical school at Lubondai and later at Kikaji also are among its institutions of training. The ministry of the Presbyterian mission progressed rapidly between 1914 and 1937 and at the end of that time the church had 94,579 members.[40] Its growth continued after 1937 and in 1968 the church reported 144,001 members and a Christian community of 175,871 members.[41]

In 1897 two brothers, Upton and William Wescott of the Plymouth Brethren began a ministry at Inkongo on the Sankaru River north of Luebo. William translated the Bible into the Luna-Inkongo. The Wescotts extended their mission's ministry to Bakwo-Mbule in 1910 and to Mitombe in 1925. They assumed the ministry from the Presbyterians at Lusambo, the transport and commerical center in 1928, and opened the Bena-Tshadi ministry in 1947. Upton Wescott rendered a valuable service by serving the medical needs of the people in a large district and traveling many miles to do so.[42] A small hospital was opened at Inkongo, and dispensaries were set up at several stations. Missionary recruits were not forthcoming to expand the ministry, and it remained quite small. Christian leaders opened places of worship in a number of villages and established a church that continued the ministry.

In 1911 the Congo Inland Mission was formed by Mennonite churches of the United States. It began its ministry in the Djoko-Punda and Tshikapa regions west of the Presbyterians. From this region the society extended its ministry south to the Angola border and west to Kikwit in Bandundu Province, establishing eight stations by 1950. Members of the society ministered to several tribes in this region and employed three languages. They translated the Bible into the Kipende language, prepared Christian literature in cooperation with the Presbyterians in the Tshiluba language, and did work with the Plymouth Brethren from Angola in the Tshokwe language. They have provided medical services at the hospitals at Djoko-Punda, Mukedi, and Kalonda; at the leprosarium at Kamayala; and at a number of other medical centers. The society provided training for church leaders at the Bible institute at Kalonda and at the School of Theology at Kinshasa. They cooperate with the medical school at Kikaji.

In 1960 the Baluba tribe moved to the Bakwanga region and

organized congregations there. As a result of the ministry of the Mennonite Christians, two church groups have formed.

Several missionary societies entered the Bandundu region between the Mennonite field on the east and the American Baptists field on the west. In 1926 the Canadian Baptists began a work that was ceded to the Mennonite missions during the 1950s and 1960s. The Congo Gospel Mission, the Unevangelized Tribes Mission, and later the Baptist Mid-Missions served this region and established small churches. The Mennonite Brethren began a work at Kafumba in 1920. Later they established their headquarters at Kikwit and extended their ministry. Valuable Christian literature was printed at Kufumba until the place was destroyed in the 1964-1965 rebellion. Serving among several tribes, the society has contributed to the development of the Kituba lanugage and the translation of the Bible into the same. It participates in the School of Theology at Kinshasa.

In 1918 the Swedish Baptists began a ministry north of the Kasai River and north of the fields of ministry of the Congo Inland Mission and the American Baptist Mission, occupying the area south of the Disciples of Christ. Dividing responsibility for the country among themselves, the missions attempted to bring the gospel to all the people. The Swedish Baptists extended their ministry to five stations by 1939, using a staff of thirty-two missionaries and many evangelists and teachers. They opened a teacher-training school at Semendua and a Bible school at Bendela. They have cooperated in the Christian institute at Bolenge and the School of Theology at Kinshasa. Their efforts have been successful and the church has been well established.

The United Methodist Board of Missions, under the direction of John M. Springer, began a station in 1913 at Kapanga and another one at Kambove, to the east of the Presbyterians. Missionaries of this board extended their ministry throughout the mining region to Lubumbashi. Together with the Garanganze Evangelical Mission, they have served the southeastern part of Zaire. They developed an important ministry and church. Church leaders have been trained at the Springer Institute at Mulungwishi. The Methodist Church of Zaire is serving in nineteen districts and is divided into two annual conferences. The southern conference is serving in a number of mining cities, and the central conference is serving a chiefly rural population.

The Methodist Episcopal Church of the United States began a ministry in the central part of Zaire, to the northeast of the Presbyterian work, under the direction of Bishop Walter Russel Lambuth in 1914. The work was begun at Wembo Nyama and extended into the surrounding territory. In 1940 the beginning of the annual conference was established and the districts, one after another, were placed in the care of African pastors. In 1952 the society cooperated with the Presbyterians in opening the Union Secondary School at Katubwe. The Lewis Memorial Hospital at Tunda is one of the many medical services offered by the Methodist missions. John Wesley Shungu became the first African bishop of the Methodist Church.

The Congo Evangelistic Mission began a work at Muanza among the Baluba tribe in 1915. Its staff served to the east of the Garanganze Evangelical Mission and established a large work in this region.

The Africa Evangelistic Band moved into the territory north of the Presbyterians and Methodists in 1936. A number of small tribes live in this relatively poor area. Church growth has been slow.

A number of missionary societies undertook to serve the people in the lakes region of eastern Zaire. The Swedish Free Mission began its ministry in 1921. It established eight stations and reported a membership of 23,966 in 1968. The Norwegian Free Mission entered the field in 1922 and established a ministry to the north of the Swedish Free Mission. Progress was slow, and during World War II the Norwegian Church was unable to help. After the war the ministry was strengthened and by 1968 a church of 12,755 members had been established.[43] The British Pentecostal Mission began a ministry among the Babembe in 1922. Because of limitations of personnel and finances and being surrounded by other societies starting work, the society has not witnessed significant growth. Its church reported 13,456 members in 1968.[44]

The Evangelization Society Africa Mission began its ministry in 1922 and established four stations. It opened a dispensary and a leper colony at Kama and a teacher-training school at Shabunda. It ministers to four small tribes and by 1968 a church of sixty-five hundred had been established.[45]

The Berean African Missionary Society began a ministry to the Balega tribe in 1938. In 1954 it extended its ministry to the

Bakumu. Although services have been held at a number of centers, the church has remained relatively small. In 1960 the Maniema Evangelical Mission also began work among the Balega. It established small churches in four centers of its activities.

The Seventh-Day Adventists began a ministry in the lakes region in 1921. They opened ten stations with two hospitals and two leper colonies. They instructed many children in their Christian day schools and reported a church of 14,134 members in 1968.[46]

In 1946 the Conservative Baptist Foreign Mission Society assumed the responsibility for the ministry begun by the Unevangelized Africa Mission in 1927. It opened a Bible school at Katwa and hospitals at Ruanguba and Katwa. The society extended its ministry to Goma and Bukavu.

The Africa Inland Mission established one of the largest ministries in the northern part of Zaire. It began its ministry in Kenya in 1895 with the intent of planting a chain of stations to Lake Chad. In 1912 John Stauffacher opened this mission's first station in Zaire at Kakenga. The society extended its ministry over some twelve hundred miles of Zaire territory and proclaimed the gospel to about twenty tribes. It has engaged a large foreign and national staff. It developed a large educational work, which included five high schools, a teacher-training college, a number of Bible schools, and the School of Theology which the society operates in cooperation with other societies of northern Zaire. Medical services are offered at five hospitals and twenty-two dispensaries.[47] A large Christian community has come into being through this ministry.

A number of missionary societies devoted themselves to bringing the gospel to the people of northern Zaire. In 1913 Charles Thomas Studd and A. B. Buxton began the work of the Heart of Africa Mission at Niangara on the banks of the Uele River. The society ministered to the tribes west of the area served by the Africa Inland Mission. The Assemblies of God of America began a ministry to the west of the Africa Inland Mission in 1921. They have ministered to the military camps and to different ethnic groups, as well as treating lepers at three colonies. In 1920 the Norwegian Baptist Mission commenced work in northern Zaire, west of the Africa Inland Mission. It reported a church of 16,000 members in 1968.[48] The Immanuel Mission undertook a work in the northeastern part of Zaire. The Press at Nyankunde and the paper *Words of Life* have made a significant contribution. The ministry has remained small and reported a church of 7,804 members in 1968.[49]

In 1931 the Unevangelized Fields Mission began its ministry to the west of the Heart of Africa Mission. It had established a significant ministry and had a large staff in the Kisangani region at the time of the Simba rebellion in 1964. It sustained the heaviest of all Protestant losses.

The Evangelical Mission of Ubangi is serving the northwestern part of Zaire. Titus M. Johnson of the Free Church began a ministry at Karawa in 1923. The Covenant Church of America joined the Free Church in this ministry. Eleven centers of activity were opened and a church of 22,273 members was reported in 1968.[50] The society trains its leaders at the Bible institute at Kayongo. Thus the Christian ministry has been established in every part of the large territory of Zaire.

The Salvation Army came to Zaire in 1934. It did not assume the responsibility to evangelize a certain region, but undertook ministries in cities like Kinshasa, Kisangani, Lubumbashi, Kolwesi, and Likasi. The society has been successful in ministering to the people of the cities and enlisting many in its service.

The Christian fellowship has closely united the missionaries of the different societies serving in Zaire. They inherited a worthy tradition of a spirit of comity, of mutual trust, and of fraternal relationship from the pioneers. The societies have helped each other. The stations along the routes became resting points for all who traveled along them. The societies coming to Zaire sought the counsel of those already established there.

The First United Missionary Conference was held in Kinshasa on January 18, 1902. Nine such conferences were held between 1902 and 1924. They provided opportunities for fellowship and consultation and were appreciated by the missionaries. The publishing of the *Congo Mission News* was begun in 1912. It has served as a source of information for the societies and as a bond uniting them. At the 1924 conference a constitution for the Congo Protestant Council was adopted. Although it remained a consultative body, the council gave the Protestants an organ to serve as liaison between the societies and foster unity and cooperation. The council also serves to represent them to the government and offer counsel wherever needed. The secretariat was established in

Kinshasa in 1928. The societies have greatly benefited from the services of the general secretary. Eventually the departments for evangelism, education, and medical services were organized and personnel were provided for these services. At the 1960 conference, Joel Bulaya was elected president for the coming year, while the Rev. Pierre Shaumba was chosen to serve as general secretary of the Congo Protestant Council. In 1970 the Congo Protestant Council was changed to become the organ of the Church of Christ of Zaire.

The task of entering Zaire and establishing the Christian ministry was no small one. The adverse climate and tropical diseases speedily removed many missionaries from their service. But progress in modern medicine, the improvement of transportation, better living conditions, and the cooperation of the Christians, who soon became the messengers of the gospel, have contributed to the establishment of the church in Zaire. As the national workers outnumbered the missionaries, the expansion of the church increased its momentum. The Zaire Christians have taken the gospel to their people. The catechists have made an inestimable contribution in proclaiming the gospel in the villages and teaching the children. School chapels were soon seen in thousands of villages.

Even though Protestant missionaries were concerned to train Christians for leadership, they were unable to fully realize this desire. The absence of a written language greatly retarded progress. Many languages were put into writing and literature and schoolbooks were printed in scores of languages. Because of distances between mission centers and often because of tribal differences, each society opened its own leadership-training schools. The Protestants were at a disadvantage because until 1948 they did not receive government subsidy for their educational efforts and even after that time, they frequently waited for long periods for government permission to open schools.

Some noteworthy cooperative efforts were undertaken. The School for Pastors and Teachers was opened at Kimpese in 1908 by the British and American Baptists. Reference has already been made to the Congo Christian College at Bolenge and other schools for theological, normal, and medical training. Among the larger united efforts in leadership training was the opening of the Free University at Kisangani, the School of Theology at Kinshasa, the

School of Theology of the North at Bunia, the Medical Institute at Kimpese, and the Faculty of Theology, established in relationship with the Free University at Kisangani. When the government nationalized the universities, the Faculty of Theology was transferred to Kinshasa. In 1975 the government excluded religious education from the university program and the Faculty of Theology transferred its classes to the campus of the School of Theology of Kinshasa.

From the beginning of their ministry in Zaire, the Protestants have devoted much effort to the preparation of Christian literature, especially the Scriptures, in the vernacular languages. No sooner had the British Baptists settled at San Salvador, when W. Holman Bentley began to prepare a grammar and a dictionary in the Kikongo language. Nils Westlind completed the translation of the New Testament in Kikongo in 1891. Bible translations in Zaire have exceeded those of other countries of Africa. The Bible has been translated into twelve languages, the New Testament into twenty, and portions into another thirty-four languages.[51] Many societies also established a printing press. In a number of regions literature committees were chosen to unify the efforts of several societies employing the same language.

In 1934 the storehouse for Bibles was opened in one of the rooms of the Union Mission House and was called the Library of Evangelical Missions. In 1946 forty missionary societies and two Bible societies cooperated to construct a large building to serve as the Evangelical Library of Congo. When the demands for Christian literature increased, the building was enlarged and larger presses were installed. The large enterprise is now known as the Center of Publication and Diffusion.

The British and Foreign Bible Society established an agency in Zaire in 1954. The American Bible Society joined that agency in 1956. The Bible Society of Zaire was established in 1969. From the large Bible house it distributes the Scriptures to the congregations of Zaire. During the last decade the Roman Catholics have also utilized its services.

Though the local people had various herbs and made some medicines that helped to combat illness, there were many diseases that were not conquered and the mortality rate was high. This prompted missions to move into medical work. All Protestant missions aimed to provide a medical missionary and, if possible, a dispensary or a hospital at every station. In 1959 there were 186 hospitals, 345 dispensaries, and many leper colonies operated by Protestants in Zaire. Nursing schools were opened to train medical personnel. At first this training was on an elementary level, but as general education progressed, more advanced medical training was offered at some of the larger medical centers. Unfortunately, programs for registered nurses and doctors were not realized until almost the end of the colonial period. Zaire has had its own doctors only during the last decades.

The medical work in Zaire has fought sleeping sickness and leprosy. Leprosy was widespread, especially in the equatorial forest region. The missions established many leper colonies, treated the patients, and provided better living conditions for them. Some patients were taught crafts, giving them some income. The lepers who did not live in a colony were advised to come regularly for treatment. With financial assistance from the American Leprosy Mission and the government, the societies have rendered a significant ministry.

Missionary doctors have cooperated with the state to halt the population decline and to watch for outbreaks of diseases that required massive action. When tests or examinations were required, they received help from government laboratories. Because of the shortage of staff, doctors were often required to travel many miles to see patients at different treatment centers or hospitals. To facilitate their services, the use of small planes was introduced by several societies. In 1960 Missionary Aviation Fellowship came to their assistance, transporting personnel to places where their services were needed.

The Zaire churches experienced difficult times from 1960 to 1965, when the country passed through political disturbances. The people were not prepared for the agitations that came with independence. Some Christians neglected the fellowship of the churches, whereas others drifted from the Christian faith. The churches were not prepared to give strong leadership and to guide their members through this period effectively. Then, before the churches were fully reestablished, the Simba rebellion erupted. The outbreak was Communist-inspired and anti-religious in nature. The rebels' attack on the churches varied from one region to another. The most severe onslaught was in the Kisangani area in which many Christians and missionaries were ruthlessly massacred. Pastors, evangelists, and teachers were killed because their Christian principles did not condone the inhuman cruelties and immorality of the rebels. The latter saw many educated Christians as a threat. The Unevangelized Fields Mission sustained the loss of nineteen of its thirty missionaries and children—the greatest loss of the Protestant societies from 1960 to 1965. The Roman Catholic losses were considerably greater. They lost 179 workers during this period. In some regions the activities of the churches ceased for about eighteen months. When order was restored to the disturbed regions, some churches were unable to resume their activities because so many church workers had been killed. It was some time before they were able to reestablish their ministries.

The destruction of school buildings, dispensaries, hospitals, the printing establishments with their equipment, and the church buildings disrupted the activities of some churches. Some have not fully recovered from the loss they sustained. The churches, however, dedicated themselves to the spiritual ministry. They resumed their spiritual outreach after the persecution quite rapidly.

Some churches felt the necessity of strengthening the spiritual life of the Christians and they prepared for a deeper-life emphasis. In 1966 the general assembly of the Protestant council, meeting at Matadi, decided to launch a "Christ for All" campaign. This campaign lasted for five years. It has become a model for evangelistic outreach, has greatly edified the Zaire churches, and has added new members to their ranks. Although the Christian ministry in Zaire has been successful and the Church of Christ of Zaire has a large membership, the Christians are confronted with the large task of bringing the gospel to the rest of the people.

A significant religious movement in Zaire has been the establishment of the Church of Jesus Christ on Earth through the "prophet" Simon Kimbangu. This movement began with the profound experiences of Kimbangu, a member of the Baptist Church at Ngombe-Lutete, in the Mbanza-Ngungu region of Zaire. After his baptism in 1915, Kimbangu went to work in Kinshasa and established a Christian home. Several years later he felt called to the Christian ministry. He returned to his village of Nkamba and began to preach and heal in 1921.[52]

The report of Kimbangu's ministry spread throughout the territory and the people flocked to him. He expounded the Scriptures, prayed, and healed the sick in the name of Christ.[53] As a result of Kimbangu's ministry, a revival spread through the territory and started a people movement to Christianity. Many people purchased Bibles and song books and disposed of their fetishes. Kimbangu requested a faithful Christian life from his followers. His popularity attracted the opposition of the Roman Catholics, for the people were leaving their services and flocking to the Kimbanguist meetings. They requested the state officials to intervene. The Belgian officials were uneasy about the movement, but hesitated to intervene. The Baptist missionaries advised the Belgian officials not to intervene, for Kimbangu had been a faithful church member and a loyal citizen.

Kimbangu chose and ordained twelve collaborators whom he authorized to preach, to heal, and to install others in the ministry as local leaders. Through this action the proliferation of local leaders and would-be prophets began. Soon Kimbangu was unable to control the movement. Many of the men chosen were not of the noble spirit of Kimbangu. The movement spread throughout the Lower Zaire region.

The Belgian officials feared political repercussions and Catholic losses as a result of the movement. They arrested Kimbangu in September 1921 and sent him to prison in Lubumbashi, where he died in 1951. Kimbangu participated in the services and was polite and cooperative during all the years of imprisonment. His Christian character never came into question.

While Kimbangu was in prison, his disciples continued the movement. In spite of persecution and deportation of about thirty-seven thousand members to other parts of Zaire, the movement continued to grow. The deported members witnessed to their faith wherever they were, and Kimbanguist groups were formed in other parts of Zaire. After 1950 the Belgian authorities relinquished the persecution, and the movement grew rapidly. Emmanuel Bamba gave leadership in reuniting Kimbanguist efforts and brought Joseph Diangienda, Kimbangu's third son, to Nkamba in 1951 to assume the leadership. Diangienda tried to bring the widely scattered groups with divergent emphases in their teachings together in some sort of affiliation, encouraging them to adhere to one doctrine. The request for legal recognition was not granted until 1959. When the Kimbanguists were able to function legally, they organized their ministries and grew very rapidly.

Since 1963 they have received subsidy from the government for their schools just as do the Protestants and Catholics.

The structure of the organization, the mode of the services, and the literature of the Kimbanguist Church reveal its Protestant origin. Pastors, catechists, and laymen gave leadership to its ministries. The last catechism published by the church presents its faith systematically. It resembles the catechism used by Protestants. However, in its declarations concerning the origin of the movement, it honors Kimbangu, the founder of the church, in much the same way as the Holy Spirit is honored. The communion service was not observed until the fiftieth anniversary of the movement. The Kimbanguist Church is among the largest of the Separatist Churches in Africa. However, although it has been established independently and maintains its independence rather than join with the Church of Christ in Zaire, it became a member of the World Council of Churches in 1968.

The early efforts of Roman Catholic missions in Angola did not affect the people of Zaire. The Roman Catholic missions were slow in entering the Zaire basin. However, after Zaire came under the jurisdiction of King Leopold II of Belgium, they entered the country and put forth much effort to establish themselves and acquire concessions from the chiefs. They received substantial concessions and favors from the Belgian authorities, and this enabled them to make rapid progress.

In 1865 the Holy Ghost Fathers serving in Gabon were given the responsibility for the Zaire River region. Representatives of the society were sent to Boma on the estuary of the Zaire River. By 1877 they had placed personnel at Landana, Banana, and Boma on the north bank of the Zaire River and at St. Antonio in the former Kingdom of Congo, but made no effort to advance into the interior. However, after W. Holman Bentley and E. A. Crudgington of the Baptist Missionary Society had successfully reached Kinshasa via the north bank of the Zaire River, Father Philippe Prosper Augouard of the Fathers of the Holy Ghost was sent on a mission to Zaire in April 1881. He started out for Stanley Pool in July, after having secured George Grenfell's help at Masuka to enlist porters for the journey.[54] He followed Stanley's route, arriving there toward the end of July, five days later than Stanley, after the latter's return from Europe. Savorgnan de Brazza had visited Stanley Pool by way of Congo-Brazzaville and had placed the sergeant Malamine at the Pool. Food was scarce at the Pool. Consequently, after a brief visit, Augouard returned to the coast. The Catholics returned to establish a station at Linzolo near Brazzaville in 1883. Leopold II expressed his wish to Pope Leo XIII that Zaire be reserved for Belgian missionaries.

In 1888 Leo XIII created the vicariate apostolic of the Belgian Congo and entrusted it to the Congregation of the Sacred Heart of Mary. The vicariate included all the Zaire territory except the northern Zaire region, which had been entrusted to the White Fathers, who entered Zaire from their field in Uganda in 1886.[55] The Congregation of the Sacred Heart of Mary had headquarters at Scheutveld near Brussels, and its missionaries therefore also were called the Scheutveld Fathers. Four missionaries, led by Gueley, established the station Berghe-Sainte-Marie at the confluence of the Kasai and the Zaire Rivers. The society expanded rapidly. They readily received concessions at choice locations. Their supplies and building materials were transported by vessels of the Congo Independent State for reasonable rates, if not entirely free of charge. In 1908 the society reported having begun activities at twenty-three head stations with 68 priests and 22 lay brothers serving a Christian community of 8,753 members.[56] In 1912 they had a larger foreign staff than all the other Roman Catholic missions in Zaire combined.[57] However, parts of their large field were assigned to other Catholic missions. They adopted the principle of establishing Christian colonies to which they brought children and freed slaves. They received extensive grants of land from the government and developed farms with significant plantations. Their ministry made much progress in the cities where the people in the service of the state and commercial companies were influenced by the Europeans with whom they associated.

In response to Lavigerie's vision to evangelize Africa, the pope entrusted Central Africa to the White Fathers under Lavigerie's direction. Challenged by Stanley's appeal for missionaries for Uganda, Lavigerie sent some missionaries to the court of Mutesa and to the region around the northern end of Lake Tanganyika. When Zaire came under Leopold's jurisdiction, he saw this as an opportunity to enter Zaire from the east. Leopold II disapproved, however, of having French Catholic missionaries in Zaire. Consequently, the pope created the vicariate apostolic of Upper Congo in 1886 and Lavigerie constituted a Belgian branch of the White

Fathers and entrusted the vicariate to it.[58] The large-visioned and ambitious Lavigerie pressed forward, establishing stations at strategic locations in eastern Zaire and Ruanda.

In 1892 the Roman Catholic Church instituted a Kwango mission to the east of Kinshasa and entrusted it to the Jesuits of the Belgian province. The first party of four, under the direction of Emile von Henexthoven, reached the Kwango in 1893. The Sisters of our Lady, teaching the girls, served side by side with the Jesuits. The work prospered and in the course of the years they opened a number of stations. In 1903 the prefecture apostolic of the Kwango was created and entrusted to them. By 1908 thirty-four Jesuits were serving at six stations.[59]

The Baptist Missionary Society began a ministry at Yakusu, just below Kisangani, in 1896. In December 1897 the Fathers of the Sacred Heart of Jesus began a station called St. Gabriel between Yakusu and the government post. This was a new organization and the work was their first missionary endeavor. They stressed residential schools and opened orphanages. In 1901 Franciscan Sisters took charge of the girls' orphanage and engaged in educational and medical services. By 1908 eight stations had been opened and the vicariate apostolic was created.

Roman Catholic missions as well as Protestant missions made special efforts to establish their work in all parts of Zaire. In 1898 the prefecture apostolic of Welle was erected to cover that part of the unoccupied territory of Zaire and was entrusted to the Premonstrantensians. In 1899 the prefecture of Matadi was created and entrusted to the Redemptorists. The prefecture apostolic of the Upper Kasai was created between the prefecture apostolic of the Kwango and the Lualaba River. It was entrusted to the Scheutveld Fathers and the Sisters of Charity of Ghent. By 1910 they had established eleven stations and nineteen Christian villages (fermes-chapelles) in which the people lived, cultivated their gardens and fields, and received religious instruction. In 1911 the prefecture apostolic of Upper Katanga was created and entrusted to the Congregation of the Holy Ghost. As the work progressed and additional missionary agencies came to Zaire, the Catholic Church created additional prefectures to fill the gaps in the large areas of service in order to occupy the country more completely.

In 1900 W. Holman Bentley reported that the Protestants had opened 40 stations served by 230 missionaries.[60] After the country had been opened to the outside world, the Roman Catholics took advantage of opportunities for navigation on the Zaire rivers and established their work at strategic towns and cities along their banks. The Congo Independent State readily granted new sites to the Catholics, whereas it did not permit the Protestants to expand. The British Baptists' efforts to expand from Yakusu were turned down. Because the Disciples of Christ were unable to secure a site, the American Baptists transferred Bolenge to them. Zaire came under Belgian jurisdiction in 1908, and in 1909 the restrictions on Protestant missions were removed. The Belgian administration willingly granted new sites with large tracts of land to the Roman Catholics and also transported their supplies to these posts on state vessels, greatly helping them in expanding their activities. The Catholics received subsidies that enabled them to open and operate many large elementary and high schools. Two-thirds of the children attending schools in Zaire in 1971 were in Roman Catholic schools.[61] In many missions it was customary to baptize children while they were attending the fourth or fifth year in the elementary school. The government engaged Roman Catholics in the state hospitals and entrusted the spiritual ministry to them. They gained many adherents through these opportunities. However, many of the children who had been baptized while attending school and patients who had consented to baptism while in physical need did not become active church members.

In 1914 more Roman Catholic societies were working in Zaire than in any other country in sub-Saharan Africa.[62] The majority of the Roman Catholic missionaries were Belgians, but British, French, Dutch, Italian, and other nationalities also served in Zaire. By 1914 the work was getting under way and it made remarkable progress after that date.

The Roman Catholic missions sent large foreign staffs to Zaire. They engaged teachers for station and village schools. However, they did not ordain the first priest until 1917, and the number of priests in 1950 was quite limited. The first bishop was consecrated in 1956, but in 1971 the majority of the thirty-four bishops were still foreigners.[63] During the last decades more effort has been made to train and install African church workers. It has been observed that in most parts of Africa this work has not been accorded the importance it deserves except in the last thirty

s.[64] Whereas in England one priest is responsible for an aver-
of 644 members, in Africa one priest is responsible for 1,800
members.[65] The Roman Catholic Church has established a
number of seminaries in which priests are being trained at the
expense of the church, and this encourages many young men to
consider this training. In addition to the seminaries, the Roman
Catholic Church opened the Lovanium University near Kinshasa,
which was legally recognized in 1949 and also had a theological
faculty. But the university was nationalized in 1971, and in 1975
the government discontinued theological education as an integral
part of the university program. Consequently, Catholics as well as
Protestants had to relocate and reestablish this aspect of training.

Helped by the government, the Roman Catholic missions
worked in close collaboration with the state. Through this collaboration the work progressed in earlier days, but many people
mistrusted the sincerity of the Catholic missions at the time of
independence and even more so during the Simba rebellion.
Catholic missionaries lost their rapport, and 179 lost their lives
from 1960 to 1965. Thus the work received a severe setback.[66]
However, the work has been reestablished in the last decade.

Until 1960 the Catholic missionaries regarded the Protestants
with disfavor. After 1960 the new political atmosphere in Zaire and
the attitude of Vatican II brought about a new relationship between the two Christian communions. Roman Catholic observers
came to the translation consultation of the Bible societies in
Kinshasa in 1963. From that time the Roman Catholics have made
the Scriptures available to their people and cooperated in some
translation or revision efforts. Fraternal meetings of seminaries
and other aspects of the ministry have been held. Under the
government's present political attitude toward religious bodies,
the Roman Catholic, the Protestant, and the Kimbanguist
Churches have equal rights. The suppression of religious teaching
in the schools requires a large reorientation on the part of the
churches in order to bring the Christian faith to the next generation and guide it in the Christian life.

CHRISTIAN MINISTRY EXTENDED TO CONGO-BRAZZAVILLE

The territory to the north of the Zaire River was formerly known
as French Congo. It came under France's influence in 1880 as a

result of Savorgnan de Brazza's voyage through the country to Stanley Pool and the treaties he made with the chiefs, who accepted a relationship with France. It was a part of French Equatorial Africa until 1960, when it became an independent state known as the Republic of Congo. The population in this territory was relatively small. It was estimated at 860,000 in 1967.[67] In the course of time two cities, Pointe-Noire on the Atlantic coast and Brazzaville on the north bank of Stanley Pool, have become the most significant cities, in which one-fifth of the population of Zaire lives.

The Roman Catholic missionary agencies established contacts with the Kingdom of Congo during several centuries, but they did not establish a ministry among the people along the Zaire River. In 1865 the Roman Catholic Church entrusted the apostolic prefecture of Congo to the Holy Ghost Fathers. By 1877 they had established centers of ministry at Landana, Banana, and Boma on the north bank of the Zaire River. But only after Stanley, and later de Brazza, had explored the territory around Stanley Pool and the Protestant missionaries had established contacts with the people at Stanley Pool, did Philippe-Prosper Augouard proceed to the Pool and establish a station at Linzolo, near Brazzaville, in 1883.

The Roman Catholic Church formed a vicariate apostolic of Loango in 1886 and entrusted it to the Holy Ghost Fathers. They instructed the people in handicrafts and agriculture on large plantations. They established a number of agricultural stations to introduce new plants.[68] To establish its ministry on the Zaire River, the Catholic Church formed the vicariate apostolic of Ubangi or Upper Congo in 1890. This embraced a large area on the north bank of the Zaire River. This vicariate apostolic, as well as those of Loango and Gabon, was entrusted to the Holy Ghost Fathers. Augouard was made archbishop and was placed in charge of the work. The ministry was supported by the French government from its inception. By 1908 some forty-two priests and twenty-four brothers were active at twelve stations.[69]

The financial assistance of the French government enabled the Holy Ghost Fathers to develop the ministry rapidly. After 1914 the work expanded rather quickly. The Catholics opened many schools and exercised a large influence in education. By 1965 there were three dioceses, which claimed a Catholic community of 350,933 people.[70] After the country became independent, Communist influence was such that the government took over the schools and did not permit religious instruction in them. The foreign Catholic teachers left the country in protest in 1965. But the government maintained its position and also forbade youth meetings. The government has not been favorable to Christianity but has not intervened in church services. Thus the church's ministry has been quite successful.

The Svenska-Missions-Foerbundet began the Protestant ministry in Congo-Brazzaville by extending its ministry on the north side of the Zaire River into this country. It was a natural extension, as parts of a tribe and of villages were on both sides of the frontier drawn up by European powers. The society commenced work at Mukimbungu and extended it to Ponte-Noire on the Atlantic coast and to Brazzaville, the capital, where it established its headquarters for the ministry in Congo-Brazzaville. At the beginning, the work in Zaire and in Congo, were parts of one ministry directed by one general assembly. But in due time the society placed the ministry in each country under a separate general assembly that related to the country. The population of Congo-Brazzaville is concentrated in the southern part where the society is serving.

The Svenska-Missions-Foerbundet has rendered significant educational and medical ministries, as well as having an evangelistic outreach. It has operated several high schools, and the industrial school at Brazzaville has trained many craftsmen who have given valuable service to society and have become faithful laymen in the church. The society trained church workers at the School of Theology at Nguedi and recently has been transferred to Brazzaville. The School of Theology has contributed greatly to the life of the church. A renewal movement began in the school during the 1960s and spread throughout the church, edifying its members and leading them to dedicate themselves to witness and service. The Evangelical Church of Congo is the largest Protestant church in the country and one of the largest in West-Central Africa. In 1968 services were held at 575 places. The church reported 59,318 members and a Christian community of 110,000 people.[71]

The Norwegian Covenant Mission began a ministry in 1940. Having entrusted its ministry in South Africa to the national church, it transferred its missionaries to Congo-Brazzaville and served beside the Swedish Covenant Mission. There was a close relationship between the two societies. When the church became independent in 1961, it merged with the Evangelical Church of Congo-Brazzaville.

The Salvation Army extended its ministry to Congo-Brazzaville from its work in Zaire in 1937. It was guided by the Zaire ministry until 1953 when it became an independent work. The Salvation Army concentrated its efforts in the cities, especially Brazzaville. The society has been successful is engaging many Christians, both men and women, in its ministry. In 1968 it reported 79 ordained leaders, 560 lay workers, and 15 Europeans serving a Christian community of 27,422.[72]

The Swedish Baptist Mission commenced work in the Ubangi-Shari region in the northeastern part of the country. By 1968 it established one hundred places of worship and gathered a Christian community of approximately ten thousand people.[73] The United World Mission seconded missionaries to the Baptist Church of the Sangha, which was establishing a ministry in the Likouala region in the northern part of the country. They opened a four-year Bible school in 1956 in which its church workers are trained. The Christian community of approximately one thousand members was organized as the Evangelical Church of Likouala in 1969.[74]

Because Congo-Brazzaville had been under French jurisdiction, the Roman Catholic society received extensive financial assistance and many privileges in its work, especially in the operation of schools and hospitals. Consequently, the Catholic community is larger than the Protestant community. As a result of the ministry of the two communions, the gospel is proclaimed throughout the country. Around 40 percent of the population is in active contact with the Christian faith, while many more are greatly influenced by it and basically consider themselves adherents to the Christian faith.

The country achieved a quasi–self-government in 1957. The government has changed hands a number of times, but a measure of stability and order has been maintained. Even though Abbe Fulbert Youlou, 1959-1963, maintained close ties with France, the influence of the Communist countries has been very strong throughout these years. Relations with France were strained in 1965 and broken off with the United States and Britain in 1966. Although the country receives aid from the Soviet Union and China, France and the European Economic Market give the most financial and technical assistance.[75]

Since the country gained its independence, the government has been under Communist influence. The government has exerted considerable pressure on the ministry of the churches, forbidding religious instruction in the schools and youth meetings. The schools had been established and operated largely by church agencies. The schools were nationalized and often teachers who did not adhere to the religious convictions of the founders were assigned to them. The churches' opportunities to influence the people with the Christian faith and guide them in a Christian way of life were greatly reduced. However, despite the unfavorable political climate, the Protestant churches continue to witness to their faith and to strengthen themselves in their ministry.

SUMMARY

The expansion of the Christian faith in Central Africa since David Livingstone died alone, kneeling in behalf of Africa, has been phenomenal. A new inspiration and commitment to the Christian ministry in West-Central Africa resulted from Livingstone's death, Stanley's successful voyage down the Zaire River, the British Baptists' journey up the Zaire to Stanley Pool, George Grenfell's exploration of the Zaire and its tributaries, and the planting of a station at Yakusu in the heart of Africa.

A remarkable number of missionary agencies and missionaries responded to the call for service under very unfavorable climatic, geographic, linguistic, and even political conditions. A third of the missionaries sent to Zaire during the first decades died within one or two years of their arrival.[76] Nevertheless, new recruits came and moved forward into the interior until a Christian ministry had been established in every part of West-Central Africa.

Not only was the missionary mortality rate high in those early years, but the population mortality rate was also high because medicines to combat certain diseases had not been discovered. Missionary agencies have contributed greatly to meeting these medical needs. Dispensaries, maternity wards, hospitals, and leper colonies were opened whenever possible. Through their assistance, diseases that were reducing the population, notably malaria and sleeping sickness, were brought under control. Education in nutrition and health care have greatly benefited the population.

The rapid spread of the Christian faith throughout West Central

Africa is due to the faithful witness and service of African Christians. Beginning in the early years of the Christian ministry, until they assumed all the responsibilities for the work, faithful men like Nlemvo, W. Holman Bentley's collaborator, brought the gospel to their people and guided them in worship and service. In the early years their formal training was very limited, yet catechists, pastors, evangelists, teachers, medical workers, translators, printers, and others have greatly contributed to the establishment of the Christian ministry. As advanced training was offered to them, their gifts for the ministry were further developed. Christian missions, both Protestant and Catholic, opened elementary schools, high schools, Bible institutes, medical schools, and universities. Protestant missions served under limited privileges throughout this area, but advanced their ministry remarkably. The churches became independent and were guided by their own members, who were trained in their own schools.

The missionary agencies reduced many languages to writing and thereby contributed to the literary development in the countries. All the languages used by large tribes or throughout a region have been reduced to writing. Bibles, or Scripture portions, and much other valuable literature have been printed, making the Christian ministry and education in the vernacular possible and effective. Smaller presses were established by a number of societies and larger union efforts also have made valuable contributions. Christian and literary journals have developed from these efforts.

The Christian ministry in West Central Africa went through difficult experiences. During the Ovimbundu revolt in 1902, the Protestant work was little affected. The constant restrictions by the Portuguese administration, however, limited the progress of the Protestant work in Angola. The attitude of the administration of the Congo Independent State restricted the establishment of the Protestant ministry in many places. The coming of missionary personnel and supplies was retarded because of World War I and because of the financial crisis in many countries after the war. Then, following a brief period of expansion, World War II again restricted the progress. The political instability of Zaire in 1960 and the Simba rebellion in 1964-1965 seriously affected the Christian ministry. Nevertheless, the Christian faith has been established throughout the region, has won many adherents, and is a significant influence in the society.

Study Questions

1. Indicate briefly the contributions of the Congregational Church in Angola.
2. Evaluate the missionary policies of the Methodist Church.
3. Describe the status of Christianity in Angola.
4. Describe briefly the efforts that were put forth to begin the Christian ministry in Zaire.
5. Evaluate George Grenfell's effort to establish centers of ministry along the Zaire River.
6. Missiologists emphasize that it is important to bring into church fellowship the responsive unchurched in as great numbers as possible. How does the Baptists' experience at Vanga, Zaire, substantiate this statement?
7. Evaluate F. S. Arnot's policy of establishing rapport with the local leadership.
8. Evaluate the evangelistic and educational efforts of the Presbyterian Church in Zaire.
9. Indicate briefly the literary contribution of the churches in Zaire.
10. Evaluate briefly the missionary policy and cooperation in Zaire.
11. Describe briefly the ministry of the churches since 1960.
12. Relate briefly the establishment of the Church of Christ in Zaire.
13. Describe briefly the birth of the Kimbanguist Church in Zaire.
14. Indicate briefly the growth of the ministry of the Roman Catholic Church in Zaire.
15. Describe the development of the ministry of the Holy Ghost Fathers in Congo-Brazzaville.
16. Evaluate the people movement in the Evangelical Church of Congo.
17. How has the attitude of the government influenced the Christian ministry?

11

Christianity in
West Equatorial Africa

During the nineteenth century France acquired a huge empire that stretched from the north of Zaire and west of Sudan to Senegal on the West coast of Africa. It bordered the southern portion of the Sahara. It embraced a part of the desert and the Lake Chad and a part of the Niger valley regions. The population was a mixture of races with a large part of it of Negro blood. It is one of the most sparsely populated regions of Africa. France did not pursue an aggressive program of development. European schools were late in coming to this region, and their purpose was chiefly to train men for French government services.

Islam was strong, especially in the northern parts of this area. It had been brought in along the trade routes from the northern shores of Africa. Christianity was late in coming to this interior region of Africa and slow in making a vital contribution.

Europeans knew little of the eastern part of this region to the north of Zaire until a Frenchman, Pierre Savorgnan de Brazza, became convinced that the Ogowe River was the avenue to penetrate Central Africa. He followed this course to Stanley Pool shortly after Henry Morton Stanley passed down the Zaire River. De Brazza left his agents on the shores of Stanley Pool. France used this event to wedge into Equatorial Africa.

Active propagation of the faith seems to have been undertaken by the followers of Lavigerie. In 1868 Rome assigned the western part of this region to Lavigerie as Apostolic Delegate. Hacquard of the White Fathers was an effective pioneer in the ministry in this region during the 1890s, but there were no significant missionary endeavors in the interior until after World War I. Protestant missionary agencies engaged in evangelization among the peoples of the coastal regions. It was after 1920 that they attempted to minister to the people of these interior regions, and a decade passed before the ministry was somewhat established. Even at the time of writing certain areas have been only partially occupied and Christians constitute a very small percentage of the population. The French anti-clerical policy did not inspire progress in missionary efforts. The French made it rather difficult for Protestant missions in this area. The Roman Catholics received considerable advantages under the French jurisdiction and still enjoy them to a certain degree. But now Protestant work is established quite firmly and is witnessing increased church growth.

Central African Republic

The Central African Republic was a part of the former French Equatorial Africa and became independent under M. David Dacko's leadership in 1960. A relatively poor country, it experienced a fair degree of stability under his presidency. On December 31, 1965, Dacko was dismissed by a military coup and Colonel Jean-Bodel Bokassa took office.

The country is predominently agricultural. Cotton and coffee are the main export crops. Some minerals are adding to the resources of the country. The population is relatively small, being estimated at 1,600,000.[1] Most of the people are animists. Islam has gained a small percentage of the population, and Christianity has been gaining many adherents during the last decade.

Roman Catholic work entered this area by way of Gabon and Congo-Brazzaville. In 1886 Rome created the vicariate apostolic of Loango. In 1890 Rome created the vicariate apostolic of Ubangi, which embraced large regions north of the Zaire River. The Holy Ghost Fathers were responsible for these regions. They established a network of mission posts in Gabon and Congo-Brazzaville which were in part economic enterprises, with schools to teach the children and agriculture to help provide their livelihood. But the work did not spread into the northern part of the Central African Republic until the early part of the twentieth century. A church was founded in Bangui in 1894. The work was confined to this area until 1925 before it expanded to the surrounding regions. In 1909 the vicariate apostolic of Ubangi-Shari was added to those of Loango and Ubangi, occupying the northern part of the Ubangi vicariate apostolic and extending north and east.[2]

The Capuchins and the Jesuits came to this area between 1927 and 1947. Their arrival led to the creation of two more ecclesiastical circumscriptions, those of Berberate and Fort Lamy.[3] The Oblates of the Immaculate Mary later established a ministry in this region. The anti-clerical policy of the French government and its lack of emphasis on education had a certain retarding effect on the missionary efforts in French Equatorial Africa. But from 1945 to 1965 missions witnessed significant growth. By 1965 the Roman Catholics had established four dioceses, and they reported 189,795 adherents in 1971.[4]

The Brethren Church sent its first missionaries of the Central African Republic in 1919. The French government at Brazzaville was not interested in Protestant missions, and the party did not receive permission to work in Ubangi-Shari until 1921. The Brethren began their ministry in the western part of Ubangi-Shari among the Karre tribe. During the first twelve years they established three centers. By 1940 they had opened thirteen centers, with Bangui, the capital, as one of them. Bangui, an important river port and airline center, plays a significant role in the life of the country, drawing a large population to it.

The Brethren emphasized religious education. A Bible school was opened in each district. Some of the students from the local Bible schools were chosen for the Central Bible Institute, where some sixty students were admitted annually for advanced training. In 1970 a theological college was opened to provide further training for church workers. The society put forth much effort to prepare Christian literature. They translated the Bible into the Sanyo language and the New Testament into the Karre and Kabba languages.

The Brethren society opened a hospital in 1957, offering general medical and dental care.[5] It also serves the people at a number of dispensaries. Medical personnel are encouraged to take training at the Bible Institute at Bata so that they will be able to serve as medical evangelists.

Since 1940 there has been marked church growth. In 1968 the society reported 300 places of worship, with 45,000 church members, who are served by 60 pastors and 160 lay workers.[6] The Brethen Church (Eglise Evangelique des Freres) is the largest Protestant church in the country.

The Baptist Mid-Missions work in the eastern part of the country. The William C. Haas family came in 1912, but they had to leave in 1916 because of illness in the family. In 1920 Haas and five other missionaries returned to establish a continuing work. They developed twelve main centers, placing emphasis on evangelism, church planting, leadership training, translation of the Scriptures, and medical services. They have a number of smaller Bible schools, two more advanced Bible schools, and a seminary.[7] The 1968 statistics indicate 319 places of worship, with 40,000 members, who are served by 200 national workers and 123 missionaries.[8] However, the missionary staff is decreasing. In 1972 there were 84 missionaries serving in this field.

The Swedish Baptist mission started work in the southwestern part of the country in 1923. By 1968 they had developed 90 centers of worship, with 16,000 members served by 21 ordained pastors and 206 lay workers.[9] Their work included schools, evangelism and church work, an orphanage, and medical services. The national church is called Union des Eglises Baptistes.

The Africa Inland Mission established work in the Central African Republic in 1924 among the Zande tribe. By 1965 the church was independent and called the Eglise Evangelique Centralafricaine, or the Evangelical Church of Central Africa. In 1968 it had about one hundred places of worship, eight hundred members, and a Christian community of about five thousand, who were served by two ordained pastors and thirty laymen.[10] In 1972 there were sixteen missionaries serving with the church.[11]

The Swiss Pentecostal Church has been working in the country since 1927. Their church membership is about sixty-five hundred.[12] Recently several other societies have come to the country, but their work is small. Several separatist churches have developed among the major tribes. The largest of these is the Comité Baptiste with seven thousand members, led by Pastor Boymandja.[13] The American Bible Society has an agency in Bangui to create, publish, and distribute literature in Sanyo, which is the lingua franca, and other vernaculars used in Chad and the Central African Republic.[14]

Chad

Chad, like the Central African Republic, is a landlocked country. It lies west of Sudan, with Libya to the north and the Central African Republic to the south. It was formerly part of French

Equatorial Africa, but since 1960 has been an independent republic. It has a population of 3,900,000[15] and is divided into two principle zones. The area west of the Chari River has rich vegetation and is inhabited mostly by animists or Christians. The northern, semidesert area in inhabited by nomadic Arabs who are Muslims.[16] Between 41 and 50 percent of the country's population adhere to Islam.

The Baptist Mid-Missions started work in Chad in 1925 among the Sara. The tribe readily received the missionaires, but the chief opposed an evangelistic ministry. No progress could be made until after his death in 1937. Christian workers were prepared through the instruction of Bible courses. Church offerings increased. The church at Fort Archambauld supported 21 evangelists. The society established work at Kyabe and at Koumra in southern Chad.[17] A Christian high school was opened in 1964. Medical services are offered at a hospital and two clinics, and in 1972 there were three Bible schools.[18] The indigenous church is called Eglises Baptistes du Chad (Association of Baptist Churches in Chad). Statistics for 1968 indicate 150 places of worship and 15,000 baptized members, who were served by 25 national pastors and 57 lay workers.[19] In 1972 there were 28 missionaries assisting the church.

The Christian Mission to Many Lands extended its work from Nigeria to Chad in 1925. John R. Olley, who started working at Fort Lamey, now N'Djamena, directed the mission for thirty years. He translated the New Testament into the Mbai and Kim languages. The society established five stations. In 1968 there were 250 worship centers, 5,000 baptized members, and a Christian community of 15,000, who were served by 147 national workers and 22 missionaries.[20]

H. C. Wilkinson of the Sudan United Mission commenced a station at Koutou in 1927. At first there was strong opposition, and progress was slow. But in the 1940s there was substantial church growth. Because of the indigenous principle established since the beginning, the church is self-supporting. It is now called the Evangelical Church of Chad (Eglise Evangelique du Tchad). Church workers are trained in three Bible schools and a theological school. The New Testament was completed in the Ngambai language in 1955. The society is engaged in education and medical work as well.[21]

After World War II, a French-Swiss group united with the

Sudan United Mission. In 1945, M. Veary, general secretary of this mission at N'Djamena, presented the needs in France and Switzerland. Swiss Christians formed a committee to undertake work in Chad. The station of Massenya was turned over to the Swiss.[22] Christians from France participated in the work by sending French missionaries and thus the committee was called "franco-suisse." The missions committee of the French Mennonite Church, which supported missionaries in other countries, became vitally interested in the "franco-suisse" mission to Chad and sent a Mr. and Mrs. Eyer to participate in the work.

During an annual conference of the Sudan United Mission, the French branch was asked to take responsibility for the evangelization of a new region. This was the Quaddai, located about seven hundred kilometers east of N'Djamena and extending to the Sudan border. The evangelization of the Muslims was extremely difficult, and the workers had to be prudent to avoid arousing fanaticism on the part of religious chiefs. Work was started in Abeche. Encouraged by the response, the missionaries undertook further work at Matadjene, north of Abeche.[23]

After the war, the Sudan United Mission started work among the animist tribes of Mont Guero, four hundred kilometers east of N'Djamena. They established work in the market town of Guera and at Mongo in 1946.

The churches formed through the efforts of the Sudan United Mission with the cooperation of the French Mennonites and the Worldwide Evangelization Crusade have formed the Evangelical Church of Chad. In 1968 they had 372 worship centers, 18,871 members, and a Christian community of 50,000. There were 47 pastors, 291 laymen, and 87 missionaries.[24]

The Evangelical Church of Chad has organized the African Mission Society and is attempting to evangelize Muslims in the Lake Chad area. The church has several tribal Bible schools and a French theological school to train church workers. It also offers medical services in a hospital and in clinics. The Flambeaux and Lumieres programs for children and youth are a vital part of the church.[25]

The Lutheran Brethren Mission has done extensive work in Chad. Through its efforts the Eglise Franternelle Lutherienne (Fraternal Lutheran Church of Chad) was formed. It has 230 worship centers, 3,778 church members, and a Christian community of 5,800.[26] The Assemblies of France, working at Guera, have 7 worship centers and about 100 members.[27] Missionary Aviation Fellowship is active in providing air transportation for missions in Chad. The New Testament is available in seven languages, but the complete translation of the Bible is not printed.[28]

The Catholic Church erected its first prefecture in Chad in 1947 and developed into four dioceses in 1966. The number of Catholic church members is about 109,627, compared to about 94,000 Protestants.[29] Christians compose about 29 percent of the total population and animists about 30 percent of the population.

The Protestant churches of Chad have no united association and work independently. However, in 1968 all Protestant societies of Chad, Niger, Mali, and the Central African Republic launched an evangelistic campaign through which many converts to Christianity were recorded. The biggest problem confronting the church in Chad is Islam.[30]

Niger

Niger is a landlocked, mostly desert country, with Nigeria on its southern border and Chad to the east. It was a French colony until 1960, when it became an independent republic. It has a population of 4,100,000.[31] It is mainly Muslim. In southern Niger, agriculture is carried on mostly by the Hausa, and the northern section is inhabited by nomads who raise cattle.

Before the arrival of the French, the only formal education was a rudimentary instruction of the Koran in the Islamic regions, but there were only a few Arabs who could read.[32] The first schools were opened by the military forces when they were stationed at permanent posts. The main interest of the military was to train auxiliaries, and they were content to have schools only at administrative centers. By 1926 there were only 28 teachers in the school system. In 1948 Niger had 60 primary schools with a total of 100 classes and 4,500 students. By 1964 this number had grown to 481 schools with 1,057 classes and 52,755 students. Besides these, there were 12 private schools, with 83 classes and 3,424 students.[33]

The Sudan Interior Mission started work at Zinder, near the Nigerian border, in 1924. It is the largest work in the country, ministering primarily to the Hausa. A center was established in Tsibiri in 1928. A hospital was opened at Galmi in 1950 and serves as the center for their medical ministry. A leprosarium has been built at Maradi. Educational ministries include two girls' schools and a Bible institute.[34] The churches formed through mission efforts are called the Evangelical Churches of West Africa. In 1968 they had 12 places of worship, 69 members, and a Christian community of 422.[35]

The Evangelical Baptist Missions started work in 1929. Because the main emphasis was on reaching people in the region under French influence, they centered most of their activities in Niamey, the capital city. Later, stations were started at Dossa, Goya, Tera, and Tabla.[36] The mission has some elementary schools and plans to open a high school. Other ministries include a Bible school and a bookstore. Translation of the New Testament into the Djerma language has been completed, and the translation of the Old Testament is proceeding.[37]

Missions that came to Niger recently include the Baptist International Mission, Inc. (1970), which has fourteen workers, and the Fellowship of Independent Missions (1971), which has two workers.[38] A Methodist church has ministered mostly to expatriates but is decreasing in membership as these expatriates are gradually leaving without being replaced.

Due to strong Islamic opposition, Christian missions in Niger have had limited success. The authority of the church is in the hands of national Christians. Missions minister through educational, medical, and socioeconomic work. In addition to the schools, the leprosarium, and a hospital, a farm school is in operation.[39] An increase in the sale and distribution of Scriptures is encouraging.

The Roman Catholic Church erected a prefecture apostolic in 1942, and this is now the diocese of Niamey. There are eleven thousand Catholics in Niger. Protestants number only around five hundred.[40]

Upper Volta

Upper Volta, a country surrounded by land, has Ghana and Ivory Coast on its southern border. Mali is to the northwest. A former French territory, it has a varied political history, becoming an independent country in 1960. The population of Upper Volta is 5,600,000.[41] The Mossi tribe, the largest group, is strongly organized around the chief. The Mossi live on farms dispersed in the savanna, where an oil-producing nut called karite is found. To the east toward Ghana are the Gourmantche and the Gourounsi, and toward the south the major tribes are the Bobo and the Lobi. Cattle raising is the chief means of livelihood. Many Voltains are migrant workers in Ivory Coast and Ghana. It is estimated that about 400,000 people are migrants who leave Upper Volta to find work.[42]

Protestant mission work in Upper Volta did not commence until in 1921, when Arthur E. Wilson of the Assemblies of God established a station at Ouagadougou. Later this society opened six additional stations. In 1948 the Assemblies from France joined the work and devoted their efforts mostly to educational work. The society translated the Bible into the More language. It trained church workers in two Bible institutes. At the Bible institute near Lake Nagabaere, students cultivated fields and thus were self-supporting. The church started by the Assemblies of God Mission became autonomous in 1949 and was recognized by the state.[43] In 1966 a revival movement broke out at a mission station and spread to neighboring villages. It contributed to marked church growth in Upper Volta, where in four years the number of Christians doubled and in 1967 was 31,000.[44] The assemblies produce several weekly gospel broadcasts. In 1966 they started a Bible school for students who hold a primary school certificate. The first class had eight students with these qualifications. In 1968 a sanctuary that seats twelve hundred people was built in Ouagadougou.[45]

The Christian and Missionary Alliance commenced a work among the Bobo tribe in 1923. The Bobos were reluctant to accept a new religion. The first five adults asked for instruction in the Christian faith after ten years of work. The society established further contacts among some other tribes and opened more mission stations. The New Testament was printed in the Bobo language in 1954. It was printed in the Dogon language in 1958, the same year that the Old Testament also appeared in the Bambara language. The church is called the Evangelical Christian Church of Upper Volta. In 1968 it had 150 worship centers, a membership of 1,700, and a Christian community of 3,000 persons who were served by 100 full-time national workers and 25 missionaries.[46]

The Sudan Interior Mission came to Upper Volta in 1930 and started work at Zadan N'gourma. Later on, four other stations were opened in the Gourma region. A Bible school at Fada N'gourma provides for church-leadership training.[47] The mission is also involved in other educational work and is engaged in medical work that includes a hospital, several clinics, and a dispensary.[48] The church started by the mission is called the Evangelical Church of West Africa. In 1968 it had a total membership of 175 and a Christian community of 2,500.[49]

The Evangelical Federation of Upper Volta is composed of the Christian and Missionary Alliance, the Sudan Interior Mission, the Assemblies of God, and the Upper Volta Mission. It coordinates joint activities but does not favor ecumenism.[50]

The Roman Catholic Church created the vicariate apostolic of the two Guineas in 1842 and appointed Edward Barron as the vicar apostolic. But concentrated efforts to establish a ministry in the interior were only made by Lavigerie after he was made Apostolic Delegate of the region in 1868. At first he assigned Jesuits to this ministry, but in 1872 he replaced them by White Fathers. Hacquard, who had already served in the Sahara, was sent to this region in the 1890s. In 1898 he was consecrated Vicar Apostolic of the Sahara and the Sudan. The White Fathers opened a number of stations in the region. At one center they gained a nucleus of believers from the freed slaves who were entrusted to them. Because of the influence of Islam, they won few converts during the early years of their ministry.[51] But by 1913 they had made a beginning and reported having 1,300 adherents. After the initial beginning, the work became more productive. By 1925 the Catholic community in Upper Volta increased to 4,339 and by 1971 to 194,958.[52] In 1967 Archbishop Msgr. Zoungara of Upper Volta was named cardinal, the second African to hold that honor.[53]

The White Fathers believed that the church had contributed much toward the advancement of people in Africa and that it could also aid the newly independent nations at this time. Therefore they undertook to train personnel in the socioeconomic fields by opening a social training center in Bobo Dioulasso, Upper Volta. This center offers courses in social ethics, including economics, sociology, trade unionism, credit unions, cooperatives, and other related courses.[54]

Mali

Mali, formerly known as French Sudan, formed a federation with Senegal in 1959, but in 1960 became an independent republic. Mali is landlocked, bordering on Mauritania Senegal, and Guinea to the west, and by Ivory Coast and Upper Volta to the south. To the east is Niger, and to the north in Algeria. The population is about 5,300,000 and is composed of a variety of ethnic groups, with the Bambara in the majority.[55] Islam penetrated into Mali several centuries ago, and a large part of the population is Muslim.

The first Protestant mission society to work in Mali was the Gospel Missionary Union. Their work commenced in 1919, but because of a lack of personnel little progress was made. After 1946 more missionaries came; eight mission stations were established, with encouraging results. The New Testament translation into the Bambara trade language was completed in 1937 and the Old Testament, in 1958.[56] The mission is engaged in educational, medical, evangelistic, and church work. It also offers a Bible correspondence course, had a Bible school in Mana, and operates a bookstore. Though there is a church membership of about twenty-five hundred, the church is not independently organized, but is still part of the mission. In 1972 the society had forty missionaries in Mali.[57]

The Christian and Missionary Alliance came to Mali in 1923 and started work at Sikasso. Although there were some converts during the first years, it was not until 1931 that a special movement of the Holy Spirit was manifested. The deaths of three missionaries within one week, caused by yellow fever, influenced the movement. Shortly after this occurred, twenty young people witnessed concerning their faith in Christ and the church growth movement started and spread beyond the boundaries of Mali. The response was good among the Dogon tribe, which mostly comprised animistic people with strong traditional customs.[58] The society had opened 11 mission stations by 1940. A Bible institute was established in 1936 at Ntorosso, and later a separate girls' Bible school was commenced at Baramba. The mission conducts other short-term Bible schools at various centers. The mission is also engaged in medical work. In 1973 the organization had 27 missionaries in Mali. The church is called the Evangelical Christian Church of Mali and Upper Volta. In 1968 it had 150 places of worship, 1,700 members, and a Christian community of 3,000.[59]

The Evangelical Baptist Mission entered Mali in 1951 and started work at Gao and later at Timbuktu. Since then, several other stations have been opened. A unique part of their ministry has been the gospel boat, first operated on the Niger River in 1959.

A bookstore and medical and dental work are part of their service.

The United World Mission came to work in western Mali in 1954, with a main center in Kenieba. They operate a hospital, an orphanage, a technical school, and a Bible school. In 1968 the church had four African pastors, a membership of about 350, and a Christian community of 3,730.[60]

The Evangelical Mission Society of Paris has two worship centers in Mali and a membership of about one hundred.

The Evangelical Association of Churches and Missions was formed in 1963. This organization attempts to coordinate the work of various evangelical Christians. It has assisted in placing evangelists in the western region of Mali and has sent a pastor to Bambara-speaking people living in Abidjan, Ivory Coast. Other activities have included the establishment of a camp for students and officials of secondary schools and the production of records in various languages through "Gospel Recordings."[61]

In 1966 a desire for a deeper understanding of the Bible was witnessed by about two thousand Christians who came, some from long distances, to attend Bible weekends held periodically. Though in recent years the Christian bookstore has been affected by the governmental pressures on private enterprise and the difficult economic situation, the proclamation of the gospel has continued. In 1969 a New Life for All campaign was launched jointly by all Protestant churches and missions.

The Roman Catholic Church sent the White Fathers into Mali in the late nineteenth century, and a station was opened at Timbuktu. Progress was slow because of opposition by Islam.[62] But by 1965 there were six dioceses and the Catholic Church had a membership of 36,632.[63]

SUMMARY

Christianity was late in coming to French Equatorial Africa, a region that was not readily accessible to foreigners and concerning which Europeans had little information. Furthermore, the French anticlerical policy from the 1870s to the 1890s did not encourage Christian activities, especially those of Protestants. The Islamized emirs of the western and northern areas opposed Christianity. Consequently, the Christian ministry has not been as thoroughly established in this region as in most other parts of sub-Saharan Africa.

The French opened schools only at the military posts to train men to serve in the civil service. As a result the literacy rate remained low. France did not make significant efforts to develop the region.

The response to the Christian message has been much greater among the people in the southern regions where the Muslim faith had not already penetrated. In many regions the Christian ministry is still seeking to establish itself, win the confidence of the people, and train national workers to take the vanguard in the ministry. In the northern regions the Christians are a small minority and do not significantly influence the social and political affairs of the country. Nevertheless, indigenous churches are ministering to their fellowmen in some regions and are increasingly winning more adherents.

Study Questions

1. Indicate briefly the expansion of the Roman Catholic ministry in the Central African Republic.
2. Evaluate briefly the growth of the Protestant churches in the Central African Republic.
3. The churches serving in French Equatorial Africa emphasized training workers in Bible schools. Evaluate this principle.
4. Describe the receptiveness of the people of Chad.
5. Describe the strength of the Christian faith in Niger.
6. Indicate briefly the receptiveness of the people in Upper Volta.
7. It is important to evangelize immediately those groups who become receptive. Describe the church growth in the Christian and Missionary Alliance's ministry in Mali.
8. Evaluate the possibilities of strengthening the Christian witness in French Equatorial Africa and present strategies for a fruitful ministry.

12

Conditions Affecting the Spread of Christianity

Africa has passed through incredible changes at an unprecedented speed within the last hundred years. Changes have occurred in the physical development, scientific inventions, education, and social structures of the countries. Jet airliners fly rapidly from one city to another and to foreign countries. Big vessels sail Africa's waterways, dock in its harbors, and are unloaded with huge, modern machinery. Large hospitals with perfected equipment provide modern medical treatment. Universities offer education in various branches of knowledge. Large governments, represented by many tribes, have replaced the political unit of the tribe.

In one century Africa has witnessed the termination of the slave trade, the coming of Christianity, the period of colonialism, two world wars, and the declarations of independence of most African countries. During the last century Christianity has spread remarkably, and autonomous churches face the challenge of the Africa of tomorrow.

DEVELOPMENT

Effects of Commerce

Henry M. Stanley's voyage down the Zaire River brought to fulfillment Livingstone's desire to open the central part of the continent to the outside world for Christianity and commerce. Missionary societies and trading companies continued to respond to new challenges. Some Europeans had a sincere desire to help the African people attain a better livelihood. The Niger expeditions were a product of this concern. Robert Moffat and many other missionaries desired to bring the Bible and the plow to Africa. Henry Venn, secretary of the Church Missionary Society,

414

advocated lawful trade to replace slave trade. He maintained that profitable, legitimate commerce would cause chiefs to desist from the slave trade. He requested that missionaries send samples of products of the country to him. He presented these samples to brokers to stimulate trade with the countries. Missionary societies and governments introduced new crops, such as coffee, cocoa, cotton, and citrus fruits. The companies traded their wares for local produce, and in this way they encouraged increased production.

The scientific, economic, and political conditions in Europe favored the economic development of other countries. European brokers were looking for raw materials. The demand for minerals encouraged mining developments. The opportunities attracted men from the villages to work in the mines, interfering with the customary village life.

As trade increased, the desire for imported merchandise also increased. Factory-woven cloth soon replaced the hand-woven cloth made in the villages. Shoes, utensils, bicycles, radios, and many hitherto unknown items appeared on the market in remote areas. To a measure, commerce was also influencing a greater number of parents to send their children to school. They realized that formal education placed an individual in a higher income bracket and that this increased one's buying power. As the demand for merchandise increased, factories were built to produce products in the country. This attracted many people to jobs in the cities. Thus Westernization encroached upon the African society, bringing with it some economic changes but also creating some negative effects for African society and culture.

Influence of the Trading Companies

The concern to develop legitimate trade brought many companies with a concern for the people to various parts of Africa. The West Africa Trading Company had close relations with the Church Missionary Society. Bishop Samuel Crowther's son, Josiah, was appointed agent general of the company in 1873. In 1879 the four British companies on the Niger amalgamated to form the United African Company.[1] The French Company traded on the Niger and in Dahomey. The German Company traded on the Tanzania coast. The African Lakes Company came to supplement the missionary effort in Kenya. After establishing and guiding the industrial station at Kikuyu for some years, the company turned the station over to the Church Missionary Society.

Unfortunately, however, the philanthropic efforts to terminate slave trade and develop trade with African countries did not remain as assistance efforts. Some of the trading companies, which had come to provide means for development of the countries, made trade agreements with the chiefs of certain areas to secure the monopoly of the trade. Later the companies used these trade agreements as privileges of political influence in the areas. This influence eventually led to colonization.

Influence of Colonial Rule

For half a century before the scramble for colonies occurred, Britain and France exercised considerable influence over certain areas of Africa. In 1830 the French conquest of Algeria began. During the 1830s the expansion of British rule from Cape Province in South Africa commenced and was eventually extended to the Zaire and Tanzania borders. The British South Africa Company made agreements in Rhodesia and Zambia, permitting its presence in those areas.

The International African Association was called into being at a meeting in Brussels in 1876 by King Leopold II. This was to be for the further exploration and civilization of Africa. However, during the following decade the spirit of philanthropy gave way to the colonizing spirit. At the Berlin Conference the definition of occupation was accepted by European powers and the partition of Africa proceeded very rapidly.

The areas in which European countries had contacts and influence were generally recognized by other European powers. Governments took the activities of their trading companies, or even the presence of missionaries of their countries, as reasons to claim priority in a country and to occupy it. Thus, because the British Niger Company had the greatest involvement in Nigeria and on the Niger, the French Company on the Niger sold out to the British Niger Company. British influence in Nigeria was recognized by the European powers, and Britain granted a charter to the company to rule Northern Nigeria.[2]

The British South Africa Company acquired the property of the African Lakes Company and all the trade treaties it had concluded with the chiefs in Malawi and northeastern Zambia. In this way it extended its rule over this area. The German agent, Carl Peters, concluded treaties with some chiefs in Tanzania and took this as his right to extend German rule over Tanzania.[3] Thus the companies who began with philanthropic motives became colonizing agents.

Areas of the coast of Africa in which no European power had a definite influence or on which no power had yet established itself were quickly claimed. To the surprise and chagrin of the British, the Germans laid claim to Cameroon, where the Baptist Missionary Society of Britain had already served for forty-two years.

Some European nations put forth much effort to develop the countries they colonized. They built roads and railroads to connect strategic places. A railroad from Capetown to Bulawayo was completed in 1897. A railroad was laid from the coast to Octavi in Namibia in 1900-1901. In Tanzania the rail line from Dar-es-Salaam to Kigoma was completed in 1914 and the one from Tanga to Moshi, in 1911. In Kenya the construction of a railway from Mombasa to Lake Victoria was undertaken. In Angola a railway was laid from Luanda to Malanje. Leopold II, king of Belgium, quickly began the construction of a railway from Matadi to Kinshasa to connect the ocean transport Zaire waterways. Similar efforts were made in other parts of the continent.

Telegraph lines were constructed. The Africans were amazed that these lines going through the valleys and over the hills were able to carry messages to people at various stations along the lines. A line connecting Cape Town with Cairo was completed at the turn of the century. Other lines connected important centers of government and trade.

New crops, such as coffee and cocoa, were introduced to supply a cash income. This helped the people economically and also stimulated trade. In other areas palm nut groves were planted and the palm oil industry was developed. Saw mills were set up, and lumber was produced from the heavy wood of the tropical forests. The development of mines was no less aggressive. The European powers took for granted that the Africans would be pleased with these developments. They failed to realize the cultural differences that were involved and that the Africans were not willing to give up their independence for economic benefits or conveniences.

The activities of the colonial powers, however, had a crucial effect on the expansion of Christianity. The missionary vision of the nineteenth century was to open Africa to Christianity, commerce, and civilization. This was the purpose to which Livingstone devoted himself and to which he challenged the people of England during his furloughs. In fact, he challenged the people of the world by his example. As a result of his appeal, three missionary societies were founded with the purpose of undertaking such a ministry in Malawi. The vision of Robert Arthington and the Baptist Missionary Society was to occupy the heart of Africa, and they offered praises to God when the Yakusu station near Kisangani, Zaire, was begun. The heart of Africa had been reached. George Grenfell and his colleagues gave themselves unreservedly to the establishment of the church in this area. A tremendous task was accomplished when the God-given vision was pursued with sincere dedication. The missions, however, were soon hindered by the political ambitions of their own countries.

In some ways, conditions were favorable to missions. The slave trade was suppressed and the ritual human sacrifices were prohibited. The tribal wars were stopped. The colonial rule permitted missions to enter some regions where the people had not been friendly. Yet, in spite of these changes, the new political situation was not advantageous to the missionary endeavor. The Africans were subjected to foreign rule and often did not understand the missionaries' motives for coming to their countries. Some missionaries tried to retain cordial relationships with the government agents, and they were suspected of being agents of the foreign powers. This suspicion did not provide a basis for communicating the gospel or for establishing fraternal relationships and the unity of the spirit in the body of Christ. The African congregations were quite disturbed about the new situation. Bishop James Johnson, a native of Sierra Leone, who was appointed superintendent of the Church Missionary Society's work in the interior, was displeased and strove for a larger measure of indigeneity.[4]

The coming of the colonial powers brought a spirit of rapid economic development to Africa that disregarded the African culture. The colonial powers imposed changes. Labor was requested to develop the country but also for the benefit of trading companies. The Africans resented it. The attempts to shake off the yoke were of no avail, and they languished under it. It is unfair to generalize since some governments were concerned to improve the conditions of the populations. Yet the exploitation of some people, as in Zaire from 1895 to 1908, was incredible. Such situations were not in harmony with the Christian message, and missionaries again took up the task of defending the human rights of the African people against European exploitation. Probably the missionaries in Zaire, more than elsewhere, were obliged to oppose the policies of the administration during the early years of the twentieth century. When the complaints were voiced, public pressure motivated the Belgian parliament to intervene and assume the responsibility for the governing of Zaire.

The French were not favorable toward non-French missions in territories under their control. Their attitude affected Protestant work in Madagascar, Gabon, and Cameroon. The German administration preferred German missions but permitted non-German missions to function.[5] Protestant missions in Angola and Mozambique were under suspicion and their activities were restricted.

In the countries where the administration supported the missions, the latter were in danger of cooperating closely with the administration for the development of the country without fully realizing the deep interests, concerns, and hurts of the African people. The coming of the British colonial rule has been called the "turning of the tide" in Christian missions in Nigeria.[6] The missionary farms in East Africa were unique examples of religious, economic, and political units governed by missionaries. In some countries missions virtually operated the educational and medical programs for the government. This close relationship had a negative effect on the missionary enterprise. Many nationals regarded the missionaries as a part of the colonial machinery. The entire influence from the West represented Christianity to them. Africans do not separate the religious from the secular in their culture. Religion permeates their entire culture. Consequently, in the early period of missionary activities, many Africans did not distinguish between church and state. When they became more acquainted with the West, they were surprised at the atheistic tendencies of some people and the frequent inconsistencies between Christian faith and life in countries that they had thought were Christian.

Influence of Two World Wars

World War I had a profound influence on Africans, who were surprised at the hostilities among the Europeans. In a number of countries, the African Christians bade farewell to German missionaries, who had brought the message of peace and good will, and saw them depart under arrest. Many church leaders were confronted with the responsibility of continuing the ministry, but without financial support from abroad. They were obliged to adjust to a foreign regime, which maintained different principles and used a different language. The adjustment for civil servants was not less.

Men from almost all parts of Africa served with the European forces. Earlier, they had been taught that it was sinful to fight. Now they observed the Europeans engaging in the fiercest battles and they were called upon to do the same. It was sad enough for the European nations to engage in war, but it was even worse for European missionaries to do so.[7] Africans were baffled. Their respect for Europeans diminished. The war, however, had a positive effect on African self-awareness. They had observed the imperfections of the Europeans and realized that they were equally human.

With the progress of the missionary programs after 1918 and especially the advancement in Western education, the new political perception of many Africans also grew. The schools and the churches, even though the Henry Venn principles were not fully applied, guided the people to self-understanding and self-expression. Church activities were guided by councils composed of African Christians and missionaries. The Africans applied this principle in civil administration. In some countries, the nationals were given a greater share in government. The legislative council in Nigeria was introduced in 1923.[8] Advanced education naturally provided greater knowledge of the political systems functioning in other countries. The movement toward self-government got under way.

Unfortunately, however, the Treaty of Versailles was a dictated settlement, and the twenty-year period from 1919 to 1939 was an interlude that led to World War II. This once again exposed European failures and inconsistencies. The European superman revealed his vulnerability.[9] Winter sees the beginning of "the retreat of the West" in this display of "internal weakness."[10] Again, it was an experience of testing and growth for the Africans who had already been moving toward independence before World War II.

The war accelerated all movements and led the world into a period of unbelievable technological achievements at unprecedented speeds. African countries rapidly moved to political independence. The decade from 1955 to 1965 stands out as the period of political independence for Africa. In thirty years following World War II, almost all African nations became independent. They are taking their places in the assembly of nations. Together with other nations, they are entering into the task of shaping the future of mankind.

Influence of European Civilization

Following World War I (1914-1918), the churches in many parts of Africa were obliged to combat the moral influence of European unbelievers. Before World War I the Africans in these countries had some contacts with government agents and commercial people, but their closer contacts were mostly with missionaries. After 1920, more Europeans who were indifferent concerning morals came to live in Africa. As Westernization took place, tribal controls were less binding. Some African Christians who had marriage problems, instead of being encouraged to settle their marital difficulties biblically, found excuses for divorce or polygamy in the morals of Europeans. In some churches an upsurge of polygamy and concubinage was observed. Prostitution made considerable inroads into the society, especially in the cities. As early as 1921, the Archdeacon Lloyd of Uganda remarked that the church was obliged to combat immorality and drunkenness. He further observed that polygamy and concubinage were becoming common matters and the church was plagued with sin.[11] Formerly the polygamous family constituted a unit in society. In the situation that developed, however, freer relations were sought to satisfy sexual desires.

The liquor trade has been an indescribable evil from the time Europeans began to trade on the African coasts. The people of Africa made liquor from the products available in each region. But the quantity was quite limited. When the European traders imported liquor in large quantities, it became one of the major evils plaguing the society. It strangled trade and progress.[12] Large numbers of people, especially in the cities, have become addicted to liquor. Bars are doing a thriving business. Many children die of malnutrition and lack of medical care because addicted fathers have spent their wages on liquor. Drunkenness has become one of Africa's greatest evils.

The churches in Africa are confronted with the problem of materialism. Dr. Mbiti observed that the influences of secularism and materialism are affecting the church as much as ancestral cults and polygamy.[13] This problem has greatly influenced the work of the churches in the last several decades. The Roman Catholic secretariat for the episcopate wrote concerning Zaire that a moral disequilibrium existed. In this moral imbalance, personal interest is the guiding motif. Little consideration is given to the services required of an office. Only the personal benefit a person may gain is considered.[14] The concern for economic gains influences some people to engage in activities on Sunday rather than assist in the work of the church. Material gains are becoming more important than the personal, spiritual blessings and the ministry of the church. Without question, there is a faithful core in the church, but various influences are making inroads, and the church has every reason to consider its life seriously. Rural life with the particularistic traditions is fast being superseded by urban influences.

Materialism seriously impairs the ministry of some churches. Some congregations provide for their financial obligations. They offer their pastors a reasonable remuneration and provide for other expenditures to permit the ministry to continue effectively. But the ministry of some churches bogs down because of the lack of financial resources. Whereas members of the congregations are earning a reasonable livelihood, the church offerings are small, and a concern to reach the unevangelized is lacking.

African society is confronted with secularization, and this spirit is affecting the work of the church. In placing emphasis on science, the religious or sacred in many of the ceremonies performed in the past is neglected. Secularization refers to the desacralization of objects formerly thought to have supernatural influences. When scientific inquiry into cause and effect is made and the object is found to be a natural element, desacralization takes place in the investigator's conception. This discovery may lead the investigator to question the existence of the supernatural altogether. At the same time, the African emphasis is on man's potential. The African is reassuring himself. He is responsible to improve his condition. When the emphasis on the human blinds people to the sacred in the universe, a secular humanism develops. Man finds himself surrounded by a material universe that he tries to manipulate. God is no longer important to him. Thus the church in Africa is in a strategic position, challenged with keeping the balance between scientific knowledge and religious devotion.

E. Bolaji Idowu refers to the influence that Africans have brought from Europe and America and which professors from abroad are disseminating in the universities as "humanistic secularism."[15] Professors and lecturers have different moral and spiritual standards. All kinds of literature is being distributed throughout the continent. This is considered authoritative. It is baffling to some, confusing to others, and an ideal way of life to others. The church has the task of guiding people through the maze of information to acknowledge Christ and live faithfully under His lordship in this scientific age.

URBANIZATION
The Extent of Urbanization

Various cities in North Africa have existed for many centuries, but there were few cities in sub-Saharan Africa before the modern period. Those cities that existed grew at a normal rate over a period of years. The population of Ibadan, Nigeria, was sixty thousand in 1852[16] The African culture, however, was basically rural. But toward the end of the nineteenth century the growth of mining and industrial cities increased at an unusual rate. Cape Town and Johannesburg in South Africa and Kinshasa, Zaire, and Lagos in Nigeria have grown exceptionally and exceed the five hundred thousand population mark. The cities of over one million people are situated along the coast, except for some cities in Nigeria and South Africa. Nigeria is the most urbanized country in tropical Africa. The other major urban concentration in sub-Saharan Africa is South Africa, where over five million people live in cities of over one hundred thousand inhabitants and over 30 percent of the population lives in towns of over fifty thousand people.[17]

The movement of the population from the rural to the urban areas is general in most parts of Africa. It is less, however, on the southern fringe of the Sahara and stretching to the southeastern part of the Central African Republic and into Sudan; and again along the Kalahari covering a part of Angola, Botswana, Zambia, the southern part of Tanzania, and the northern part of Mozambique. There are no large cities in these areas.

Intensive urbanization in Africa began with the mining and industrial development and moved forward at an accelerated speed. Johannesburg, which was founded in quite an unproductive area, had a population of over one hundred thousand in 1895.[18] The rapid growth of cities is continuing. In recent years Kinshasa, Zaire, has been growing at an annual rate of 11 percent. Sociologists, who write on urbanization in Africa, foresee that African cities will continue to grow rapidly. Modern industrialization fosters the growth of cities. Although mining has influenced the growth of cities, except for Johannesburg, it has not produced large cities.

A significant reason for the rapid growth of the cities has been the failure of rural development. The jobs in the cities and in the mines provide immediate cash, whereas the underdeveloped rural projects often bring only subsistence returns. In many areas the poor roads and the high cost of transport make farming unprofitable, and, although every country and every area faces unique situations, the low income from agriculture has to a large degree influenced people to move to the cities. Even though agricultural agencies have been active, rural development has not made significant progress and many young people hesitate to undertake agriculture.

Contrasts in the level of economic development greatly influence urbanization. In areas of low economic development, even if they are densely populated—such as in Rwanda, Malawi, Lesotho, and Upper Volta—the extend of urbanization has been slight. The centers of advanced economic development and of political influence are attracting the masses.

Problems Created by Urbanization

The rapid movement to the cities created various problems. Many men went to work in the mines or cities, leaving their families or fiancées in the villages. There were long periods of separation. Those who took their families with them often lived in inadequate quarters. Frequently the towns sprang up before the streets had been plotted. Running water and electricity were not available. Educational, medical, and religious services did not keep pace with the growing cities.

Unemployment is another problem of urbanization. In 1963 John Taylor, African secretary of the Church Missionary Society, realized the responsibilities the society confronted in the cities of Nigeria. Taylor asked R. S. O. Stevens to consult with the Nigerian Christian Council. In his report Stevens notes that immense tasks are being accomplished by a few people with big machines, while multitudes are unemployed. There are one hundred men waiting for every job.[19] Unemployment is an insurmountable problem in many African cities. People are attracted to the cities by the salary a fortunate relative or friend is receiving and hope to have the same opportunities. But only a few are so fortunate. The extended family helps the unemployed. Consequently, the employed person frequently has a number of relatives or friends staying at his home while they look for a job, which may take months or even years to find. This causes social and moral problems. Overcrowded quarters tend to cause tensions. The financial drain on the family economy may become excessive.

Unemployment may drive people to engage in unwholesome activities. Many cities have a high rate of thievery. People sometimes resort to thievery out of desperation and eventually make it a way of life. Some women and girls use prostitution as a means of income and readily find clients in cities where the male population exceeds the female population.

In the traditional life situation in Africa, the extended family and the clan act as a system of moral guidance and control. The principles of the clan are generally observed, the spirits of the ancestors are respected, and the clan taboos exert a controlling influence. The person who moves to the city has left these controls. He is away from the clan, and no one will report his acts. The moral restraints have been removed, and he feels free to indulge in whatever seems satisfying to him.

The marriage relationship is obliged to adjust to city life. In traditional village life there are values that stabilize it. The members of the family mutually share responsibilities. A couple is part of the clan; the clan participates in arranging for and in shaping the marriage.[20] The family forms a significant unit in the clan structure. Husband and wife have their roles in the family economy. In the city the husband becomes the sole breadwinner. The wife is unable to find ground to make a garden and has more leisure time than she had in the village. The city setting may be pleasing if she can associate with other members of the tribe or friends; however, it may be difficult if she is a stranger and is afraid of city life. Some women try to supplement the family income by being small market merchants. They spend the day selling wares at the market while the children are left to shift for themselves. Married life in the city requires significant adjustments. Divorce is on the increase. Crowded residential areas encourage adultery and prostitution.

In the village, the families and clan play a vital role in the life of every member. In the city a couple may be isolated from all members of the tribe and may be obliged to arrange for the customary ceremonies. If they are church members, they will contact their pastor for child dedication, baptism, or other religious observances relating to the family. If, however, they observe traditional customs, birth, death, and other events will be disturbing experiences if no other members of the tribe are there for support.

The Church's Concern for Urbanization

The extent of urbanization is not great in comparison with the size of the continent. Yet the problems in the cities are very real, and the cities have a strong influence on the people. The church must recognize and cope with this situation. Whenever the church has developed from within the urban community, it has tended to be successful. In some cities large numbers have been added to the congregations and new congregations have been started in rapid succession.

Some churches have been aware of both the needs and the potential of ministries in the cities. When the Kimberley, South Africa, mines were opened, most of the Catholic Fathers serving in the area went to Kimberley and concentrated their efforts in the city, which was growing rapidly. A number of Protestant missionary societies went to Johannesburg with the miners. The United Mission of the Copperbelt was organized to minister to the multitudes that flooded the area, not confining their ministry to only one city.

Churches, however, have failed to realize fully the tremendous needs of the multitudes who left their homes and went to the cities. Not infrequently, Christians have moved to the cities before the church did so. They arranged for places of worship on Sundays on their own initiative and asked their home congregation to send a pastor to serve the new Christian community. If one or more of the group were leaders, they requested to be recognized as a congregation. The testimony of these faithful Christians has greatly contributed to the establishment of the Christian faith in the cities, but generally it has been insufficient. When people come to the cities, they may look for the Christian fellowship and community relationships they had in the villages. During the initial period they are responsive and may readily be led into a vital relationship with a church. When tribal controls have been removed, individual decisions are made more readily than in the village social structure. Consequently, when people move to the city they may be won through the fellowship of the church. The churches have not recognized this factor sufficiently.

The churches were conscious of their responsibilities to some degree. The All-Africa Church Conference at Ibadan, Nigeria, in 1958 devoted its considerations to the subject "The Church in Changing Africa." The conference considered various aspects of the life of the church. In addressing itself to the problem of industrialization, the conference noted that the family solidarity of the village life was disrupted. The church needed to seek new forms of outreach and provide a teaching mission relevant for the situation, which includes the strengthening of family life. The conference was also aware of the needs of the landless people and advocated assistance in rural resettlement, hoping that it would provide a livelihood for many people in Kenya. This would prevent them from moving to the cities and becoming subject to an immoral way of life.[21]

The ministry of the church in the urban setting was further considered by the Urban Africa Consultation, which convened at Nairobi, Kenya, in 1961. The consultation recommended insights for an effective ministry to urban industrial people, the training of pastors, the training of the laity, and effective methods of conducting urban ministries.[22]

The Association of Evangelicals in Africa and Madagascar has expressed its concern for the ministries of churches in the cities. The Christian education commission is willing to help the churches in Africa strengthen their teaching ministries.

The churches realized that the ministry in the cities could not be an extension of the ministry of a station located in a rural area. Nor could the pastor with little academic or theological education, having spent his life in a rural community, adjust to and minister effectively to a city congregation. Training centers have been opened in the cities and the ministries in the cities have been intensified. However, the growth of the cities calls for increased efforts.

Some churches have recognized and grappled with the needs of the youth in the cities. Many churches have provided little Christian fellowship or opportunities of service, while others are conducting significant youth programs.

The churches are obliged to recognize and deal with tribal loyalties in the city. People seek out and associate with members of their tribe and prefer to worship in their own language. Churches have tried to bring in Christians from several tribes together into one congregation to avoid perpetuating tribalism. The services were translated into a second language to permit all people to understand. However, in some cities they have found their ministry more effective by offering services for tribal units. In northern Nigeria the Anglican Church provides services for the Yoruba people and also for the Ibos. They preserve denominational unity while providing congregations for every tribe. In Kinshasa, Zaire, the churches from a number of regions have established a work in the city, ministering in the tribal language chiefly to people coming from their rural area. Wherever one language is used by all people, separate services are less important.

Urbanization is rapidly increasing throughout the world. The church is called to minister to those who live in the high-rise apartment buildings. These complexes will become a more important mission field in the future and a greater challenge to the church. The church is called upon to recognize the needs of the city dwellers, provide a culturally relevant ministry, and lead the Christian community in testimony and service.

Study Questions

1. State the changes that influenced Christian missions.
2. Evaluate the effects of colonialism on Christian missions.
3. How has European civilization affected Christian missions?
4. Suggest strategies to cope with the problems caused by urbanization.

13

Methods of Promoting
the Expansion of Christianity

EVANGELISM

Missionary Efforts

The universal church is called to proclaim the gospel. It ministers so that men will acknowledge Jesus Christ as their Savior and Lord and join the fellowship of the church to glorify God through it. The believers so joined to Christ and His church become self-sufficient, reproducing churches. Motivated by the love of Christ and guided by the Holy Spirit, Christian missionaries dedicate their lives to obey the Lord's commission to proclaim the gospel to all people. Those who felt called to Africa knew very well that tropical diseases might bring death soon after their arrival. In His own time and according to His unfathomable wisdom, God called His messengers and empowered His divine gospel. He revealed Himself and brought millions of Africans into blessed fellowship with Himself and His Son Jesus Christ. Missions in Africa during the last two centuries can be understood only when God's immeasurable grace is acknowledged.

The first endeavors to proclaim the gospel were complicated by the tropical diseases of Africa. In the early period of missions, these diseases were still unknown and no medicines had been discovered to counteract them. In the equatorial regions of Central Africa, most Europeans could not tolerate the climate. The life expectancy in this area was very low. The first efforts of the Moravians in Ghana ended with the deaths of the members of several parties. Other attempts also ended in failure because of the heavy death toll. Even as late as the 1880s and the 1890s a large percent of the workers in the equatorial regions of Zaire and West Africa died within a few years of their arrival. But God was

429

calling the churches to the task, and new recruits came to replace those who gave their lives for the sake of the gospel. God revealed Himself, and congregations came into being in various parts of the continent.

Christian Witness

Some Africans who accepted the Christian faith dedicated themselves to proclaiming the gospel to their fellow-men. The testimony of the converts contributed greatly to the expansion of the Christian faith and to the growth of the church. Very often the faithful believers told their families and the people of their village about the joy and satisfaction they had found through the Christian faith. People were converted and groups of believers were formed. In much the same way as the church was born in Antioch, according to Acts 11:19ff., the church has been born through the testimony of the believers in many towns, villages, and hamlets of Africa.

The evangelization of Africa has mostly been through the testimony and ministry of African Christians. The missionaries brought the Christian message to an area and won the first converts to the Christian faith. However, generally little church growth took place until the converts took the Christian message to their people.

Evangelistic Methods

Church growth has been different in most places. It would be presumptuous to generalize, but several tendencies in church growth became apparent. Whenever the response was limited, or the workers expected few converts, individuals accepted the Christian faith and formed a group from the society. When this situation continued over a period of time, this Christian group tended to form a small elite society separated from the people. This tendency was especially strong wherever the Christian farms or compounds were maintained by the missionary societies. The formation of a small elite society generally impaired church growth. These Christians were soon regarded as a special group by the people rather than as a part of them. Consequently, the separation disrupted the effective communication of the gospel and the spontaneous witness to the people. Wherever this unfortunate situation continued, the Christians became a misunderstood minority group in the society and the people as a whole were not evangelized.

Another tendency has been for the first believers, overwhelmed by the joy they found in the Christian faith, to witness to their people and bring about a movement toward Christianity that resulted in the conversion of most of them. Whenever this movement has been guided effectively, the Christian faith has spread from community to community, and group after group of believers has been formed.

The people movements of Africa have been instigated especially by the testimony of lay Christians, who, by their testimony and daily Christian life, have influenced their neighbors and friends to accept the Christian faith. The faith was transmitted from one person to another and from one village to another. Frequently, entire villages accepted the Christian faith and requested Christian instruction. Although not all people have been receptive, and there have been some remarkably unresponsive tribes, yet the great expansion of Christianity is largely the result of people movements.

Unfortunately, all too often missionaries and African church leaders have not expected the Holy Spirit to convict entire peoples and move them to accept Christ as their Lord. They have failed to give leadership and guidance where the Holy Spirit worked in an exceptional way, and so they have stalled the people movements. Other missionaries compared African people movements to the mass conversions and baptism ordered by authorities in Europe in the Middle Ages. These leaders failed to recognize the decision-making patterns of the African culture. Through their lack of understanding, they stifled the ministry of the Word and the Holy Spirit, which they themselves had come to bring and for which they sincerely prayed. The people movement in Uganda during the 1890s is an example. When the movement began through the Bible study and prayer sessions in the Church Missionary Society, the White Fathers said Pilkington was a visionary missionary. Later, however, when they realized the effectiveness of the movement, they also promoted the Bible study sessions in their ministry. Fortunately, they acknowledged the situation and changed their attitude. In other cases, workers did not change their attitude and suppressed the people movements.

The vision of the missionaries for the evangelization of Africa has to a large degree determined the outcome of their ministry. Some were constrained to evangelize all the people in the area assigned to them. They established a ministry, lived with the people, visited village after village, spoke with people, listened to their concerns, and planted many churches. They entrusted them to the care of catechist-evangelists, while they continued to evangelize other villages. Frequently this brought about a people movement and the evangelization of an entire area or clan. On the other hand, some missionaries considered themselves pastors rather than missionaries. They served the people at the place of their residence and became pastors of small, elite groups of believers. Furthermore, this class of workers tended to separate themselves from the people and their need. This type of ministry has generally resulted in a small, one-by-one ingathering of believers.

In some countries, there have been large evangelistic campaigns. Prior to these campaigns, areas were exposed to much publicity, special literature was produced to aid in the campaigns, counselors were trained, and prayer cells were formed. Outstanding evangelists and much music attracted crowds to these meetings and many conversions were recorded. Just how much these campaigns have contributed to church growth depends on the follow-up, which may vary for different areas.

The churches have used the mass media to proclaim the Christian faith. In the earlier period, slide projectors and literature were used. Both were fascinating elements in their day and created interest that could be followed up. Missionaries reduced many African languages to writing, produced Christian literature, and distributed it widely. The translation of the Bible into a people's own language has always had an important effect. The people eagerly awaited the day of its appearance. For many tribes the printing of the Bible in their language was synonymous with Christianity having become indigenous. The biblical message was meaningful and captivating. The Old Testament reflected a culture familiar to them. The fascinating stories of the patriarchs and other personalities in the Bible held the interest of the people. The Bible stimulated their thinking and brought new ideas to them.

The radio became uniquely powerful during the 1950s. With the coming of transistor radios, the gospel was transmitted into the remote villages and hamlets. Ownership of a radio indicated social status. The people gathered near the radio to listen to it. The gospel programs reached many people in this way. The gospel has been transmitted from Christian stations in Liberia and Ethiopia and also from government-operated stations in other countries. More recently, television is becoming a powerful medium of communication in the larger cities.

Music is a part of everyday life in Africa. Christian songs, especially those composed by African song-writers in keeping with the rhythmic style and the pentatonic scale of most African music, have enriched the services and greatly enchanced the diffusion of the gospel. The gospel has been transmitted in song by Christians sitting around the evening campfires. The many choirs and musical groups, singing to the beat of drums, have greatly influenced the people.

Evangelists' Ministry

The credit for the evangelization of Africa south of the Sahara goes largely to the teacher-evangelists. They became the central figures in the extension of Christianity. They lived with their families as members of the village communities and found their sustenance by means of gifts of locally produced items and food, including produce from the fields, which usually were worked by the women.

These faithful servants of the Lord frequently had little formal training, but they were motivated by the love of Christ for the people and they presented Him. They led many people to the Lord whom they acknowledged, loved, and served. They have been the pioneers, going to villages where the gospel was not known. They have conducted services every day, especially on Sunday, and have offered elementary instruction to the children. In these elementary schools, the Christian message had a central place. Through the ministry of the teacher-evangelists, many groups of believers have been formed.

The groups of believers constituted the church in the towns and villages. They gathered to worship God, to nurture the believers, and to proclaim the gospel. They testified to the Christian faith in their daily relationships with the people. Some of these groups continued to grow and became self-sufficient, reproducing churches. The ability of the leader often played an important role in the growth of the church. Some groups, however, lost their "first love" and inspiration. Instead of evangelizing the people about them, they relied on outside sources for leadership and the maintenance of their spiritual life.

Pastoral Vocation

During the first years of the existence of many Christian groups, the sense of Christian vocation was quite apparent. They were constrained to witness to their fellow-men. The little Christian groups had a dynamic evangelistic outreach. In some churches this missionary spirit continued until the entire population was evangelized. Wherever the spirit of evangelism prevailed, Christians have volunteered for the ministry. There has been no shortage of Christian workers, and generally the concept of the priesthood of believers has received significant emphasis.

In some Christian groups, however, the concern for evangelism did not manifest itself. The Christians expected a greater consecration and a greater sacrifice on the part of the church workers, as compared with the laity. These groups witnessed little, if any, church growth. This attitude has often retarded the establishment of indigenous churches in an entire region. All too often the first Christians built chapels, proclaimed the gospel, and sent evangelists to other areas. The second generation of Christians, however, who were in a better position to promote the work of the church and to guide the churches toward autonomy, lacked the interest and vitality of the previous generation and failed to guide the church in a fruitful ministry.

In a large part of sub-Saharan Africa, rapid church growth took place after the gospel had been proclaimed for a number of years and the people had become acquainted with the Christian faith. But the churches failed to call a sufficient number of leaders to instruct all the new believers in the Christian faith. Furthermore, many of the catechists who were to instruct the believers had not received theological training and found the task beyond their capacity. Consequently, the task of strengthening and nurturing the new believers was not accomplished successfully. This has been quite crucial for many churches. Some of these Christians did not grow in the Christian faith or participate in the ministry of the church. Frequently the spontaneous expansion of the church stalled at this stage.

WESTERN EDUCATION

Missionary Purpose

Missions serving in Africa have devoted considerable efforts to the teaching ministry. Some societies were determined to maintain evangelism as their priority and not to dissipate their time and effort in education. However, they readily realized the necessity of preparing pastors, evangelists, teachers, and other personnel for the ministry of the church in order to establish congregations. All too frequently, however, the balance between a leadership-training program and general education has not been maintained. The desire for Western education promised to bring quick results in evangelizing and educating the young people of Africa. It seemed likely to produce a literate, Christian laity. Missionaries reflected on the biblical principle of training a child in the way he should go and the promise that later he will not depart from this training (Prov. 22:6). This text easily led to a strategy of what McGavran calls "redemption and lift," which involved much missionary personnel and the larger part of mission funds. Missionaries felt that a Western education would form a literate laity and would thus contribute to church growth and equip the people to participate in the activities of society.[1] The missionaries, however, did not recognize the indigenous systems. Instead, they transplanted on African soil schools that were suited to prepare students for Western society. Africans were thus alienated from the indigenous systems instead of being taught how to graft the essentials of Christianity into African forms of thought and into African culture.

African Desire

The desire on the part of Africans for Western education soon became evident wherever the missionaries won the confidence of the people. A strong, motivating factor in the eagerness for Western education was the desire to receive power to meet the daily situations of life. Africans came to regard the ability to read and write as a source of the Europeans' power. Therefore, they wanted to acquire this power that was a means for them to become like Europeans. A young man who was literate could find employment in a government office or with a trading company. He could soon wield considerable power in society and his salary would contrib-

ute to the financial resources of the clan. This circumstance promoted the desire for Western education. The clamor for education
was not prompted by the desire for a new culture as much as the
search for a tool to share the white man's power.[2] To the masses,
Western education was the key that could unlock countless opportunities in the new world that was being created.[3] They were
convinced that education, not religion, was the white man's source
of strength. Often they did not consider education in a church
school a guide to a better life, but rather as a means to attain the
power and prestige of the West.[4] Consequently, the motive of the
pupils and the purpose of the schools were quite different. This
caused disappointments.

The different purposes for education held by the churches and
the people frequently caused much confusion. The church leaders
were basically concerned with training personnel for the ministries
of the church, whereas the church members expected the church
schools to provide their children with the best tools for a good
livelihood. This tension between the lay Christians and the church
leadership caused Samuel Crowther some difficulties in his ministry in Nigeria.[5] In some instances church council members placed
the emphasis on secondary education and neglected the religious
education, both in the public schools and in the church schools.
This attitude evidently carried over to the pupils, and often their
participation in the religious instruction was half-hearted. Many
pupils were of the opinion that education and Christianity were
interchangeable terms. To acquire the European's knowledge
meant to have his religion. To have a Western education meant to
be a Christian. The Christian faith became a scientific knowledge.
Many young people studied the Christian faith on the same basis
as any other subject.

The desire for Western education was phenomenal. Whenever a
mission or church post was established, the village would soon
request teachers. There were regional variations, but the desire
was quite general. The teacher-evangelists entered and opened
new areas, which the mission and church later occupied. The
number of classes and pupils increased rapidly. An educational
effort among the Ibo people indicates that the schools increased
from 5 to 46 and the pupils from 392 to 4,066 between 1901 and
1912. At the Sakbayeme station of the Basel missionary society in
Cameroon, the number of pupils rose from 100 in 1904 to 2,500 in

1910 and to 6,600 in 1914. In Malawi the Reformed Church reported 110 classes in 1903 and 865 classes in 1910.[6] The reports from other countries are similar. In their desire for education, every village requested a catechist. Village chiefs and elders walked fifty miles and more to request a teacher for their villages. Western education became a necessity to them.

Educational Methods

The children came to the mission school and received secular and religious education at the same time. The missionary societies were not prepared for the clamor for Western education. They sent inadequately trained catechists to conduct classes and services. Many Christians were sincere in their interest to instruct the people, and it was an honor to be a messenger of the mission. The sincere catechists were a testimony to the Christian faith, but not all were able to transmit the message effectively. The people heard the gospel, and the pupils received religious instruction. Many believed and were baptized. Their understanding, however, was very limited, and they needed further instruction. The education offered was quite elementary. In the early years the pupils hardly became literate. Gradually, one-room schools in the rural areas offered a number of classes.

The regional schools were established early in the educational program. Most of the elementary education has been carried on at these schools. They were established in rural areas where the pupils could easily obtain food. The education was basically carried on in a rural setting before the large cities made their appearance.

In the early period of missions, the village and regional, or district schools functioned in close relation with the evangelistic ministry of the societies. The missionaries gave counsel to the teacher-evangelists when they visited the districts. As the educational program was more fully developed, a missionary was appointed to supervise the educational endeavor.

The need for more advanced training for a select number of students who had the ability to become teachers, pastors, or teacher-evangelists soon became evident. The training of professional workers was emphasized and special schools, serving large areas, were established.[7] The latter served as educational centers during the developing years of the country. Eventually they became universities or seminaries for pastoral training, or they offered both general and theological training. Some of these institutions offered training adapted to the common life and according to the academic level of the people. They have continued to offer training relevant to the actual situation. Others, however, have followed an European curriculum and have failed to give due consideration to the students' geographical and cultural milieu. Mention can be made of only several of the institutions that have made a vital contribution. It was noted in Chapter 4 that the Fourah Bay College in Sierra Leone has sent workers to various parts of West Africa. That school was affiliated with the University of Durham in 1876 and offered university degrees in arts and theology. The Lovedale Institute in South Africa became a model training center for South and East Africa. Representatives of the Lovedale Institute helped to establish institutions of learning at the Livingstonia Mission in Malawi and at the East Africa Scottish Industrial Mission in Kenya. The Kafue Training Institute in Zambia, established by the Methodist mission and several other ecclesiastical groups has had an important influence in the training of youth in Central Africa.[8]

The students for the vocational training schools were carefully chosen by the church councils. In the earlier period they generally had had some teaching experience and were more advanced in age than the average student. The new training schools were frequently quite small with only a few teachers, but they laid the foundation for education in Africa. They resulted in the introduction of new teaching methods that improved the educational system. The teachers generally prepared the texts in the vernacular and they often adapted the texts that were written in another language.

The fundamental assumption that the parents, the church, and the society are responsible for the child's education underlies the Roman Catholic policy of education.[9] The Roman Catholic Church has been successful in receiving full government financial support for its educational programs. Thus it has been able to expand its educational ministry greatly and operate high schools. Belgium, France, and Portugal did not grant the same privileges to Protestant missions. The children who have enrolled in Roman Catholic schools have been added to their communities and have been taught to consider themselves Catholics. The church's emphasis on its saving ministry and of the saving efficacy of the sacraments has greatly influenced them to remain loyal to the church.

The Roman Catholic bishops gave direction to the educational programs and sent a large European and American staff to Africa for its educational endeavors. To a certain degree they have modeled the programs according to what they were familiar with in the countries from which they came. Because of the large foreign staff, Africanization of the education offered became significant only when African bishops and teachers assumed the responsibilities toward the end of the colonial period.

Educational Contributions

The mission schools made a most significant contribution in the Westernization of sub-Saharan Africa. They constituted the modern educational system until quite recently. When the British administrators arrived in Nigeria, they found that missions had already developed a system of education.[10] In 1823 there were six thousand recognized mission schools compared to one hundred government schools in Africa under British rule.[11] In Zaire the proportion was very much the same, but more of the schools were operated by the Roman Catholics. The French were mostly interested in training clerks, secretaries, and other personnel for administration. They did not emphasize general education for the population at large. Beginning in 1923, the British government subsidized the education offered by the mission schools. In principle this policy was adopted by several European countries. However, France and Belgium chiefly subsidized Roman Catholic schools until 1948, and after 1948 the subsidy given to Roman Catholic schools was much greater than that given to Protestant schools. Consequently, even though the Roman Catholics entered the work in Africa at a late date, at the All-Africa Ministers of Education Conference at Addis Ababa in 1961 it was estimated that 68 percent of the children in school were in church-related schools, of which 35 percent were in Roman Catholic schools.[12] The governments counted on men trained at mission schools to serve in the clerical and administrative responsibilities of the administration.

Those who received their education in mission schools served in the administration of the countries and with commerical enterprises throughout Africa. Although some secondary schools were established and several institutions offered university training, the mission schools offered basically elementary education, with the emphasis on religious education in order to create a literate laity in the churches. Mostly mission-trained teachers offered the instruction. Secondary (high school) education was late in coming because personnel was scarce and government grants to construct the facilities and to operate the schools were not easily obtained. Consequently, even today secondary schools cannot accept all who want this training.

The church schools have had a good reputation. Having high academic standards, they continue to attract many students. Pupils are given individual counsel, and parents are notified if a student has serious problems. Discipline is for the purpose of forming the character of the pupils. Some city dwellers drive their children to church schools from as far away as 150 miles.

Most church agencies serving in Africa have considered education a means of evangelization. Through the systematic teaching of the Scriptures, the pupils could gain significant knowledge of the biblical message. The success, however, was not as remarkable as they had anticipated. Many pupils considered the religious instruction merely another subject. Their comprehension of the Christian faith was similar to their understanding of a scientific study. Many failed to come to a personal relationship with Christ. They participated in the religious instruction classes and were baptized and became church members. They increased the church register, but the grace for service in the church was not manifested.

The large educational programs of the churches involved much personnel and funds. Although the educational program contributed significantly to the development of the country and provided leadership for the activities of the churches, it must be evaluated in light of the limitations it placed on direct evangelism and also on pastoral training.

PASTORAL TRAINING

Pastoral Call

Many Protestant churches in Africa called pastors from among the church members who indicated gifts for this service and a sincere devotion to the Lord. From the very beginning of the formation of the church, believers were encouraged to bring the message of salvation through faith in Jesus Christ to their fellow-men. Native workers were asked to proclaim the gospel even though they had only a limited formal education. The growth of the church has been effected through both spontaneous and structured efforts.

Pastors, evangelists, deacons, and catechists were chosen from among the faithful Christians. They had received such formal education and training as the mission offered. The early workers came from within the life of the church. This pattern of choosing the leaders from among the church members has often been maintained. The pastors have not been kept from full participation in the ministry of the Word and the sacraments because of their limited education. However, in some churches the ordination of pastors is the responsibility of a commission on the ministry. In other churches it is the responsibility of the bishop.

Although the policy of choosing church leaders from among the members has generally been maintained, there has been a tendency that has not been entirely in harmony with this policy. Pastoral candidates were expected to manifest intellectual, social, and spiritual qualifications as judged by Western standards in order to qualify to serve as pastors. Consequently, only a relatively few men have been ordained. In recent years the churches have generally tended to require theological training for ordination. This new policy has further limited the call of pastors. Because of this tendency, men who have secondary or university training tend to withdraw from Christian service. Churches looked for persons who had the spiritual and natural leadership gifts. They realized that they needed men with various levels of pastoral training to communicate the gospel effectively in the cultural setting and according to the people's comprehension. Sincere dedication and leadership gifts were important qualifications for rural congregations. The leaders who relate to the cultural setting and who consider that the congregations belong to them have generally given valuable service. The people had confidence in their message, and many accepted the Christian faith.

The Roman Catholic missions, however, have made clerical training the basis for the ministry. The person who expresses the desire to become a priest and has a good rapport is accepted in a seminary and trained for the priesthood. Those qualifying after training are ordained.

Inadequate Pastoral Training

In the early years the church leaders were the men with the best training in the society. However, the pastoral training did not keep pace with general education. The pastors were not able to speak the foreign language employed by the colonial power effectively or to communicate with the students regarding modern scientific knowledge. The people began to look up to the teachers and officials rather than to the pastors for leadership. The progress of the churches has been greatly affected by this situation. In order to receive government subsidies for their educational programs, the churches emphasized the training of teachers and neglected the training of pastors.

The respect for the pastoral vocation also decreased because of the low remuneration pastors received in comparison to teachers, secretaries, accountants, and other office personnel. People tend to respect a person according to the salary he receives, the clothes he wears, and the car he drives. The people wanted their children to study in programs that would lead them to a good remuneration rather than prepare them for the pastoral ministry.

The growth and development of many congregations and Christian groups have been retarded because of a lack of qualified leaders. In some villages the Christians had no leader, while in other villages a catechist gave leadership. A number of catechists were assisted by an evangelist. However, in many cases the ordained pastor visited the village several times a year to administer the sacraments.

The training of church leaders has been somewhat limited because many older men who are serving the church in one capacity or another have been unable or unwilling to leave their places of service and their homes to go to a distant place for several years of training. Their property and family responsibilities made their departure difficult. Consequently, some men who served congregations for many years received no training to equip them to serve better.

The cost of training men in the conventional residence program has limited the number of people who could be trained for the pastoral ministry. The method of training is becoming increasingly more expensive and more difficult for the churches to support. Therefore, whereas the number of congregations is increasing, the number of students the congregations are able to send and support is decreasing, especially the older men with large families. Thus the shortage of qualified leaders is increasing.

Since few older men are volunteering for the pastoral ministry, younger men with less experience are sent to the theological schools for training. However, after some of the younger men complete their training, some congregations are not willing to accept them for leadership positions. Some men who have received pastoral training in a residence program in a city during the last decades are having difficulties in adjusting to the rural, less-developed areas and to the meager remuneration offered by the congregations. Some men seek employment in addition to the pastoral ministry in order to supplement their income. This limits the time they are able to devote to the pastoral ministry.

The progress of many churches has been impaired by the importance that has been placed on the intellectual accomplishments rather than on the leadership abilities of students. Therefore, the younger men who were fluent in the language used in the classroom replaced the older men who had not had the opportunity to study that language but who were leaders among their people. The churches would have benefited by training both the older and the younger men on their level of education. They would have greatly benefited by offering training to the men who were in the service of the church, either by offering refresher courses, by providing opportunities to take courses during their holidays (vacations), or by offering theological education by extension.

As a result of their contribution in education, missionary societies were in positions of influence that were advantageous to further their cause. Representatives of church agencies served as members of education commissions in the countries in which they worked. In this way they had occasion to guide the development of education in the country. This involvement was an incentive to continue the educational ministry of the society. As a result of the large involvement in education, pastoral training was generally neglected.

Some churches emphasized the training of church leaders and also of teachers for the educational ministry. However, they were the exception rather than the rule. The training of teachers was necessary if the churches were to receive government subsidies for church schools. Consequently, many churches gave priority to teacher training. Relatively few men were trained for the Christian ministry, especially on the university level of theological training. In 1965 the Protestant churches had very few men with degrees in theology.[13]

Nature of Pastoral Training

The churches have varied considerably in their emphasis on leadership training. Some have emphasized choosing leaders from the members of the congregations and offered pastoral training in the cultural setting with a culturally relevant program. These leaders remained in their cultural setting and in communication with their people while they received training for service. Consequently, their training helped them to communicate the gospel effectively. These pastoral training schools were conducted in the language of the people. As early as 1893 the missionary societies were concerned to produce teacher-evangelists who would communicate the gospel effectively to their people.[14] Quite frequently, however, instead of developing programs of church-leadership training adapted to their particular culture, programs of leadership training that were not relevant for the local situation were introduced from Europe or America. They were inclined to develop a professional program. Frequently courses were taught or not taught simply on the basis of the availability of a text and resource materials. Both the cultural patterns of education and the contents of the program received insufficient consideration. This need is now being rectified in some places through the participation of African professors in the instruction and in the preparation of culturally relevant teaching resources.

The purpose of the Bible school and theological training has generally been to train church workers. The training was for a specific need. The churches chose the students for pastoral training. They came to the residence school with their families, and most of them were supported by the sending church.

Some of the churches realized the necessity of training leaders on several academic levels. In order to serve the more educated people of the cities and centers of learning, they offered advanced theological training. They offered Bible-institute training to pastors of the larger congregations and a more elementary Bible-school training or brief courses to leaders of less-developed areas. Whereas the men of the first two categories were generally ordained and salaried, those of the latter group were often laymen who received some remuneration but basically provided for their livelihood through another occupation.

Missionary educators who have played a leading part in the development of education were not ignorant of the cultural implications of their educational programs.[15] They continually reevaluated the education they were offering in order to develop more culturally relevant programs of education. Out of the search for theological education that would be instrumental in furthering church growth and planting new churches, Theological Education by Extension (TEE) was envisioned and implemented by Ralph Winter in Guatemala. The valuable ministry of this new method of education soon became known. Theological-education-by-extension workshops were conducted at strategic centers in Africa, and the program was adopted by various churches in Africa. Fred Holland of the Brethren in Christ in Zambia has given leadership to theological education by extension in English-speaking countries of Africa, especially in Southeast Africa.

Interested people may participate in theological education by extension in their own locality and do the self-study on their level of education by means of material prepared for this purpose.[16] This program permits the church workers or interested laymen to improve their knowledge of biblical truth and methods of ministry and to apply the newly found truths in their service while they continue their ministry. Through the practical application of the studies, the functional view of the ministry is supported.

Many churches are adopting theological education by extension as their basic method of leadership training because it enables more people to participate in this education. Consequently, it augments the number of church workers. Furthermore, it eliminates the problem of cultural dislocation, which often occurs when students go to a residence program in a city for a number of years.

The materials used in extension studies have been adapted for the culture in which they are used and to meet the needs of the communities in which the men serve. The discussions are related to the activities within the local congregations. The course work provides motivation for the practical work, and the practical work provides motivation for the course work. Consequently, this method of training is proving to be very relevant.

The Roman Catholic Church was late in establishing missionary work in Africa and also in training a priesthood. When it established work in sub-Saharan Africa, of which the work of the White Fathers in Central Africa was notable, it sent a large European staff. Since the 1930s, however, it devoted more effort to the training of priests. By 1966 it had trained some 2,500 priests and was preparing about 150 a year.[17] This is a significant figure, but quite insufficient to serve the needs of the Catholic communities.

The Catholic training program is patterned after the European model. The two central defects in the existing seminary system are remoteness from general life and ineffectiveness.[18] For six or seven years the students are segregated in the seminary, frequently in a remote rural area, and they lose contact with the people and with the rapidly developing African society. The program of studies includes much scholastic theology and philosophy. These studies have been criticized as largely irrelevent to the ministry the men will be engaged in;[19] hence a reshaping of the course seems necessary.

The Roman Catholic ministry was based on a priesthood remunerated by the central organization of the church. Indigenous principles were not emphasized. During the last decades, however, the church has also moved toward indigeniety.

MEDICAL SERVICES

When missionaries came to Africa, they found the mortality rate appalling. Lack of knowledge concerning many diseases and the absence of medicines against them permitted these diseases to spread and cause a heavy death toll among Africans and foreigners. In the most unhealthy regions, four out of five children died before they were two years old. Malaria, dysentery, and sleeping sickness were some of the major causes of death. Missionaries felt compassion for the people and did what they could to alleviate their suffering.

At this point, however, it is important to note that there were African medicine men who had a surprising knowledge of herbs and locally prepared cures that were effective in treating many ailments. Early missionaries did not understand the contributions of these men and thus failed to give due credit to them, often labeling their treatments witchcraft. Though at the time missionaries may have been unaware of it, a certain competition between these men and Western medical workers arose. This caused problems to many Africans who felt pulled between the two. Since missions did not recognize the value of native medicines, African Christians often sought help from the medicine men secretly, lest they be accused of reverting to witchcraft. In retrospect, medical missions might have contributed more to Africa if they had respected the knowledge of the medicine man. They could have recognized their practice in areas where they could serve and supplemented it with Western medical knowledge. This would have alleviated tensions and helped to plant a sound medical practice in the culture of the people.

There were no hospitals in the early years of missionary activities, and many missionaries had only a box of medicine and a rudimentary knowledge of medical science. Nevertheless, the missionaries' services have often helped the sick and prevented death. Christianity is interested in the here-and-now and in the physical and spiritual well-being of the people. Its expression of concern and love for them and its willingness to help wherever possible made a profound impression on them. In the early days the Africans questioned the missionaries' purpose for coming. The medical services helped to establish relations and confidence in addition to helping them.

The causes of many of the diseases were not known. At that time the people thought malaria was caused by a certain vapor that came from humid soil. Consequently, Europeans frequently built their houses on elevated places and about eighteen inches above the ground. It was discovered only at the beginning of the twentieth century that the mosquito transmits the malaria parasite from one person to another. Consequently, the disease swept through the villages, causing many people to die at a young age.

It was necessary to minister to the healing of the soul together with the healing of the body, for much illness is the result of tension in the clan and fear of witchcraft. The people needed mental and spiritual rehabilitation in order to recover physically.

Motivation for Medical Ministry

The Church of Jesus Christ has considered healing the sick and helping the needy as an integral part of its redemptive ministry. Jesus Christ stated that He had come "to proclaim freedom for the prisoners and recovery of sight for the blind" (Luke 4:18 NIV). He went about healing the diseases of the people and sent the disci-

ples with power to cure diseases (Luke 9:1). When the early
church began its ministry, healing was an integral part of that
ministry (Acts 3). Moved by compassion, the church has responded to the need and promoted medical missions, including
clinics, dispensaries, hospitals, and medical schools.

The churches responded to the medical needs the missionaries
confronted in Africa. Medical workers soon were a part of the
personnel of many missionary societies. John Theodore van der
Kemp, a member of the first party of the London Missionary
Society to go to South Africa in 1799, had studied medicine at
Edinburgh. Forty-two years later, David Livingstone followed him
under the auspices of the same society. They followed in the
tradition of the church's ministry and of outstanding medical
pioneers like John Scudder, missionary to India, and Peter
Parker, missionary to China.

Magnitude of the Medical Services

Many missionaries served with their box of medicine, as David
Livingstone had done. They realized, however, that a more concentrated effort was needed in order to make an impact on the
medical needs. David Livingstone stirred the European population
with his reports on the needs of the African peoples. Bishop
Lambuth of the Methodist Church appealed to the churches for
medical missionaries, stating that they were more imperatively
needed in Zaire than on any other field.[20] Similar appeals came
from other parts of Africa, especially from the tropical regions.

Most of the Protestant missionary societies tried to place at least
one person with some medical knowledge at every station. The
pioneers offered their services under very inadequate conditions.
There were no dispensaries or hospitals to use as medical centers.
They treated contagious, tropical ulcers in a room in their house
that was set apart to serve as a doctor's office. Sometimes the
doctor had to make the necessary improvisations. Dr. Jaggard of the
Disciples of Christ of Zaire was obliged to perform operations on
his dining room table and to sterilize his instruments on the
kitchen stove.[21] Even more recently, Dr. Albert Schweitzer was
confronted with an operation before his supplies had been un-
packed or a building had been constructed for medical service.

Many stations put forth much effort to offer medical services at
a dispensary and, if possible, at a hospital. The first hospitals

constructed with permanent materials were thought of very highly. The societies realized that satisfactory services could not be offered without adequate facilities. Consequently, they constructed buildings and supplied them with modern equipment. The societies' devotion to serve is illustrated by the United Brethren in Christ of Sierra Leone. Whereas the people had murdered the workers at Rotfunk during the 1898 war, the society built the Hartfield-Archer Medical Dispensary there in 1907 and enlarged its services.[22] In Zaire, Dr. Paul Carlson was killed during the 1965 rebellion. In his memory the Paul Carlson Medical Center was established; it offers a wide range of medical services. The extent to which medical services were offered may be noted in Zaire where the Protestant societies operated 171 hospitals and dispensaries, served by 56 doctors, 166 foreign nurses, and an African staff of 1,097 persons.[23] The missionary societies pioneered in medical services. It was some time before the governments made significant contributions in this area of service.

In addition to bringing relief for the general diseases, the churches have contributed greatly to the care and healing of the lepers. Leprosy is very prevalent in parts of the equatorial forest belt of Africa. From West Africa through to East Africa, the societies established leprosy colonies with hospitals where systematic treatment was given. The American Leprosy Missions, Inc., has greatly helped the societies in this ministry. Among the many services that have been offered is the leprosarium of the Assemblies of God at Hope Town, Liberia. The colony has 350 acres of land on which the leprosy patients are settled.[24] In the Central province of Liberia the Baptists offer treatment to those who have leprosy. The Worldwide Evangelization Crusade treats the leprosy patients in Ghana.[25] The Lutheran Brethren operate a leprosarium at Lere, Cameroon. In 1970 some 195 outpatients from the surrounding area came for treatment, while 95 patients resided at the colony. Similarly, in one country after another, those with leprosy are treated in order to alleviate their deplorable condition and, if possible, to reintegrate them into society. The extent of the ministry may be observed in that there were 35 leperosy colonies with 6,600 patients in Zaire in 1950[26] The present trend is to treat lepers at treatment and rehabilitation centers but let them stay with their families rather than isolate them at leperosy colonies.

In addition to ministering to the physical suffering of the people, the medical services have contributed to the breaking down of the power of fear and the belief in witchcraft. To Africans, events do not just happen. In regard to illness, there must be a person or force that disturbs the person. The people interpreted every event in the framework of their magic or religious background, and the event may cause agonizing and disturbing fear.[27] As long as the people lacked scientific knowledge, they considered any act of healing an act of magic. For some time European medical science did not commend itself to large sections of the population because the people were suspicious of European medical skill. The Africans continued to have more faith in indigenous medical facilities.[28] But as compassionate help and scientific knowledge were brought to the people, the understanding and the world view of many changed. They began to share the knowledge and to apply it in accurate diagnosis and effective treatment. They realized that the old magic was more limited than they had assumed. Through the understanding of the causes of the diseases and difficulties, the activities of the demonic forces became less important. Then, as the Christians realized that they could entrust themselves to Christ, their fear of the demonic forces diminished considerably. The activities of the medical workers in service to the people is helping to drive out fear and build faith in its place.

In recent years medical authorities are recognizing the validity of many African cures through the use of native herbs. Serious study of specific remedies is being made. Late as this recognition is, it is valuable for the future development of more natural cures.

Perpetuating the Medical Services

The medical services have not only treated the patients but have also trained nationals to serve their people. In the earlier years of medical services, the doctors rarely had qualified medical assistants. They encouraged nationals to help care for the patients and thus relieve the doctors of some of the time-consuming routine work. Accordingly, almost every hospital became a training center. Classes were offered to nurses' aides. They were taught how to give medicine and to help a doctor. These instruction classes led to elementary training courses for nurses. This instruction was continuously enlarged until medical faculties to train more advanced medical personnel were established. The ministry that was begun on a very limited scale and under inadequate conditions is developing into one in which national doctors are able to serve their people.

The societies did not only care for the sick at the stations but also established rural dispensaries served by mission-trained nurses. In many countries the churches are still offering large medical services, even if the governments are assuming more responsibilities. The task is too large for the churches, and it is quite natural for the governments to assume this responsibility.

Moved by compassion, missionaries did what seemed quite natural to them. They could not turn a deaf ear to the cries that surrounded them. To do so would have been a denial of the faith they proclaimed and of the purpose for which they came to Africa. They believed in witnessing to their faith by administering medicine and showing Christian concern. The medical services have frequently broken down barriers of communication. They have caused people to consider a dimension of the Christian faith that they had not observed in other religions, even though conflicts with African medicine men existed. Many Christians have rendered this service as to the Lord, their Master. They have served tirelessly in situations where the staff was much too small in comparison to the needs. Even today there is an enormous amount of unrelieved suffering in many countries. The churches in cooperation with other agencies address themselves to this need.

Study Questions

1. Prepare a strategy for effective evangelism for your church.
2. Christian missions engaged in education in order to prepare a literate laity and to train church workers. The governments are now assuming responsibility for education. What strategy should the churches pursue in presenting Christian education to the people?
3. Outline a strategy for pastoral training.
4. Christian missions engaged in medical services because the people needed medical care. The governments are now assuming the responsibility for medical services. How should the Christian communities assist the people in need?

14

Outgrowth of the
Christian Movement

THE AFRICAN INDEPENDENT CHURCH MOVEMENT

The African Independent churches constitute a significant portion of Christianity in Africa and a unique spirit in African Christianity. The development of the Independent churches has attained a dimension unprecedented in the history of the Christian church. These independent church movements have been founded by separation from parent churches, missions, or independent churches—in a few cases, under the initiative of a dynamic leader. The ministry of William Wade Harris in Ghana and the Ivory Coast, the Kimbanguist Church in Zaire, and Independent churches in South Africa and some other countries have been referred to. Such ministries may be found in many countries of Africa, especially south of the Sahara; these ministries have a large influence on the population.

Beginning of the Movement

The beginning of separation took place in 1872 by members of the Paris Evangelical Church in Lesotho (formerly Basutoland). They eventually returned to the church. Six years later, a pastor of the Wesleyan mission began a separate Tembu church, which was again affiliated with the original church.

One of the first Independent churches was founded in Pretoria in 1892, when a pastor of the Methodist Church formed the Ethiopian Church. He hoped to establish an inclusive, native church to which most Africans would adhere. However, his church remained quite small, but the movement that was started has brought some five thousand distinct ecclesiastical and religious bodies into existence. After a beginning had been made, many secessions occurred; by 1966 the separatists numbered one-quarter of all the Bantu Christians in South Africa. Joseph Booth, an Australian, brought the Watch Tower movement to Zambia in 1908, beginning the separatist movement in that region. Men who went to work in other areas came in contact with these movements and took ideas with them to their homes. In this way the Watch Tower movement, the African National Church, the Last Church of God and His Christ, and other independent groups were started in Tanzania.

The Luo people of western Kenya live around the shore of Lake Victoria Nyanza and have a population of one and one-quarter million. From 1902, Christian missions, Roman Catholics, Anglicans, Seventh-Day Adventists, and Africa Inland Mission have worked among them. By 1967 both Protestants and Catholics had won more than 20 percent of the total population. African catechists and pastors played an important role in the expansion of Christianity. The missions maintained good relations with the Luo society, but opposed polygamy and the ancestral cult with its magic and divination. In 1914 Johana Owalo formed the Momiya Luo Mission. In 1916 Alfayo Odongo formed the Roho movement, which stayed in the church until 1934. After his death his followers formed the Dini ya Roho (Religion of the Holy Ghost). It soon spread to Tanzania.

In 1957 the JoHera (People of Love) separated from the Anglican Church and were registered in 1958 as the Church of Christ in Africa. In 1967 the Holy Trinity Church in Africa separated from the Church of Christ in Africa. In 1966, thirty-one distinct Luo separatist churches had registered with the Kenya government. The separatist movement had begun and continued to proliferate.

While independent churches were being formed in South and East Africa, the Native Baptist Church seceded from the American Southern Baptist mission in Lagos, Nigeria, in 1888. The Aladura (praying church) began in 1918 during the influenza epidemic and has given rise to many separate groups.

Simon Kimbangu of Zaire proclaimed the gospel, beginning a people movement in 1921. He did not separate from the Baptist church, but the government drove the movement underground. It then became one of Africa's largest Independent church movements.

Thus independent churches and groups came into existence. It is difficult to estimate the number of the adherents to these reli-

gious bodies. *The World Christian Handbook* of 1968 gave their
number as 6,849,959. They grew rapidly during the next seven
years and by 1975 may have had approximately ten million adherents. The 1968 statistics for South Africa indicate 3,200,000 adherents; for Kenya, 500,000; for Nigeria, 225,000; and for Ghana,
175,000. Their proliferation across Africa has been increasing.
Many movements of renewal or protest are constantly appearing.[1]

The secessions, varying in size from a single congregation to half
a million adherents, have arisen out of remarkably similar patterns
of background circumstances in each ethnic group concerned. Yet
usually there have not been conscious links or visible coherence.[2]

Nature of the Independent Movement

There is no impenetrable screen between mission churches and
African Independent churches. The same holds true of the three
types of Independent churches because there is a constant exchange of ideas and evaluations between representatives of all
those different groups, whereby one group contributes to the understanding of the other.[3] Most of the movements have emerged
spontaneously in areas where Christian missionary activity has
been effective and some of the stronger groups have come from a
renewal movement. The independent religious movement reveals
a dynamic working of the Spirit that transcends the doctrinal and
organizational partitions of denominations. In many cases, it
brings the people to acknowledge Christ and to follow Him in
faithful discipleship. However, the Christian movements are surrounded by a syncretistic fringe consisting of movements with
non-Christian religious systems at their center.

Barrett divides the religious movements as follows: renewal
movements claiming to be basically Christian and remaining
within the mission churches; those that separate from the mission
churches and become independent churches; and heterodox
movements that are sycretistic and basically non-Christian.[4]

The African Independent churches may be classified into three
general categories: Ethiopian, Zionist, and Bantu Messianic
movements.

Ethiopian Churches. During the early period following the translation of the King James Version of the Bible, from 1611 to 1871,
the term *Ethiopian* was widely used to designate the people of

sub-Saharan Africa. The people cherished all references in the Bible that presented the Africans in a dignified light. The Ethiopian churches applied this mystical character to themselves.[5] A similar movement of "Ethiopian" sentiment was manifested in America among the American Negroes during which the Negro churches were called Abyssinian churches.[6]

In West Africa, Ethiopianism became fundamentally racial. The basic underlying thought was the conversion of Africa and the establishment of a Christian theocracy that would embrace all of Africa. Ethiopianism incited Negro racialism and gave the educated Africans a hope they thought would be fulfilled someday.[7]

Among the Ethiopian churches, there are those that have separated from mission churches. This has been chiefly on racial grounds or because a person's desire for leadership prompted him to withdraw and form an independent church. Other churches in turn separated from the already independent churches. The Ethiopian churches have largely retained the church organization and the Bible interpretation that they adhered to in the Protestant churches from which they seceded. The following characteristics have been ascribed to the independent Christian churches: they accept the historical Jesus as Lord and give Him a central position in their faith, even though this may be expressed in new African forms; they manifest a resurgence of the traditional African world view and customs; and they strongly affirm the right to be fully African and fully Christian, yet independent.[8] In their worship services, the Ethiopian churches portray the African character.

Zionist Movement. The Zionist movement had its origin in the United States of America in 1912 when John A. Dowel founded the Catholic Apostolic Church of Zion. Officially they recognize Jesus of Nazareth as being somehow the Messiah of the Bantu. However, the fact that Jesus is the Messiah is not enough for the Bantu, as far as Shembe's group, and the followers of George Khambule, Lekganyane, or John Masowe are concerned. In these groups the prophet himself becomes the Messiah and Moses, leading his people into the promised land.[9] They believe in faith healing, practice triple baptism by immersion, and are awaiting the parousia in the near future. They insist on the work of the Holy Spirit in the revelations and healings. The prophet is the head and bishop of the church. His calling comes from above. But the

succession of the leadership follows the dynastic pattern, passing
from the father to the son. These groups are also designated as
Spirit churches because they maintain that the Spirit moves
the prophet. In West Africa they are also known as praying
churches.[10]

   The Zionist churches are, however, syncretistic and retain such
traditional practices as reverence of ancestral spirits, purification
rites, and polygamy. Although they are syncretistic, they combat
certain elements of animism, such as demons and magic. The
nativistic section of the Zionist movement tends to draw the people
back to their former religious practices.[11]

   Messianic Groups. The Messianic groups are formed through
adherence to a dominant person or prophet. The distinction between the Zionist and Messianic groups is somewhat vague. However, the Messianic group attribute special power to the prophet
—a power that to a certain extent elevates him to the position of
Christ. He guards the door to heaven and becomes the mediator
and savior and virtually replaces Christ. Consequently, the movement falls short of guiding people to faith in Christ and therefore
of being a Christian movement.[12]

   Some groups seem to be a combination of the Zionist and Messianic tendencies. Furthermore, each category exerts a certain
influence on the others. The Ethiopian churches tend to exercise a
stabilizing influence on the others as it brings a more thorough
teaching of the gospel to bear on the faith and practice of the
adherents. The results of its influence are multiplied by the tendency of every new movement to establish its doctrine.

   Heterodox Groups. Among the separatist movements are a
number of groups that do not claim to be Christian. They are
syncretistic and combine elements of traditional religion with
Christian teachings to the extent that the revelation in Jesus Christ
is fully obliterated. They are heterodox movements that are
specifically non-Christian and cannot be called Christian; several
thousand of them have erupted during the twentieth century.[13]

Causes of the Independent Movement

   There are various causes that may instigate an independent
movement. Barrett notes that a number of factors produce the

tribal "Zeitgeist" (spirit of the times), with its tendencies toward independence. As these factors exert their influence, the level of separation is reached.[14] One of these factors is the failure of one party to be sympathetic to another party's point of view. Missionaries have sometimes not fully understood or appreciated the African's point of view, which is deeply rooted in his culture. Some also have not recognized that area of the African culture that is compatible with the Christian message. Thus differences in cultural orientation may cause tensions that lead to the formation of an independent church. Another significant factor is the desire of a strong personality to be independent and direct his own group according to his own interests. The feeling of being restricted in one's activities by a church council has enhanced this tendency and caused separation.

Some Independent churches have been formed because of church discipline in the established church. When some people are disciplined, they gather others in similar circumstances to form an independent group.

Barrett notes a correlation between the length of the period the people have had the Scriptures in their language and the inclination toward independence. The liberation the Scriptures bring to the individual and the opportunity they present to him to be in direct communion with Christ seem to have been interpreted to offer independence to them. Many new groups have been started because their members failed to find the Christian love they sought in the older church.[15] The failure to understand the people's deep concern with sympathetic, Christian love has motivated some people simply to forsake the fellowship of believers, while others have looked for the loving fellowship in another group. The church will want to give careful consideration to this matter.

The spirit of renewal is manifested in the more sincere separatist groups. It is unique to note that this concern has caused the formation of new groups throughout the history of the church. This spirit has expressed itself through dynamic evangelism and sacrificial service.

Life and Worship in the Independent Movement

The reasons for secession of the separatist groups do not include a concern for changes in liturgy. The larger Independent churches basically retain the liturgic patterns of the church from which they

seceded. However, they give expression to their faith and emotions in culturally relevant forms. Naturally, songs composed by
Africans and set to African tunes are used more extensively.
Frequently African music enriches the worship service. In the
large Kimbanguist Church in Kinshasa, Zaire, the participation of
a large orchestra adds significantly to the worship service. In some
of the smaller groups the services become quite emotional, involving expressions of ecstacy. Because of the antiritualistic tendencies of some smaller groups, some of the larger independent
churches emphasize ritual more strongly.

The separatist groups reveal a sense of togetherness among
themselves. The members express the desire for a sense of belonging. The individualism of Western civilization did not satisfy their
needs. Even in the East Africa Revival Movement and in the
Christ-for-All evangelistic emphasis, the prayer cells and the small
group fellowships are meeting a need. The desire for belonging is
an element in the formation of the group, and it is expressed in the
spirit of the group both in worship and in daily fellowship.

In the Ethiopian-type churches the sermon still plays an important role. The Scriptures are held in high esteem. The centrality of
the Bible is striking. Earnest Bible study is one of the characteristics of this group. They purchase Bibles and distribute them. Thus
the proclamation of the Word has a central place in the worship
service. Many of the members, however, are illiterate, and their
knowledge of scriptural truth is limited.

Prayer in the Ethiopian churches, both in worship services and
in prayer fellowships, readily expresses the community's and the
individual's sincere relationship to Christ. Prayer in the Ethiopian
churches resembles the spontaneous expression of the Pentecostal
churches. The Zionist churches place more emphasis on prayer
and are frequently called the "praying churches." However, they
are sometimes criticized for being controlled by the emotions
instead of the intellect. The sincerity of their faith and prayer
brings many people to a personal relationship with Christ. The
positive results of their ministry and testimony may not be
overlooked.

Baptism and purification rites are important activities in the
Zionist churches. They are preceded by confession of sins and
followed by instruction in the Word of God. Faith healing is practiced in relation to the needs of people. They accept the injunction

of the Scriptures (James 5:14-15) to lay hands on the sick person. They place much emphasis on the Holy Spirit. Everyone is to receive the Holy Spirit and speak in tongues.

Dreams are considered important by Africans and also by the Zionist and Messianic movements. Dreams are believed sent by ancestors. The people act according to their interpretation of the message they feel they have received. They share these dreams with each other as significant messages. The community regards the dreams as such.

The expression of worship in the Messianic groups is usually much more emotional and unstructured. Several people may be speaking, singing, or dancing at the same time. In the smaller groups the leader plays an especially large role in the activities of the community.

Role of Women in the Independent Movement

Women receive due consideration in the Ethiopian and Zionist churches. The women's societies serve in various functions in the church. Some women serve both as lay and as ordained preachers and administer the sacraments in the church. Women are active in these churches, as they are in many established churches. The women's societies organize their social activities, hold meetings, have choirs, gather offerings and help needy people, visit neighbors, especially the sick, and cater at festival gatherings. The women often indicate greater interest and devotion to the work of the church than the men. In their financial contributions they do not take a second place. In South Africa and Rhodesia women have a significant influence because of their large number in the communities, as the men work in the mines.[16] Yet women are in the majority in the churches in other countries of Africa, even where the men have not gone off to the mines, and are vitally interested in the activities of the churches.

The presence of the women in the church is observed when the opportunity for participation and expression of the spiritual gifts is given. Motivated by a concern for their families and their neighbors, many women have devoted themselves to guide them in the Christian faith. They have fulfilled a spiritual ministry that has been less observed by the community, but was nevertheless very important. In other groups, deaconesses have contributed significantly to the life of the church. Again, in the Zionist groups, and even more in the Messianic groups, women serve both as lay preachers and as ordained preachers and administer the sacraments. Most preachers or leaders of these groups have not received theological or pastoral training. They serve in response to their personally felt call and with the natural gifts they have received. Consequently, it is not unusual for a gifted woman who has won respect and recognition in a community to be granted this office of service in the group.

Attitude of the State to the Independent Movement

The Independent churches have had considerable difficulty in obtaining legal status in most countries. Some have been severely suppressed and existed as an illegal movement for some decades. A number of them have been severely persecuted. From 1960 to 1973 some of the larger, older, and more established of these churches received legal status. More recently some countries have outlawed the formation of separatist groups. The new groups are obliged to affiliate with one of the legally recognized churches.

Attitude of the Christian Councils to the Independent Movement

The Independent churches have not been readily accepted by the established churches. Their motives have been misinterpreted. Churches have opposed their existence because they considered division and separation a denial of the unity of the body of Christ. Consequently, little fellowship has been cultivated between the established churches and the new groups that separated themselves. The churches viewed the action of the separatist groups as having rejected them and as undermining their ministry. The separatist groups wanted to establish their identify and were afraid of being drawn into the former fold once more.

After years of separate existence, however, many of the larger groups have made efforts to win recognition from major churches and Christian councils in Africa and beyond. Most independent bodies have a desire for ecumenical fellowship with other Christian churches. The largest success has come through their participation in educational and medical concerns, in service agencies like relief help and Bible societies in the country, and by affiliating with national and international ecclesiastical organizations. Only a few Christian councils have been willing to accept separatist churches into their organization. The National Christian Council of Kenya has accepted a good number of these churches, and they comprise a significant portion of the membership represented by the council. The councils of Rhodesia and Malawi have accepted Independent churches as members. The Christian Council of Ghana accepted three churches that started independently and then called on American Negro Missions to serve with them. However, some Christian councils have not been willing to accept Independent churches, and some Independent churches have not been interested in joining a Christian council. In Nigeria, the Interdenominational Church Council has been formed, and most of its member bodies are separatist.

The hesitancy of the national Christian councils and the governments to recognize the separatist churches has motivated them to form councils or federations of separatist churches. As larger ecclesiastical bodies, they have applied for legal status. This movement has given birth to many councils of separatist churches. The councils give them a sense of belonging and a relationship with other bodies. Generally, however, they have not been successful in attaining legal status, except where the older bodies already had legal status that then covered the younger churches.

Some Independent churches expected to find opportunities to fellowship and work with other ecclesiastical bodies in the All-Africa Council of Churches. A number of them applied. But the international body has been motivated by its relationship to the national Christian councils and has acted quite slowly in accepting Independent churches. The Harrist Church (Eglise Harriste) of Ivory Coast and the Kimbanguist Church (Eglise de Jesus Christ sur la terre par le prophete Simon Kimbangu) of Zaire were the first Independent churches to be accepted by the World Council of Churches.

Contributions of the Independent Movement

The Independent churches have generally maintained the centrality of the historical Jesus as Lord and Savior. The knowledge of the Christian faith of some of the members has been limited. Consequently, some discrepancy may exist between the doctrine accepted by the group and the practice of some believers. Nevertheless, they affirm faith in Christ in traditional African forms.

The future will reveal to what extent the independent movement will serve as a movement of renewal and reform. The intimate fellowship in, and the radiant witness of, some of the Independent churches are important contributions to Christianity. The indigeneity of the Independent churches, by which the Christian faith is expressed in forms relevant to the culture and African music and forms of worship are used, is significant in establishing Christianity in Africa. The movement is very complex, but the general effect of the movement has been to make Christianity indigenous.

The established churches, however, note a denial of the oneness in Christ and of the love that the movement forcefully proclaims for there are continuous divisions in the independent movement. The tendency for the leader to seek personal recognition instead of exalting Christ is a constant danger. When disciplined church members begin their own group in which Christian discipline is neglected, their testimony of Christianity bears a negative effect.

The African Independent churches have made a significant contribution in evangelizing unbelievers. Their members often witness to their faith with a radiant joy and an assurance of conviction that testifies to their relationship with Christ and is very convincing. They are often in a close relationship with their fellow-men and witness to them in the everyday situations of life. They have a great potential for winning their fellow-men. The future will reveal the contribution they will make to the advancement of Christianity in Africa.

Some of the traditional churches are conscious of the importance of the Independent churches and of the contribution they may make. They are also conscious of their obligation toward these churches and are establishing fraternal relations with them. They are assisting them with teaching personnel and instructing their future leaders in order that they may proclaim the gospel more effectively. The collaboration of the two Christian movements, the traditional and the independent, may contribute significantly to the establishment of the Christian faith in Africa.

FORMATION OF CHRISTIAN COUNCILS
Missionary Fellowship

The missionaries serving in various countries of Africa were concerned for fellowship with fellow workers who were involved in the same task and confronted with similar problems. The mis-

sionaries in Zaire esteemed the fellowship so valuable that the first
conference of representatives of the missionary societies met at
Kinshasa (formerly Leopoldville) in 1902, twenty years after the
beginning of the Christian ministry in that country. These representatives decided to hold periodic conferences of missionaries of
Zaire at which the fellowship in the common task could be established and the ministry considered together. Because the
meetings were invaluable, they have been conducted almost
annually. The fellowship became more intimate, and the cooperation between the societies increased. The conferences were
only consultative, but the discussions of the issues helped them
understand the problems at stake and plan for effective ministries.

The desire of missionary societies to share their concerns for the
evangelization of the non-Christians brought about the formation
of the Foreign Missions Conference of Missionary Societies of
Great Britain and Ireland.

International Missionary Council

The growing interest for fellowship with missionaries from other
continents and to work unitedly for the evangelization of the world
brought into being the World Missionary Conference at Edinburgh
in 1910. The Edinburgh Conference recommended that the relationship established at that meeting be maintained through a continuation committee and that regional committees or Christian
councils be organized in the mission fields and in the sending
countries. The only official action taken by the Edinburgh Conference was the formation of the continuation committee of which
John R. Mott became president and Joseph H. Oldham the full-
time secretary.

World War I broke out before the continuation committee organized a further meeting. The activities of the continuation committee basically ceased during the war, and the world-wide fellowship established at Edinburgh almost came to an end. In 1921 the
committee was reorganized and became the International Missionary Council.[17] However, the war and the dictated peace had
disturbed the Christian fellowship experienced at Edinburgh, and
it was not easy to revive it fully.

The International Missionary Council sponsored a special session at LeZoute, Belgium, in 1926 to study Christian missions in
Africa. This was the only meeting entirely devoted to Africa until

the meeting at Ibadan, Nigeria, in 1958. The International Missionary Council sponsored five world conferences as follows: Jerusalem, 1928; Madras, 1938; Whitby, 1947; Willingen, 1952; and Ghana, 1957-1958.[18] However, they were not of the same nature and scope as the Edinburgh Conference.

The missionary inspiration and the concern for world evangelism of the Edinburgh Conference gave rise to the Faith and Order Movement and the Life and Work Movement. Consequently, the International Missionary Council, the Faith and Order Movement, and the Life and Work Movement existed simultaneously. The Faith and Order and Life and Work movements merged in 1938 and formed the provisional committee of the World Council of Churches, which was inaugurated at Amsterdam in 1948.

Christian Councils

In response to the recommendation of the Edinburgh conference, a continuation committee, a missionary conference, or a Christian council was formed in a number of African countries. The Congo General Conference endorsed the recommendation and adopted the name Congo Continuation Committee in 1911. The General Missionary Conference of Northern Rhodesia (Zambia) was founded in 1914. By 1938 Christian or missionary councils or conferences were formed in Zaire, Zambia, Rhodesia, Malawi, Mozambique, Tanzania, Kenya, South Africa, Angola, Nigeria, Ghana, and Sierra Leone.[19] However, only the Congo (Zaire) Protestant Council (as it was called in 1924) and the Christian Council of South Africa qualified as national councils in representing most of the churches serving in the country. The other Christian councils represented a number of missionary societies but had no national representation. Later Christian councils were also formed in Burundi, Cameroon, Ethiopia, Madagascar, and Rwanda.

In some countries several organizations, representing areas or theological tendencies, were formed. Thus the Christian Council of Nigeria represented missionary societies and churches of the central part of Nigeria. The Evangelical Union of Missions represented Christian agencies serving east of the Niger. The Miango Conference represented Christian communities in the northern provinces. These merged in 1928 to form the United Conference of Protestant Missionary Societies in Nigeria.[20]

The ministry and contribution of the Christian councils has been on the national level. Consultations among the Christian councils on a continent-wide basis was almost nonexistent. The councils took part in the meetings of the International Missionary Council and in meetings of missionary conferences in Europe and America, but no gathering of Christian councils in Africa took place.

The Christian councils or conferences have established closer fellowship among the Christian bodies serving in a country. They have given valuable suggestions for strategy, methods, and purpose and have helped create a sense of unity of purpose. They have presented the concerns of the Christian bodies to the government and thereby greatly facilitated their ministry.

Every council has served the needs of the Christian bodies in its country. In relation to the Evangelical Alliance of Angola, Eduardo Moreira of the Portuguese League of Missionary and Educational Action, served as liaison officer in Lisbon for the American, British, and Swiss missions serving in Portuguese colonies.[21] The Congo (Zaire) committee expressed its concern about the treatment of Africans by the rubber gatherers during 1902-1908, thus contributing to the appointment of the Investigating Commission. Christian councils have expressed their views on injustice.

Christian Cooperation

Cooperation has permitted church bodies to undertake significant responsibilities that one body could not undertake alone. The churches in Kenya and Nigeria appointed an educational counselor. The Kenya counselor was designated by the Christian council. The bishops of the Upper Nile and Uganda solicited his services for their districts also. The counselor for Nigeria was designated for southern Nigeria by the Christian council. The council in Zaire established an educational bureau through which government subsidies for church schools were obtained. This collaboration significantly aided the education efforts.

The cooperation has enabled church agencies to begin institutions of advanced learning in order to train personnel. They have cooperated in establishing high schools, colleges, seminaries, and universities. In West Africa the Anglicans and Methodists have cooperated at the Fourah Bay College in Sierra Leone and at Igbabi College, Lagos. The Lovedale Institute, one of the early centers of training in South Africa, has served a number of

churches. When the government took over the Lovedale Institute
in 1953, the Anglicans, Methodists, Presbyterians, and Congregationalists founded the Federal Theological Seminary. The
Evangelical School of Theology in Kinshasa was founded by eight
church bodies serving in the western part of Zaire. The Alliance
High School of Kikuyu, Kenya, was opened in 1926 and has been a
successful joint enterprise. The Theological College of Northern
Nigeria at Bukuru trains pastors for various participating
churches. More recently the Theological Seminary at Yaounde,
Cameroon, was opened as a cooperative venture. These are but a
few of the many significant cooperative efforts.

Large cooperative efforts in preparing, printing, and distributing
Christian literature have been made. Regional committees for the
preparation of Christian literature were formed. The production of
Christian literature was an important aspect of the proclamation of
the Christian faith. In order to minister to this need, the Conference of British Missionary Societies in 1923 established its Africa
Literature Committee, which produced the *Bibliography of African
Literature*. The delegates at the Le Zoute conference in Belgium in
1926 recognized the great need for printed material in the vernacular and the several European languages. The conference recommended cooperation by the societies working in Africa to promote
the production of literature. The International Committee on
Christian Literature was formed. It focused attention on the needs
and stimulated concern for adult education and for the production
and distribution of reading materials for African Christians.[22]

The translation of the Bible had led Protestant missionaries to
collaborate with each other.[23] The Christian Councils of Africa in
cooperation with the Bible societies have made significant contributions in translating the Bible or portions of the Bible into the
African languages and making them available to the people.

In 1963 the Catholic Church sent observers to a meeting of Bible
translators. Since that time it has participated in Bible translation
and distribution.

The fellowship that has led to local cooperation has also led to
national and international cooperation. The cooperation of all the
churches in a country or an area increased the influence of the
evangelistic campaigns, such as Christ for All or New Life for All
conducted in several countries. The help given by members of
churches of one area or country made it possible to launch cam-

paigns in other areas or in other countries. In Zaire, Pastor Makanzu was released by the church and for several years he conducted evangelistic campaigns in various places of the country. Willis Braun traveled to many African countries, helping churches to organize evangelistic efforts. These campaigns have greatly edified and refreshed the churches.

The Christian fellowship and the cooperation in common causes has drawn some Christian communities toward union. In a number of instances where several agencies of the same confession served in one area, they have united into one church. Examples of the results of Christian cooperation include the following: the union of the Livingstonia and the Blantyre communities in Malawi; the union of the Lutheran churches in Tanzania and in Ethiopia; the union of the United Protestant Church of Madagascar (1934); the formation of the United Church of Zambia (1961); and the formation of the Church of Christ of Zaire (1970).

The International Missionary Council and the World Council of Churches

The second assembly of the World Council of Churches at Evanston, Indiana, in 1954 took steps leading to the integration of the International Missionary Council and the World Council of Churches. Some of the member councils of the International Missionary Council were not in favor of this move. The plan of integration was nevertheless "accepted in principle" at the international gathering of the International Missionary Council at the University College, Legon, Ghana, in 1957-1958. The integration of the International Missionary Council and the World Council of Churches was accepted by the assemblies of both bodies in New Delhi, India, in 1961. The Congo (Zaire) Protestant Council and the Norwegian Missionary Council declined to be members of the new organization. Max Warren, general secretary of the Anglican Church Missionary Society, opposed the merger because it implied that missions were only the responsibility of the church structures and no representation was given to interdenominational and international mission societies and evangelistic associations. Such missionary and evangelistic agencies are not represented in the assembly of the World Council of Churches.[24]

The World Council has put forth efforts to enlarge the cooperation with the African churches, the Roman Catholics, and the

Independent churches, but the results have been limited. The Independent churches formed the African Independent Churches Association.[25] Some of the Protestant churches of Africa have become members of the World Council of Churches, but only the Christian Council of Rhodesia and the South Africa Council of Churches became members of the World Council of Churches.[26] The overtures of the World Council of Churches to the Christian Councils of Africa caused tensions in some countries. Through integration of the International Missionary Council with the World Council of Churches, its relationship with the African churches was less intimate. This, in part, gave rise to the formation of the All-Africa Conference of Churches and the Association of Evangelicals of Africa and Madagascar. Most of the Protestant churches are members of one of the two associations. The danger of dividing the Protestants into two camps is apparent.

During the years following the Tambaran Assembly (1938), the International Missionary Council gave much attention to the training of the ministry in the younger churches. It sponsored a series of surveys covering Africa and Madagascar. These studies revealed the urgent need to strengthen the theological training programs. Through the initiative of Charles Ranson, the then general secretary of the International Missionary Council, the Theological Education Fund was created. The resources of the Theological Education Fund were made available at a time when the churches realized the need for improved theological training. The renewed effort on the part of the churches with the resources of the fund, brought about a significant change in the quality and extent of theological education of the churches in Africa.

The All-Africa Conference of Churches

The first All-Africa Christian Conference was held at Ibadan, Nigeria, in January 1958. The African representatives of the Protestant churches felt the conference provided valuable fellowship and contributed to their understanding of the churches in Africa. They recommended the appointment of a continuation committee to implement the report of the conference. This committee instigated the formation of the All-Africa Conference of Churches.[27] D.S.G. M'Timkulu, formerly lecturer at Fort Hare University, South Africa, was appointed secretary. He guided the activities of the committee and called the Kampala, Uganda, sessions.

At the Ibadan conference, the delegates were pleased with the discussions on various aspects of the life and ministry of the church that were conducted under the chairmanship of Sir Francis Ibiam of Nigeria. These considerations led to the further valuable consultations and conferences on an all-Africa basis.

The continuation committee prepared a constitution and guidelines for the work of the commissions. The All-Africa Conference of Churches established its offices at Kitwe, Zambia, at the Mindolo Ecumenical Center, founded by the Copperbelt Christian Service Council during the same year. In 1965 the secretariat of the All-Africa Conference of Churches was transferred to Nairobi, Kenya. The first assembly of the All-Africa Conference of Churches convened at Kampala in 1963, and the second assembly convened at Lusaka, Zambia, in 1974.

The All-Africa Conference of Churches is an autonomous organization with a fraternal relationship with the World Council of Churches. Because of this relationship, only the churches favorably inclined to the World Council of Churches have joined the All-Africa Conference of Churches. The goal set by the founders to affiliate all African churches with the organization has not nearly been realized.

The All-Africa Council of Churches seeks to give guidance to all aspects of the life and ministry of the church. The representatives at the Ibadan conference in 1958 were concerned that the profitable discussions be presented to the churches and implemented. This is also the concern of the All-Africa Council of Churches. It accepted the responsibilities to administer the Ecumenical Program for Emergency Action in Africa, for which the division attempts to raise $10 million outside Africa in ten years.[28]

The Association of Evangelicals in Africa and Madagascar

The Association of Evangelicals for Africa and Madagascar was formed at Limuru, Kenya, in 1966 by delegates representing evangelical churches and mission societies in twenty-three African nations. It gathers the Christian agencies that are not favorably inclined toward the World Council of Churches. The general assembly has met at Limuru in 1969 and in 1973.

The Association of Evangelicals of Africa and Madagascar headquarters in Nairobi is a service agency to the national fellowships, churches, and theological schools. It is active in sponsoring such activities as seminars promoting church growth, church management, New Life for All, and Theological Education by Extension.

The theological commission of the Association of Evangelicals of Africa and Madagascar assumes the responsibilities of the former Association of Evangelical Bible Institutes and Colleges in Africa and Madagascar and gives guidance to the theological education of the member churches. The Christian commission is to assist cooperative projects of curriculum development, encourage Christian education leadership conferences and training programs, and try to make the teaching of the Scriptures more effective.

The All-Africa Conference of Churches and the Association of Evangelicals of Africa and Madagascar are promoting closer fellowship and understanding among the Christians of their respective fellowships. The representatives of the various countries serve together in the ministries to the people of Africa, and the Christians may participate in the ministries to their fellow-men through the Christian council or fellowship of each country. In so doing, an awareness of the African Christian community is fostered. Intimate relationships are established as Christians serve together. The All-Africa Council of Churches and the Association of Evangelicals of Africa and Madagascar seek a closer fellowship between the two communities and greater cooperation in the common task they have under the one Lord.

Ecumenical Relations With the Roman Catholic Church

In the Protestant communion the ecumenical attitudes have grown the quickest in the mission territories and then have spread back to the home countries. Among the Catholics this has not been the case. Following Vatican II, the Catholic Church has taken a seemingly conciliatory attitude toward other Christian communions and has brought about a new relationship between Christians. However, inasmuch as the Catholic Church maintains that it is the true Church and since it only invites reconciliation with other Christian communions, most of what has been done is in the nature of a preecumenical phase rather than a real expression of ecumenism. The activities have attempted to bring disunity to an end and replace hostility between denominations with a good-neighbor attitude, but ecumenical relationships are exceptions rather than the norm.

In Africa and Asia on the whole, the Catholics have lagged behind from the ecumenical viewpoint. In large parts of Africa the ecumenical spirit did not begin to be felt until the latter years of the 1960s. Even some of the more forward looking priests considered ecumenism inopportune.[29] Others, however, recognized the importance of Christian fellowship. Protestant and Catholic seminaries conducted Bible study and prayer fellowships. They have conducted studies concerning the Christian life and have cooperated in Scripture translation. The fellowship and cooperation has brought the two Christian communions closer together.

The Anglican Church, especially in East Africa, has made efforts to bring the disunion with the Catholics to an end. The two churches have maintained cordial relations for some time. The presence of three official observers of the Catholic Church at the meetings of the All-Africa Conference of Churches in Kampala, Uganda, in 1963 was a sign of a new attitude.[30] In January 1964 the two churches formed Uganda's Christian council. The council enables the churches to take united action in several important spheres, especially in dealing with the government.

Study Questions

1. State the most significant reasons for the independent movement.
2. Evaluate the Independent church movement in relation to church growth in Africa.
3. Indicate what contribution the Independent church movement may make to church growth in Africa.
4. How can the established churches assist the Independent churches and establish ecumenical fellowship?
5. Indicate briefly the contribution of the International Missionary Council to the development of ecumenical relations.
6. Outline a strategy for effective ministry for the Christian councils.
7. Suggest avenues of ecumenical cooperation for your church.
8. Outline a strategy of action for the All-Africa Conference of Churches and for the Association of Evangelicals of Africa and Madagascar.

15

Conclusion

Two very amazing and significant facts of history are the sweep of Christianity over North Africa during the early centuries of the Christian era and, after a millennium of difficulties and setbacks, its flowering throughout sub-Saharan Africa. Christianity was established in North Africa during the apostles' lives. It spread rapidly, won the allegiance of the overwhelming majority of the population, and contributed most significantly to the life and ministry of the Christian church during the first five centuries. Able church leaders, teachers, apologists, theologians, and writers came from its ranks. They witnessed to their faith with a dynamism that eventually won the support of the Roman state, causing Christianity to become the predominant religion of the Greco-Roman civilization.

Christianity established itself in Egypt, and the monks proclaimed the gospel to the rural population. During the persecutions monks and Christians fled into the interior, witnessing to their faith and winning converts wherever they went. The gospel was proclaimed in the vernacular, and the Scriptures were translated into it. The church was indigenized and became the national church of Egypt. In part because of its national character, the church in Egypt continued to serve under Muslim pressure.

Northwest Africa has been plagued with invasions by foreign powers. Phoenicians, Romans, Vandals, and Byzantines in turn invaded and ruled the territory. The foreign element exercised a dominating role in the society. Latin was used extensively by the Christian community. The Bible was not translated into the vernacular, and Christianity did not really take root in the culture. The Christians were divided into the Roman Catholic, Donatist, Arian, and Monophysite churches. When the Muslims invaded the territory, many people fled to Europe, greatly weakening the

472

Christian community. Without the resource of the Scriptures in the vernacular, the Christian community rapidly declined under the Muslim pressure until the church became practically nonexistent.

As a result of the fall of the Roman Empire and the decay of the Greco-Roman civilization, the Roman and Byzantine churches chiefly devoted their efforts to evangelize the peoples of Europe. Their attempts to minister in North Africa were opposed by the Muslims, and their contacts with West and South Africa had not been established. The Ethiopian Church strove to establish itself and to guard the country against Arab invasion. The threat of an Arab invasion and an attempted revolt by the Agau influenced a close association between church and state. The status and power of the Ethiopian Church was elevated, and again the emperor was called "Defender of the Faith." Christianity assumed a passive stance. Consequently, Christianity in Africa witnessed little growth until the nineteenth century.

A resurgence of spiritual life in Western Europe in the sixteenth century inspired interest in missions and brought into existence missionary agencies. In the fifteenth, sixteenth, and seventeenth centuries Christianity was planted on the fringes of Africa south of the Sahara.

The Dutch settlement in South Africa and the Moravian missionary efforts inspired further Protestant contacts with Africa. These efforts attained a significant dimension during the latter part of the nineteenth century and produced the flowering forth of Christianity throughout sub-Saharan Africa in the twentieth century. The Roman Catholic Church was somewhat later in its missionary thrust in that part of Africa, but when it renewed its efforts, it sent a large staff to the ministry.

The missionary thrust overcame the obstacles of disease, climate, and communication; a phenomenal expansion of the Christian faith took place. Christian communities arose throughout sub-Saharan Africa. They witnessed to their faith, winning many people and integrating the Christian faith in the life of the people. Christianity made a profound influence on the people. The Christian faith liberated from fear and gave a hope for the future. The nineteenth century witnessed the abolition of slavery and the introduction of Western medicine and Western education; the people were taught new handicrafts and plants and methods of agriculture were introduced to assist them. Many languages were reduced to writing, and literacy increased rapidly. The people were anxious to acquire the knowledge and the tools that came with Christianity and Western civilization. The introduction of aspects of Western culture, however, discredited many valuable aspects of the indigenous culture and led to a degree of disintegration of the old culture. In time, however, a degree of momentum was gained by the process of integrating new teachings and new ways of life into the African culture with a strong concern to develop a culture that is Christian and authentically African.

The unity of spirit and cooperation among the churches serving in various countries of Africa was outstanding. The churches formed Christian councils, which in several cases represented almost all the Christian agencies serving in the country. Thus in effect these councils became national councils. Some Christian councils were of a regional character. The cooperation led to closer affiliation in many aspects. The Christian councils in Zambia and Zaire led to the formation of churches in which all the Protestant bodies are represented. The concern of the churches and councils to fellowship on an international basis and to strengthen the Christian witness led to the formation of the All-Africa Conference of Churches (AACC) and the Association of Evangelicals of Africa and Madagascar (AEAM). Some churches of Africa affiliated with non-African Christian bodies. The churches of Africa assumed their places in the world-wide Christian fellowship.

Many Independent churches have been formed. They have gained numerous adherents and are exerting a significant role in African Christianity. Some groups have come into existence through the personal interest of one person and represent only a family or clan. However, several Independent churches report a membership exceeding one million. The older churches have maintained that proliferation of new groups is a denial of the spirit of unity of the church. Yet they are recognizing the Christian love and the indigenous Christian vitality that the Independent churches are manifesting. Also, the older churches are recognizing the contributions these churches are making in integrating the Christian faith in the African culture and in establishing Christianity on the continent.

The growth of the Christian community in Africa during the past one hundred years has been phenomenal. The Christian faith has been accepted, and an indigenous Christianity has taken its place in the world-wide Christian fellowship. In the next phase of growth and ministry, it is confronted with the challenge to assume responsibility in world mission.

Footnotes

Notes on Chapter 1

1. Harnack (1908), 2:58-62.
2. Walker (1918), p. 67.
3. Schaff (1910), 2:27.
4. Groves (1948), 1:32.
5. Cornevin (1964), p. 100.
6. Neander (1871), 1:83.
7. Walker (1918), p. 80.
8. Ibid., p. 137.
9. Latourette (1943), 5:227.
10. Cornevin (1964), p. 79.
11. Ibid., p. 80.
12. Walker (1918), p. 67.
13. Schaff (1910), p. 28.
14. Duchense (1965), p. 286.
15. Groves (1948), 1:60.
16. Monceaux (1901), p. 15.
17. Newman (1957), p. 207.
18. Duchense (1965), pp. 296-99.
19. Latourette (1937), 1:93.
20. Duchense (1965), p. 402.
21. Walker (1918), pp. 58-59;
    Qualben (1942), pp. 86-88.
22. Newman (1957), pp. 98-202;
    Neander (1871), 1:575-93.
23. Neander (1871, 1:478-481;
    Duchense (1965), pp. 404-11.
24. Frend (1952), pp. 142-145;
    Lietzmann (1953), 3:82-86.
25. Frend (1952), pp. 193-200.
26. Cornevin (1964), p. 90.
27. Frend (1952), p. 193.
28. Walker (1918), p. 176.
29. Hodges (1915), p. 286.
30. Neander (1871), 1:228-30.
31. Groves (1948), 1:63.
32. Schaff (1950), 3:792-94.
33. Newman (1957), pp. 362-64.
34. Schaff (1950), 3:793.
35. Walker (1918), pp. 187-88.
36. Schaff (1950), 3:857-58.
37. Groves (1948), p. 65.
38. Frend (1952), pp. 303-6.
39. Cornevin (1964), p. 92.
40. Ibid., p. 294.
41. Groves (1948), p. 68.
42. Cornevin (1964), p. 95.
43. Newman (1957), pp. 348-49.
44. Ullendorf (1968), pp. 97-98.
45. Cornevin (1964), p. 97.
46. Neander (1871), 2:143-45.
47. Groves (1948), p. 53.
48. Latourette (1970), 1:234.
49. Cornevin (1964), p. 103.

Notes on Chapter 2

1. Corneivin (1964), p. 109.
2. Oliver (1962), p. 69.
3. Groves (1948), p. 74.
4. Ibid., pp. 74-75.
5. Cornevin (1964), p. 114.
6. Groves (1948), p. 80.
7. Cornevin (1964), p. 116.
8. Oliver (1962), pp. 69-70.
9. Groves (1948), p. 107.
10. Page (1908), pp. 10-15.
11. Groves (1948), p. 93;
    Kane (1974), p. 214.
12. Groves (1948), p. 105.
13. Ibid., p. 114.

14. Ibid., p. 116.
15. Neander (1871), 4:63.
16. Oliver (1962), pp. 95-96.
17. Groves (1948), pp. 110-11.
18. Cornevin (1964), p. 144.
19. Kane (1972), p. 57.
20. Neill (1973), p. 140.
21. Cornevin (1964), p. 185.
22. Bane, (1956), p. 42.
23. Schmidlin-Braun (1933), p. 241.
24. Latourette (1939), 3:242; Bane (1956), pp. 41-45.
25. Groves (1948), p. 126.
26. Latourette (1939) 3:242.

27. Schmidlin-Braun (1933), p. 281.
28. Groves (1948), p. 129.
29. Latourette (1939), 3:243.
30. Groves (1948), p. 129.
31. Latourette (1939), 3:243.
32. Oliver (1962), pp. 95-98.
33. Groves (1948), pp. 132-33.
34. Cornevin (1964), p. 196.
35. Ibid., p. 199.
36. Ibid., p. 228.
37. Oliver (1962), p. 100.
38. Groves (1948), p. 136.
39. Latourette (1939), 3:244-45.
40. Groves (1948), p. 137.

Notes on Chapter 3

1. Neill (1973), p. 141.
2. Latourette (1943), 5:423-24; Walker (1918), pp. 245-46.
3. Neill et al. (1971), p. 498.
4. Leonard (1964), 3:466.
5. Warneck (1901), pp. 32-34.
6. Leonard (1964), p. 471.
7. Neill et al. (1971) p. 557.
8. Ibid.

9. Paden et al. (1970), p. 199.
10. Ayandele (1966), p. 331.
11. Paden et al. (1970), p. 253.
12. Debrunner (1965), p. 21.
13. Paden et al. (1970), p. 200.
14. Foster (1961), p. 1.
15. Groves (1948), p. 196.
16. Oliver (1966), pp. 17-25.

Notes on Chapter 4

1. Groves (1948), 1:185.
2. Foster (1961), p. 2.
3. Ibid.
4. Ibid., p. 3.
5. Stock (1899), 2:100.
6. Groves (1954), 2:15-19.
7. Stock (1899), 2:102-3.
8. Ibid., p. 101.
9. Warneck (1901), p. 101.
10. Groves (1955), 3:183.
11. Olson (1969), pp. 87-88.
12. Ibid.
13. Ibid., pp. 89-91.
14. Bane (1956), p. 120.
15. Lovett (1899), 1:480.
16. Groves (1948), 1:212.
17. Ibid., pp. 215-17.
18. Foster (1961), p. 7.
19. Stock (1899), 1:157-61.
20. Latourette (1943), 5:459.
21. Bane (1968), p. 46.
22. Groves (1954), 2:216.

23. Schwager (1907), pp. 87-88.
24. Groves (1954), 2:217.
25. Glover (1960), p. 260.
26. Bane (1968), p. 74.
27. Ibid., pp. 75-76.
28. Ibid., pp. 76-77.
29. Ibid., p. 53.
30. Wold (1968), p. 20.
31. Latourette (1943), 5:450.
32. Groves (1948), 1:296.
33. Latourette (1943), 5:451.
34. Warneck (1901), p. 193.
35. Du Plessis (1930), p. 99.
36. Groves (1948), 1:297.
37. Kane (1971), p. 328.
38. Debrunner (1965), pp. 26-27.
39. Groves (1948), 1:173.
40. Ibid., p. 301.
41. Ibid. (1954), 2:227.
42. Gareis (1901), p. 239.
43. Groves (1954), 2:229.
44. Neill (1973), p. 307.

45. Southon (1934), pp. 33-35.
46. Debrunner (1965), p. 64.
47. Southon (1934), p. 43.
48. Debrunner (1965), p. 64.
49. Ibid.
50. Neill (1973), p. 308.
51. Debrunner (1965), pp. 68-73.
52. Cornevin (1960), 2:468.
53. Debrunner (1965), p. 87.
54. Cornevin (1960), 2:468.
55. Groves (1954), 2:231.
56. Debrunner (1965), p. 98.
57. Cornevin (1969), pp. 126-29.
58. Latourette (1943), 5:445.
59. Groves (1954), 2:233.
60. Ibid., pp. 231-33.
61. Page (1908), p. 51.
62. Crowder (1962), p. 143.
63. Page (1908), p. 84.
64. Ajayi (1969), p. 31.
65. Groves (1954), 2:47.
66. Ibid., p. 48.
67. Latourette (1943), 5:437.
68. Stock (1899), 2:103.
69. Neill et al. (1971), p. 309.
70. Crowder (1962), p. 144.
71. Stock (1899), 2:104-5.
72. Ibid., p. 451.
73. Ibid., p. 452.
74. Ajayi (1969), p. 38.
75. Stock (1899), 2:109.
76. Ibid., pp. 109-11.
77. Groves (1954), 2:61.

78. Stock (1899), 2:118-19.
79. Bowen (1875), pp. 175-76.
80. Pinnock (1918), p. 100.
81. Bowen (1875), pp, 203-4.
82. Ibid., pp. 183-204.
83. Stock (1899), 2:442-43.
84. Ibid., p. 444.
85. Crampton (n.d.), p. 23.
86. Ajayi (1969), p. 211.
87. Latourette (1943), 5:439.
88. Neill (1973), p. 309.
89. Warneck (1901), p. 199.
90. Goldie (1890), p. 210.
91. Groves (1954), 2:240.
92. Richter (1922), p. 157.
93. Groves (1955), 3:218.
94. Latourette (1943), 5:440.
95. Groves (1955), 3:218-19.
96. Ajayi (1969), p. 51.
97. Kwast (1971), p. 66.
98. Johnston (1908), 1:27-28.
99. Van Slagaren (1969),
    pp. 57-58.
100. Kwast (1971), pp. 70-76.
101. Hawker (1909), p. 77.
102. Kwast (1971), p. 77.
103. Ibid., p. 79.
104. Ibid., p. 84.
105. Groves (1954), 2:70.
106. Leonard (1964), p. 499.
107. Ibid., p. 500.
108. Bane (1968), p. 106.

Notes on Chapter 5

1. Cornevin (1964), p. 234;
   Du Plessis (1911), pp. 3-4.
2. Cornevin (1964), pp. 234-36.
3. Latourette (1943), 5:338.
4. Groves (1948), 1:155.
5. Sales (1971), p. 18.
6. Groves (1948), 1:156.
7. Sales (1971), p. 20.
8. Ibid., pp. 12, 21.
9. Hinchliff (1968), pp. 3-5.
10. Du Plessis (1911), p. 27.
11. Sales (1971), p. 19.
12. Hinchliff (1968), pp. 6-7.
13. Thompson (1904), p. 354.
14. Sales (1971), pp. 25-27.

15. Du Plessis (1911), pp. 56-57.
16. Sales (1971), p. 28.
17. Thompson (1904), p. 366.
18. Groves (1948), 1:220-21.
19. Thompson (1904), pp. 368-72.
20. Groves (1948), 1:236.
21. Thompson (1904), pp. 372.
22. Walker (1959 ed.), pp. 122-28.
23. Hinchliff (1968), pp. 13-16.
24. Oliver (1962), p. 163.
25. Hinchliff (1968), pp. 16-21.
26. Groves (1948), 1:222.
27. Ibid.
28. Sales (1971), pp. 33-34.
29. Hinchliff (1968), p. 24.

30. Ibid., pp. 24-25.
31. Sales (1971), p. 64.
32. Groves (1954), 2:137.
33. Groves (1948), 1:224-25.
34. Sales (1971), p. 37.
35. Groves (1948), 1:225-26.
36. Sales (1971), pp. 57-58.
37. Groves (1948), 1:227-28.
38. Hinchliff (1968), p. 27;
    Du Plessis (1911) pp. 145-47.
39. Du Plessis (1911), pp. 168-69.
40. Groves (1948), 1:245, 249.
41. Hinchliff (1968), p. 31.
42. Findlay (1923), 4:252.
43. Ibid.
44. Latourette (1943), 5:351.
45. Groves (1948), 1:240.
46. Thiessen (1954), p. 247.
47. Groves (1948), 1:259.
48. Blaikie (1903), p. 68.
49. Braekman (1961), p. 49.
50. Groves (1954), 2:166.
51. Braekman (1961), pp. 50-51.
52. Cornevin (1960), 2:121.
53. Walker (1959 ed.),
    pp. 180-210.
54. Cornevin (1960), 2:128.
55. Sales (1971), p. 94.
56. Hinchliff (1968), p. 39.
57. Ibid., p. 48.
58. Latourette (1943), 5:349.
59. Groves (1954), 2:252.
60. Du Plessis (1911), p. 354.
61. Groves (1954), 2:258.
62. Brown (1960), pp. 202-5.
63. Du Plessis (1911), p. 370.
64. Sales (1971), pp. 84-86.
65. Groves (1954), 5:282.
66. Sales (1971), p. 88.
67. Latourette (1943), 5:363.
68. Blanc (1970), pp. 50-51.
69. Ibid., p. 63.
70. Ibid., p. 72.

71. Leonard (1964), 3:494-95.
72. Du Plessis (1911), p. 371.
73. Sales (1971), p. 110.
74. Ibid., p. 112.
75. Ibid., p. 115.
76. Brown (1960), pp. 41-42.
77. Sales (1971), pp. 118-19.
78. Du Plessis (1911), p. 370.
79. Brown (1960), pp. 242-46.
80. Hinchliff (1968), p. 62.
81. Du Plessis (1911), pp. 285-86.
82. Cornevin (1960), 2:135.
83. Groves (1955), 3:242-43.
84. Warneck (1901), p. 216.
85. Sales (1971), p. 128.
86. Ibid., pp. 129-30.
87. Cornevin (1964), p. 383.
88. Warneck (1901), p. 216.
89. Sales (1971), p. 134.
90. Latourette (1953), p. 1436.
91. Hinchliff (1968), pp. 90-91.
92. Barrett (1968), p. 3.
93. Turner (1967), p. 16.
94. Baeta (1968), pp. 249ff.
95. Sales (1971), p. 144.
96. Groves (1958), 4:197-99.
97. Hinchliff (1968), pp. 101-2.
98. Groves (1958), 4:227.
99. Sales (1971), p. 146.
100. Ibid., pp. 145-46.
101. *World Almanac* (1976), p. 652.
102. Groves (1954) 2:154-55.
103. Latourette (1943), 5:379.
104. Ibid., p. 380.
105. Groves (1954), p. 250.
106. Carnevin (1960), 2:564.
107. Groves (1954), p. 251.
108. Brown (1960), p. 150.
109. Ibid., p. 151.
110. Latourette (1943), 5:380.
111. Gerdener (1958), p. 124.
112. Glover (1960), p. 297.
113. Neill et al. (1971), p. 564.

Notes on Chapter 6

1. Carter (1963), pp. 361-63.
2. Smith (1928), p. 38.
3. Pascoe (1901), p. 362.
4. Smith (1928), p. 38.
5. Ibid., p. 44.

6. Carter (1963), p. 366.
7. Groves (1948), 1:259.
8. Oliver (1962), pp. 166-69.
9. Groves (1955), 3:100.
10. Pascoe (1901), p. 362b.

11. Ibid.
12. Ibid.
13. Latourette (1943), p. 384.
14. Groves (1958), 4:90.
15. Du Plessis (1911), pp. 287-89.
16. Kane (1971), p. 402.
17. Smith (1928), pp. 64-65.
18. Kane (1971), p. 400.
19. Glover (1960), p. 286.
20. Latourette (1943), 5:385.
21. Schwartz (1974), pp. 13-16.
22. Kane (1971), p. 401.
23. Neill et al. (1971), p. 525.
24. Kane (1971), p. 402.
25. Rotberg (1965), p. 12.
26. Groves (1955), 3:139.
27. Braekman (1961), p. 83.
28. Rotberg (1965), p. 16.
29. Leonard (1964), p. 499.
30. Blanc (1970), p. 116.
31. Smith (1928), pp. 44-45.
32. Leonard (1964), 3:499.
33. Randall (1970), p. 49.
34. Ibid., p. 27.
35. Latourette (1943), 5:386.
36. Rotberg (1965), p. 31.
37. Smith (1928), pp. 80-81.
38. Ibid., p. 88.
39. Randall (1970), p. 48.
40. Latourette (1943), 5:388.
41. Randall (1970), p. 50.
42. Smith (1928), p. 90.
43. Randall (1970), p. 51.
44. Glover (1960), p. 291.
45. Smith (1928), p. 91.
46. Ibid., pp. 82-83.
47. Rotberg (1965), p. 31.
48. Latourette (1943), 5:390.
49. Randall (1970), p. 49.
50. Ibid., p. 51.
51. Kane (1971), p. 405.
52. Smith (1928), p. 90.
53. Kapella (mid.), p. 41.
54. Groves (1954), 2:180-81.
55. Anderson-Morshead (1909), pp. 10-12.
56. Ibid., pp. 32-40.
57. Groves (1954), 2:204.
58. Rotberg (1965), pp. 10-11.
59. Groves (1954), 2:303.
60. Rotberg (1965), pp. 10-11.
61. Groves (1954), pp. 306-7.
62. Latourette (1943), 5:393.
63. Jack (1901), pp. 148-49.
64. Ibid., pp. 150ff.
65. Groves (1954), 2:310.
66. Robinson (1930), p. 339.
67. Latourette (1943), 5:394.
68. Johnston (1898), p. 52.
69. Groves (1954), 2:312.
70. Johnston (1898), p. 68.
71. Groves (1954), 2:313.
72. Latourette (1943), 5:395.
73. Alexander (1969), p. 22.
74. Latourette (1943), 5:396.
75. Jack (1900), p. 215.
76. Groves (1954), 2:315.
77. Jack (1900), p. 217.
78. Oliver (1966), p. 61.
79. Latourette (1943), 5:396.
80. Heanley (1888), pp. 138-42.
81. Anderson-Morshead (1909), p. 153.
82. Ibid., p. 162.
83. Latourette (1943), 5:397.
84. Alexander (1969), p. 167.
85. Kane (1971), p. 408.
86. IRM 32 (March 1943): 48.
87. Glover (1960), p. 294.
88. Moreira (1936), p. 18.
89. Latourette (1943), 5:401.
90. Moreira (1936), pp. 18-19.
91. Glover (1960), p. 294.
92. Moreira (1936), p. 22.
93. Ibid., p. 23.
94. Groves (1955), 3:180.
95. Moreira (1936), pp. 40-41.
96. Copplestone (1973), pp. 557-58.
97. Ibid., pp. 559-61.
98. Latourette (1943), 5:402.
99. Groves (1955), p. 182.
100. Neill et al. (1971), p. 427.
101. Descamps (1965), pp. 36ff.
102. Ibid., pp. 39ff.
103. Jacobsen (1968), pp. 20ff.
104. Leonard (1964), 3:501.
105. Matthews (1904), p. 21.
106. Ellis (1869), p. 39.
107. Blanc et al. (1970), p. 171.

108. Leonard (1964), 3:502.
109. Ellis (1869), pp. 114-17.
110. Blanc et al. (1970), p. 172.
111. Leonard (1964), 3:502.
112. Ibid.
113. Stock (1899), 2:473.
114. Ibid., p. 474.
115. Latourette (1943) 5:307-8.
116. Blanc et al. (1970), p. 177.
117. Leonard (1964), 3:502.
118. Blanc et al. (1970), p. 179.
119. Latourette (1943), 5:309.
120. Blanc et al. (1970), p. 181.
121. Leonard (1964), 3:502.
122. Latourette (1943), 5:308.
123. Stock (1899), 2:476.
124. Leonard (1964), 3:502.
125. Blanc et al. (1970), p. 184.

126. Sibree (1907), pp. 288-94.
127. Leonard (1964), 3:505.
128. Blanc et al. (1970), p. 194.
129. Ibid., p. 201.
130. Latourette (1945), 7:219.
131. Blanc et al. (1970), p. 204.
132. Neill et al. (1971), p. 363.
133. Latourette (1945), p. 220.
134. Blanc et al. (1970), p. 207.
135. Latourette (1943), 5:314.
136. Neill et al. (1971), p. 375.
137. Stock (1899), 2:468.
138. Ibid., pp. 468-72.
139. Thompson (1951), p. 334.
140. Stock (1916), 5:266-68.
141. Thompson (1951), p. 334.
142. Ibid., p. 573.

Notes on Chapter 7

1. Cornevin (1960), 2:179.
2. Groves (1955), 3:222.
3. Groves (1954), 2:97.
4. Krapf (1860), pp. 126-30.
5. Ibid., pp. 159-60.
6. Ibid., pp. 232-36.
7. Ibid., pp. 423-31.
8. Stock (1899), 2:129-30.
9. Krapf (1860), p. 210.
10. Ibid., pp. 311-50.
11. Ibid., pp. 367-408.
12. Stock (1899), 2:135.
13. Ibid.
14. Oliver (1966), p. 61.
15. Groves (1954), 2:285-86.
16. Latourette (1943), 5:407.
17. Anderson-Morshead (1909), p. 43.
18. Stock (1899), 3:80.
19. Oliver et al. (1963), pp. 215-18.
20. Cornevin (1964), p. 290.
21. Wilson (1936), p. 35.
22. Latourette (1943), 5:404.
23. Groves (1954), 2:330.
24. Ibid., p. 287.
25. Krapf (1860), p. 45.
26. Groves (1954), p. 317.
27. Stock (1899), 3:94-95.
28. Ibid., pp. 100-101.
29. Ibid., pp. 105-7.

30. Ibid., pp. 108-12.
31. Marsh and Kingsnorth (1963), p. 101.
32. Oliver (1952), pp. 64-66.
33. Marsh and Kingsnorth (1963), p. 35.
34. Ibid., p. 53.
35. Oliver (1952), p. 108.
36. Ibid.
37. Ibid., p. 110.
38. Calvert (1919), pp. 40-50.
39. Marsh and Kingsnorth (1963), pp. 227-28.
40. Calvert (1919), p. 105.
41. Oliver (1952), pp. 95-97.
42. Groves (1955), 3:77-78.
43. Latourette (1943), p. 406.
44. Hamilton (1912), pp. 197-98.
45. Lovett (1899), 1:649ff.
46. Groves (1955), pp. 80-81.
47. Oliver (1952), p. 163.
48. Ibid., pp. 164-65.
49. Marsh and Kingsnorth (1963), p. 228.
50. Groves (1958), 5:88.
51. Bernander (1957), p. 15.
52. Ibid., p. 24.
53. Ibid., p. 133.
54. Oliver (1952), p. 240.

55. Gann and Duignan (1970), p. 390.
56. Oliver and Fage (1962), 2:10-15.
57. Stock (1916), 4:76.
58. Ibid., p. 77.
59. Ibid., pp. 280-81.
60. Latourette (1943), 5:412.
61. Groves (1955), 3:224.
62. Groves (1954), 2:130-31.
63. Oliver (1962), p. 233.
64. Barrett et al. (1973), p. 32.
65. Ibid., p. 129.
66. Stock (1899), 3:412-13.
67. Ibid., p. 415.
68. Ibid., pp. 416-17.
69. Marsh and Kingsnorth (1963), pp. 131-32.
70. Stock (1899), 3:453-54.
71. Ibid., pp. 451-54.
72. Stock (1916), 4:94.
73. Groves (1955), 3:227-29.
74. Ibid., p. 228.
75. Ibid., pp. 228-29.
76. Stock (1916), 4:94.
77. Ibid., p. 97.
78. Groves (1955), p. 229.
79. Oliver (1952), pp. 186-88.
80. Latourette (1943), 5:418-19.
81. Taylor (1958a), pp. 91-95.
82. Ibid., p. 100.
83. Ibid., pp. 103-4.
84. Neill et al. (1971), p. 533.
85. Groves (1955), 3:228-29.
86. Neill et al. (1971), p. 553.
87. Ibid., p. 75.
88. Bamori (1972), pp. 7-8.
89. Kane (1971), p. 368.
90. McGavran (1970), p. 216.
91. Ibid., p. 213.
92. Cf. Tippett (1973), pp. 328ff.

Notes on Chapter 8

1. Glover (1960), p. 320.
2. Budge (1970), p. 582.
3. Ullendorf (1968), p. 74.
4. Erickson (1973), p. 7.
5. Groves (1948), 1:138-42.
6. Greenfield (1965), p. 79.
7. McLeish (1927), pp. 148-51.
8. Ibid., pp. 152-53.
9. Groves (1954), 2:291.
10. Cornevin (1964), p. 270.
11. Groves (1954), 2:292.
12. Cornevin (1964), p. 312.
13. Groves (1954), 2:83.
14. Ibid., p. 85.
15. Groves (1964), pp. 170-71.
16. Cornevin (1960), p. 289.
17. Ibid.
18. Latourette (1944), 6:30.
19. Groves (1955), 3:256, Stock (1899), 3:218-19.
20. Groves (1955), 3:258.
21. Latourette (1944), 6:30.
22. Glover (1960), p. 318; Latourette (1944), 6:30.
23. Coxill and Grubb (1968), p. 91.
24. Glover (1960), p. 318.
25. Coxill and Grubb (1968), p. 91.
26. Neill et al. (1971), p. 574.
27. Kane (1972), p. 373.
28. Neill et al. (1971), p. 559.
29. Glover (1960), p. 324.
30. Thiessen (1955), p. 278.
31. Kane (1971), p. 379.
32. Latourette (1944), 6:35.
33. McLeish (1927), p. 185.
34. Neill et al. (1971), p. 559.
35. Latourette (1944), 6:35.
36. Neill et al. (1971), p. 178.
37. Glover (1960), p. 227.
38. Latourette (1944), 6:22.
39. Thiessen (1955), p. 166.
40. Stock (1899), 3:514-15.
41. Glover (1960), p. 228.
42. Ibid.
43. Latourette (1944), 6:26.
44. Groves (1955), 3:165.
45. Ibid.
46. Thiessen (1955), p. 167.
47. Latourette (1944), p. 27.
48. Thiessen (1955), p. 167.
49. Glover (1960), p. 229.
50. Ibid., pp. 229-30.
51. Thiessen (1955), p. 168.
52. Kane (1972), p. 283.

53. Neill et al. (1971), p. 187.
54. Ibid.
55. Ibid., p. 347.
56. Glover (1960), p. 310.
57. Coxill and Grubb (1968), p. 75.
58. Neill et al. (1971), p. 348.
59. Ibid., p. 337.
60. Groves (1955), p. 155.
61. Latourette (1944), 6:17.
62. Groves (1954), 2:210.
63. Groves (1955), 3:157-58.
64. Kane (1972), p. 312.
65. Coxill and Grubb (1968), p. 94.
66. Kane (1972), pp. 313-14.
67. Latourette (1944), 6:18.
68. Thiessen (1955), p. 69.
69. Kane (1972), p. 314.
70. Neill et al. (1971), p. 610.
71. Latourette (1944), 6:12.
72. Ibid., p. 13.
73. Neill et al. (1971), p. 13.
74. Groves (1955), 3:158-60.

75. Rutherford and Glenny (1900) pp. 162-75.
76. Coxill and Grubb (1968), p. 59.
77. Glover (1960), p. 314.
78. Neill et al. (1971), p. 13.
79. Thiessen (1955), p. 170.
80. Glover (1960), p. 315.
81. Coxill and Grubb (1968), p. 78.
82. Glover (1960), p. 316.
83. Coxill and Grubb (1968), p. 78.
84. Glover (1960), p. 316.
85. Coxill and Grubb (1968), p. 78.
86. Kane (1972), p. 318.
87. Thiessen (1955), p. 171.
88. Coxill and Grubb (1968), p. 78.
89. Kane (1971), p. 318.
90. Coxill and Grubb (1967), p. 78.
91. Neill et al. (1971), p. 423.
92. Ibid., p. 365.
93. Thiessen (1955), p. 173.
94. Neill et al. (1971), p. 374.
95. Groves (1955), 3:162.

Notes on Chapter 9

1. IRM 57 (March 1968): #36.
2. Coxill and Grubb (1968), p. 84.
3. Kane (1972), p. 320.
4. Latourette (1943), 5:459.
5. Latourette (1945), 7:249.
6. Neill et al. (1971), p. 548.
7. Ibid., p. 223.
8. Kane (1972), p. 321.
9. Coxill and Grubb (1968), p. 69.
10. Dayton (1973), p. 406.
11. Kane (1972), p. 222.
12. Stock (1899), 3:157.
13. IRM 55 (March 1966): #57.
14. Kane (1972), p. 322.
15. IRM 57 (March 1968): #36.
16. Kane (1972), p. 222.
17. Neill et al. (1971), p. 237.
18. Latourette (1943), 5:457-58.
19. Dayton (1973), p. 575; Neill et al. (1971), p. 237.
20. Groves (1955), 3:183-84.
21. Ibid., p. 209.
22. Coxill and Grubb (1968), p. 85.

23. Groves (1955), 3:247-48.
24. Neill et al (1971), p. 551.
25. Coxill and Grubb (1968), p. 85.
26. Olson (1969), pp. 186-87.
27. Ibid., pp. 189-93.
28. Turner (1967), p. 11ff.
29. Kane (1972), p. 326.
30. IRM 57 (March 1968): #37.
31. Ibid.
32. Groves (1955), 3:211-12.
33. Wold (1968), pp. 84-86.
34. Coxill and Grubb (1968), p. 74.
35. Wold (1968), pp. 99-101.
36. Coxill and Grubb (1968), p. 74.
37. IRM 57 (March 1968): #38.
38. Wold (1968), pp. 113-14.
39. Kane (1972), p. 329.
40. Coxill and Grubb (1968), p. 74.
41. Wold (1968), pp. 66ff.
42. IRM 56 (March 1967): 60.
43. Neill et al. (1971), p. 298.

44. Thompson Adolff (1951), pp. 581-82.
45. Neill et al. (1971), p. 298.
46. IRM 55 (March 1966): 56.
47. Neill et al. (1971), p. 298.
48. Glover (1960), p. 270.
49. Kane (1972), p. 332.
50. Coxill and Grubb (1968), p. 71.
51. Thiessen (1955), p. 189.
52. Coxill and Grubb (1968), p. 71.
53. Latourette (1943), 5:448.
54. Latourette (1945), 7:249.
55. Neill et al. (1971), p. 298.
56. IRM 46 (March 1957): #38.
57. IRM 57 (March 1968): 38.
58. Kane (1972), p. 33.
59. Dayton (1973), p. 520.
60. Groves (1964), p. 213.
61. Neill et al. (1971), p. 227.
62. Kane (1972), p. 337.
63. Coxill and Grubb (1968), p. 70.
64. Groves (1955), 3:214.
65. Glover (1960), p. 271.
66. Kane (1972), p. 337.
67. Coxill and Grubb (1968), p. 70.
68. E. Grau in Baeta (1968), p. 61.
69. Groves (1948), p. 176.
70. Latourette (1943), 5:248.
71. Glover (1960), p. 272.
72. Ibid.
73. Coxill and Grubb (1968), p. 70.
74. Ibid.
75. Ibid.
76. Kane (1972), p. 338.
77. Neill et al. (1971), p. 227.
78. Oosthuisen (1972), pp. 371-79.
79. IRM 57 (March 1968): 39.
80. Neill et al. (1971), p. 226.
81. Dayton (1973), p. 590.
82. Grove (1955), p. 215.
83. Cornevin (1969), p. 200.
84. Müller (1904), p. 88.
85. *Missionary Review* (1901), p. 145.
86. Cornevin (1969), p. 200.
87. Latourette (1945), 7:247.
88. Cornevin (1969), p. 324.
89. Debrunner (1965), p. 172.
90. Dayton (1973), p. 362.
91. IRM 58 (March 1969): 41.
92. IRM 56 (March 1967): 55-56.
93. Debrunner (1965), p. 270.
94. IRM 58 (March 1969): 41.
95. Neill et al (1971), p. 602.
96. Latourette (1943), 5:445.
97. Groves (1958), 4:19.
98. Debrunner (1965), p. 166.
99. Ibid., p. 172.
100. Neill et al. (1971), p. 602.
101. Legum (1969), pp. 352-56.
102. Cornevin (1962), p. 452.
103. Walker (1929), pp. 160-79.
104. Glover (1960), p. 274.
105. Cornevin (1962), p. 452.
106. Coxill and Grubb (1968), p. 67.
107. Dayton (1973), p. 130.
108. Ibid., p. 365.
109. Coxill and Grubb (1968), p. 67.
110. Latourette (1943), 5:445-46.
111. Neill et al. (1971), p. 159.
112. IRM 58 (March 1969): 40.
113. IRM 61 (March 1972): 148-49.
114. Ajayi (1969), p. 134.
115. Latourette (1943), 5:441.
116. Glover (1960), p. 277.
117. Kane (1971), p. 343.
118. Coxill and Grubb (1968), p. 81.
119. Groves (1955), 3:187.
120. Coxill and Grubb (1968), p. 81.
121. Groves (1955), 3:187-88.
122. Ibid., p. 220.
123. Ibid., pp. 185-86.
124. Grimley and Robinson (1966), pp. 42-43.
125. Ajayi (1969), p. 234.
126. Grimley and Robinson (1966), p. 42.
127. Kane (1971), p. 344.
128. Grimley and Robinson (1966), pp.47-51.

129. Ibid., p. 61.
130. Ibid., p. 60.
131. Kane (1971), p. 345.
132. Groves (1958), p. 189.
133. Coxill and Grubb (1968), p. 80.
134. Ibid., p. 81.
135. Kane (1971), p. 346.
136. Grimley and Robinson (1966), p. 69.
137. Oosthuisen (1972), pp. 360-64.
138. Ibid., p. 370.
139. Kane (1971), p. 346.
140. Latourette (1943), 5:443.
141. Grimley and Robinson (1966), p. 294.
142. Coxill and Grubb (1968), p. 98.
143. Grimley and Robinson (1966), pp. 301-2.
144. Ibid., p. 303.
145. Van Slagaren (1969), p. 86.
146. Latourette (1943), 5:434.
147. Kwast (1971), p. 88.
148. Glover (1960), p. 337.
149. Latourette (1943), 5:434.
150. Van Slagaren (1969), p. 107.
151. Groves (1955), 3:60.
152. Latourette (1943), 5:434-35.
153. Kwast (1971), pp. 91-93.
154. Ibid., p. 93.
155. Kane (1971), p. 351.
156. Blanc et al. (1970), p. 238.
157. Van Slagaren (1969), p. 73.
158. Kane (1971), p. 351.
159. Glover (1960), p. 337.
160. Kane (1971), p. 350.
161. Van Slagaren (1969), p. 117.
162. Ibid., p. 120.
163. Ibid., p. 122.
164. Ibid., p. 126.
165. Michelson (1969), pp. 196-97.
166. Neill et al. (1971), p. 79.
167. Kane (1971), p. 352.
168. Latourette (1970), 6:428.
169. Groves (1955), p. 270.
170. Neill et al. (1971), p. 223.
171. Latourette (1943), 5:434.
172. Groves (1955), p. 123.
173. Neill et al. (1971), p. 223.
174. Grimley and Robinson (1966), pp. 318-52.
175. McGavran (1970), pp. 260ff.; Wold (1969), pp. 99-101.

Notes on Chapter 10

1. Jadin I. (1970), pp. 165-66.
2. Braekman (1961), pp. 31-32.
3. Axelson (1970), p. 172.
4. Fullerton (1928), p. 32.
5. Bentley (1907), p. 20.
6. Hartland 20.05.1880.
7. Comber 30.01.1887.
8. *Missionary Herald* (1893), p. 17.
9. Fullerton (1928), p. 116.
10. B.M.S. statistics.
11. Groves (1955), 3:126.
12. Ibid., p. 127.
13. Ibid., pp. 127-28.
14. Groves (1958), 4:205.
15. Kane (1971), p. 394.
16. Braekman (1961), p. 129.
17. Ibid., p. 133.
18. Coxill and Grubb (1968), p. 59.
19. Latourette (1943), 5:400.
20. Latourette (1945), 7:234.
21. Ibid., p. 233.
22. Dayton (1973), p. 600.
23. Comber 5.7.1878.
24. Lagargren (1970), p. 5.
25. Guinness (1899), pp. 179-80.
26. Bentley (1900), 1:124.
27. Comber 24.7.1882.
28. Carpenter (1952), p. 8.
29. Braekman (1961), p. 65.
30. Ibid., pp. 91-95.
31. *Missionary Herald* (1890), pp. 219-53.
32. Coxill and Grubb (1968), p. 64.
33. Groves (1954), 2:120.
34. Carpenter (1952), p. 24.
35. Braekman (1961), p. 174.
36. Kane (1971), p. 361.
37. Carpenter (1952), p. 2.
38. Coxill and Grubb (1968), p. 65.

39. Slade (1959), p. 104.
40. Braekman (1961), p. 179.
41. Coxill and Grubb (1968), p. 65.
42. Braekman (1961), pp. 147, 181.
43. Coxill and Grubb (1968), p. 64.
44. Ibid.
45. Ibid., p. 65.
46. Ibid.
47. Kane (1971), p. 361.
48. Coxill and Grubb (1968), p. 65.
49. Ibid., p. 66.
50. Ibid., p. 65.
51. Kane (1971), p. 364.
52. Hollemweger (1973), p. 4.
53. Bertsche (1964), p. 2.
54. W.H. Bentley 19.8.1881.
55. Groves (1955), 3:123.
56. Ibid., p. 124.
57. Neill et al (1971), p. 142.

58. Latourette (1943), 5:421.
59. Groves (1955), 3:124.
60. Ibid., p. 125.
61. Neill et al. (1971), p. 142.
62. Latourette (1943), 5:422.
63. Neill et al. (1971), p. 142.
64. Hastings (1967), p. 189.
65. Ibid., p. 207.
66. Kane (1971), p. 363.
67. Neill et al. (1971), p. 140.
68. Latourette (1943). 5:428.
69. Groves (1955), 3:123.
70. Neill et al. (1971), p. 140.
71. Coxill and Grubb (1968), p. 64.
72. Ibid.
73. Ibid.
74. Kane (1971), p. 358.
75. Legum (1969), pp. 397-99.
76. Carpenter (1952), p. 11.

Notes on Chapter 11

1. Dayton (1973), p. 502.
2. Groves (1955), 3:227.
3. Thompson (1960), p. 303.
4. Neill et al. (1971), p. 94.
5. Hill (1969), pp. 85-87.
6. Coxill and Grubb (1968), p. 63.
7. Kane (1971), p. 355.
8. Coxill and Grubb (1968), p. 63.
9. Ibid.
10. Ibid.
11. Dayton (1973), p. 106.
12. Kane (1971), p. 356.
13. Neill et al. (1971), p. 94.
14. IRM 55 (March 1966): 54.
15. Dayton (1973), p. 503.
16. Legum (1969), p. 406.
17. Glover (1960), p. 338.
18. Dayton (1973), p. 503.
19. Coxill and Grubb (1968), p. 63.
20. Ibid.
21. Glover (1960), p. 339.
22. Blanc et al. (1970), p. 369.
23. Ibid., p. 370.
24. Coxill and Grubb (1968), p. 63.
25. Kane (1971), p. 354.
26. Coxill and Grubb (1968), p. 63.
27. Ibid.
28. Kane (1971), p. 354.

29. Neill et al. (1972), p. 96.
30. IRM 56 (March 1967): 54.
31. Dayton (1973), p. 564.
32. Sere de Rivieres 1965:280.
33. Ibid., p. 18.
34. Glover (1960), p. 282.
35. Coxill and Grubb (1968), p. 79.
36. Glover (1960), p. 282.
37. Kane (1971), p. 348.
38. Dayton (1973), p. 564.
39. IRM 56 (March 1967): 55.
40. Neill et al. (1971), p. 443.
41. Dayton (1973), p. 595.
42. Legum (1969), p. 392.
43. Glover (1960), p. 281.
44. IRM 56 (March 1967): 54.
45. IRM 57 (March 1968): 37.
46. Coxill and Grubb (1968), p. 96.
47. Glover (1960), p. 280.
48. Dayton (1973), p. 365.
49. Coxill and Grubb (1968), p. 96.
50. IRM 56 (March 1967): 54.
51. Latourette (1943), 5:460.
52. Neill et al. (1971), p. 630.
53. IRM 56 (March 1967): 55
54. Baeta (1968), p. 360.
55. Legum (1969), p. 371.
56. Glover (1960), p. 281.

57. Dayton (1973), p. 247.
58. Neill et al. (1971), p. 367.
59. Coxill and Grubb (1968), p. 77.
60. Ibid.

61. IRM 56 (March 1967): 55.
62. Latourette (1943), 5:460.
63. Neill et al. (1971), p. 367.

Notes on Chapter 12

1. Ajayi (1965), p. 233.
2. Ibid.
3. Marsh and Kingsnorth (1963), pp. 104-6.
4. Ajayi (1965), pp. 233-35.
5. Oliver (1952), pp. 167-69.
6. Ajayi (1965), p. 233.
7. Groves (1958), pp. 74-77.
8. Ayandele (1966), p. 342.
9. Groves (1958), 4:73-74.
10. Winter (1970), p. 11.
11. Groves (1958), 4:222.
12. Prof. Ayandele of the University of Ibandan treats the subject in detail. Ayandele (1966), pp. 307ff.

13. Baeta (1968), p. 147.
14. Consultation (1972), p. 51.
15. Baeta (1968), p. 432.
16. Groves (1954), 2:60.
17. O'Conner in Cugler, ed. (1971), pp. 5-12.
18. Cornevin (1964), p. 303.
19. Stevens (1963), pp. 2-3.
20. Taylor and Lehmann (1961), p. 73.
21. AACC Report (1958), pp. 34-45.
22. Consultation (1961), pp. 43-45.

Notes on Chapter 13

1. Beaver (1966), p. 48.
2. Groves (1955), 3:239.
3. Ayandele (1966), p. 289.
4. Smalley (1974), p. 207.
5. Crampton (n.d.), p. 81.
6. Groves (1955), 3:236.
7. Beaver (1966), p. 49.
8. Rotberg (1965), pp. 119-24.
9. Walsh in Beaver (1966), pp. 32-34.
10. Crampton (n.d.), p. 78.
11. Beetham (1967), p. 32.
12. Ibid.
13. Ibid., p. 39.
14. Ayandele (1966), pp. 292-294.
15. Farrelly in Barrett et al. (1973), p. 49.

16. Covell and Wagner (1971), pp. 101ff.
17. Hastings (1967), p. 189.
18. Ibid., p. 192.
19. Ibid., p. 193.
20. Stonelake (1937), p. 115.
21. Carpenter (1952), p. 46.
22. Groves (1955), 3:247.
23. Carpenter (1952), p. 46.
24. Glover (1960), p. 267.
25. Groves (1958), 4:19.
26. Carpenter (1952), p. 51.
27. Oosthuisen (1968), p. 87.
28. Ayandele (1966), p. 343.

Notes on Chapter 14

1. Coxill and Grubb (1968), p. 98.
2. Barrett (1968), pp. 4-5.
3. Sundkler (1948), p. 20.
4. Barrett 1968.18,32,34.
5. Shepperson (1958), p. 249.

6. Sundkler (1965), p. 54.
7. Ayandele (1966), p. 178.
8. Barrett (1968), p. 273.
9. Sundkler (1948), p. 204.
10. Turner (1967), 1:16.

11. Sundkler (1965), p. 35.
12. Olson (1972), p. 209.
13. Barrett (1968), pp. 34-35.
14. Ibid., pp 109ff.
15. Ibid., pp. 154ff.
16. Hayward (1963), pp. 66ff.
17. Latourette (1944), 6:29.
18. Beetham (1967), pp. 171-72.
19. Groves (1958), p. 226.
20. Ibid., p. 22n

21. Ibid., p. 228.
22. Hogg (1952), pp. 277-79.
23. Neill (1964), p. 245.
24. Winter (1970), pp. 68-69.
25. Hinchliff (1968), p. 103.
26. Fey (1968), p. 104.
27. Beetham (1967), p. 173.
28. Fey (1968), p. 246.
29. Hastings (1966), p. 238.
30. Fey (1968), p. 77.

Glossary

Apologist—one who speaks or writes in defense of a faith, a cause, or an institution

Archdeacon—a clergyman having the duty of assisting a diocesan bishop in ceremonial functions

Asceticism—the practice of strict self-denial as a matter of personal and especially of spiritual discipline

Bishopric—the office of bishop or the administrative division for which a bishop is responsible

Calif or *caliph*—a successor of Muhammad as temporal and spiritual head of the Muslims in a region

Catechist—a national in a missionary district who teaches Bible doctrine

Diocese—an administrative division; the territorial division of a bishop

Dynasty—a succession of rulers of the same line of descent; a powerful group or family that maintains its position for a considerable time

Edict—an official public proclamation having the force of law

Gnostic—one who adheres to the conviction, especially during the late pre-Christian and early Christian centuries, that matter is evil and that emancipation comes through knowledge

Hermit—one who lives in solitude, especially for religious reasons

Mandate—an authoritative command; in this book: an order or commission granted by the League of Nations to a member nation for the establishment of a responsible government over a former conquered territory

Millennium—a period of one thousand years

Nous—the mind as rational; the highest intellect; God regarded as the World Reason

489

Patriarchate—office, jurisdiction, or time in office of a patriarch

Philanthropic—characterized by good will to fellow-men

Polemist—one who makes an aggressive attack on, or refutation of, the opinion or principles of another

Predestinarians—those who believe in the doctrine that God in His sovereignty infallibly guides those who are destined for salvation

Prefecture—district governed by a prefect or the office or term of office of a prefect

Presbyter—a member of the order of priests in churches having episcopal hierarchies, including bishops, priests, and deacons

See—(noun) a cathedral town; a seat of a bishop's office, power, or authority

Simony—buying or selling a church office or ecclesiastical preferment

Treatise—a systematic exposition or argument in writing, including a methodical discussion of facts and principles involved and the conclusions reached

Vicar Apostolic—a Roman Catholic titular bishop who governs a territory not organized as a diocese

Bibliography

Ajayi, J.F. Ade. *Christian Missions in Nigeria. 1841-1891. The Making of a New Elite.* Evanston: North Western University Press, 1969.

Alexander, Frank. "Missions in Malawi." Unpublished M.A. thesis. Pasadena: Fuller Theological Seminary, School of World Mission, 1969.

All-Africa Church Conference

    Ibadan, Nigeria, "The Church in Changing Africa," New York: International Missionary Council, 1958.

    Kitwe, Zambia, "The Urban African Consultation," Kitwe: Mindolo Ecumenical Center, 1961.

    Kitwe, Zambia, "All Africa Seminar on the Christian Home and Family Life," Kitwe: Minsolo Ecumenical Center, 1963.

    Kampala, Uganda, "Drumbeats from Kampala," London: Lutterworth, 1963.

    "Christian Education in Africa," London: Oxford University Press, 1963.

American Board of Commissioners for Foreign Missions, Annual Report, Fall, 1958.

Anderson, E. *Messianic Popular Movements in Lower Congo.* Uppsala: Almquist & Wiksells Boctrycker, 1958.

Anderson, Efraim. *Churches at the Grass-roots; A Study in Congo-Brazzaville.* London: Lutterworth, 1968.

Anderson, L.K. *Bridge to Africa.* New York: Board of Foreign Missions of the Presbyterian Church in U.S.A., 1952.

Anderson, W.H. *On the Trail of Livingstone.* Mountain View, Colo.: Pacific, 1919.

Anderson-Morshead, A.E.M. *The History of the Universities Mission to Central Africa 1859-1909.* London: Universities Mission, 1909.

Axelson, Sigbert. *Culture Confrontation in the Lower Congo*. Falkoeping, Sweden: Gummerssons Boktryckeri A.B., 1970.

Ayandele, E.A. *The Missionary Impact on Modern Nigeria 1842-1914*. London: Longmans, 1966.

Baeta, C.G. *Christianity in Tropical Africa*. Oxford: University Press, 1968.
          Prophetism in Ghana. London: SCM, 1962.

Bamori, Jean. *"Apercu historique de l'Union des Eglises Baptistes du Burundi."* Unpublished thesis. Kinshasa, Zaire: Ecole de Theologie Evangelique de Kinshasa, 1972.

Bane, M.J. *Catholic Pioneers in West Africa*. Dublin: Clonmore and Reynolds, 1956.

Barrett, David B. *Schism & Renewal in Africa*. Oxford: University Press, 1968.

Barrett, D.B., Mambo, G.; McLaughlin, J., Malcom, J.M., eds. *Kenya Churches Handbook*. Kismu, Kenya: Evangel, 1973.

Bartels, F.L. *The Roots of Methodism*. Cambridge: University Press, 1965.

Beaver, R. Pierce. *Ecumenical Beginnings in Protestant World Mission: A History of Comity*. New York: Nelson, 1962.
          Envoys of Peace. Grand Rapids: Eerdmans, 1964.
          The Gospel and Frontier Peoples. South Pasadena; William Carey Library, 1966.

Beetham, T.S. *Christianity and the New Africa*. London: Praeger, 1967.

Bentley, H. Holman. *Pioneering on the Congo*. 2 vols. London: Religious Tract Society, 1900.

Bentley, H.M., and Bentley, W. Holman. *The Life and Labour of a Congo Pioneer*. London: Religious Tract Society, 1907.

Bernander, Gustav. *The Rising Tide: Christianity Challenged in East Africa*. Rock Island, Ill.: Augustana, 1957.

Berry, L.L. *A Century of Missions of the Africa Methodist Episcopal Church 1840-1940*. New York: Gutenberg, 1942.

Bertsche, J.E. *"Kimbanguism: A Challenge to Missionary Statesmanship."* Unpublished paper, 1964.

Beyerhaus, Peter. *Missions: Which Way?* Grand Rapids: Zondervan, 1971.

Beyerhaus, Peter, and Lefever, Henry. *The Responsible Church and the Foreign Mission*. Grand Rapids: Eerdmans, 1964.

Blaikie, W.G. *Personal Life of David Livingstone*. New York: Revell, 1903.

Blanc, Rene; Blocher, Jacques; and Kruger, Etienne. *Histoires des Missions Protestantes Francaises*. Bruxelles: Le Phare, 1970.

Bonn, Alfred. *Ein Jahruhundert Rheinische Mission*. Barmen: Missionshaus, 1928.

Bontinck, F. *Aux origines de l'Etat Independent du Congo: Documents tires d'archives americaines*. Louvain: Editions Nauwelaerts, 1966.

Booth, Newell S. *The Cross Over Africa*. New York: Friendship, 1945.

Bowen, J.F. *Adventures and Missionary Labors in Several Countries in Africa From 1849 to 1856*. Publisher unknown, 1875.

Braekman, E.M. *Histoire du Protestantisme au Congo*. Bruxelles: Librairie des Eclaireurs Unionistes, 1961.

Brown, Arthur Judson. *One Hundred Years. A History of the Foreign Missionary Work of the Presbyterian Church in the U.S.A.* New York: Revell, 1937.

Brown, W.E. *The Catholic Church in South Africa*. London: Burns and Oates, 1960.

Budge, Sir E.A. Wallis. *A History of Ethiopia*. The Netherlands: Anthropological Publications, 1970.

Calvert, Albert F. *German East Africa*. New York: Negro University Press, 1919.

Carpenter, G.W. *Highways of God in Congo*. Leopoldville: LECO, 1952.

Carter, Gwendolen M. *Five African States*. London: Pall Mall, 1963.

Christian Council of Nigeria. *"Christian Responsibility in an Independent Nigeria."* A Report. Ibadan: Abiodun, 1962.

Comber, Thomas. Unpublished letter written to the Baptist Missionary Society on 30 January, 1887.

Conference at Salisbury, Rhodesia. "A Conference Report." London: Oxford University Press, 1963.

Consultation 1961: Urban Africa Consultation, Nairobi, Kenya, March 1961. Nairobi: All-Africa Church Conference.

Consultation on the Church in Zaire. Kinshasa: Roman Catholic Church, 1972.

Copplestone, J. Tremayne. *History of Methodist Missions, Vol IV: Twentieth Century Perspectives.* New York: United Methodist Church, 1973.

Cornevin, R. and M. *Histoire de l'Afrique des Origines a la 2e Fuerre Mondiale.* Paris: Petite Bibliotheque Payot, 1964.

Cornevin, Robert. *Histoire de L'Afrique.* 2 vols. Paris: Payot, 1960.
Histoire de Dahomey. Paris: Berger-Levrault, 1962.
Histoire du Congo. Paris; Berger-Levrault, 1966.
Histoire du Togo. Paris; Berger-Levrault, 1969.

Covell, Ralph R., and Wagner, C. Peter. *An Extension Seminary Primer.* South Pasadena: William Carey Library, 1971.

Cox, Emmet D. *The Church of the United Brethren in Christ in Sierra Leone.* South Pasadena: William Carey Library, 1970.

Coxill, H. Walklin, and Grubb, Sir Kenneth. *World Christian Handbook.* London: Lutterworth, 1968.

Crampton, E. Patrick T. *Christianity in the North of Nigeria.* Publisher unknown, n.d.

Crawford, John R. *Temoignage Protestant au Zaire.* Kinshasa: CEDI, 1972.

Crooks, J.J. *A History of the Colony of Sierra Leone, Western Africa.* Dublin, Cork, Belfast: Brown and Nolan, 1903.

Crowder, Michael. *A Short History of Nigeria.* New York: Praeger, 1962.

Crowther, Samuel A. *Journal of an Expedition up the Niger and Tshadda Rivers.* London: Cass, 1970.

Dayton, E.R., ed. *Mission Handbook.* Monrovia, Calif.: MARC, 1973.

Debrunner, Hans W. *A Church Between Colonial Powers. A Study of the Church in Togo.* London: Lutterworth, 1965.
A History of Christianity in Ghana. Accra: Waterville, 1967.

Delury, George E., ed. *World Almanac and Book of Facts.* New York: Newspaper Enterprise Association, 1976.

Descamps, Baron. *Histoire Generale Comparee des Missions.* vol. 8. Paris: Librairie Plon, 1932.

Diswasani, A. "*L'Eglise evangelique au Zaire.*" Unpublished report. Kinshasa: Ecole de Theologie Evangelique de Kinshasa, 1970.

Duchense, Louis M.O. *Early History of the Christian Church, From Its Foundation to the End of the Fifth Century.* Translated by Claude Jenkins. London: Murray, 1912.

> *Early History of the Christian Church From Its Foundation to the End of the Fifth Century.* Translated by C. Jenkins. (1st ed. 1912). London: Murray, 1965.

Du Plessis, J. *A History of Christian Missions in South Africa.* New York: Longmans, 1911.

> *The Evangelization of Pagan Africa, A History of Christian Missions to the Pagan Tribes of Central Africa.* Cape Town and Johannesburg: Juta, 1930.

Ellingworth. *Bulletin for the Society of African Church History.* vol. 2, 1967.

Elliot, W.A. *South Africa.* London: London Missionary Society, 1913.

Ellis, William. *The Martyr Church: A Narrative of the Introduction, Progress and Triumph of Christianity in Madagascar.* London: Snow, 1870.

Erickson, Edwin. "The Church in Ethiopia," Unpublished paper. Pasadena: Fuller Theological Seminary, School of World Mission, 1973.

Fey, Harold E., ed. *A History of the Ecumenical Movement: 1948-1968.* Philadelphia: Westminster, 1968.

Findlay, G.G. and Holdsworth, W.S. *The History of the Wesleyan Methodist Missionary Society.* vols 1-5. London: Epworth, 1921-22.

Fisher, W.S. and Hayte, J. *Africa Looks Ahead.* London: Pickering & Inglis, 1948.

Foster, Raymond Samuel. *The Sierra Leone Church. An Independent Anglican Church.* London: SPCK, 1961.

Fox, William. *A Brief History of the Wesleyan Missions on the Western Coast of Africa.* London: Ayllot and Jones, 1851.

Frend, W. *The Donatist Church, a Movement of Protest in Roman North Africa.* Oxford: Clarendon, 1952.

Fullerton, W.Y. *The Christ of the Congo River.* London: Carey, 1928.

Fyfe, Christopher. "West African Methodists in the Nineteenth Century," *Sierra Leone Bulletin of Religion.* vol. 3, pp. 22-28, 1961.

A *History of Sierra Leone.* London: Oxford University Press, 1962.

Galbraith, John S. *Mackinnon and East Africa 1878-1895.* Cambridge: University Press, 1972.

Gann, L.H., and Duignan, Peter, eds. *Colonialism in West Africa.* Cambridge: University Press, 1970.

Gareis, Reinhold. *Geschichte der Evangelischen Heidenmission.* Emmishofen, Switzerland: Hirsch, n.d.

Garrett, T.S. and Jeffrey, R.M.C. *Unity in Nigeria.* London: Edinburgh House, 1965.

George, Claude. *The Rise of British West Africa.* London: Cass, 1968.

Gerdener, G.B.A. *The Story of Christian Missions in South Africa.* Johannesburg: Linden Christian Church, 1950.
    Recent Developments in the South Africa Mission Field. London: Marshall, Morgan & Scott, 1958.

Gilis, C.S. *Kimbangu: Fondateur de l'Eglise.* Bruxelles: Librairie Encyclopedique, 1960.

Glover, Robert Hall. *The Progress of World-Wide Missions.* New York and London: Harper and Row, 1960.

Goldie, Hugh. *Calabar and Its Mission.* Edinburgh: Oliphant, Anderson & Ferrier, 1890.

Goodall, Norman. *History of the London Missionary Society.* Oxford: University Press, 1954.

Greenfield, Richard. *Ethiopia: A New Political History.* New York: Praeger, 1965.

Grenfell, George. Correspondence with the Baptist Missionary Society, London.

Griffith, Robert. *Madagascar, A Century of Adventure.* London: London Missionary Society, 1919.

Grimley, John B., and Robinson, Gordon E. *Church Growth in Central and Southern Nigeria.* Grand Rapids: Eerdmans, 1966.

Groves, C.P. *The Planting of Christianity in Africa 1840-1954.* 4 vols. London: Lutterworth, 1948-58.

Grubb, Norman P., and Studd, C.T. *In Congo Forests.* Grand Rapids: Zondervan, 1956.

Guinness, Mrs. H. Grattan. *The New World of Central Africa. With a History of the First Christian Mission on the Congo.* New York: Revell, 1899.

Hamilton, J. Taylor. *Twenty-Five Years of Pioneer Missions in Nyasaland: A History of Moravian Missions in German East Africa*. Bethlehem, Pa.: Bethlehem, 1912.

Harnack, Adolph. *The Mission and Expansion of Christianity in the First Three Centuries*. Translated and edited by James Moffat. New York: Putnam. 2nd ed., 2 vols., 1908.

Hastings, Adrian. *Church and Missions in Modern Africa*. London: Burns and Oates, 1967.

　　　Mission and Ministry. London: Sheed and Ward, 1971.

Hawker, George. *The Life of George Grenfell*. Publisher unknown, 1909.

Hayward, Victor E. *African Independent Church Movements*. London: Edinburgh House, 1963.

Heanley, R.M. *A Memoir to Edward Steere, Third Missionary Bishop in Central Africa*. London: George Bell, 1888.

Hemmens, H. L. *Congo Journey*. London: Carey, n.d.

　　　George Grenfell, Pioneer in Congo. London: SCM, 1927.

Hening, Mrs. E. F. *History of the African Mission of the Protestant Episcopal in the United States*. New York: Stanford and Swords, 1850.

Herzkovits, M.J. *Dahomey*. Locust Valley, N.Y.: Augustin, 1938.

Heseltine, Nigel. *Madagascar*. London: Pall Mall, 1971.

Hill, Robert W. "The Christianization of the Central African Republic." Unpublished M.A. thesis. Pasadena: Fuller Theological Seminary, School of World Mission, 1969.

Hinchliff, Peter. *The Church in South Africa*. London: SPCK,

Hodges, George. *The Early Church From Ignatius to Augustine*. New York: Houghton Mifflin, 1915.

Hofmeyer, Jan H. *South Africa*. London: Benn, 1931.

Hogg, W.R. *Ecumenical Foundations. A History of the International Missionary Council and Its Nineteenth Century Background*. New York: Harper, 1952.

Hohensee, Donald Wilhelm. "Church Growth in Burundi." Unpublished M.Th. thesis. Pasadena: Fuller Theological Seminary, School of World Mission, 1975.

Holden, W. Clifford. *A Brief History of Methodism, and of Methodist Missions in South Africa*. London: Wesleyan Conference Office, 1877.

Hollenweger. *Christianity in Tropical Africa*. Oxford: University Press, 1973.

Hubbard, David A. "The Literary Sources of the Kebra Negast." Unpublished Ph.D. thesis. Edinburgh: St. Andrews University, 1956.

Hutton, J.E. *A History of Moravian Missions*. London: Moravian Publication Office, 1923.

Idowu, E. Bolaji. *Towards an Indigenous Church*. London: Oxford University Press, 1965.

International Review of Missions. Editorials, 1966, 1967, 1968, 1969, 1972.

Jack, James W. *Daybreak in Livingstonia. The Story of the Livingstonia Mission, British Central Africa*. Edinburgh: Oliphant, Anderson & Ferrier, 1901.

Jacobson, Leonard. *"Church Growth on the Island of Madagascar."* Unpublished M.A. thesis. Pasadena: Fuller Theological Seminary, School of World Mission, 1968.

Jadin, Louis. *"Les Survivantes Chrétiennes au Congo au XIXe Siècle," Etudes d'Histoire Africaine*. Louvain: Editions Nouwelaerts, 1970.

Johnson, T.S. *The Story of a Mission. The Sierra Leone Church: First Daughter Church of C.M.S.* London: SPCK, 1953.

Johnston, Harry H. *British Central Africa. An Attempt to Give Some Account of a Portion of the Territories under British Influence North of the Zambezi*. London: Methuen, 1898. *George Grenfell and the Congo*. London: Hutchinson, 1918.

Jones, Rufus M. *The Quakers in the American Colonies*. London: Macmillan, 1962.

Kane, Herbert J. *A Global View of Christian Missions*. Grand Rapids: Baker, 1971. *Understanding Christian Missions*, Grand Rapids: Baker, 1974.

Kapella, G. M. "Histoire de l'Eglise en Zambie," *L'Ecrivain Africain*, No. 15, n.d.

Kerr, Robert. *Morocco After Twenty-Five Years. A Description of the Country, Its Laws and Customs and European Situation*. London: Murray and Evenden, 1912.

Krapf, J.L. *Travels, Researches, and Missionary Labours During an Eighteen Years' Residence in Eastern Africa*. London: Trueber, 1860.

Kwast, Lloyd E. *The Discipling of West Cameroon*. Grand Rapids: Eerdmans, 1971.

Lagargren, David. *Mission and State in the Congo*. Uppsala: Almquist & Wiksells, 1970.

Latourette, Kenneth Scott. *The Thousand Years of Uncertainty*. vol. 1., 1970.

    The Thousand Years of Uncertainty. vol. 2, 1971.

    Three Centuries of Advance. vol. 3, 1970.

    Europe and the United States. vol. 4, 1971.

    The Great Century: The Americas, Australasia, and Africa. vol. 5, 1974.

    The Great Century: North Africa and Asia, vol. 6, 1970.

    Advance Through Storm. vol. 7, 1974.

    Grand Rapids: Zondervan. (First published 1937-1945 by Harper and Row, New York.)

Legum, Colin, ed. *Africa Handbook*. Harmondsworth, Middlesex: Penguin, 1969.

Leonard, E.G. *A History of Protestantism*. Edited by H. H. Rowley. Translated by Joyce M. H. Reid. London: Nelson, 1965.

Lerrigo, P.J. *Rock-Breakers, Kingdom Building in Kongo Land* (ABFMS). Philadelphia: Judson, 1922.

Lewis, Cecil, and Edwards, G.E. *Historical Records of the Church of the Province of South Africa*. London: SPCK, 1934.

Libert, E. *Etudes d'histoire Africaine, Vol. II: Missionaries Chretiens et Kimbanguisme*. Kinshasa: Universite Louvanium, 1971.

Lietzmann, H. *A History of the Early Church*. Translated by Bertram Lee Wolf. London: Lutterworth, 1953.

Loewen, Melvin. *Three Score, The Story of an Emerging Mennonite in Central Africa*. Elkhart, Ind.: Africa Inter-Mennonite Mission, 1972.

Lovett, Richard. *The History of the London Missionary Society 1795-1895*. vols. 1 and 2. London: Henry Trowede, 1899.

Lugard, Lord. *The Dual Mandate in British Tropical Africa*. London: Cass, 1965.

Macaw, Mrs. Alexander. *Congo, The First Alliance Mission Field*. Harrisonburg, Pa.: Christian Publications, 1937.

Marsh, Zoe, and Kingsnorth, G.W. *An Introduction to the History of East Africa*. Cambridge: University Press, 1963.

Matthews, T. T. *Thirty Years in Madagascar.* London: Religious Tract Society, 1904.

Maurice, Albert. *Stanley: Letters Inedites.* Bruxelles: Office de Publicite, S.A., 1955.

Maxwell, J. Lowry. *Nigeria, the Land, the People and Christian Progress.* London: World Dominion, 1927.

McFarlan, Donald M. *Calabar, The Church of Scotland Missions, 1846-1946.* New York: Nelson, 1946.

McLeish, Alexander. *Light and Darkness in East Africa.* London: World Dominion, 1927.

Meyers, John Brown, and Comber, Thomas J. *Missionary Pioneer to the Congo.* New York: Negro Universities Press, 1969.

Michelson, Clifford S. "The Evangelical Lutheran Church of East Cameroon." Unpublished M.A. thesis. Pasadena: Fuller Theological Seminary, School of World Mission, 1969.

Missionary Herald. The 1890s are bound in one volume and designated "1890," 1890.

Missionary Review of the World. Vol. 14, 1901.

Modjumvela, Avongola. "*Oeuvre de la Mission Baptiste Suedoise chez les Basakata.*" Unpublished thesis. Kinshasa: Ecole de Theologie Evangelique de Kinshasa, 1973.

Monceaux, Paul. *Histoire litteraire de l'Afrique chretienne depuis les origines jusqu'a l'invascion arabe.* Paris, 1901.

Moreira, Eduardo. *Portuguese East Africa.* New York: World Dominion, 1936.

Mullin, Joseph. *The Catholic Church in Modern Africa.* New York: Herder, 1965.

Müller, Gustav. *Geschichte der Ewe-Mission.* Bremen: Norddeutschen Missions-Gesellschaft, 1904.

Myers, John Brown. *The Congo for Christ.* London: Partridge, 1895.

Neander, August. *General History of the Christian Religion and Church.* Translated from German by Joseph Torrey. 5 vols. New York: Hurd & Houghton, 1871.

Neill, Stephen. *A History of Christian Missions.* Middlesex, England: Penguin, 1973.

Neill, Stephen; Anderson, Gerald H.; and Goodwin, John, eds. *Concise Dictionary of the Christian World Mission.* New York: Abingdon, 1971.

Nelson, Robert G. *Congo Crisis and Christian Mission.* St. Louis: Bethany, 1961.

Newman, Albert. *Manual of Church History.* Vols. 1 and 2 (original 1894). Philadelphia: Franklin, 1957.

Nichols, James H. *History of Christianity 1650 - 1950.* New York: Ronald, 1956.

North American Assembly on African Affairs. *Africa is Here.* Springfield, Ohio: Wittenberg College, 1952.

Northcott, C. *Livingstone en Afrique.* Neuchatel: Delachaux et Niestle, 1960.

O'Conner, Anthony M. "The Distribution of Towns in Subsaharan Africa," in Cugler, Joseph, ed., *Urbanization in Subsaharan Africa.* Oxford: University Press, 1971.

Oliver, Roland. *The Missionary Factor in East Africa.* London: Longmans, 1966.

Oliver, Roland, and Fage, I.D. *A Short History of Africa.* Baltimore: Penguin, 1962.

Olson, Gilbert W. *Church Growth in Sierra Leone.* Grand Rapids: Eerdmans, 1969.

Olson, Jeannine. *Histoire de l'Eglise, Vingt Siecles et Six Continents.* Yaounde: Editions Cle, 1972.

Oosthuisen, G.C. *Post-Christianity in Africa.* London: Hurst, 1968.
   Theological Battleground in Asia and Africa. New York: Humanities, 1972.

Paden, John N., and Soja, Edward W., eds. *The African Experience, Vol. I: Essays.* Evanston: Northwestern University Press, 1970.

Page, Jesse. *The Black Bishop Samuel Adjai Crowther.* New York: Revell, 1908.

Parrinder, Geoffrey. *West African Religion.* London: Epworth, 1961.

Pascoe, C.F. *Two Hundred Years of the S.P.G. 1701-1900.* London: Society for the Propagation of the Gospel, 1901.

Philip, Horace R.A. *A New Day in Kenya.* London: World Dominion, 1936.

Pinnock, S.G. *The Romance of Missions in Nigeria.* Richmond, Va.: Foreign Mission Board, 1918.

Platt, W.J. *An African Prophet.* London: SCM, 1934.

Qualben, Lars P. *History of the Christian Church.* London: Thomas Nelson, 1942.

Randall, Max Ward. *Profile for Victory, New Proposals for Missions in Zambia.* South Pasadena: William Carey Library, 1970.

Record of the Third All-Africa Lutheran Conference, Oct. 12-21. Addis Ababa, Lutheran World Federation, Department of World Mission, 1965.

Richter, Julius. *Geschichte der Evangelischen Mission in Africa.* Gueterslop: C. Bertelsmann, 1922.

Riddle, Norman G. "Church Growth and the Communication of the Gospel in Kinshasa." Unpublished M.A. thesis. Pasadena: Fuller Theological Seminary, School of World Mission, 1971.

Robinson, Charles H. *History of Christian Missions.* New York: Scribner, 1930.

Rotberg, Robert I. *Christian Missionaries and the Creation of Northern Rhodesia.* Princeton: Princeton University Press, 1965.

Rutherford, J., and Glenny, Edward H. *The Gospel in North Africa.* London: Percy Lund, Humphries, 1900.

Sales, Jane M. *The Planting of Churches in South Africa.* Grand Rapids: Eerdmans, 1971.

Sadler, George. *A Century in Nigeria.* Nashville: Broadman, 1950.

Schaff, Philip. *History of the Christian Church,* 3 vols. Grand Rapids: Kregel, 1950.
    History of the Christian Church. (Reprint of 1910 ed.) 8 vols. Grand Rapids: Eerdmans, 1960.

Schermerhorn, R. *Christian Missions in the Modern World.* Publisher unknown, 1933.

Schlatter, Wilhelm. *Geschichte der Basler Mission 1815-1915.* vols. 1-3. Basel: Basler Missionsbuchhandlung, 1916.

Schmidlin, Joseph. *Katholische Missionsgeschichte.* Steyl: Missions-druckerei, 1924.
    Catholic Mission History. Translated by Matthias Braun. Techney, Ill.: Mission, 1933.

Schwager, Friedrich. *Die Katholische Heidenmission der Gegenwart im Zusammenhang mit Ihrer Grossen Vergangenheit.* Stegl: Missionsdruckerei, 1907.

Schwartz, Glenn J. "Crucial Issues of the Brethren in Christ in Zambia." Unpublished M.A. thesis. Pasadena: Fuller Theological Seminary, School of World Mission, 1974.

Selby, John. *A Short History of South Africa.* London: Allen & Unwin, 1973.

Sere de Rivieres, Edmond. *Histoire du Niger.* Paris: Berger Levrault, 1965.

Shepperson, George. *Church and Sect in Central Africa.* Rhodes Livingstone Journal, Manchester (no. 33), 1963.

Shepperson, G., and Price, T. *Independent Africa:* John Chilembwe and the origins, setting, and significance of the Nyasaland native rising of 1915. Edinburgh, 1958.

Sibree, James. *The Madagascar Mission.* London: London Missionary Society, 1907.

    Fifty Years in Madagascar: Personal Experiences of Mission Life and Work. London: Allen & Unwin, 1924.

Slade, Ruth E. *English-Speaking Missions in the Congo Independent State.* Brussels, 1959.

    King Leopold's Congo. London: Oxford University Press, 1962.

Smalley, William A., ed. *Readings in Missionary Anthropology.* South Pasadena: William Carey Library, 1974.

Smith, A.C.S. *Road to Revival: The Story of the Rwanda Mission.* London: Church Missionary Society, 1945.

Smith, E.W. *The Way of the White Fields in Rhodesia: A Survey of*

Smith, E.W. *The Way of the White Fields in Rhodesia. A Survey of Christian Enterprise in Northern and Southern Rhodesia.* London: World Dominion, 1928.

    African Ideas of God. A Symposium. London: Edinburgh House, 1950.

Smith, Herbert. *Fifty Years in Congo, Disciples of Christ at Equator.* Indianapolis, Ind.: United Christian Missionary Society, 1949.

Southton, Arthur E. *Gold Coast Methodism.* Cape Coast: Methodist Book Depot; London: Corgate, 1934.

Springer, John M. *Pioneering in the Congo.* Methodist Book Concern, 1916.

    Christian Conquests in the Congo. Methodist Book Concern, 1927.

Stevens, Canon R.S.O. *The Church in Urban Nigeria.* Birmingham: Juckes, 1963.

Stock, Eugene. *The History of the Church Missionary Society: Its Environment, Its Men, and Its Work.* vols 1-4. London: London Missionary Society, 1899-1916.

Stonelake, Alfred R. *Congo Past and Present.* New York: World Dominion, 1937.

Sundkler, Bengt G. *Bantu Prophets in South Africa.* London: Lutterworth, 1948.

    The World Mission. Grand Rapids: Eerdmans, 1965.

Swann, Alfred J. *Fighting the Slave-Hunters in Central Africa.* London: Cass, 1969.

Taylor, James Dexter. *The American Board of Missions in South Africa.* Durban: Singleton, 1911.

Taylor, John V. *The Growth of the Church in Buganda.* London: SCM, 1958.

    Processes of Growth in an African Church. London: SCM, 1958.

Taylor, John V., and Lehmann, Dorothea. *Christians of the Copperbelt.* London: SCM, 1961.

Thiessen, John Caldwell. *A Survey of World Missions.* Chicago: Inter-Varsity, 1954.

Thompson, A. C. *The Moravian Missions.* New York: Scribner, 1904.

Thompson, H. P. *Into All Lands: A History of the Society for the Propagation of the Gospel in Foreign Parts, 1701-1900.* London, 1951.

Thompson, Virginia, and Adolff, Richard. *The Emerging States of French Equatorial Africa.* Stanford, Calif.: Stanford University Press, 1960.

    French West Africa. Stanford, Calif.: Stanford University Press, 1967.

Tippett, Alan R. *Peoples of Southwest Ethiopia.* South Pasadena: William Carey Library, 1970.

Tippett, Alan R., ed. *God, Man and Church Growth.* Grand Rapids; Eerdmans, 1973.

Tucker, Alfred R. *Eighteen Years in Uganda and East Africa.* vols. 1 and 2. London: Arnold, 1908.

Turner, H.W. *African Independent Church.* Oxford: Clarendon, 1967.

Ullendorf, Edward. *Ethiopia and the Bible*. London: Oxford University Press, 1968.

Van Slageren, Jaap. *Histoire de l'Eglise en Afrique*. Yaounde, Cameroon: Editions Cle, 1969.

Wagner, C. Peter. *Frontiers in Missionary Strategy*. Chicago: Moody, 1971.

Walker, Eric A. *A History of South Africa*. London and New York: Longmans, 1928.

Walker, F. Deaville. *Thomas Birch Freeman*. London: SCM, 1929.
> *The Romance of the Black River. The Story of the C.M.S. Nigeria Mission*. London: Church Missionary Society, 1930.
> *A Hundred Years in Nigeria: The Story of the Methodist Mission in West Nigeria 1842-1942*. London: Cartage, 1942.

Walker, Williston. *A History of the Christian Church*. New York: Scribner, 1918 (1959, 1970).

Warneck, Gustav. *History of Protestant Missions*. New York; Revell, 1901.

Warren, T.J.P. *North Africa Today*. Tunis: North Africa Mission, 1947.

Weaver, W.B. *Thirty-Five Years in Congo*. Chicago: Congo Inland Mission, 1945.

Welbourn, F.B. *East African Rebels*. London: SCM, 1961.
> *Religion and Politics in Uganda, 1952-1962*. Nairobi: East African, 1965.

Whiteside, J. *History of the Wesleyan Methodist Church of South Africa*. London: Stock, 1906.

Willoughby, W.C. *The Soul of the Bantu*. New York: Doubleday, 1928.

Wills, S.J. *An Introduction to the History of Central Africa*. London: Oxford University Press, 1966.

Wilson, George Herbert. *History of the Universities' Mission to Central Africa*. Westminster: Universities' Mission, 1936.

Wilson, William J., ed. *The Church in Africa. Christian Mission in a Context of Change. A Seminar*. New York: Maryknoll, 1967.

Wiltgen, R.M. *A Gold Coast Missionary History 1471-1880*. London, 1956.

Winter, Ralph D. *The Twenty-five Unbelievable Years.* Pasadena: William Carey Library, 1970.

Wold, Joseph Conrad. *God's Impatience in Liberia.* Grand Rapids: Eerdmans, 1968.

Wright, Marcia. *German Missions in Tanganyika, 1891-1941. Lutherans and Moravians in the Southern Highlands.* Oxford: Clarendon, 1971.

Indexes

Index of Persons

Geographical Index

Subject Index